P9-CDS-622

LIVING IN STYLE

INSPIRATION AND ADVICE FOR EVERYDAY GLAMOUR

LIVING IN STYLE

INSPIRATION AND ADVICE FOR EVERYDAY GLAMOUR

RACHEL ZOE

WITH MONICA CORCORAN HAREL

GRAND CENTRAL
Life & Style
NEW YORK · BOSTON

Copyright © 2014 by Rachel Zoe, Inc.

Additional copyright information can be found on page 272.

Grand Central Life & Style

Hachette Book Group

237 Park Avenue

New York, NY 10017

www.GrandCentralLifeandStyle.com

Designer: Erika Oliveira

Printed in the United States of America

WOR

First Edition: March 2014

10 9 8 7 6 5 4 3 2

Grand Central Life & Style is an imprint of Grand Central Publishing.

The Grand Central Life & Style name and logo are trademarks of Hachette Book Group, Inc.

The Hachette Speakers Bureau provides a wide range of authors for speaking events. To find out more, go to www.HachetteSpeakersBureau.com or call (866) 376-6591.

The publisher is not responsible for websites (or their content) that are not owned by the publisher.

Library of Congress Cataloging-in-Publication Data

Zoe, Rachel.

Living in style: inspiration and advice for everyday glamour / Rachel Zoe; with Monica Corcoran Harel. — First edition.

pages cm

ISBN 978-1-4555-2358-0 (hardcover) — ISBN 978-1-4555-2360-3 (ebook)
1. Fashion. 2. Beauty, Personal. 3. Zoe, Rachel. I. Harel, Monica Corcoran. II. Title.

TT507.Z638 2014
746.9'2—dc23

2013028161

To my idols and mentors, my mother and father; my sister and best friend, Pamela; and my angels, Sophie and Luke. Most of all, to my partner in life and my love, Rodger, and to the light in my life and my heart, my beautiful sons, Skyler Morrison and Kaius Jagger.

CONTENTS

FOREWORD

by Diane von Furstenberg

Everyone wants a glamourous life. To me, glamour isn't just about gold lamé and fancy things. It's shine and confidence. It's a certain independence that comes with experiences that aren't always so glamourous. And sometimes when you look back, those are the moments you value the most. A lifestyle is not just a reflection of what you own or how you travel. It's learning how to create a life that will make you happy.

Rachel loves glamour and she has great taste. She and I first got to know each other when I relaunched my iconic wrap dress about twelve or so years ago. We had lunch in Los Angeles one afternoon and I liked her energy right away. Of course, she and I both share a love for the seventies. But Rachel isn't just my kind of woman because she is chic. She's always on the go and so excited about everything she does. Whenever I see her, she's happy to be part of that particular moment.

That spirit comes through in the way she lives and her talents as both a stylist and a designer. She's a modern woman who listens to the needs of modern women. This book is cleverly broken down to include fashion, beauty, home décor, and family rituals. Let it all inspire you to define your own glamourous life.

INTRODUCTION

THE NEW GLAMOUR

It's hard to believe that I wrote my first book, *Style A to Zoe: The Art of Fashion, Beauty & Everything Glamour* seven years ago. At that time, as a stylist, my days and nights involved everything from high-profile client fittings to red-carpet premieres to late-night fashion parties. It was frantic, nonstop, and exciting—I definitely didn't get enough sleep! But in hindsight, I now see that I was often focused so much on the details that I forgot to step back and see the big picture. It's not that I didn't realize what an exciting career I had. Believe me, I did. I just rarely slowed down to take a moment and appreciate it all.

> "THERE ARE NO ABSOLUTES IN LIFE. I'LL ALWAYS BE THE FIRST ONE TO TELL YOU TO BREAK A STYLE RULE—EVEN ONE OF MY OWN."

My life has dramatically shifted since then. Along with being a wife and a stylist, I'm now a fashion designer, a CEO to nearly thirty employees, and a mom to our toddler son, Skyler. You would think that with all this, I would be even more sleep-deprived. Surprisingly, my day-to-day is more manageable now. That's because taking on these new roles and responsibilities has forced me to become extremely efficient—whether it's streamlining my wardrobe to be versatile or reconfiguring my living room for more warmth and comfort. I also had an epiphany along the way. It dawned on me that while my work has always revolved around making people look fantastic (which I truly love to do), I needed to focus on living in style, too. And while my first book focused mostly on the red carpet, the chapters here are a reflection of my own chic world. Since my life evolved dramatically, I've had to redefine some of my own sensibilities and expectations.

Make no mistake—I still love glamour. I will always love glamour. But I have reinvented it in different ways that suit my new lifestyle. My definition of glamour is now a bit more—gasp!—practical. Maybe even a little relaxed, too. And this new outlook applies to everything from my fashion choices to my free time. I now see how denim with a fantastic statement jacket can be as glamourous as a sequined evening dress or why an intimate Sunday supper with friends can be as chic as an over-the-top cocktail party.

What's most important is that I have learned there are no absolutes in life. I'll always be the first one to tell you to break a style rule—even one of my own. I wouldn't be where I am right now if I didn't ignore most conventions and take risks every day.

I'm so excited to share my personal stories, inspirations, and advice with you—not to mention, to help you define glamour in a way that works overtime for you, too. It's been twenty years since I started working in fashion. This book feels like a celebration of my two decades in the industry!

CHAPTER 1

FASHION IS MY EVERYTHING

People always ask me how I got my start in fashion. I'll get to that, I promise. But what comes to mind when I think about where my passion for beautiful clothes and my obsession with being a part of this industry began is my very first fashion show. Front row? Please. I literally crashed that runway show. It was Marc Jacobs's spring collection in New York, about fifteen years ago; I had no invitation. In fact, I recall feeling incredible anxiety as I stood in line on the street for hours, not knowing whether I would get in at all.

Of course, I can still remember exactly what I wore that day—a vintage black Alaïa dress with six-inch black Manolos. My favorite lipstick at the time was MAC Chili, so my pout was a fiery red. There was no way I was going to miss that show—I was so starry eyed. I would have camped out overnight on the sidewalk, if necessary. A Marc Jacobs show was—and still is—one of the highlights of every Fashion Week. Everyone who was culturally relevant and cool was there, from Sofia Coppola to Winona Ryder, and half of New York wanted a ticket. In my mind, *no* was not an option. A well-known event photographer named Patrick McMullan noticed me lingering outside and snapped my picture—a little black dress can go a long way. He said that he expected to see more of me, which made me feel like I belonged there even more. As soon as the doors opened, I ran to the front and charged through. I even managed to scam a seat, though I was so far back that I couldn't see the looks on the models below the waist. I didn't care.

The runway, the lights, the electricity in the room! I was totally hooked. My next stop *had* to be Paris to see the haute couture shows. I had saved up enough money to finance a weeklong stay in the fashion mecca. "This is my dream. I need to do this," I said to Rodger, who has always supported me. We had just married—I was twenty-six—so I guess you could call the trip my fashion honeymoon. It sounds exciting, but I have to admit I was pretty lonely over there. Working as a freelance stylist in New York, I hadn't yet met a lot of magazine editors or designers. Fashion circles can feel impenetrable.

But once I finagled my way into some of the shows—again, after lots of waiting around and practically begging for tickets—it didn't matter at all. I held my breath as supermodels like Naomi Campbell and Gisele Bündchen paraded down the runways in unbelievable confections of every fabric imaginable. The sheer architecture of Alexander McQueen's collection for Givenchy stunned me. When I glimpsed the elegant, avant-garde gowns and outrageous hairpieces at the Chanel show, my heart literally stopped. Skipped a few beats. Remember your first crush—that rush? For me, this was true love. And I fell hard.

My infatuation wasn't just with the amazing, intricately constructed clothes, though; the fantasy and the glamour and the theatrics made me gasp and even tear up a little. More than anything, the shows reminded me of the transformative power of fashion: you can put on a red dress and take on a whole new identity, or slip into a pair of shoes that alter your horizon in every way.

Top: In one of my
favorite dresses, age 3.
Bottom: In one of my
favorite dresses, age 4.

Even as a little girl, I daydreamed about fashion. I would dash to my mother's closet as soon as I woke up each morning. Who needed cereal and cartoons? I preferred her trove of designer high heels, jewelry, scarves, furs, and jumpsuits. But it wasn't just about playing dress up for me—I didn't even need a mirror. As soon as I layered myself in her chunky tribal necklaces and stood in her chic Maud Frizon heels, I felt instantly like a glamourous woman.

When I was about thirteen, my parents took my older sister, Pamela, and me to Europe for the first time. In Saint-Tropez, I spotted these incredibly elegant women meticulously tanned right down to their ankles and dripping with gold jewelry. Each one of them looked so effortlessly chic, as though she had stepped right off the beach into a little black dress and piled her hair into a messy topknot. Voilà! I knew in that moment that I wanted to be that woman. Always.

And what I realized when we returned home to our traditional suburb of Short Hills, New Jersey, was that I *could* be that woman—well, sort of—if I dressed the part. Pictures from my early teens show me wearing that topknot and as much gold jewelry as I could "borrow" from my mom. Like many others, I also turned to Madonna as my saint of style and sometimes wore rubber bangles up my arms and teased my hair into a wavy bob. All the while, I pored over fashion magazines such as *Vogue, Elle,* and *Harper's Bazaar* for inspiration. I wanted to know everything about new designers and trends. My friends became my models, too. Girls would come to my house after school for their makeovers. I would restyle their clothes with scarves and belts, or roll up their jeans and add new shoes—I even redid their hair and makeup. We called it "Dress up with Rachel."

One day, I decided to work my magic on a neighborhood boy who always wore tracksuits. It drove me insane, because his parents dressed so well and I knew that he had fantastic clothes in his closet. I went over to his house and I laid out outfits—Ralph Lauren cable-knit sweaters and khakis to loafers and matching belts—for the entire school week, Monday through Friday. The next day, he showed up looking like he had walked right out of a Polo ad. To see him looking so good made me feel proud and incredibly happy. It was obvious that he felt a whole new sense of confidence.

Back at that time, I had no idea that I could build a career around my love for making people look their best. The closest I came to working in fashion in my teens was a part-time job at Nine West, where I sold the most shoes out of all the employees each week. Even then, I had this contagious enthusiasm for fashion. I would slip a pump onto a woman's foot and say, "This shoe is going to change everything for you." After I graduated high school, I went to George Washington University and majored in psychology and sociology. How we think and behave has always fascinated me; that education has proven to be a great foundation for what I do now.

As a stylist, I understand how fashion can affect your mood and your perspective. It's not *just* about clothes. What you wear is a visual extension of your self-expression. A velvet tuxedo jacket or a vintage caftan can help identify who you are and how you want to be seen. And now, as a designer, I contemplate that power whenever I sketch the strong lines of a suit or test the weight and feel of one of my bold cuffs. Fashion excites me today as much as it did when I sat in the back row and watched that first magical Marc Jacobs show. I still literally get goose bumps when the lights go down and the music starts—whether it's the show of a new and upcoming designer or my own collection coming down the runway.

Left: On set with the Backstreet Boys, 2000. Right: With Lanvin creative director Alber Elbaz.

STARTING OUT

Would you rather win the lottery or have dinner with Lanvin designer Alber Elbaz? Does the sight of a vintage architectural Christian Dior cocktail dress from the fifties make your hands shake a little? Me, too. I rarely meet people who are on the fence about fashion and style. Either you love it and breathlessly look forward to the new looks every season or you don't.

My first real foray into this world was styling shoots in New York at the now defunct teen magazine *YM.* At that time, I didn't even realize there was such a thing as a stylist. A friend of a friend told me about a fashion assistant position at the magazine. I was so nervous in the interview, but my obsession with style and designers came through and I got the job. There, I was insanely devoted to making everyone featured in the magazine look chic and cool. I worked long and hard and within two years jumped from assistant to fashion editor to senior fashion editor. The work exhilarated me and I learned so much about the process of creating beautiful looks for editorial covers and photographs. But I also discovered that I wanted to operate more autonomously and creatively. I decided, after two and a half

years, to make a huge leap and go out on my own as a freelance stylist. I was terrified, but at the same time, I was lucky that I had such supportive parents and Rodger on my side.

For me, working required a lot of discipline and a lot of faith. Some days, I worked with musical artists like Backstreet Boys, Stone Temple Pilots, and Jessica Simpson. Other days, when I didn't have a gig, I willed my phone to ring with another assignment. Making money wasn't my priority; I was just happy to be doing what I loved on my own terms. I really believe that people who love fashion don't dream of becoming rich—they just thrive on the creativity of the business and fantasize about gorgeous clothes.

In the end, a stylist's job is to make everything look effortless. If you flip through a magazine and skim a fabulous editorial spread, it's easy to assume that the process is as glamourous as those amazing photos, and the same goes for watching a beautiful actress swan down the red carpet in a breathtaking gown. But trust me—a tremendous amount of work precedes those gorgeous fashion moments.

> "PEOPLE WHO LOVE FASHION DON'T DREAM OF BECOMING RICH—THEY JUST THRIVE ON THE CREATIVITY OF THE BUSINESS AND FANTASIZE ABOUT GORGEOUS CLOTHES."

You can't even imagine how many racks of clothes and cartons of shoes and bags get lugged to a photo shoot. I typically call in anywhere from twenty to fifty dresses for an award show; fittings begin about two months ahead of time. It's hard work, no doubt, but I often stop in the middle of a crazy job to take a deep breath and appreciate the wonder of it all, whether I'm choosing which amazing vintage cocktail ring adds pop to a 1960s-inspired photo spread or pinning a couture Chanel gown on an award-nominated actress.

But the true emotional payoff comes when my team and I order in Chinese food to watch the Oscars and I see one of my clients looking ravishing and confident on the red carpet. Later that night, Rodger and I will hit the party circuit and stop by Madonna's legendary after-party. Still now, the chance to be part of such an iconic and glamourous event is always a highlight.

Breaking into fashion is one thing. Climbing up the ladder—in five-inch platforms, no less—requires fanaticism, a great sense of style, and a willingness to learn everything about the business and do anything to prove yourself. Here are my tips for proving that you live (and maybe die a little) for fashion.

BE ABLE TO PRONOUNCE: Azzedine Alaïa (A-zuh-deen Ah-lie-ah), Rochas (Row-shah), Balenciaga (Bah-lehn-see-ah-ga), Givenchy (Gee-von-shee), Rodarte (Row-dar-tay), and Prabal Gurung (Prah-bahl Goo-rung). These and plenty of other designer names will make you stumble. It may require some practice in the mirror, but it's a sign of respect to properly reference someone and not bludgeon a name.

NEVER CARRY: Anything fake. Counterfeit bags with slightly askew logos or mismatched hardware are an affront to designers and editors alike. So much creative thought and hours upon hours of hands-on work go into manufacturing a piece of fashion. Buying a faux anything really is ripping off an artist. If you can't afford a current authentic purse and crave a luxurious designer bag, score a cool, vintage Gucci knapsack or Vuitton bucket bag at a thrift store or an amazing bag without a logo. I love to see someone carrying a unique bag by an up-and-coming designer or a customized satchel that speaks to her own personal style. Your bag should say more about you than just how much you have in your bank account. Be creative in your choice and feel confident about it.

> "MY MOTTO HAS ALWAYS BEEN THIS:
> 'NO TASK IS TOO SMALL.'"

DO CARRY: An emergency style kit that will endear you to everyone, whether you work at a magazine, alongside a stylist, or with a fashion photographer. I keep an SOS kit in my office, too, just in case a colleague snags a dress or spills a latte. The essentials that I always have on hand: safety pins, mini Static Guard spray, travel-sized deodorant, travel-sized lint roller, stain remover pen, wipes, top stick tape, sewing kit, hair elastics or rubber bands, and bobby pins.

DON'T SAY "NO": Making a run for lattes may not be the most glam task, but it will endear you to the VIPs and show some initiative. The same goes for shouldering huge duffels crammed with dozens of ankle boots. My motto has always been this: "No task is too small." Back in the early days, I fetched everything from coffee to packages for a client. On one of my first independent styling jobs, I flew to Monaco alone—for one night!—with six trunks of clothes for Britney Spears. It may have been one of my most difficult and strenuous jobs early on (both mentally and physically), but I felt such pride when I saw her looking so fantastic onstage. I didn't even mind that the customs agents wanted to strangle me.

With designer Prabal Gurung

DON'T SAY "YES": If you have agreed to work on a shoot or a fitting and then a better last-minute opportunity arises, pass it up. In a business dominated by trends, fierce loyalty can trump experience and expertise. Fashion is a bit like high school: Word gets around. Plus, the industry is a giant revolving door with editors and publicists and photographers changing jobs frequently. People will remember that you went that extra mile when they move on to a new job. I have worked with the same editors for over fifteen years and still watch them leapfrog from one title to another.

PLAY NICE AND PLAY HARD: Movies such as *The Devil Wears Prada* have depicted the fashion world as a snippy war zone of oversized egos and prickly personalities. Um, that can be true. And I have seen plenty of young people start out with a sense of entitlement that doesn't serve them in the least. In my company, it's the genuinely good and committed people who get ahead. I call my colleagues my "team," because we all pitch in. Important e-mails get answered after hours and on the weekends. We don't worry about whose job it is—or isn't—when something needs to get done. Even I still sometimes do our coffee runs on my way into the office!

ALWAYS HAVE AN ANSWER: When anyone asks me what I seek most in a prospective colleague, my top response is a point of view. I constantly look to my team for their opinion and I value a confident eye. Know your aesthetic, trust it, and speak it. If you have an interview for a fashion assistant position at a magazine or to intern for a designer, be sure to do your homework. I always ask prospective employees to name their favorite designers and to tell me how they stay on top of what's happening in the industry. My advice is to read *WWD*—the daily trade newspaper/bible of fashion—to be in the know. During Fashion Week, be sure to check out all the shows on Style.com so you know what's on trend for the upcoming season.

With Skyler

A DAY IN MY LIFE

As a mother, wife, designer, stylist, author, entrepreneur, and obsessive fashion enthusiast, I constantly struggle with the art of balance. There never seems to be enough time in the day to devote myself entirely to each of my passions and responsibilities. Every hour is scheduled with meetings that range from reviewing prototype handbags for my collection to discussing potential partnerships. In the height of award season, I'm dashing to clients' houses for fittings and drinking twice as much tea as my usual three cups a day! But, with all that said, I wouldn't trade any of it for the world. Here is a peek at the schedule I try to keep for the most part, day-to-day.

7:00 A.M.: I wake up and before anything else, go immediately to my son, Skyler, and cover him with morning kisses. Then, I make him breakfast and play with him a bit. That time together is crazy important for me. I like to be with him before Europe and New York start calling.

7:30 A.M.: I'm usually stationed at my kitchen table with a very, very large cup of English breakfast tea and a bowl of berries with Greek yogurt. I get on my computer and begin to filter through my e-mails. I usually wake up to more than a hundred of them—and often, I won't check certain ones before I go to bed the night before, because then I would never fall asleep. In between e-mails I love to skim *WWD* to see what's happening in the world of fashion.

8:30 A.M.: I go upstairs for a three-minute shower and then take thirty minutes to get ready from start to finish—no longer. I typically slip into tailored black trousers or crisp denim with a soft tee and a cashmere duster or structured jacket. I don't lay it all out; I just go by instinct and then grab a pair of heels and sunnies to complete my look. Moisturizer, mascara, concealer, cheek tint, lipstick. A spritz of Tom Ford's Santal Blush and I'm off.

9:30 A.M.: I get into the office, which is always fun, because I love my team so much. First, I check in at the styling studio, which is a floor below my office. I like to work my way up in the building. Together, we skim the racks, discuss past shoots, upcoming editorials, and clients' schedules. We may be pulling for a premiere, a press tour, an editorial shoot, or an ad campaign.

11:00 A.M.: Next, I wander up a floor to meet with my product development office to check if the latest collection samples have arrived yet, or to show them a vintage picture that inspires me. (I get in trouble if I try to sneak by them!) Then, I wander over to my digital team. Typically, I'll meet with the editors of my daily fashion, beauty, and lifestyle website and newsletter, *The Zoe Report,* to discuss upcoming content, trends, likes, and dislikes. I love this part of my day, because I'm surrounded by dozens of twentysomethings who have their fingers on the pulse of everything that has to do with fashion and beauty. It's fascinating to hear about the new street trends and amazing products they discover. After that, I check in with the graphic design team to go over layout and imagery for the website and newsletters. You would be amazed at how much time and effort goes into selecting the size and placement of each headline, border, and image you may breeze over on any given morning. I'm picky…in a good way, of course.

12:30 P.M.: I typically break for lunch around this time, and Sky almost always joins us for the meal. As a mom and my own boss, I'm fortunate to be able to take a little time for lunch each day. Everyone needs what I call a "sanity break," because it gives you clarity when you go back to work. Lunchtime is now one of the most important and satisfying moments in my day—plus, I get to spend some time with Sky! Pre-Sky, lunch was always a walking meal.

1:00 P.M.: On any given day, I might jump right into a footwear sketch review or a resort color and concept preview. During this time, my team and I make edits to the collection while conceptualizing designs for upcoming seasons. I might choose between gold or silver hardware for a bag or examine how a certain fabric falls in a jumpsuit. I love making these creative decisions.

3:30 P.M.: The meetings continue, focused on bigger, broader business issues with the brand and the company. Even though Rodger and I work together, his office is around the corner from mine and we don't visit each other that much. We might walk into a meeting and say "Hi, babe"—but really it's all business during the day. We act like colleagues and always keep it professional. But every once in a while, I like to duck into his office and be a little silly to break up the day. Laughter is very important to me, and I think that's why our nine-to-five relationship works so well. During these larger brand meetings we might discuss prospective partnerships, strategic opportunities, or upcoming appearances at department stores or conferences, which I love to do, because I get to meet the women who wear my clothes.

6:00 P.M.: There are exceptions, of course, but I always try to go home to feed Skyler his dinner. Then later, when Rodger gets home, we give Sky a bath—both of us get splashed—and put him to bed together. Bath time and reading books is a family ritual that brings me so much happiness. Growing up, I remember my mom combing knots out of my hair after bath time and my father singing "Good Night, Ladies" every night to me before bed—until I was thirteen!

7:30 P.M.: In a perfect world, my husband and I sit and have dinner. I order in take-out and we drink a glass of white wine and try not to talk about work. Sometimes we are both in bed by 11:00 p.m. and watch reruns of *Friends* and *Will & Grace* while returning e-mails. But it's more likely that we go out to dinner or have an event three times a week. It's important to make time to support my peers by attending everything from editorial dinners to store openings to product launch parties.

Next spread, left: Fitting a model. Center: Rachel Zoe styling studio. Right: In the design studio.

GET IN THE MOOD

Sometimes, the seed of one of my collections is an image. Mick Jagger pouting in a purple velvet slim-cut suit helped me conceptualize my designs for my Fall 2012 looks. Brigitte Bardot frolicking in the South of France with Serge Gainsbourg inspired my dresses for Spring 2013. I will stare at a shot and absorb its spirit—whether it is flirtatious, it has a sense of unbridled sensuality, or something else. It could also be a swatch of caramel leather that piques my creativity. Or a simple stud on a shred of corduroy. In essence, inspiration comes in so many forms, both visual and tactile. So when I sit down to design, I always try to capture the essence of my collection with the help of a mood board. What begins with a few random photos and pieces of fabric might eventually come together as the sensibility and texture of a cropped leather jacket or a pair of pintuck pants.

> "WHEN I SIT DOWN TO CONCEPTUALIZE A
> COLLECTION, MY MIND ALWAYS TIME TRAVELS
> TO FASHION MOMENTS THAT INSPIRE ME."

Inspiration boards make great starting points for refining your own personal style, too. If you admire Kate Moss's look, tack up a few shots of her in outfits and study her choice of color, silhouettes, and accessories. This can help you focus on the feel and look of an overwhelming event such as a wedding. You don't need fancy supplies to make one—I rely on basic black bulletin boards and clear pushpins, but a blank wall and a roll of tape works in a pinch. There are so many great digital and online tools for making mood boards now, too. And don't be intimidated by a blank one. Nothing is permanent. I post things and then shift them around or replace them all the time. Have fun with it.

POWERFUL INSPIRATIONS

I'm fascinated by the history of fashion and its standout moments. The silhouettes, fabrics, and even hemlines say so much about the cultural currency of the time. It's no shock that the miniskirt made a splash in the sixties just as women were joining the workforce and reveling in their new-found independence. Mary Quant, reportedly the original designer of the miniskirt, once said that she was inspired to shorten the skirt so girls could run to catch the bus. How cool is that?

When I sit down to conceptualize a collection, my mind always time travels to fashion moments that inspire me. I might reflect on Cristóbal Balenciaga's nod to architecture or Elsa Schiaparelli's passion for whimsy and vibrant color. But you don't need to be a designer to appreciate the past through a prism of style. I often think about a certain decade and its fashion highlights when I get dressed in the morning. If I want to feel particularly empowered, I might think about how a sleek three-piece suit inspired by the late sixties with gold accessories instills me with confidence. Or I might gravitate toward something sequined and off the shoulder that feels more deco as I get ready for a splashy cocktail party. Certain moments in fashion history always influence my personal style and runway collections.

LE SMOKING BY YVES SAINT LAURENT

Catherine Deneuve once said, "The thing about a tuxedo is that it is virile and feminine at the same time." For sure. Yves Saint Laurent's strong-shouldered, formal pantsuit, which debuted in 1966, is always in the back of my mind when I design. It's the most iconic way for a woman to dress, in my opinion. Put on a tux and you suddenly feel strong, confident, and sensual. Like Deneuve observed, it's a unique juxtaposition of the soft and strong.

Make it modern: Go ahead and gender bend. A tailored velvet blazer always looks timeless with great trousers or even denim—high-waisted or skinny. It's an androgynous kind of sexy that reads cool and bold. I love to juxtapose the formality of a tuxedo jacket or trousers with a satin side stripe alongside the casual look of a white tee.

Clockwise from left: The bias cut by Vionnet. The "New Look" by Christian Dior. The Missoni caftan.

THE BIAS CUT BY VIONNET

This Parisian couturier reinvented sensuality with her mastery of the bias cut: a technique of halving fabric on a diagonal so that it skims every curve of the body. Those 1930s liquid silk gowns worn by screen legends Jean Harlow and Carole Lombard come to mind whenever I think of Madeleine Vionnet, who pinned and draped her dresses on a form instead of sketching designs. She was really the first "body-con" designer—her figure-hugging creations are discreetly sexy as any bandage dress.

Make it modern: I love to juxtapose the proportions of an elegant bias-cut silk chiffon gown with a cropped marabou or faux fur chubby—it's very old Hollywood. Or you can add some street chic to the silhouette with a leather bolero jacket.

THE "NEW LOOK" BY CHRISTIAN DIOR

In February 1947, Christian Dior shocked and awed Paris when he debuted his spring-summer collection. The designer showed accentuated and hourglass silhouettes in decadent fabrics as a tribute to the female form. There were full skirts and jackets with nipped-in peplum waists and sensually rounded shoulders. It was so well received that women attending the fashion show actually mobbed him afterward—and I would have been right there with them. I love the structure in the peplum jackets and the corsetry in the skirts. And I'm always amazed by how he used a form like a figure eight in his clothes to highlight feminine curves.

Make it modern: Every woman should own one blouse or jacket with a peplum waist, which looks great with skinny jeans or a pencil skirt to vary the proportions. I see peplum as a shortcut to looking polished—that cinch instantly delivers a bombshell silhouette. I like to accessorize it with a bold necklace or statement pendant.

THE MISSONI CAFTAN

My dad had a major thing for Missoni sweaters when I was growing up. Every time he went to Italy, he would come home with a new one. I always admired the colorful knits and patterns, but I didn't become a true fan until my first visit to Italy. I saw the scarves and sweaters and caftans and realized that the brand was more about a bohemian lifestyle than it was just about the label. It's amazing to think that this fashion empire began in the early fifties, with the husband and wife founders, Ottavio and Rosita Missoni, creating their own knits. They revolutionized sportswear, inventing that signature zigzag knit on a special machine. I bought my first vintage Missoni caftan when I was nineteen and have since acquired too many to count.

Make it modern: You can spot a Missoni caftan from a mile away—once you get closer, you're intrigued by the intricacies of the knits. I'm not sure how in the world they make some of those unexpected disparate color palettes work, but they always do. I sometimes like to pair mine with a skinny belt or structured jacket to contrast its etherealness. To look a bit more polished, pull your hair into a sleek topknot or wear it down and straight instead of opting for beachy waves or a more tousled style.

THE DIANE VON FURSTENBERG WRAP DRESS

Diane von Furstenberg captured exactly how women wanted to feel in 1972: empowered but at ease. Her jersey knit wrap dress couldn't be more flattering or comfortable. I marvel at the fact that the shoulders are unstructured and yet the silhouette is so strong. This dress looks great on any body type, never wrinkles, and wears as easily as a bathrobe. I also love that DVF once said of her inspiration for the iconic dress: "Well, if you're trying to slip out without waking a sleeping man, zips are a nightmare." That statement in itself epitomized female empowerment at the time of its creation.

Make it modern: The genius of this style of dress is its classic, timeless appeal. You can buy vintage DVF prints from the seventies, which I adore, or you can invest in one of her contemporary versions. I like to wear mine with a stacked wood heel and two bold cuffs on either arm to heighten its power-dress appeal.

THE TURBAN BY ELSA SCHIAPARELLI

The Italian-born aristocrat had a penchant for shocking avant-garde creations. She was the first one to put zippers on the outside of her designs; she collaborated with the surrealist Salvador Dalí; and she established hot pink as her signature color. That's quite a life. She was ahead of her time, so it's no wonder she also had a thing for turbans, one of my favorite daring fashion accessories. They just add instant allure to any look.

Make it modern: I love a simple black satin turban with a long white dress or casual denim worn with a tee and a fitted blazer. The headband version is the easiest and most current way to wear one. A few years ago, I wore a satin turban on Thanksgiving and cooked my turkey looking like a 1940s screen siren. I know it's silly, but why not feel super glamourous while chopping vegetables? I paid homage to Schiap (as she is known) at the 2012 Metropolitan Museum of Art Costume Ball when I designed a rose-gold gown and matching turban for model Karolina Kurkova—it was one of the most surreal moments of my career.

THE COCOON COAT BY CRISTÓBAL BALENCIAGA

Leave it to the genius Spanish couturier to revolutionize proportions and upend the hourglass silhouette with the sack dress, balloon skirt, and my favorite, the 1957 cocoon coat. Thanks to him, geometric forms became fashion. His statement coat with oversized buttons and shorter sleeves allowed a woman to showcase jewelry and elegant leather gloves. The jumbo collar also elongated her neck. Ah, what a difference a few cuts can make!

Make it modern: Oversized silhouettes in outerwear like cocoon coats appear on runways with regularity. I like to see the voluminous shape contrasted with formfitting separates like slim-cut trousers or skinny jeans tucked into knee-high boots. Steer away from pairing the style with an A-line frock, which can swallow you whole and look too retro.

THE ANDRÉ COURRÈGES SPACE AGE COLLECTION

The French designer, who studied civil engineering and favored the architect Le Corbusier, took his cues from technology and futurism in 1964 when he introduced a lunar mission–inspired fashion line. Tunics and minidresses with clean lines, cutouts, and geometric adornments were paired with flat white boots that skimmed the knees. Courrèges made wearing white fashionable all year round, which I believe in, too.

Make it modern: Somehow, the streamlined sixties-inspired dresses and suits still look incredibly modern—fifty years later. The trick to making the styles feel current is to accessorize with on-trend accents like ankle boots or a motorcycle jacket. You don't want to overdo it and emulate all the iconic beauty looks of that era with both pale pink lipstick *and* Twiggy-style over-the-top eyelashes.

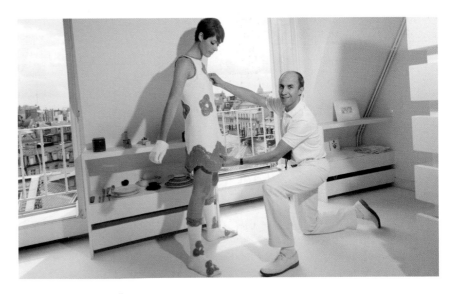

Coco Chanel in her suit

COCO CHANEL'S SUIT

The iconic designer once called her suit "the fashion statement of the century" and I couldn't agree more. She wore her first one in 1910 and at the time, it was a groundbreaking move to challenge the norms of femininity. She even bobbed her hair to further flip off what was socially acceptable for women at that time. When I wear this style, I feel unstoppable. To me, this look is forever. I have said that if I could be known as a designer for great suiting, I would be happy. Every season, I focus on creating these eclectic ensembles that are both classic and current.

Make it modern: The beauty of a well-cut suit—Chanel or otherwise—is that you can wear it thirty different ways. I think it's the best investment a woman can make, in fact. Wear the trousers with a simple silk tank or a sequined top; anchor a flowing day dress or a long caftan with the jacket. You can also pair the jacket with shorts or a miniskirt. It's such a versatile staple.

"THE BEAUTY OF A WELL-CUT SUIT—CHANEL OR
OTHERWISE—IS THAT YOU CAN WEAR IT
THIRTY DIFFERENT WAYS. I THINK IT'S THE BEST
INVESTMENT A WOMAN CAN MAKE, IN FACT."

THE MINIMALISTIC GLAMOUR OF HALSTON

At first glance, a Halston design looks so simple. But when you get closer and dissect its construction, you see that it's actually quite complex. To me, that assessment sums up Halston's talent and appeal on so many levels. This man—with his perpetual tan, cashmere turtlenecks, and movie-star smirk—managed to make glamour feel effortless, accessible, and super easy. There's nothing fussy or overly structured about his draped dresses and pleated pantsuits. He understood that women want to look sexy but not distasteful. A Halston one-shoulder jersey dress or cowl back jumpsuit do that perfectly.

Make it modern: Because the designs appear so minimal, I love to pair Halston with bold gold jewelry such as oversized earrings or a collar. Obviously, the pieces are all different, but you can avoid looking like you just left Studio 54 by wearing your hair in a contemporary chignon or side part. But if you want to pay full homage to retro chic, go for it with straight hair parted down the middle and a strappy sandal. I'm such a sucker for that look.

FEAR FACTOR

People often ask me why it took so long for me to launch my eponymous line. My first collection debuted to editors and retailers in spring of 2011 (when I was seven months pregnant) and hit stores that fall. The truth is this: I knew—from consulting with many designers over a dozen years—just how much focus and devotion creating a signature line would entail. Being a designer is a full-time job. I already had a full plate with styling clients such as Anne Hathaway, Kate Hudson, and Jennifer Garner.

"MY PERSONAL CAREER ADVICE IS THAT FEAR CAN BE A WONDERFUL MOTIVATOR. ONCE YOU FEEL COMPLACENT OR TOO COMFORTABLE, FIND A NEW HURDLE."

And did I mention I was also terrified? Just the idea of putting myself out there gave me emotional hives. I entered this business as a stylist, which kept me behind the scenes. This role reversal meant everyone in the front row would now be critiquing *my* designs. What motivated me, besides my fantastic creative team, was taking on a new challenge. Oscar de la Renta has often told me that he is still nervous before his runway shows—although he appears totally calm. This is a man who trained with Balenciaga and dressed Jackie Kennedy! He said that if he ever stops feeling nervous, it's time to find a new job.

Ironically, just days before that conversation, I had said the very same thing at a conference for fashion and beauty bloggers. My personal career advice is that fear can be a wonderful motivator. Once you feel complacent or too comfortable, find a new hurdle. When I first went out on my own as a stylist, there was no safety net. The hustle was endless, and on days that no work came my way, I channeled my anxiety into drive and ambition. And those same feelings—though in a different context—still motivate me today.

With every collection, I wonder, "Will the editors and critics like it?" and "Will women buy it?" It's not quite a full-on panic, but I can tell you that at times, it's a form of adrenaline that wakes me in the middle of the night with my heart thumping. It also sometimes drives me to act out—like cutting bangs the night before my New York runway show in fall 2012. But in the end, every ounce of anxiety is worth it: I am living my dream. And

I hope that my unconventional path and honesty inspire you, too. Apply for that fashion editor job, launch a style blog, sit down and sketch a ball gown. Remember: If it makes you a little anxious, that's a good thing.

IN EVERY COLLECTION

There has been so much written about building a closet around must-have basics. Fashion editors insist that you should own a navy blazer; friends will tell you that no closet is complete without a pencil skirt. My take? As a new designer, I'm always thinking about the anchors of my collections that work for *every day* and for *forever.*

No matter the season, there are about ten pieces that I will always send down the runway. I strive to make glamorous *wearable* clothes for modern women, whether they're working overtime or jet-setting through time zones. That's my mission. My idea of a basic is a trusted look that works with almost everything—and is anything but basic.

> "I STRIVE TO MAKE GLAMOROUS *WEARABLE* CLOTHES FOR MODERN WOMEN…THAT'S MY MISSION."

SOMETHING SEQUINED: There is no easier way to cheat glamour than with a little sparkle. Sequins don't need to be overly glitzy or precious. They might be leather or suede or even clear paillettes. But I use them in myriad forms and you'll always find a sequined jacket, dress, or blouse in my designs. They go with everything!

CRISP DENIM: Nothing beats a great pair of jeans. I love a denim look that is clean and modern. Find a denim silhouette that works for you—whether it be a skinny- or wide-leg—and dress those jeans up with stilettos and a silk blouse.

A VERSATILE JUMPSUIT: I slip on a one-piece and instantly feel casually elegant. Every one of my collections includes a carefree and relaxed jumpsuit with pockets for keys and a phone, as well as a more structured, sophisticated version. It's my take on loungewear.

THE LEATHER JACKET: It could be a bomber, a biker, or a blazer, but you should own one for the cool factor alone. Its versatility will astound you once you start experimenting. Wear it with a mini and a tank or even with an evening gown—a contrast I adore. I'm a fiend for all stylish outerwear, whether it's a peacoat or a swing style or a fitted one with military flair such as epaulets. I don't subscribe to the old rule that a coat hem has to exceed that of a dress or skirt beneath it. In fact, a floor-length skirt looks fantastic with a cropped winter coat. One trick I have learned is to wear thin layers underneath so I don't get overheated if I want to keep it on inside.

A TYPE OF TUXEDO: The first piece I ever designed was a double-breasted button-front tuxedo minidress with a notched collar. (I almost did a cartwheel when Jennifer Lopez was later photographed in it.) Dating back to the late 1800s, this tailored formalwear always looks elegant, but modern, too. I particularly like a nontraditional approach, like a tuxedo jumpsuit or dress.

THE WHITE BUTTON-UP SHIRT: I can never get enough of this staple, even though we have seen more than a million incarnations of it. Every season, I design one with a different collar, cuff, or sleeve. This versatile piece looks great with skinny jeans, leather pants, a pencil skirt, and even a maxi skirt.

A CHUNKY KNIT: I think there is a misconception of sweaters being frumpy and conservative. As a designer and stylist, I believe I can make knitwear sexy. That might come across in a sweater dress or a cropped chunky knit worn with a white tank and leggings. I also love an oversized sweater, which can be cozy and luxurious, especially when traveling.

THE THREE-PIECE SUIT: There's a bit of an equestrian and a Victorian feel to this amazing look that takes androgynous femininity to a whole new level. Whether it's a downtown pinstripe skinny suit worn with biker boots or a Park Avenue camel hair ensemble with wide-leg pants, a three-piece suit always looks confident and cool. Best of all, you have great separates to play with.

THE "SURE THING" DRESS: For most women, a no-brainer look is a fit and flare dress that flatters every body type—it gives you a waist and makes your legs look longer. I like one in a neutral tone that you can change up completely with different accessories like boots or lots of metal jewelry or a bolero jacket. Every season, I do a fit and flare and it has become a favorite among my friends.

A MAXI SKIRT: I have lived by this staple for as long as I can remember and I own at least a dozen of them. It's the best way to look glamourous *and* feel comfortable. You never have to be self-aware in a maxi because you are wearing a floor-skimming silhouette that allows you to move freely without being self-conscious about flashing anyone. In essence, it's chic loungewear that looks great with almost everything, from a classic button-down to a slouchy tee to a boyfriend blazer.

I can go on about the art of fashion—from the amazing and pivotal designers to their standout pieces—for hours. But it's the way in which *you* personalize a dress with a bold enamel pendant or a brightly printed scarf that makes it memorable. Yves Saint Laurent once said, "Fashions fade, style is eternal." He knew that even his most exquisite designs called for interpretation by whoever wore them. I couldn't agree more.

When I sketch a suit or a dress, it's just the first step to creating a fantastic look. Even when I see my collection on hangers, it looks incomplete in a way. Why? Because it's up to you to take fashion to a new level by making it your own. Now that we have explored how I became obsessed with beautiful clothes and why certain designers will forever inspire me, it's time to talk about style. Your style.

CHAPTER 2

DEFINE YOUR STYLE

I'm not staring at your shoes. Really. People who don't know me assume that I judge everyone's outfits, from head to toe—not true. In fact, I'm never critical. I appreciate individual style and that has little to do with who can collect the most expensive designer bags or ankle boots. In the art world, you need a ton of money to become a major collector. In fashion, anyone can put together an amazing look—even on a dime. And I love that sense of democracy. All you need is a go-to signature style.

Top: My mom, Leslie.
Bottom: Modeling,
age 18.

Growing up, my older sister, Pamela, and my mom both unwittingly helped me to shape my style. In my eyes, they were both so effortlessly glamourous. My sister and her friends all ran around in sky-high heels and lots of makeup. My mother, as dramatic in her everyday look as Elizabeth Taylor, never left the house without deep crimson lips and a dozen accessories. She layered sculptural gold necklaces, favored oversized cocktail rings, and wore of-the-moment designers like Norma Kamali and Thierry Mugler. As a little girl with a big personality in suburban New Jersey, all I wanted to do was establish my own personal style like they had, and stand out for it. I still wear many of the accessories that I have "borrowed" from my mom over the years. Her affinity for layering pieces is one of her signatures that became my own, too.

My look was probably at its most creative in my early twenties. I scoured Manhattan thrift stores with a vengeance and experimented with wearing clothes every which way. I often say that the most inventively stylish people I know are the ones on a tight budget. An intern in my office might wear a great vintage locket as a chain belt or a bold ethnic scarf as an obi. I always notice and appreciate that type of ingenuity when it comes to fashion. Never mind a picture—in my opinion, an outfit is worth a thousand words. I encourage you to take some time to evaluate your own look and make sure it's an extension of your personality.

When anyone asks me how to find or even refine her signature style, I offer a few simple suggestions that always help me. Yes, I even reexamine my style now and again to make sure that it suits my current lifestyle. My first tip is to look to anyone whose style you admire. It could be a friend, colleague, sibling, or celebrity. My own look is always grounded in that of the late sixties and early seventies and if I had to name my singular fashion idol from that period, it would be Jane Birkin. (Later on in this chapter, we'll break down her iconic style.)

Be sure to immerse yourself in your icon's style. Look for pictures of her online if she is famous and peruse her fashion habits. If your icon is a friend, ask her to define her personal style and even tour her closet. Does she wear a lot of bohemian peasant tops with skinny jeans and equestrian boots? Or is she more polished, in herringbone suits with silk chiffon blouses and platform pumps? Either way, after you take notes on her nuances, you can look to see if you have similar pieces in your own wardrobe. It's so much easier to shop once you know exactly what you need!

Figure out your fashion comfort zone. Every woman I know and client I style has an excess of one thing in her closet. You do, too, no doubt. Look at your own clothes and see which piece or pieces dominate. If my closet could talk, it would scream "Stop buying jackets, Rachel!" But I can't help myself! Tailored jackets are my happy place. And more important, they work for me. You need to determine if your staple does the same for you. If you have a surplus of chunky knit cardigans or pencil skirts, you can assume that these pieces comprise that sartorial comfort zone. We tend to buy the same piece over and over—in different shades and fabrics—because it's safe and familiar. Hopefully, these particular items are major assets to your style.

One easy way to find out is to do this: Try on a few of them in front of a full-length mirror and truthfully assess how they look on you from every angle. Take pictures so that you can be as objective as possible. Be sure to pair them with a number of other pieces to gauge how they work within your daily wardrobe. You should also access how you feel emotionally when you wear these clothes. If you're hiding under oversized sweaters, you probably broadcast insecurity when you wear them; it might be time to experiment with tops that accentuate your natural silhouette and *don't* swallow you up. If you put on a pencil skirt and immediately feel like you can ask for a promotion, that's a powerful piece in your fashion arsenal and one you should keep.

Trust your instincts, but don't be afraid to ask a friend or a spouse to step in as reinforcement. Just make sure it's someone who has great taste and won't be too harsh in the critique. When I'm on the fence about my outfit, I turn to Rodger. Let's face it: I've been with this man for more than twenty years and he knows me better than anyone. So much of looking fantastic comes from feeling truly confident in your look. Rodger can tell in a second if I'm pulling on the bodice of a vintage silk dress or tugging at the sleeves of a knit caftan. He knows from my anxious pout and furrowed brow if I want to turn around and change. So I trust him when he tells me I look unforgettable or uncomfortable. Then again, there are times when he scratches his head at one of my fashion-forward getups and I say, "Babe, this is a fashion thing and I don't need a straight man's opinion. I'm not trying to look hot today."

My final tip for developing your individual style involves a little word play. Think of an adjective—or even a few—that describes how you want to look and feel. *Glamourous* is always on the forefront of my mind when I get dressed. That doesn't mean I walk out the door every morning in Grecian-inspired Halston gowns and faux fur stoles. I also want to look and feel *effortless* and *strong*. For me, these words don't need to be translated literally with specific pieces. They more summon the spirit of my style. I might access *glamourous* with one of the bold deco-chic cuffs I designed with enamel, jade, and pavé rhinestones. Once I slip it on, I immediately feel more cosmopolitan. I get to *effortless* by wearing my hair in loose Brigitte Bardot–esque waves or throwing a tuxedo jacket over my shoulders. *Strong* might come from an oversized structured bag or a tailored suit. You can also think about how you would want someone else to describe your style in a few choice words. If *polished* and *classic* come to mind, go for timeless pieces like wool crepe day dresses and silk chiffon blouses. Craving a *bohemian* aura? Think about amassing printed maxi dresses, caftans, and silk-gauze wide-leg pants.

Once you have your look down, you can build a wardrobe that embodies your signature style—and also edit out the pieces that don't complement your fashion personae. The major payoff to cultivating your signature style is the confidence you feel because your look says it all: "This is who I am."

*In Wolford tights, Paris
Fashion Week, 2011*

ACCENTUATE WHAT'S GREAT

Coco Chanel once said that showing your knees was "hardly ever pretty." (I love it when my all-time idol and I think alike!) I don't like my knees. I can't even pinpoint why, exactly, except to say that they look a little chickeny. In fact, you won't find a recent picture of me in shorts or a minidress unless I'm also wearing opaque tights. Rationally, I know that my joints are totally normal, of course. But the reality is that I am uncomfortable when I expose them. So I don't.

Instead, I dress to highlight my upper body, thanks to a long torso, defined, feminine shoulders, and an elongated neck. I showcase these favorite features by wearing open necklines and off-the-shoulder dresses or tanks. Long necklaces also give the illusion of extending the upper body. Once you know which areas you want to accentuate, focus on necklines, silhouettes, sleeves, and hemlines that do just that. Fashion is a lot like magic, and over years of styling dozens of women, I have developed more than a few tricks for highlighting your best features.

GIVE AN INCH: When it comes to hemlines, even a half-inch alteration can extend the line of the leg. Experiment with the length of a skirt or dress to see where your hem falls best. Just above or below the knee is usually the sweet spot, but trust your eye and instinct.

THE PRICE OF GOLD (AND SILVER): As much as I adore metallic fabrics, their reflective quality can make you appear larger if you have va-va-voom curves. By the same token, that effect may be something you're going for, depending on your body type. Examine how light hits a metallic dress or consider a separate such as gold lamé capri pants or a silver sequined top.

CINCH EFFECT: If you want your torso to appear longer, wear a belt on the lowest point of your natural waistline. Or, a wide belt worn a little higher than your waist always creates more of a classic hourglass silhouette.

MAX OUT: Do not fear the maxi dress. I swear, it works for everyone. If you're petite, wear it with heels (and be sure the hemline still touches the floor) or opt for one that is more fitted with less volume.

BETWEEN THE LINES: Contrary to what people say, horizontal stripes do not always add bulk. I find that skinnier stripes—such as the ones on a French sailor sweater—are the most flattering. Trust me: Stripes actually make you look taller. Also, a racer stripe on the side of a pair of pants tricks the eye and makes you look leaner by elongating the leg.

LEAN LIMBS: A bishop's sleeve, which is fitted from the shoulder to the elbow and then flares slightly, always looks elegant and leans out the upper arms.

NECKLINE KNOW-HOW: A choker worn just above the collarbone will make your neck appear longer. I swear by this one. Long necklaces—with a dress or separates—also extend the line of the body, so you look taller and slimmer overall.

GO NUDE: To create the illusion of longer legs, slip into a pair of nude platform wedges or pumps—the higher, the better. Be sure to match the shade to your skin tone—whether it's a true taupe or more of a dusky pale rose—so that the pumps appear to be an extension of your gams. Avoid T-straps, which bisect the line and shorten the leg.

WHITE HOT: I adore white all year round because it brightens the skin. It makes you look fresh and stand out in a sea of black. Experiment with different shades to find what complements your complexion. Stark snow white can wash out someone fair, but works best for darker skin tones. A silk white, winter white, or off-white—*blanc cassé* in French—could be much more flattering for you.

KICK OFF: Dark denim is *always* more slimming than a lighter wash. A pair of midrise jeans with a kick or flare below the knee—whether it is a wide-leg or a boot-cut style—is elongating for everyone, I promise you. I love skinny jeans, but the reality is they are not universally flattering; tall, boyish figures fare best in the silhouette.

MY FASHION UNIFORM

The idea of a uniform may sound drab to you, but it's actually the best-kept secret of every stylish woman. If there's one thing I learned as a stylist, it's that no one—not even movie stars with outrageous bodies—wakes up super excited to get dressed every single morning. Even some of the most gorgeous actresses have issues with their bodies. Besides, some days you just feel exhausted or uninspired. Maybe you danced until 3:00 a.m. Maybe your precious toddler crawled into your bed and said, "Wake up, Mommy!" in the middle of the night.

"WHETHER YOU'RE A WORKING WOMAN, A FULL-TIME STUDENT, OR A NEW MOM, YOU SHOULDN'T COMPROMISE YOUR STYLE. FOR SURE, FUNCTIONAL CAN BE FASHIONABLE."

I have a few different uniforms, depending upon where I am working and whom I will see on any given day. On a usual day in Los Angeles, my go-to look is basically a pair of wide-leg or bell-bottom jeans worn with a T-shirt, tunic, or tank and a statement jacket. For footwear, it's usually platform wedges that allow me to move around fast and comfortably. I definitely have a practical sensibility, but still always aim to look chic. Whether you're a working woman, a full-time student, or a new mom, you shouldn't compromise your style. For sure, functional can be fashionable. Before I even enter my closet in the morning, I ask myself three questions.

Left: A typical NYC "uniform."
Right: A typical LA "uniform."

WHAT'S ON MY SCHEDULE? First, I muse on my entire day—from tasks to appointments—and consider which clothes will carry me through every hour. If I know I will be running from one meeting to another or standing all day at a fitting, I opt for outfits that move with me. No fussy silk blouses or heavy accessories. You might see me in a maxi skirt with a soft tee and a knit duster.

WHO AM I SEEING TODAY? Am I tweaking a collection all day in the showroom with my team? My outfit can be stripped down and easy: high-waisted denim with a cashmere sweater and heels. But if clients are coming into the office or I'm styling an actress for an event, I add a structured jacket with a lot of hardware. It's smart to save those super-chic accents for days when you really need them.

HOW LONG IS MY DAY? It's very rare that my working day ends at sunset. I always make time to run home to feed Skyler and put him down to sleep before I head back out for a dinner or fashion event. Still, I get dressed in the morning with my evening agenda in mind. You might dash to drinks, a business dinner, or a date right from work. To make that transition from office to after-hours as seamless as possible, wear an outfit that transforms easily. A simple black jumpsuit, for instance, gets an upgrade with a fur vest, higher heels, and a few gold cuffs. And don't forget to add a smoky eye or a red lip.

Of course, I always infuse my day-to-day look with a little glamour. My fashion talisman is a pair of black tuxedo pants. I swear, they are magic when it comes to amping up a simple outfit. My preference is a pair in a good crepe or georgette that won't wrinkle during the day and I always insist on a little stretch so that they give when I'm dashing around. A pair of great dark jeans that look crisp and clean can always work for me, too. Once you nail your uniform, it's easy to shop for chic variations on it.

WHEN IN DOUBT, EVOLVE

Yes, finding a signature look is key. But never straying from that look or updating it will land you in a rut. Your style is a lot like any long-term relationship. If you don't shake things up once in a while and experiment, boredom sneaks in. If I look at pictures of myself over the past decade, I can see a decided shift in my style.

At any given moment five or so years ago, you would have found me wafting around in an ethereal floor-length caftan with huge sunnies, eighteen necklaces, and strappy brown sandals—even in the middle of January. I was going for this South of France vibe all year round. Maybe I took living in L.A. too literally. Nowadays, my style is a lot less bohemian and slightly more practical—I like to think that it's more refined and polished. For inspiration now, I look to street style in cities like Paris and London instead of far-flung beaches. I can think of six great reasons to reevaluate your closet.

> "YOUR STYLE IS A LOT LIKE ANY LONG-TERM RELATIONSHIP. IF YOU DON'T SHAKE THINGS UP ONCE IN A WHILE AND EXPERIMENT, BOREDOM SNEAKS IN."

HAVING A CHILD: I can't even begin to list the many wonderful ways motherhood has changed my life, but I will say that my clothes are no longer as precious. Most outfits must be more durable and able to withstand tugs from tiny hands and sticky fingerprint smears. I choose soft cottons and crepe wools over delicate fabrics such as silk chiffon or crochet knits. Maybe that's why I wear so much black now, too!

FALLING IN OR OUT OF LOVE: Clearly, a life pivot like going solo after a long-term relationship calls for a fresh eye on your wardrobe. Maybe it's time to reinvent your look—even dress up a little more. Similarly, a new romance—or a sudden crush—is a great excuse to take stock of your sartorial staples or try something new.

CAREER MOVE: When I added fashion designer to my résumé, I needed to revamp my look for meetings with conservative investors and buttoned-up buyers. My urban boho style begged for more architecture and edge with an infusion of sophisticated and tailored pieces. I added structured bags to my accessories and swapped teetering sandals for more empowered platform pumps and ankle boots. The metamorphosis didn't just alter my appearance, though. With my new career—and a staff of thirty executives, editors, stylists, and assistants to oversee—I needed pieces that made me feel more effectual and authoritative.

SCALE FLUCTUATION: Obviously, pregnancy calls for roomier clothes. For me, maternity wear consisted mostly of bubble dresses, leggings, long caftans, and lots of scarves to deflect the focus from my expanding waist.

Still, any time you gain or lose more than ten or fifteen pounds, you should try on your clothes and reassess the fit. A tailor can nip in or let out a seam if you go down or up a size. If it requires more than a quick fix, decide if you plan to stay at this new weight and shop accordingly. Wearing clothes that constrict will only gnaw at your self-esteem, and the same goes for garments that are now too large and barely skim your figure.

NEW HOME: A major move calls for a wardrobe check. When I first moved from Manhattan to Los Angeles, my all-black staples from power suits to body-con dresses suddenly felt severe and forced. On the West Coast, effortless chic rules. No one wears tights or conservative black pumps or even pleats. I have seen film executives in flip-flops! Back in New York and other East Coast cities, breezing into a boardroom in an ikat silk maxi dress and gold gladiator sandals will get you demoted. So if you relocate from a small town to a city or to a whole new time zone, be sure to take note of the style of your new locale. You don't have to conform, but you might find some surprising and flattering new additions to your look if you're open to adapting. Of course, a dramatic climate change requires new staples.

MILESTONE BIRTHDAY: Whether you're turning twenty-five or forty, a significant birthday is an ideal time to scrutinize your inventory. First of all, you can figure out what you want to splurge on and think of it as a gift to yourself. Do you need a leopard-print belt or a pair of riding boots? Treat yourself. Second, there's a chance that you have outgrown—both figuratively and literally—a few items. Ten years ago, I wore tailored shorts, which I no longer do. That's not to say that you should toss your short skirts or shorts when you say hello to forty as a rule. It's more of a personal comfort level and yes, a matter of taste. At forty, it may be time to retire the midriff-baring tops and cut-off denim shorts. But then again, some women still manage to pull it off, so maybe not. A milestone is a good time to reassess, nonetheless.

VINTAGE: HUNTING AND GATHERING

Without a doubt, my love for vintage has formed the foundation of my signature style. Even as a teenager, I had no interest in wearing the latest trend or designer du jour. If it was cool to wear what everyone else wore, I bypassed cool. While my friends in New Jersey bought Benetton sweaters and Guess jeans, I browsed the flea market stands in Soho for mod shifts and major costume jewelry.

One reason for collecting vintage is simply that in most cases, no one else will have it. When I first started styling, I knew that adding vintage accessories and pieces into my clients' red-carpet looks would make them stand out. But wearing a midcentury modern big brass cuff or a vintage biker jacket also relays this instinctive sense of style. It shows that you can breeze into a retro boutique or thrift shop or estate sale and strike gold (sometimes literally).

When I was younger, buying vintage was also a way to access fantastic pieces on a meager budget. Some of my favorite looks cost under fifty dollars. I can still recall this architectural military jacket I found in a thrift shop that I wore to death. There was a leather bomber jacket, too. (Clearly, my jacket fetish started early on.) But my biggest vintage coup back in the day was a seventies Gucci coat with original horse-bit accents. It's still hanging in my closet and looks as glamourous today as it did twenty-five years ago.

It's easy to go crazy and buy everything chic in sight. Trust me, I know. These days, I seek out only seminal designer pieces that bear a stamp or label. (That was Rodger's advice after watching me take over every single inch of closet space in our home.) My friend William Banks-Blaney in London has an insane vintage boutique and he drops me a line if he gets in a breathtaking Dior cocktail dress, a YSL piece from one of his most famous collections, or an amazing Courrèges jacket. Over the years, I have willed myself to think twice, even three times, before I purchase yet another caftan or cocktail ring. In Chapter 3, my mom, Leslie, will share her tried-and-true tips on shopping vintage, but here's what goes through my head before I get to the register.

DOES IT FIT? A great but ill-fitting piece might be inexpensive, but I always consider the cost of tailoring, too. Reconstructing a dress or jacket can add up, so I never buy anything that will cost as much as its price tag to tailor to my measurements. In essence, ask yourself, "Is it more work than it's worth?"

IS IT IN GOOD CONDITION? I recommend that you avoid damaged pieces—especially if they date back to the pre-fifties, when fabrics were manufactured differently. A small tear is an easy fix for a tailor; obvious stains or elbows that have frayed or thinned require costly cosmetic surgery—and even then, they may never look exactly right.

WILL IT UPDATE? Some vintage pieces can easily be modernized with the addition of a contemporary top, jacket, or shoes. But certain looks—like thick polyester jackets from the seventies or heavy brocade column dresses—will always look costumey and should be avoided.

IS IT REALLY AN INVESTMENT? I have heard many stories of fake designer labels being sewn into marginal designs. If you're looking to splurge on a piece for its heritage, be sure that the label matches the time period—e.g., YSL updates its label every decade—and that the vintage seller has a stellar reputation. Websites such as VintageFashionGuild.com offer authentication resources like a directory of designer labels such as Loris Azzaro and Gilbert Adrian for cross-reference. I also love 1stdibs.com and RessurectionVintage.com, because they give you a little history about a particular piece and you know everything is authentic.

MY STYLE ICONS

It's no surprise that I look to the past for style cues. As I've said, my own aesthetic is anchored in a carefree elegance that reigned in fashion during the sixties and seventies. When I'm musing on my next collection or dressing a client for the red carpet, I always think about the amazingly stylish women who constantly influence me. Each of these icons inspires me in a completely different way, whether it's to play up the sexy appeal of androgyny or to steer more toward an ethereal romanticism. Meet my top ten women of style and enjoy some tips on how you can emulate their glamour with a few key pieces.

THE EVERYDAY BOMBSHELL: BRIGITTE BARDOT

"Every age can be enchanting, provided you live within it."

If only we all woke up looking like my absolute idol. Somehow, Bardot—with her sensually tangled hair and dramatic cat-eye makeup—always nailed effortless glamour. It was as though she had just stepped out of a Mercedes convertible after doing her hair and makeup at seventy-five miles per hour. Even wearing a simple sundress with casual sandals around the South of France, she managed to look extremely sexy without ever looking cheap.

Closet must-haves: An off-the-shoulder sundress, striped bateau sweater, and ballet flats. Accent the look with a thick headband and delicate gold chains.

THE SCENE QUEEN: BIANCA JAGGER

"I don't want to wear what every other woman wears. I won't be dictated to."

Leave it to the Studio 54 staple and Mick Jagger's former muse to wink at masculinity and look even more feminine for it. Jagger wore a custom white Yves Saint Laurent skirt suit to her 1971 Saint-Tropez wedding, and had a penchant for strong lines and tailored silhouettes. But she knew to dabble heavily in Halston's buttery, fluid sheaths whenever she hit the dance floor. She not only defines glamour and sexiness, but disco, too. I reference her often when I'm styling or getting dressed for a night out.

Closet must-haves: A tailored slim-cut suit to wear with pumps and a lace camisole. One vintage seventies disco dress, preferably sequined or threaded with gold Lurex. A long pendant necklace and an envelope clutch make great finishing touches.

THE MIDCENTURY MOD WAIF: EDIE SEDGWICK

"It's not that I'm rebelling. It's that I'm just trying to find another way."

I never get tired of staring at pictures of the socialite whom *Vogue* once called a "youthquaker." With her pale lips, outrageous lashes, and striped blond pixie hair, she defined that whole era of linear sixties mod. I particularly love that she trotted around New York in a black leotard, tights, and a T-shirt because she practiced ballet twice a day—and that this simple look became an "it girl" costume. It's a perfect example of how a signature style can identify you and become a classic.

Closet must-haves: Opaque black tights with a metallic minidress and a mod leopard print coat. Add tassel earrings and lots of Lucite cuffs as points of interest, too.

*Edie Sedgwick on set
with Andy Warhol*

THE CHIC PREP: ALI MACGRAW

"Looking at beautiful things is what makes me the happiest."

With that sleek curtain of shiny black hair and strong, striking features, this classic beauty epitomized the best of Ivy League style. Sure, her role in *Love Story* created a camel hair craze, but her bohemian tomboy look offscreen is worthy of a once-over, too. Her preppy wardrobe staples included knit caps, sleek trousers, and peasant blouses. MacGraw's early style always reminds me of modern-day Ralph Lauren. She really mastered androgyny, but added her own feminine flair with turbans and velvet chokers. I love the photos of her pre-actress days as a model and an assistant to Diana Vreeland at *Vogue*.

Closet must-haves: A long fitted sweater vest and a well-worn pair of brown equestrian boots. Add a knit cloche and chunky Navajo jewelry as accessories.

THE FRENCH CHANTEUSE: JANE BIRKIN

"Keep smiling. It takes ten years off!"

Never mind her huge caramel eyes and those long blunt bangs, this gorgeous woman had an innate sense of personal style that everyone still tries to emulate. It was schoolgirl poet in her short, sweet dresses mixed with nonchalant street chic with her high-waisted denim and peacoats. She's one of my biggest influences when I design. In fact, I think every fashion designer has at least one Jane Birkin moment. She had this habit of never matching and yet her outfits always came together so perfectly. Hermès named what's become their most iconic bag after her—what could be cooler than that?

Closet must-haves: A sixties-style A-line shift, cropped velvet pants, and a pair of Parisian-chic leather ankle boots. Look for a long vintage pendant necklace and slender gold bangles to complete the look.

THE FOLK HEROINE: MARIANNE FAITHFULL

"I wear Chanel. It doesn't go in and out of fashion at all."

There is so much soul to this woman's look, whether she's outfitted in a peasant dress and floppy hat or a miniskirt and silver Mary Janes. Faithfull battled a lot of demons in her early life and her style reflected her struggles and identities—from the happy hippie songbird to the raw, exposed rocker chick. You can see both those sides in her shaggy protective bangs, leather frocks, and high boots. She screams retro rock-and-roll London to me and I can't get enough of that.

Closet must-haves: A lace minidress, flat black ankle boots, and a floral print blazer. Accessorize with a distressed leather backpack and a floppy felt fedora.

THE THINKING WOMAN'S SUPERMODEL: IMAN

"I believe in glamour. I am in favor of a little vanity. Looking good is a commitment to yourself and to others."

Iman and I first bonded over our shared obsession with the disco era and that decade's unabashed celebration of chic. No one rocks a metallic jumpsuit like this multitalented woman, I swear to you. When she wore a maxi skirt and blouse from my resort collection to accept a prestigious award in Beverly Hills in 2011, I nearly melted. Like me, Iman is obsessed with caftans and relies on statement accessories like bold jewelry and knockout shoes to complete her look. But it's her generous spirit and the way in which she carries herself that comes to mind when I look to her for inspiration. She's invincible—the strongest woman I know.

Closet must-haves: A velvet suit with flared pants and fitted jacket and a leather pencil skirt. A chain belt and a graphic choker are signature Iman accents, too.

THE SCREEN SIREN: SOPHIA LOREN

"Sex appeal is fifty percent what you've got and fifty percent what people think you've got."

Was there ever a time that this Italian superstar did not look drop-dead glamourous? I once saw her outside a Golden Globes party at the Beverly Hilton in Los Angeles, walked right up to her, and said, "I never, ever do this, but I have to say that you are AMAZING!" She smiled and replied in her silky Italian accent, "Thaaaank you so much." Loren, with her curves and exotic beauty, has sensuality and elegance down to a science. She wears a flouncy floral frock like it's a bandage dress and always manages to make cleavage a classy accessory in deep scoop necks and plunging V-necks.

Closet must-haves: A sleeveless dress with a flared skirt and fitted bodice. Of course, a few pieces of classic lingerie like satin tap pants and a tulle and lace corset. You can't go wrong with an oversized black straw sun hat and classic nude stiletto pumps as well.

THE DESIGNER MUSE: ANJELICA HUSTON

"Nothing I buy ever looks new, because I have my look down and it's classic."

Models with perfect symmetrical faces couldn't compete with Huston and her bold Cubist features. I love that she highlighted her face as if it were a canvas by wearing her long raven hair in a sleek chignon. Back then, she stood out amid the blond-haired and blue-eyed models, and inspired women who didn't fit the all-American ideal of beauty. Her Irish roots showed in the way she wore tweed separates as eveningwear, and Huston never met a fitted blazer she didn't like. She was a muse and model for both Halston and Valentino in the sixties and seventies—enough said. I also named a pair of high-waisted wide-leg trousers after her in my first collection.

Closet must-haves: A black crepe jumpsuit with a deep V-neck that shows off your clavicle and a one-shoulder party dress. Vintage geometric scarves, a sleek structured bag, and don't-mess-with-me sculptural cuffs all make perfect add-ons.

THE POWER VIXEN: DIANE VON FURSTENBERG

"Your clothes are your friends. Be the woman you want to be."

Let me just say that this woman is the epitome of everything I strive to be—she's a personal hero for so many reasons. Beyond her unique beauty and dynamic sense of style, she exudes this strength and confidence that are just so captivating. She wears everything—from a sequined gown to denim and a tunic—with such authority and ease. If you look at pictures throughout her career, you can see that she has never feared splashy prints and color. Her outfits, even now, always skim her curves and suggest (rather than announce) her sexuality. She's extraordinary in that she's an icon to so many generations of women, even inspiring today's younger set.

Closet must-haves: A wrap dress, of course, long printed dresses, and a sleek fitted blazer that you can push up at the arms. An animal-print cashmere scarf and a clutch with bold hardware work perfectly as accents.

Diane von Furstenberg

CAMERA READY

The red carpet terrifies me. I have been photographed many times at this point, but I would be lying if I said I feel at ease with flashbulbs in my face. That said, I try to follow the tips I pass along to my clients for nailing a photo op.

Bypass the shimmer and glitter. That dewy look we all love often reads as perspiration in a photo.

When posing, to avoid coming across as stiff and very pageantlike, just keep your arms relaxed at your sides to show off your outfit.

Berry lips with a blue undertone make teeth look whiter. Nude and magenta hues aren't as flattering.

Small prints have a tendency to strobe or blur in a photo, so go with a solid or a larger graphic print.

Play Mario Testino. I take pictures of my clients from every angle—the back, the front, the side, from above and below—before I send them off to face the paparazzi. You can check your makeup by taking a quick shot in natural light and then ask a friend to photograph you full-length as I do for my clients.

While a sleek chignon can be the most elegant of coifs, it can look severe in a photo because you can't see the actual bun. I always pull out a few wisps around the face to soften the style.

TAKE A FASHION LEAP

Once you have found your fashion comfort zone, take a risk. If you always wear long sleeves, I dare you to slip into a strapless dress. Think you loathe the color red? Stop by a makeup counter and experiment with a berry lip. When it comes to style, my mantra is: "Just try it once." That applies to my own daily wardrobe decisions as well as to my work as a designer and a stylist. I once wore a vibrant yellow velvet Marc Jacobs gown to the Met Gala.

"ONCE YOU HAVE FOUND YOUR FASHION COMFORT ZONE, TAKE A RISK."

Yes, I had stepped out of my fashion comfort zone. But in the end, I felt really special wearing my friend's dress on such a major fashion night. It was definitely a "moment" for me.

When I first meet with an actress as a stylist, I always ask her if she's "highly allergic" to any colors and which silhouettes scare her. I sit and I nod—like a therapist—and then I start to plot her first big fashion risk. My client Jennifer Garner once told me that she would never wear a one-shoulder dress. Guess what? The vintage one-shoulder tangerine Valentino gown she wore for the Oscars in 2004 still stands as one of her favorite looks to date. Anne Hathaway, another longtime client and dear friend, told me when we first met that like me, she would not wear yellow. You know where this story is going, right? And the list goes on and on.

"WHEN IT COMES TO STYLE, MY MANTRA IS: 'JUST TRY IT ONCE.'"

Fashion should be thrilling and unpredictable and fun. All my icons have become forever memorable because they loved to express themselves through their style. If you're cultivating your signature look, enjoy every ounce of the experimentation. Laugh at your reflection when you try on something unflattering. Squeal a little if a dress or a pair of jeans makes you look utterly fantastic. And be sure to take a risk every now and again. Go ahead. I dare you.

CHAPTER 3

DETAIL ORIENTED

Black patent ankle boots or nude platform pumps? A bold enamel pendant necklace or a pair of geometric cuffs? In my opinion, an outfit is only half complete without accessories. When I get dressed in the morning, I think about all the possibilities—from a hat to the necklace to the shoes—as I decide on a look. Sometimes, I like to start backward and select my jewelry first. Then, I might choose a simple black sheath or a crisp white button-down with flared trousers as the perfect canvas for a bold piece. It's no wonder I have been known to say "I dream in jewelry." Leaving the house without accessories would feel to me like walking out the door naked.

As I mentioned earlier, my mother always had a fabulous arsenal of accessories. If you look at pictures of her from when she was in her twenties and thirties, she is consistently decked out in oversized sunnies and huge necklaces. As a little girl, I swear that I could practically cover my whole body in all her bold chokers, pendants, strands of beads, cuffs, and cocktail rings. I never liked dainty pieces either. When I was sixteen, I bought my first piece of collectible costume jewelry: a Chanel charm bracelet at a vintage boutique in Paris. It was a big deal, because I had saved up for the thick gold chain, with a dangling Eiffel Tower and rue Cambon. I can still recall how it felt on my wrist—it was very heavy!—and sparkled in the sunlight. After that, I spent time saving up for a Louis Vuitton monogram purse. My parents thought I was crazy to splurge on a designer bag, but I already knew then that a chic, timeless investment like that would transform my day-to-day look.

"I SEE BOLD ACCESSORIES AS A WOMAN'S ARMOR."

Since then, my taste in accessories has undergone plenty of incarnations. My preteen obsession with everything gold led me to pile on stars, hearts, and lots of other flashy charms. During the early eighties, I had a thing for fingerless lace gloves, headbands, and white Ray-Bans. Later on in my college years, I went through a tribal phase of wearing chunky, Navajo-inspired jewelry, lots of turquoise and coral rings, and heavy silver necklaces. But no matter my style at any given time, I never, ever thought small. In the past decade or so, I have returned to my roots. I adore gold, especially chains with heft and oversized pendants. You can upgrade any look, from a bathing suit to a classic black turtleneck, with oversized accents of rich, lustrous gold.

I see bold accessories as a woman's armor. Look at Wonder Woman, with her chic gold cuffs, tiara, and those amazing red go-go boots. Cleopatra, known for her opulent accessories, adorned her headdresses with gold cobras and precious scarabs to convince all of Egypt she was a divine goddess. I could stare at pictures of Elizabeth Taylor from the 1963 film *Cleopatra*—not to mention, in general—all day for inspiration. Great accessories have their own special powers for me, too. A cool fedora is always my go-to on a bad hair day. If I need to feel confident for a meeting, I wear my stunning Van Cleef & Arpels Jackie O cuff, a molten eighteen-karat gold piece from 1977 that the jeweler reissued in a limited edition. Its weight and shine alone instill me with extra courage.

In a necklace by Chanel

When I style an actress for the red carpet, the right jewelry or shoes can be the last piece of the puzzle. It might add a splash of color or a sense of texture—even a bit of avant-garde edge. The focus is almost always on the dress, but the right accessories always add a point of interest. In fact, they can even change the personality of a look. Here's an experiment: Take a little black dress out of your closet and model it in front of the mirror with different shoes, jewelry, and even a scarf or a hat. Add layered pearls and chains with lizard-skin sling-backs and you have the epitome of ladylike style. Change it up completely to nail downtown glamour with a chunky collar necklace, leather jacket, and ankle boots. Now you see why I sometimes pick my accessories first!

TRINKETS TO SUIT YOUR STYLE

Jewelry always tells a story. Rings, necklaces, and earrings often have some sentimental value and help us assume our style identities. One of my first prized pieces as a kid was a gold ring with little dangling hearts that announced my girly, flirtatious side. It was a gift for my bat mitzvah and I still have it in my jewelry box. When you start to collect jewelry or sit down to evaluate what you already own, think about your style. Do your pieces complement, even enhance, your fashion persona? Here are some style profiles to help guide your jewelry choices.

BOHEMIAN SPIRIT: You own a dozen peasant blouses, fringed purses, and never met a caftan you didn't adore. Your signature will probably be sizable gold hoops—think about the diameter of a silver dollar—that will stand out against your romantic waves. Long beaded chains or link necklaces that you can layer atop those ethnic prints are key. A few chunky turquoise, coral, or bone rings add some gypsy flair, too. But don't overdo it or you might look like you're wearing a costume!

"JEWELRY ALWAYS TELLS A STORY."

CHIC MINIMALIST: Clean simple silhouettes, streamlined proportions, and symmetry appeal to your love of only the bare essentials. The subtlety and architecture of a pair of pyramid studs will work perfectly when your hair is pin straight or pulled back into a tight chignon. An oversized men's watch, be it a Rolex or a Timex, and simple gold bands on your fingers also complement your pared-down style.

FASHION REBEL: Gwen Stefani is your style icon and your friends marvel at how only you can make leggings work with shorts in the office. A trio of cool huggies, studs, and spikes on your ear accent your unconventional street style. An oversized pendant necklace with geometric adornments, studded bangles, and a thick snake ring complete the look.

DRAMA QUEEN: You love metallic sequins for day and a one-shoulder dress is your go-to frock on any vacation—including a ski weekend in Aspen. Gold tassel drop earrings that sway with every head toss on a dance floor are essential. A few statement rings, a flashy gold choker with diamonds, or a group of oversized cuffs will get you noticed—in a good way.

UPTOWN GIRL: Cashmere cardigan in the closet? Check. Riding boots, too? Check. Headband? You're wearing it right now. Diamond studs are the classic, polished girl's best friend. I like them in baguettes, a princess cut, or even tiny flower configurations. A chic tank watch with an Hermès orange or rich cognac band looks great on your wrist, alongside a link bracelet with a monogrammed circle pendant.

Discovering your style narrative doesn't mean that you can't dabble in other profiles. I always say that every uptown girl should experiment, at least once, with an edgy downtown vibe. If you're a devout bohemian, take off a few bangles and pull that wild mane of hair into a sleek, straight ponytail. The most unique looks are actually a blend of a few contrasting elements.

Opposite: Eva Mendes in Dior Haute Couture and a Van Cleef & Arpels necklace, Golden Globes, 2009. This page, clockwise from top left: Van Cleef & Arpels' "Jackie O" cuff; in Rachel Zoe Collection jewelry; Cartier's Panthere ring.

PRECIOUS CARGO

Once you have determined your jewelry persona, the fun really begins; you have a focus when you shop. As a collector of fine and costume jewelry, I am always looking for architectural pieces and those with unique embellishments. Many of my most cherished bracelets and necklaces—like a Lanvin interchangeable jade or tiger-eye pendant and a pair of vintage Dior crystal cuffs—are plated and studded with simple stones.

Before I became a mom, my jewelry philosophy could be summed up as: More is more. I often layered a half-dozen chains around my neck and adorned my wrists and fingers with chunky gold panther rings, snake cuffs, and sometimes even angled pieces with studs. Clearly, you can't hug a toddler if you're wearing a spiked piece of jewelry. Now, I rely on one or maybe two dramatic pieces in my everyday style, like a vintage gold Givenchy circle pendant on a heavy link chain. I think this mandatory lifestyle edit has forced me to become even more creative about my choices.

When it comes to rules, I really have only one "don't": If your ears are pierced, don't forget to wear earrings always—even just a simple pair of studs. Seeing an unadorned hole in an earlobe is just a personal pet peeve of mine; it looks so odd. I'm all for mixing metals like yellow gold with silver or even rose gold and for wearing pieces from different decades. (When it comes to hardware on bags and shoes, however, I like to see unity in gold or silver. More on that later.) I sometimes pair my bold YSL gold chain from the seventies with a pair of classic diamond studs. What I love most about jewelry is that if you're suddenly not feeling a piece, you can just take it off.

LESLIE ROSENZWEIG ON COLLECTING VINTAGE JEWELRY

How do I know Rachel inherited my love for accessories? Since she was ten or eleven, she would take pieces from my collection of jewelry and say, "Oh, Mom will never miss this." Little by little, things would disappear. When she first started styling, she used many of my accessories, such as antique clutches and bracelets on her clients. I once saw Keira Knightley wearing my vintage earrings in a magazine!

I began buying dramatic jewelry in the seventies, when I was in my early twenties. My husband had started an international company and we would often visit Europe—particularly Paris—on business. I always went to a little shop on the Left Bank called Utilité Bébé to pick up runway-inspired costume jewelry that was more affordable than pieces by Dior and Yves Saint Laurent.

As with vintage clothing, Rachel invests only in special designer jewelry that bears a signature or stamp. That label usually means the piece was manufactured in limited edition or sold as high-end costume or fine jewelry—and typically, a piece like that will appreciate in value. But if you're collecting for yourself and don't necessarily look at pieces as investments, you can buy anything and enjoy it. Early on, I collected Miriam Haskell jewelry just because I liked her shapes and ornate styles. I gave a lot of them to Rachel, and now, they are worth a lot more. My taste ran to statement earrings and bracelets that resembled artwork. I loved dramatic pieces and looked for original designs and interesting shapes.

I got to know one vintage dealer named Sandi Berman very well and she supplied me with many wonderful bracelets, necklaces, and earrings. She now owns a fantastic shop in New York on the Upper East Side called Catwalk Couture. I recommend you find a dealer or a shop and buy regularly from that source. The dealer will look for pieces that he or she knows you like and you might even get better deals. Nowadays, the price of vintage jewelry by designers such as Chanel and YSL is outrageous.

I have found interesting pieces at antique shows and flea markets where vendors have booths full of great jewelry. My best advice for finding pieces, signed or not, is to go to country fairs where people are selling estate pieces. I still buy for Rachel every now and again—and she still "borrows" whenever she comes home to visit. ■

In 2012, Tiffany & Co. asked me to decorate five different windows at their Fifth Avenue flagship store to celebrate the history of Hollywood glamour from the 1930s through the 1970s. My creations were displayed at Tiffany boutiques around the world. Never mind the fact that this was a dream-come-true opportunity, it also turned out to be an educational experience. To convey the spirit of each era, I explored Tiffany's vast archives and studied the jewelry innovations and design trends within each decade. And I often use what I learned—from how to recognize certain date and purity hallmarks to what innovations came about in design—when I shop for vintage jewelry, fine or costume.

1920s: This is easily one of my favorite decades for jewelry. Deco pieces never become dated. The liberated fashion of the Prohibition era created the need for modern styles of jewelry. Women who bobbed their hair wanted long, sleek geometric earrings and lots of clanking bangles to adorn their newly bare arms. Coco Chanel wore a mismatched pair of black and white earrings in 1926 and started a trend in asymmetrical sets. Because of the discovery of King Tut's tomb in 1922, Egyptian influences were reflected in jewelry's carved gemstones, garland curves, and exotic pharaoh motifs. Cartier's Trinity ring—interlocking yellow, white, and rose gold bands—debuted in 1924 and the style encouraged women to mix metals. Almost a century later, it's still wildly popular and has spurred plenty of similar styles.

Look for: Long necklaces studded with faux pearls or lariats finished with tassels; resin bangles, cuffs, and earrings featuring jade, coral, and onyx. Check out hair ornaments like tiaras and bandeaus worn lower on the forehead.

1930s: The 1929 stock market crash and subsequent Depression put a dent in spending. Costume jewelry was marketed to be worn for just one or two seasons and then tossed away. Can you imagine? Luckily, many of the well-crafted pieces like faux pearl and paste chokers, marcasite pins, and celluloid armlets remain today. The same applies for cuffs that feature huge natural stones. I'm always surprised by their quality and creativity, too.

Look for: I love sparkly clip brooches, which often come in pairs to be worn on the straps of a dress, and elegant compacts inlaid with enamel and gemstones. Swarovski crystals for jewelry date back to the thirties, so seek out lozenge-sized faceted stones in earrings, necklaces, and rings.

1940s: As the popularity of cinema hit an all-time high, Hollywood glamour took hold of the nation, and huge feminine bows, knots, ballerinas, and floral motifs appeared in brooches and bracelets. Van Cleef & Arpels introduced its signature snowflake diamond designs in rings, necklaces, and earrings. Cocktail party trends called for oversized rings with semiprecious stones. Just look at any screen siren of that decade—Ava Gardner, Bette Davis—and you'll see bold diamond earrings and tiered jeweled necklaces.

Look for: Huge topaz and citrine rings that overtake your hand in rose gold mounts and links; ruby and diamond combinations in bands and earrings. Star sapphires and other cabochons or shaped gemstones in rings and pendants are great finds, too.

1950s: Thanks to a savvy marketing campaign for De Beers, diamond engagement rings became de rigueur. And because of their popularity, certificates that graded their quality and value were introduced in 1957. Pearls—both natural and cultured—became all the rage, with fans in Jackie Kennedy and Grace Kelly. Women invested in matching sets of earrings and bracelets and necklaces, rather than in individual pieces. Motifs of the time included animals, bumblebees, butterflies, and flowers—along with the starbursts and Sputniks associated with advances in space exploration. In 1958, America sent its first satellite skyward.

Look for: Highly textural gold pieces with braided and Florentine accents. Abstract modernist midcentury pieces—inspired by Pablo Picasso and Salvador Dalí—in brass or silver make an interesting conversation starter.

1960s: Unconventional elements like uncut crystals and elaborate clawed settings in gold were introduced. Mod pieces in black or white and Day-Glo colors inspired by optical art became the focal point of an outfit in pendants, giant hoop earrings, and multi-strand necklaces.

Look for: Statement button earrings in black or white and huge enamel pendants on snake chains. Thick Lucite cuffs in Day-Glo or saturated colors or with a graphic checkerboard motif.

1970s: The "Me Decade" of individualism brought about a craze for ethnic styles and bold, showy pendants made of horn, bone, and wood. Splashy primary colors seen in enamel pieces mirrored the optimism of Pop Art and disco fever fueled a trend in bright yellow gold. I love the big gold hoops that women wore with their hair straight and parted down the center and lots of bangles on each arm.

Look for: Cool zodiac-inspired pieces and signed costume necklaces by YSL, Givenchy, Lanvin, and Pierre Cardin. Gold or wooden bangles look great in a dramatic stack, and I am always on the lookout for huge link chains and pendants with earthy elements.

Next spread: Windows styled by Rachel Zoe for Tiffany & Co.

1930s

1940s

1950s

1960s

The 1970s represent effortless glamour
— it's the era of my favorite style icons.

xoxo
Rachel Zoe

1970s

SHOES: THE GREATEST HITS

It's funny that shoes are often the last things we slip on before we head out the door, because women usually notice them first. High heels mean everything to me, because they make me tall. My first were a pair of simple black Charles Jourdan pumps that I snagged from my mom when I was thirteen and I never looked back—and I didn't stumble once either. I swear I was born to wear high heels. My father loves to talk about how athletic I was as a teen. (I played a lot of tennis.) Then, he will laugh and add that I quit sports because I was finally allowed to buy crazy heels and I refused to wear sneakers. He's right!

Now, I don't own a single pair of flats. I even went to the hospital to deliver Skyler in eight-inch Givenchy wedge boots! Yes, I definitely received a few double takes as I teetered into the maternity ward. But it was important for me to feel as chic and pretty as possible as I embarked on the exciting journey to motherhood. It was also the one element of that experience I could control, in a way. And when I left, I was wearing a Halston duster cardigan, floppy hat, big sunglasses, and those same eight-inch heels while cradling my newborn son. By the way, little Sky now has his own share of accents: fedoras, beanies, sunnies, and dozens of pairs of tiny shoes, too. I like to joke that I will accessorize him until the day he puts his foot down and says "No." And on that day, I *at least* know he will be wearing amazing shoes!

Of course, shoes are subjective for everyone—little boys aside. One woman's ballet flat is another's satin stiletto peep-toe. When I design shoes for my collection, I always strive to create classic styles with a little sex appeal—that might be a peek of toe cleavage or a cut that reveals the sensuous line of an arch. In my years of working in fashion, I have developed a sacred list of essential styles that will carry you through any occasion.

BLACK ANKLE BOOT: All hail the bootie. This here-to-stay style of low-cut boot, whether it's a patent platform or a studded suede stiletto, is the new black pump, in my opinion. It can be flat or it can be five inches high. The anklet is modern and versatile, and can infuse a pencil skirt or a little black dress with some edge.

NUDE PUMP: Once again, this shoe will make you love your legs, as they add inches to the line of your silhouette by matching your skin tone. I love to pair nude pumps with minidresses, skinny jeans, and short skirts. Take advantage of their elongating effect and show some skin.

ALL-SEASON WEDGE: What a way to cheat glamour! With a wedge—be it a canvas espadrille or a metallic peep-toe—you get a boost of four to five inches without any discomfort. I rely on them for my busiest days. You can wear this style with a maxi dress, tailored shorts, or even a slim-cut suit. They are amazingly versatile.

RIDING BOOT: There's a reason Gucci has been designing equestrian boots since its inception in 1921. These flat boots that skim just below the knee are both classic and sophisticated. Wear them with skinny jeans and a tweed jacket or a day dress and belted coat. If I weren't petite and determined to be taller than I am, I would wear flat classic riding boots all the time. Thankfully, there are many great high-end and midlevel brands out there with their own versions of the iconic style.

BALLET FLATS: Paired with cropped trousers and a white shirt or a chunky knit, these classic slip-ons always read fresh and youthful. And they remind me of Audrey Hepburn, of course. I love the design of these shoes, because they truly marry fashion and function. Opt for bright colors, embellishments, or even pony hair for a more glamourous finish.

THE ESSENTIAL HANDBAGS

My philosophy on handbags has always been to splurge on a few fantastic investment pieces that you will hopefully own forever—especially since a fabulous handbag can salvage a boring outfit. Besides, cheap leather, hollow hardware, and flimsy construction not only don't last, but are also easy to spot and quickly detract from even the most stylish ensemble. I usually advise against buying the "it" bag of any particular season. A handbag like that can sometimes become passé when a new one takes its place. Of course there are exceptions like the elegantly rounded YSL Muse, Givenchy's Nightingale, Proenza Schouler's chic PS1 satchel, and the uniquely structured Celine Phantom tote. Each of these bags transcends trend in its modern take on an iconic design. But unless you can handle the seasonal splurge, save up for something that's classic and of the best quality you can afford. It doesn't have to be a designer brand either. These are the five styles you should eventually own, because each one will serve you well.

CLUTCH: The options are endless, from a frame to a box to a fold-over to an envelope. Sizes vary, too—small minaudières and oversized clutches that can carry as much as a shoulder bag. I am attracted to a metallic or exotic skin such as python or stingray, because it adds a little drama to any ensemble and works for day or night. You will get the most bang for your buck out of a neutral-hued clutch, but satin or Lucite for special events will get a lot of mileage, as well.

Be sure that: The design you choose can accommodate your necessities. If you're a woman who carries three lipsticks and a spare set of keys, choose accordingly. In fact, it will be helpful to take your essentials with you when you shop for a clutch so you can size correctly.

STRUCTURED TOTE: Depending on your agenda, a sensational tote can land you a business deal or get you through a layover without losing your mind. I opt for black, dark brown, or burgundy—preferably in patent and with feet underneath, as this bag usually takes a beating and often ends up sitting on the floor of a restaurant or plane. Look for one with striking hardware that adds some luxe.

Be sure that: The straps can handle your load. Lugging around a laptop, over time, will wear on the handles and seams—and not to mention your shoulder. Organized pockets, like those for a phone or sunglasses, make it easiest to access everything on the go.

CROSS-BODY OR MESSENGER: Once you go hands free, it can be hard to return to carrying a traditional handbag. If you're a multitasking mom or someone who's constantly on the go, this utilitarian purse will become your chic salvation—especially if it has a smart interior. I always add a cross-body strap to the more classic styles when I'm designing handbags for my collection. Look for soft, luxurious leathers that will wear well over time.

Be sure that: The chain or strap always lies flat. You want the bag itself to sit right above your hipbone and not add unnecessary bulk, so be sure you can adjust it as needed. Most well-designed bags have straps that can be made longer or shorter.

SLOUCHY HOBO: This is the one you'll grab eighty percent of the time—trust me. I thought long and hard before I designed a hobo with a front magnetic snap and an eight-and-a-quarter-inch strap that we tested around the office on women of all different heights. This handbag is really all about the engineering. Gauge the comfort of a few bags, because different shapes and sizes will fall differently on your body.

Be sure that: The body of the bag rests comfortably under your bent elbow. A roomy hobo can easily turn into a black hole, so make certain there are adequate places to stash things you might need to find fast. Or you can use your own individual pouches to keep things organized.

SHOULDER BAG: A ladylike bag always reads grown-up and sophisticated. I like a more structured body with a chain strap, which transforms jeans and a long-sleeved tee into a more polished look. Think of this bag the way you would a tailored jacket and look for great lines and rich embellishments like miniature gold padlocks or horse bits.

Be sure that: This retro-inspired silhouette doesn't look too fussy if you opt to buy vintage. Color blocking, animal prints, and exotic skins will make it feel younger and more modern.

Next page, top: Carrying a Ferragamo clutch. Bottom: A line up of clutches from my closet. Opposite: Carrying a structured Hermès Kelly bag, Fashion Week 2011.

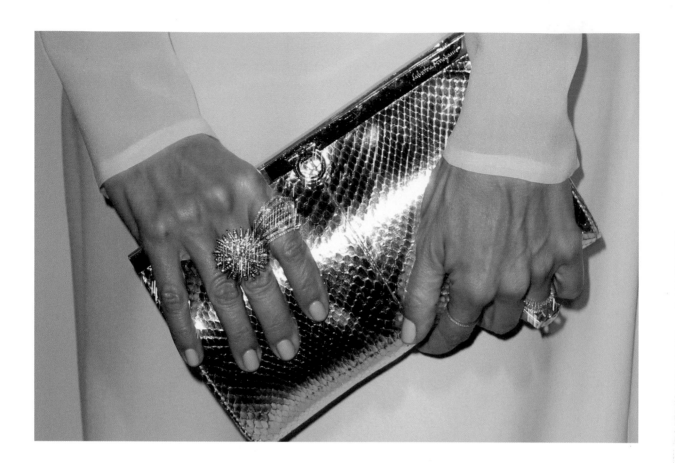

OPTICAL OBSESSION

In my opinion, sunglasses can make just as much of a statement as jewelry—I never leave home without two pairs. They can disguise the aftermath of a late night, or just allow you to be a little mysterious. I like to think of sunnies as "do not disturb" signs. Plus, a fabulous pair of shades can upgrade a simple look to super stylish and sophisticated.

My addiction to sunglasses might explain why I have three drawers filled with them in my closet! Here in Los Angeles, shades are essential—especially since my light green eyes are extremely sensitive to bright light. When I'm in a rush to get out the door, I rely on big dark sunglasses and bold red lipstick for instant glamour. And unless I'm wearing a semitransparent lens, I always remove them inside. When it comes to choosing a frame, it's important you set aside time to try on at least a dozen pairs. My favorite frames have distinctly different personalities and I rotate them depending on my mood or outfit. Some busy days call for an easy, casual look with aviators, while a pair of oversized dark frames can make a sleek suit look even more cosmopolitan.

WAYFARER: Being a fan of midcentury architecture, I love that this style was designed to reflect the cool minimalism of Charles Eames. And the fact that Bob Dylan, John F. Kennedy, and Audrey Hepburn all wore them says it all. Bold colored frames are fun for a contemporary take on this classic look.

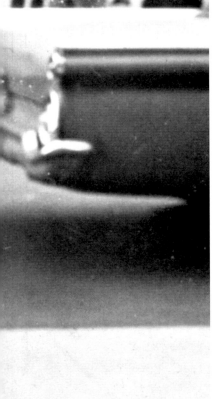

Audrey Hepburn

Left to right: Jacqueline Kennedy Onassis, Carole Lombard, Julie Christie, and Elizabeth Taylor

OVERSIZED: There is just no faster or easier way to access high-impact glamour than slipping on a pair of huge sunnies—and this is the style that you'll catch me in most often. Jackie Onassis actually commissioned Nina Ricci and Parisian optical designer François Pinton to create unique oversized frames for her back in the 1960s. Clearly, she knew they would help camouflage her identity, but I suspect she knew she would start a trend, too.

AVIATOR: These lightweight teardrop-shaped specs convey classic cool and exude a sense of adventure—they were originally developed by Ray-Ban for pilots in 1936. You can experiment with the lens size, hue, and material of frame. I love the traditional gold metal with a dark green lens, but you should also check out tortoiseshell or horn frames with blue, yellow, or even a mirrored lens. I'm forever a fan of Ray-Bans, too.

ROUND: What can I say about a style that both Coco Chanel and John Lennon popularized in their day? They can read either mod hippie or gamine chic, depending on your outfit. Wear them in the compact size of a silver dollar or go as huge and dramatic as Elton John, which I have done on many occasions. I love an ombré lens with an acetate or Lucite frame.

CAT-EYE: For me, this shape summons the glamour of the fifties with visions of Marilyn Monroe and Elizabeth Taylor. If the pointed eyes feel too retro, choose a subtler take on the shape with a rounder version. Or go all out and over-the-top with an animal print frame.

TIE ME UP

Hermès sells one of its signature scarves every twenty-five seconds, which is no surprise to me. The iconic silk square, with its plump hand-rolled hems, has become one of the most versatile accessories since it debuted in 1937—so versatile that Grace Kelly wore one as a chic sling when she broke her arm in 1956, while Sharon Stone multitasked with the scarf in a bondage scene in *Basic Instinct*. But one of my favorite interpretations of the scarf comes courtesy of Madonna, who wore one as a bandeau top in *Swept Away*.

But you don't have to splurge on designer scarves. I'm always on the lookout for fantastic prints—whether it's the Pucci-inspired geometrics of the fifties or a vivid colorful floral—when I visit vintage shops or flea markets. And there are plenty of styles beyond the classic silk scarf. Long skinny knit scarves, chunky wool ones, fur stoles, and larger cashmere wraps can refine any look, too. I love a fringe, an animal print, or bold colored knit to add a point of interest. There are so many ways to wear one.

BEACH DAY: A vibrant scarf looks fantastic and ultra-glamourous at the beach, especially when you wear it with a black, white, or neutral bathing suit. Fold the scarf into a triangle and wear it pirate- or handkerchief-style with soft beach waves or a long braid.

JOB INTERVIEW: The classic button-down white shirt and fitted blazer get upgraded to elegant with a colorful scarf worn tucked inside the shirt-front like an ascot. It's a great way to show some personality and style to a potential employer, while still being conservative enough to come off as professional.

FIRST DATE: When the scarf is folded into a tie and worn as a sixties-style headband, it always reads mod and feminine with a touch of innocence. Look for a pop of color that contrasts with your hair.

BUSINESS DINNER: Europeans have mastered the pull through, and it's an effortlessly chic way to wear any scarf. Simply fold a scarf in half and tug the ends through the U of the loop. You're set! Wear it with a fitted knit cardigan and pencil skirt or more casually, underneath a peacoat.

WINTER STROLL: Thicker scarves, fur stoles or collars, and large cashmere wraps not only prevent a chill but also add a vibrant, textural layer to a black, camel, or winter-white coat. I like to wear an oversized, featherweight cashmere scarf since the volume of the fabric adds interest to any winter coat. Wraps can look a bit dated if worn like shawls, so I artfully drape one so that one end sits just over the shoulder.

TOP IT OFF

Hats are such an easy shortcut to chic. I think part of their appeal for me is the fact that so few people wear them nowadays. I'm not talking about baseball caps, of course—my taste veers toward sophisticated felted fedoras that inject a dash of androgyny, or a faux fur fez that makes you look totally jet set. Just donning a hat makes a statement in itself. When a woman walks into a restaurant in a great ivory linen suit with a jaunty Panama, everyone stops and looks her way. It feels almost cinematic.

My own personal hat collection runs the gamut from black oversized floppy ones banded with grosgrain ribbon to chunky knit gray cashmere beanies. I love the elegance and simplicity of a cloche, which adds an elegant deco touch to modern skinny jeans and a cropped jacket. Some women say that they don't look good in hats, or that they don't feel comfortable in them. My philosophy on wearing hats is, the more you sport them, the more you grow to love them. Experiment with different brims and shapes; there is a style out there for everyone. To add a little flair to a hat band (the edging just above the inner-brim), I sometimes pin on a vintage pearl brooch or a couple of pheasant feathers. You can even circle a skinny belt around the band to add some texture or a pop of color, too.

Clockwise from left: In a vintage Dior turban. In a vintage straw fedora. In a Rachel Zoe Collection hat.

As a designer, I incorporate my hats into every runway show. For a Spring presentation, a model might wear a raffia newsboy cap with a sleek denim shorts suit. It's a hat style that can read casual with denim and a cardigan or dressed up with a floral day dress. A black floppy straw hat on a model in an ethereal white dress for spring screams "South of France!" I wear mine whenever I hit the beach. For autumn, I love a structured felt fedora, like the one I paired with a gray plaid, slim-cut suit for my Fall 2012 collection. The hat lends a little tomboy street cool to a ladylike silhouette. But probably one of my favorite looks is the Russian fur hat. As you probably guessed, my inspiration for it was Julie Christie in *Doctor Zhivago*. If you live in a climate that calls for one of these amazing—and warm—hats, go for it.

GET A GRIP

Don't forget your fingers! Gloves, too, can make an equally stylish statement. I own a small stockade of leather gloves in rich earth tones such as caramel and mahogany. I love anything in suede, leather, embossed, or crocodile. The shot of texture and color looks elegant peeking out from the three-quarter sleeves of a winter-white cocoon coat or the cuffs of a traditional cashmere cardigan. Studded black leather gloves or even fingerless ones imbue a ladylike look with a little grit and edge.

Honestly, mittens are not part of my cold weather accessories repertoire. They are too bulky for me—and how does one text? Muffs, on the other hand, couldn't be more elegant and retro chic, whether in faux or real fur. A muff is one of those accessories you may question initially, but wear one on a chilly day and you'll be collecting compliments.

GETTING GORGEOUS

People may compliment your shoes or bag, but their gaze will invariably settle on your face. And while a dramatic red pout will make you stand out in a crowd, it's all that you radiate in that split-second of being noticed that counts. My philosophy on beauty is that it comes more from an inner confidence than from any cosmetic. If you feel fantastic, you look it. You don't need to smile at your reflection whenever you pass a mirror—but you definitely shouldn't scowl either. Admire yourself. Appreciate yourself.

THE ALLURE OF ASYMMETRY

Perfection has never appealed to me—especially when it comes to beauty. What you may perceive as an imperfection can actually become an asset. I love to see a gap in the front teeth, à la Lauren Hutton. Fun fact: Hutton refused to succumb to pressure from modeling agencies to fill the space in her smile and went on to land the very first million-dollar contract with Revlon in 1974. And Cindy Crawford's beauty mark—which was airbrushed off her debut cover for *British Vogue*—has become as much a part of her natural beauty as her insanely high cheekbones and beautiful smile.

"MY PHILOSOPHY ON BEAUTY IS THAT IT COMES MORE FROM AN INNER CONFIDENCE THAN FROM ANY COSMETIC. IF YOU FEEL FANTASTIC, YOU LOOK IT."

When I admire someone's looks, it's always because of a standout feature. Maybe it's a strong jawline that accentuates a full mouth, or wide-set eyes that make the composition of a face all the more arresting. A sincere smile can make a pronounced difference, too. Even in choosing models for my own runway shows, I am not seeking complete symmetry or an utterly perfect profile. What's more fascinating to me is a confident gaze and sense of self that comes with appreciating your own beauty.

If you look in the mirror and find yourself focusing on a high forehead or a crooked nose, you're overlooking the entire package. I always say with a laugh that I have oversized features—big lips, big cheeks, big eyes. But I embrace what I have and focus on enhancing my assets. Take a peek at your own face and do the same. Instead of zeroing in on your least favorite features and trying to downplay them, focus on what you love and play up those areas.

Love your lips? Make them the focal point of your face with a statement red, coral, or berry. If you want to highlight your eyes, begin your makeup routine by emphasizing them with mascara and bold liner so that

"PERFECTION HAS NEVER APPEALED TO ME—
ESPECIALLY WHEN IT COMES TO BEAUTY.
WHAT YOU MAY PERCEIVE AS AN IMPERFECTION
CAN ACTUALLY BECOME AN ASSET."

they take center stage. Amazing cheekbones deserve a dab of shimmer to accentuate their contours. The same applies to hair. You can spotlight shine with a pin-straight style or underscore your mane's untamable nature with sexy beach waves. Once you start focusing on your best feature, it will quickly become the first thing you notice when you spot your reflection in the mirror.

ABOUT FACE

You might think you need to use more makeup as you get older, but the opposite is true. I wear about half as much now as I did when I was a teen-ager. Back in the horrifying eighties, I went overboard with the Sun In and frosty pink lipstick. When I look at photographs from that era, I shudder. How did I not see that a head of brassy highlights and turquoise eyeliner aged me a decade?

In those days, taking care of my skin was hardly a priority. I rarely washed off my makeup before I went to bed, let alone applied any sort of moisturizer. At this point in my life, you would never catch me wearing a smoky eye from the night before in the morning. I'm obsessive about cleansing, exfoliating, and adding moisturizer to every inch of my face and body. If you spent a day with me, you would see me applying hand lotions and lip balm almost every hour. You should think of your skin as your most important investment; you can grab a chic fedora to disguise a bad hair day, but no amount of concealer or foundation will camouflage neglected skin.

"YOU MIGHT THINK YOU NEED TO USE MORE MAKEUP AS YOU GET OLDER, BUT THE OPPOSITE IS TRUE. I WEAR ABOUT HALF AS MUCH NOW AS I DID WHEN I WAS A TEENAGER."

In Chapter 2, I talked about my uniform—that go-to outfit that never lets me down. I have one for beauty as well. My reliable everyday look always centers on a fresh, healthy complexion and I alternate between a statement lip and a dramatic eye. Through experience, I have learned these will fight for attention on your face. That's never good. I pick one, like a matte berry pout or cat-eye, and then make that emphasis the point of interest on my face. How to decide which? It all depends on the day. If I know that my schedule calls for running around the city and I want to look more glamourous than I feel, I apply a bright red lip and add huge sunnies. Meanwhile, a statement eye with bold liner and mascara serves me better at important meetings where I'm making eye contact with a lot of people.

"YOU SHOULD THINK OF YOUR SKIN AS YOUR MOST IMPORTANT INVESTMENT; YOU CAN GRAB A CHIC FEDORA TO DISGUISE A BAD HAIR DAY, BUT NO AMOUNT OF CONCEALER OR FOUNDATION WILL CAMOUFLAGE NEGLECTED SKIN."

In my everyday makeup look

I always keep a few day-to-night necessities at my office—and in my car—for a quick transformation. I add another coat of mascara and thicken my eyeliner or slightly smudge it for a smoky effect; I dab a little shimmer on my cheekbones, and finally, I deepen my lip, whether it's taking it from a pinky brown to a plum or overlaying vibrant red with a vampy Bordeaux shade.

"MY RELIABLE EVERYDAY LOOK ALWAYS CENTERS ON A FRESH, HEALTHY COMPLEXION AND I ALTERNATE BETWEEN A STATEMENT LIP AND A DRAMATIC EYE."

My day and night looks definitely vary depending upon my mood, but I never veer too far from my goal of looking effortlessly glamourous. Some women have made their distinctive beauty choices a personal trademark. Think of Gwen Stefani with her vivid red lips and platinum blond pompadour. I love this story: Gwen's grandmother gave her a crimson lipstick in high school and she has been fiercely loyal to the color ever since. Or Jennifer Lopez, who always radiates a natural sensuality with her light chestnut tresses, flawless complexion, and nude lips.

Finding your signature look is just a matter of practice and patience. I should know. After years of flirting with caramel highlights, I finally went honey blond a few years ago. And every once in a while, I try on a lipstick shade that's the complete opposite of my usual hue—that's how I discovered my love for a deep plum. Experimenting is exciting. Be bold. Have fun. Define beauty in your own way.

JOEY MAALOUF'S THREE EASY STEPS TO FLAWLESS SKIN

I share Rachel's fixation with radiant skin. Luckily, you can cheat a bit and get there with the right products and tricks. While you might think you should test your foundation on your wrist or jawline, your décolletage is really the best match for skin. This way, your face and body colors won't clash or be off at all. When choosing a color for your base products, always be sure to match the shade in natural light.

> "EXPERIMENTING IS EXCITING. BE BOLD. HAVE FUN. DEFINE BEAUTY IN YOUR OWN WAY."

For a flush of color that stays put until you wash your face—and you had better wash that face before bed!—opt for cream blush. Unlike powder, it blends right into the foundation and actually stains the skin. Don't be afraid of vibrant cream pinks and peaches. These go on sheerer than they appear and tone down with blending, complementing your skin's glow.

To finalize your look after you've filled in the details, colorless finishing powder, loose or pressed, goes on invisibly and will set your foundation all day. The minerals also absorb any oil or shine and give skin a silky finish. I recommend looking for one in a light reflecting formula for an extra dewy effect. ■

RED-CARPET GLAM

A lipstick shade is as important as a shoe. A coif—whether it's a side-parted high ponytail or a sexy waterfall of waves—should complement a gown as much as a clutch. When I style a client during award season, the fittings don't end with her outfits and accessories. My team—aka "the glam squad"—and I put together a head-to-toe look, because an ensemble requires the right makeup and hair to be really fabulous. I have seen the most stunning dress overshadowed by a messy mane or an overdone smoky eye that clashed with the final aesthetic too many times.

Most of the time, my input on makeup for my clients is instinctual. I'm always partial to a berry lip with dewy skin and major lashes for a formal evening event, or a dramatic topknot that can be softened with loose tendrils. Finding the right hair and makeup isn't a science, but certain elements of a dress should be considered.

COLOR: Matching your eye shadow exactly to your dress is risky business and often reads as too monochromatic. Instead, pick a shade within that color family—for instance, a muted khaki looks fabulous with emerald green. An accent of gold or bronze on your cheeks will break up the color conformity. Any neutral hue on your eye—gray, black, navy, or brown—always complements any jewel-tone or pastel dress. Don't forget the dozens of gorgeous tonal browns to choose from, like fawn, mocha, and nutmeg. Dresses in black or white make the perfect palette for "wow" eye shadow colors like deep purple or even an electric blue liner. Similarly, don't coordinate your lip color exactly to the hue of your dress—go a few shades deeper or lighter.

FABRIC: The weight and texture of your outfit should also dictate your beauty moment. A light silk chiffon or lace look calls for a romantic transparent wash of color rather than major statement makeup. Velvet, leather, brocade, or wool crepe can carry a more dramatic eye or strong lip. You can mimic texture like braiding on a gown in your hair, too. Of course, shine should also be considered. A silk-satin gown looks great with a polished, glossy hairstyle.

DECADE: If you're wearing vintage or a dress inspired by another era, keep your makeup and hair contemporary—at least avoid the over-the-top looks that defined that same time period. Pairing a midcentury mod shift with a dramatic cat-eye and backcombed bouffant will look more costumey than chic. Instead, keep it modern: pin straight and parted down the middle coif or a casual ponytail.

STYLE AND MOVEMENT: Off-duty mini or workplace shirtdress? A minimalist sheath or a flowing macramé maxi dress? Clean lines cry out for similar hair and makeup, like a fresh face and coral or deep plum lip, depending on the season. Also, you don't want to pair a seriously smoky eye with a day dress for the office or an afternoon event. I think a neat side braid or a high, tight ponytail always works with an architectural dress. A long maxi or more ethereal style that floats looks amazing with "Juliet" hair, romantic waves, or a tousled topknot.

My obsession with vintage doesn't stop at twenties art deco jewelry and mod shifts from the Kennedy era. Beauty trends from previous decades are a great source of inspiration, too. When I contemplate a look, I sometimes scan photos of movie stars like Elizabeth Taylor back in the fifties or Faye Dunaway from *Chinatown* in 1974.

Every decade has its beauty trends and some become more memorable than others. Here's my cheat sheet to the glamour moments worth revisiting from the past.

1920s: The dark berry heart-shaped lip—popularized by the silent screen actress Clara Bow—which overaccentuates the V or cupid's bow of the upper lip. A toned-down version of this bold lip can look totally modern.

1930s: Sultry Greta Garbo popularized the pencil-thin arched brow, which was often drawn on. Lashes were always curled outward and upward, too, which really adds pop—this is my preferred way to accentuate my eyes.

1940s: Pinup glamour took hold in Veronica Lake peekaboo waves and dramatic red lips with matching nails. I can't even tell you how often we re-create old Hollywood for the red carpet, mimicking that look to a tee. You don't need to update this classic.

1950s: Makeup became softer, as Christian Dior introduced pink and coral lipsticks. Liner always had a slight kick to elongate the eye and add subtle drama—a still-fantastic day look now.

1960s: This is one of my favorite eras for beauty, with its emphasis on over-the-top lashes, bold liner, and a pale, nude lip. Monochromatic mod that continues to work now!

1970s: Natural, fresh-faced beauties like Farrah Fawcett brought the focus to bronzed skin, feathered hair, and light makeup. Who didn't want to look like one of Charlie's Angels back in the day? The natural, sun-kissed look is now timeless, thanks to them.

1980s: Big hair and yellow eye shadow aside, the eighties had some redeeming beauty moments, too. Contouring cheeks with blush, bold brows, and navy eyeliner were trends with staying power that I still love.

1990s: Minimalistic beauty—a revolt against eighties excess—ruled the runways and overtook the streets. Sleek chignons and low ponytails replaced big hair; a dewy complexion with a natural flush and scant eye makeup became perfect in its simplicity. This emphasis on the face, which has always encouraged me to take great care of my skin, never goes out of style. It's an unexpected and fresh look for evening, too.

Opposite: Faye Dunaway.

Next spread, top row: Clara Bow, Greta Garbo, Veronica Lake, Sophia Loren. Bottom row: Jean Shrimpton, Farrah Fawcett, Christie Brinkley, Kate Moss.

1920s

1930s

1960s

1970s

1940s

1950s

1980s

1990s

My "hero kit"

YOUR "HERO KIT"

You know the lipstick that always does the trick when you dig it out of your purse for a touch-up? I do. There are products I literally can't live without and I call that collection my "hero kit." My loyalty to these exceptional items is so deep that I buy them in bulk and divvy them up for at-home use, on-the-go touch-ups, and travel. I probably own a half-dozen NARS Orgasm blushes—and I'm okay with that.

Of course, editing can be as crucial as accumulating. Sometimes, you discover your heroes by singling them out of your own collection. Empty out your makeup bag and decide if every product deserves its place. Does your concealer glide on effortlessly and stay put? Do you always achieve the perfect winged eye with that liquid liner? I like to keep the extra products that I use only occasionally in a drawer by my bathroom sink. Every three months or so, I go through the goods and throw away anything that I haven't touched in a while. Unfortunately, makeup usually

doesn't come with an expiration date, but many products are susceptible to bacteria and lose their effectiveness over time. I'm pretty meticulous about regularly replacing items like mascara, which needs to be changed out at least every three months. Eye and lip pencils can be used for a year as long as you sharpen them every week to keep the tip hygienic. Liquid foundations last about six months before the formula breaks down, while lipsticks and glosses have a lifespan of about a year. I use only organic skincare and body creams, which tend to expire within six months because they don't contain preservatives.

Storage is important, too. There's nothing worse than not being able to zipper a bag shut because of product overload. I stash my "heroes" in a roomy canvas cosmetics pouch that's lined with a material that can be easily cleaned. Here's what you will find inside:

EGYPTIAN MAGIC: Ever since hearing about this moisturizing balm a decade ago, I have been addicted. I use it on my face, my hair, and even dab a little on my leather bags to soften them or remove a stain. It was my go-to product throughout my pregnancy for dry skin.

TATCHA BEAUTY PAPERS: These fragrance- and powder-free blotting sheets are life changing. They remove the oil from your face without smudging your makeup. At the end of the day, I always blot my face before adding more products for an evening event.

NARS ORGASM BLUSH: This peach-pink shade with gold flecks delivers the perfect dose of sun-kissed shimmer on my cheekbones. I even keep a compact in my kitchen for a quick pick-me-up! During the summer, I also use the Multiple version of the product—a cream blusher in a chubby stick—for my lips and cheeks.

TOM FORD LIPSTICKS: I love all of his lipsticks—from the deep purple of Black Orchid to the autumnal brick red of Deep Mink—for their rich consistency and vibrant pigments. They never dry your lips or bleed beyond the pucker line. And the packaging is insanely chic, of course.

SKYN ICELAND EYE GELS: I never get dressed for an event without applying these patches first. They have a cooling effect and dissolve any puffiness. Wear them for ten minutes and you'll look like you slept for an extra hour. Fashion Week essential!

ARMANI LUMINOUS SILK FOUNDATION: Ask any makeup artist to name a favorite product and this liquid magic will top the list. It is soft and light on your skin and you don't need much of it for great coverage.

TARTE MASCARA: It drives me crazy when a mascara becomes dry and clumpy within a week of use. Tarte's Lights, Camera, Lashes formula has conditioning ingredients, so it always feels soft and looks natural. For those tiny inner and lower lashes, I also use Givenchy Phenom, which has an ingenious ball-shaped applicator.

ARCONA TRIAD PADS: The scent of these cranberry toner pads instantly makes me happy. They cleanse away makeup, tone, and hydrate skin with antioxidants, too. I never travel without them—they're a lifesaver on a long flight.

SMASHBOX LIMITLESS LIQUID LINER PEN: For me, it's all about precision. I love this pen applicator, because you can hold it and draw a line with a steady hand. It doesn't move or run or clump. Plus, it's waterproof.

ZOYA NAIL POLISH IN RILEY: This is the perfect deep Bordeaux for a high-impact manicure. It's my must-have shade for fall and winter. I discovered this line of toxin-free polishes when I was pregnant and now I'm a forever fan.

Of course, these are *my* personal heroes. They work with my lifestyle and complement my features. To find your own lifesaving products, go to makeup counters and experiment, read up on the runway trends every season, and check out beauty blogs. I stay on top of what's hot by contributing to *The Zoe Report,* my daily newsletter, and reading fashion magazines every month.

HANDS ON

Manicures have become masterpieces, with all the new nail art and creative techniques out there. Personally, I tend to play it pretty straightforward, but you will never catch me with chipped or peeling polish. I talk with my hands a lot, so my nails are always front and center. When I don't have time for a professional manicure, I make sure to take a moment to do my own. My preferences in polish go in two distinct directions: a clean, pinkish nude or rich, sumptuous Bordeaux.

I've learned some simple ways to extend a mani or pedi a few extra days, though. First, always use your own polish. Salons sometimes add thinner to make a bottle last longer, but the polish becomes less resilient. This way, you can quickly touch up at home if you get any chips. Also, be sure to polish the tip of the nail with both your color and topcoat to prevent chips. This step alone can double the life of a manicure or pedicure.

Believe it or not, it takes about twelve hours for nails to completely dry. Avoid washing your hands with hot water or even blowing on your nails. Though the latter seems instinctive, warm breath stalls the process. I know sitting idly can be frustrating, but try to take a few minutes to let your nails dry initially, and then before you leave the salon, apply oil to avoid surface smudges. A little later you can run them under cold water to set.

BRUSH UP

When it comes to application, the right brushes are essential—and must be washed with brush cleaner or a mild shampoo every couple of weeks. I have a weakness for Tom Ford's line of brushes, because the white bristles are so soft and dense, but there are many options out there. I rely on five essentials, day to day.

SHADING BRUSH:
With its angled tip and long handle, this brush is perfect for highlighting cheekbones or brow bones with a swath of shimmer.

BRONZER BRUSH:
Ideal for applying loose or compact powder; use it in a circular motion to evenly distribute mineral foundation or bronzer.

CHEEK BRUSH:
I like a slightly rounded brush head with very soft bristles and long, tapered handle to hit the entire apple of my cheek with color.

EYE SHADOW BRUSH:
Use its small, slightly rounded tip for expertly tucking eye shadow into the crease, shading the lids, and sweeping color onto the brow bone.

EYE SHADOW BLEND BRUSH:
Never underestimate the power of blending. I love this brush's ability to diffuse eye shadow color and soften the line of a smoky eye.

Makeup brushes by Tom Ford

MANE ATTRACTION

My hair has been at my shoulders or longer for as long as I can remember. And as much as I adore the look of a gamine pixie cut and its easy maintenance, I doubt that I will ever go short. Personally, I like the infinite options that come with length, as well as the ability to hide behind a curtain of hair. But in order to preserve these long locks, I'm very keen on maintenance.

Like most women, I adore a professional blowout. Having shiny, silky hair that you can flip over your shoulder is as empowering as a new pair of shoes or a great handbag. Just last year, I partnered with a friend to open DreamDry, a New York salon that offers blowouts and hair styling until 10:00 p.m. every night. (Tell me, who has time to see a hairdresser before sunset during the week?) And while I must admit that I'm an amateur when it comes to blow-drying my own hair, I have learned a few tips and secrets from our stylists. First of all, you shouldn't attempt to blow-dry super wet hair. Have you ever noticed how your hairdresser spends a good ten minutes "predrying" your hair before he or she starts the process? That's because moisture plus heat equals frizz. Let your hair air dry or add low heat with a blow-dryer to get your mane about seventy-five percent dry before you really start styling.

Next, divide hair into multiple three- or four-inch sections. Start with the hair on the crown or around the face—that's what people see first, after all. And if you're like me, your arm is going to start aching soon! Using a round brush, pull the hair taut and aim the nozzle downward on top of the hair to seal the shaft and create shine. Repeat on each section.

Finally, mist your fingers with a holding spray that adds shine and then gently tousle your sleek mane. You can also gently run your palms around your part to flatten flyaways with the residual product.

It's always hard for me to wash my hair after a great blowout. I just want it to last forever—I prolong it as long as four days. I wash my hair only once or twice a week, and many stylists have told me that my mane is amazingly healthy as a result of that habit. You can get away with it if your hair tends to be dry like mine; or you can extend time between washing like I do by adding a little dry shampoo to your roots. It may sound crazy, but women washed their hair once a month back at the turn of the century. That's a long time between shampoos!

I rotate my shampoo and conditioner every month or so in order to avoid buildup. And as someone who colors her hair, I occasionally use a clarifying shampoo to strip away natural buildup from the environment. Chemical and color treatments like straightening or highlighting make hair very porous and absorbent. Every Sunday night, I do a deep conditioning treatment while I watch TV or answer e-mails. When I go to bed, I use a clip to coil it up in a topknot instead of leaving it down. Why? The oils in your hair, not to mention the product buildup from shampoos and serums, can irritate your face and cause breakouts.

While I recommend experimenting to find your favorite products, these are my current ones for healthy hair.

KÉRASTASE CRISTALLISTE SHAMPOO AND CONDITIONER: This line is specially formulated for fine, lengthy hair, which is my exact match. It reduces frizz and makes my hair incredibly shiny.

BYRON WILLIAMS SPIRULINA HAIR SPRAY: I love that this holding spray is certified organic and contains blue algae, which prevents damage and strengthens hair. I use it on flyaways or a topknot to make hair stay put.

GLOSS MODERNE HIGH-GLOSS MASQUE: When my hair needs a spa day, I slather on this treatment to restore its natural luster and hydrate. It can be a lifesaver if you use a lot of heat on your hair with flat irons, curling irons, or blow-dryers.

ORIBE DRY TEXTURIZING SPRAY: I can extend a blowout by three days with this dry hair spray that absorbs oil at the roots and adds body. Keep it in your office for instant day-to-night volume.

HAMADI ORGANICS HEALING SERUM: Scented with ylang-ylang and bergamot, this moisturizing spray treatment for dry, overprocessed tresses refreshes dry ends and leaves my hair incredibly soft. I spritz my entire mane and then comb through to the ends at least twice a week.

PHYLIA CONNECT LEAVE-IN TREATMENT: This spray-on blend of organic ingredients treats both the hair and the scalp. I use it right out of the shower and it lifts my hair at the roots and makes my hair look twice as thick.

ADIR ABERGEL'S THREE STEPS TO AMAZING HAIR

Rachel and I collaborate often on looks for her clients. We have similar beauty sensibilities—we never want a woman to look "done"; rather, she should always exude a fluid, effortless look. To achieve that, we focus first on volume. To get the body that makes hair look so healthy and full, always use a volumizing product on your roots before you start styling. You will see a boost right away. You should invest in a backcomb, which creates height that lasts all day. The secret here is to take very small sections and gently tease or compact the hair at the root before styling.

Next, you need movement. Spray on dry shampoo, even if you just washed your hair. It sounds crazy, but it's a red-carpet secret. This step creates texture, which is the key to movement. During a blow-dry, be sure to let the round brush cool down for about twenty to thirty seconds before you remove it from your hair. That way, you will get some long-lasting bounce.

Finally, shine is a must. It truly makes hair look youthful. Do a weekly deep masque, which will pay off with amazing shine. When you blow-dry your hair, be certain that you flatten the cuticle by using a boar bristle round brush and aiming the nozzle downward. A flat cuticle really reflects light. ■

Obviously, we all have different hair profiles and needs when it comes to styling. But there are a few basic tools that will always come in handy for the health and manageability of your mane.

ROUND BRUSHES:

I like a small one-inch boar bristle version for my bangs and a larger one, about three inches in diameter, for the rest of my hair. Natural bristles make your hair much shinier.

POWERFUL HAIR DRYER WITH ACCESSORIES:

More wattage can cut your blow-dry time in half, so look for those with no fewer than 1300 watts. Right now, I'm using Sultra's 1650-watt powerful ionic dryer, which does the job fast and makes my hair glossy. A good diffuser is essential if you have curly or wavy hair—it helps to prevent frizz by minimizing the intensity of the airflow. A nozzle, which always comes with a dryer, will direct the air and prevent hair from burning.

WIDE-TOOTHED COMB:

Hairstylists always say "Never brush wet hair,' because it will cause breakage. Instead, I use a wide-toothed comb right out of the shower.

MINI FLAT IRON:

Personally, I avoid using too much direct heat on my hair, because I don't trust my hand. But I do like the miniature version for taming flyaways or getting a kink out of my bangs. Flat ironing is a good way to achieve a super-sleek look.

CURLING IRON OR ROLLERS:

For achieving sexy beach waves or adding some volume to the crown of your hair, a curling iron or wand with a one-inch barrel or hot rollers will come in handy.

CLEAR ELASTICS:

Sometimes you just don't have those extra twenty minutes to style your hair. For that reason, I think a few handy clear elastics are as essential as a blow-dryer. Ponytails, braids, a half updo—the possibilities are endless!

Left: Jerry Hall. Right: Kate Moss.

ICONIC BEAUTY LOOKS

Trends come and go, but there are a handful of hair and makeup effects that never swerve out of style. When in doubt, try one of these looks with staying power.

RED LIPS

Love it: Every woman must wear bombshell red lipstick for one day in her life, at least. It's the pinnacle of glamour.

Get it: Experiment with undertones such as blues or corals to find your most flattering shade. And be sure to shape lips with a nude pencil first to keep the bold color in place.

GLOWING SKIN

Love it: Who doesn't want to radiate health and natural beauty? It makes you so approachable.

Get it: Moisturize your skin and then add just a touch of concealer beneath the eyes. Finish with a light bronzing powder that has a hint of shimmer.

THE SMOKY EYE

Love it: There is no trick I love more for transforming a look from day to night. Your eyes instantly become the focal point of your face.

Get it: I like to see variations on the traditional black liner. Experiment with colors like a slate blue or olive green. Even a rich mocha brown can stand out as much as black. Trace your top lash line with liquid liner and then dot liner between the lower lashes. Immediately begin smudging the lines for a soft, smoky effect. Then, brush the upper lid with a shadow and blend the color right to the line above the upper lashes.

MAJOR LASHES

Love it: This sixties-inspired look reads ultra modern and allows you to go full force with a dramatic lip in any hue.

Get it: Whether it's with a few coats of mascara or faux lashes, be sure to hit the lower lash line, too. You can also curl your lashes for more drama. I like to add individual fake lashes just to the upper outer corners for an extra upward kick.

STATEMENT BROW

Love it: A full brow can alter the whole composition of your face and gives you options on how to define them, from thick arches to strong arrows. I once overplucked my own brows, so now I tweeze them rarely and very carefully. If yours tend to grow thick and unruly, plan to groom them monthly.

Get it: You can always bolster your brow with a pencil or an angled brush and powder. Or, gently brush naturally dark hairs upward and outward and then set with a clear brow gel before shaping.

STICK-STRAIGHT HAIR

Love it: I love that this classic style can feel retro or modern, depending on the rest of your look. It also brings all the attention to your neck and face.

Get it: Whether you blow it out yourself or visit a salon, don't forget to finish with a shine serum to prevent flyaways and create depth.

TOPKNOT

Love it: The young girls in my office are
fanatics of this chic high bun, and vary
it by incorporating a French braid or even
a cool clip.

Get it: I like the old-school method of coiling
a high ponytail and securing it with pins.
To make it more free spirited, I pull some
tendrils around my face and grab a few ends
out of the knot so it appears a little undone.

BRAID

Love it: I've been obsessed with braids
ever since I was a little girl. A braided
updo manages to look both youthful and
sophisticated at the same time.

Get it: Whether it's a fishtail, French, or the
milkmaid style across your crown, this will
become your new favorite look, I swear.

PONYTAIL

Love it: Never mind the fact that pulling your hair off your face gives you an instant facelift—there is something so sleek about a ponytail.

Get it: Experiment with the possibilities, from a high one with lots of volume and movement to a low pony with a center part and a pin-straight tail.

BEACH WAVES

Love it: A cascade of textured waves that frames the face always looks effortlessly sensual. The look works equally well with a bathing suit and ball gown. Sometimes I go to sleep with my damp hair in a few braids in order to get those sexy ripples.

Get it: Thankfully, you don't need to live by an ocean to get these waves. There are texturizing products galore that make your hair look like you just went for a swim—many of them are even called "beach waves." To get the look with a curling iron, be sure to vary the direction of the waves you create so it doesn't look too uniform. You want the end result to be windswept and a little messy, which you can achieve by bending over and flipping your hair a few times.

CHAPTER 5

THE WHITE HOUSE

It took me years to come to appreciate my parents' amazing taste. Growing up, I didn't think of them as design savvy and forward thinking. In fact, I considered them eccentric and kind of weird. We lived in a suburb of Manhattan and the prevailing décor in my neighborhood was anything but contemporary and sleek. Most of my friends' houses featured traditional French or colonial furniture sets, wing chairs, heavy floral drapery, and lots of oriental rugs. Our house, however, could have been described as a stark tribute to streamlined, midcentury modern design.

My childhood home in
Short Hills, New Jersey

The entire interior was neutral, including our walls, B&B Italia sofa, and natural fiber rugs. My dad relaxed and read the *New York Times* in a cognac-colored Eames leather recliner with a matching ottoman, but most of the other pieces fell into a muted palette of ecru, linen, and blond wood. Then, there was the art. Our neighbors favored glossy oil paintings in ornate gilt frames. Hunt scenes, portraits, ships at sea—that kind of thing. The Rosenzweig house? Photo collages layered with aggressive text by Barbara Kruger, graphic political prints that commented on apartheid by Keith Haring, and disquieting paintings by modern realist Mark Tansey. My parents followed the art scene closely and collected pieces by the most talented up-and-comers—my dad will elaborate on how to start collecting art on page 166. It all seems so cool now, but back then I wondered why we couldn't hang just one watercolor of flowers.

Even my bedroom was a study in clean aestheticism. It, too, was entirely neutral with a big white trundle bed in the corner, except, of course, for my own art: bright Technicolor posters of boys—the likes of Erik Estrada and Shaun Cassidy—graced my walls until I was eight. Later, Duran Duran and George Michael were my crushes du jour. I think I became boy crazy before I could even talk! My focus centered on my bedroom closet even then. Let's just say there was never enough room for all my thrift store finds and accessories. And much like today, I organized my clothes and shoes according to color. Truth be told, my school outfits were more of a priority than my homework. Shocking, right?

In my junior year of college at George Washington University in D.C., I met Rodger. He was a waiter at a restaurant where I started working as a hostess; we became inseparable after our first date. (Much more on that magical night in Chapter 6.) As soon as I graduated, we both moved to New York. My first apartment was a thousand-square-foot studio that I decorated with stray hand-me-downs from my parents and pieces like shag rugs and lamps I found at flea markets. Working nonstop, I didn't put too much time or thought into my décor. All my energy went toward my career—and my clothes. When Rodger and I moved in together, we never really established a home. We relocated every two years to better rentals, because that's what New Yorkers do. I distinctly remember going through my "shabby chic" phase at our place on Thirty-fifth and Park with its overstuffed country French chairs and distressed furniture. It was beautiful and trendy, but it never felt like a reflection of me. I would walk into my apartment and, quite honestly, feel a bit uncomfortable. I realized that if my home didn't embrace my true aesthetic, I would always feel like a guest.

*The lobby of the Delano
Hotel, Miami*

At that point, though, I hadn't yet figured out my own design sense. Thankfully, a visit to the Delano Hotel in Miami's South Beach when it first opened helped me solve that dilemma. The lobby, designed by Philippe Starck and conceived as an indoor-outdoor space, was an airy haven of little enclaves separated by sheer white curtains that led out to the pool. The natural light alone made it feel like a beautiful beach with blond hardwood floors and scattered cabanas. The lobby instantly brought me back to our family vacations to the South of France. Statement pieces by Starck and Marc Newson and art by Man Ray added distinction. It was my idea of heaven. I looked at Rodger and said, "I want our home to be like this…for-ev-er."

Once we returned to New York, we even brought in a decorator—Delphine Krakoff—to transform our loft on Ninety-fifth Street into an East Coast urban facsimile of the Delano. Too bad it was just a rental.

When we moved to Los Angeles in December 2002, my clean and contemporary design sense was right on the mark. Midcentury modern houses beckoned with their uniform lines and floor-to-ceiling glass windows. I could finally rely on bright natural light instead of lamps and fixtures. Thankfully, the furniture we already had suited the architecture of our first house. Especially since Rodger and I had carted so much of it—from an Arco lamp to a Philippe Starck sofa to a Christian Liaigre bench—across the country. Each of those pieces, except for the Arco lamp, which broke during the move, is still in our current house in Beverly Hills.

And now, decades later, the midcentury ranch I thought was so odd as a kid is a muse. That sparse and modern aesthetic my parents always embraced appeals to me on so many levels. Our first big investments were a neutral B&B Italia sofa and an Eames lounger in white leather that I bought for Rodger. Maybe our son will look around one day and think we're a bit weird, too. That's just fine.

PASSION AS INSPIRATION

Decorating a home—or even a room—requires confidence and vision. To me, it's a lot like the process of putting together an outfit. You're using different elements to create one overall, cohesive look. Of course, furniture and rugs and window treatments often require much more financial output than earrings or a pair of skinny jeans. But if you focus on your personal style and your passions, you already have a jump on how to create a setting.

> "DECORATING A HOME—OR EVEN A ROOM—REQUIRES CONFIDENCE AND VISION. TO ME, IT'S A LOT LIKE THE PROCESS OF PUTTING TOGETHER AN OUTFIT."

Clearly, my first love has always been fashion. My dad likes to say "Fashion is Rachel's art." He's right. Almost every accent in our house relates to my obsession. A collection of Visionaire vinyl dolls by Kidrobot—from a mini Karl Lagerfeld to a tiny Vivienne Westwood—all speak to my worship of and respect for my favorite fashion icons. On my coffee table in the living room, a pair of silver-plated shoes sits atop a stack of fashion books. These fashion tomes, by the way, make great statement pieces on a table or mantel. Plus, guests can flip through them during a cocktail party. It's no surprise to me that so many museums around the world, from the Met in New York to the Grand Trianon at Versailles, have exhibited fashion as conceptual art. When I was in my twenties in New York, I hung vintage flapper dresses on my apartment walls and displayed a Versace chainmail dress on a coffee table. It still seems silly to stash all my fabulous pieces in a dark closet. I want to see my "art" and be inspired by it throughout the day.

Now, I surround myself with fashion photographs and prints. In the master bedroom, an entire wall is covered by a dozen art deco antique Hermès ads from the 1920s and 1930s. Right now, I'm coveting the 1963 "Bubble" series of models suspended in giant plastic balls above the River Seine in Paris by Melvin Sokolsky. His black-and-white photographs are absolutely breathtaking both in their composition and design.

"MY CLOSET IS MY IDEA OF A FANTASTIC MUSEUM."

As much as I love accessories, you won't find random knickknacks in my house. However, people who know me well have noticed my array of designer ceramic trinket trays and vibrant ashtrays by the likes of Hermès, Gucci, and Bulgari. In fact, my collection continues to expand, thanks to thoughtful contributions from friends and family. They look stunning all grouped together or scattered throughout the house. If you find a particular object that speaks to you, such as vintage decanters or Murano glass pieces, start amassing and make them the centerpiece of a table or shelves.

My closet is my idea of a fantastic museum. Sometimes, I artfully arrange my clutches on shelves so I can step back and admire them like Rembrandts. Printed silk scarves, especially designer vintage ones, look so chic and add a splash of color to a wall in any room. You can either iron one and mat it yourself or have a professional framer handle the job. I love to see a scattering of shoes on bookshelves or an étagère. A pair of vintage Ferragamo wedges used as bookends? Adorable! Another great nod to fashion is a vintage dress form, which you can buy online for under a hundred dollars. It becomes a colorful and textural sculpture when you add a fantastic piece like a vintage Pucci dress to it, or an architectural Thierry Mugler gown. It's art you can refresh or change out as often as you like.

RON ROSENZWEIG ON BUYING ART

As Rachel mentioned, Leslie and I have been collecting art since the 1960s. Sometimes we buy a major painting to celebrate our anniversary, such as the Frank Stella we acquired to celebrate ten years together. It's a true passion.

If you're looking to start collecting, first of all, buy what you love. We didn't even realize that art could be an investment when we purchased our first pieces, which were African sculptures and American Indian art; we were just drawn to the works. Later, we realized that we both had a passion for abstract modern artists and so we started educating ourselves.

It's important to learn about different periods—you never know whom or what you might discover along the way. I think it's a good idea to subscribe to art magazines to see as much as you can. Early on, Leslie and I would go to different galleries in Soho to get a sense of the landscape; she even took contemporary art classes at a local museum. Another great way to expand your knowledge—and collection—is to meet other people looking to buy art. In the early eighties, we joined a group affiliated with the New Museum in New York and we all shared information on new artist studios and exhibits. Galleries, art walks, and the young patron programs at museums are great places to socialize, too.

Once you purchase your first major piece, make it the centerpiece of your décor. What we have found over the years is that rather than buy something to match the palette or style of the room, we let the art become the focal point. A painting can bring a whole space together with its size, colors, and tone. ■

COMMIT, INVEST, REJOICE

Decorating can be daunting, because interior design is all about commitment. Big-ticket items like couches and dining room tables require a lot of consideration. Before we bought the B&B Italia sofa that is now in our family room, Rodger and I visited it in the showroom and discussed it countless times. The same goes for our Philippe Starck marble-topped table and white couch.

Before settling on a large piece that will greatly affect your surroundings, I suggest that you contemplate the purchase just as you would an expensive designer handbag or coat. I ask myself a few questions before I begin acquiring major furnishings.

CAN I LIVE WITH THE COLOR AND DESIGN FOR A DECADE?
I always opt for neutral, because we can accessorize with color in throws and cushions. On the other hand, you might crave colorful major furnishings and temper the overall palette with muted accents. In deciding on the design, we tend to invest in well-crafted pieces with timeless modern design instead of on-trend furniture. Pieces that boast "great bones" retain their value and last a lifetime.

HOW DOES IT WORK WITH MY OTHER PIECES?
Take a picture of the piece in question and then take it home and look at in the context of your space. You don't want to invest in a major item that might force you to redo your entire interior to make it flow well.

IS IT A SHOW PONY OR A USABLE PIECE?
I have been to homes in which certain furniture is completely off-limits. Maybe it's an original Hans Wegner chair or a spindly antique side table that's unsteady. My personal feeling on "don't touch" pieces is that they can intimidate your guests. You always want to make sure your furniture makes people feel comfortable.

WILL I HAVE A STROKE OVER A STAIN?
As someone with mostly white décor, I have learned to pray and look the other way when a guest sips red wine while sitting on my tufted white Chesterfield couch. You can only be so vigilant, right? Be sure you have such investment pieces pretreated for any spills. Legend has it that Coco Chanel let only certain visitors sit on her neutral suede couch!

DO I ABSOLUTELY LOVE, LOVE, LOVE IT?
It's my go-to rule whenever I buy something valuable. I usually ask myself if I would be absolutely heartbroken if I didn't take it home. Sometimes, I even wait a week before purchasing to see if I am truly obsessed or just infatuated.

Left to right: The lobby of the Claridge's Hotel, London. Suites at the Claridge's Hotel, London.

MY INSPIRATIONS

Gorgeous hotels and restaurants can make excellent sources for décor ideas, because they're designed to be both elegant and inviting. So much thought is funneled into every detail, from the comfort and configuration of the seating to the placement of simple accents. If you visit a fantastic location—whether it's a cool café or a chic private home—be sure to take notes. Throughout the years, I have found a few favorite places to stay, dine, visit, and glean ideas.

CLARIDGE'S HOTEL LOBBY AND SUITES: This art deco setting manages to marry masculine and feminine to stunning effect. The lobby features a black-and-white checkerboard floor with leather club chairs and a graceful ornate crystal chandelier by Dale Chihuly. Each suite feels decidedly different, but shares a few hallmarks of deco design like geometric mirrors and piped furniture. Your house can be eclectic from room to room, too. Rather than try to extend an overall theme throughout, infuse each area with its own personality and carry over one element, like a color or a chevron print.

Left to right: Restaurant Le Dalí, Paris. Hotel Du Cap, Eden Roc, France. Coco Chanel's Paris apartment.

RESTAURANT LE DALÍ AT LE MEURICE: Philippe Starck oversaw the design of this gorgeous eatery with its mismatched bergère chairs, Doric columns, and whimsical touches like a lamp with drawers and seating with ladies' shoes as legs. A dining table with an assortment of chairs always looks unique and more eye-catching, in my opinion. And the best part is that you can nab a collection of different styles at a flea market. I also appreciate the bold statement that a suede or velvet banquette in a smoky gray or pale mink brown makes as seating at the table.

HOTEL DU CAP: Built originally as a private mansion for writers, this château-style hotel perched on the coast of the French Riviera has become an outpost for actors, designers, and artists. But it's the twenty-two acres of towering pines, tropical gardens, topiaries, and the saltwater infinity pool that make me gasp whenever I visit. People say that Marc Chagall sketched the impressive view from one of the cabanas back in the 1960s. Think of your backyard as a giant living room and set up little pockets of

inviting furniture. You can use chaise lounges, overstuffed outdoor cushions, and even colorful towels. We set up a dining table beneath an arbor in our back space and occasionally dine al fresco on warm nights.

COCO CHANEL'S PARIS APARTMENT: When I had the honor of visiting Coco Chanel's apartment at 31 rue Cambon (it's closed to the public!) I didn't know where to look first. From the interlocking Cs chandelier to the mirrored spiral staircase to the huge Chinese screens etched with camellias, every inch of this four-room flat above the original Chanel boutique is impossibly ornate and elegant. Believe it or not, she only entertained here—she had a suite at the Ritz, where she slept most nights. I love that as a Leo, Chanel adorned her space with lions. Picking a motif meaningful to you makes it much easier to choose small treasures for display. If you favor a certain animal, flower, or even decade, look for interesting pieces that express your particular taste.

COMMUNAL CHEER

The rooms where people gather become the most beloved and most frequently used. It may be the kitchen, where a few friends chat at the table while you make scones, or a family room that plays host to the bustling kids' dinner table every Thanksgiving. In my house, these two, along with the living and dining areas, must be warm, stylish, and functional.

TO LOOK OVER AND SEE MY TWO FAVORITE GUYS
WITH BEDHEAD SLEEPILY WATCHING ME MAKE
OATMEAL OR TOAST BAGELS MAKES ME SO HAPPY."

In the living room—which we originally deemed the "white room"—a giant sofa languishes across from a set of deep, cozy Mario Bellini chairs. A console with two vintage French blown-glass lamps that feature black-and-white shades lend a little Parisian flair to the space. I think our guests have always been a little leery of tracking in wet leaves or accidentally spilling coffee on the white silk rug—I wanted the space to feel more welcoming. To do that, I turned one corner into a parking lot for Skyler's vintage toy cars and planes and boats. It's funny to spot his playthings in this otherwise pristine space, but it definitely makes the room feel more lived in.

Our family room happens to house quite a few of Skyler's playthings, too. Are you seeing a theme here? In this area off the kitchen, a huge sectional faces a media center and we have a cool little bar space to the left that is strictly Rodger's domain. I swear, I have never gone back there. When friends or family come over to watch a movie or casually hang out, we overtake the sofa and a tufted white Barcelona ottoman and even a few poufs. Leather poufs can serve as a glamourous alternative to additional seating. The whole room is an organic environment for sharing a few glasses of wine or passing around a bowl of popcorn.

But isn't it always the kitchen that becomes the unofficial clubhouse? No matter how many candelabras or bouquets of fresh flowers you put in the dining room, a crowd congregates around wherever the host can be found cooking. I love our eat-in kitchen—I make breakfast for Rodger and Skyler every morning. To look over and see my two favorite guys with bedhead sleepily watching me make oatmeal or toast bagels makes me so happy.

Selecting paint colors makes me nervous, because it requires a major leap of faith. In our current home, we had the interior painted a shade of white recommended to us by a dear friend, who happens to be a brilliant designer. But we bought the shade from a different brand of paint than she suggested. Guess what? Every wall ended up a blush color that reminded me of pale pink roses. I felt like I was trapped in a sixteen-year-old girl's bedroom!

What we learned the hard way was simply to do this: Always paint a wide swatch of your wall in a chosen paint color and sit with it for at least twenty-four hours. You want to see the effect during full sunlight *and* at dusk. Personally, I like white only because I view walls as a blank canvas for art and a backdrop for beautiful furniture and accessories. I have dreamed of painting a wall a rich emerald green, but I can't bring myself to deviate from my neutral aesthetic. That's not to say that I don't appreciate a colorful room in another home, of course. I envy people who have the guts to go over the top with a vibrant blue or deep plum in a dining room.

During the aforementioned painting fiasco, I also learned about the different finishes, since they profoundly affect the end result, too. Each of these different types of paint works best in a particular area.

MATTE:
I like the flat, nonreflective look of this finish, which best covers the imperfections of an old house. It works on ceilings and in living rooms or bedrooms. Caveat: Smudges won't clean off with a sponge—you have to touch up spots.

EGGSHELL:
The slightest sheen makes this velvety finish easier to wipe away, but it also marks up easily, so avoid using it in the kitchen or bathrooms.

SATIN:
This finish with a pearl-like sheen works well for bathrooms and kitchens, because it withstands humidity best.

SEMIGLOSS:
All our crown moldings, casings, and doors are painted in this slightly shiny coat that makes trim stand out from walls. I love the slight luster.

GLOSS:
Some people adore the high drama of this seriously shiny paint, which can reflect light like a mirror. Be careful with this one, though: If your walls aren't completely smooth, every blemish will be magnified.

My bedroom

BEDROOM BLISS

A bedroom should be the most serene and comfortable room in your home—a zen area where you emotionally shed the day's hurdles. In past apartments and houses, this room often doubled as a work zone for me. I never intended to do business at the end of the night or first thing in the morning, but invariably I woke up, grabbed my laptop, and started returning e-mails. With technology so mobile today, it's easy to snuggle up next to your phone and check your messages in the middle of the night. Don't do it. Trust me, you don't want to feel anxious or frustrated in bed because of a work situation. That feeling will carry over and affect your sleep. I created a sitting area in my bedroom to ensure that I don't do business between the sheets. A couple of mod club chairs and a small marble end table in front of the fireplace make the perfect configuration for flipping through magazines and sipping a cup of English breakfast tea or taking a fashion emergency call from a client. If your bedroom real estate is limited, a side chair in a corner with a Moroccan pouf can become a viable workspace, too. Add a floor lamp to create a special area to write notes or to make a packing list for an upcoming vacation.

In keeping with my fixation on natural light and an ambient setting, our bed faces a wall of windows with shutters that we rarely close. When we do, there are Lucite lamps on the nightstands and a vintage hanging pendant light above the sitting area that all create a soft hue. I'm a fiend for facing windows from my bed, because I like to see stars and wake up to the sun. But I'm also intrigued by floating a bed in the middle of a room instead of abutting a wall—but try it only if you have enough space to anchor the bed in the center without creating an obstruction.

Some say that the secret to a successful marriage is separate bathrooms. Maybe that's what accounts for Rodger and my twenty-plus years together! We are lucky enough to each have our own private domain off the master bedroom. (We have separate closets, too, which I think may be the *real* secret to a happy marriage.) In my mind, a bathroom should be a serene setting, because it's where you start your day, for the most part. It's the last stop before bed, too. You can make it a more chic and personal setting with beautiful perfume bottles arranged like art pieces and fresh flowers. I display my scents on a mirrored tray, which highlights the curves of each bottle and flacon. A pair of midcentury modern leather cube chairs—plus one miniature version for Skyler—face a mirrored vanity where I do my hair and makeup every morning. I always put away my cosmetics or creams and hair tools. We all work hard in front of the mirror to look effortlessly gorgeous and glamourous. Why leave all the incriminating evidence behind?

Sleep On It

When it comes to linens, I am of two distinct minds. I love the crisp clean look of all white sheets and duvet with a simple border, such as the classic Frette Hotel line. An ivory sheepskin throw strewn at the end of our four-poster mahogany bed makes it cozy, too. But I'm also crazy for the infusion of color a room gets with a vibrant knit Missoni coverlet or chevron throw pillows. My solution? Invest in two different bedding sets that satisfy your different moods. That way, you won't feel so pressured to pick the perfect comforter and sheet set.

Still, choosing colors and prints can be overwhelming. Good bedding is an investment, for sure, as the price of a luxury Egyptian cotton flat sheet can rival the cost of a great pair of sunglasses, though there are great lesser-priced options, too. One way to whittle down choices is to consider possibilities from a fashion perspective. Look in your closet and let your wardrobe help dictate which hues and textures will suit you. If you favor clean lines and unadorned fabrics in clothes, a Versailles-inspired brocade comforter doesn't fit your aesthetic. Do you have a peasant blouse for every day of the week? Look for Moroccan-inspired bedding with Moorish motifs. You want to invest in bedding that you can live with for at least a year or so. I always opt for the more classic, even basic, styles for that very reason.

Designers like Missoni, Diane von Furstenberg, Donna Karan, and Ralph Lauren all offer coordinating sets that reflect their sartorial sense. Ralph Lauren's pieces, as you can imagine, evoke a more equestrian club setting with muted paisleys, while Donna Karan's collection is as minimalist and sleek as her clothes. I dream of designing linens some time soon, because I believe a bed should be a visual and physical sanctuary. Technically, you spend about twenty-five percent of your life in your bed, right? In that case, it should be perfect. My set will most likely embrace my passion for great tailoring with crisp lines, clean stitching, and glamour. Stay tuned.

Skyler's nursery

A Chic Nursery

I probably had the most fun when I designed my son's room. All I knew when I first started conceptualizing it was that I wanted Skyler's space to feel dreamy and oasislike to kids and adults alike. The conventional color scheme—pink for a girl, blue for a boy—didn't speak to me. No surprise there, right? Instead, I envisioned a neutral palette with functional modern furniture and accents. His sleek Spot On Square crib was reminiscent of a streamlined Minotti chair, sitting atop a huge sheepskin rug. I can't tell you how many hours the whole family has spent cuddling and reading books on that cloud of a rug, surrounded by his menagerie of plush animals. In addition to a taupe glider, we added an oversized white leather couch that faces the crib from across the room. When

Sky was just a baby and people would come over to see him, I wanted guests to have a place to relax while he played or napped in his crib. Otherwise, everyone lingers around the crib—it can get a little crowded and uncomfortable. It's nice to have a conversation nook in a nursery if you have the space.

What I love most is that his nursery mimics the soothing colors and modern design of the rest of the house. Though that's not to say you won't find stocked bookshelves and rows of his tiny adorable shoes—he also has a stuffed polar bear on display that's almost as big as an armchair! I like to see his silly toys and silver piggy bank when I walk in the door. But his room does feel like a seamless continuation of our décor and as much a part of the house as every other room.

CLOSET CONFIDENTIAL

Nothing makes me more anxious than a disorganized closet, strewn with inside-out clothes, scattered shoes, and puddles of accessories on the floor. Seriously, I hyperventilate. Here's why: As a stylist, one of the first things I learned was the importance of organizing my fashion inventory. Not to mention, ill-handled pieces can easily be damaged. There's nothing more frustrating than trying to untangle a knot of gold chains or discovering that an unworn silk dress needs to be dry-cleaned because it wasn't hung properly.

"NOTHING MAKES ME MORE ANXIOUS THAN A DISORGANIZED CLOSET."

At my headquarters, we have an entire four-thousand-square-foot studio filled with borrowed clothes, shoes, and accessories for red-carpet styling and editorial photo shoots. Every item is categorized according to style, size, designer, and project. We keep files on who wore which piece to what event and when. Jewelry is meticulously logged so that an earring or necklace never gets overlooked. The system must be military in its precision—otherwise we wouldn't be able to operate efficiently.

"THE FIRST THING YOU WOULD SEE IF YOU STEP INTO THE CLOSET OFF MY MASTER BATHROOM IS MY COLLECTION OF CHANEL JACKETS."

Many of the same rules apply to my own closet at home. I'll get into the details of how my closet is arranged in a moment, but I'm not suggesting you must act like a drill sergeant, too. I do know a well-organized wardrobe will make you a more stylish woman, though. If your belts are all raveled into a ball in a bin, it's unlikely you will be able to take the time to pick the best one in the morning. (Instead, hang them from hooks.) Same goes for shoes that can't easily be eyeballed or sweaters that are crammed haphazardly in a stacking cube. Being able to see everything at once makes you more discerning—and who doesn't love options?

The first thing you would see if you step into the closet off my master bathroom is my collection of Chanel jackets. I like them to be front and center, and I suggest you do the same with your most prized pieces. It's a good rule to spot your favorites right away. New purses that I want to admire are also displayed prominently, outside their dust bags. (I call them "sleeping bags," because I like to think that my purses are cozy and happily resting when they're not with me.) Each pair of shoes sits on a rack with one heel and one toe facing forward so I can assess a shoe's whole look when I'm getting dressed.

Accessories like jewelry and sunglasses have their own shallow slide-out drawers in my closet. My system is built into the closet in matching dressers, but you can invest in valet boxes or clear plastic units with drawers. In my first book, *Style A to Zoe*, I talked about my mom's method of organizing her jewelry in hardware store compartment boxes meant for sorting screws and nails and bolts; I still stand by that practical system.

In addition to my everyday closet, I have racks of clothes that make up my archival collection: vintage pieces with heritage like a Pucci gold lamé gown or a Courrèges peacoat. Some of these clothes are extremely precious and date back more than fifty years. As you can imagine, I handle them with great care and store them accordingly. Sequined pieces are protected with padding on the shoulders so they don't snag other knits and antiquated silks are rolled in acid-free paper.

My overall rules for closet organization are pretty simple and straightforward:

HANG: Choose a uniform hanger style so that all your clothes display at the same level. Wooden ones gobble up inches of space; I prefer a thin version covered in black velvet that prevents slippage. Also, be sure to remove any plastic dry cleaner bags, which trap clothes in the chemicals used in the process. For pants with a center pleat, fold on the crease and clip to hang from the waist.

COORDINATE: Arranging everything—from shoes to dresses to blouses to belts—by color has always worked for me. I find it the easiest way to locate a piece and quickly decide if it suits my palette of the day. Prints and items with sequins, diamantés, or other special embellishments get categorized separately. You might prefer to categorize your pieces according to style, such as skirts or jackets, or to group work and casual wear separately. There are no absolutes when it comes to coordinating your looks, as long as you devote yourself to a system.

FOLD: Certain basics like T-shirts, sweaters, and even jeans are easier to find if you fold and stack them in open-faced cubes rather than pile them in dresser drawers. Just be sure that the stacks you create are not so high they'll topple—I think a maximum of twelve inches is a manageable measure.

STORE: I categorize my intimates and lingerie according to style and then by color and in a drawer, separated with dividers especially made for them. (Fabric-lined organizers are best for delicates.) An open bra clasp can snag on lace, so be sure always to secure them.

PROTECT: I prefer lacquered shelves, but wooden ones should always be covered in paper to avoid splinters and snags. My closet has a few windows, so I'm overly conscious of what's in the path of sunlight. No hats, bags, shoes, or other leather pieces are ever left out to fade. Instead, a pair of white orchids atop my two dressers soaks up the sun.

CHERISH: I know not everyone has a walk-in closet. A few of my apartments in New York had closets with barely enough room for my clothes, let alone me! But if you have the space for a small chair or even an ottoman or bench, I suggest that you create a little perch. It will make you feel all the more glamourous as you decide which shoe or jacket looks major.

Left: A selection of Chanel jackets from my collection. Right: A selection of sequin pieces from my wardrobe.

WORKED UP

For years, I worked from my kitchen table wherever I lived. Picture creative colleagues and fashion assistants all sitting in a rectangle, pecking at laptops and taking calls. It was fun, but it's a wonder we ever got anything done at all! A couple of years ago, with my business expanding to include media properties and other ventures, we relocated Rachel Zoe, Inc., to a proper corporate space: a giant, airy loft in an amazing fashion area in West Hollywood on a charming street with chic boutiques and cafés. Suddenly, I had a new all-important challenge: How do I decorate my very first office?

Right away, I knew it had to be a calm, soothing environment. Our days get insane, so I wanted the space to deflect that. My employees would all work at sleek table desks with modern floor lamps and white lacquered credenzas on hand for storage. My own office, situated in a far corner with three walls of glass, needed to be a chic refuge where I could sit and conceptualize a day dress, review my newest collection, or just recharge creatively with a cup of tea. To whittle down my options, I looked to the decades that inspire me as a fashion designer for ideas.

For my own seating, I chose a Knoll wire chair designed by Warren Platner in the 1960s for its comfort and sculptural grace. It also contrasts nicely with my smoked glass table desk, which I try not to clutter. On it, I keep a stack of inspirational art and fashion books alongside a potted cactus and a white orchid. Visitors who pop in can choose between sitting in a Milo Baughman caramel suede and chrome chair from the 1970s or lounging on an off-white Mario Bellini Bambole sofa with peaks like meringue. Thanks to all the natural sunlight and glass walls, I rarely turn on the overhead lights unless I am working late.

My Knoll desk chair

The accents here all reflect my taste and infuse my workspace with personality. A white sheepskin rug adds texture and tactile softness, while a throw in black and fuchsia makes for a cheerful pop of color. Adding a small area rug or brightly hued blanket can really help to individualize your area, no matter how large or small the space. A scattering of vintage Gucci ashtrays from the seventies act as little points of interest on my side tables. I do not smoke, but the design of these logo enamel pieces reminds me of that glamourous decade.

Choosing art was a matter of framing inspiration. I knew that I wanted to be able to look up and see some of my style icons. It ultimately came down to black-and-white portraits of Twiggy and Marianne Faithfull, separated by a shot of Halston and Yves Saint Laurent. The collection reminds me to push myself as a fashion designer, and to trust my instincts, too. When you decide on art for your own office or workspace, include images that speak to your creativity. I think a snapshot or two of your family or pet is appropriate, but an entire wall of dog or baby pictures screams that your mind is elsewhere. If you work in a creative field, hang a few portraits of your career idols or of pieces that wow you. As an employer, I like to get a sense of the aspirations and inspirations of my team. Your boss definitely notices those little things.

MARTYN LAWRENCE BULLARD
ON HOW TO BUILD A ROOM

With a roster of clients like Cher and Elton John, I have certainly created dramatic and glamourous spaces as an interior decorator. Rachel asked me to share my tips for making a room come together. When I design, I always like to start with the statement piece. In the living room, it's the main sofa, which must be comfortable, inviting, and strong of shape and presence. In a bedroom, it's the bed; in the dining room, it's the table; and so on. Next, I look to the flooring. If possible, I like floorboards dressed with a rug, which adds texture and color. Your floor covering is a great place to pull all the colors in the room together. A fantastic area rug can be put on top of a carpet to add a splash of bold color or a point of interest, too.

Then, start collecting furnishings and don't be afraid to be eclectic. Midcentury modern tables with eighteenth-century chairs on a Pottery Barn sisal rug can be the chicest of combinations. Color, shape, scale, and form are the elements to consider when mixing styles. Color in particular is vital to an interior. It immediately embeds your personal stamp on a space. If your room is dark by nature or has low ceilings, pick a bright color to bring in the sunshine. Consider a brilliant white gloss, Mediterranean turquoise, sunflower yellow, or crisp celadon green. If your room is bright, intense colors will diffuse with the daylight and become inviting at night. Crimson, emerald, cobalt blue, and other jewel tones are great possibilities.

Window dressings add glamour, comfort, and style to a room. Even the most modern abode looks better with some form of window covering, be it glass beads or a sheet of polished steel. Just be sure that they fit in with the character of the space. And lighting is everything. It changes the mood and atmosphere of a room instantly. A statement chandelier or table lamp is truly the jewelry of the space. A dimmer switch, by the way, is an interior designer's best friend!

Personal style is the only real ingredient in a room that matters. Adding personal mementos—like framed photos or trinkets picked up in an exotic market on vacation—is an amazing way to give your room a stylish and inviting vibe. ■

THE GOOD LIFE

Time flies. I know that sounds cliché, but it sometimes feels like just yesterday that I was starting out as a stylist and calling in a couture gown for the first time (twenty years ago!), or that Rodger and I were talking until dawn on our very first date (I was nineteen then, by the way). Of course, those two moments became amazing life milestones—discovering my passion and meeting my best friend—so they will always resonate with me. And thankfully, I met a man who is as crazy about celebrating life as I am. We also savor the more low-key happenings, too. Rituals and traditions have always been a big deal for us.

Left: With Skyler at the farmer's market, 2012. Center: With Rodger and Skyler on Halloween, 2012. Right: With Brian Atwood, 2010.

These days, it's harder for people to commit to quality time, because we are all so incredibly busy. You might be juggling the demands of a job with the needs of your family. Or you may be spending every free hour updating a style blog—and I just might be following it, too. Technology has forced us all to become master multitaskers. We work, we sleep, we worry about what we didn't manage to do! Who isn't always playing catch-up? Trust me, I know what it's like to overschedule yourself.

"SOMETIMES, THOUGH, YOU HAVE TO PUT ASIDE THE TO-DO LIST AND RAISE A GLASS TO ALL THE GOOD THINGS IN LIFE."

Sometimes, though, you have to put aside the to-do list and raise a glass to all the good things in life. I'm not talking just about major holidays or anniversaries. Growing up, my family sat down for dinner together almost every night. At the time, it was hard for me to understand why we needed to spend an hour at the dining room table when I could have been on the phone with my friends or flipping through *Vogue*. Now, as an adult, I understand why my mom and dad insisted on this time and I have carried it on to my own family.

It's the simplest rituals that you come to value the most in life. Every Sunday, for instance, Rodger, Skyler, and I all go to our local farmer's market in Beverly Hills and spend an hour or so browsing the stands and picking up fresh fruit and vegetables for the week. Sky nibbles on ripe berries while I shop for orchids and organic greens like mesclun and arugula. Not only has this become a regular family outing, but also one of the highlights of my week.

"IT'S THE SIMPLEST RITUALS THAT YOU COME TO VALUE THE MOST IN LIFE."

No doubt, every year will bring new traditions. My feelings toward certain occasions have changed, too. I never used to care about Halloween, but once you have a child, it becomes very important, as you can imagine. When Sky was one and a half, we all dressed up as cowboys and visited a pumpkin patch. We had the best time! And I imagine we'll keep it up until he outgrows it. But of course, I reserve my chic flapper costume for the nighttime parties.

We also recently started hosting a major family Thanksgiving feast at our house. And the same goes for Passover—I'm talking up to twenty people. Full disclosure: I may not cook all day (you'll learn more about how I entertain in Chapter 7), but I've found my own way to honor these holidays. When I look around the table and see my family and friends, I feel lucky to have such amazing people in my life. In the end, it's all about enjoying as much as we possibly can.

Obviously, I can't stop time, but I *can* make every moment as memorable as possible. The past few years have brought more responsibilities for me as a mom and within my career. And the busier I get, the more I realize how important it is to appreciate life and make the most of it. I hope you will be inspired by this peek into how I make merry on some of my favorite occasions.

LOVE ALWAYS

As I said earlier, I can still recall every minute of my first date with Rodger—even though it lasted almost eight hours! The cutest part? When he dropped me off after we talked most of the night, he asked, "Do you want to see me tomorrow?" (I said yes!) We haven't been apart many days since that night on August 29, 1991.

Over the years, so much has changed. We moved across the country, built a company together, and started a family. I like to say that Rodger and I are both codependent and independent. We completely live for each other and need each other, but we can also exist separately. In my mind, that independence is the most important aspect of a successful relationship or marriage. In order to thrive independently, you need to have a solid and unshakable trust—an assurance that allows you always to be yourself. Rodger has seen a vulnerable side of me that I rarely show to anyone and sometimes I need to be strong for him, too. In my experience, you must take turns being strong and supportive for each other.

As you could probably guess, romantic holidays are a big deal for us. Every year, we celebrate both the night of our first date and our wedding anniversary. In August, we're usually away on vacation and enjoy a simple dinner out together. But our wedding anniversary is a little more of a tradition: Because we got married on February 15, we usually skip going out on Valentine's Day and opt for a night of pizza and movies with our single friends. Little did I know when I married Rodger that our anniversary would fall right in the middle of Fashion Week and so close to Oscar season—not exactly a low-key time for me. For the past decade or so, we've had a New York tradition of going to see Marc Jacobs's runway show and then dashing over to Babbo—Mario Batali's fantastic flagship restaurant—for a romantic late-night supper.

A couple of years ago, Rodger wowed me with a romantic getaway to the Beverly Hills Hotel for our twenty-first anniversary, post–Fashion Week. Okay, so the hotel is only a few blocks from our house, but it's a rare night that we aren't with Skyler. I walked into a gorgeous suite to find Champagne, chocolates, and rose petals scattered everywhere. What an amazing night. I even quoted Julia Roberts from *Pretty Woman* and said to my husband, "If I forget to tell you later, I had a wonderful time tonight."

*With Rodger in
Santorini, 1991*

After all these years and celebrations, you might think that Rodger and I have run out of ideas for gifts. No way. I'm fanatical about buying presents for everyone in my life, so each year I listen for clues on what my husband might want. (Keep in mind that the stakes are high, as this is a man who left a trail of rose petals that led to a giant orange Hermès box on my thirtieth birthday—it was my first Birkin.)

Over the course of our relationship, I have surprised Rodger with simple silver jewelry, vintage watches, golf bags, and engraved ID bracelets. One of my most recent gifts to him was a chic Linus roadster bicycle, modeled after a 1950s French design. He nearly cried when I wheeled it out, because he had casually mentioned that he wanted a bike, but didn't think that it registered with me. One year I gave Rodger a chic picture frame with a photo of him holding Skyler. He later gave me the same style of frame with a picture of Sky and me. In a way, we were acknowledging that our son was the ultimate gift that we gave to each other. Just thinking about those frames reminds me that exchanging gifts is really more about being thoughtful than buying something extravagant.

THE BIG DAY

Everyone is entitled to their own red-carpet moments, and your wedding is definitely the most important. It's your day to be the center of attention and shine. Initially, I thought I wanted to marry Rodger somewhere exotic with family and just a few friends. I envisioned a beach or cliff side in the South of France or Positano. But my father was so excited for us and wanted to celebrate with an unforgettable event. In the end, we decided to throw a black-tie party at the Rainbow Room in Manhattan in 1998. My bridesmaids wore black velvet gowns with gloves and my wedding dress was this gorgeous Isaac Mizrahi gown with a fitted bodice and tulle skirt. I had seen the gown in red on the cover of *Vogue* and I called Isaac to beg him to make it for me in white. (I was on hold for thirty minutes pacing back and forth while I waited for his decision. It felt like hours!)

"IF I CAN SHARE ANY ADVICE, IT'S SIMPLY TO MAKE SURE YOU HOLD HANDS WITH YOUR PARTNER AS MUCH AS YOU CAN AT YOUR WEDDING."

In hindsight, I'm glad our wedding was a glamourous affair. I felt like a princess during every moment of it. Everywhere I turned, our dearest friends and family were dancing and toasting our happiness. It was truly the most magical night of my life. If I can share any advice, it's simply to make sure you hold hands with your partner as much as you can at your wedding. It's easy to get separated when you're making the rounds and greeting your guests. Everyone wants to talk to you! Rodger and I even stepped away right after the ceremony to enjoy a private moment and look out at the people who were there with us. I can't even remember what we said to each other—only that neither of us could stop smiling.

BRIDAL CHIC

Obviously, I couldn't mention weddings without discussing *the dress*. When you flip through your photo album thirty years from now, you should still love it as much as you did on your special day. I have styled all different types of brides, from a friend who married in a slip dress in a Kansas cornfield to an actress who literally toppled over trying on a giant tulle ball gown. Of course, the silhouette and style you choose should suit your personality and the ambience of the wedding itself—but I always suggest going more classic than contemporary.

How to find the perfect gown? Before anything else, go through tons of magazines and books to look at as many gowns as you can. I also advise you to begin pulling clips from magazines about six months before you even start shopping. A bridal salon can be incredibly overwhelming if you don't have a general sense of what you want to wear. *But,* at the same time, be open to anything. Yes, in essence, you are preparing to ultimately change your mind. It sounds crazy, but I have found that most women wear the opposite of what they assumed would feel right on them.

"WHEN IT COMES TO ACCESSORIES, I HAVE THREE WORDS FOR YOU: WEAR A VEIL."

When it comes to accessories, I have three words for you: Wear a veil. My philosophy is that you have one day in your life to do it, so take advantage of that opportunity. It's romantic and timeless and makes the walk down the aisle a true Cinderella moment. If you're worried about comfort, you can always take it off right after the ceremony. Wear a pair of shoes that are comfortable, too, so that you can dance all night. Stash wedges or lower heels under the table if you think you'll need to make a quick switch. As for jewelry, choose classic styles over dramatic pieces. It's tempting to wear an over-the-top necklace or chandelier earrings, but you don't want your gems to compete with your wedding dress. Even a simple slip dress shouldn't be upstaged by big jewelry. I typically recommend that brides select accessories close to their everyday style. If you always wear gold hoops, try on a pair with pavé diamonds. I opted for classic diamond solitaire studs.

With bridal beauty, again, be true to your style. If you don't typically wear a lot of makeup, do a natural, glamourous look for your wedding—just amp it up a little bit. Remember: You want to feel comfortable and look like yourself.

You may be seduced by trends, but on this occasion, I always recommend that you veer more toward traditional. Believe me, I have seen brides make outlandish decisions just because they saw it on a runway or in a bridal magazine. You just might regret the purple leather opera gloves or that mini top hat. If you feel the need to distinguish yourself with a unique accent, opt for a subtle highlight like a colored sash or shoes. When it's right, you'll know it.

Next spread: Our wedding day, February 15, 1998

VIP DAYS

Every year, I insist that I am doing something "small" for my birthday—no matter my age. "I don't want anything over the top," I will say to Rodger. But then, about a week before the big day, I suddenly realize that I miss my friends and want to throw a huge, amazing party just to see them all. At this point, Rodger is so used to my indecisiveness that he scouts out a space and reserves it for when I decide I do want to have a party. If you're on the fence about whether or not to make something into an occasion, I say go for it. You never want to regret a missed opportunity to make a lasting memory—for yourself and for the people you love.

"IF YOU'RE ON THE FENCE ABOUT WHETHER OR NOT TO MAKE SOMETHING INTO AN OCCASION, I SAY GO FOR IT. YOU NEVER WANT TO REGRET A MISSED OPPORTUNITY TO MAKE A LASTING MEMORY—FOR YOURSELF AND FOR THE PEOPLE YOU LOVE."

For my fortieth birthday—a big deal, I know—we took over a bungalow at the Chateau Marmont in West Hollywood. This effortlessly chic and legendary hotel has always been a favorite of mine. Rodger and a few friends even put together a slide show of photos that made me cry and then laugh and then cry again. (Why didn't I burn those pictures of me from the eighties when I had the chance?) We all got dressed up and danced until our feet ached. When the moment felt right, I stood up and gave a quick toast to my guests. At any event I host, I try to express my gratitude to my guests by letting them know how much they all mean to me. It's been a tradition of mine for as long as I can remember—I believe I even spoke at my birthday parties when I was a little girl! I don't think you ever need a reason to be thankful for your health and happiness. When it comes to public speaking, my motto is this: Speak from the heart. When Rodger speaks at a party, the whole room freezes, because he's so captivating. His roast to my mom at her sixtieth birthday had people laughing all night and his toast to me on my thirty-fifth birthday received a standing ovation.

RODGER BERMAN ON GIVING A GREAT TOAST

Rachel's birthday party every year is a chance to publicly acknowledge what she means to me and tell her how proud I am of her evolution. I don't write down what I plan to say, but I do spend a few hours thinking about it beforehand and try to formulate a beginning, middle, and end.

HIT ON A COMMON THEME. The most important thing to remember is that you want the audience to feel included. If you tell a personal story about someone, make sure you tap into a known personality trait or experience that is familiar to everyone.

SURPRISE EVERYONE. Sometimes, I also like to reveal a side of someone's nature that might not be so evident. For instance, one year, I thanked Rachel for making breakfast for me every morning. Not everyone realizes that she's such a caretaker; it was nice to be able to point that out.

HUMOR ALWAYS WORKS. Everyone loves to laugh at a party or wedding. My toasts are usually more heartfelt than humorous, but I am known for making some sly references and gently poking fun at someone or a situation.

READ YOUR AUDIENCE. Rachel keeps her speeches to a minute or two, but I tend to go on longer. I don't think you want to talk for more than five minutes, though. It's always smart to look out at the guests and read their faces and body language. If people are fidgeting or not making eye contact with you, wrap it up. ■

Top and bottom, left:
Skyler with his family on
his first birthday. Bottom
right: With Rodger and
Skyler at our Memorial
Day barbecue.

KID STUFF

Why is it that children's birthday parties have become a competitive sport? I like to think it's because parents want their kids to have *the* best day. My philosophy is this: Children are happy with simple snacks, some upbeat music, and lots of smiling faces. Ponies and petting zoos are fun, but certainly not essential. When Skyler turned one, we planned a little party in the backyard that soon ballooned to a hundred guests. What was that I said about going big? But when it rained that morning, we moved it indoors at a nearby restaurant and brought in a face painter and a music teacher who got everyone jumping around and dancing. Trust me, my son is an excellent dancer! If you want to go for it, that's fine, but no one should feel pressured to spend a small fortune to hire a circus for a group of toddlers. At the end of the day, a balloon and cake make any kid happy.

THE ANNUAL BBQ

Remember how much you loved sleepovers and pool parties as a kid simply for the joy of spending time with your friends? It didn't matter that you saw them every day at school. As adults, we sometimes outgrow that urge to invite people over just because we love them, but you never need a reason to gather your friends and family.

Every year, about three weeks before Memorial Day, Rodger and I start to get e-mails asking, "What time is the barbecue?" and phone messages like, "Can't wait! What can we bring?" It's a running joke—or rather, known fact—among our friends that we will host a BBQ on the inaugural summer holiday every year. We've been throwing this bash for about five years now, and I have a feeling it will be a lifelong Berman family tradition.

Initially, this barbecue was a small, intimate gathering of eight or ten close friends. But every year, it never fails that the guest list expands, making our small barbecue into an all-day soiree for fifty! (Are you seeing a theme here?) Truthfully, it's better this way—we get to spend the afternoon with so many people we adore. I always say if you're going to do the prep work for a party, you may as well make it a major one! We get to see everyone we care about all at once, and include them as part of what has become one of our favorite rituals, too.

Top: Rodger's first
Father's Day gift.
Bottom: Rodger's first
Father's Day.

FATHER'S DAY

Growing up, Father's Day was always a big deal for me. I had a "Daddy's Little Girl" nightgown that I wore until I outgrew it. Every year, I woke up early to make my father a special omelet and pancakes. Now that my husband is a father, too, I like to thank him for being such an incredible dad to Skyler. That usually means a special brunch and a day at the park. For his first Father's Day, a group of friends joined us for brunch and we made him wear a goofy "Number One Dad" sash and hat. In true Rodger form, he wasn't embarrassed in the least. And Skyler giggled nonstop!

FRIENDSHIPS FOREVER

As important and fun as these big gatherings are, my close girlfriends also mean everything to me. Unfortunately, with our insane schedules, it's difficult for us to find time to get together. And I know that we're not the only women who need to send at least a dozen e-mails to organize a dinner. Since our free time is so limited and we want to make the most of our few hours together, we usually make it a "girls' night in." If it's at my house, I might order a spread of Mexican food and make flavored margaritas. If we decide to bring in pizzas and chopped salads, I'll open a few bottles of Chianti and Pinot Grigio. Some nights, we just lounge around and catch up on what's happening with each other. But I have a few more fun ideas for making the most of your girls' night.

RED WINE, RED NAILS. If you're like me, you can barely find time to get to a nail salon. Hire a few local nail technicians who can do quickie manicures for an hour or two. Catching up with friends while you sip wine and get pampered feels so luxurious and decadent.

PUSH PLAY. My girlfriends and I used to meet every week to watch *Gossip Girl* together at one of our houses. We would order takeout and hit pause a million times to discuss every amazing outfit and steamy scene. (I actually did a cameo in one episode, in which a vat of chocolate ended up on my head and my Pucci dress. Insane!) Now that show has ended, but we try to get together for a regular movie night instead. I love to screen a favorite film like *Almost Famous.* Who doesn't love Kate Hudson's fabulous seventies groupie costumes?

DO GOOD, FEEL GOOD. Every once in a while, we gather to talk about charities or causes that are important to us. We might discuss how to raise awareness or brainstorm on planning an event. A few times, we have even volunteered together as our girls' night activity. One organization in particular, Baby2Baby, is close to my heart, because they supply families in need with baby gear and essentials. I'm also an ambassador to the incredible foundation Save the Children. Why not have a little fun with philanthropy?

"BANANAS" BREAD RECIPE

When I need to get zen, I bake—maybe it's the precision required in measuring and mixing ingredients that soothes me. During the frantic weeks leading up to Fashion Week and award season, I have been known to bake dozens of cookies and brownies for my office. It has become such a tradition that my team starts to drop not-so-subtle hints like "Where is your apron?" No matter what, it's always my chocolate chip banana bread that disappears the fastest.

½ cup softened unsalted butter, plus more for greasing the pan
1 cup sugar
2 eggs
1 cup mashed bananas (about 3 medium overripe)
2 cups all-purpose flour
1 teaspoon baking powder
½ teaspoon baking soda
½ teaspoon salt
1 cup milk chocolate or semisweet chocolate chips (optional)
½ cup walnuts, peanuts, or pecans (optional)

- Heat oven to 350°F. Lightly grease the bottom of a 9 x 5 x 3–inch loaf pan (do not grease sides).

- Beat the ½ cup butter and the sugar in large bowl with electric mixer on medium speed until fluffy (about one minute). Beat in the eggs and bananas until smooth (about one more minute). Add the flour, baking powder, baking soda, and salt, and beat, just until mixed. Stir in the chocolate chips and nuts with a spatula, if using.

- Pour the mixture into the prepared pan. Bake for 1 hour and 10 minutes or until a toothpick comes out clean.

- Allow the bread to cool in the pan for 10 minutes and then remove it to a wire rack. Allow it to cool completely, about 1 hour.

For an even more decadent finish, I sometimes add a crumble topping:

½ cup sugar
⅓ cup all-purpose flour
½ teaspoon cinnamon
¼ cup softened unsalted butter

"Bananas" Bread ingredients

Mix all the ingredients together until crumbly, then sprinkle over the loaf for the last 30 minutes of baking.

CHAPTER 7

LET'S HAVE A PARTY

Someone at a dinner party once asked me to name my top five wish-list dinner guests alive or not. What a great question, right? My mind somersaulted because there are *so many* people I would want to invite!

To me, creating a guest list is a lot like building your wardrobe. You want to include your trusted go-tos and something a bit unexpected while always maintaining a perfect balance. Those are my considerations when I fantasize about my dream dinner party.

First of all, Brigitte Bardot would *have* to come—she's so private. but I think she would really open up in this intimate setting. Coco Chanel would receive an invite, too. She led an unbelievably fascinating life and I could ask her all sorts of questions about her philosophies on fashion, men, and Paris society. I would absolutely include Jane Birkin, and seat her to my right. She's the most fabulous woman in the world without even trying. I would ask her about the swinging sixties in London—she and Bardot could reminisce about the sexy film *Don Juan* that they made together in 1973. Of course, I would be a fool to pass up a chance to invite a Beatle. Paul McCartney is my pick. He could even sing a few songs during dessert. Then, there's Johnny Depp. I have had a crush on this brilliant actor since I was thirteen and I know he's a perpetually captivating person. He has managed to maintain his personal style and integrity as an actor—an amazing and admirable feat.

This imaginary dinner party would be amazing, but how would I prepare for such fabulous guests? In my last chapter, I shared my favorite rituals and holidays. Now, it's time to talk about *how* to throw together a gathering—and why parties for no particular reason might be my favorite ones of all.

THE ART OF BEING AN EXCELLENT HOSTESS

When it comes to entertaining, I learned a long time ago that trying to accomplish everything invariably leads to a disaster. You know that hostess, the one who's smiling a little too wide and looks like she is about to have a nervous breakdown in the kitchen? Maybe she just burned the risotto and she's trying to keep it together. Or she was so busy that she never had a chance to shower and she's wearing last night's mascara. Unfortunately, guests pick up on that energy and then feel like they're imposing. I should know, because I have been that frazzled hostess once or twice—but not anymore.

The key to being a fantastic entertainer is to look like you are having an amazing time—because you really *are* enjoying yourself, of course. If that means ordering in a spread and just mixing the cocktails and pouring the wine, do that. Your friends don't come to your home to judge you on your ability to whip up foie gras or make the perfect roast chicken. One Thanksgiving, I dashed around the kitchen like a crazed French chef and served a twelve-pound turkey with a slew of side dishes. (Of course, I was

Brigitte Bardot at a dinner party

wearing a turban, but no apron.) It was rewarding, but completely exhausting. Though I hope my guests did, I didn't get to enjoy the occasion as much as I would have liked, because I was so busy.

Lately, my party MO is to oversee a few hors d'oeuvres—including my grandmother's insanely beloved baked salami roll—and to roast almonds in the oven, which makes the whole house smell welcoming and festive. Instead of creating the entire menu, I usually have the main dishes catered so that I can enjoy myself, especially now that I have Sky on my hip and everyone wants to play with him. I also set out what I can early in the day so there's time to shower and to dress up before guests arrive.

Still, even the most meticulous groundwork doesn't guarantee everything will go as planned. I have burned that baked salami a few times—but a little char actually makes it taste better, believe it or not. Even if I do make a mistake (and we all do), I don't let it destroy my night. I just laugh and admit to my guests that I dried out the chicken and that we need to order out. I'm the first to ask "Okay, who wants Thai?" You have to see the humor in any situation—whether it's a sudden downpour at your barbecue or a salty soufflé. Everyone else will follow your lead and laugh, too.

As a hostess, my entertaining checklist is fairly simple and straightforward. I try not to focus on the little details—which no one else notices anyway—and direct my energy to the elements that matter most to me.

KEEP THE LIGHTING DIM AND FLATTERING. Unless it's natural sunlight, an overly bright setting is not only unkind to anyone over the age of twenty-five, but it also makes you feel like you're dining in a department store. Candlelight—from dainty flickering votives to magnificent pillars—always delivers a warm glow that makes everyone look like they just returned from a weekend in Saint-Tropez. For fixtures in the dining room, look for incandescent bulbs that emit a soft amber light instead of harsh white with blue undertones. I'm a huge fan of dimmers, which are fantastic for adjusting mood lighting. If you don't have dimmers, opt for lamplight instead of overhead, and strategically place floor and table lamps around the room for ambience.

"THE KEY TO BEING A FANTASTIC ENTERTAINER IS TO LOOK LIKE YOU ARE HAVING AN AMAZING TIME—BECAUSE YOU REALLY *ARE* ENJOYING YOURSELF, OF COURSE."

CREATE A DECIDED FLOW. Everything I do, from designing a collection to decorating a living room, calls for an easy energy. I don't care for anything that feels fussy or constricting in the end. The overall cadence carries over into my entertaining, too. A party should have a natural flow that you might have to gently nudge if it ambles off course. For instance, start everyone off with cocktails in one spacious room. Then, beckon them into another area—maybe a dining room—for supper, or outside for al fresco nibbles. By moving the party, even from one end of a room to another, you create some fluidity and energize people with a new setting. If my guests are all gridlocked in the kitchen during a party at our house, I'll motivate the crowd by saying "Everybody go outside and get some air!" Place candles, food, and fresh flowers wherever you want people to congregate. Otherwise, they may randomly stand in hallways.

INVIGORATE THE MOOD. Unfortunately, there is no foolproof recipe for inviting guests who always have excellent chemistry. And if people aren't mingling or having fun, I'll admit that I used to go into emotional cardiac arrest. How are you to know that two jewelry designers might not want to talk shop or that a usually gregarious couple will arrive sulking after an en route spat? When I detect a social lull among my guests, I do one of two things: recount an embarrassing personal moment that will loosen everyone up or whisper "Rodger, change the music." Believe me when I say that his music can make even the most uptight people shimmy a little in their seats.

RODGER'S PARTY PLAYLIST

Rachel and I both love a lot of the same music from the late sixties and early seventies. It's one of the interests we bonded over early on and I even convinced her to come to some Grateful Dead shows back in the day. If you come to a dinner party at our house, you're bound to hear these songs.

"Love Street," The Doors

"Lay Lady Lay," Bob Dylan

"All I Want Is You," U2

"Green Eyes," Coldplay

"Peggy-O," The Grateful Dead

"Landslide," Fleetwood Mac

"Everybody Hurts," R.E.M.

"Angie," The Rolling Stones

"Don't Tell Me," Madonna

"Get Together," The Youngbloods

SERVE LOW-KEY, UNCOMPLICATED FOOD. I won't try to dissuade you from adding a chilled gazpacho or a steaming bouillabaisse to the menu. But for me, the easiest way to feed a crowd without worry is with items that are best enjoyed at room temperature—especially at a casual dinner party. You'd be surprised how many different dishes fall into that category, from grilled rosemary chicken breast to sliced steak to poached salmon. When you are not tied to a menu that must be scheduled to accommodate temperatures, you're not hovering over a hot stove or oven and blotting at your face in between courses. Also, there is no urgency about eating. Your guests can dig in when they're ready and they don't feel compelled to end a fascinating conversation because the braised short ribs are getting cold. And everyone can come and go as they please.

DRESS FOR THE OCCASION

Part of the fun of playing hostess is deciding what to wear when you open the door. If your outfit includes a tiara at a dinner party, you set a silly and decadent tone. Similarly, your bare feet at a brunch immediately put everyone at ease—and might even encourage other guests to shuck off their shoes. For my own quick touch-ups, I tuck away a lipstick in my guest bathroom or kitchen so I can refresh my pout in seconds. My overall philosophy on what to wear when entertaining is that you should dress up and even take a few fashion risks. Wear that bold purple dress or the satin turban. Do a bright red lip. After all, everyone is looking at you—you should be stunning when you host. I love to finish my look with a statement piece like a choker, long chains, or bib necklace that infuses glamour. Of course, what you wear depends somewhat on the type of party. Here are some suggestions by occasion.

CHIC COCKTAILS. A jumpsuit is a cool and easy silhouette that can easily be amped up with sky-high heels and a few layered accessories.

CANDLELIT DINNER PARTY. Time for a little black dress that shows some décolletage with a gold choker that will reflect flickering tapers. If you're going to be popping up a lot to serve, avoid too many layers and fabric that might make you overheat.

CASUAL WEEKEND BRUNCH. Tailored dark denim with a fitted white tee and a boyfriend jacket looks effortlessly polished. I love to juxtapose the effect with a slightly messy topknot.

LATE-AFTERNOON BARBECUE. You can't go wrong with a bright, colorful maxi dress and gold gladiator flats. Keep in mind that heels and grass don't mix and that you may be sitting on a lawn, so anything super short could become X-rated. If you like a little extra height, opt for a comfortable wedge.

DIVIDE AND CONQUER

Have you ever attended an amazing party and wondered "How does she do it?" If she's savvy, she doesn't do it all alone. Delegating is imperative to pulling off a spectacular event—with your sanity intact. It could be that you divvy up the duties with your partner or a good friend. You might even consider cohosting a party; that way, you all share the work and cost and, in the end, bring new faces together.

Over the years, Rodger and I have developed and refined a system for entertaining that keeps us both busy and out of each other's path while we prep. He stocks the bar and does all the heavy lifting, from inching furniture around to fetching ice. I'm in charge of the cuisine, from shopping for ingredients to cooking or ordering and then setting the table.

We always create a timeline for an event, whether it's a Sunday supper for eight friends or a Studio 54–inspired dance party.

THREE WEEKS OUT: Think about your invitations, which can set the initial tone. I spend an hour or so on Paperless Post and gravitate toward a palette of white, black, and gold or tan. My wording—always in Century Gothic font, because it's timeless and strong—is typically minimal and to the point. Theme invites, with a grill for a barbecue or Champagne flutes for a celebration, are always fun.

TWO WEEKS OUT: Create a menu. Rodger and I start planning our dishes and a signature cocktail. We might serve festive sangria with blood oranges or a clear whiskey iced tea.

With Rodger at my birthday party, 2011

ONE WEEK OUT: Stock up on nonperishables. We shop for items such as tapered candles for the dining room table and spirits and mixers for the bar. If we are hosting a barbecue, we pick up plastic cutlery and recyclables. This is also a good time to assess seating and/or tables; look into rentals if necessary.

ONE TO TWO DAYS OUT: Time to double-check recipes and shop for essentials. We buy all the perishables—from charcuterie to fresh vegetables—within forty-eight hours of a party. Pick up any fresh flowers you'll want, and be sure you have appropriate vases. I also lay out my outfit at this point so I won't have to think about it on the day of the event.

THREE HOURS BEFOREHAND: Get glam. Though it might seem logical to wait until that last hour to shower and change into your outfit, something always comes up. I have learned to get ready earlier and then do the last minute tasks such as arranging cheese plates in my hostess wear.

ONE HOUR BEFOREHAND: Now that Rodger and I are cohosting with a toddler, it's not easy to control the schedule! Skyler runs around the house in a diaper while I chase him with his outfit, or put him to bed if we are entertaining in the later evening. I like to put platters out on the buffet table and pull out any last-minute items. We go through our checklist one last time and inevitably run to the local market for anything outstanding.

THIRTY MINUTES BEFOREHAND: Rodger deals with the beverages that need to be chilled and then puts on the music. I light candles. We always strive to be done with prep about a half hour before guests arrive. That way, we can relax and have a chill moment together before the doorbell rings.

Left and right: The décor at my non-traditional baby shower, hosted by Pamela Skaist-Levy. Center: A formal table setting.

A TABLE IS A RUNWAY

By now, you might have already gathered that our décor aesthetic is rooted in a soft, neutral palette. Not shockingly, the same goes for my take on a beautifully set dinner table. I like a muted palette here, because it reminds me of a fashion runway. The vivid colors and varied textures of food and bright décor accents pop on this canvas. Most of my dishes are white; my Tiffany wedding china bears only a discreet platinum edge. A classic border on a plate, whether it's chevron or chain links, makes an interesting side note to the meal. My mom taught me to sometimes use chargers as dinner plates. That way, everyone has enough room on their dishes to try everything on the table. On occasion, though, I love to mix up my plates and juxtapose formal with casual accents. Simple stemware looks cool next to ornate china; modern flatware adds some edge to antique patterned dishes. Colored or clear glass bowls inject a little whimsy to a table, too. My collection of oversized square simple white dinner plates are unexpected and look graphic and bold.

If I want to create a more formal and elegant setting, I break out the silver-ware, occasion glasses, soup bowls, and bread plates. A few easy rules for setup: Linens should be placed on the center of the plate or folded and to the left. Plates should be layered according to use, e.g., the first-course plate—be it a salad or soup—will rest on top. A bread plate goes above the forks, which are to the left of the plate. Forks start at the outside according to use, so have a salad fork to the left of the main utensil. The knife sits to the right of the plate, with the blade facing inward. Finally, glasses go above the knife, starting with water and then wine stems.

We have an immense zebra wood rectangular table that seats twelve, but it was custom-made to be extra wide. I like an expanse of space, because I often serve meals family style. If I am going to put out huge bouquets of fresh-cut flowers—such as peeled back roses made famous by my favor-ite floral designer, Eric Buterbaugh—and giant serving platters of delicious food, I can't bear a cramped, cluttered table. A few dramatic candelabras or a row of votives can take up precious real estate on a table. But be as creative with your table as you are with your personal style. Bright neon fruit like lemons or limes pop in a glass cylinder vase or even artfully scat-tered down the center of the table. Rosemary or lavender tied around a napkin or centered on a plate always looks romantic.

DRAMATIC BLOOMS

Flowers are one of my favorite indulgences for entertaining, but they don't always cooperate. I'm partial to these temperamental ones in monochromatic single varietal bunches, so I know how to care for them.

HYDRANGEAS:
These clouds of blossoms are hearty and gorgeous, but can also wilt suddenly. Place stems in very hot water for 30 seconds if flowers droop—they should perk up and stay fresh for up to five more days.

PHALAENOPSIS ORCHIDS:
I love that these exotic plants are dramatic, yet affordable. You can even buy them at some grocery stores. They bloom only once or twice a year, but their flowers last up to three months if you add three ice cubes to the container per week and keep them out of direct sunlight.

CALLA LILIES:
Fluted like Champagne glasses, these graceful flowers tend to bend at their stems in the same direction. I'm crazy for the "black" variety, which are actually a deep, rich red. In arranging them, be gentle so as to avoid bruising.

PEONIES:
High season for these spectacular round blooms is spring—sadly, they're scarce in winter. If the buds won't open, place them in warm water and on a sunny ledge.

TULIPS:
Keep these fragile slender-stemmed blooms away from direct sunlight and heating vents. You can add a penny or two to the water to make them last a few days longer.

Peeled back roses by Eric Buterbaugh

Opposite: The dining room

For seating, we have a dozen white fiberglass Eero Saarinen tulip swivel chairs designed for Knoll back in the mid 1950s. Each one, with its fluted lines and pedestal base, looks like a piece of sculpture. The architect and designer once said that he created the one-legged chair to minimize clutter—a man after my own heart. It's also easy to be able to turn to talk intimately with someone on your left or right.

I rarely assign seating because I trust that my guests are all outgoing and inclusive. But if you invite a group of people who don't know each other at all and feel anxious about it, think ahead and use cute place cards to put together people who have common interests. That way, you won't have to worry about hovering and igniting conversations all night. Some hosts don't like to let couples sit next to each other—but not me. I understand that my dinner party might be the only time they have together all day or even all weekend. When it comes to conversation, I always encourage my guests to tell personal stories and talk about current events. If you're seated next to someone you don't know at a dinner, a smart, original inquiry always ignites a dialogue. It can also be a lively icebreaker for a hostess to throw out to the table between courses. My only forbidden topic? Politics. People get extremely heated over hot-button issues—especially after a few glasses of wine—and suddenly, half the table could be heading out the door.

SCENTS AND SENSIBILITY

Fragrance is an accessory for your home and it always impacts the ambience of a party. Perfumed candles do double duty, but be sure the scent isn't too overpowering. The same rule applies to room sprays and artfully placed potpourri. You can have different fragrances from room to room, reserving a spicy, sensual fragrance for the cocktails area and a floral one for the bathroom. My favorites?

AMBER:
Spicy, exotic, warm notes make the perfect olfactory palette for a get-together on a cold night. Fantastic for an Oscar party.

FIG:
I adore the subtly sweet earthiness of this fragrance with its milky accents. Keep one candle flickering in the foyer to set the tone for a dinner party.

LAVENDER:
No matter the occasion, this gentle herbal scent always soothes the scene and helps people relax. I love it for daytime events.

TUBEROSE:
This highly intoxicating floral feels romantic and mysterious—it's also known for its aphrodisiac properties, making it the perfect redolence for a sexy cocktail party.

SANDALWOOD:
It's no surprise that Tom Ford has a fragrance called Santal Blush. Super sensual with a strong woodsy finish, it's the ideal backdrop for a first date at the house or romantic night in.

With friends attending Carine Roitfeld's "Black Tie, Smoky Eye" event in Paris

ATTIRE: BLACK-TIE, SMOKY EYE

Los Angeles might be the epicenter of unfathomable dress codes. I have seen invitations that call for bizarre attires like "denim dazzle" (two words that should never collide, in my opinion) and "corporate elegant." Suggested party attire should never confuse guests or, worse, force them to panic and spend a week's pay on an elaborate costume or a cocktail dress in a specific hue like pale lemon or Vreeland red.

Instead, take a cue from my style icon Carine Roitfeld, former editor-in-chief of French *Vogue* and now the global fashion director at *Harper's Bazaar*. In Paris, during Fashion Week fall 2012, she hosted a blowout party called Le Bal with a "black tie, smoky eye" dress code. What I loved about this particular directive is that everybody could kohl their eyes and raid their closets for a stunning getup—it didn't require any additional hassle or effort. Rodger even played along and borrowed my eyeliner!

When Rodger and I got married at the Rainbow Room in New York in 1998, our wedding was a black-tie affair—even though we walked down the aisle to the Grateful Dead's iconic anthem, "Truckin'." (My dad and I danced to Stevie Nicks's "Landslide," a favorite song of mine.) But other than that occasion, I can't think of a time I asked my guests to style themselves a certain way. I'm not averse to sensible theme parties or dress codes at all; rather, I just appreciate my friends' collective and individual style so much that I let them handle their own attire.

TIMING IS EVERYTHING

I try to be on time, if not early, for everything—especially when I am in New York, where you can set your watch by certain people. In Los Angeles, punctuality is considered a lost art, but I still think it's a sign of respect to show up at an appointed time. When people have to wait for you, they can't help but feel you assume their time isn't valuable. That's never a solid foundation for any relationship—personal *or* professional.

When I throw a dinner party, I typically call for cocktails an hour or so earlier than the time we sit down to eat. That gives everyone a cushion for when to arrive—but still, some people always seem to show up during dessert. At the age of eighty-six, Coco Chanel complained in an interview that people were sauntering into dinner parties two hours late in Paris; she called it vulgar. Coco would go insane if she lived in L.A.!

There is, however, a social drawback to being punctual: Sometimes you get to an event before the room fills. Walking into a party and not seeing any familiar faces used to give me a panic attack. Seriously, I would exit as soon as I politely could. But after years of attending luncheons and cocktail parties and lavish European-style business dinners, I have learned that it's better to get to a party when it's already in full swing and then leave just after the party has peaked. (Plus, I now devote my early evening to feeding my son and tucking him in before I go out.) I always ask ahead for the nod to bring a guest along so I can be sure I will know at least one person there, but sometimes, a plus one is impossible and you have to respect that request. Besides, flying solo is a great opportunity to socialize outside your comfort zone.

When you're out alone, look for a familiar face—even if you have met a person only once—and strike up a conversation. You can even be honest and admit you don't know anyone else and plan to shadow him or her. Another idea is to seek out the host and insist on helping out, whether that's opening a bottle of wine or putting out a platter. It's a great way to meet other guests, as the host will be greeting people as they arrive and make introductions. People will flock to where there is food and drink, so try stationing yourself there. Or, you can try to flatter a guest who looks interesting. A well-aimed compliment will endear you to someone every time—but be sure it's sincere. Look for the person wearing an amazing dress or killer jewelry and ask about it. If you're just not feeling super out-going, plan to arrive at the end of the cocktail hour or mingling portion of an event. That way, you can take your place at the table and instantly have someone to talk to on either side.

GIVING AND RECEIVING

Whenever I entertain, I always instruct my guests not to bring anything at all. It's a good policy, because it takes the pressure off people to find the perfect token of thanks. Still, many of my friends arrive with *something.* In my opinion, the best hostess gifts are ones that can be enjoyed later. For instance, I will never thrust a layer cake or bouquet of fresh flowers into the hands of the host, because either offering requires immediate attention and might not complement what she or he had planned. Instead, a box of exotic chocolate truffles or a set of designer playing cards tops my list.

Sometimes, Rodger and I will give our host a classic game such as Monopoly or Scrabble as a gift. (After a few cocktails, board games can get very, very interesting.) I'm also partial to gorgeous coasters, elegant serving trays, and oversized glossy fashion or photography books like *Halston: An American Original* or *Poolside with Slim Aarons.* A box of gold embossed note cards is a thoughtful token, too. (Just insist that the host needn't use one as a thank-you note to you!) A cute or funny apron can be an unexpected and functional offering. But at the end of the day, you can never go wrong with an incredibly great bottle of wine or Champagne. Put it in a gold or silver wine sleeve with a little note or just tie on a ribbon to personalize it.

A recent study revealed that more than half the country feels fine about regifting. That's great, but I'm not one of them. I support recycling, but I think it's bad karma to pass along a present someone gave to me. I will, however, pay forward a sweater or scarf or accessory that doesn't work for me. I always preface it with "Someone gave this to me, but I can't use it. It's more you than me." That way, it's clear that I am regifting.

Top: A set of playing cards by Tiffany & Co. Bottom: Macaroons by La Duree.

Next spread: A selection of keepsake thank-you notes

*Left: Bianca Jagger,
Halston, and Liza Minnelli.
Right: Margherita Missoni
on her wedding day.*

MERCI IN THE NEW MILLENNIUM

Never underestimate the value of a thank-you. In an ideal world, I would be known for my handwritten notes of appreciation on embossed stationery with tissue paper–lined envelopes. To me, they are incredibly thoughtful and personal, and make a distinctive keepsake. I keep a collection of letters and notes I have received from friends, designers, and clients in a special box just because I treasure them. The paper stock is creamy and thick and the scrawled messages are sometimes witty and sly. They feel like pieces of art.

"NEVER UNDERESTIMATE THE VALUE OF A THANK-YOU."

But my own go-to for gratitude is electronic. It's not only better for the environment, but I can pen a sincere thank-you anywhere, whether I'm waiting for a dinner date or sitting in an airport. Within forty-eight hours of receiving a gift or attending a dinner, I make a point to send an e-mail with a heartfelt message. Because e-thanks can seem impersonal, it's important to call out something specific. I might gush about the design of a piece of jewelry someone has given to me or mention how much I loved discussing the agony of getting my son to nap over lunch. I draw the line at thank-you texts, though. Seven characters of gratitude just doesn't cut it.

INFORMAL, BUT UNFORGETTABLE

Fashion people love any excuse to wear beautiful clothes. Look back at photos from Studio 54's heyday and you'll spot Halston, in a white silk scarf, laughing uproariously on the arm of Liza Minnelli.

Or a tuxedoed and bespectacled Yves Saint Laurent doing a social lap with the divine Catherine Deneuve. Don't get me started again on how much I long to have lived in the seventies and hit the scene at the venerable hot spot. That whole moment epitomizes this unforced glamour and verve to me. There was an ease to the way people entertained and enjoyed themselves.

Of course, the modern-day fashion world knows how to celebrate, too. And in my twenty years in the business so far, I have been lucky enough to attend dozens upon dozens of over-the-top, fantastic events. Valentino's forty-fifth anniversary extravaganza comes to mind: a black-tie party on the grounds of the Villa Borghese with aerialist ballerinas pirouetting in front of the Colosseum. I must have gasped a dozen times during the thirty-six-hour event!

Casual gatherings can be just as impressive. Some of my favorite stylish entertainers and dear friends have managed to make low-key get-togethers feel equally special, even opulent, in an organic way. The Missoni family, for instance, hosts weekends in Italy with kids frolicking in and out of their villa, amid mismatched plates and all sorts of eclectic cuisines.

Diane von Furstenberg invites her dear friends over to her Paris apartment to sit around in a circle on overstuffed ethnic floor pillows. The supremely witty Marc Jacobs prefers a close-knit dinner party of four or six guests who wouldn't ordinarily come together; he loves to choreograph the conversation of a disparate group. Stella McCartney inspires me because she adheres to her lifelong activist ideals when she throws a party. The menu is always vegan and delicious. Above all, the takeaway is to remember that it's all about the company you keep and your own style of entertaining. No matter what you serve or how you set a table, your guests will always have an amazing time if you relax, be yourself, and have fun, too.

GOING PLACES

Travel was a huge part of my childhood. My parents strongly believed that seeing other parts of the world and learning about the cultures of other countries made a person more well rounded and savvier about life. I couldn't agree more. When I was twelve, they took my sister and me on an unforgettable vacation to Italy. I can still remember walking around Venice, astounded by the beauty of the city. On this particular trip, I also fell hard for chic European style and discovered my obsession with fashion. I noticed how the women relied on simple, well-cut silhouettes, luxurious fabrics, and dramatic accessories to look elegant. Still, whenever I travel, I take note of the local style and nuances. I also make a mental note of the colors and shapes of the landscapes. When I sit down to conceptualize a collection, I envision those women and their surroundings. It's hardly shocking that many of my style icons are European.

With Skyler in Saint Bart's

I even save all my old passports and the colorful currencies from different countries. Rodger and I have this dream to rent a villa for a month on the Amalfi Coast of Italy or in Tuscany when Skyler gets a little older. In my fantasy, I see us walking into the nearby little village to buy fresh pasta, Parmesan, a bottle of Pinot Grigio, and a loaf of bread for dinner. We will learn some Italian while Skyler makes new friends. Unlike my breathless and busy trips to Paris, our European family hiatus will be snail-paced, quiet, and a bit like a Bertolucci film—until the pipes burst in our eighteenth century villa, of course.

It's as important to take do-nothing vacations as it is to soak up culture. Our lives are overscheduled enough. You shouldn't underestimate the value of spending one day being lazy. My MO when we head to Saint Bart's every year is to do absolutely nothing but gaze out at the ocean, play with Skyler in the sand, and meet up with friends for casual dinners. I recharge while I'm there and come back to work feeling refreshed and even inspired by the vivid hues of a dramatic sunset or the way a light fabric billows in an afternoon breeze.

PACK LIKE A PRO

Every year, I take at least two major trips. In August, it's off to New York and then Europe for almost six weeks of runway shows, including my own shows and events during fashion season. And at the end of the year, it's the getaway to Saint Bart's. The first is not an easy pack, as I'm in New York when we show the collection in early fall and the weather can be unpredictable—think humid and sunny one morning and a dreary downpour an hour later. Then, I head to Paris, London, and Milan, where I might need a coat and lots of cold weather accessories. Since I'm jet-setting through time zones and different climates, I have learned to begin organizing my wardrobe weeks ahead of time. Saint Bart's—where I mostly live in caftans, sarongs, and wide-brimmed hats—calls for some thought about day-to-day looks and evening outfits. Last-minute packing always results in overdoing it—just ask Rodger. Now, I have a tried-and-true timeline for packing smart, no matter the destination:

TWO WEEKS OUT: I like to create an "outfit itinerary" after looking at the schedule of my trip, especially with business travel. Note the time and nature of each event and then lay out a potential look—including accessories—for that occasion. I might mark down velvet tuxedo with booties for an afternoon meeting with a retailer or a printed maxi dress, leather jacket, and platform wedges for a cocktail party. If you notice any gaps, you have plenty of time to find new pieces before you go. And you can always ask friends to fill in the blanks with a borrowed evening clutch or a cashmere scarf.

This is also a good time to set aside pieces that need to be dry-cleaned or shoes that could use a new heel or sole. The same goes for accessories—check clasps on necklaces or bracelets and make sure that all the earrings you plan to pack are in pairs. I always photograph my options with my phone so I have an easy-to-access reference guide.

If you're taking a lengthy trip or packing beyond what you can manage at the airport, consider shipping items ahead of time. By planning a few weeks in advance, you can send a suitcase across the country via FedEx Ground and pay about sixty-five dollars for a fifty-pound bag that arrives in four business days; but overnight service runs closer to three hundred dollars.

ONE WEEK OUT: Check the weather report for any unexpected climate changes and alter your outfit lineup accordingly. Review the photos of your looks if you took them, and make notes on any necessary tweaks. I always swap out a few pieces or experiment with different accessories—it's the stylist in me. If you purchased a new pair of shoes for the trip, wear them for an entire day to break them in and to ensure that they are comfortable. There is nothing worse than blisters on a vacation!

Refill any prescriptions that may be low and assess all your beauty products to be sure that you won't run out of moisturizer or foundation while away. Pick up three-ounce travel bottles to transfer liquids for carry-on use. I like to schedule a manicure, pedicure, and blowout for the day or so before I travel. I always pick up my chosen nail polishes so I will have them handy for on-the-go touch-ups. Who hasn't chipped a nail at the airport?

THREE DAYS OUT: I call ahead to the hotel to request extra hangers. You can also ask if they offer steamers to guests. (If not, put a handheld one aside to pack.) Contact your credit card companies to alert them of your trip—especially when traveling overseas—so that none of your charges will be declined. Arrange to have your mail handled and suspend your newspaper subscription if need be.

TWO DAYS OUT: Finalize your outfits and put all shoes, clothes, and accessories aside. As a stylist, this is what I call the "big edit." Make sure your pieces are truly versatile: a cool leather jacket and a sleek black dress are items you can accessorize a few different ways. Look at your shoe picks through the same prism: Can you wear that pair of suede over-the-knee boots with a few outfits? Do you really need two pairs of black pumps? I would rather overpack accessories like scarves, hats, bags, and statement jewelry. Not only do these accents take up less space, but they also complete your signature style. At this point, also load up with reading material and make a mellow playlist for the flight.

THE DAY BEFORE: Pack! I have learned not to wait until the day of a trip to organize my suitcase. Packing your suitcase the day before allows you to make last-minute tweaks and substitutions. My method is to use the dust bags that come with handbags to separate all my essentials. Undergarments go in one, scarves in another; same with T-shirts and tights. Shoes, of course, go in their own dust bags as well. (Any

*Arriving in Paris with Skyler
and lots of luggage*

soft pouches will work.) I place all the heaviest items like bags, shoes, and belts in the bottom and then layer clothes on hangers on top. My sequined pieces, silks, and any other fragile garments stay in dry cleaner bags to prevent any snags or pulls.

THE DAY OF: Set aside at least thirty minutes more than you think you will need to get out the door—there are always a few stray things to do, and you don't want to panic about missing a flight. Stow certain last-minute carry-on items such as a cell phone charger and any snacks for the plane. Your travel outfit could profoundly affect your comfort over a span of hours, so be sure to wear clothes that won't constrict you. I typically choose roomy, even slouchy pieces like a sweater dress or leggings with a jersey tee and duster. You won't catch me in any color but black, which can camouflage both stains and wrinkles. My secret weapon is an over-the-knee boot that ties the whole ensemble together.

Left: Didier Ludot, Paris.
Right: Four Seasons
Hotel George V, Paris.

J'ADORE PARIS

Every visit to Paris feels like the very first one—even though I have been there almost forty times. I always see something new in the architecture, the museums, the cafés, or even the little shops on the side streets. Then, there are the people. They look so poised and stylish. Even the Parisian children carry themselves with elegance. I swear to you, the babies are born inherently chic over there. I get more inspired in Paris than in any other city in the world.

Because I have a finite amount of time to visit the boutiques and flea markets, I become anxious to shop as soon as I arrive. A word of advice: If you fall in love with a dress, a painting, or a purse while traveling, buy it. First of all, that item will always remind you of your trip and spur a little nostalgia. Second, it's likely you won't be able to find it stateside—and there's nothing worse than retail regret. (Rodger and I have shipped home vintage lamps from Paris and a rug from Saint Bart's for that reason!) You don't want to think of Rome as the place where you *didn't* buy those amazing equestrian boots.

In Paris, I usually hit my favorite vintage shops first. I love a boutique in the Saint Germain called Les 3 Marches de Catherine B. It's like going

to a museum to shop, completely stocked with pristine Chanel pieces. Browsing vintage haute couture at the gorgeous emporium Didier Ludot in the gardens of the Palais Royal is a must, too. If I'm there over the weekend, I always go to the big antique flea market called Les Puces de Saint-Ouen, where you can find everything from a vintage Rolex to the most incredible deco light fixture.

Where to stay? I like to get to know at least one neighborhood of a foreign city as much as possible, so I make it a point to pick hotels in a specific area whenever I visit. That way, you can stake out your favorite café and visit every morning for a coffee or at sunset for a glass of wine. Pretty soon, the owner starts to recognize you and smiles or winks when you walk in; maybe his little French bulldog trots over, too. You can feel like a local even when you're away from home. I adore the Four Seasons Hotel George V off the Champs-Elysées and near avenue Montaigne. There are the most fabulous flower installations by the brilliant Jeff Leatham that he changes out almost every day and many of the rooms have beautiful terraces.

With Marc Jacobs at his
home in Paris

The courtyard at Hôtel Costes on rue Saint-Honoré is where I eat lunch almost every day during Paris Fashion Week. You literally see every designer there—I used to spot Yves Saint Laurent eating in the corner with his partner. I would shake with excitement just catching a glimpse of him! When I'm not people watching, I love to visit the Louvre, and the Opéra National de Paris, where Stella McCartney has shown her collections in the past few years, is a beautiful building, too. It was built in the 1600s by Louis XIV, so it's incredibly opulent and over the top.

"EVERY VISIT TO PARIS FEELS LIKE THE VERY FIRST ONE."

If I'm taking a trip to somewhere I don't know quite as well, I typically forgo travel books for word-of-mouth suggestions from friends. That way, your itinerary is more personal. A few weeks before a vacation, I e-mail friends who I know have visited my planned destination and ask for their favorite cafés, secret beaches, and vintage or antique stores. Sometimes, I am more specific and ask what the best spot is to catch a breathtaking sunset, or say "Tell me about the flea market where you got that amazing vintage clutch." I rely on this method of planning so heavily that I asked some of my most stylish and well-traveled friends to contribute insight on their favorite places in the world—from London to Buenos Aires. Their suggestions make me want to pack a bag and go!

In Paris

Left: Nammos restaurant, Mykonos. Right: The Cotton House hotel, Mustique.

SHOE DESIGNER BRIAN ATWOOD ON MYKONOS

In Mykonos, the energy, the light, and the sea are all intoxicating. It's a traveler's utopia, unlike anywhere else in the world. There is a sensuality about the people and the island and the food that has me hooked. Kiki's, a taverna with no electricity situated under a tree, has the best octopus I've ever eaten. Everybody waits for a table—there are no reservations. The beachside restaurant Nammos is the place to see and be seen. Arrive preferably by yacht and plan to dance on tables by the end of your meal. The best hotel is the Belvedere, but I have rented the same villa for the past several years.

Staying in a home away from it all makes my time in Mykonos more relaxing and intimate. Usually the house is packed with ten to fifteen of my family members and friends. We often go to Kapari Beach—it's private, has a chic crowd, and even some nudity!

You can't leave Mykonos without an evil eye souvenir. You can find a colorful multi-wrap bracelet for two euros, or really high-end handmade pieces that are exquisite. ∎

FASHION DESIGNER MATTHEW WILLIAMSON ON MUSTIQUE

The remote private island of Mustique is an idyllic paradise, with endless stretches of white sand, turquoise waters, and lush greenery. Its isolated nature is a huge part of its appeal. When I'm feeling social, I go to Basil's Bar, which is an institution that serves impeccably fresh fish and seafood. They do an amazing lime daiquiri, too.

I like to stay at the Cotton House hotel, which has beautiful rooms and exceptional service—they host a cocktail party for the island's inhabitants each week. If I have an hour to kill, I might take a boat and explore some of the secluded bays and coves around the island. The waters around Mustique are full of beautiful reefs and tropical fish. It's a wonderful aquarium! ∎

Left: The Bowery Hotel, New York. Right: Old district of Recoleta, Buenos Aires.

CALVIN KLEIN DESIGNER FRANCISCO COSTA ON NEW YORK CITY

I love the forwardness and constant energy of New York—its adrenaline, fresh ideas, and driven people are all inspiring. Because of the vertical nature of the city's architecture, you're always looking up. The High Line is the perfect place to go for a walk and escape. This elevated public park provides the best of both worlds, combining the city with its natural surroundings.

When I am down on the Lower East Side, I enjoy eating at The Fat Radish and visiting all the modern galleries, like Lisa Cooley and Orchard Windows Gallery. Casa in the West Village has the most delicious, authentic Brazilian food in New York City—their okra and chicken stew always remind me of home.

You can't go wrong staying at The Carlyle, because it is super chic, but if you are looking for something more downtown, then The Bowery Hotel is a cool option. ■

POLO PLAYER NACHO FIGUERAS ON BUENOS AIRES

Buenos Aires is known as the Paris of South America because of its European design, dating back to the beginning of the twentieth century.

Palermo Viejo is an older neighborhood that's great for discovering hip restaurants and small boutiques. I love the restaurants Sucre, La Panaderia de Pablo, and an amazing little coffee shop called I Love Café in the Recoleta area. If you want to sound like a local, order a *fernet con Coca,* an herbal Italian liquor mixed with Coca-Cola.

On a lazy afternoon, I like to walk around the old district of Recoleta, a beautiful historic neighborhood that is one of the highest points of the city. Before you leave Buenos Aires, you must pick up a beautiful handcrafted maté, which is a silver-trimmed calabash gourd used for drinking tea from the leaves of yerba maté. It comes with a silver straw called a *bombilla.* ∎

Krishnarpan
restaurant, Nepal

FASHION DESIGNER PRABAL GURUNG ON NEPAL

Nepal sits between two powerful nations—India and Japan—and it embodies and embraces both cultures, but maintains its own strong identity. The landscape of mountains, hills, and plains is stunning and inspiring. It's truly remarkable to have such diversity in a country of its size, between the religions practiced and the languages spoken. My favorite cultural touchstone is the Patan Museum, which is actually an old royal palace with a fantastic Asian art collection. I also love the Garden of Dreams—a magnificent neoclassical garden with pavilions, pergolas, and fountains—because it has such a rich history and is breathtakingly beautiful.

Dining is intimate. There is a strong culture of either going to friends' and families' homes or hosting a dinner and cooking a large meal. I go home for my mother's cooking, so I rarely go to the restaurants. However, Tukuche is great for traditional Nepalese fare and the dishes at Krishnarpan are absolutely exquisite.

For shopping, Thamel Street—also known as "Freak Street"—is where you can buy clothes, crafts, food, and even music. The hippie movement moved through India to Nepal and left such a mark on this street. What to bring home? Pashmina shawls originated in Nepal, so you can never go wrong with one! Also look for a thangka painting, which depicts a Buddhist deity on silk. ∎

Above: Caffè Florian, Venice.
Opposite: Hotel Danieli, Venice.

PUCCI DESIGNER PETER DUNDAS ON VENICE

As a Norwegian, I love places on the water and Venice is one of my favorite cities. It has to be one of the most romantic places on the planet. A weekend there is an almost guaranteed successful getaway. I usually like to stay at the Hotel Danieli, which is right on the main canal—the sunrises and sunsets are unparalleled. It's nice to sit and have a coffee at Caffè Florian in Piazza San Marco, which opened in 1720. The café sells some of the best home fragrances; Sala Orientale is one of my favorites and it is a staple at my Florence offices.

When it comes to culture, the Fortuny Museum is a well-hidden treasure. It has a great collection of pleated Fortuny delft dresses, a rare editions bookshop, and small exhibitions like one on Roberta di Camerino. Before I leave the city, I make sure to stock up on gold and silver crucifixes from the San Marco Cathedral. I wear them in my ear and seem to lose them in various beds all over the world! It's also one of the best places to buy Murano glass, which is multicolored and reminds me a bit of Pucci patterns. You can find it throughout the city. ■

Left: Buca Mario
restaurant, Florence.
Right: Beverly Hills Hotel.

RODARTE DESIGNERS KATE AND LAURA MULLEAVY ON FLORENCE

Florence is one of the most beautiful cities in the world because of its art and architecture. If we have a free morning or afternoon, we always visit the Galleria dell'Accademia di Firenze, which holds Michelangelo's *David* and the unfinished *Prisoners*. Our favorite museum is San Marco, where you can see the Fra Angelico frescoes. We always pick up Botticelli T-shirts as souvenirs!

We love dining at Buca Mario, which opened in 1886 and has an amazing cellar space. For bellinis, we go to Harry's Bar, which overlooks the Arno. They use the most aromatic peaches from northern Italy, and the last time we were there, we received never-ending bowls of the ripest cherries. ■

JUICY COUTURE COFOUNDERS PAM SKAIST-LEVY AND GELA NASH TAYLOR ON LOS ANGELES

There is an incredible light that only a sunny day in Los Angeles can bring. It makes you feel like anything is possible and happiness is abounding. Where else can you jump in your car and drive to the sunny shores of Malibu or check out the desert in Two Bunch Palms—just two hours outside the city? There are dozens of great places to stay in the city, but we love the Beverly Hills Hotel. It feels like home because we have been going there our whole lives. When you walk through those doors, you feel like Eloise. Be sure to check out the coffee shop downstairs—it is truly an institution.

For a shot of culture, we are huge fans of the Museum of Contemporary Art (MOCA), which is downtown. It doesn't feel like a corporate museum and never disappoints. We also love its bookstore and gift shop for artsy finds. The funky neighborhood of Echo Park is where you find the most killer vintage shops that have great prices and are well curated. But if you're looking for an authentic souvenir, pick up anything from Olvera Street, which is a historical Mexican marketplace downtown. ■

Bond Street, London

BURBERRY CHIEF CREATIVE OFFICER CHRISTOPHER BAILEY ON LONDON

I am constantly inspired by London on so many levels and I particularly love its people, its architecture, and the wonderful parks and gardens that add green to our city. There's a beautiful hidden English garden in the middle of Battersea Park that is a real gem and gives a moment of calm in the city. You have the well-known, elegant, and bustling shopping areas such as Bond Street, Knightsbridge, and Regent Street—but don't forget to explore the wonderful little streets off the beaten track, too.

When I'm craving culture, I absolutely love the National Portrait Gallery. The portraits take your breath away as they transport you through different periods of time, culture, and politics. Step outside again and you'll find yourself in one of the most bustling, vibrant, and dramatic parts of London: Trafalgar Square. The energy in the air in this part of town simply buzzes.

London is home to some of the best antique bookstores in the world and I like whiling away the hours looking for something special. Try Pottertons in Chelsea for art and design, Peter Harrington on Fulham Road for exquisite and rare first editions, or simply wander along Charing Cross Road and dip into the many bookshops there to bring home a unique reminder of your stay. ■

DESTINATION LUGGAGE

Now that I know about all the hidden gems in these fantastic places, what to bring? Obviously, a week in a cosmopolitan city calls for completely different packing than a jaunt to the slopes. I categorize my trips according to weather, landscape, street style, and activities.

URBAN ESCAPE. City vacations or business trips call for the most versatile clothes and accessories. If you're out all day, you might not want to run back to your hotel to change for dinner. Instead, you can amp up your look with bold jewelry, red lipstick, and heels. For jewelry, think big—or, at least, as big as you can pack. Oversized cuffs can inject texture, color, or a flash of metal to a little black dress or jeans and a tee. I love to top off my metropolitan look with a felt fedora.

When I travel to New York or London, I always bring along a structured bag with a cross-body strap that looks polished but gives me easy, on-the-go access. Cities mean a lot of walking, so cool motorcycle boots or classic riding boots—flat or with a modest wedge or chunky heel—are perfect. Wayfarer sunglasses always feel spot on in the city because they're sleek and architectural.

Denim, skinny or wide in a dark wash, can transition easily from day to night with a pair of platform pumps. A silk button-up blouse also works around the clock—just undo another button and add a statement necklace for an evening out. I like to bring along at least one tuxedo-inspired dress, because it looks androgynously chic in a cosmopolitan setting and also exudes a little rock-and-roll vibe. On windy days or chilly nights, a leather peacoat or bomber jacket is perfect.

BEACH GETAWAY. What I love most about our annual Saint Bart's trip is that I can pack light. If you're heading to a tropical setting or a beach destination, it's all about easy, ethereal pieces like caftans and maxi dresses that mirror the casual vibe. An eyelet sundress that you can wear with gladiator flats during the day or metallic espadrilles at night is key. An oversized raffia tote that can hold my swimsuit, sunscreen, and other beach necessities is my go-to. I like to wear cat-eye sunglasses on the beach, because they make me feel especially glamourous.

Silk harem pants are comfortable and they ripple in a sexy way with a gentle island breeze. Similarly, a printed peasant blouse feels right in line with the atmosphere and pairs well with a lightweight linen blazer. And always be sure to pack a classic black bikini. Jewelry with turquoise, coral, or tiger-eye pops with sun-kissed skin and a bright headscarf or headband is essential for taming an ocean-tousled mane.

WINTER WEEKEND. Cold-weather locales can pose a few packing dilemmas. It's easy to get stuck on shoes when you want to look stylish, but also might encounter ice or snow. My solution is faux fur–lined wedge boots with rubber soles that are both fashionable and functional. They look cute with thick black knit leggings or a cable-knit cashmere sweater dress with a cozy cowl neck.

I opt for a well-worn leather tote or knapsack that can stow a knit beanie and a pair of mirrored aviator sunglasses. You won't have to sacrifice your silhouette, either, in a belted puffer jacket that will keep you warm. Underneath, go with a warm, fitted cashmere sweater and accessorize with an oversized men's watch and quilted leather gloves.

CARRY-ON CHIC

What you bring on a flight in your carry-on bag can make or break the first and last leg of your journey. Over the years, I have learned to pack all my beauty products—from skincare to cosmetics to hair needs—in separate zip pouches so I can stay moisturized in the air and do a quick touch-up before the plane lands. (I transfer certain lotions to three-ounce containers to comply with TSA rules.) I also stash a set in my tote that includes slippers, an eye mask, a small throw, and a miniature pillow. A lot of airlines don't stock enough blankets and pillows for every passenger. You're better off being prepared!

Since checked luggage can often be delayed, I also fold a pair of leggings and a sweater into a pouch so that I have an outfit in a pinch. If I'm heading to the beach, I also include a bathing suit for the same reason. All of my jewelry comes with me in a separate holder, too. Never check valuables, and protect them from scratches by packing each piece in its own velvet pouch. Storing necessary credit cards, airline paperwork, and my passport and license in an accessible zip pocket in my tote makes the process of boarding that much simpler, too. Chargers for tech accessories and sanitizer get pockets as well. Finally, I always pack enough fashion magazines to keep me busy through the entire flight.

AU REVOIR

Well, that was fun! By now, I hope you feel inspired to begin or end your day with more confidence in who you are—or who you want to be. Perhaps you'll spend an extra minute or two in the morning applying a new bold red lipstick or set aside an evening to throw a chic dinner party and tackle a new recipe. Writing this book certainly has reminded me that even a little effort goes a long way.

What I have laid out for you is merely a blueprint. Now, it's your turn to experiment and rewrite the pages. There truly are no rules when it comes to defining your signature style. Be fearless. Trust your creative instincts. Take fashion risks! You only live once—so make every day glamourous.

RACHEL ZOE

Thank you for your tremendous support throughout my career. I hope you enjoyed reading this book as much as I relished working on it. Here's to life, love, & endless glamour!

XoRachel Zoe

ACKNOWLEDGMENTS

TEAM ZOE

Monica Corcoran Harel—You are incredibly talented and such a dream to work with! Your enthusiasm and dedication to this book have meant everything to me.

Mandana Dayani—There are not enough words to describe my love and gratitude for who you are and what you mean to me. My friend and my sister, I love you.

Marisa Runyon—It's been a very long road together and I can't thank you enough for always staying by my side and being my champion and my family.

Kelsey Berlacher—You are a star that keeps shining brighter every day. I am eternally grateful to you, my Kels Kels.

Kendall Cohan, Shannon Nash, Jessica Amento, and Mel Chalian—To the greatest team on earth: Thanks for always being my cheerleaders and for making me smile when I didn't think I could. I am forever grateful for your dedication to this project.

Justin Coit—Thank you doesn't say enough for your immeasurable patience and kindness. You always capture the best of me. You are a true friend and my family. You will go so far!

Byron Williams—You are my brother and a genius. I am endlessly grateful to you for helping me find myself.

Joey Maalouf—I cannot thank you enough for always making me feel beautiful and being the most extraordinary uncle to my son. My love for you is immeasurable.

Amanda Englander—Your patience and attention to every page, photo, and very last comma helped shape this book immensely. Thank you!

Andy McNicol—Many thanks for envisioning a follow-up book and convincing me that I had so much more to say.

CONTRIBUTORS

I am so lucky to have such witty, thoughtful, talented, and well-traveled friends who shared their collective brilliance with my readers. Thank you so much for your time and input. You are the everyday inspirations in my life.

Adir Abergel

Brian Atwood

Christopher Bailey

Rodger Berman

Martyn Lawrence Bullard

Francisco Costa

Peter Dundas

Nacho Figueras

Prabal Gurung

Joey Maalouf

Kate Mulleavy

Laura Mulleavy

Leslie Rosenzweig

Ron Rosenzweig

Pam Skaist-Levy

Gela Nash Taylor

Diane von Furstenberg

Matthew Williamson

Beautiful images helped bring this book to life. Thanks to everyone who generously provided art.

Bowery Hotel

Buca Mario

Chanel

Claridge's Hotel

The Cotton House

Didier Ludot

Dorchester Hotel Collection

Dwarika's Hotel

Eric Buterbaugh

Foundation Pierre Berge—Yves Saint Laurent

Four Seasons Hotel George V

Hachette Filipacchi Photos

Hôtel Costes

Hotel Danieli

Hotel Du Cap

La Duree

Le Meurice and Le Dalí

Margherita Missoni and Missoni

Morgans Hotel Group

Nammos

ShoeDazzle

Tiffany & Co.

Tom Ford

Van Cleef & Arpels

RACHEL ZOE

An unparalleled fixture in the fashion world, Rachel Zoe is a distinguished designer, stylist, and editor, renowned for her effortless take on glamour. Having immersed herself in fashion and design for two decades, Rachel has been heralded as one of the most influential forces working in fashion today.

Rachel's first book, *Style A to Zoe*, was published in 2007 and was a *New York Times* bestseller. Very shortly after the success of her book, Rachel debuted *The Rachel Zoe Project* on Bravo in 2008. The show catapulted her from behind-the-scenes stylist to a household name and ran internationally for five successful seasons.

In an effort to further expand her direct relationship with her audience and share her knowledge and expertise, in 2009 Rachel launched *The Zoe Report*, a free daily newsletter featuring her latest obsessions in the ever-evolving worlds of fashion, beauty, and lifestyle. In 2011, she debuted two additional daily newsletters, *Zoe Beautiful* and *AccesZOEries*, focusing on beauty and accessories.

Rachel launched her eponymous contemporary collection in 2011. Drawing on vintage-inspired fabrics, patterns, and the spirit of her style icons from the sixties and seventies, her line introduced separates, footwear, handbags, and jewelry evocative of her modern take on timeless glamour.

Most recently, Rachel co-founded the newly opened chain of blowout salons, DreamDry, launched a television production company, Rachel Zoe Productions, and has aligned with several brands to lend her face, name, and expertise to their initiatives.

She has been the recipient of numerous prestigious industry awards, including The Fashion Group International's Fashion Oracle Award, the Accessories Council Fashion Influencer Ace Award, *Hollywood Life Magazine*'s Star Stylist Award and *Hollywood Reporter*'s Most Influential Stylist. And perhaps most notably, Rachel was the recipient of 2011's Launch of the Year Award from the Footwear News Association and in 2012 was inducted into the Council of Fashion Designers of America (CFDA). She was named Stylist of the Year at the 10th Annual Style Awards at Mercedes-Benz Fashion Week in 2013.

Rachel Zoe currently resides in Los Angeles with her husband and business partner, Rodger Berman, and their sons, Skyler and Kaius.

MONICA CORCORAN HAREL

Monica Corcoran Harel is a writer and consultant who covers fashion, design, and culture. She contributes to the *New York Times*, *ELLE*, *Marie Claire*, *Deadline Hollywood*, and *InStyle*. Her reported essay on cosmetic treatments was part of a 2013 National Magazine Award–winning package for *Los Angeles Magazine*. She has advised on *Project Runway* and co-authored the style book *The Fashion File* with *Mad Men* costume designer Janie Bryant. Corcoran Harel lives in Los Angeles with her husband, Gadi, and their daughter, Tess.

PHOTO CREDITS

Page 4: Justin Coit; page 9: Justin Coit; page 11: Getty Images Entertainment; page 15: Justin Coit; page 16, top: Justin Coit, bottom: Gamma-Rapho via Getty Images; page 17: Gamma-Rapho via Getty Images; page 19, top and bottom, Rachel Zoe; page 20, left: Rachel Zoe, right: Joe Shildhorn/BFAnyc.com; page 23: Rachel Zoe; page 24: Justin Coit; pages 28–29, Justin Coit; page 31: Rachel Zoe; page 32: ©Foundation Pierre Bergé—Yves Saint Laurent; page 35, left: Roger Viollet/Getty Images, top right: Gamma-Keystone via Getty Images, bottom right: Courtesy of Missoni—photo by Giampaolo Barbieri for Vogue Italy, 1969; page 36: Burt Glinn, Magnum Photos; page 37: Popperfoto/Getty Images; page 39: WireImage; page 40: Getty Images; page 41: Paris Match via Getty Images; page 43: ©Hachette Filipacchi Photos—Photo: Kammermann; page 44: WireImage; page 48: Billy Farrell/BFAnyc.com; page 51: Justin Coit; page 53, top and bottom: Rachel Zoe; page 55: Billy Farrell/BFAnyc.com; page 57: Getty Images: page 59, left: BuzzFoto/FilmMagic, right: FilmMagic; page 60, left: Getty Images, right: WireImage; page 62, left: Getty Images, right: Getty Images; page 66: Gamma-Rapho via Getty Images; page 69: Popperfoto/Getty Images; page 70: NY Daily News via Getty Images; page 73: WireImage; page 74: Gamma-Keystone via Getty Images; page 77: Getty Images; page 78: WireImage; page 81: Gamma-Keystone via Getty Images; page 82: Time Life Pictures/Getty Images; page 85: Getty Images; page 87: Gamma-Rapho via Getty Images; page 88: WireImage; page 91: Justin Coit; page 93, left and right: Getty Images; pages 94–95: Justin Coit; page 98: Getty Images; page 71, top left: Courtesy of Van Cleef & Arpels, top right: Getty Images, bottom: Getty Images; pages 104–105: All photos courtesy of Tiffany & Co.; page 106: Justin Coit; page 109: Getty Images Europe; page 112, top: WireImage, bottom: Justin Coit; page 113: WireImage; page 115: Getty Images North America; page 116: Getty Images; page 118, left: Popperfoto/Getty Images, right: Time & Life Pictures/Getty Images; page 119, left: Mondadori via Getty Images, right: Getty Images; page 120: Popperfoto/Getty Images; page 122: FilmMagic; page 123, top: FilmMagic, bottom: Getty Images; page 125, top left: Getty Images, bottom left: Justin Coit, right: WireImage; page 127: Justin Coit; page 129, left: FilmMagic, right: WireImage; page 130: Rachel Zoe; page 132: WireImage; page 135: Bill Farrell/BFAnyc.com; page 136: Mondadori via Getty Images; page 138, top left: Getty Images, top right: Getty Images, bottom left: Fairfax Media via Getty Images, bottom right: ABC via Getty Images; page 139, top left: Getty Images, top right: Getty Images, bottom left: WireImage, bottom right: WireImage; page 140 Justin Coit; page 143: Courtesy of Tom Ford; page 144: Justin Coit; page 149, left: Lichfield/Getty Images, right: Getty Images; page 150, left and right: Getty Images; page 151, left: Getty Images, right: ABC via Getty Images; page 152, left: Gamma-Keystone via Getty Images, right: Gamma Rapho; page 153, left: Michael Ochs Archives, right: Getty Images; page 155: Justin Coit; page 156: Rachel Zoe; page 158: Courtesy of Morgans Hotel Group; page 160–161: Justin Coit; page 162: Justin Coit; page 163: Justin Coit; page 165: Justin Coit; pages 168–169, All photos courtesy of Claridge's; pages 170–171, left: Courtesy Le Dali, middle: Courtesy of Hotel Du Cap, right: © Hachette Filipacchi Photos—photo: Kammerman; page 174: Justin Coit; page 177: Justin Coit; page 178–179: Justin Coit; pages 180–181: Justin Coit; page 183: Justin Coit; pages 186–187: Justin Coit; page 188: Justin Coit; page 191: Justin Coit; pages 192–193: Justin Coit; page 195: Courtesy of Martyn Lawrence Bullard; pages 196–197: Courtesy of Martyn Lawrence Bullard; page 199: Justin Coit; pages 200–201: All photos, Rachel Zoe; page 203: Rachel Zoe; pages 206–207: All photos, Rachel Zoe; page 209: All photos, Rachel Zoe; page 210: Rachel Zoe; page 213: All photos, Rachel Zoe; page 214: All photos, Rachel Zoe; page 217: Justin Coit; page 219: Justin Coit; page 221: Gamma-Rapho via Getty Images; page 225: Mark Woodworth/BFAnyc.com; page 227: Justin Coit; 228–229: All photos, Justin Coit; page 230: Justin Coit; page 231: Justin Coit; page 233: Rachel Zoe; page 235, top: Courtesy of Tiffany & Co., bottom: Courtesy of La Duree; pages 236–237: Justin Coit; page 238, left: Getty Images, right: Courtesy of Margherita Maccapani Missoni; page 241: Justin Coit; page 242: Rachel Zoe; page 245: Rachel Zoe; page 246, left: Courtesy of Didier Ludot, right: Courtesy of Four Seasons, George V; page 248, Rachel Zoe; pages 250–251: Rachel Zoe; page 252: Courtesy of Nammos ; page 253 Courtesy of The Leading Hotels of the World; page 254: Photo by Gregory Goode; page 255: Copyrights by Sigfrid López; 256:Courtesy of Dwarika's Hotel; page 258: Courtesy of Caffé Florian; page 259: Courtesy of Hotel Daneli; page 260: Courtesy of Buca Mario; page 261: Courtesy of Dorchester Collection ; page 262: Getty Images Europe; page 267: Photo by Justin Coit.

Streams of Living Water

Richard J. Foster

Streams of Living Water

Celebrating the Great Traditions of Christian Faith

HarperSanFrancisco

A Division of HarperCollinsPublishers

For information about Renovaré write to Renovaré, 8 Inverness Drive East, Suite 102, Englewood, CO 80112–5624.

HarperCollins books may be purchased for educational, business, or sales promotional use. For information please write: Special Markets Department, HarperCollins Publishers, Inc., 10 East 53rd Street, New York, NY 10022.

HarperCollins Web Site: http://www.harpercollins.com

HarperCollins®, ▰ ®, and HarperSanFrancisco™ are trademarks of HarperCollins Publishers Inc.

FIRST EDITION

Library of Congress Cataloging-in-Publication Data

Foster, Richard J.
    Streams of living water : celebrating the great traditions of
  Christian faith / by Richard J. Foster. — 1st HarperCollins ed.
      p. cm.
    Includes index.
    ISBN 0–06–066743–5
    ISBN 0–06–062822–7 (pbk.)
    1. Spiritual life—Christianity. I. Title.
  BV4501.2.F6546   1998
  248—dc 21   98-22646

---

99 00 01 02 ❖/RRD 10 9 8 7 6 5

To Lynda L. Graybeal
who believed in this project from the beginning and has been its
most faithful and steady advocate. Lynda and I have worked together
professionally for well over a dozen years now, and I dedicate this
book to her in gratitude for her perseverance, patience, and
resilience.

Contents

Acknowledgments

N O ONE WRITES in isolation. Always we stand on the shoulders of those who have gone before and hope against hope that present and future readers will give attention to our efforts. When a work gives special attention to history, the debt increases doubly and triply. And so I must begin by expressing profound gratitude to all those through the centuries who have lived so faithfully and to all those who have so faithfully recorded the experiences of their lives.

In addition, many people have helped me think through the issues and structure of this book. In particular, the early members of our RENOVARÉ team have worked with me by teaching, preaching, and clarifying the themes of this book. I thank them each one: Edward England, Marti Ensign, Roger Fredrikson, James Bryan Smith, Donn Thomas, William L. Vaswig, Dallas Willard.

Editors are indispensable members of the writing team. They encourage, guide, prod, console. I thank Patricia Klein of Harper-SanFrancisco, who has been the editor for this project. As a labor of love several individuals read through the entire manuscript, sharing their thoughts, insights, and corrections. I thank them for helping to make this a better, more readable book: Bruce Demarest, Carolynn Foster, Lynda Graybeal, and Gayle Withnell. Special thanks to Joan Skulley for caring for many office details during the last months of writing. In addition, Tim Boyd with his expertise in church history, Bill Griffin with his understanding of Roman Catholicism, and Warren Farha with his knowledge of Eastern Orthodoxy helped make the appendices more accurate than they would have been otherwise.

I must add that Carolynn was far more than just a reader of the manuscript. She has lived with my obsession of many years with the ideas of this book. In the pressured final months of writing she took over literally all the responsibilities of home and family. Whenever I was convinced the project was too daunting, she urged me on. Whenever I was convinced the writing was so bad that it would be a mercy to consign it to the fireplace, she said it was good and would be better. Whenever I got too cocky, thinking I was producing a *magnum opus*, she found the words to bring me back to reality. (Actually, words often were unnecessary; a quizzical look or a slight lift of the eyebrows was sufficient.) She is the most precious person in my life—I thank her.

I am keenly aware that words are, at best, "frozen thought" and cannot adequately express the life of the streams of devotion described in this book. Only Jesus, the living Word of God, transcends this limitation. I can only pray that he will take these words and use them to breathe life into your soul.

Richard J. Foster
Ash Wednesday 1998

Foreword

"**I** *hate* organized religion. I've moved way beyond it."
"I *despise* the institutional church. I don't need institutions to depend upon."

"I *don't believe* in communities of worship. I am strong enough to be on my own."

"I *don't like* religion at all. Hypocrites and selfish people invent it to serve their own purposes."

"However, I'm *very* spiritual."

You will hear such language over coffee in the browsing rooms of the giant bookstores. It is commonly voiced when celebrities chatter about themselves on late night television. College students will flock to religious studies courses but avoid chapel before they go off variously on their own to find the meaning of life or to commune with the spirit in the woods or get connected with the energy in the universe or be touched by angels.

Helping you become very spiritual—no italics, please, for the word "very" this time—is a goal Richard Foster has set for himself in *Streams of Living Water*. But every page shows that he means something different than do authors of the best-sellers found on bookstore shelves marked "Spiritual-Occult-Metaphysical-Holistic-Wholistic-Alternative-Ancient-New Age." Too many pages show that he and those authors only coincidentally use the same words—*Spirit, spiritual*, and *spirituality*—as they attempt to convey very different things.

Think of the self-acquired, self-advertised spirituality as a kind of vapor: thin, particled, almost invisible, shapeless, hard to grasp. Whoever boasts the possession of it can escape criticism or judgment. You cannot make congregations out of the clientele that buy into it; they despise concrete community. Think of the kind of spirituality Foster is encouraging as thick, rooted, concrete, always seeking shape, graspable by anyone who would appraise it and reject or improve it.

What are the differences between the two sorts? Many, of course, but at the core is the fact that the first kind is unmoored and the second is moored. The unmoored makes up reality as it goes along; it flits and is fleeting, leaving one at sea. The moored sort, on the other hand, has a harbor and an anchor, a home port from which one heads forth into the storms or to outlast the calms and to which one returns for replenishment.

Moored spirituality is responsible to textual traditions and the communities that attempt to live by them. Those who relate to it may come from any number of religious traditions. They spend their lives studying the Qur'an or the Upanishads or living in connection with communities that derive from Torah. In the present case, the texts and the communities are Christian, rooted in the Bible and, especially, in Jesus Christ. Foster is not ungenerous to others, but this is the place he knows and advocates, having no choice in the matter because he has been called there.

Richard Foster does not talk about moorings and place. His metaphor is "streams," with Jesus Christ as the source. Some French writers have coined a wonderful word for what this is about: *ressourcement*. That means resuming to the source, the headwaters, dipping deeply, and coming forth refreshed. To do this in the present case Foster asks us in each chapter to visit a number of classic Christian people who can serve as paradigms and then to visit some people in the Scriptures. And in each chapter there is also someone from our time, to assure that we understand that the source still pours forth streams in which we can bathe or from which we can drink.

Foster cannot not be the teacher. I note how often he needs "first," "second," and "third" sequences (and many longer than that) in order to help us find our ways into the disciplines of faith and to find ways to make them memorable. While those numbers are cold and abstract, warmth and clarity come when he talks about people in the tradition, the stream.

And how varied are these people. I think that some of the unmoored spiritual people—it's time to pay them a compliment now—who are often more adventurous and imaginative than many stolid Christians, reject the faith because it is bland and boring. Its saints and heroes seem outclassed in a head-to-head encounter with the guru of the week, the shaman of the season, the channeler of the half-decade.

Bland? Boring? Right off Foster says or shows "Not so!" as he takes us out to the desert with crazy Antonius and shows that that monk was not all crazy. Foster is ecumenical; his streams flow together. Here is William Seymour, a black Pentecostal founder, who gets rejected even by white Pentecostal pioneers. Here is Phoebe Palmer, not a "mainstream" character in the kind of church history I started out to teach four decades ago. Yet here she is, up there with high-class literary figures, martyrs, and founders.

Asking us to learn from such an assortment of characters who might often have wondered how Foster gets to see their streams of influence flowing together takes some nerve on his part. No one is likely to find all the paradigms congenial. But it is likely that readers will end up learning more from the surprising and abrasive misfits than from the congenial people who fit so smoothly into our preconceived ways.

Foster belongs to a small but I think and hope a growing company—I see Kathleen Norris and Nancy Mairs in it and before them, Henri Nouwen and more—a company of those who ask us to be more patient than the readers of the "spirituality" books at the megastores are. He wants us not just to pick and choose but to be judged by what we read, always with the possibility in mind that we will change and be changed. When some of those who have rejected Christian community start turning away from the "spiritual" people because now *they* have come to look bland and boring, when they start looking for streams of living water, I think they will find Foster and, behind his stories and lessons, their source both congenial and durable. Having a mooring at that source does not mean getting to stay at home while the winds would blow into the sails. It means knowing where the lighthouses and beacons are, where the harbor is into which to return for momentary retreat before the next sailing forth into the turmoil of the world.

Knowing such a mooring and finding the streams are acts that, according to his book title, we should "celebrate." Whoever reads these pages and walks in their way is likely to do precisely that. I invite you to accept the mentoring of a reliable, seasoned guide in Richard Foster and, several paradigms back behind him and his other subjects, the figure of Jesus Christ.

Martin Marty

Introduction

TODAY A MIGHTY river of the Spirit is bursting forth from the hearts of women and men, boys and girls. It is a deep river of divine intimacy, a powerful river of holy living, a dancing river of jubilation in the Spirit, and a broad river of unconditional love for all peoples. As Jesus says, "Out of the believer's heart shall flow rivers of living water" (John 7:38).

The astonishing new reality in this mighty flow of the Spirit is how sovereignly God is bringing together streams of life that have been isolated from one another for a very long time. This isolation is completely understandable from a historical perspective. Over the centuries some precious teaching or vital experience is neglected until, at the appropriate moment, a person or movement arises to correct the omission. Numbers of people come under the renewed teaching, but soon vested interests and a host of other factors come into play, producing resistance to the renewal, and the new movement is denounced. In time it forms its own structures and community life, often in isolation from other Christian communities.

This phenomenon has been repeated many times through the centuries. The result is that various streams of life—good streams, important streams—have been cut off from the rest of the Christian community, depriving us all of a balanced vision of life and faith.

But today our sovereign God is drawing many streams together that heretofore have been separated from one another. It is a little like the Mississippi River, which gains strength and volume as the Ohio and the Missouri and many other rivers flow into it. So in our day God is bringing together a mighty "Mississippi of the Spirit."

In this book I have tried to name these great Traditions—streams of spiritual life if you will—and to note significant figures in each. The naming is not perfect, I know, but I hope it will give you the major thrust of these Traditions: The Contemplative Tradition, or the prayer-filled life; The Holiness Tradition, or the virtuous life; The Charismatic Tradition, or the Spirit-empowered life; The Social Justice Tradition, or the compassionate life; The Evangelical Tradition, or the Word-centered life; The Incarnational Tradition, or the sacramental life.

In reality these different Traditions describe various dimensions of the spiritual life. We find their emphasis throughout the teaching of Scripture—from the Pentateuch to the prophets, from the wisdom literature to the Gospels, from the Epistles to the Apocalypse. And many are the lives that illustrate these themes: Abraham, Sarah, Jacob, Moses, Ruth, David, Hannah, Samuel, Isaiah, Jeremiah, Mary, Peter, Elizabeth, Paul, Tabitha, Lydia, John . . . the list could go on and on.

But no one models these dimensions of the spiritual life more fully than Jesus Christ. If we want to see this river of life in its most complete form, it is to Jesus that we must turn.

Streams of Living Water

Chapter 1

◦

Imitatio:
The Divine Paradigm

Looking to Jesus the pioneer and perfecter of our faith.

—*Hebrews 12:2*

We must imitate Christ's life and his ways if we are to be truly enlightened and set free from the darkness of our own hearts. Let it be the most important thing we do, then, to reflect on the life of Jesus Christ.

—*Thomas à Kempis*

CRITICAL TURNING POINTS IN CHURCH HISTORY*

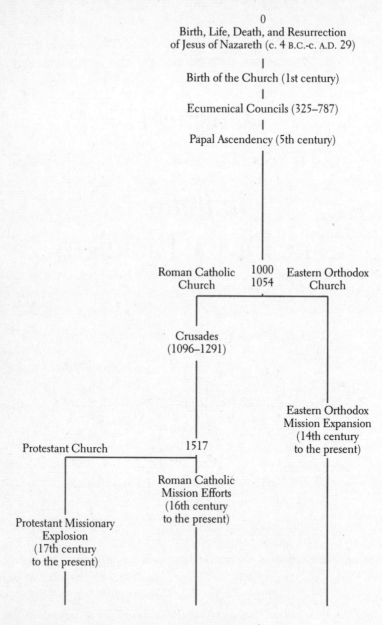

0
Birth, Life, Death, and Resurrection
of Jesus of Nazareth (c. 4 B.C.-c. A.D. 29)

Birth of the Church (1st century)

Ecumenical Councils (325–787)

Papal Ascendency (5th century)

Roman Catholic   1000   Eastern Orthodox
Church   1054   Church

Crusades
(1096–1291)

Eastern Orthodox
Mission Expansion
(14th century
to the present)

Protestant Church   1517

Roman Catholic
Mission Efforts
(16th century
to the present)

Protestant Missionary
Explosion
(17th century
to the present)

*See Appendix A for an overview of church history.

1

As Jesus walked this earth, living and working among all kinds and classes of people, he gave us the divine paradigm for conjugating all the verbs of our living. Too often in our concern to make doctrinal points we rush to expound upon Jesus' death, and in so doing we neglect Jesus' life. This is a great loss. Attention to Jesus in his living gives us important clues for our living.

Jesus lived in this broken, painful world, learning obedience through the things that he suffered, tempted in all the ways we are, and yet remaining without sin (Heb. 5:8, 4:15).[1] We are, to be sure, reconciled to God by Jesus' death, but even more, we are "saved" by his life (Rom. 5:10)—*saved* in the sense of entering into his eternal kind of life, not just in some distant heaven but right now in the midst of our broken and sorrowful world. When we carefully consider how Jesus lived while among us in the flesh, we learn how we are to live—truly *live*—empowered by him who is with us always even to the end of the age. We then begin an intentional *imitatio Christi*, imitation of Christ, not in some slavish or literal fashion but by catching the spirit and power in which he lived and by learning to walk "in his steps" (1 Pet. 2:21).

In this sense we can truly speak of the primacy of the Gospels, for in them we see Jesus living and moving among human beings, displaying perfect unity with the will of the Father. And we are taught to do the same, taking on the nature of Christlikeness—sharing Jesus' vision, love, hope, feelings, and habits.

One of the best things we can do for one another, then, is to encourage regular immersion in the Gospel narratives, helping each other understand Jesus' perceptions into life and his counsels for growth and then making constant application to our daily experience. The dimensions of this task are infinite, of course. However, for the sake of our concern here we want to consider how Jesus *in his living* provides us a clear paradigm for *our* living, especially as Jesus' living relates to the several streams of devotion that frame the structure of this book.

PRAYER AND INTIMACY

Let's consider the Contemplative Stream, the prayer-filled life. Nothing is more striking in Jesus' life than his intimacy with the Father. "The Son can do nothing on his own, but only what he sees the Father doing; for whatever the Father does, the Son does likewise" (John 5:19). "I can do nothing on my own. As I hear, I judge" (John 5:30). "The words that I say to you I do not speak on my own; but the Father who dwells in me does his works" (John 14:10).

Like a recurring pattern in a quilt, so prayer threads its way through Jesus' life. As Jesus was baptized by John, he "was praying" (Luke 3:21). In preparation for the choosing of the Twelve he went up the mountain alone and "spent the night in prayer" (Luke 6:12). After an exhausting evening of healing "many who were sick" and casting out "many demons," Jesus got up early in the morning "while it was still very dark . . . and went out to a deserted place, and there he prayed" (Mark 1:35). Jesus was "praying alone" when he was prompted to ask his disciples, "Who do you say that I am?" (Luke 9:18–20). When Jesus took Peter, James, and John "up on the mountain to pray," it led to the great transfiguration experience, and Luke notes that the appearance of Jesus' face was changed "while he was praying" (Luke 9:28–29). After the disciples had failed to heal a sick child, Jesus took care of the matter for them, explaining their failure in these words: "This kind can come out only through prayer" (Mark 9:29). Jesus' fiercest anger came when he saw how people had turned the temple, which he said was to be a house of prayer, into a den of robbers (Matt. 21:13). It was after Jesus finished "praying in a certain place" that the disciples asked him to teach them to pray (Luke 11:1).

And teach them he did. Not only the now famous Lord's Prayer, which is found here, but teaching layered upon teaching. Jesus taught them to come to God in the most intimate of ways, saying, "Abba, Father" (Mark 14:36). He gave parables about the "need to pray always and not to lose heart" (Luke 18:1). He taught his disciples to pray "in secret," to "pray for those who persecute you," when praying to "forgive, if you have anything against anyone," to "believe that what you say will come to pass," to petition "the Lord of the harvest to send out laborers into his harvest," and much more (Matt. 6:6, 5:44; Mark 11:25, 23; Matt. 9:38).

And the teachings are matched by continual practice, not only of prayer itself but of intense times of solitude. Jesus was led by the Spirit into the wilderness for forty days (Matt. 4:1). He "withdrew . . . to a deserted place by himself" after learning of the beheading of his dear friend and cousin, John the Baptizer (Matt. 14:13). Following the incredible experience of feeding the five thousand, Jesus immediately "went up the mountain by himself to pray" (Matt. 14:23). When the disciples were exhausted from the demands of ministry, Jesus told them, "Come away to a deserted place all by yourselves and rest a while" (Mark 6:31). After Jesus' healing of a leper Luke seems to be describing more of a habitual practice than a single incident when he notes that Jesus "would withdraw to deserted places and pray" (Luke 5:16).

Without question, the most intense and intimate of recorded prayers is Jesus' high priestly prayer in the Upper Room, where he poured out his heart to the Father on behalf of his disciples and "also on behalf of those who will believe in me through their word" (John 17:20). And of course any discussion of Jesus' prayer life and intimacy with the Father must culminate in the holy work of Gethsemane, where Jesus' sweat became like great drops of blood and his anguished words, "Let this cup pass," reached completion with, "Not my will but yours be done" (Luke 22:42).

Jesus, who retreated often into the rugged wilderness, who lived and worked praying, who heard and did only what the Father said and did, shows forth the Contemplative Tradition in its fullness and utter beauty.

If you are anything like me, even this cursory look at Jesus' love and intimacy with the Father stirs within you longings for a deeper, richer, fuller experience of the divine milieu. No doubt you too ache for a steadfast faith, a boundless hope, an undying love. Jesus points the way.

Purity of Heart

Consider with me the Holiness Stream, the virtuous life. It is simply a marvel to watch Jesus move among children and women and men—always timely, always appropriate, always capable. How did this come to be?

We cannot understand the holiness and ingrained virtue in Jesus without carefully examining those forty days of temptation in the wilderness. In that single event we see a lifetime of practiced virtue coming to the fore. Throughout those forty days Jesus fasted from food so that he could all the more fully enter the divine feast. Then, when his spiritual resources were at their maximum, God allowed the Evil One to come to him with three great temptations—temptations that Jesus undoubtedly had dealt with more than once in the carpentry shop and that he would face again throughout his ministry as a rabbi. Yet these were not just personal temptations; they were temptations for Jesus to access for his own use the three most prominent social institutions of the day—economic, religious, political.[2]

The economic temptation was for Jesus to turn stones into bread (Matt. 4:1–4). This was more than a taunt to ease private hunger pangs; it was a temptation to become a glorious miracle baker and provide "wonder bread" for the masses. But Jesus knew how short-lived all such solutions are and rejected the live-by-bread-alone option: "One does not live by bread alone, but by every word that comes from the mouth of God" (Matt. 4:4).

The religious temptation was for Jesus to leap from the pinnacle of the temple and, by having angels catch him in mid-flight, receive God's stamp of approval on his ministry. Divine certification inside the sacred boundaries of temple territory would surely have guaranteed the fervent support of the priestly hierarchy. But Jesus saw the temptation for what it was, and he directly confronted institutionalized religion—not only here in the wilderness but throughout his ministry, wherever and whenever it became idolatrous or oppressed the faithful. He knew that in his person, "something greater than the temple is here" (Matt. 12:6).

The political temptation was the promise of "all the kingdoms of the world and their splendor" in exchange for Jesus' own soul (Matt. 4:8–10). This mountain temptation represented the possibility of worldwide political power—not only coercive force, but also the glory and acclaim of sitting on the world's highest pinnacle of influence and status. It was a temptation that fit perfectly the messianic hopes of the day for a Savior who would cast off the oppressive Roman occupation. But Jesus knew that domination and force were not God's ways. He rejected coercive structures because he intended to demonstrate a new kind of power, a new way of ruling. Serving, suffering, dying—these were Jesus' messianic forms of power.

In those forty days in the wilderness Jesus rejected the popular Jewish hope for a Messiah who would feed the poor, bask in miraculous heavenly approval, and shuck off oppressive nations. And he undercut the leverage of the three great social institutions of his day (and of ours)—exploitative economics, manipulative religion, and coercive politics. What we see in those forty crucial days is someone who understood with clarity the way of God and who had the internal resources to live in that way, instinctively and without reservation. Jesus' actions were a living embodiment of the Holiness Stream.

But action, by itself, is not enough. It needs to be accompanied by adequate teaching on the virtuous life to lead ordinary people into genuine progress in holiness. Jesus clearly understood this—hence his abundant instructions on life as it is meant to be lived.

The heart of this teaching is the Sermon on the Mount, and the heart of the Sermon on the Mount is the law of love—the "royal law," as James calls it. Nothing more fully or more beautifully describes the life of holiness. Love is so compact a word that it needs unpacking, of course, and this is what Jesus does in his famous sermon. The life of virtue reflected in that teaching is governed by the maturity of love rather than the immaturity of binding legalism. It is a teaching that takes us beyond the "righteousness . . . of the scribes and Pharisees" (Matt. 5:20).

Now, the righteousness of the scribes and Pharisees consisted primarily in externals that often involved manipulative control of other people. Instead of this sort of righteousness, Jesus points to an inner life with God that transforms the heart and builds deeply ingrained habits of virtue. If we develop those habits, we will have the interior spiritual and moral resources with which to respond righteously when we are faced with temptations of any and every sort, as Jesus was in the wilderness.

If you seek holiness of life, I encourage you to make a good friend of the Sermon on the Mount. It is an expanded commentary on the royal law of love. And Jesus' life is an expanded commentary on the Sermon on the Mount. I find it endlessly moving to watch how Jesus walked among people, healing the sick, giving sight to the blind, bringing good news to the oppressed. Always appropriate. Always able. Always giving the touch that was needed. Always speaking the word that was needed. It is a wonder and a marvel.

We see Jesus consistently doing what needs to be done when it needs to be done. We see in him such deeply ingrained "holy habits" that he is always "response-able," always able to respond appropriately. This is purity of heart. This is the virtuous life. To see the vision of the Holiness Tradition in all its robust dynamic, we need look no further.

This brief look at the holiness of Jesus calls out to us. It calls us to a more consistent life, a more obedient life, a more fruitful life. Jesus, who lived fully every teaching of the Sermon on the Mount long before he taught it, shows us the way.

LIFE IN THE SPIRIT

Let's ponder together the Charismatic Stream, the Spirit-empowered life. Nothing is more satisfying to observe than how Jesus lived and moved in the power of the Spirit. As Jesus arose out of the baptismal waters, "the Holy Spirit descended upon him in bodily form like a dove. And a voice came from heaven, 'You are my Son, the Beloved; with you I am well pleased'" (Luke 3:22). Directly on the heels of this dramatic event, "Jesus, full of the Holy Spirit, returned from the Jordan and was led by the Spirit in the wilderness"

(Luke 4:1). Then, after the temptation encounters, Jesus returned to Galilee "filled with the power of the Spirit" (Luke 4:14). Such is the refrain that echoes down through his entire ministry: "full of the Holy Spirit" . . . "led by the Spirit" . . . "filled with the power of the Spirit."

It is a wonder to watch Jesus moving among people, exercising spiritual charisms* with ease and aplomb. The charism of wisdom was absolutely legendary in Jesus. People listening to his teachings were utterly dumbfounded, "for he taught them as one having authority, and not as the scribes" (Mark 1:22). In fact astonishment was the standard response to his teachings. The reason for this response is that when Jesus taught he did far more than what we think of as teaching. He spoke life into each heart and soul. Wisdom as a charism of the Holy Spirit is far more than knowledge or information, more even than truth; it is truth applied to the heart and the mind in such a living way that the person is transformed.

The charism of discernment is another of the gifts Jesus used frequently. Any number of times he refused to entrust himself to particular people because, as John puts it, "he himself knew what was in everyone" (John 2:25). Do you recall that when the paralytic came to Jesus for healing, Jesus first forgave his sins? This threw the scribes into a tailspin, "questioning in their hearts" about Jesus' authority to do something only God could do. Their hearts, however, were an open book to Jesus: "At once Jesus perceived in his spirit that they were discussing these questions among themselves" (Mark 2:1–8). This is the charism of discernment at work, and evidence of a Spirit-empowered life.

We must not leave out the charism of miracles. Consider the miraculous catch of fish and the equally miraculous multiplying of fishes and loaves. Consider also the turning of water into wine to bless a wedding couple and the cursing of the fig tree to teach a lesson in

---

*A "charism" is a divinely inspired spiritual gift that God bestows upon individuals for the good of the community of faith and the advancement of the kingdom of God upon the earth.

faith. Consider further the amazing calming of a storm at sea and the even more amazing walking on the waters of the sea. Finally, consider the most astonishing of all the miracles, the transfiguration of Jesus and the appearance of Moses and Elijah with him.

Another spiritual charism Jesus exercised—one we are rather uncomfortable with today—was exorcism. Evil spirits could not hide from him. Again and again Jesus discerned the spirit controlling people and spoke to it authoritatively. The experience following the healing of Peter's mother-in-law is typical of his work of exorcism: "That evening they brought to him many who were possessed with demons; and he cast out the spirits with a word, and cured all who were sick" (Matt. 8:16).

This link between exorcism and healing is seen frequently in the Gospels, and the charism of healing is far and away the most prominent spiritual gift we see in Jesus' ministry. He heals the centurion's servant. He heals the paralytic. He heals Jairus's daughter, raising her from the dead. He heals a man blind from birth. He heals Peter's mother-in-law. He heals two blind men. He heals a mute demoniac. He heals the man with the withered hand. He heals the Gerasene demoniac. He heals the deaf man with a speech impediment. He heals the blind man of Bethsaida. He heals the epileptic boy. He heals the woman suffering from hemorrhages. He heals the man with dropsy. He heals ten lepers. He heals the blind beggar Bartimaeus. He heals Lazarus, raising him from the dead. And more than once we read that, as crowds pressed in upon him with their great need, "he cured all of them" (Matt. 12:15).

At a critical point in his work Jesus commissioned seventy disciples to go on ahead of him, preaching the good news of the kingdom and healing everywhere. This they did, returning with the astonishing news that "even the demons submit to us!" Upon hearing this, "Jesus rejoiced in the Holy Spirit" (Luke 10:1–21). The word we render "rejoice" here means literally "to leap for joy." Jesus, you understand, was leaping for joy in the Spirit, for now it was clear to him and the others that the power ministry of the promised Holy Spirit was transferable to ordinary disciples.

And Jesus' definitive teaching on the coming of the promised Holy Spirit is given to us in his famous Upper Room Discourse (John 13–17). Here we learn that the Spirit will come alongside Christ's disciples as Advocate, Helper, Comforter, and Strengthener. We learn that he will be our Teacher, guiding us into all truth. We learn that he also comes to convict the world of "sin and righteousness and judgment" (John 16:8).

For those disciples so long ago, Jesus' departure was a great sadness. But it was a necessary sadness—necessary for ushering in the fullness of the Spirit. "It is to your advantage that I go away," Jesus told them, "for if I do not go away, the Advocate will not come to you; but if I go, I will send him to you" (John 16:7).

On the last day of the Festival of Booths, Jesus cried out, "Let anyone who is thirsty come to me, and let the one who believes in me drink. As the scripture has said, 'Out of the believer's heart shall flow rivers of living water.'" Then, by way of commentary on this great statement, John adds, "Now he said this about the Spirit, which believers in him were to receive; for as yet there was no Spirit, because Jesus was not yet glorified" (John 7:37–39). The fullness of the Spirit had to await Jesus' death, resurrection, and ascension. Those events have since occurred, Jesus has been glorified, and the fullness of the Spirit is now available to all. This is the great heritage of the Charismatic Tradition, the Spirit-empowered life.

This is the life that is open to you and to me. A life flowing with rivers of living water. Rivers of love and joy. Rivers of signs and wonders. Rivers of peace and power. Jesus shows us the way.

JUSTICE AND SHALOM

Let's look at Jesus and the Social Justice Stream, the compassionate life. At the inauguration of his ministry, Jesus stood in the synagogue at Nazareth and declared,

The Spirit of the Lord is upon me,
  because he has anointed me to bring good news to the poor.

He has sent me to proclaim release to the captives
   and recovery of sight to the blind,
      to let the oppressed go free,
to proclaim the year of the Lord's favor. (Luke 4:18–19)

These words, which Jesus took from Isaiah, are rooted in the prophetic vision of the Hebrew Year of Jubilee.[3] In his message and person Jesus was, in effect, announcing a perpetual Jubilee in the Spirit. The social ramifications of this were profound indeed: the land was to be healed, debts were to be forgiven, those in bondage were to be set free, capital was to be redistributed. With these words Jesus delivered a war cry for social revolution. No wonder his friends and neighbors—who understood perfectly well what he was saying— were "filled with rage" and tried to "hurl him off the cliff" (Luke 4:28–30).

Jesus' shorthand for this perpetual Jubilee life is the cryptic message, "Repent, for the kingdom of heaven is at hand" (Matt. 3:2, RSV). And Jesus fully intends that this "kingdom of heaven" will constantly confront and pull down the kingdoms of this world. His is an alternative social vision—a vision of an all-inclusive people, gathered in the power of God, filled with the love of God, and empowered to do the works of God. It is a vision of Jubilee sharing, Jubilee caring, and Jubilee compassion for all who are crushed and broken by social and economic structures.

Jesus underscores the incompatibility of his Jubilee life with the institutional structures of this world when he says, "No one puts new wine into old wineskins; otherwise the new wine will burst the skins and will be spilled, and the skins will be destroyed. But new wine must be put into fresh wineskins" (Luke 5:37–38). Jubilee life demands Jubilee structures.

In the Beatitudes we see the Jubilee inversion in which Jesus takes all those kinds and classes of people that in the natural order of things are thought to be unblessed and unblessable and shows that in the forgiving, receiving, accepting life of God's kingdom they too are blessed. He tells us to "bless those who curse you," "love your enemies," "lend, expecting nothing in return," "do not judge," "do not condemn," "forgive," "give" (Luke 6:27–38). What kind of a vision is this? What kind of a life? An impossible ideal, a utopian dream?

Perhaps. And yet this is exactly how Jesus himself lived. Notice his compassion in cleansing the leper and healing the paralytic, people who were outcasts of his day (Luke 5:12–26). Look at his relentless tenderness in healing a centurion's slave and in raising a widow's only son from the dead. Note too the response of the people—"A great prophet has risen among us!"—which aligns Jesus' deeds here with the ancient prophetic tradition of social righteousness (Luke 7:1–17).

When John the Baptizer sends two of his followers to find out from Jesus whether he embodies the messianic expectation, Jesus responds, "Go and tell John what you have seen and heard: the blind receive their sight, the lame walk, the lepers are cleansed, the deaf hear, the dead are raised, the poor have good news brought to them. And blessed is anyone who takes no offense at me" (Luke 7:22–23). Yes, says Jesus, the messianic kingdom of perpetual Jubilee is indeed coming, but in a way that no one would have guessed. People, especially the Zealots, had been looking for military conquest. But Jesus flatly rejects the Zealot option and shows instead another kingdom and another power—the kingdom of love and the power of the divine community.

Notice how Zacchaeus embraces this Jubilee life, accepting its call to generosity (Luke 19:1–10). Notice too the Jubilee attitude of the widow who puts her two copper coins in the offering, giving "out of her poverty" (Luke 21:1–4).

Look at the Jubilee events in the Upper Room: they are rich in social righteousness. Jesus begins by showing the Jubilee inversion of greatness with a towel and a basin. Next he helps his disciples see that the primary social structure God uses to change the power structures of this world is the divine community. Finally, he offers up the uniting Jubilee prayer for the divine community: "that they may all be one" (John 17:21).

We dare not omit the struggle in the Garden. It too helps us understand social justice. Remember, Jesus could have called down ten thousand angels to obliterate the political structures of his day. The Zealots were hoping he would. But in the Garden Jesus gives his final rejection of the Zealot option and turns his face toward the cross. And in the cross we see the Jubilee way, the way of conquest by suffering.

The Jubilee vision of Jesus culminates in the Apocalypse, the last book of our Bible, where justice and righteousness prevail, where the divine community lives in a new heaven and a new earth, and where God "will wipe every tear from their eyes" and "mourning and crying and pain will be no more" (Rev. 21:4). This is Jesus' social vision of perpetual Jubilee. It embodies all we mean and desire when we speak of the Social Justice Tradition.

Jesus' living out of justice and shalom challenges our vested interests. It rebukes our rugged individualism and selfish hoarding. And it invites us to be the kind of people in whom justice and compassion flow freely. Jesus, who lived in the virtue and power of that Jubilee life that pulls down the kingdoms of this world, points the way.

PROCLAIMING THE EVANGEL

Let's consider the Evangelical Stream, the Word-centered life. Jesus, the Christ, came proclaiming the good news of the kingdom of God and was in his very person the embodiment of the good news of the kingdom of God. Jesus was, and is, the living Word of God enfleshed among us, standing in his person as the very good news he proclaimed.

And what is this good news? It is, very simply, that people—*all* people—can enter into a living and abundant life with God in his kingdom of love now, and that this reality will continue on, and indeed intensify, after death. How is this possible? It is not that God's kingdom of love did not exist before Jesus, or that it had been postponed somehow. No. But before the incarnation its availability had, in the nature of things, been restricted and mediated through a special people and a special religious class. In Jesus' person all that changed. In Jesus the doors were thrown wide open: "Whosoever will may come." The kingdom of God's love has been made available to all. Whenever, wherever, whoever. In Jesus' person.

Jesus himself was absolutely clear about these matters. "I am the way, and the truth, and the life," he declared. "I am the bread of life." "I am the light of the world." "Before Abraham was, I am." "I am the good shepherd." "I am the gate for the sheep." "I am the resurrection and the life." "I am the true vine" (John 14:6, 6:35, 8:12, 8:58, 10:11, 10:7, 11:25, 15:1). The good news is that in Jesus himself the way has been opened for you and for me to come freely into God's great kingdom of love.

But how? Very simply. By grace through faith we receive God's love for us and enroll as Jesus' disciples, or students, or apprentices. That means we follow him in all things, learning from him, receiving his strength, and living as he would live if he were in our place. By grace through faith.[4]

Now, Jesus went about proclaiming the gospel of the kingdom and its availability to all. He also demonstrated the reality of its presence. This dual action of proclamation and demonstration is found throughout the Gospels. "Jesus went throughout Galilee, teaching in their synagogues and proclaiming the good news of the kingdom and curing every disease and every sickness among the people" (Matt. 4:23). There it is: the proclamation of the presence of the kingdom and the demonstration of its life, in this case by the ministry of healing. He gave the same commission to the Twelve: "He sent them out to proclaim the kingdom of God and to heal," which is exactly what they did. "They departed and went through the villages, bringing the good news and curing diseases everywhere" (Luke 9:1–6). Again, proclamation and demonstration. He gave exactly the same mission to the larger group of seventy: "Cure the sick who are there, and say to them, 'The kingdom of God has come near to you'" (Luke 10:9). Proclamation and demonstration. In this dual action we catch a glimpse of how the Evangelical Tradition is integrated with the Charismatic Tradition. (Of course, in Jesus *all* the Traditions function as one.)

It is a wonder to watch how people responded to Jesus' wonderful good news about God's kingdom of love and its accessibility. They came pouring in. In Matthew's Gospel we read that "from the days of John the Baptist until now the kingdom of heaven has suffered violence, and the violent take it by force" (11:12). As we compare this with its parallel text in Luke, we see that Matthew is using the language of "violence" to describe the rush of people pressing into God's kingdom of love. Jesus had brought people such good, great news that they were all but knocking down the doors to get in! They had found the treasure in the field and were willing to sell everything they had to get it. They had seen the pearl of great price and nothing would stop them from having it. They were "violent" men and women—violent in the sense that they would not allow anything to keep them from coming into this abundant life in God's kingdom of love.

Zacchaeus came rushing in, as we noted above. When the word of the gospel penetrated his heart, it opened up a great river of generosity that compelled him to give away half of his goods to the poor and to repay four times over anyone he had defrauded. Jesus commented on his action, "Today salvation has come to this house" (Luke 19:1–9).

Mary Magdalene came rushing in. When Jesus freed her of seven demons, her life was forever changed and gratitude flowed out of every pore in her body. At great personal risk she gathered with the little band at the foot of the cross, watching and waiting and praying. Then, after the burial stone was put it place, entombing Jesus, she stayed there with "the other Mary," sorrowing. But that sorrow turned to joy when, on the third day, Easter morning, Mary was the first witness to the resurrection, and the first to be addressed by the risen Christ, who called her by name, "Mary!" (John 20:16).

Nicodemus came rushing in. True, at first he came under cover of darkness, but even this act threatened his position and standing among the leaders. And later, when the religious authorities were about to seize Jesus, Nicodemus posed just the right question to stop them in their tracks: "Our law does not judge people without first giving them a hearing to find out what they are doing, does it?"—that phrase "does it?" making it clear to all that by now Nicodemus "was one of them" (John 7:45–52). Then, following the crucifixion, Nicodemus provided the spices for Jesus' burial. Now frankly, Nicodemus had nothing to gain by this action and much to lose. But the touch of Jesus upon his life had been so transforming that he risked all in this simple act of courtesy.

Oh, there were so many others. The woman at the well in Samaria came rushing in. Little children came rushing in. The Syrophoenician woman came rushing in. The thief on the cross came rushing in. The poor came rushing in. Such was the response of so many.

But not *everyone*. The rich young ruler held back. He had great wealth, and (more important) his great wealth had him. Jesus saw into his heart and called him to total divestiture so that discipleship might be possible. But the young ruler could not bring himself to carry out this radical act and went away sad.

The leader of one of the synagogues held back. When Jesus went to the synagogue to teach one sabbath, a woman who had been crippled for eighteen years was among the crowd. Jesus, overcome with compassion for her, called her over to him and said, "Woman, you are set free from your ailment" (Luke 13:12). And as he laid his hands on her, immediately she stood up straight. Well, you can imagine the utter joy in this woman. You would think, when she began praising God, that everyone else would praise God with her. But not this leader of the synagogue. No, he became "indignant," says Scripture (Luke 13:14). And why? Here was a woman who had just been freed from an eighteen-year affliction. Why was this leader unable to join in her joy? Well, because Jesus had done this good work *on the sabbath*. The rigid religious observances of this leader kept him from entering into God's great kingdom of love.

Judas held back. He had charge of the money for the apostolic band, and that money had eaten a hole in his heart. In addition, he was a Zealot, and he had hoped to force Jesus' hand to join the Zealot cause. If Jesus were to be confronted by violent force, surely he would respond with supernatural violent force, or so Judas thought. So he betrayed his Master.

Yes, some turned back. Jesus welcomed them to the great banquet of God's love, and they declined the offer. Their excuses for refusing the invitation of love were lame indeed—new land, new oxen, new bride. So Jesus turned from them and went out into the streets and lanes, the highways and byways, and welcomed in the outcasts—"the poor, the crippled, the blind, and the lame"—and they simply flooded in (Luke 14:15–24).

This, then, is the evangel message of Jesus. And he calls all who follow him to share his invitation with others. "Go," he says, "and make disciples of all nations." Notice that he calls us not to make *converts* but to make *disciples*. And part of the task of making disciples is "teaching them to obey everything that I have commanded you" (Matt. 28:18–20). This is our call and our commission. And it is the great heritage of the Evangelical Tradition.

I am sure that you, like me, desire to bring the good news of God's kingdom of love to your neighbors and friends and welcome them to enter in. If so, then we are to follow Jesus. He shows us the way.

THE SACRAMENT OF THE PRESENT MOMENT

Let's think together about the Incarnational Stream, the sacramental life. Incarnation is right at the heart of the Jesus story, of course. The wonder and the glory and the majesty of Christmas is that at one pinpoint in history the great God of the universe stooped to take on human form. God came to us as a baby in swaddling clothes in a manger in an obscure village in a backwater of civilization. Incarnation!

One of the earliest attempts to express the enormity of this divine invasion declares to us that Christ Jesus,

> who, though he was in the form of God,
>   did not regard equality with God
>   as something to be exploited,

but emptied himself,
  taking the form of a slave,
  being born in human likeness.
And being found in human form,
  he humbled himself
  and became obedient to the point of death—
  even death on a cross. (Phil. 2:6–8)

Nothing can ever approach this perfect and unrepeatable reality of incarnation. Jesus, the Christ, is incarnation itself. We bow under the mystery of it.

But as wonderful as the doctrine of divine incarnation is, it cannot provide us with a paradigm for *our* living. It is an unrepeatable reality in holy history. Therefore, Jesus in his divinity cannot give us the paradigm we need. Jesus in his *humanity* can, however.

It is easy for us to overlook this human paradigm because the substance of it is centered in Jesus' hidden years. We are given very little information about those growing-up years, but what we *are* given is highly suggestive. Not *suggestive* in the fanciful "sandbox miracles" kind of way that some have used to fill in those hidden years. No, *suggestive* in a much more ordinary way. But precisely because it *is* ordinary, it is all the more helpful to us. Following the birth events we are told quite straightforwardly that "the child grew and became strong, filled with wisdom; and the favor of God was upon him" (Luke 2:40). A parallel statement is given later, following Jesus' interaction with the leading teachers in the temple when he was twelve: "And Jesus increased in wisdom and in years, and in divine and human favor"(Luke 2:52). Most instructive of all is the simple comment of Luke after Joseph and Mary had found Jesus in the temple: "Then [Jesus] went down with them and came to Nazareth, and was obedient to them" (Luke 2:51).

A whole world is carried in that unadorned observation that Jesus was "obedient to them." Jesus grew up under the tutelage of his parents, Joseph and Mary. And while Joseph is not heard from again, we can be confident that Jesus learned the carpentry trade from him and worked in that trade until he began his public rabbinic ministry at roughly the age of thirty.

We would do well to ponder those years Jesus spent as a carpenter, working in what we today would call a blue-collar job. Where do you imagine Jesus learned to walk in perfect harmony with his heavenly Father? Where do you suppose he learned to "give to everyone who begs from you, and do not refuse anyone who wants to borrow from you" (Matt. 5:42)? Where do you imagine he came to experience such a life of single-minded devotion to God that he knew that "no one can serve two masters" (Matt. 6:24)? Where, I ask you, did he learn such a deep, intimate life of prayer that he could confidently teach us, "Ask, and it will be given you; search, and you will find; knock, and the door will be opened for you. For everyone who asks receives, and everyone who searches finds, and for everyone who knocks, the door will be opened" (Matt. 7:7)? Where do you think he learned to live out the words, "In everything do to others as you would have them do to you" (Matt. 7:12)? Where did he learn all these things and so much more? I will tell you where. He learned them in his carpentry work and at home with his parents and his brothers and sisters. Jesus did not all of a sudden one day start spouting nice sayings about God. No, when he began his public ministry, he was speaking out of a life that had been tested and tried. He had proven the teachings to be true over and over again as he sawed wood and assembled chairs and built cabinets.

It is critical that we understand the significance of this. Today we tend to confine Jesus and his work to stained glass and high altars and silent retreats, or perhaps to intercessory prayer work and revival meetings. And clearly there was a specifically religious or liturgical dimension to Jesus' incarnational living. He went to synagogue "as was his custom" (Luke 4:16). As a faithful Jew he recited the Shema twice a day: "Hear, O Israel: The LORD our God, the LORD one" (Deut. 6:4, NIV). In addition, he observed the three hours of prayer that were part and parcel of Jewish practice: morning, afternoon, and evening.

But as good and essential as these things were (and are), we must recognize that the majority of Jesus' life—and of ours—is found in our families and homes, in our work and play, among our neighbors and in our everyday surroundings. This tangible world is the place we most fully express the meaning of incarnational living. This is where we experience the outflow of love, joy, peace, and all the fruit of the Spirit. Here and nowhere else. It was true for Jesus; it is true for us. This is the Incarnational Tradition.

This way of sacramental living calls out to us. It calls us to make all our waking and sleeping, all our working and playing, all our living and loving flow out from the divine wellspring. It can; Jesus points the way.

IMITATIO

When Jesus walked across the pages of human history, people—astonished by what he did and what he said—exclaimed, "Never has anyone spoken like this!" (John 7:46). And it is appropriate to add, "Never has anyone lived like this!" Jesus captivates our imaginations and wins our hearts because he was, and is, the very Son of God with the power and the life to transform and empower our lives.

During his years in the flesh Jesus called out his disciples, saying, "Follow me." That call had specific and immediate content, and it had specific and immediate results: those disciples left their nets and other business activities and literally followed Jesus. They traveled with him. They listened to what he taught. They watched what he did. And they tried to do things the way Jesus himself did them. They were his students, his apprentices in the life of the Spirit.

Jesus, alive and among his people today, calls to us exactly as he did those disciples so long ago, saying, "Follow me." Now, we do not follow Jesus in precisely the same way those early disciples did. We cannot walk the dusty roads of Galilee with him. No, we follow him in the Spirit, but the basic principle and pattern is the same. This is why the study of the Gospel records is such a help to us. In their pages we see how Jesus lived and what he did while he was enfleshed as we are. We see, for example, that he trained himself in prayer, solitude, worship, and like disciplines. And we are to imitate him in this, as in all central aspects of his living.

But it is right here that we face a problem—for some an insurmountable problem. How can we imitate Jesus' pattern for living when we do not live in first-century, rural Palestine? We repair automobiles or work at computer terminals or teach school or raise children, and we have responsibilities and demands that simply were unheard of two thousand years ago. How can we imitate the life of Christ in our day and age?

It is precisely at this point that I have encouraging news. We are not the only ones from a different culture and age who have wanted to imitate the life of Christ. Others—myriads and myriads of them—have sought to imitate the way of Christ and to translate that way into their own settings and surroundings. We are helped immensely by looking at their efforts and learning their stories. Furthermore, it is a genuine act of humility to realize that we can learn from others who have gone before us. To be sure, they made mistakes, but even so they have much to teach us. In the midst of all their stumbling and fumbling they sought to imitate the way of Christ and to grow in Christlikeness. Their stories have been—and remain—a rich source of joy, inspiration, and instruction. It is to some of those stories that we now turn.

Chapter 2

∽

The Contemplative Tradition: Discovering the Prayer-Filled Life

As a deer longs for flowing streams,
    so my soul longs for you, O God,
My soul thirsts for God,
    for the living God.
                    —*Psalm 42:1–2a*

Deep within us all there is an amazing inner sanctuary of the soul, a holy place, a Divine Center, a speaking Voice, to which we may continuously return.
                    —*Thomas Kelly*

THE CONTEMPLATIVE TRADITION*

Notable Figures   *Significant Movements*

0

Jesus of Nazareth
(c. 4 B.C.–c. A.D. 29)

John the Apostle (1st century)

| Antony of Egypt (c. 251–356) | Desert Fathers and Mothers |
| Pachomius (290–346) | (4th century) |

Macrina the Younger (c. 330–379)

Gregory of Nyssa (330–c. 395)
Euthymius the Great (c. 378–473)
Benedict of Nursia (c. 480–c. 547)   Benedictines
(6th century to the present)
John Climacus (579–649)
Maximus the Confessor (c. 580–662)

Cuthbert (634–687)
Vulmar (?–c. 700)

Benedict of Aniane (c. 750–821)

Simeon the New Theologian (949–1022)
Antony of Kiev (?–c. 1073)

1000

Aelred of Rievaulx (c. 1110–1167)
Clare of Assisi (c. 1193–1253)   Poor Clares
Gregory Palamas (c. 1296–1359)   (13th century to the present)
Sergius of Radonezh (1314–1392)   Brothers & Sisters of the Common Life
Julian of Norwich (c. 1342–1413)   (14th–15th centuries)
Catherine of Siena (c. 1347–1380)
Nil Sorsky (1433–1508)   Moravian Movement
John of the Cross (1542–1591)   (16th century to the present)
Brother Lawrence (1611–1691)

Pietist Movement
Madame Guyon (1648–1717)   (17th century to the present)
François Fénelon (1651–1715)
Nikolaus Ludwig von Zinzendorf
(1700–1760)
Nicodemus the Hagiorite (1748–1809)
Friedrich von Hügel (1852–1925)
John Hyde (1865–1912)
Thérèsa of Lisieux (1873–1897)
Evelyn Underhill (1875–1941)
Frank Laubach (1884–1970)
John Baillie (1886–1960)
Thomas Kelly (1893–1941)
Catherine de Hueck Doherty (1900–)
Thomas Merton (1915–1968)
Henri Nouwen (1932–1996)

*See Appendix B for brief biographies and histories.

WE ALL HUNGER for a prayer-filled life, for a richer, fuller practice of the presence of God. It is the Contemplative Stream of Christian life and faith that can show us the way into just such intimacy with God. This reality addresses the human longing for the practice of the presence of God.

SEEKING A HISTORICAL PARADIGM

The life of Antonius—a Christian who lived many centuries ago—is for me a powerful example of the Contemplative Stream of faith and witness. Let me tell you his story, and in the telling we will catch a fuller picture of the Contemplative Tradition.

Antonius grew up in a rather well-to-do family in Egypt. His parents were committed Christians, and from everything we can learn, he had an excellent upbringing. But tragedy struck when Antonius was only a teenager: both of his parents died suddenly. As a result, the responsibilities of caring for the home and providing for his younger sister fell upon Antonius—a tough assignment for any young person! But he rose to the occasion.

Into the Desert

Antonius's life vocation arose out of prolonged meditation on the book of Acts. For some months he had been prayerfully considering the moving stories of the disciples being of one mind and heart, holding all things in common, and giving to those in need. Then, one Sunday when the Gospel lesson was read—"Go sell all that you have and give to the poor and you shall have treasure in heaven"—the words spoke directly into Antonius's heart. And he obeyed that Scripture quite literally. After making provision for his sister, he sold off his parents' estate and gave the money to the poor. Another Scripture that deeply affected him at this same time was a sentence of encouragement from Jesus: "Do not be anxious for tomorrow." On the strength of those two Gospel passages, Antonius went out into the Egyptian desert, seeking God.[1]

Antonius's literal understanding and application of Scripture may embarrass us today. And certainly some of the things he did were a bit excessive, to say the least. But we need to understand that he was living at a time when Christians were becoming increasingly secularized. Seeing this, Antonius, and others like him, tried desperately to keep the Church from forgetting its first love. In the only way he knew, Antonius shouted, "No! Somehow, someway, Christians ought to be different; somehow, someway the Church ought to be different!"

Almost instinctively Antonius understood that the followers of Christ were the *athletae Dei*, the athletes of God. And, like a good athlete, Antonius had a single-hearted devotion toward the goal of Christlikeness. And so he renounced possessions in order to learn detachment; he renounced speech in order to learn compassion; he renounced activity in order to learn prayer.

So off he went into the solitude of the Egyptian desert, not just for a few days or weeks but for twenty years. Please understand, he did not do this to avoid responsibilities at home or to get away from people. Antonius went into the desert to discover God ... and to fight the devil.

And fight the devil he did! The stories of his struggles with demonic forces are voluminous and fantastic—strange, perhaps, to modern sensibilities. But before we jump to analyzing the experiences, we would do well first to listen to them.

His first temptation experience, we are told, happened because the devil "wished to cordon him off from his righteous intention." And so he paraded before Antonius a host of memories about what he was leaving behind: "the guardianship of his sister, the bonds of kinship . . . the manifold pleasure of food," and the like. At first all of this raised "a great dust cloud of considerations" in Antonius's mind. But his resolve stood firm. Next the devil "hurled foul thoughts" at him, but Antonius "overturned them through his prayers." So the devil "resorted to titillation," but Antonius, "seeming to blush, fortified the body with faith." So, turning to more blatant sexual temptation, the devil decided to "assume the form of a woman and to imitate her every gesture," but Antonius "extinguished the fire of his opponent's deception." Back and forth the fight went, Antonius winning round after round until the devil "fled, cowering at the words and afraid even to approach the man." Concerned that we understand whose power was behind these victories, Antonius's biographer writes, "This was Antonius's first contest against the devil—or, rather, this was in Antonius the success of the Savior."[2] Well it may have been "his first contest," but it was far from his last.

Another confrontation underscores the dramatic character of these stories. Antonius was visiting some above-ground tombs when demonic spirits attacked him and threw him to the ground. Not just once or twice, but again and again. Battered and exhausted, Antonius shouted out, "Here I am—Antonius! I do not run from your blows, for even if you give me more, nothing shall separate me from the love of Christ." He then broke into song: "Though an army should set itself in array against me, my heart shall not be afraid."

The demons, astonished by this courage, retreated. But at night they attacked again, violently shaking Antonius's room. With terrifying noises the spirits took on the form of "lions, bears, leopards, bulls, and serpents, asps, scorpions, and wolves." In the midst of the commotion, Antonius declared, "If there were some power among you, it would have been enough for only one of you to come. But since the Lord has broken your strength, you attempt to terrify me by any means with the mob; it is a mark of your weakness that you mimic the shapes of irrational beasts." To this the demonic spirits had no defense. Defeated, they scattered.

Then Antonius was given a vision, "a certain beam of light descending toward him." Humbled by the divine Presence, he nevertheless sought to understand why God would let him go through such terrible struggles: "Why didn't you appear in the beginning, so that you could stop my distresses?" The response he heard spoke not only to his present situation but also to his future ministry. "And a voice came to him: 'I was here, Antonius, but I waited to watch your struggle. And now, since you persevered and were not defeated, I will be your helper forever, and I will make you famous everywhere.'"[3]

These are the kinds of stories that are sprinkled throughout those first twenty years of solitude Antonius spent in the Egyptian desert. They show us that desert life was as much warfare as it was serenity. In fact, Antonius became known as a warrior against demons.*

The demonology in these stories is subtle and psychologically suggestive. The stories deal with far more than the conquering of demons; more profoundly, they deal with the conquering of the self—the demons within. Throughout the stories there is a penetrating element of self-scrutiny, self-knowledge, self-mastery. The demonic stood not only for what was *hostile* to human nature but for what was *incomplete* in human nature. Always the demons seemed to manifest themselves in exactly those guises that would make the desert monks the most needy and the most susceptible to temptation. All of the stories carry with them the sense of growth in grace, of character formation, of clarifying the motives and intents of the heart. For Antonius the issue was not so much conquest over particular demons as progress in virtue. In this we see how the Contemplative and Holiness Traditions interface with one another.

Throughout this process of desert temptation the role of spiritual discipline (*askesis*) was prominent. In fact, the very purpose of going into the desert was for training in spiritual discipline. This life involved solitude and fasting for the sake of intense, internal focus; meditation and prayer for the sake of deepening spiritual communion; Scripture study and reflection for the sake of the transformation of the mind; and manual labor and exorcism for the sake of doing the works of the Father.[4]

Now, the purpose of these Disciplines of the Spiritual Life was to train the body and the soul in righteousness. This, in turn, produced

---

*In light of the renewed interest today in "spiritual warfare," we might do well to study carefully the life of one who had become a master in it long before any of us came on the scene.

established men and women who could stand firm in the time of trial.

We find this kind of character formation in abundance in Antonius. His biographer writes, "It was not his physical dimensions that distinguished him from the rest, but the stability of character and the purity of the soul. His soul being free of confusion, he held his outer senses also undisturbed, so that from the soul's joy his face was cheerful as well."[5] Antonius became characterized as "tolerant in disposition and humble of soul."[6] In fact, so striking was the transformation of his life that "simply by seeing his conduct, many aspired to become imitators of his way of life."[7] This was the fruit God produced in him from the years of solitude in the desert.

Into the World

Evidently this interior formation was not for Antonius alone, for after his twenty years in the desert God catapulted him into one of the most remarkable ministries of that day. Proclaiming the everlasting gospel of Jesus Christ, he moved freely among both society's elite and its rejects—teaching, counseling, healing, expelling demons, and more. The Emperor Constantine Augustus sought out his counsel, but Antonius also ministered tirelessly among the poor in the mines and in the prisons.[8] He confronted unjust judges and preached the gospel with great power. His speech was full of grace, often bringing reconciliation between hostile groups.

Antonius's healing ministry was known throughout the region. Once, a count—Archelaus by name—asked Antonius to pray for a saintly and desperately ill woman, Polycratia, who lived across the Mediterranean Sea in the city of Laodicea. Moved by her need, Antonius did pray for her, "and the count marked the day on which the prayer was spoken." Returning to Laodicea, Archelaus found Polycratia in perfect health. When he inquired about this dramatic change of circumstances, the people mentioned the day she had been healed. Immediately Archelaus "pulled out the sheet on which he had marked the time of prayer. And checking it, he at once

showed the writing on the paper, and everyone was astonished to realize that the Lord had freed her from her pains just when Antonius was
praying and appealing on her behalf to the goodness of the Savior."[9]

Often the healing work was accompanied by a well-nigh-amazing
discernment. On one occasion a man named Fronto came to Antonius
seeking healing. He had multiple maladies, among them a growing
blindness. Antonius discerned that Fronto was inordinately attached
to him. So, rather than pander to his dependency needs, Antonius
counseled Fronto to take responsibility for his own life, saying,
"Leave, and you will be healed." But Fronto did not leave, *could* not
leave, *would* not leave, so attached was he to the master. As a result,
no healing occurred. Time went by, and Antonius continued to resist
Fronto's lavish subservience. "You will not be able to be healed while
staying here," Antonius warned him again. "Go out, and when you
arrive in Egypt you will see the sign accomplished in you." At last, in
desperation over his physical illnesses and with great sadness, Fronto
turned to leave his master. As he walked away, he was healed![10] Such
was the wisdom and discernment of Antonius. Indeed, wisdom and
discernment are among the natural results of a prayer-filled life.

Though the stories of divine healing through the hands of Antonius
are many and varied, not everyone was healed. We are told that with
those who suffered, Antonius "sympathized and prayed." He was
"neither boastful" when healing occurred "nor disgruntled" when no
healing occurred. "He encouraged those who suffered to have
patience and to know that healing belonged neither to him nor to
men at all, but only to God. . . . The ones who suffered therefore
received the words of the old man as healing, and learned not to
dwell on their infirmities but to be patient. And the ones who were
cured were taught not to give thanks to Antonius, but to God
alone."[11]

The healing aspect of Antonius's ministry reminds us of the tie
between the Contemplative and the Charismatic Traditions. And the
sensitivity in the exercise of that healing work teaches us many
things. The stories of Antonius's wisdom in teaching and disputation

were legendary. Once two Greek philosophers came up the mountain to visit him, hoping for an opportunity to cross intellectual swords with him. When they arrived, Antonius said through an interpreter, "Why did you go to so much trouble, you philosophers, to visit a foolish man?" Respectfully, they responded that he was not foolish, but wise, and that they had come to him because of his wisdom. He replied, "If you came to a foolish man, your toil is superfluous, but if you consider me wise, become as I am, for we must imitate what is good. If I had come to you I would have imitated you; but since you came to me, become as I am; for I am a Christian." At this the two philosophers knew they had met their match.[12]

On another occasion he was disputing with some Greeks who were ridiculing the cross of Christ. After considerable argumentation Antonius said to them, "Look, there are some here suffering from demons (for there were some who came to him distressed by demons, and he said, bringing them into their midst)—you cleanse them, either by your syllogisms, or by any skill or magic you might wish, summoning your idols! Or, if you are not able, end the war you wage with us, and behold the power of the cross of Christ!" Whereupon Antonius called upon Jesus in prayer and made the sign of the cross over those who were afflicted by demons. Immediately "the men stood and were sound, coming to their senses and giving thanks to the Lord."[13]

The effect of his teaching ministry is expressed well in the words of his biographer: "All rejoiced while Antonius talked about these things. In some, the love of virtue increased, in others carelessness was discarded, and in still others conceit was brought to an end. And all were persuaded to hate the demonic conniving, marveling at the grace given by the Lord to Antonius for the discernment of spirits."[14]

It is interesting to note that toward the end of his life Antonius returned to the solitude of the Egyptian desert, free from any compulsive attachments to "his ministry."

Have you by now recognized that I have been telling the story of St. Antony, or Abba Antony, the founder of the Desert Fathers and

Mothers? He lived in the third and fourth centuries (c. 251–356), and his story has been immortalized for us by Athanasius in *The Life of Antony*, a famous fourth-century biography that became something of a literary sensation in its day.

At the end of his biography Athanasius powerfully summarized the force of Antony's life:

> It was as if he were a physician given to Egypt by God. For who went to him grieving and did not return rejoicing? Who went in lamentation over his dead, and did not immediately put aside his sorrow? Who visited while angered and was not changed to affection? What poor person met him in exhaustion who did not, after hearing and seeing him, despise wealth and console himself in his poverty? What monk, coming to him in discouragement, did not become all the stronger? What young man, coming to the mountain and looking at Antony, did not at once renounce pleasures and love moderation? Who came to him tempted by a demon and did not gain relief? And who came to him distressed in his thoughts and did not find his mind calmed?[15]

That was Abba Antony. What about you and me? We live in very different times and in a very different place. But even so, we can still learn much from Abba Antony about the contemplative life, about the gaze of the soul upon God.

SEEKING A BIBLICAL PARADIGM

All the Traditions that form the structure of this book are deeply rooted in Scripture. And our understanding of each Tradition is immeasurably enriched by giving attention to its biblical expression. Examples of the Contemplative Tradition abound—from the Psalmist, who meditated upon God's character, Law, and creation, to Mary, the mother of Jesus, who pondered all things in her heart; from Elijah, who kept a lonely vigil over earthquake, wind, and fire, to Mary of

Bethany, who chose to sit at Jesus' feet. But certainly one of the most glowing illustrations of the Contemplative Stream is John the Beloved, one of the original apostolic band.

John was one of the first to follow Jesus and one of the last at the foot of the cross (John 1:35–39, 19:26). Between those two events he was with Jesus almost constantly throughout his earthly ministry. And following Jesus' death, resurrection, and ascension, John lingered longer and contemplated more deeply than most on the Christ event. New Testament scholar Everett F. Harrison notes that John was "more alert than the others to the greatness of Jesus and was conscious of being at the center of an epochal, transforming movement in human history."[16]

John is a model of the Contemplative Tradition for several reasons. The Gospel that bears his name has all the marks of an author who had spent a lifetime meditating upon Jesus' life and ministry.[17] This is most assuredly why A.H.N. Green-Armytage speaks of the Gospel of John as "the work of a contemplative."[18] Then too, if we can identify the Seer of Revelation with the Apostle John, as I believe we can, we have a powerful example of how God could use the solitude of Patmos to bring forth perhaps the most profound apocalyptic visions in the entire Bible. But most important of all is John's teachings, especially his teachings on love. Entering into God's great love for us and our responding love toward God is the abiding gift of the Contemplative Tradition. As Green-Armytage has written, "A contemplative ... makes the love of God his main, his only object in life."[19]

A Son of Thunder

The outline of John's life, such as we have it, is straightforward enough. He was a fisherman, working for his father, Zebedee. The fishing business was prosperous enough that they had employees—Peter was likely one of them (Mark 1:20, Luke 5:7–9). Salome was John's mother, and it is possible that this is the Salome who was the sister of Mary, the mother of Jesus (Matt. 27:56, Mark 16:1). If so, that would make John a cousin to Jesus.

On three occasions the Gospels present John in a rather unfavorable light—certainly far from the kind of person we picture as a shining example of the prayer-filled life. Once Jesus is traveling toward Jerusalem, and he sends some disciples on ahead to a village in Samaria, evidently to make arrangements for the night's lodging. The village people refuse the request, and John and his brother James are incensed by their lack of hospitality. They ask Jesus, "Lord, do you want us to command fire to come down from heaven and consume them?" (Luke 9:54b). Now, in asking this, John is clearly within the tradition of Elijah, who had a knack for casting fire upon his enemies. But in Jesus, one greater than Elijah has arisen, and the young John has yet to understand the difference between the fiery denunciations of Elijah and the everlasting gospel of peace that Jesus brings. Jesus rebukes him.

On another occasion we detect a harsh intolerance in John. Evidently, upon seeing an "uncertified exorcist" casting out demons, John tries to stop his work. Rather proudly, it appears, he announces to Jesus, "Master, we saw someone casting out demons in your name, and we tried to stop him, because he does not follow with us." Again John fails to understand the all-inclusive nature of Jesus' mission and kingdom, and the Master has to rebuke him, saying, "Do not stop him; for whoever is not against you is for you" (Luke 9:49–50).

A third occasion gives hints at the personal ambition that drives John and his brother James. They approach Jesus with a rather audacious request: "Grant us to sit, one at your right hand and one at your left, in your glory." Of course, they have no idea what they are really asking, and Jesus tells them as much in his kind but firm rebuke (Mark 10:35–40; cf. Matt. 20:21). These occasions may well explain the nickname that Jesus gave to John and his brother James: "Boanerges, that is, Sons of Thunder" (Mark 3:17).

The Inner Circle

I imagine that these three events caused John genuine embarrassment in later years, but they are counterbalanced by three events in which only the inner circle—Peter, James, and John—had the privilege of participating. In the first, a synagogue leader, Jairus, begs Jesus to come to his little daughter, who is near death. But before Jesus arrives, messengers come, saying that the child has already died. Jesus continues on nonetheless, and we are told specifically that he "allowed no one to follow him except Peter, James, and John" as he went into the home of Jairus. Once there, he made everyone at the house leave except for the child's mother and father. He then took the child "by the hand and said to her, 'Talitha cum,' which means, 'Little girl, get up!' And immediately the girl got up and began to walk about" (Mark 5:35–43). Think of it: John was one of only five to witness this overwhelming event. Can you imagine the effect it must have had upon him?

The second event is the well-known transfiguration, and only "the three" are allowed to accompany Jesus. "Jesus took with him Peter and James and John, and led them up a high mountain apart, by themselves. And he was transfigured before them, and his clothes became dazzling white, such as no one on earth could bleach them. And there appeared to them Elijah with Moses, who were talking with Jesus." We are told that the disciples "were terrified" at what transpired (Mark 9:2–8). (I am sure we would have been terrified too!) Think of it: John was one of only three to witness this all-consuming event. Can you imagine the effect it must have had upon him?

The third event occurs following the Last Supper. Jesus takes his disciples down and across the Kidron Valley and up to the Mount of Olives. When they come to the entrance to Gethsemane, he instructs the other disciples to "sit here while I pray." But craving the company of "the three" for his moment of greatest agony, he "took with him Peter and James and John, and began to be distressed and agitated. And said to them, 'I am deeply grieved, even to death; remain here, and keep awake.' And going a little farther, he threw himself on the ground and prayed" (Mark 14:32–35). Throughout that dark night Jesus prayed the agonizing prayer of relinquishment; and Peter, James, and John, overcome with sorrow and confusion, slept. But evidently they were awake long enough to overhear Jesus' torturous prayer and to watch his physical struggle, perhaps even to see the bloodlike sweat. Think of it: John was one of only three witnesses to this excruciating event. Can you imagine the effect it must have had upon him?

"The Disciple Whom Jesus Loved"

These events, and others like them, produced a change in John that was altogether amazing. We see in him a deepening, settling, contemplative love. But I have yet to mention what was certainly the single most important influence in producing this transformation— namely, Jesus' notable love for John. Five times in the Gospel of John the author speaks of "the disciple whom Jesus loved" (John 21:7).[20]

The first occurs in the Upper Room. As they gather for the Passover meal John sits next to Jesus, certainly a position of high privilege. John's head is resting easily on Jesus' chest as the two recline on cushions, John being on the right side and leaning to the left, according to custom: "One of his disciples—the one whom Jesus loved—was reclining next to him."

Jesus then makes the startling announcement, "Very truly, I tell you, one of you will betray me." John bolts upright with the announcement, and all the disciples begin looking around, wondering who it could be and what this could mean. Peter, thinking of a way to discover the culprit, motions to John to ask Jesus who he is referring to. John reclines back near Jesus and quietly, privately, asks, "Lord, who is it?" Quietly, privately, Jesus tells him, "It is the one to whom I give this piece of bread when I have dipped it in the dish" (John 13:21–30). John alone among the disciples now knows the identity of the betrayer. It is a wonder that Jesus is willing to trust John with this privileged information, and an even greater wonder that John can remain calm (and silent) as the evening wears on.[21]

Following Jesus' arrest, only two disciples overcome their fear sufficiently to watch the trial, "Simon Peter and another disciple." We are not given the identity of this other disciple, but John is the likely candidate. Because of his acquaintance with the high priest, John has access to the hall where the trial is being held. John, in fact, speaks to the woman guarding the gate and is able to get Peter inside. Peter evidently stays back with the servants, where, as you may recall, he gets into considerable trouble. But John is able to go in close where he can hear the proceedings and thus becomes an eyewitness to details that are otherwise inaccessible to the followers of Jesus. Perhaps he is close enough to look into the Master's eyes and see the giving and forgiving love Jesus has for him (John 18:12–16).

And perhaps it is John's answering love that draws him irresistibly to the foot of the cross. From atop the cross Jesus "saw his mother and the disciple whom he loved standing beside her." Jesus' next words both honor John's love and care for Mary's need: "Woman, here is your son. . . . Here is your mother." From that point on, we are told, "the disciple took her into his own home" (John 19:25–27).

On Easter Sunday morning Mary Magdalene rushes up to Peter and "the other disciple, the one whom Jesus loved" with the news that the grave stone has been removed and the body is missing. Together Peter and John run toward the tomb. John, younger and more agile perhaps, outruns Peter and arrives at the tomb first. He hesitates at the tomb's entrance, but Peter brushes past him and goes inside. Taking courage, John joins Peter inside the tomb. Together they see the linen grave cloths lying in orderly array, bearing no sign of pillage or violence. A little distance from them rests the *soudarion* that had been around the head of Jesus. Looking at these things, John "saw and believed" (John 20:2–10). John, "the disciple whom Jesus loved," was the first one to believe in the resurrection of Jesus.

On one last occasion we find the double use of that intriguing phrase. That occasion occurs beside the Sea of Tiberias. Seven of the disciples decide to go fishing together. But fishing, the one thing they know how to do well, they cannot do that night. Then, through the early-morning mists, they catch a glimpse of a form on the shore. A voice calls out, inquiring about their success. Grudgingly they shout back that there *was* no success, only failure. "Cast the net to the right side of the boat, and you will find some." And they oblige. I wonder whether John, as they cast the nets again, is thinking about another time when he heard those same words (see Luke 5:1–11). Immediately, the net is filled to the breaking point, and just as quickly John knows who spoke to them. "That disciple whom Jesus loved said to Peter, 'It is the Lord!'" (John 21:1–8).

John has been called the Seer of Patmos, and so he was, but long before Patmos he was the Seer of Galilee. He saw, he knew, he spoke. Commenting on John's discernment in this situation, Everett Harrison writes, "the understanding of the many comes through the contemplation of the few whose hearts have been attuned to the Lord."[22]

The haunting phrase we have encountered four times now — "the disciple whom Jesus loved" — does not speak of a love past or terminated. The tense suggests a continuous flowing of Jesus' love, and John reciprocates in love. John's heart-love needs no scrutiny that day beside the Sea of Tiberias. That is Peter's need, not John's. Once Peter's heart has been probed and the prophecy has been given about his martyrdom, Jesus begins to walk along the shore, speaking to Peter in words that come like an echo from the past: "Follow me."

As the two of them walked away together, "Peter turned and saw the disciple whom Jesus loved following them; he was the one who had reclined next to Jesus at the supper and had said, 'Lord, who is it that is going to betray you?'" (John 21:20). Peter, amazingly free from morbid preoccupation about his own future death, cannot help asking about the future of his friend and comrade. Patiently, lovingly, Jesus helps Peter see the question as a diversion from his own marching orders: "If it is my will that he remain until I come, what is that to you? Follow me!" (John 21:22). As events unfolded, we know that Peter served Jesus through a martyr's death and John served Jesus through old age, but both served in answering love.

"Little Children, Love One Another"

God's great love for us, and our answering love, is a prominent theme in John's writings.[23] His Gospel, as you know, contains one of the most treasured passages in all the Bible about God's love: "For God so loved the world that he gave his only Son, so that everyone who believes in him may not perish but may have eternal life" (John 3:16).

The theme of love is a guiding feature of the Upper Room Discourse. In it we hear articulated Jesus' new commandment: "I give you a new commandment, that you love one another. Just as I have loved you, you also should love one another. By this everyone will know that you are my disciples, if you have love for one another" (John 13:34–35). In the marvelous teaching on "abiding," the theme of love again appears: "As the Father has loved me, so I have loved you; abide in my love. . . . This is my commandment, that you love one another as I have loved you. No one has greater love than this, to lay down one's life for one's friends" (John 15:9–13). And at the conclusion of Jesus' high priestly prayer for unity, we hear the theme of love reiterated: "I made your name known to them, and I will make it known, so that the love with which you have loved me may be in them, and I in them" (John 17:26).

But it is in John's Epistles that we find the greatness of his teaching on love. The First Epistle especially reverberates with the theme of love, and through it we hear the echoes of the fourth Gospel: "For this is the message you have heard from the beginning, that we should love one another" (1 John 3:11).

Please understand, John's call to love does not refer to some warm feeling or an abstract ideal. He is talking about clear-headed action toward God and others that is rooted in Jesus' sacrificial action on our behalf.

From the outset John makes it clear that our love is not an *originating* love but a *responding* love: "We love because he first loved us" (1 John 4:19). Nor is God's love toward us vague or ethereal. From years of contemplating the divine condescension, John saw that "God's love was revealed among us in this way: God sent his only Son into the world so that we might live through him. In this is love, not that we loved God but that he loved us and sent his Son to be the atoning sacrifice for our sins" (1 John 4:9–10). In this emphasis on responsive love John helps us see something of the interplay between the Contemplative and the Incarnational Traditions. Divine love (which is at the heart of the contemplative life) must be given visible expression (which is at the heart of the incarnational life).

Therefore, the incarnation—and most specifically Jesus' sacrificial death on the cross—becomes the visible sign of God's love toward us. This is one reason that John placed such importance upon confessing "that Jesus Christ has come in the flesh." For John, the failure to make this confession is a certain sign of "the spirit of the antichrist" (1 John 4:2–3).[24] In this emphasis on the incarnation John again helps us see something of the interplay between the Contemplative and the Incarnational Traditions. To repeat: divine love (which is at the heart of the contemplative life) must be given visible expression (which is at the heart of the incarnational life).

With the source and spring of our love clear, John then proceeds to make the action of our love clear: "We know love by this, that he laid down his life for us—and we ought to lay down our lives for one another. How does God's love abide in anyone who has the world's goods and sees a brother or sister in need and yet refuses help?" (1 John 3:16–17). No teaching could be more straightforward and clear than that. Or this: "Those who say, 'I love God,' and hate their brothers or sisters, are liars. . . . The commandment we have from him is this: those who love God must love their brothers and sisters also" (1 John 4:20–21).

Now, with these concrete expressions of love clearly before us, we are prepared to hear what must be considered the high-water mark of John's teaching on love: "God is love, and those who abide in love abide in God, and God abides in them. Love has been perfected among us in this: that we may have boldness on the day of judgment, because as he is, so are we in this world. There is no fear in love, but perfect love casts out fear; for fear has to do with punishment, and whoever fears has not reached perfection in love" (1 John 4:16b–18). Clearly, John deserves the title history has given him: the Apostle of Love.

During the reign of Domitian (A.D. 81–96), John was banished to the island of Patmos, where in complete solitude he received the mystic visions that form the core of his Apocalypse, the last book of our Bible. Released from Patmos, John spent the remaining years of his long life as Bishop in Ephesus.[25] Tradition tells us that when John was no longer able to walk, disciples would carry him into the worshiping community, where he would urge the people again and again, "Little children, love one another."[26]

And so, from the intimacy of the Last Supper, to the contemplative teachings on love, to the solitude of Patmos, to the pastoral ministry in Ephesus, John provides us with an exemplary model for the Contemplative Tradition. Deepest intimacy and abiding love, prayerful meditation and discerning contemplation—these are the marks of John's life and ministry.

SEEKING A CONTEMPORARY PARADIGM

Regardless of how inspiring the stories of Abba Antony and the Apostle John might be, they are far removed from our day. Can this contemplative way of life be experienced in our time, especially among those of us who must constantly face the demands and pressures of ordinary life? To find an answer to this pressing question, we can do no better than to consider the life of Frank C. Laubach.

A man of prayer and a man of action, he was the Apostle of Literacy to "the silent billion," as he referred to those who could neither read nor write. Earning degrees from Princeton University, Union Seminary, and Columbia University, he was highly sophisticated theologically and psychologically.

Laubach's greatest work grew out of the ashes of a bitter disappointment. He had been a missionary educator in the Philippines for over ten years, helping establish Union Seminary in Manila and serving as dean of the School of Education at the University of Manila. Then in 1925 the seminary decided to establish a separate administration for its growing college in Manila. Laubach, a member of the board, desperately wanted the new position of college president, but out of chivalry he voted for his opponent. He lost the presidency by one vote.[27]

The Solitude of Mindanao

His educational career now in shambles, Laubach spent two years in bitter self-recrimination, and an onslaught of illnesses left him a semi-invalid. Finally, realizing that his emotional self-flagellation was affecting his health, he sought a deeper devotional life. Even though this did not take root, eventually his health did return, and in 1929 he accepted the call to evangelistic work in the area surrounding beautiful Lake Lanao on the island of Mindanao, Philippines. Since Lanao was isolated, dangerous, and lacking in health services, Laubach's wife, Effa, and their only surviving child—three children had died from malaria—stayed in Baguio, nine hundred miles to the north.

Hence, with only the companionship of his dog, Tip, Laubach labored among the Maranao people. Success was elusive at first. Each evening, with Tip at his side, Laubach would climb Signal Hill back behind his cottage. On top of that hill overlooking Lake Lanao, disheartened and utterly alone, he sought companionship with God.

One December evening in 1929 on Signal Hill, Frank Laubach had a transforming experience. His own words describe it best:[28]

> One evening I was sitting on Signal Hill looking over the province that had me beaten. Tip had his nose up under my arm trying to lick the tears off my cheeks. My lips began to move and it seemed to me that God was speaking.
>
> "My Child," my lips said, "you have failed because you do not really love these Moros. You feel superior to them because you are white. If you can forget you are an American and think only how I love them, they will respond."
>
> I answered back to the sunset, "God, I don't know whether you spoke to me through my lips, but if you did, it was the

truth. . . . Drive me out of myself and come and take possession
of me and think Thy thoughts in my mind. . . ."

My lips spoke to me again: "If you want the Moros to be fair
to your religion, be fair to theirs. Study their Koran with them."

Climbing down Signal Hill, Laubach told some local priests that
he wanted to study their Koran. "The next day," he notes, "they
crowded into my little cottage, each with a Koran under his arm.
They were bent upon making a Moslem out of me! So we went to
work with great zeal."

Of that pivotal event Laubach said, "After that night on Signal Hill,
when God killed my racial prejudice and made me color-blind, it
seemed as though He were working miracles at every turn." From this
watershed experience two great pioneering efforts emerged—one
internal and the other external—both inextricably bound together.
The first explored the growth of the soul under God. The second
involved the development of a literacy movement that eventually
reached an estimated sixty million people.

Journey Inward

Laubach's letters and journal notations on his inward journey are
endlessly moving. Fortunately he preserved his early experiences on
Signal Hill in what could arguably be his most important piece of
writing, *Letters by a Modern Mystic*. These letters to his father describe
the "open windows and swinging doors" into a vastly deeper and
fuller spiritual life than he had ever known.

One glorious experience occurred on 24 May 1930: "The day had
been rich but strenuous, so I climbed 'Signal Hill' back of my house
talking and listening to God all the way up, all the way back, all the
lovely half hour on the top. And God talked back! I let my tongue go
loose and from it there flowed poetry far more beautiful than any I
ever composed. It flowed without pausing and without ever a failing
syllable for a half hour. I listened astonished and full of joy and gratitude. I wanted a dictaphone for I knew that I should not be able to

remember it—and now I cannot. . . . 'Why,' someone may ask, 'did God waste his poetry on you alone, when you could not carry it home?' You will have to ask God that question. I only know He did and I am happy in the memory."[29] Stories like this, reflecting the vibrancy and excitement of Laubach's spiritual growth, are legion.

On 10 February 1931, Laubach evaluated what had been happening to him: "If there is any contribution that I have to make to the world that will live, surely it must be my experience of God on Signal Hill."[30] And the reaction of the people was a constant source of amazement to him. "I do nothing that I can see excepting to pray for them, and to walk among them thinking of God. They know I am a Protestant. Yet two of the leading Moslem priests have gone around the province telling everybody that I would help the people to know God."[31]

This led Laubach into many experiments in prayer. His "Game with Minutes" is the delightful spiritual exercise of forming a habit of having God in mind each minute we are awake. "Impossible," you may say. Laubach himself wondered about its feasibility: "Can I bring God back in my mind-flow every few seconds so that God shall always be in my mind as an after image, shall always be one of the elements in every concept and percept? I choose to make the rest of my life an experiment in answering this question."[32]

While going through busy days filled with literacy development, he was constantly "learning the vocabulary of God" (a phrase that he later used as a book title). On 1 January 1937, from Nagpur, India, he wrote, "God, I want to give You every minute of this year. . . . I shall try to learn Your language as it was taught by Jesus and all others through whom You speak—in beauty and singing birds and cool breezes, in radiant Christlike faces, in sacrifices and in tears."[33]

One of the most stunning lessons Laubach learned was how prayer and work blend into one. On 11 March 1937, while working on a literacy plan for the Urdu Dihate Indian dialect, he wrote, "Of all today's miracles, the greatest is this: To know that I find Thee best when I work listening, not when I am still or meditative or even on my knees in prayer, but when I *work* listening and co-operating."[34]

This, you see, is a marvelous contemporary expression of the ancient Benedictine rule *ora et labora*, "work and pray."

Everywhere he went Laubach experimented with what he called "flash prayers." At a station in Allahabad, India, he wrote, "This morning, as I came from the train and prayed for all the people on the street, I felt new energy surge into me. What it does to all of them to receive that instant prayer I may never know. What it does for me is electrical. It drives out fatigue and thrills one with eager power."[35]

He attempted many similar experiments. Once, after what seems to have been a tennis match, he wrote, "Yesterday, Lord, I saw how an experiment in prayer may be tried by athletes! I tried to put my arm in Thy control and my playing improved so much that instead of losing, I won. I tried to put my opponent's arm under Thy control and believe he did better. We humans have not begun to suspect what a field for useful scientific research prayer is!"[36]

Laubach's prayer experiments constantly turned him to the needs of others. On 27 April 1937, at Kikuyu, Kenya, he felt God speaking to him: "My child, when you pray to Me of your own little troubles and doubts, your prayer is pretty thin and small. When you reach out to help other people by offering yourself as a channel for Me, your prayer becomes at once large and noble."[37]

Often intercession for others filled his diary notations. On 22 May 1937, at Dar-es-Salaam, Tanzania, he wrote, "Sitting in the church alone for a long while trying to give Thee out to many people, I *wanted* to become that way *habitually*, so that to see a man would be *more* than to pray; it would be to *give him my soul filled with Thee*, O Christ. Can I become that way to the English with their insufferable snobbery? Can I ignore it? Can Love and I draw a circle to take them in and to understand them and to give my soul to them full of Christ? That is a good test!"[38] Always he kept trying to learn how intercessory work could be done better. He wrote, "Father, am I not learning that the best way to pray for people is to go and sit near them and pray while there? Perhaps holding their letters or photos in my hand is as effective. This experiment which I began May 8 with letters and photos, recording the hour when I pray, may answer this

question."[39] All of Laubach's manifold experiences in prayer rein-
force to us that at its center the Contemplative Tradition is a prayer-
filled life.

Journey Outward

It would be possible to go on and on with these many experiments
in growing a soul that Laubach felt were his greatest gift to humanity.
Equally significant, however, is how he brought the life of contemplative prayer directly into the world of action and social concern. This is
seen most fully in the worldwide volunteer movement he developed
for promoting literacy—a movement informally known as "each one
teach one." In time, this work, which was a direct outgrowth of his
inward spiritual explorations, extended to two hundred different languages and dialects in over one hundred countries. But the work did
not begin as a worldwide movement. In 1929, in total obscurity beside
Lake Lanao, Laubach began learning the Maranao language. Up to
that point almost no work had been done in the field of adult literacy
education.* Lanao proved to be the perfect laboratory, for the
Maranao language was uncomplicated and perfectly regular. Before
long, with the help of several paid staff members, Laubach had large
numbers of adults reading, and he was publishing a bimonthly newspaper, the *Lanao Progress*. Then, in December 1932, Laubach
received word that mission funds for the program were being cut
because of the Depression. Sadly he called his crew together and
explained that he could no longer pay salaries for the teachers. At this,
one of the most influential chieftains on the island, Kakai Dagalangit,
stood and said, "This campaign shall not stop. It's Lanao's only hope."
Then, staring directly at the teachers with fierce eyes, he declared, "I'll
make everybody who knows how to read teach somebody else, or I'll
kill him."[40] Laubach wisely modified this "teach or die" approach into
"each one teach one," and the Laubach Literacy Movement was born.

---

*The Russian literacy campaign had been launched in 1921, but Laubach was
unaware of it.

Word of Laubach's literacy program in Lanao spread quickly, and numerous groups interested in trying to duplicate his efforts elsewhere wrote him, seeking help. Attempts to respond by correspondence produced only meager results, so Laubach determined that he would arrange to visit missionary educators at sites along his route home on his next furlough to the United States. He paid all expenses of this first literacy tour himself, a tour that took him to Singapore, Ceylon, India, Egypt, Palestine, Syria, and Turkey.

Once in the United States Laubach met with friends to consider the potential for developing a worldwide literacy program. This led to the founding of the World Literacy Committee, which provided the financial backing for his vision.

Laubach returned to India and tried to tackle the problem of 325 million illiterate Indians, a far more formidable task than he had faced in Lanao. While the Maranao language had only sixteen letters, some of the Indian languages had hundreds of letters and letter combinations. In addition, almost all printed material in India was written in a literary style far different from the common, spoken language. Traveling sixteen thousand miles and conducting conferences throughout India, he finally developed a technique of "picture-word-syllable" correlations that could teach illiterate peoples to read in Hindi, Urdu, and Marathi. He met with Mahatma Gandhi and Jawaharlal Nehru and was involved in over two hundred promotional and organizational meetings for the literacy of India.

In 1938 Laubach published *Toward a Literate World*, the first in a host of literacy development writings, the most famous being, *Forty Years with the Silent Billion*. His burning passion for literacy took him to every continent of the globe, where he worked both within and outside Christian settings. He met with kings, prime ministers, presidents, generals, and colonial administrators from Lebanon to Malaya. He developed literacy in Afghanistan, Nepal, Dutch New Guinea, and nearly one hundred other countries. He worked with President Harry Truman to build broad-based support in the United States for increased international aid for literacy efforts. He developed an

English literacy program—*Streamlined English*—which continues to be used to this day. And on and on it goes.

Perhaps one event can stand as a paradigm for hundreds of similar stories. In 1950 Laubach decided to develop a literacy program in Dondi, Angola. The news of Laubach's coming spread, and by the time he arrived, thousands of people were waiting. To reduce the group to a manageable size, Laubach told the crowd that literacy training would be given only to those who had walked twenty miles or more. Twelve hundred people remained! In three days Laubach and his team created an Umbundu language literacy primer. Large charts of each lesson were used to teach four hundred schoolchildren, each of whom in turn taught two others. Under every tree as far as the eye could see, "teachers" and students were hard at work.

By the end of the week the young teachers began presenting their students to five examining boards who were in continuous session. Nearly four hundred new readers received diplomas at a graduation ceremony attended by more than four thousand people. Of this event Laubach wrote, "The emotion and exclamations of those new literate graduates beggars all description." Cheers rose as Laubach announced a gift of five hundred dollars to translate his graded reader, *The Story of Jesus*, into Umbundu. Upon leaving Dondi, Laubach found himself torn between "gratitude for what had been accomplished and regret that we could not stay there the rest of our lives."[41]

In the Contemplative Stream Frank Laubach stands as a shining star. His profound and multifaceted prayer experiences catapulted him into a worldwide literacy mission. What can we say about his life and his work? Perhaps his own words speak most eloquently: "God, what is man's best gift to mankind? To be beautiful of soul and then let people see into your soul."[42]

DEFINING THE CONTEMPLATIVE TRADITION

"Beautiful of soul." Certainly this is one of the deepest descriptions of the Contemplative Stream, the prayer-filled life. But all of us are painfully aware of how far we fall short of that description. How do we become "beautiful of soul"? The devotional masters struggle to describe this process to us: "This divine, loving fire of contemplation . . . this burning of love . . . the fire and wound of this forceful love . . . this very fire of love . . . love aflame . . . the fire of divine love."[43] In fact, the two most common words used to describe the contemplative way of life are *fire* and *love*. Purging, purifying fire. Enveloping, comforting love. This is the stuff of the contemplative life.

fire + love

Put simply, the contemplative life is the steady gaze of the soul upon the God who loves us. It is "an intimate sharing between friends," to use the words of Teresa of Avila.[44] Let me describe for you some of the contemplative life's most fundamental characteristics and movements.[45]

Love. Through time and experience we sense a delicate but deepening love for God that feels more like a gift than an achievement. In the beginning this love is so quiet and unobtrusive that it is hardly perceptible. John of the Cross calls it a "secret and peaceful and loving inflow of God."[46] This is a great encouragement to us, for early in our prayer life—try as we might—we are unable to truly love God. This love comes little by little, and at first we experience a great deal of fluctuation in its intensity. High and low, hot and cold. In time, however, our love grows deeper, stronger, more steady.

Peace. At the same time, in slips a peace that cannot be analyzed or dissected—"a peace that passes understanding," as Paul puts it (Phil. 4:7). This quiet rest, this firmness of life orientation, is not due to the absence of conflict or worry. In fact, it is not an absence at all, but rather a Presence. This peace is interrupted often by a multitude of distractions, especially in the beginning. But no matter—it is still there, and it is still real. And in time its quiet way wins over the chatter and clatter of our noisy hearts.

Delight. Another movement we begin to experience is delight. A very wise woman—one who had been through great hardship in her life—captured the essence of this quality for me when on one occasion she declared, "Fun ahead, saith the Lord!" There is pleasure, friendship, joy—deep joy. And playfulness. God laughs into our soul and our soul laughs back into God. John of the Cross calls it "the sweet and delightful life of love with God ... that delightful and wondrous vision."[47] But it is not uninterrupted delight. We experience an ebb and flow, an exquisite delight mingled with a painful yearning.

Emptiness. Which brings us to an opposing, almost contradictory movement in the contemplative life: emptiness. At the very moment we are entering a loving delight, we are also pulled into intense longing, yearning, searching—searching and not finding. Well, there *is* a finding of sorts, but not a complete finding. Perhaps we could call it a dissatisfied satisfaction. John of the Cross calls it "a living thirst ... [the] urgent longing of love."[48]

Often the emptiness is a darkness as well. We experience *Deus Absconditus*, the God who is hidden from us. Dryness too—a Sahara of the heart. Throughout these experiences solitude is our welcome companion, for we are learning to be alone with the Alone. Please understand, this emptiness, this darkness, this dryness is itself prayer. It is a heavenly communion of an ascetic sort. While delight is a feasting, emptiness is a fasting, and both are needed for the growth of the soul.

Fire. Still another reality we experience as we grow in the contemplative life is fire. Not literal fire, of course, but real fire nonetheless—in some ways more real than literal fire. The initial movement of love now intensifies, becoming a steady, flaming passion. Anything that causes distance or separation from God—disobedience or perhaps mere neglect—is painful in the extreme. So we feel, and even welcome, the purifying fire of God's love burning out the dross: all stubbornness, all hate, all grasping need for self-promotion. And as the self-sins are burned away, the seeds of universal love blossom and flower.

Wisdom. This leads to a still deeper movement of the Spirit: wisdom. No sterile intellectualism or impersonal awareness, this is a knowing and inflowing of God himself. We are filled with "the knowledge of the glory of the LORD, as the waters cover the sea" (Hab. 2:14). We know as we are known. We enter that eternal life which is to "know you, the only true God, and Jesus Christ whom you have sent" (John 17:3b). Prayer turns into the deepening self-communication of the Trinity, a self-communication we are privileged to listen in on and even participate in.

Transformation. Through it all, God gradually and slowly "captures" the inner faculties: first the heart and the will, then the mind, the imagination, and the passions. The result is the transformation of the entire personality into the likeness of Christ. More and more and more we take on his habits, feelings, hopes, faith, and love.*

DISCOVERING THE MAJOR STRENGTHS

The Contemplative Tradition brings many strengths to our Christian walk. Let me mention four.

The first and most fundamental contribution of the Contemplative Tradition is that it constantly fans the flames of our "first love" (Rev. 2:4). Its message is this: "Love God with all your heart . . . love God with all your heart . . . love God with all your heart. Without heart-love you have nothing." The contemplative life is always calling us back to our beginnings, always forcing us to the root, always reminding us of our foundation. It keeps saying to us, "Fall in love with Jesus over and over and over again."

Now, we must not let the simplicity of this message fool us. Maintaining our "first love" demands ceaseless vigilance. We need habitual reminders that the Christian life comes not by gritting our teeth but by falling in love.

Second, the Contemplative Tradition forces us beyond merely a cerebral religion. It insists on the insufficiency of intellectual formulation alone. Thomas Merton writes, "The contemplative is . . . he who has risked his mind in the desert beyond language and beyond ideas where God is encountered in the nakedness of pure trust, that is to say in the surrender of our own poverty and incompleteness in

---

*We will look at the process involved in transforming the personality in Chapter 3 ("The Holiness Tradition: Discovering the Virtuous Life").

order no longer to clench our minds in a cramp upon themselves, as if thinking made us exist."[49]

This emphasis is important because of our perennial tendency to keep faith at arm's length—even from ourselves. If all this gets too close to us, we might lose our objectivity, our perspective. And our independence. (Oh, how we fear the loss of our independence!) It is the Contemplative Stream that teaches us the truth of George Matheson's prayer:

> *Make me a captive, Lord,*
> *And then I shall be free;*
> *Force me to render up my sword,*
> *And I shall conqueror be.*[50]

The stress upon the centrality of prayer is a third contribution of the Contemplative Tradition. Contemplatives do not think of prayer as a good thing, or an important thing, but as the *essential* thing, the *primary* thing. Theophan the Recluse put it well: "If prayer is right, everything is right."[51]

But the Contemplative Tradition offers more than an insistence upon the pivotal nature of prayer. It also offers a distinctive angle on prayer: a stress upon silence and a call to unceasing prayer. Brother Lawrence shares with us his practice of the presence of God: "I do nothing else but abide in his holy presence, and I do this by simple attentiveness and an habitual, loving turning of my eyes on him. This I should call . . . a wordless and secret conversation between the soul and God which no longer ends."[52]

Fourth, more than other approaches to faith the Contemplative Stream emphasizes the solitariness of our life with God. In the language of the old folk spiritual, we must travel this "lonesome valley" alone. "No one else can walk it for me,/ I have to walk it by myself." Solitariness does not mean individualism, but it does mean that there are limits to the role of the community. I am responsible for developing a personal history with God. You too. That is not something others can do for us. So, while we always want to affirm the importance of the Christian community, we need to understand that our growth in grace must contain a good dose of solitude.

This is a rocky, desert spirituality. We are summoned to explore the desolate, barren landscape of the soul—landscape that most people studiously avoid (except perhaps in their nightmares). It is the place where we find true hope, but only after we see how like despair hope is. It is the place where we discover that the cross means mercy and not cruelty, life and not death. These are some of the things that we learn from the Contemplative Tradition.

UNDERSTANDING THE POTENTIAL PERILS

Not everything in the Contemplative Tradition is positive, however. Every movement has its dangers and perils, and the Contemplative Stream is no exception. But forewarning will help forearm us, help us avoid dangerous shoals and riptides. (I should add that these dangers are caused by distortions of the Tradition; they are not essential ingredients in it.)

Certainly the most obvious danger encountered in any exploration of the Contemplative Tradition is the tendency to separate it from ordinary life. This problem is exacerbated by the fact that much of our literature in this field is written by monastics. It is easy to wonder, for instance, if the contemplative life is applicable or relevant to computer programmers and machinists and stay-at-home dads and moms with clothes to wash and floors to clean. Let's be honest: the desert monastics did not have to concern themselves with diapers or baby-sitters or PTA meetings.

But we need to be absolutely firm in our insistence that smack in the middle of everyday life is precisely where prayer and intimacy with God need to be developed. True, some may have special callings to intense expressions of contemplative living that are separate and apart, but the vast majority of us build a history with God right in the midst of our families and our places of living and working and among our neighbors and friends. These places comprise the "holy ground" where we are to find God. Church attendance and Bible reading and other "religious" activities will find a place in our overall experience, but the truly holy place for us will be at our office or workbench, at the playground with our children, in the quiet sanctuary of our home or apartment, with our spouse or in profound solitude (if we are single).

A subtle form of this same danger is seen in the way an intense focus upon the contemplative life keeps some people from serious engagement with the pressing social issues of our day.[53] When prayer and piety are used as a dodge from responsible action, we must expose this twisted and deformed spirituality as an impostor. White-hot love for God is necessarily tied to a concern for the broken and bleeding of humanity. A genuine prayer life powerfully connects us with the suffering and pain and injustice of our fallen world.

A second peril is a kind of "consuming asceticism."[54] Asceticism itself simply means "training"; we derive our English word "athlete" from the same root. And we all need to train in the spiritual life. But just as we can find people who are obsessed with exercise, so we can find people suffering from "spiritual gluttony."

While modern people are seldom in danger of this temptation—our temptation runs in the opposite direction!—it certainly plagued Christians in earlier generations. For instance, Simeon Stylites, the famous Egyptian "pillar saint," lived for thirty years on a sixty-foot-high column, binding himself to the pillar by a rope so that he would not fall. "The rope became embedded in his flesh, which putrefied around it, and stank, and teemed with worms. Simeon picked up the worms that fell from his sores, and replaced them there, saying to them, 'Eat what God has given you.'"[55]

In Europe and the British Isles we find examples of the same kind of consuming asceticism, with every practice more fantastic than the one before. St. Ciaran mixed his bread with sand. St. Kevin remained in a standing posture for seven years. St. Finnchua spent seven years suspended by his armpits from iron shackles. St. Ite caused his body to be eaten into by beetles.[56]

We today are appalled at these excesses—and in truth they *are* appalling. But are they all that different from today's excesses? We find people, for example, whose entire lives revolve around having "buns of steel." Consuming asceticism and inordinate exercise are opposite ends of the same obsession.

We avoid a consuming asceticism by clearly understanding the true purpose and right place of ascetical practices. We train in the spiritual life so that we have the ability to live rightly. It is not fasting for fasting's sake, for example, but fasting so that we can learn feasting upon God. The Disciplines of the spiritual life are a means, not an end. The end is "to glorify God, and to enjoy him for ever."[57] The end is "righteousness and peace and joy in the Holy Spirit" (Rom. 14:17). The end is a wild, hilarious love relationship with God in which we freely live and do the will of God.

The third peril in the Contemplative Tradition is the tendency to devalue intellectual efforts to articulate our faith. This can sometimes border on (or plunge headlong into) anti-intellectualism. We can see this in the various mysticisms that are divorced from solid theology. And even completely orthodox writers in this Tradition can sometimes inadvertently contribute to this problem in their zeal to stress heart-faith.

It is not hard to understand why this danger emerges. We have all seen the kind of cold, obtuse theology that cannot engage the will or touch the heart. However, in our attempts to correct intellectualism devoid of life, we must not debunk the necessity of right reason and clear thinking. We love God with both the mind and the heart, and these two must ever be inseparable twins for us. (This is an issue we will revisit in a later chapter, for it is a danger that emerges in many guises.)

The fourth and final peril I want to discuss with you—how I wish it truly was the *final* peril; these dangers are legion—is the tendency to neglect the importance of the community of faith. Now, this is a checkerboard peril, for many contemplatives are part of intentional communities that show forth some of the most sterling examples of loving, nurturing accountability. But, as we will see more than once, a Tradition's greatest strength has the potential to become a serious weakness. The contemplative stress upon our solitariness before God—

a message we desperately need to hear—can lead us, especially in Western cultures, into an individualism that thinks only in terms of "God and me." Certain mystical expressions—especially those tinged with an anti-institutional spirit—are particularly susceptible to this danger. Sometimes it is tied to the anti-intellectualism noted above, which causes people to ignore the rigorous theological work of the past. The result: a doctrinal naïveté that frequently leads to an unknowing heterodoxy.

Suffice it to say that we need connections. True, God may call out an occasional Elijah or John the Baptist, but these exceptions only prove the rule. The vast majority of us are not meant to live out our faith in isolation.* We need the community of faith, the body of Christ. We need other sisters and brothers who love us, support us, and give us their discernment. And we need to be connected to the heavenly community of the past—"the communion of saints." We are empowered by learning their stories, sharing their struggles, gaining strength from their courage, learning from their mistakes, and being instructed by their teaching.

PRACTICING THE CONTEMPLATIVE TRADITION

Always, with each and every one of these Traditions, we must answer the question of how to translate it into practice in everyday life. Here, then, we must ask how the contemplative way can be experienced as part of our daily routine. Because the answer could comprise an entire volume, let me be suggestive rather than exhaustive.

First, experiment with varied venues for solitude. Take a pre-dawn walk, listening to the awakening sounds of your world (whether city or country). Limit your speaking for one day and see what you learn about yourself and others. Sit in an airport or bus station and observe

---

*If you feel that you are the rare exception to this rule, my only counsel is to be sure your divine authorization is repeatedly confirmed. (If I were in that position, I would go so far as to ask the Authorizer for identification papers!)

people carefully, reflecting on what you see. Take a one-day silent retreat—or a three-day retreat, a seven-day retreat. Go to the city for a social justice retreat. Make your next plane flight or bus trip a personal retreat. For one month leave your car radio off and make your morning commute a mini-retreat. Arise at 2:00 A.M., light a single candle as a reminder of the presence of Christ, and for one hour listen to the sounds of the night. You will, I am sure, think of many more ways to discover wilderness time for yourself.

Second, for a time set aside your normal Bible reading and _try praying_ the Scripture. This is prayerful reading in which we turn our heart and mind and spirit ever so gently to the divine Center. All of our external and internal senses swing like a needle to the polestar of the Spirit. We read slowly, quietly, prayerfully, pausing at any word or phrase where we feel the Spirit's drawing.

Perhaps we come upon Nehemiah's wonderful statement, "The joy of the LORD is your strength" (Neh. 8:10). We stop and wait, yielded and still. The Spirit may plumb the depths of our weakness, exposing reasons for our lack of strength and giving us intense longings for a strength that is not our own and not dependent upon the winds of circumstances. We begin praying the Scripture, "Lord, help me to enter into your joy . . . forgive my hankering after joy in things that never fully satisfy—food and superficial talk and frivolous things. Let me soak in your joy." Instruction from the Spirit may come. Or song and dance. Or joy-filled prayer in a language unknown to the conscious mind. And more. I am giving only hints here; you, I know, will find your way as you pray the Scripture.

Third, undermine that perennial, everlasting human itch to get ahead with intentional times of "holy leisure." Take a nap. Spend an hour visiting with your neighbor about nothing important. Help each other watch the sun go down. Take a walk, not for exercise or to study plant life but for the sheer joy of walking. Stop praying for a day. Listen to the birds—not to get some "message" from them but to hear them. Sit in the silence, doing nothing, having nothing, needing nothing. Take a bath instead of a shower. Waste time for God. The ideas are endless.

THE CALL TO PRAYER-FILLED LIVING

QUESTION: What is the Contemplative Tradition?
ANSWER: A life of loving attention to God.
QUESTION: Why should we explore it?
ANSWER: Because through it we experience the divine rest that
           overcomes our alienation.

Every one of us is called to be a contemplative—not in the sense of a particular vocation we call "the contemplative life," but in the sense of a holy habit of contemplative love that leads us forth in partnership with God into creative and redeeming work. Thomas Merton writes, "I have not only repeated the affirmation that contemplation is real, but I have insisted on its simplicity, sobriety, humility, and its integration in '*normal Christian life*.'"[58] I invite you to the adventure of exploring in "normal Christian life" a loving attention to God and a growing union with God.

Chapter 3

~

The Holiness Tradition: Discovering the Virtuous Life

Train yourself in godliness, for, while physical training is of some value, godliness is valuable in every way, holding promise for both the present life and the life to come.

—*1 Timothy 4:7b–8*

Holiness is goodness on fire.

—*Walter Rauschenbusch*

THE HOLINESS TRADITION*

Notable Figures   *Significant Movements*

0
Jesus of Nazareth
(c. 4 B.C.- c. A.D. 29)

James the Apostle (1st century)

Hermas (2nd century)

Tertullian (c. 160–c. 225)

Cyprian of Carthage (c. 200–258)

Gregory of Nazianzus (c. 330–389)

John Cassian (c. 360–c. 435)
Caesarius of Arles (?–543)
Gildas the Wise (?–c. 570)

Medericus (?–c. 700)
Corbinian (670–725)

1000

Bernard of Clairvaux (1090–1153)	Cistercians
	(12th century to the present)
Athanasios of Constantinople (c. 1230–c. 1323)	
Thomas à Kempis (1379–1471)	
Girolamo Savonarola (1452–1498)	Roman Catholic Reformation
Ignatius of Loyola (1491–1556)	(16th century)
Menno Simons (1496–1561)	Anabaptists
Teresa of Ávila (1515–1582)	(16th century to the present)
Jeremy Taylor (1613–1667)	
Richard Baxter (1615–1691)	Puritan Movement
Blaise Pascal (1623–1662)	(16th–18th centuries)
William Law (1686–1761)	
John Wesley (1703–1791)	Holiness Movement
Francis Asbury (1745–1816)	(18th century to the present)
Phoebe Palmer (1807–1874)	
Hannah Whitall Smith (1832–1911)	
	Keswick Movement
E. Stanley Jones (1884–1973)	(19th–20th centuries)
Dietrich Bonhoeffer (1906–1945)	

*See Appendix B for brief biographies and histories.

THE CONTEMPLATIVE TRADITION—the prayer-filled life—forms the foundation for holy living. It is through an ever-deepening intimacy with God that we are enabled to enter into an ever-deepening re-formation of heart and mind. The Holiness Stream of Christian life and faith focuses upon the inward re-formation of the heart and the development of "holy habits." We can rely upon these deeply ingrained habits of virtue to make our lives function appropriately and to bring forth substantial character formation. This addresses the erosion of moral fiber in contemporary society.

SEEKING A HISTORICAL PARADIGM

A moving example of the Holiness Stream is found in the life of Phoebe, an extraordinary teacher, humanitarian, and theologian. A powerful preacher of "the holiness way," she has been called "the most influential female theologian the Church has yet produced."[1] Because of her commanding personality and remarkable teaching and speaking abilities, Phoebe's influence spread far and wide. One story from her extensive ministry illustrates something of the power of her personality.

While in Scotland preparing to hold special meetings at a rather staid Presbyterian church, Phoebe noted that there was no altar for people to come to in surrender of heart and will to God. Phoebe requested that an altar be built immediately and was told in no uncertain terms that, even if the trustees were favorable to such an action (which they were not), it would take a full week just to receive their approval. Undaunted, she insisted, warning that if the church wanted these meetings and desired to experience the blessing of God, an altar had to be built without delay. Her stubborn determination won out, and at 4:00 A.M. a crew of construction workers arrived at the church, finishing their work just in time for the afternoon meeting. The new altar was quickly packed with people earnestly offering their lives in perpetual sacrifice to God.

Phoebe's teaching and speaking ministry began in the most unassuming manner—a weekly meeting (in her lower Manhattan home) called "the Tuesday Meeting for the Promotion of Holiness." Initially confined to women, the meeting proved so popular that her home had to go through several renovations to accommodate the ever-increasing numbers—four hundred at its peak. Conducting this Tuesday Meeting for nearly forty years, Phoebe attracted some of the most gifted and significant Christian leaders of the day: the philosopher Thomas Upham; the founder of the Free Methodist Church, B. T. Roberts; the leader of the Women's Christian Temperance Union, Frances Willard; the founder of Boston University, John Dempster; and a host of others.

Transcending the limitations of both gender and denomination, she brought together Methodists and Baptists and Presbyterians and Episcopalians and Catholics and Quakers and United Brethren and Messianic Jews. People far and wide copied her format so that eventually over two hundred Tuesday Meetings were going on in such distant places as England, India, and New Zealand.

Methodist Beginnings

Phoebe's father was a young convert of John Wesley, and so the history and teachings of prominent Methodist leaders dominated the family's religious life. At nineteen Phoebe married a physician and fellow Methodist. Phoebe bore six children to the union, though sadly three died in infancy. The third child, Eliza, died under especially tragic circumstances: a maid accidentally dropped a lit oil lamp on the gauze curtain covering the baby's crib, causing a terrible flash fire. Rushing upstairs, Phoebe "grasped my darling from the flames. She darted one inexpressible look of amazement and pity, on her agonized mother, and then closed her eyes forever on the scenes of earth."[2]

The loss was a critical turning point. In what she called her "inexpressible bewilderment of grief," Phoebe turned to her Bible—and to her God—for consolation. Her own words best describe the agony of that time:

> While pacing the room, crying to God, amid the tumult of grief, my mind was arrested by a gentle whisper, saying, "Your Heavenly Father loves you. He would not permit such a great trial, without intending that some great good proportionate in magnitude and weight should result. . . . In the agony of my soul I had exclaimed, "O, what shall I do!" And the answer now came,—"Be still and know that I am God." I took up the precious WORD, and cried, "O teach me the lesson of this trial," and the first lines to catch my eye on opening the Bible, were these, "O, the depth of the riches, both of the wisdom and knowledge of God! How unsearchable are his judgments and his ways past finding out!" . . . The tumult of feeling was hushed. . . . "What thou knowest not now, thou shalt know hereafter," was assuringly whispered. Wholly subdued before the Lord, my chastened spirit nestled in quietness under the wing of the Holy Comforter. . . . And now I have resolved, that . . . the time I would have devoted to her, shall be spent in work for Jesus. And if diligent and self-sacrificing in carrying out my resolve, the death of this child may result in the spiritual life of many.[3]

In this single, ecstatic event Phoebe was "weaned from the world" and given an unquenchable zeal to do the work of Christ.

"Christ the Altar"

Her spiritual struggles, however, far from being over, had just begun in earnest. Phoebe longed for "entire sanctification" and was troubled by the teaching John Wesley gave in his *Plain Account of Christian Perfection* that believers should not consider themselves sanctified "till there is added the testimony of the Spirit, witnessing his entire sanctification, as clearly as his justification."[4] Phoebe's quandary actually had less to do with Wesley's teaching itself than it did with testimonials from the pantheon of Methodist leaders—which for her was a kind of "lives of the saints"—which all but universally spoke of an acute awareness of personal sinfulness as part of this "testimony of the Spirit." But, try as she might, Phoebe could never experience an epiphany of wretchedness. Indeed, her own inward searching succeeded only in drawing her all the more intimately into God's love, hence deepening her dilemma!

Interestingly, the horns of this "dilemma" were broken as Phoebe listened to the varied testimonies of sanctifying grace from women at the Tuesday Meeting. Moved by the great diversity of their experiences, Phoebe came to see that God's means of sanctifying grace were far richer than merely personal awareness of sinfulness. "I purpose from this hour," she declared, "to leave no means unused that I may know the same grace."[5]

Long hours of prayerful searching and of biblical study led her to what she would later call her "day of days." It was almost exactly one year after the terrible death of Eliza that Phoebe had a decisive experience of total consecration and sanctifying grace—one that would energize the remainder of her life. Again her descriptive powers are so great that they cannot be improved upon:

> Between the hours of eight and nine (in the evening)—while pleading at the throne of grace for a present fulfillment of the exceeding great and precious promises; pleading also the fulness and freeness of the atonement, its unbounded efficacy, and making an entire surrender of body, soul, and spirit; time, talents, and influence; and also of the dearest ties of nature, my beloved husband and child; in a word, my earthly *all—I received the assurance that God the Father, through the atoning Lamb, accepted the sacrifice*; my heart was emptied of self, and cleansed of all idols, from all filthiness of the flesh and spirit, and I realized that I dwelt in God, and felt that he had become the portion of my soul, my ALL IN ALL.[6]

This profound "Valley of Decision," as she called it, led to the development of her "altar theology." That teaching, in brief, says that Christ himself is the altar upon which we rest our all in sacrifice, and since everything that touches the altar is holy, we are holy when we place everything we are upon the altar. We, therefore, live in a state of holiness and sanctification as we continually give ourselves as a living sacrifice to Christ, our altar. And in a flurry of exegetical license Phoebe often quoted these words of Jesus: "The altar sanctifieth the gift" (Matt. 23:19, KJV).

This imagery of Christ as the altar upon which we offer ourselves gave Phoebe the freedom she needed to have personal certainty of "sanctifying grace."[7] It also became a significant addition to the vocabulary of the Holiness movement; as one historian put it, "The altar motif became a permanent part of evangelical spirituality."[8]

Throughout her life Phoebe continued to develop and popularize her "altar theology" until it become her most unique contribution to American theology. And, as things turned out, it was a genuinely important contribution, substantially influencing the Pentecostal understanding of the work of the Holy Spirit at the turn of the twentieth century.[9]

"The Promise of the Father"

But Phoebe spoke and wrote on many other themes as well, themes that often arose out of the give-and-take of human need and faithful ministry. At a Tuesday Meeting one woman expressed her heartfelt desire for a holy life but said that an obstacle hindered her—an insurmountable obstacle, it seemed to her. One of the conditions Phoebe had established for receiving "entire sanctification" was to give public witness to this "blessing,"* and this woman

---

*The practical outworking of Phoebe's "altar theology" involved three clearly defined steps: entire consecration, faith, and testimony. This woman, you understand, felt hindered from fulfilling the third step.

belonged to a denomination that barred women from speaking in church! So what was she to do?

Everyone turned to Phoebe for an answer to this dilemma—a dilemma that was, in part, of her own making. Her response was surprisingly succinct and pragmatic: at Pentecost the Holy Spirit was poured out upon all those gathered in the Upper Room, both men and women, and they were empowered to testify to Christ. Hence women were not only *allowed* to speak but were *impelled* to do so by the very Spirit of God. This concise answer ultimately led to a more detailed response—a four-hundred-page book entitled *The Promise of the Father*.[10] In this book Phoebe anticipated numerous contemporary feminist concerns, addressing them without mincing words: "We believe that hundreds of conscientious, sensitive Christian women have actually suffered more under the slowly crucifying process to which they have been subjected by men who bear the Christian name than many a martyr has endured in passing through the flames."[11]

A total of eight other books followed. The most famous, *The Way of Holiness*, succeeded in catapulting Phoebe onto an international platform. She later edited a magazine, *Guide to Holiness*, which at its zenith had thirty-seven thousand subscribers, one of the largest circulation lists among religious journals in America at that time.

Perhaps by now you have guessed that I have been telling the story of Phoebe Worrall Palmer (1807–1874). On the other hand, maybe you had no clue who I was discussing, since her story is little known today.

This is most regrettable, for Phoebe Palmer's impact has been substantial. The Second Evangelical Awakening (1857–1865), which brought over a million genuine converts into American churches, can be traced to her ministry. And in the wake of her work in the British Isles from 1859 to 1863, more than seventeen thousand individuals professed conversion to Christ and thousands more claimed sanctifying grace. Indeed, those meetings proved so popular that special trains were scheduled to accommodate the crowds.[12]

Phoebe helped launch one of the earliest inner-city ministries to the poor in America—"The Five Points Mission"—and she was the principal founder of the Methodist Church's mission to China. A direct progenitor of a dozen different Protestant denominations that are still active today, she also influenced the founders, early presidents, or key leaders of some of the major universities in America, including the University of Michigan, Northwestern University, Syracuse University, Wesleyan University, Boston University, the University of Georgia, American University, and Drew University. She significantly influenced the embryonic development of major international religious groups such as the Salvation Army, the Wesleyan Church, the National Camp Meeting Association for the Promotion of Holiness, the Free Methodist Church, the Keswick Movement in England, the Church of the Nazarene, the Assemblies of God, and the worldwide Pentecostal movement.[13]

At a time when women generally were not accorded positions of authority, literally tens of thousands looked to Phoebe Palmer for leadership and instruction. She embodied the personal piety and energetic spirituality that marked the Holiness movement of the nineteenth century. She was impelled by holy fire, sterling convictions, and boundless zeal. Sustained attention to her life and teaching is well worth the investment.

SEEKING A BIBLICAL PARADIGM

How can I pick a single model of the Holiness Stream from the New Testament? The examples are myriad. Not that these women and men which dot the landscape of our New Testament were perfect. Of course not, but, then, perfectionism is not what the Holiness Tradition is about. It is about . . . well, that comes later.

The Pillar of Jerusalem

The one personage I want to lift up as the biblical example par excellence of the Holiness Stream is James*, the blood-brother (half-

---

*Not to be confused with the Apostle James, the son of Zebedee and brother of John.

brother, if you will) of Jesus and the author of the Epistle that bears his name.[14]

What a story James has to tell! Throughout Jesus' earthly ministry James rejected his older brother's messianic mission.* In fact, his disapproval of Jesus' activities probably bordered on genuine hostility. At one point, when the people were declaring that Jesus "has gone out of his mind," James (along with his mother, his brothers, and his sisters) tries "to restrain him" and make him return home. But Jesus rejects the embarrassed solicitations of his family, declaring, "Whoever does the will of God is my brother and sister and mother" (Mark 3:21, 31–35).

So James decidedly was not numbered among those who left all at the outset to follow Jesus; he was not even among the curious crowds who were amazed at his teachings and still more amazed at his healings. And yet when the disciples are gathered together waiting for the promised Holy Spirit, to our astonishment we discover James among them (Acts 1:14). And we find that in just a few short years he is recognized as a "pillar" of the church, eventually authoring the Epistle that bears his name (Acts 12:17, 15:1–29, Gal. 2:9, James 1:1).

This is a complete turn of events. What could possibly have happened to change James the scoffer into James the believer and ultimately into "James the Just," the leader of the Jerusalem church? I believe the answer is nothing less than Jesus' personal appearance to his younger brother following his resurrection from the dead. The documents mention this fact in such an unconscious, almost offhanded manner that, unless we are careful, we easily miss it. Right in the middle of a cataloging of postresurrection appearances we read, "Then he appeared to James, then to all the apostles" (1 Cor. 15:7). How gracious of Jesus! How utterly kind! It is the only postresurrection appearance we know of where Jesus made himself known to someone who did not believe in him.

---

*It is interesting to note that James's younger brothers—Joses, Judas, and Simon—and his sisters—whose names are unknown to us—followed James's lead in refusing to believe in Jesus (Matt. 13:55; Mark 6:3; John 7:5).

Just imagine that meeting, brother to brother. James's older brother—the brother he had played with, eaten with, worked with—now stood before him in resurrected form. What a transforming confrontation! This single encounter erased all the embarrassments of the past, all the objections, all the doubts. Jesus, his own brother, was—and is—the hoped-for Messiah!

Quickly the believing fellowship welcomes James, and before we know it he is the acknowledged leader of the church at Jerusalem. Just look at his enormous influence. Paul, following his conversion and a three-year "study leave," meets with James in Jerusalem, recognizing his status as an apostle (Gal. 1:19). Peter, after his miraculous deliverance from prison, instructs those gathered for prayer at "Mary's house" (the mother of John Mark) to tell the whole story to James, indicating, in effect, that James is the one person who *must* be notified of the situation (Acts 12:17). It is James who presides over the great "Jerusalem Council" of Acts 15. He led the believing community through the thorny issue of whether a person had to become a Jew before they could become a Christian. James alone brings the council's findings to a decisive conclusion: "Therefore I have reached the decision that we should not trouble those Gentiles who are turning to God." Then he guides the growing church to declare with one voice, "It has seemed good to the Holy Spirit and to us to impose on you no further burden . . . " (Acts 15:19, 28). And finally, Paul, on his last trip to Jerusalem, makes a point of meeting with James in what sounds like an all-but-official reception: "The next day Paul went with us to visit James; and all the elders were present" (Acts 21:18). Clearly James was a man of enormous influence in the early Christian community.

And his influence was rooted in the most profound devotion. Eusebius records that James "used to enter alone into the temple and be found kneeling and praying for forgiveness for the people, so that his knees grew hard like a camel's because of his constant worship of God. . . . So from his excessive righteousness he was called the Just."[15] Indeed, one of his traditional titles was James the Just (or James the Righteous—the Greek word can be translated either way).

Josephus, in his *Antiquities of the Jews*, tells us of the earthly end to James: Ananus, the high priest, ordered his death by stoning around A.D. 62. Josephus further notes that many Jewish leaders vigorously protested this unjust act of Ananus, which gives us some inkling of the high regard accorded James even by the non-Christian Jewish community.

Purifying the Source

Perhaps the greatest legacy James gives us is the small Epistle that bears his name. This letter, addressed to Jews dispersed throughout the Mediterranean, says less about Jesus than any other New Testament book, but its speech is more like Jesus' than any of them. Indeed, its closest parallel is Jesus' own Sermon on the Mount, from which it quotes (5:12). It also has many affinities to the ancient Hebrew wisdom literature. Of course, both of these writings center on the formation of moral character, and this is the focus of James's Epistle as well.

Contrary to popular opinion, the Epistle of James is not a book about action. It is a book about the *source* of action, the heart of virtue. Even the most frequently quoted saying from the book— "Faith without works is dead"—is not about action. We do not respond to this verse by jumping up and doing some works, for, you see, we can do all kinds of works without faith. No, James shows us how we can be hooked into a different kind of reality, a spiritual reality that in turn produces a different kind of person, which in the natural course of things produces a different kind of action. Forming this "different kind of person" is the burden of James's Epistle and the reason he is such a moving example of the Holiness Tradition.

Different in what way? James shows us a person who can face trials of all kinds with rock-solid joy, a person who is plugged into a divine wisdom that sees "bitter jealousy" and "selfish ambition" for the impostors they truly are, a person who instinctively relates to all peoples on the basis of the "royal law" of love, a person who out of divine resources is able to "tame the tongue," a person who eschews "fightings and wars" because the inner wellspring of the life is so purified that from it naturally flows blessing and not cursing.

James, you see, understands that what is on the inside of a person will come out. If the central core of who we are is "earthly, unspiritual, devilish," what flows out will be "disorder and wickedness of every kind." Conversely, if the central core of who we are is "pure, . . . peaceable, gentle, willing to yield, full of mercy and good fruits, without a trace of partiality or hypocrisy," then what flows out will be "a harvest of righteousness [which] is sown in peace for those who make peace" (James 3:15–18).

This is why James gives so much attention to *purifying the source* out of which all action flows: "Does a spring pour forth from the same opening both fresh and brackish water? Can a fig tree, my brothers and sisters, yield olives, or a grapevine figs? No more can salt water yield fresh" (James 3:11–12).

A divinely transformed heart, by its very nature, will produce right action. It simply cannot do otherwise. James learned this from his Master and older brother. Jesus, in his Sermon on the Mount, gave us the world's most complete teaching on how right action flows from the wellspring of a right heart, and the Epistle of James is a beautiful commentary on this teaching.

This explains why James can sum up "pure and undefiled" religion in a simple two-fold action: "to care for orphans and widows in their distress, and to keep oneself unstained by the world" (James 1:27). These two actions show what is in the heart. "Look at the action," says James, "and you will know the heart. Pure action, pure heart. Defiled action, defiled heart." So he identifies for us the kind of action a pure heart *will do*—namely, care for the most helpless in the culture—and the kind of action a pure heart will *not do*—namely, accept the death-giving pollution of a world system in rebellion against divine Love. In the most simple and straightforward manner possible, James gives us the *via positiva*, what we *do* do, and the *via negativa*, what we do *not* do.

Purity of heart is the fountainhead of all right action—this is the message of James. And this is why he is such a rich source for us of the Holiness Tradition, the virtuous life.

Seeking a Contemporary Paradigm

On the day Dietrich Bonhoeffer heard that the 20 July 1944 attempt to assassinate Hitler had failed[16]—the day he knew that his own fate and the fate of his friends was sealed—he wrote an account of his life in a poem entitled "Stations on the Road to Freedom." Brooding in his Tegel prison cell, he set forth the four great dimensions of a spiritual life that lead to freedom in all its facets—freedom from ingrained habits of sin, freedom from cowering inaction and irresponsibility, freedom from fear of a monstrously demonic and immensely powerful nation-state. Listen carefully and prayerfully to his words, for they speak of the holiness of life:

Stations on the Road to Freedom

July 21, 1944

Discipline

If you set out to seek freedom, then learn above all
discipline of soul and senses, so that your passions
and your limbs might not lead you confusedly hither and yon.
Chaste be your spirit and body, subject to your own will,
and obedient to seek out the goal that they have been given.
No one discovers the secret of freedom but through self-control.

Action

Dare to do what is just, not what fancy may call for;
Lose no time with what may be, but boldly grasp what is real.
The world of thought is escape; freedom comes only through
    action.
Step out beyond anxious waiting and into the storm of events,
carried only by God's command and by your own faith;
then will freedom exultantly cry out to welcome your spirit.

SUFFERING

*Wondrous transformation! Your strong and active hands
are tied now. Powerless, alone, you see the end of your action.
Still, you take a deep breath and lay your struggle for justice,
quietly and in faith, into a mightier hand.
Just for one blissful moment, you tasted the sweetness of freedom,
then you handed it over to God, that he might make it whole.*

DEATH

*Come now, highest moment on the road to freedom eternal,
Death, put down the ponderous chains and demolish the walls
of our mortal bodies, the walls of our blinded souls,
that we might finally see what mortals have kept us from seeing.
Freedom, how long we have sought you through discipline,
    action, and suffering.
Dying, now we behold your face in the countenance of God.*[17]

This poem, written under the shadow of almost certain execution, is one of the finest expressions of the Holiness Tradition ever penned. And the Lutheran pastor and theologian who penned them is a sterling contemporary model of that Tradition.

"Costly Grace"

The outline of Bonhoeffer's story is well known. In 1927 he was a *student* earning a doctorate in theology from Berlin University at the age of twenty-one. In 1930 he was a *debater* crossing theological swords with the liberal establishment at Union Theological Seminary, New York. In 1931 he was a *teacher* exegeting issues of Christian ethics and the nature of the Church at Berlin University. Bonhoeffer, it seemed, was destined for the life of an academic. But the ominous storm clouds of the Third Reich changed everything.

By 1933 Dietrich Bonhoeffer was an *activist* attacking the idolatrous "Aryan Clause," which excluded Jews from civil service. By 1934 he was a *leader* in the newly formed "Confessing Church," prophetically denouncing the heretical defections of the "German Christians." * By 1935 he was a *professor* establishing a clandestine seminary at Finkenwalde—an institution where "pure doctrine, the Sermon on the Mount, and worship can be taken seriously."[18] By 1937 he was an *author* attacking "cheap grace"—that is, "grace without discipleship, grace without the cross, grace without Jesus Christ, living and incarnate."[19] By 1939 he was a *double agent* seeking the defeat of his own nation and deeply involved in the conspiracy to assassinate the Führer. By 1943 he was a *prisoner* living out the days of misfortune "equably, smilingly, proudly, / like one accustomed to win," and at the same time feeling "restless and longing and sick, like a bird in a cage."[20] By 1944 he was a *theologian* from a prison cell, searching, ever searching, for a "religionless Christianity" in which "man is summoned to share in God's sufferings at the hands of a godless world."[21] And finally, in the gray dawn of Sunday, 8 April 1945, Dietrich Bonhoeffer became a *martyr*, whispering to his fellow prisoners as he left his cell to be hanged on the Flossenbürg gallows, "This is the end—for me, the beginning of life."[22]

Bonhoeffer's biographer, Eberhard Bethge, summarizes the self-sacrifice and prophetic vision of this young pastor-theologian when he speaks of him as "that fighter on behalf of the First Commandment against the idolatrous syncretisms of his time and of our time as well; the composer of devout prayers and inspiring sermons; the fascinating author of spiritual literature; the exciting writer of the letters from prison; the sophisticated analyst of the Christian situation in the post-Enlightenment era; the witness to faith in Jesus Christ both now and in the future."[23]

---

*"German Christians" was the term used for Protestants who supported Hitler. The "Confessing Church," of which Bonhoeffer was a key figure, arose as a witness to Christian faithfulness and became the chief opposition to the German Christians.

"Christ the Center"

Bonhoeffer's life as a churchman in Germany and in broader ecumenical circles is a model of courage and compassion. His work in the resistance movement is endlessly fascinating. His death is moving beyond words. But why would I consider him an example of the Holiness Tradition? He was far from perfect. He made mistakes, some of them serious. What is it that makes me single him out as a model for the virtuous life? Six things. The first three, which we turn to now, are tied to his conviction that Christ is the absolute center of all things.

First, Bonhoeffer took Jesus seriously. It is hard to overestimate how fully the christological question affected everything for him. If Jesus truly lived, died, rose, and is among his people today, it makes all the difference in the world. We simply cannot consider the earth apart from Christ's footsteps imprinted upon it. "Christ's manger stands on the earth, his cross is rammed into the earth, his grave is dug into the earth."[24] This being so, the community of faith must come to recognize Christ's personal presence in the world today and set out to follow him in all things.

This emphasis emerged most powerfully in his lectures at Berlin University in 1933, a period Eberhard Bethge calls "the high point of Bonhoeffer's academic career."[25] The message of those lectures is captured for us in *Christ the Center*. Here we find Bonhoeffer's unswerving call for "one complete Christ." "I do not know," he says, "who this man Jesus is unless I say at the same time 'Jesus Christ is God', and I do not know who the God Jesus Christ is unless I say at the same time 'Jesus Christ is man'. . . . This one God-Man is the starting point of christology."[26] From this solid vantage point Bonhoeffer could critique both the reigning liberal reduction of dogmatics to a humanistic domestication of God and the Church's worship of a Christ-replica of its own lust for privilege.

By means of this rigorous christological critique of all political, theological, and ecclesiastical pretensions, Bonhoeffer found a Christ who constantly offends our sensibilities, much like "the idiot" in Dostoyevsky's writings: "The idiot does not keep himself apart, but clumsily causes offense everywhere. He has nothing to do with the great ones, but with the children. He is mocked and he is loved. He is the fool and he is the wise man. He endures all and he forgives all. He is revolutionary, and yet he conforms. . . . Christ goes through the ages, questioned anew, missed anew, killed anew."[27] Christ stood at the very center of Bonhoeffer's vocation and was the interpretive key to his understanding of Scripture and his critique of Church and society.[28]

Second, Bonhoeffer took Jesus' call to discipleship seriously. He felt this call most powerfully compressed in Jesus' robust and prophetic Sermon on the Mount. Throughout his life he stoutly refused to do what is so common today—namely, to see Jesus' Sermon as an "impossible ideal," or merely as nice words that are not meant to be obeyed, or perhaps as instructions for some future dispensation. No, he understood the Sermon on the Mount to be Jesus' universal call to obedience—a call issued to all peoples, at all times, in all places. In a letter to his brother Karl-Friedrich he wrote, "I have begun to take seriously the Sermon on the Mount. That is the only source of power capable of blowing up the whole phantasmagoria* once and for all."[29]

The most systematic treatment of this matter is found in *The Cost of Discipleship*, where Bonhoeffer argues for "costly grace": "Such grace is *costly* because it calls us to follow, and it is *grace* because it calls us to follow *Jesus Christ*."[30] This he contrasts with "cheap grace," by which he means "grace sold on the market like a cheapjack's wares. . . . Cheap grace is the preaching of forgiveness without requiring repentance, baptism without church discipline, Communion without confession, absolution without personal confession."[31]

The German title for *The Cost of Discipleship* is the single word *Nachfolge*—"discipleship." Discipleship is a theme Bonhoeffer wrestled with throughout his life. That theme can be seen in his seminars, sermons, and study groups from as early as 1932. But it was in

---

*Translator's note: "i.e., Hitler and his rule."

the seminary life at Finkenwalde that he was able to give concrete shape to the hold that the Sermon on the Mount had on his life. His lectures on discipleship became the "nerve center" of the curriculum, and the seminarians felt the exhilarating experience of being drawn into a revolutionary movement. They knew that they were "witnessing a theological event."[32] The future of Christianity in Germany was at stake—indeed, the future of the Christian faith itself. In those lectures, which later became *The Cost of Discipleship*, Bonhoeffer gave the world a "catholic" or universal exposition of obedience.

For Bonhoeffer personally, Jesus' call of discipleship freed him from the lust for position and status, turned him from "phraseology to reality," and led him in time to relinquish the secure life of academia.[33] It also led him to his uneasy pacifism: desiring to be obedient to the peace commandment of Jesus while at the same time standing in firm resistance to the tyranny of Hitler.[34]

Third, Bonhoeffer took spiritual discipline seriously. It is no accident that his lectures often returned to the *disciplina pietatis*.[35] He was training for a life in which the powers of body and soul are placed entirely in the service of Christ. His life was built on "a new kind of monasticism . . . a life of uncompromising adherence to the Sermon on the Mount in imitation of Christ."[36]

While always rejecting "any escapism disguised as piety," he unquestionably understood the nature of spiritual formation: "We must be assimilated to the form of Christ in its entirety, the form of Christ incarnate, crucified and glorified." And again, "To be conformed with the Incarnate—that is to be a real man. . . . 'Formation' . . . means in the first place Jesus' taking form in his church."[37] And Bonhoeffer's personal habits of daily meditation, prayer, and sacrament intensify his teaching on "formation."

Consequently, God had so built within Bonhoeffer such ingrained habits of virtue that he had the inner spiritual resources for appropriate action. As we learned from our study of James, a divinely transformed heart will, by its very nature, produce good fruit. This is what enabled Bonhoeffer to stand firmly against the idolatrous cult of the Führer when so many around him were caught up in the seductive siren of patriotism. This is what enabled him to make the heart-wrenching decision to leave the security of the United States and "live through this difficult period of our national history with the Christian people of Germany."[38] This is what enabled him to describe (and truly experience) his imprisonment and suffering and loss as a "wondrous transformation."

Action in the World

The remaining three reasons for holding Bonhoeffer up as a model of the virtuous life are tied to his conviction that Christian faith must, of necessity, result in action in the milieu of contemporary society.

Fourth, Bonhoeffer *took free, responsible, obedient action seriously.* He rejected all legalistic systems for defining moral norms. He refused to reduce Christ and Scripture to ethical principles and rules. Instead, he stressed the ongoing, relational dialectic of encountering God's will, often against our will, and, in Christ, receiving the freedom to act responsibly in any given situation. When the center is clear, the boundaries of responsible action can be open to meet the demands of the present moment. "It is therefore impossible," he wrote from prison, "to define the boundary between resistance and submission on abstract principles: but both of them must exist, and both must be practised. Faith demands this elasticity of behaviour."[39]

This matter is most fully developed in his *Ethics.*[40] In that text we are warned of the delusion of grasping for a Pharisee-like knowledge of good and evil in hopes that we can discern when we are "right" and when we are "wrong." No: ethical action, he insisted, is not found in this way. Rather, every changing situation of need becomes the specific locus of God's will and command.

In taking this stance, Bonhoeffer framed an ethic that was responsive to the present moment and so could engender responsible resistance to the growing Nazi horror. For example, at the outset of the

Jewish deportations, Bonhoeffer wrote, "An expulsion of the Jews from the West must necessarily bring with it the expulsion of Christ."[41]

Bonhoeffer's purpose in centering ethical action in God's will and directive in the crisis of any given moment was not to validate some "easy way out"—a strategy common today in the various versions of situational ethics. Rather, he attempted to marshal a vigorous social ethic that can "see the great events of world history from below, from the perspective of the outcast, the suspects, the maltreated, the powerless, the oppressed, the reviled—in short, from the perspective of those who suffer."[42]

In one of the most moving passages of *Ethics*—a passage written when Germany was smack in the middle of ecstatic celebration over its greatest military victory, the fall of France—Bonhoeffer called the Church to a corporate "confession of guilt." "The church," he declared, "confesses that she has witnessed the lawless application of brutal force, the physical and spiritual suffering of countless innocent people, oppression, hatred and murder, and that she has not raised her voice on behalf of the victims and has not found ways to hasten to their aid. She is guilty of the deaths of the weakest and the most defenseless."[43]

Fifth) Bonhoeffer *took the purity of the Church seriously*. Consistently he called the Church to *be* the Church. His was a purifying voice warning the Church against violating the First Commandment to "have no other gods before me" (Exod. 20:3).

Two days after Hitler became chancellor of Germany, Bonhoeffer gave a radio address in which he warned against the possibility of Germany slipping into an idolatrous cult of the *Führer* (leader), who might very well turn out to be a *Verführer* (misleader) mocking God himself.[44]

In response to the passage of the Aryan Clause that excluded Jews from civil service, Bonhoeffer wrote a document titled "The Church and the Jewish Question." His insistence in this paper that "the church has an unconditional obligation to the victims of any ordering of society, even if they do not belong to the Christian community," so infuriated some of his colleagues that they walked out on his speech. Here also Bonhoeffer first considered aloud the possibility that, if the state fails in its obligation of justice for all, the Church has a responsibility "not just to bandage the victims under the wheel, but to put a spoke in the wheel [of the state] itself."[45]

The national church election of 23 July 1933 brought the issue of church and state to a head. The German Christians were victorious, capturing key positions in the church. It was a time begging for a renewed confession of faith, which is precisely what Bonhoeffer called for in his Sunday sermon of 23 July: "Church, remain a church! . . . [C]onfess, confess, confess."[46]

And confess they did, at least in the beginning. In August the Council of Young Reformers deputized Bonhoeffer and Professor Hermann Sasse to retreat to the Christian community of Bethel to produce a confession of faith that would challenge the German Christians. What they produced—the Bethel Confession—solidly and uncompromisingly stated the theological foundation of the struggle and gave a spirited defense of the Jews: "This 'holy remnant' bears the indelible stamp of the chosen people," and they must never be "exterminated by Pharaoh-like measures." "We oppose," continued Bethel, "the attempt to deprive the German Evangelical church of its promise by the attempt to change it into a national church of Christians of Aryan descent."[47] This amounted to the sharpest possible repudiation of Nazi Aryanism.

A line had been drawn in the sand! Or had it? The Bethel Confession was sent to some twenty theologians, who proceeded to dilute any criticism of the state and to whittle away at its uncompromising call for obedience to Jesus Christ. The final toothless product had so emasculated the challenge to resist the Third Reich that Bonhoeffer refused to sign it.

The Bethel Confession, so promising in the beginning, failed to provide any genuine challenge to the German Christians.[48] Nevertheless, it highlights Bonhoeffer's role as a purifying force in the Evangelical Church of Germany.

But Bonhoeffer's concern for the Church was not confined to confessional purity alone. He sought a living fellowship of Word and sacrament, confession and forgiveness, prayer and worship. This brings us to perhaps his most moving piece of devotional writing, *Life Together*.

At Finkenwalde Bonhoeffer established an "Evangelical House of Brethren" where precisely this kind of life could be lived out. When the Gestapo closed down the Finkenwalde Seminary, Bonhoeffer saw the need to record for posterity the rationale and daily regimen of this community and to call the Church to an authentic community life if it was to know genuine renewal. Thus, with a compelling sense of urgency, he completed *Life Together* in just four weeks. In it we find some of the finest writing anywhere on mutual submission out of reverence for Christ, reciprocal confession under the cross, and a daily life of Scripture, meditation, prayer, and intercession.

Sixth, Bonhoeffer took the world seriously. What he saw so clearly was the need for righteousness in action in the midst of a secular and secularizing world. The reality that gripped him so totally was that we must live in "existence for others." "Jesus," he wrote, "is there only for others. . . . Our relation to God is not a 'religious' relationship . . . but our relation to God is a new life in 'existence for others,' through participation in the being of Jesus. . . . The church is the church only when it exists for others."[49]

This brings us to Bonhoeffer's powerful notion of "religionless Christianity." The aspect of this teaching that is especially relevant to our study of holiness is his insistence that we "must live a 'secular' life, and thereby share in God's sufferings." This is a life that is "freed from false religious obligations and inhibitions" and open to serve all people—whoever and wherever they are. It is a life, not of religious acts, but of "participation in the sufferings of God in the secular life." It is a life of repentance that is less concerned with our own needs, problems, sins, and fears than with being "caught up into the way of Jesus Christ," suffering with those who suffer and rejoicing with those who rejoice. And we do all of this right in the middle of the vicissitudes of everyday life.[50]

Bonhoeffer did not live to flesh out his concept of religionless Christianity. In his *Letters and Papers from Prison* we have only the barest outline. Even so, the outline is most suggestive and challenging:

> To make a start, [the Church] should give away all its property to those in need. The clergy must live solely on the free-will offerings of their congregations, or possibly engage in some secular calling. The church must share in the secular problems of ordinary human life, not dominating, but helping and serving. It must tell men of every calling what it means to live in Christ, to exist for others. In particular, our own church will have to take the field against the vices of *hubris*, power-worship, envy, and humbug, as the roots of all evil. It will have to speak of moderation, purity, trust, loyalty, constancy, patience, discipline, humility, contentment, and modesty.[51]

Bonhoeffer here is calling for a world-affirming spirituality of the first order, and its implications for the life of holiness are profound indeed. We long for more. We can only wonder where Bonhoeffer would have taken this creative line of thinking had he lived. Nevertheless, we can be genuinely grateful for one who lived so courageously and taught so profoundly.

DEFINING THE HOLINESS TRADITION

Holiness means the ability to do what needs to be done when it needs to be done. It means being "response-able," able to respond appropriately to the demands of life. The word *virtue* (*arete*) comes into our New Testament from a long history in Greek philosophical tradition, and it means simply to function well. Virtue is good habits we can rely upon to make our life work. Conversely, vice is bad habits we can rely upon to make our life not work, to make it dysfunctional, as we say. So a holy life simply is a life that works.

How contrary this is to our popular notions of holiness. Frankly, it is rarely considered a compliment to be seen as "holy" these days.

And certainly no one wants to be thought of as "holier-than-thou." To most minds the concept of holiness carries with it an air of arrogance and judgment. Furthermore, it is often associated with trivialities of behavior that we all know have little or nothing to do with a virtuous life. Because these misconceptions are so pervasive in our culture, it is crucial that we learn what holiness *is not* as well as what it *is*.

Holiness *is not* rules and regulations. Elaborate lists of dos and don'ts miss the point of a life hidden with God in Christ. No single standard of behavior is dictated by the word *holy*. All external legalisms fail to capture the heart of holy living and holy dying.

Holiness *is* sustained attention to the heart, the source of all action. It concerns itself with the core of the personality, the well-spring of behavior, the quintessence of the soul. It focuses upon the formation and transformation of this center.

Holiness *is not* otherworldliness. Its life is not found by developing logic-tight compartments of things sacred and things secular. We do not come into it by studiously avoiding contact with our manifestly evil and broken world.

Holiness *is* world-affirming. The holy life is found smack in the middle of everyday life. We discover it while being freely and joyfully *in* the world without ever being *of* the world. Holiness sees the sacred in all things. It is integrative, synoptic, incarnational.

Holiness *is not* a consuming asceticism. It is not punishment for the sake of punishment. It neither despises nor depreciates the human body. And it never locates virtue or merit in ascetical exercises themselves.

Holiness *is* a bodily spirituality. It affirms the goodness of the human body and seeks to bring it into working harmony with the spirit. It utilizes appropriate Spiritual Disciplines for training the body and mind in right living. It is, in this sense, ascetical—but never for the sake of the asceticism, always for the sake of the training.

Holiness *is not* "works-righteousness." We cannot muster up our willpower to do good deeds and thereby become righteous. Sanctifying grace, just like justifying grace, is utterly and completely a work of . . . well, grace. It is unearned and unearnable. It is a God-initiated and God-sustained reality; *we* cannot do it, conjure it up, or make it happen.

Holiness *is* a "striving to enter in," as Jesus tells us. *Effort* is not the opposite of grace; *works* is. Works has to do with merit or earning, and the effort we are called to undertake has nothing whatever to do with meriting or earning anything. In fact, the classical Disciplines— fasting and prayer, for example— have no virtue or merit whatsoever in and of themselves. They merely place us before God in such a way that he can begin building the kingdom-righteousness within us. (I say "merely" because I want to underscore that the virtue is all of God, but I certainly do not want to give the impression that our effort is nothing. In the economy of God it is a very important something. We will come to this presently.)

Holiness *is not* perfectionism. We do not by some act of divine fiat become sinless creatures incapable of any wrong action. As holy persons we can still make mistakes—and we do, with sorrowful regularity. We fail. We fall. Even so . . .

Holiness *is* progress in purity and sanctity. We are set apart for divine purposes. Holy habits deepen into fixed patterns of life. We experience a growing preponderance of right actions flowing from a right heart. We are ever in the process of becoming holy.

Holiness *is not* absorption into God. It does not mean the loss of our identity, our personhood. Through holy living we do not become less real, less whole, less human. Quite the opposite.

Holiness *is* loving unity with God. It is an ever-expanding openness to the divine Center. It is a growing, maturing, freely given conformity to the will and ways of God. Holiness gives us our truest, fullest humanity. In holiness we become the persons we were created to be.

DISCOVERING THE MAJOR STRENGTHS

The Holiness Tradition feeds us in many ways: focusing on personal transformation, emphasizing purity of heart, assuring progress in character formation, fostering growth in grace, and more.

The Ultimate Goal

First of all the Holiness Tradition constantly holds before us the ultimate goal of the Christian life: an ever deeper formation of the inner personality so as to reflect the glory and goodness of God; an ever more radiant conformity to the life and faith and desires and habits of Jesus; an utter transformation of our creatureliness into whole and perfect sons and daughters of God.

You see, the goal of the Christian life is not simply to get us into heaven, but to get heaven into us! God is intent upon making you and making me into "a dazzling, radiant, immortal creature, pulsating all through with such energy and joy and wisdom and love as we cannot now imagine, a bright, stainless mirror that reflects back to God perfectly (though, of course, on a smaller scale) His own boundless power and delight and goodness."[52]

To be sure, the full reality of this "perfect reflection" awaits glorification. But even now we need to hear the ultimate goal spoken over us again and again so that we may enter into the process that leads to this goal. God does not wait until death to initiate this process of complete and total transformation. Oh, no. It begins now, and God can and will do far more here and now than we can possibly imagine. If we are not perfect yet, we can be a whole lot better.

We, you see, are terribly prone to settle for less than what God desires for us. We are glad enough for God to remove an irritating behavior from our personality (a sour disposition, for example), or a destructive addiction (like alcoholism), but it is a very different thing for him to begin restructuring our inner affections. We may be willing to give up honors and possessions and even friends, but it touches us too closely to disown ourselves. And yet we simply must understand that God is seeking not to improve us but to transform us. C. S. Lewis writes, "The goal towards which [God] is beginning to guide you is absolute perfection; and no power in the whole universe, except you yourself, can prevent Him from taking you to that goal."[53]

The Wellspring of Action

A (second) major strength we find in the Holiness Stream is its intentional focus upon the heart, the wellspring of action. All of the best writers in this Tradition constantly (almost monotonously) call us toward purity of heart. The great Puritan divines, for example, gave sustained attention to this "heart-work," as they dubbed it. In *Keeping the Heart,* John Flavel, a seventeenth-century English Puritan, notes that the "greatest difficulty in conversion, is to win the heart *to* God; and the greatest difficulty after conversion, is to keep the heart *with* God. . . . Heart-work is hard work indeed."[54]

For the Holiness Tradition, external actions—this set of ethical practices or that set of observances—are never the center of attention. Specific actions are a consequence, a natural result of something far deeper, far more profound. The scholastic maxim *Actio sequitur esse* reminds us that action is always in accordance with the essence of the person who acts.[55] This does not reduce good works and acts of charity to insignificance, of course, but it does make them matters of secondary significance, *effects* rather than *causes.* Of primary significance is our vital union with God, our "new creation" in Christ, our immersion in the Holy Spirit. It is this union that purifies the heart. When the branch is truly integrated into the vine—united with the vine and receiving its life from the vine—then good spiritual fruit is a natural consequence (John 17). Action follows essence.

It is so easy for us to center virtue in the action itself. If an individual does this particular thing or refrains from doing that particular thing, we think he must be virtuous. Now, it is true that virtuous persons will do virtuous actions, but it is not the actions that make those persons virtuous. Rather, those persons do the actions because they are virtuous. It is a little like the star tennis player who consistently makes good shots; she makes good shots precisely because she is a good tennis player. By sheer luck I might make a good shot, but that would not make me a good tennis player, as the shots before and after the lucky shot would amply prove.

This is why the moral philosophers can say, "Virtue is easy." When the heart is purified by the action of the Spirit, the most natural thing in the world is the virtuous thing. To the pure in heart, vice is what is hard.

So the constant appeal to heart-purification by the voices from the Holiness Tradition are welcome words. It is no vain thing to be returning to our first love over and over and over again. It is an act of faith to continually cry out to God to search us and know our heart and root out every wicked way in us (Ps. 139:23).

We are—each and every one of us—a tangled mass of motives: hope and fear, faith and doubt, simplicity and duplicity, honesty and falsity, openness and guile. God knows our heart better than we ever can. He is the only one who can separate the true from the false; he alone can purify the motives of the heart. But he does not come uninvited. If chambers of our heart have never experienced the healing touch, perhaps it is because we have not welcomed the divine scrutiny.

The most important, the most real, the most lasting work is accomplished in the depths of our heart. This work is solitary and interior. It cannot be seen by anyone, even ourselves. It is a work known only to God. It is the work of heart purity, soul conversion, life transfiguration.

Though we cannot see the work itself, we can detect some of its effects. We experience a new firmness of life-orientation. We experience a settled peace that we do not fully understand and cannot fully explain. We begin seeing everything in the light of God's overriding governance for good. And, most amazing of all, we begin to feel abiding, unconditional warm regard for all people.

The Assurance of Progress

Third, the Holiness Tradition gives us hope for genuine progress in character transformation. This hope is a grace-filled gift, for there are many people who have simply given up on any movement forward in the spiritual life. Often such people devise elaborate justifications for their lack of growth—some suggesting that any real change must await another dispensation, others suggesting that since we are covered by the righteousness of Christ, we do not need and should not expect any character formation.[56]

But the salvation that is in Jesus Christ is not limited to the forgiveness of sins; it is also able to break sin's power. We are "created in Christ Jesus for good works, which God prepared beforehand to be our way of life" (Eph. 2:10). Sin no longer needs to reign in our mortal bodies. We *can* walk in newness of life. We *can* yield our arms and legs and eyes and ears and brain to God as "instruments of righteousness." We *can* be "conformed to the image of his Son," Jesus (Rom. 6:12–14, 8:29).

Growth in Grace

And that leads me to the fourth strength of the Holiness Tradition—namely, its tough-minded, down-to-earth, practical understanding of how we "grow in the grace and knowledge of our Lord and Savior Jesus Christ" (2 Pet. 3:18). The foundational structure for this growth in grace involves a training of body, mind, and spirit by means of the disciplines of the spiritual life. These Disciplines are well-recognized activities of prayer and meditation and study and fasting and solitude and service and worship and celebration and much more. All these activities are ways by which we quite literally present our bodies as "a living sacrifice" to God (Rom. 12:1).

This is a seeking after the righteousness of the kingdom of God through indirection. By undertaking Disciplines of the spiritual life that we *can* do, we receive from God the ability to do things that under our own steam we simply *cannot* do, such as loving our enemies. The Disciplines, you see, place us into the divine stream of things in such a way that God is able to build within us deeply ingrained habits of "love, joy, peace, patience, kindness, generosity, faithfulness, gentleness, and self-control" (Gal. 5:22b–23a).

While the classical Disciplines of the spiritual life are the foundational means for our formation, they are far from the only means. Often God uses the various difficulties and trials we face in life to produce in us a kind of patience endurance (James 1:2–3). At other times God uses the interactive exchange that goes on between ourselves and the Holy Spirit to develop a dependent spirit within us. Or to grow our faith. Then again, God will often use human beings and other physical means to mediate his life to us. All of these things shape us, form us, and make us substantively different persons, to the extent that we are willing participants in this work of grace. We can stop our growing conformity to Christ at any point. God in his wisdom and sovereign freedom has given us veto power over our own formation. This is the dignity he bestows upon us as free moral agents.

And the Spirit is most patient, waiting for us to come to our senses and see the goodness of rightness. But believe me, God is determined to pursue this good work in us to the very end. C. S. Lewis observes, "The command *Be ye perfect* is not idealistic gas. Nor is it a command to do the impossible. [God] is going to make us into creatures that can obey that command. . . . He meant what He said. Those who put themselves in His hands will become perfect, as He is perfect—perfect in love, wisdom, joy, beauty, and immortality."[57]

The transformation of ourselves into the likeness of Christ will not be fully completed in this life, for, as Lewis notes, "death is an important part of the treatment."[58] How far each one of us moves forward into godliness here in this life depends upon a whole host of complex factors, not the least of which is the emotional, mental, and psychic package we were given at birth. Such factors can either give us a good running start or handicap us enormously. Yet even with all the complex interplay between heredity, environment, and other factors too numerous to mention, we can and should expect substantial movement forward into a life of "righteousness and peace and joy in the Holy Spirit" (Rom. 14:17b).

I want to make two comments about this growth in grace—comments that will sound strangely contradictory but that in fact fit together quite nicely. First, in our thinking and our living we need to make generous allowance for divine infusions of grace that produce in us quantum leaps forward.[59] These (as best I can understand) are utterly sovereign acts of God. We in no way cause them to happen, and they appear unconnected to our strivings in any discernible way. Perhaps you have been grappling with a particular addiction—say, pornography—and at some point all distorted sexual desires simply and totally disappear. Or maybe in some simple worship context you experience wave after wave of supernatural Love washing over you in a paroxysm of hope and wonder and joy and peace. These are glorious acts of God for which the only sane response is to fall to our knees in worship, adoration, and praise.

My second comment stresses the other side of the coin. We have a part to play in this "growing in godliness" (as the Puritans were fond of calling it). We have work to do. And it is exceedingly important work, for God has ordained it to be the normal and most common means of our formation. Graciously God invites us to work in cooperation with the Spirit through spiritual Disciplines appropriate to our need and through the various other means of grace. Paul so beautifully brings together these two sides of the same coin when he states, "Work out your own salvation with fear and trembling; for it is God who is at work in you, enabling you both to will and to work for his good pleasure" (Phil. 2:12b–13).

Now, this ordinary, everyday means of character transformation lacks the fireworks of the special infusions of overwhelming grace. Furthermore, it seems painfully slow, though it always proceeds at a rate consistent with the nature of the virtue being sought. Francis de Sales writes, "The ordinary purification and healing, whether of the body or of the mind, takes place only little by little, by passing from one degree to another with labor and patience. . . . The soul that rises from sin to devotion may be compared to the dawning of the day, which at its approach does not expel the darkness instantaneously but only little by little."[60]

It is easy for us to undervalue this most fundamental means of grace. It appears so commonplace, so quiet, so modest, so unimpressive. But it is *the* primary way we grow. God has ordained that it be so. Through it God invites us to be participants in the work of grace, "labourers together with God," as Paul puts it (1 Cor. 3:9, KJV).

In any event, these two realities actually work hand in glove. Our bodies, our minds, our souls need shaping and preparing for any special infusion of grace. On our own we are not sufficient receptacles to contain the divine Blessing. We would simply blow apart, or something worse. Therefore, we should always value this ordinary way (this intolerably slow way) of growth, for through it God prepares us for things we can hardly imagine.

UNDERSTANDING THE POTENTIAL PERILS

Every Tradition has its zealots—those who, not fully understanding the Tradition, push some aspect of its teaching into a distortion. I want to mention three such distortions in the Holiness Stream that can easily become serious pitfalls in our lives.

The first is legalism. This comes any time we turn our center of attention away from the heart and onto externals of one sort or another. Usually these externals are tied to particular standards of culture or modes of behavior. When this shift of focus happens, we reduce virtue to custom and thereby trivialize it.

Once we define holiness solely by external matters, we are, of necessity, plunged into legalisms of one sort or another. Why? Because now we have hoops for people to jump through. We have a way to manage and control ourselves and others. (And usually we are the hardest on ourselves.)

Now, external actions are not unimportant, which is why this matter is often confusing to people. We solve our confusion by seeing how Jesus gave central attention to the heart out of which flow the issues of life. When the heart is set right, then the actions that are good and true will flow naturally. So external action is of importance, but it is of secondary importance. External action is derivative, not primary.

Please understand. It is not wrong for us to study the issue of appropriate action as we do in ethics courses. Nor is it wrong to have lists of right actions as we do in the Decalogue and many other biblical passages. These show us how love acts in given situations. But they are never the center of our attention, only the byproduct, and, by their very nature, they can never fully encompass a virtuous life.

Righteousness, holiness, the life of virtue is centrally and primarily a matter of "heart work." This is why Jesus gave such sustained attention to the rightness of the heart out of which flow the issues of life.

But (and here is the rub), if holiness is primarily a matter of the heart, how can we know who is holy and who is not, who has it and who doesn't? Legalism, with its external standards, majors in answering this question. I suggest to you that it is a virtue to ignore the question.

The second great peril for the Holiness Tradition is _Pelagianism_ (a teaching named after Pelagius, a fourth-century monk).[61] It is a big word with a long history, but it refers primarily to any form of earning or meriting our standing with God. Sometimes it is called "works righteousness," that is, attempting to attain righteousness by means of our own works.

The reason Pelagianism is such a great danger to the Holiness Tradition is that inherent in any serious call to holy living is the temptation to believe that any progress forward is somehow our doing. It is the arrogance of feeling that we are in charge after all, that we really can pull ourselves up by our bootstraps. You see, the ancient Adamic temptation to "be as gods" is ever with us.

Because this temptation is so great, some groups have rejected the possibility of any moral progress in this life. They tell us that the only righteousness we should look forward to is the "imputed righteousness" * of Christ on our behalf. Now, the doctrine of imputed righteousness is a precious truth. Our standing with God is an act of grace alone. We can do nothing to improve that standing. Because of the work of Christ on our behalf we are loved and accepted just the way we are. This is a reality we simply receive and embrace without any attempts to add to or improve upon it.

---

*Sometimes this is also called "alien righteousness," for it is a righteousness that comes from the outside and is alien to our sinful nature, which is in rebellion against God. At other times the term "objective righteousness" is used to underscore the objective nature of God's declaring us righteous through the shed blood of Jesus Christ.

Having said this, I must go on to say that all the writers of the New Testament would find it completely ludicrous to think that the imputed righteousness of Christ leaves us locked into the same patterns of viciousness and destruction. "God forbid," as Paul puts it (Rom. 6:2, KJV). No, the righteousness of Christ that is imputed to us so generously and freely also places us on the path of discipleship, where we learn to "grow in grace" (2 Pet. 3:18). We become apprentices to Jesus so that slowly but surely (no doubt with many slips and falls along the way) we begin to "follow in his steps."

So there are things for us to do, but what we do does not make us righteous. We could imitate the life of Christ down to the minutest detail and still not be righteous. Our actions, in and of themselves, contain not a single iota of righteousness. All that the actions of discipleship do is place us before God so that he can begin to build the righteousness of the kingdom within us. Purity of heart, indiscriminate love, a peace that transcends understanding—these, and so much more, are the things built into the heart of the disciple.

Now, once again we must underscore in the most complete way possible that this heart-work is God's work alone. We simply cannot program our heart; only God can, and God only. It is *sola gratia*, grace alone. Jesus, in his Sermon on the Mount, says, "Let your light shine before others, so that they may see your good works and give glory to your Father in heaven" (Matt. 5:16). Now, some inquisitive mind might wonder, If it is "*your* light" and "*your* good works," then why don't *you* get the glory? The reason is simple: we know that we have done nothing more than receive a gift. Our transformation of heart is utterly and completely a work of grace.

It is time now to look at the third peril, *perfectionism.* This danger is largely derivative from a failure to deal successfully with the first two. If my focus remains upon external standards of behavior, and if I feel that I am the one who has attained those standards, I am going to be sorely tempted to see myself as perfect.

This pitfall is especially dangerous because it cuts us off from our essential humanity. Often it forces us to deny who we really are and what is actually in us. When this happens, we begin to pretend that we are what we are not. And the resulting inner contradiction is destructive indeed.

Perfectionism is almost routinely understood in legalistic terms. The reason for this is easy to see. In order to know who is perfect and who is not, we need an external criterion by which we can judge others. And most deadly of all is the way this approach to life necessitates a rigid, condemning, judgmental spirit. If you doubt what I have just said, simple observation will give ample and regrettable testimony that this is the case.

Now, the impulse to be perfect is not wrong. We are to be perfected in love even as our Father in heaven is perfect (Matt. 5:48). We should intend to be perfect. And we should make plans to be perfect. But no matter how far we go into perfection, there will always remain room for growth.

Paul captures this paradox so beautifully in his Epistle to the Philippians. First, he makes it quite clear that he has room for growth: "Not as though I had already attained, either were already perfect." Then he gives the lifestyle posture of the disciple of Jesus: "Forgetting those things which are behind, and reaching forth unto those things which are before, I press toward the mark for the prize of the high calling of God in Christ Jesus." And finally he shows us that this very process is itself perfection: "Let us therefore, as many as be perfect, be thus minded" (Phil. 3:12–15a, KJV). So, as we constantly recognize how far we have yet to go, and as we constantly press forward toward all that God has for us, we are in fact entering into a kind of perfection.

You see, God meets us at the point of our effort. We do not sit back and expect God to pour righteousness on our heads. There are things for us to do. But the effort is always in a spirit that is nonlegalistic, nonworks, nonjudgmental, noncondemning. And always we realize that we do not have anything that we have not been given.

How, then, do we deal with the perils in the Holiness Tradition? By replacing legalism with love. By replacing Pelagianism with grace. By replacing perfectionism with growth. If we do this with true and honest hearts, we will be kept on the right path.

PRACTICING THE HOLINESS TRADITION

Holiness never involves works, as we have seen, but it most assuredly ✗
involves effort. Hence we cannot ignore the question of practice.
How do we go about moving forward in holiness?

First, we train. And in our training we remember the principle of
indirection. Rather than tackle the issues of virtue and vice head-on, we
undertake activities of body, mind, and spirit that in time will build spiritual resources within us to act appropriately when the situation
demands it. As athletes of God we plan a regimen of spiritual Disciplines that will stimulate our growth in grace. If we are struggling with
pride, we learn service, which leads us into the many little deaths of
going beyond ourselves. If we are needing hope, we learn prayer and
meditation, which usher us ever deeper into the heart of the Holy. If
compulsions of one kind or another obsess us, we learn fasting, which
teaches us to control all the senses by the grace of God. If we want faith,
we learn worship, which shows us the Lord high and lifted up. And on it
goes. Throughout we are training for holiness, planning for perfection.

Second, we invite others to travel the journey with us. Such persons become both companions and mentors. They provide us with
discernment, counsel, and encouragement. Often we are too close to
our own training plan to see that we are overachieving and setting
ourselves up for failure. Or to see that sloth is setting in and we need
encouragement to venture out into the depths. Furthermore, others
often can detect our growth and development better than we, and
their reassuring words help us see the footprints of God in our lives.

Such spiritual companionship also provides a loving accountability. A trust relationship is built in which it is the most natural thing in
the world to answer honestly and fully the query, "How is it with your
soul?" In the best of worlds we can identify persons who are giving us
spiritual direction and persons to whom we give spiritual direction.
But even where the best is not possible—and often it is not—we can
still find loving relationships that nurture our spiritual growth.

Third, when we stumble and fall, we get up and start again.
Appropriate confession and restitution are always in order, but we

never spend too much time lamenting our failures and shortcomings. Where we are not yet perfect, we know that we have a perfect Friend who will never leave us, never forsake us. Besides, we are in this for the long term. We are looking ahead to the perfection that is coming and is to come. We keep pressing on.

I wish that this simple counsel did not sound so trivial, for it is a profound truth for our growth: stumbling is part of our growing. Our mistakes and failures teach us the right way to live—and that the right way is the good way. And after stumbling it is no small thing for us to start at the beginning once again. We are learning that by starting again and again and again something firm and lasting is being built in us. The old writers called this something "fortitude," and fortitude builds habits, and habits build character, and character builds destiny.

THE CALL TO VIRTUOUS LIVING

QUESTION: What is the Holiness Tradition?
ANSWER: A life that functions as it should.
QUESTION: Why should we explore it?
ANSWER: Because through it we are enabled to live whole, functional lives in a dysfunctional world.

Every one of us is called to holiness of heart and life. Anthony Bloom reminds us that *"All holiness is God's holiness in us*: it is a holiness that is participation and, in a certain way, more than participation, because as we participate in what we can receive from God, we become a revelation of that which transcends us. Being a limited light, we reveal the Light."[62] How wonderful to think that as we become partners with God, participating in this ongoing work of Christian perfection, our little light (which is not the source of light but only a reflection of the Light—and often a distorted and faint reflection at that) might lead others all the more fully to see Jesus, the Light of the world.

Chapter 4

~

The Charismatic Tradition: Discovering the Spirit-Empowered Life

Be filled with the Spirit, as you sing psalms and hymns and spiritual songs among yourselves, singing and making melody to the Lord in your hearts.

—*Ephesians 5:18b–19*

Now is the Lord appearing in this day of his mighty power, to gather His elect together, out of all forms and observations, kindreds, tongues and nations; and is making up his jewels, his mighty host, and exalting Jesus Christ to be King of Kings, to lead his Army . . . in the mighty power of the living Word of God.

—*William Dewsbury, 1655*

THE CHARISMATIC TRADITION*

Notable Figures   *Significant Movements*

0
Jesus of Nazareth
(c. 4 B.C.- c. A.D. 29)

Notable Figures	Significant Movements
Paul the Apostle (1st century)	
Montanus (2nd century)	Montanist Movement
Perpetua (c. 180–203)	(2nd–3rd centuries)
Gregory Thaumaturgus (c. 213–c. 270)	
Ephraem the Syrian (c. 306–c. 373)	
Flavian (c. 320–404)	
Samson (c. 485–c. 565)	
Gregory the Great (c. 540–604)	Gregorian Liturgical Movement
	(7th century to the present)
Alcuin of York (c. 732–804)	

1000

Notable Figures	Significant Movements
Hildegard of Bingen (1098–1179)	
Lutgarde of Aywieres (1182–1246)	
Francis of Assisi (1182–1226)	Franciscans
Richard Rolle (c. 1300–1349)	(13th century to the present)
Bridget of Sweden (c. 1303–1373)	
Joan of Arc (1412–1431)	
George Fox (1624–1691)	
Charles Wesley (1707–1788)	
Seraphim of Sarov (1759–1833)	
Pastor Hsi (1830–1896)	
C. H. Mason (1866–1961)	
William Seymour (1870–1922)	
Evan John Roberts (1878–1951)	
Sundar Singh (c. 1889–1929)	
Aimee Semple McPherson (1890–1944)	Pentecostal Movement
David du Plessis (1905–1987)	(20th century to the present)
Kathryn Kuhlman (c. 1910–1976)	
Demos Shakarian (1913–)	Charismatic Renewal
Dennis Bennett (1917–1991)	(20th century to the present)
Oral Roberts(1918–)	
John Wimber (1934–1997)	Modern Liturgical Renewal
David Yonggi Cho (1936–)	(20th century to the present)

*See Appendix B for brief biographies and histories.

WHILE THE HOLINESS TRADITION centers upon the power *to be*, the Charismatic Tradition centers upon the power *to do*. While this distinction is important, we must not make too much of it, for—as we shall see presently—these two Traditions are most healthy when they refuse to function independently of one another. (So it is with *all* the Traditions.) The Charismatic Stream of Christian life and faith focuses upon the empowering charisms or gifts of the Spirit and the nurturing fruit of the Spirit. This Spirit-empowered way of living addresses the deep yearning for the immediacy of God's presence among his people.

SEEKING A HISTORICAL PARADIGM

Every time I consider the Charismatic Stream I think of Francesco, a young man who lived at the height of the Middle Ages. He was born and raised in Italy, but French influences were also prominent from the outset. His given name at birth was actually Giovanni, but when his father, Pietro Bernadone, returned from a business trip to France, he immediately changed the child's name to Francesco, "the Little Frenchman." His mother, Pica, was French, and Francesco learned his mother's native tongue at her knee. He particularly loved the French ballads popularized by roving troubadours.

Before the Hound of Heaven conquered his heart, Francesco was the fun-loving leader of a frolicking group of young men from the area. His first biographer notes, "Up to the twenty-fifth year of his age, he squandered and wasted his time miserably. Indeed, he outdid all his contemporaries in vanities and he came to be a promoter of evil and was more abundantly zealous for all kinds of foolishness."[1]

In his early twenties Francesco left home to fight in a bloody skirmish with a neighboring city, where he was taken as a prisoner of war. A one-year incarceration there, along with a one-year convalescence back home, proved to be a critical turning point. During these dark, lonely months Francesco experienced an ever-growing, ever-deepening, converting grace. Living as a hermit beside the tumble-down, nearly abandoned church of San Damiano, he heard the *debar Yahweh* (the word of the Lord)—"Rebuild my church"—coming from the church crucifix. This Francesco did, at first by literally repairing the ruined walls of San Damiano and then by undertaking the far greater task of rebuilding the spiritual heart of the church—a rebuilding that was desperately needed.

Pietro Bernadone was livid about Francesco's new life, especially the young man's lavish generosity to the poor with Pietro's hard-earned money. Finally, in an act of desperation, he hauled his recalcitrant son before the local bishop, demanding justice. Francesco responded by renouncing all claims to his father's estate and returning all goods—including the clothes off his back, so that he stood naked before the bishop. He then turned to Pietro Bernadone, saying, "Until now I called you my father, but from now on I can say without reserve, 'Our Father who art in heaven.' He is all my wealth and I place all my confidence in him."[2]

And so, mindful of the jugglers that accompanied the French troubadours, Francesco declared that he was *Le Jongleur de Dieu*, living in utter poverty and wandering through the towns and villages, preaching the gospel. Many of the young men who had been part of his thrill-seeking circle in earlier days joined him. Another person joined him too—Clare Favarone, a well-to-do young lady from Francesco's hometown. Thus began one of the great spiritual movements of history.

The story of that movement is so well known that by now you have probably guessed that the Francesco I have been telling you about is none other than the little, poor man of Assisi, St. Francis. What an extraordinary story! What a powerful influence! But why would I think of Francis as a pivotal figure in the Charismatic Tradition?

Power in the Spirit

Well, first of all, because of the striking power in the Spirit that surrounded all that Francis did and said. Perhaps one story will suffice. Clare—who by this time had established the "Second Order" of the Franciscans, "the poor Clares"—had often requested the opportunity to eat with Francis, but he had never granted her request. Finally some of the brothers urged him to consent, saying, "Father, it seems to us that this strictness is not according to divine charity . . . especially considering that she gave up the riches and pomp of the world as a result of your preaching." In the end Francis was persuaded, and so a meeting was arranged at the little church of St. Mary of the Angels. Francis had a meal prepared and spread on the ground, as was his custom. Meeting at the appointed hour, "St. Francis and St. Clare sat down together, and one of his companions with St. Clare's companion, and all his other companions were grouped around that humble table." As they ate, Francis "began to speak about God in such a sweet and holy and profound and divine and marvelous way that he himself and St. Clare and her companion and all the others who were at that poor little table were rapt in God."

In the meantime the people of Assisi were horrified to see in the distance St. Mary of the Angels and the entire forest around it enveloped in flames. They rushed up the hill, hoping to put out the blaze before everything was lost. But upon arriving at the little church, they found nothing amiss. No church on fire. No forest ablaze. Nothing. Entering the church they discovered Francis, Clare, and the others "sitting around that very humble table, rapt in God by contemplation and invested with power from on high." They then realized that the fire they had seen was not a material fire, but a spiritual fire. The blaze they saw was "to symbolize the fire of divine love which was burning in the souls" of these simple servants of Christ. The end result of this astonishing event was that the people of Assisi returned home "with great consolation in their hearts and with holy edification."[3]

I know I said that one story would suffice, but how can I leave out the most famous Francis story of all: the taming of the ferocious wolf of Gubbio? It seems that a huge wolf had been terrorizing the citizens of Gubbio, killing several children. The people were so traumatized that they would hardly venture out of their homes, and certainly not beyond the town's boundaries. Hearing this, Francis immediately determined to find the wolf. He struck out on the road to the area where it was often found, his companions following along at a safe distance. Seeing them coming, the wolf charged at them, open-mouthed and menacing. Francis firmly and gently called out to him, "Come to me, Brother Wolf. In the name of Christ, I order you not to hurt me or anyone." His companions, at first frightened, were astonished to see the wolf stop in its tracks, close its jaws, lower its head, and lie down at Francis's feet like a lamb. As it lay in front of him, Francis addressed the wolf: "Brother Wolf, you have done great harm in this region, . . . and this whole town is your enemy. But, Brother Wolf, I want to make peace between you and them, so that they will not be harmed by you any more." He then proceeded to propose a peace pact between the wolf and the people of Gubbio: the wolf would promise not to terrorize and kill, and the people would promise to treat the wolf with courtesy and provide it with food. As the people watched in astonishment, "The wolf showed by moving its body and tail and ears and by nodding its head that it will- ingly accepted what the Saint had said and would observe it." At this all the people "shouted to the sky, praising and blessing the Lord Jesus Christ."

In this dramatic act the shalom of God descended upon that city, for we are told that "from that day, the wolf and the people kept the pact which St. Francis made. The wolf lived two years more, and it went from door to door for food. It hurt no one, and no one hurt it. The people fed it courteously. And it is a striking fact that not a single dog ever barked at it."[4]

Francis's entire ministry was rich in miracles and healings, signs and wonders, revelations and visions. Once he encountered a blind girl from the city of Bevagna in the Spoleto Valley. Seeing her inward heart-devotion, he "marked the eyes of the blind girl with his spittle three times in the name of the Trinity and restored to her the sight she desired."[5] One man from the city of Orte had a tumor between his shoulders "the size of a large loaf of bread." Francis, seeing his condition, laid hands on him and blessed him, and "he was suddenly so completely healed that no trace of the tumor remained."[6] The stories go on and on.

Growth in the Spirit

But these things, by themselves, do not make Francis a paradigm for the Charismatic Stream. Power is not an end in itself, it was never intended to be. Healthy spiritual power is, of necessity, tied to spiritual growth. And it is right here, at the linkage between spiritual power and spiritual growth, that we see how intimately connected are the Charismatic and the Holiness Traditions. That interconnection is exactly what we would expect. These two traditions *should* work hand-in-glove and *should* fuel each other. What makes Francis so important for our study, then, is the way he integrated in his person the empowering gifts of the Spirit with the nurturing fruit of the Spirit—love and joy and peace and patience and kindness and generosity and faithfulness and gentleness and self-control. We are drawn to the sheer beauty of his personality.

All of the wonder-working events in Francis's life had this soul growth as their objective. We are told that after one astonishing miracle Francis remained in the area "because of the great good which he saw the Lord was performing in the souls of the people who came there, for he saw that many of them . . . were inebriated with the love of God and converted to heavenly longings." This is the point of all the miracle stories. Nor were all the miracles of an outward nature. Many, in fact, were deeply interior, involving unusual discernment and wisdom. Whether outward or inward, the results were always the same, however: deeper love of God, greater holiness of life, fuller freedom in the Spirit.

Bonaventure said of Francis, "By the range of virtues which shone forth in his life, he stood head and shoulders above all others."[7] Francis wandered the hills and villages, constantly preaching conversion to the values of the gospel. He taught his followers to greet everyone with the salutation "Peace and good!" Now, for us to realize how dramatic this statement was, we must recover some sense of the violence and carnage of the age; these people lived under constant threat of blood vendettas and murder and pillage. Against that backdrop the greeting of peace and goodness from these humble "friars minor" came as a blessed shock.

Perhaps this focus upon goodness can be best gathered up in Francis's "Salutation of the Virtues." Francis made these simple statements in praise of the various "strengths"—which is what the word *virtues* means—that make a moral life possible. These strengths, he says, are rooted in God and come forth from God. They are the energies of the converted life. The more we ponder this simple text, the more we see Francis as a theologian of the Spirit, for it is the Spirit who brings us into ever-deeper, ever-fuller purity of heart.

> *Hail, Queen Wisdom! May the Lord preserve you*
> *with your sister holy pure Simplicity!*
> *O lady holy Poverty, may the Lord save you*
> *with your sister holy Humility!*
> *O lady holy Charity, may the Lord save you*
> *with your sister holy Obedience!*
> *O all you most holy virtues,*
> *may the Lord save you all,*
> *from Whom you come and proceed.*[8]

Joy in the Spirit

Holy joy is one of the most common marks of those who walk in the power of the Spirit, and Francis and his merry band possessed it in abundance. Their joy must have been a wonder to watch; just reading about it quickens the heart. These young troubadours of the Lord went from town to town, inebriated with holy joy. Even when Francis stood in front of the pope, he all but danced. Thomas of Celano wrote of this event noting that Francis "spoke with such great fervor of spirit, that, not being able to contain himself for joy . . . he moved his feet as though he were dancing."[9]

My favorite of the stories that illustrate the joy in the Spirit felt by Francis and his band centers on Francis putting together the very first Christmas crèche in the little town of Greccio. (Manger scenes are so common today that it is hard for us to imagine the feelings that must have accompanied that original experience. The story is preserved for us in Thomas of Celano's *First Life of St. Francis*.)

The year was 1223. Francis by now had resigned as the head of the order that bears his name and was three years away from his death. The Christmas feast was nearing, and in delightful spontaneity Francis declared, "I wish to do something that will recall to memory the little Child who was born in Bethlehem." So in merry abandon he found a nearby cave and made the necessary arrangements. Just imagine the mystery and intrigue as the people of Greccio wondered what Francis was up to in that cave at the edge of town. Then Christmas Eve—"the day of joy . . . the time of great rejoicing"—arrived. The people of the neighborhood lit candles and torches "to light up that night" and made their way to the cave "with glad hearts." Standing at the edge of the cave, they saw revealed by their lights a tiny baby in a manger—a baby wrapped snugly in strips of cloth and warmed by the hot, steamy breath of a half-dozen cows and sheep. What in the world?!

Then Francis appeared, and "he saw it and was glad." Ah, now the people caught the point: "Greccio was made, as it were, a new Bethlehem." They were "filled with new joy over the new mystery. The woods rang with the voices of the crowd and the rocks made answer to their jubilation. The brothers sang . . . and the whole night resounded with their rejoicing." Francis stood over the manger scene, "uttering sighs, overcome with love, and filled with a wonderful happiness." Francis sang to the people in "a sweet voice, a clear voice, a sonorous voice." He preached, speaking "charming words."

Then a member of the crowd had a vision that he shared with those gathered around this simple manger scene. His vision was of a little child lying in a manger, lifeless. But in the vision Francis went up and touched the child and the child awakened "as from a deep sleep." The lesson of the vision was not lost on the assembled crowd, "for the Child Jesus had been forgotten in the hearts of many; but, by the working of his grace, he was brought to life again through his servant St. Francis and stamped upon their fervent memory." What a reverent, jubilant, solemn celebration! And what a wonder-filled pageant for illiterate people who did not have the luxury of reading and rereading the story for themselves. On that night the joy of Christmas became palpable to the people of Greccio. Each observer, Thomas noted, "returned to his home with holy joy."[10]

I commend Francis of Assisi to you as a model of charismatic jubilee.

SEEKING A BIBLICAL PARADIGM

The Apostle Paul is without doubt one of the finest models of the Charismatic Stream in the entire Bible. He had a well-nigh amazing balance between the rational, objective apprehension of the gospel and the ecstatic, subjective charisms of the Spirit—enveloping both in the nurturing, maturing fruit of the Spirit. He could boldly declare, "I thank God that I speak in tongues more than all of you," and at the same time confess, "If I speak in the tongues of mortals and of angels, but do not have love, I am a noisy gong or a clanging cymbal" (1 Cor. 14:18, 13:1). He gives us both the most carefully reasoned theological treatise in the New Testament—Romans—and the finest practical teaching on exercising the spiritual gifts—First Corinthians.

The man himself was something of a wonder. Raised in Tarsus—a city created out of the combined influences of Athens and Rome, Babylon and Nineveh—he was the child of this Hellenistic/Oriental world. His family held the coveted title *civis Romanus* (or citizen of Rome), and he had a Roman name, *Paullus*, Paul. But he was also, and equally, a "Hebrew of the Hebrews," and he had the Hebrew name Saul.

A brilliant student, he was sent to Jerusalem to study under Gamaliel, the leading teacher of the school of Hillel. He quickly rose in the ranks, and some have even suggested that he took a seat on the Sanhedrin, Israel's ruling body. Be that as it may, we first encounter Paul in Acts, when Stephen was proclaiming gospel truth to "the rulers of the Jews." The Sanhedrin responded with utter rage; these dignified elders "ground their teeth at Stephen" (Acts 7:54). The Sanhedrin's "Hall of Polished Stones" reverberated with the howling of a lynch mob. Stephen was dragged to the Rock of Execution, and as this first Christian martyr was being put to death, Saul guarded the coats of the killers, nodding his approval of their killing work.

Saul's approval, in fact, went so far that he took a leadership role in the persecution that followed, "ravaging the church by entering house after house; dragging off both men and women, he committed them to prison" (Acts 8:3). Eventually this led Saul to that fateful Damascus journey during which a blinding "light from heaven" struck him to the ground and the risen Christ called him by name: "Saul, Saul, why do you persecute me?" (Acts 9:3–5).

No doubt you are acquainted with the rest of the story. Saul's three-day fast at the home of Judas on "the Street called Straight." The vision to Ananias and his obedience to that vision. Ananias's tender words to Saul: "Brother Saul, the Lord Jesus, who appeared to you on your way here, has sent me so that you may regain your sight and be filled with the Holy Spirit" (Acts 9:17b). The divine commissioning of Saul as "Apostle to the Gentiles" and the sobering reminder, "I myself will show him how much he must suffer for the sake of my name" (Acts 9:16). Saul's sight restored and his baptism into Christian fellowship. His dramatic proclamation in the synagogues: "He is the Son of God." His powerful disputation with the Jews, "proving that Jesus was the Messiah" (Acts 9:20–22).

At this point the story fades some, although we do know bits and pieces. We know, for example, that Saul went to the deserts of Arabia for three years (Gal. 1:17). This would not have been difficult logistically, since Damascus was the terminus of one of the great spice routes from southern Arabia and the Horn of Africa. And it was an essential solitude for Saul. At this critical juncture he needed, not the apostles, but the risen Jesus alone; not a city, but the wilderness. Much later he insisted that his gospel message did not come from any human or earthly source: "I received it through a revelation of Jesus Christ" (Gal. 1:12). We cannot understand all that follows in this great man's life without recognizing the importance of those three years alone in the school of the Spirit in the Arabian deserts.

We do know that he returned to Damascus briefly (Gal. 1:17). This is most likely when the plot to get rid of him once and for all was hatched and when he made his daring midnight escape over the city wall in a fish basket.[11]

We do know that he spent time in Jerusalem with Peter and James; then, when things got a bit risky, he slipped off to his home-town of Tarsus (Acts 9:26–30). There he disappeared from sight for perhaps a decade, only to reappear in Antioch ready for his famous missionary journeys.

The details become much clearer from this point on. The story of the commissioning at Antioch, the subsequent missionary journeys, and the final trip to Rome are well known and sufficiently docu-mented that I do not need to detail them here.[12] But perhaps it would be useful to highlight an incident from each of his three mission trips to illustrate the charismatic character of his effective ministry.

First Journey: Power Encounter at Cyprus

We see, at the very outset of these missionary journeys, the fre-quent and intentional mention of the superintending role of the Holy Spirit, the third member of the Trinity. When persecution scat-tered the early followers of the Way, evangelistic fires broke out in Antioch and spilled over unintentionally into the non-Jewish Greek population. Barnabas, "a good man, *full of the Holy Spirit* and of faith," was sent to look into this unusual phenomenon (Acts 11:24, italics added). Seeing that it was the work of God, he knew that Saul was just the person to help out. For a full year the two of them worked together in Antioch, and "the disciples were first called

'Christians'" here because people saw that the way of Christ was more than just a movement within Jewry (Acts 11:26). It was a perfect place to launch a mission to Gentile peoples.

While the leaders of the church at Antioch—"prophets and teachers"—were "worshiping the Lord and fasting, *the Holy Spirit said*, 'Set apart for me Barnabas and Saul for the work to which I have called them'" (Acts 13:2, italics added). This was followed by more fasting, more praying, and then a commissioning of these two with the laying on of hands. While human instrumentality was used, Luke made it quite clear who was in charge of this effort: "So, being sent out *by the Holy Spirit* . . . " (Acts 13:4, italics added).

Traveling to the island of Cyprus, Barnabus and Saul had extraordinary results—so much so that the proconsul of the island, Sergius Paulus, invited them to speak at the palace. But one man, Bar-Jesus or Elymas by name, tried to stop them. He was the local magician, and these gospel heralds were crowding in on his territory. The battle was set—occult magician versus Spirit-empowered apostle. "But Saul, also known as Paul, *filled with the Holy Spirit*," applied the gospel medicine to Elymas: "The hand of the Lord is against you, and you will be blind for a while, unable to see the sun" (Acts 13:9, 11, italics added).[13] Perhaps the Venerable Bede was correct when he commented on this event, "The apostle, remembering his own case, knew that by the darkening of the eyes the mind's darkness might be restored to light."[14]

We today may wonder at Paul's authority and power in this situation. I mean, few of us are at the people-blinding level! But Paul had learned, through a process of time and experience, that when *he* spoke, *God* spoke. He knew how to discern the movements of the Spirit, and he knew how to work in cooperation with those movements. That knowledge produced a spirit-empowered life.

Second Journey: Exorcism at Philippi

How Paul and his team ended up in Philippi in the first place is itself a charismatic wonder. Paul kept trying to go north, but he was hindered on two separate occasions: first the team was "forbidden by the Holy Spirit to speak the word in Asia," and then, when they tried to go into Bithynia, "the Spirit of Jesus did not allow them" (Acts 16:6–8). We have no hint as to the means the Spirit used to convey this restriction—a prophecy perhaps, or a vision, or simply a growing conviction that this was not the way. But by now Paul and his companions were well acquainted with walking in responsiveness to the movements of the Spirit. So instead of going north, they angled west until they came to Troas, where they waited for further guidance.

And further guidance they got in abundance. Paul had a vision in the night: "There stood a man of Macedonia pleading with him and saying, 'Come over to Macedonia and help us'" (Acts 16:9). Notice that the region, Macedonia, was specified in the vision, but not the specific city. God's guidance was for them to go west instead of north as they had wanted; that was the supernatural side of the equation. They used their sanctified common sense in choosing Philippi; it was the major city in the region and, being a port city, the easiest to get to.

As usual, Paul began his work by using the religious life of the place—whatever it happened to be—as his starting point. In the non-Jewish context of Philippi there was no synagogue, but there was a small prayer gathering of women by the river. Paul, Silas, Timothy, and Luke joined them:[15] "We sat down and spoke to the women who had gathered there" (Acts 16:13). It is moving to realize the cultural biases that these evangelists had to overcome to meet at a public site with Gentile women. Now, watch how God honors this small effort.

The first miracle was that the businesswoman in the group, Lydia, was soundly converted and then baptized—"she and her household."[16] She then urged Paul and the others to stay in her home, giving Paul a base for his operations (Acts 16:14–15).

The second miracle took place as Paul and the others were continuing in their regular practice of gathering by the river, "the place of prayer." It seems that a young slave girl "who had a spirit of divination" latched onto Paul and his company, crying out, "These men are slaves of the Most High God, who proclaim to you a way of salvation." Now, this was actually quite good—even accurate—advertising for Paul and his team. But Paul had no need for that kind of publicity. Besides, this poor possessed child needed deliverance, which is exactly what she got. Paul, whirling around, spoke directly to the spirit possessing the child: "I order you in the name of Jesus Christ to come out of her." And "it came out that very hour" (Acts 16:18). A dramatic event, to say the least.

But rather than thanking Paul for this wonderful work, the owners of the child, seeing "that their hope of making money was gone," had Paul and Silas beaten and thrown into prison on a trumped up charge of "advocating customs that are not lawful for us as Romans to adopt or observe" (Acts 16:19–21).

However, in this too God honored their efforts, for the next miraculous event came in response to their midnight prayers and praises. God, in wonder-working power, threw open the doors of the prison for Paul and Silas and threw open the door to Christ for the jailer. "Suddenly there was an earthquake, so violent that . . . all the doors were opened and everyone's chains were unfastened. . . . Then [the jailer] said, 'Sirs, what must I do to be saved?'" (Acts 16:26–34). Conversion at the riverside, the healing of a possessed child, conversion in a jail—those results are hard to improve upon.

Third Journey: Extraordinary Works at Ephesus

In Paul's third missionary journey he spent extensive time in Ephesus. He began by completing the work in some of Apollos's converts, for he laid hands on them and "the Holy Spirit came upon them, and they spoke in tongues and prophesied" (Acts 19:6). Next, he preached in the synagogue, and when he was rejected there, he set up shop at the lecture hall of Tyrannus. Perhaps sensing that it was important to stay with certain groups for extended periods in order to establish them in the faith, Paul used this hall as a base of operations for two years. It became the daily gathering place for preaching, teaching, and argumentation as "the word of the Lord" went throughout the region.

It is instructive to see that extensive teaching work and miraculous manifestations went hand in hand. Paul had a marvelous ministry of the Spirit, which exuded power in both word and deed: "God did extraordinary miracles through Paul, so that when the handkerchiefs or aprons that had touched his skin were brought to the sick, their diseases left them, and the evil spirits came out of them" (Acts 19:11–12).

Paul's work of exorcism was so stunning that some itinerant Jewish exorcists tried to imitate it by saying, over some poor individual in need of help, "I adjure you by the Jesus whom Paul proclaims." The evil spirit in the man responded, "Jesus I know, and Paul I know; but who are you?" At last this man possessed by the evil spirit "leaped on them, mastered them all, and so overpowered them that they fled out of the house naked and wounded" (Acts 19:13–16).

These "power encounters" were not infrequent occurrences in Paul's ministry. I mentioned the encounter at Cyprus, the exorcism at Philippi, and the wonderful works at Ephesus; but I could just as easily have told about the great "signs and wonders" that occurred in Iconium, or the healing of the man crippled from birth at Lystra, or Paul's supernatural vision at Corinth, or the miraculous healing of Eutychus by the hand of Paul at Troas, or Paul's encounter with an angel of God while at sea, or Paul's own healing from a viper bite at Malta (Acts 14:1–4; 14:8–18; 18:7–11; 20:7–12; 27:21–26; 28:1–6). Paul knew how to exercise spiritual authority. Furthermore, he knew that the work of God was a work of the Spirit. This is the Charismatic Tradition at its finest.

SEEKING A CONTEMPORARY PARADIGM

In the most unassuming of places in the heart of Los Angeles, a work of the Spirit broke forth in 1906 that was destined to become the fountainhead of a worldwide Pentecostal explosion. William J. Seymour was the divinely chosen leader of this work, which came to be known as "the Azusa Street Revival." By perceiving the deeper implications of Pentecostal glossolalia, Seymour stood at the forefront of one of the most revolutionary social movements in history, a movement intent upon "erasing the color line." In the midst of the most racist era of a totally segregated society, huge throngs of people from virtually every race, nationality, and class on earth came together at Azusa Street. Meeting night and day continuously for three years, Azusa Street was an all-inclusive fellowship beyond the color line. Seymour, with far-sighted leadership, harnessed the power released in glossolalic worship to break racial, gender, and nationalistic barriers and offer the world a historic opportunity for genuine healing and reconciliation. It was an explosion of Spirit-empowered, charismatic fervor at its best and most powerful. Then, right at the moment of Seymour's greatest influence, white supremacy reared its ugly head, denouncing and rejecting this grace-filled work of God. . . . But that is running ahead of my story.[17]

Searching for Freedom

In the salt tang of gulf breezes William Joseph Seymour was born 2 May 1870 in the bayou country of Centerville, Louisiana. With virtually no opportunity for formal education in this center of Ku Klux Klan violence,[18] Seymour worked hard in the fields while managing, in the frontier tradition of Abraham Lincoln, to educate himself.[19] During those years he drank deeply from the wellspring of black Christian spirituality—"the invisible institution," as it has been called.[20] Here he developed a lifelong love for the tradition of spirituals, which sprang out of the blood-soaked soil of slavery.

At the earliest possible moment Seymour left his southern roots in search of the greater freedom of the North. In 1895 he headed to Indianapolis, Indiana, the pre–Civil War center for the Underground Railroad. But even there he found only the most menial and unskilled occupations open to him, and so he took a job as a waiter in a large downtown hotel restaurant. He also joined the Simpson Chapel, a black congregation in the largely white Methodist Episcopal Church. His denominational choice is significant. A far easier option would have been the African Methodist Episcopal Church, which had a congregation closer to his residence. But by choosing the more interracial Methodist Episcopal Church, he acted on his long-held determination to seek racial reconciliation through the power of the Spirit.

In 1900 Seymour headed to Cincinnati, Ohio, where he encountered the "Evening Light Saints" (later to be called the Church of God Reformation Movement), a white denomination that reached out vigorously to African-Americans. Drawn by its racial inclusiveness and its strong holiness emphasis, Seymour joined this group and soon felt a call to enter a preaching ministry. With few (and small) congregations in the movement, such a call meant that Seymour constantly traveled. He cared for his own support during this time, since offerings were not taken at evangelistic services.[21]

In his evangelistic efforts Seymour traveled to Texas looking for his relatives who had been separated from him during slavery days. Finding family in Houston, he decided to make his home there. For a time he served as an interim pastor at a black holiness church while its pastor, the Reverend Mrs. Lucy Farrow, was in Kansas serving as governess for the family of Charles F. Parham, a well-known evangelist and Bible teacher of the day.

Upon her return to Houston, Rev. Farrow told Seymour about her Kansas experiences, giving a glowing account of having spoken in "unknown tongues." Seymour wanted to learn more, and so when Parham came to Houston to establish a Bible school, Seymour gained admission. Parham's own segregation attitudes, coupled with those generally held in the Houston area, barred Seymour from actually attending classes. But he was allowed to sit just outside the classroom door, which Parham carefully left ajar. In the afternoons Seymour and Parham preached together in the black sections of Houston. Parham, however, observed strict rules of segregation in the large evening services in Caledonia Hall downtown, so Seymour sat in the rear of the auditorium. Parham also prohibited interracial mingling at the altar afterwards, a practice that hindered Seymour from receiving any experience of glossolalia there.

While Seymour had been giving pastoral leadership to Rev. Farrow's congregation, a visitor from Los Angeles, Mrs. Neely Terry, attended a service. Very impressed with Seymour's pastoral and godly demeanor, she told her prayer group back in California all about the inspiring pastor in Houston. Sensing divine urgings to establish a "holiness congregation," the prayer group wrote to Seymour, inviting him to come as their pastor and including travel expenses. Seymour jumped at their invitation, seeing in it a "divine call," and in January 1906, after only a few weeks at Parham's school, he left Houston by train for Los Angeles and the more open racial climate of the West.

The enthusiastic little group met Seymour at the train station, and nightly meetings began immediately. Controversy soon erupted, however, when the new preacher began giving sustained attention not just to the holiness teachings of the day, but also to divine healing and glossolalia as a sign attending baptism in the Holy Spirit.* The conflict reached such heights that at one point influential members of the group literally padlocked the meeting house door, refusing entrance to Seymour and those with him. Seymour responded by undertaking a solitary vigil of prayer and fasting that continued for many days. People were moved and drawn to him by this godly example — even those who did not accept his teachings on tongues. Seymour became known as a man of deep prayer.[22]

"This Is That"

Those first months in California were intense times of spiritual searching. Finally, on 9 April 1906, the day after Palm Sunday, a spiritual breakthrough occurred. It began in the home of Edward Lee, a janitor and intimate member of the prayer group. Seymour had anointed him with oil and prayed for him with the laying on of

*These developments underscore how from a historical perspective the Charismatic Tradition grew out of the Holiness Tradition, and they illustrate some of the conflicts this relationship has engendered.

hands, when suddenly Lee burst forth into ecstatic speech. "At last," exclaimed Lee, "This is that."[23]

Astonished and awed, Seymour and Lee walked the short distance to 214 North Bonnie Brae Street, the home where the evening prayer service was to be held. Seymour began preaching to that little prayer group from Acts 2:4: "And they were all filled with the Holy Ghost, and began to speak with other tongues, as the Spirit gave them utterance" (KJV). He never finished his sermon, however, for Lee lifted his hands, opened his mouth, and electrified everyone with a torrent of glossolalia. Immediately the entire company was swept to its knees, as if by some unseen power, amid an outpouring of tongues and sudden joy. Jennie Evans Moore, who later married Seymour, went to the piano (though she did not know how to play) and played flawlessly as she sang (in a voice known for its beauty) in six foreign languages she did not know, with interpretation for each: French, Spanish, Latin, Greek, Hebrew, and Hindustani.[24]

For three days this little prayer group of cooks, janitors, laborers, railroad porters, and washwomen carried on in exuberant celebration and ecstatic worship. Of those days Douglas Nelson writes, "At times they shouted their acclaim for all to hear, at other times an awesome hush descended. Some fell into trances for three, four, or even five hours. Unusual healings were reported. Clusters of people outside whispered reverently that God's power was falling again as in the book of Acts."[25]

On the third night of this spiritual Pentecost—12 April, Maundy Thursday—Seymour himself experienced a deep touch from God. It was late and most people had already left, too tired to continue praying; but Seymour and a white friend remained on their knees, determined to "pray through." Finally his exhausted friend said, "It is not the time," to which Seymour exclaimed, "I am not going to give up." He continued on alone until suddenly

> a sphere of white hot brilliance seemed to appear, draw near, and fall upon him. Divine love melted his heart; he sank to the floor seemingly unconscious. Words of deep healing and

encouragement spoke to him. As from a great distance he heard unutterable words being uttered—was it angelic adoration and praise? Slowly he realized the indescribably lovely language belonged to him, pouring from his innermost being. A broad smile wreathed his face. At last, he arose and happily embraced those around him.[26]

Within days this jubilant, ragtag group was joined by huge crowds of both black and white, necessitating a larger facility. Quickly an old two-story building at 312 Azusa Street was secured. Clearing out the debris and sweeping the dirt floor clean, parishioners placed a pulpit—two large wooden crates—in the center of the room with a prayer altar in front of it. The pews, forming circles surrounding pulpit and altar, were redwood planks laid across nail kegs and old boxes.* Upstairs one long room was designated "the upper room" and was furnished with redwood planks set upon backless chairs for prayer. A single sign cautioned, "No talking above a whisper."[27]

A surge of interest brought huge crowds from virtually every race, nationality, and social class to Seymour's congregation. Meetings were held three times a day—morning, afternoon, and evening—often merging and flowing into one continuous worship experience from early morning to late night. The inside of the building overflowed with perhaps eight hundred persons, while four to five hundred more stood on the board sidewalk outside, squeezing together at the windows and doors in an attempt to see inside. These meetings continued on unabated for three years. The miracle Seymour had been seeking happened: by the power of the Spirit, a revolutionary new type of Christian community was born. As Frank Bartleman, a journalist who chronicled the events of Azusa Street, exclaimed, "The 'color line' was washed away in the blood."[28]

Not only were people streaming to Azusa Street, but they were going out as well. Within weeks of those Holy Week meetings the

---

*The backless pews, which represented a long-traditional preference in African-American Christianity, allowed "room to pray."

first overseas missionaries from Azusa Street departed for Scandinavia, India, and China, followed by others to Africa and elsewhere. In September 1906 Seymour launched a newspaper, *The Apostolic Faith*, which quickly grew to nearly fifty thousand subscribers and was distributed literally around the world. This humble ministry from Azusa Street was indeed "a contribution from the ghetto to the world."[29]

"For Such a Time as This"

What might account for the unusual impact of Seymour and his Azusa Street Mission? Conditions there were the exact opposite of those usually thought essential for any lasting influence. One eyewitness summarized the situation this way: "No choir. . . . No collections are taken. No bills have been posted to advertize the meetings. No church organization is back of it. . . . You find a two-storey whitewashed old building. You would hardly expect heavenly visitations there, unless you remember the stable of Bethlehem."[30] Other leaders, most particularly Charles Parham, had stressed glossolalia as a valuable experience for the Church today. These leaders had greater resources and more extensive contacts than Seymour. But it was at Azusa Street that the power fell, and it was from Azusa Street that the influence went deeper and wider than anywhere else. Why?

The only complete answer to that question, of course, can be found in the wisdom of divine Providence. Azusa Street was a supernatural work, a Spirit-empowered work, a charismatic work. God freely chose the insignificant, the unimpressive, the foolish to show forth his glory. But alongside this, and in conjunction with it, I would like to suggest four additional factors that might help us understand the amazing impact of this work.

First, Seymour understood clearly the implications of glossolalia for interracial reconciliation and community. This he saw in ways that Parham and many of the other white leaders *never* saw. As a son of slaves he understood Pentecost as a new Jubilee requiring the release of the broken and bruised from their oppression. He consistently connected what was happening at Azusa Street with the Pentecostal outpouring in the second chapter of Acts, where the result of the "tongues like as of fire" was reconciliation between nations and races and cultures. In the very first issue of *The Apostolic Faith* Seymour stated, "Multitudes have come. God makes no difference in nationality, Ethiopians, Chinese, Indians, Mexicans, and other nationalities worship together." Three months later, in December 1906, he wrote, "The people are all melted together . . . made one lump, one bread, all one body in Christ Jesus. There is no Jew or Gentile, bond or free, in the Azusa Street Mission. . . . He is no respecter of persons or places."[31] In those early years white leaders came in large numbers, repenting of their racial attitudes and working alongside Seymour.[32] Never in history had any such leadership surged into the church of a black pastor.

At the beginning of the century W.E.B. DuBois declared, "The problem of the twentieth century is the problem of the color-line."[33] In the ministry of William Seymour the color line was overcome, and a challenge of reconciliation was set before the whole world. In some ways the interracial miracle at Azusa Street was more astonishing than the miracle of glossolalia. In Seymour we see the Charismatic Tradition interfacing powerfully with the Social Justice Tradition.

Second, Seymour exercised an equality and acceptance of each person under God as potential participants in leadership. He threw the door wide open for any and all whom God gifted and anointed. In the third issue of *The Apostolic Faith* Seymour noted, "No instrument that God can use is rejected on account of color or dress or lack of education. This is why God has built up the work. . . . The sweetest thing is the loving harmony."[34]

This openness extended all through the social strata of that day, including women. Many of the most powerful leaders flowing out of the Azusa Mission were women—Julia Hutchins, Neely Terry, Jennie Moore, Agnes Ozman, Florence Crawford, and others. Women by the score would arm themselves with Bibles and anointing oil and walk from house to house, looking for people in need. If they found any who were sick, they would anoint them and pray. Then they would volunteer their services in the name of Jesus, cleaning house, doing dishes, caring for children.[35] Affirming this leadership, Seymour declared, "Before Jesus . . . organized His church, He called them all into the upper room, both men and women, and anointed them with the oil of the Holy Ghost, thus qualifying them all to minister in this Gospel. On the day of Pentecost they all preached through the power of the Holy Ghost. In Christ Jesus there is neither male nor female, all are one."[36]

Third, Seymour stressed genuine Christian love above all else. This was more important to him than glossolalia. He wrote, "The Pentecostal power, when you sum it all up, is just more of God's love. If it does not bring more of God's love it is simply a counterfeit. Pentecost means to live right in the 13th chapter of First Corinthians, which is the standard."[37]

This description of divine love as "the standard" was common with Seymour. Sometimes he called it "Jesus' standard" or "the Bible standard"; at other times he spoke of "the Azusa standard." In each case he was pointing people to divine love as the central reality of the Spirit's presence.

Seymour's stress upon the primacy of love is quite astonishing, especially in light of later historical developments in Pentecostalism. Many white leaders simply never understood his insight here, and so they made glossolalia *the* distinctive mark of Pentecostal fellowship. For Seymour, however, the primary evidence of the Holy Spirit was divine love. "Tongues are one of the signs that go with every baptized person, but it is not the real evidence of the baptism in every day life. If you get angry, or speak evil, or backbite, I care not how many tongues you may have, you have not the baptism with the Holy Spirit." "Pentecost," he said, "makes us love Jesus more and love our brothers more. It brings us all into one common family."[38]

This call to "one common family" was a practical ecumenism of the most radical sort. Never content to think of love in the abstract, Seymour felt that it must "make all races and nations into one common family." He longed for a whole Church—not just holy individuals but a divine community inseparably joined together beyond race or gender or class or nation. At one point he exclaimed, "O how my heart cries out to God in these days that He would make every child of His see the necessity of living in the 17th chapter of John, that we may be one in the body of Christ, as Jesus prayed."[39]

The fourth critical element was Seymour himself. The Azusa Street Mission, and the revival movement it spawned, had at its center a holy man. Rev. Glenn Cook, an early leader of the movement, wrote, "This man . . . really lived what we had been preaching for years, a sanctified life. It was the wonderful character of this man whom God had chosen that attracted the people to keep coming to this humble meeting."[40] William Durham of Chicago visited Azusa Street and declared that Seymour was "the meekest man I ever met. . . . He is . . . so filled with God that you feel the love and power every time you get near him."[41]

A key feature of Seymour's leadership was the power of his discernment, allowing him to instantly bring a person or group back to a sense of the holy. As Rachael Sizelove observed, "The Lord gave Brother Seymore [sic] wisdom to rule the people as he did to Moses. No one dared to get up and sing a song or testify except under the anointing of the Spirit."[42]

It was a gentle and long-suffering leadership as well. On one occasion Rev. Cook and other ministers met with Seymour to contend with him over some doctrinal matter. Afterward Cook acknowledged, "The contention was all on our part. I have never met a man who had such control over his spirit. The Scripture that reads, 'Great peace have they that love thy law, and nothing shall offend them,' was literally fulfilled in this man. No amount of confusion and accusation seemed to disturb him. He would sit behind that packing case and smile at us until we were all condemned by our activities."[43]

The impact of Seymour's life and leadership is summed up well by the effect he had on Florence Crawford upon their first meeting. Crawford, after reading the writings of John Wesley, had been seeking long and hard after "perfect love." But to no avail. The counsel she received from the leading clergy of the city had proved fruitless. Finally she visited the Azusa Street Mission:

They sang a little, but that did not seem to touch my heart. They went down in prayer but that didn't move me at all. . . . Finally a big colored man got up on his feet. He said, "Hallelujah!" It just went through my soul. He waited a minute, and again he said, "Hallelujah!" I thought, "God, I have heard the voice from heaven. I have heard it at last. . . . He has the thing my heart is reaching out after."

I forgot everything else, for I heard the voice of the great Shepherd of the sheep. . . . The one thing I wondered was, How could I get it? How could I receive that wonderful blessing on my soul that I had hungered for so long, and that this man had? . . . Oh, the hunger that God planted in my soul! It didn't matter what my people would say—my friends and all—but only, could I get it?[44]

Seymour was truly a powerful example of holy and charismatic elements of life working hand in hand.

Rejection and Obscurity

Seymour's story does not have an altogether happy ending. That ending, twisted and complicated, is a sad account of rejection and condemnation, and I can only sketch out the barest essentials here. The troubles began with Charles Parham, though they certainly did not end with him.

Seymour had invited Parham to Los Angeles, hoping that he would lead area-wide revival meetings to strengthen the movement. Such large-scale meetings were something a black leader simply could not accomplish in the dominant white society, and Seymour needed white partners who would value not only glossolalia but racial equality and Christian unity. Seymour further hoped that Parham—who was then at the height of his power and influence— might assume a leading role in shepherding the movement.

Parham did indeed go to Los Angeles, but unfortunately he was unable to rise to the occasion. Arriving at Azusa Street, he recoiled in disgust at the racial intermingling. He was aghast that black people were not in their "place," and simply could not abide "white people imitating unintelligent, crude negroisms of the Southland, and laying it on the Holy Ghost."[45] Parham made his way through the crowd, stood at the pulpit, and delivered a stinging rebuke: "God is sick at his stomach!" He proceeded to explain that God would not stand for such "animalism."[46]

Up to this point Seymour had believed that Parham's segregated work in Kansas and Texas was a temporary accommodation to local custom, but now his deep-seated social and racial beliefs were all-too clear. In reality, Parham maintained close affinities with the Ku Klux Klan, believed that the mixing of the races had caused the flood in Noah's time, and viewed the Anglo-Saxon race as the lineal descendants of the ten lost tribes of Israel.[47] Needless to say, a sharp line of demarcation appeared between the vision of Seymour and that of Parham.

When it was clear that the majority of the Azusa Street Mission would not accept Parham's leadership, Parham left with an estimated two to three hundred followers and opened a rival campaign at a nearby Women's Christian Temperance Union building. This repudiation of the Azusa work—and competition with it—undermined Seymour's position and seriously weakened the movement. In the years that followed, Parham used every opportunity to condemn the Azusa Street Mission in the strongest possible terms.[48]

Parham's separation was the first, but it was by no means the last.[49] Gradually the white leadership, many of whom had initially truly humbled themselves in the intoxicating milieu of spiritual ecstasy, found reasons to remove themselves from Azusa Street. They could live with glossolalia but not with the revolutionary interracial fellowship that Seymour insisted flowed from it. They abandoned love and reconciliation. The movement split irreparably along racial lines.

Many great and powerful days lay ahead for William Seymour, for there is triumph amid betrayal. Missionaries by the score continued to flow out from Azusa Street, spreading the message of glossolalia and reconciliation worldwide. C. H. Mason, the founder of the Church of God in Christ, came to Azusa Street and was profoundly touched. Seymour and Jennie Evans Moore were married 13 May 1908 and continued to minister together for many years.

However, after 1909 Seymour's influence was only a shadow of what it had been.[50] In 1915 Seymour published *The Doctrines and Discipline of the Azusa Street Apostolic Faith Mission*. It afforded him the opportunity to express several concerns he had about the direction of the Pentecostal movement. He urged "colored brethren" and "white brethren" to love and respect one another, adding, "I hope we won't have any more trouble and division spirit." He expressed his abiding concern for unity: "I can say through the power of the Spirit, that wherever God can get a people that will come together in one accord and one mind in the Word of God, the baptism of the Holy Ghost will fall upon them, like as at Cornelius' house (Acts 10:45–46)." Finally, he warned against viewing glossolalia as the only evidence of the baptism of the Spirit. This, he said, was a change from the beginning days of the Azusa Street Mission. He then gave what he felt were other, more essential evidences, particularly Christian love.[51] This ninety-five-page position paper only underscored the widening breach between Seymour's vision and the direction of the movement he was so instrumental in founding.

Some have suggested that Seymour's decline was due to limited abilities or weak leadership. Yet the real reason for his decline lies in precisely the opposite direction: his leadership was *too* effective, *too* successful. He had called for an all-inclusive community of loving persons beyond the color line. In 1906 Seymour's way was a direct challenge to the prevailing white supremacy. Indeed, if continued, it could well have meant a martyr church. Douglas Nelson writes, "Seymour championed one doctrine above all others: there must be no color line or other division in the church of Jesus Christ because God is no respecter of persons. He resolutely refused to segregate or Jim Crow the movement. . . . For this reason, and this reason alone Seymour was rejected and forgotten by the movement he created."[52]

On 28 September 1922 at age fifty-two William Seymour died in almost total obscurity. A heart attack was the medical cause of death. Some say he died of a broken heart.

Throughout his ministry Seymour was reticent to speak of himself, but following the painful split with Charles Parham, he shared with sixteen-year-old Frank Cummings a dream he had had before the Azusa Street Mission opened. He dreamed he was in a great forest. Small fires broke out, he said, burning and crackling and finally merging into a great wall of flame. In the dream a preacher rushed up to the fire with a wet gunnysack, desperately trying to put it out. But the fire leaped over the preacher and spread far beyond his reach. "Frankie, son," Seymour confided, "this teaching is meant to spread over the entire earth."[53] And so it has.

DEFINING THE CHARISMATIC TRADITION

We do not live our lives "under our own steam"; we were never created to do so. We were created to live our lives in cooperation with another reality. The Charismatic Tradition gives special attention to this other reality, which is, quite simply, life in and through the Spirit of God.

Frankly, there are no "noncharismatic Christians." I understand what is meant by that term, and I see the historical and sociological reasons for it, but the Christian life is by definition a life in and through the Spirit.

The Charismata

Now, the charismata are identifiable expressions of that life in specific forms for specific purposes. Every follower of Jesus is endowed by the Spirit with one or more of these spiritual charisms. These are not the same as natural talents, though they sometimes fit together with them.

The sign of the presence of the charismata is that the effect of one's actions greatly exceeds the input of the human being. In other words, if we knew only what the human being put in, we could not imagine the outcome. The results are always incommensurate to our efforts. It is, you see, a work of the Spirit.

We are fortunate that Paul addressed in considerable detail many practical matters relative to exercising the spiritual gifts. No biblical writer has given us more. The bulk of this teaching is concentrated in three crucial passages: Romans 12, Ephesians 4, and especially 1 Corinthians 12–14. We would do well to meditate at length upon these teachings. In all three we find lists of gifts—lists that, while they vary somewhat, all contain the same essential features: gifts of leadership, such as apostleship, evangelism, and preaching/teaching; ecstatic gifts, such as tongues, discernment of spirits, and prophecy; and gifts that build community life, such as wisdom, faith, and helps.

A person with the charism of apostleship, for example, is endowed with spiritual abilities to pioneer in new areas, planting churches cross-culturally. A person with the charism of evangelism has special spiritual enablement to touch those outside of the community of faith with the evangel, the good news of the gospel. A person with the charism of faith has spiritual abilities to see creative, new possibilities and trust God for them. And so forth.

We must always remember this threefold function of the charisms of the Spirit: leadership, ecstatic empowerment, and community-building. Any efforts to restrict the work of the Spirit to leadership gifts only, or ecstatic gifts only, or community-building gifts only, simply miss the point. This temptation toward restriction arises because of the vested interests and particular histories of differing groups. But it is a temptation that must be resisted if we are to be faithful to the biblical witness.

The ecstatic gifts are most often given to show us that God is present where we assume that he is not. At Pentecost everyone assumed that those disciples huddled together were outlaws. But by supernatural visual aids and heavenly sound effects God demonstrated in no uncertain terms that he was with them (Acts 2:1–13). The same was true at the home of Cornelius. The Jewish Christians, you understand, had assumed that God could not be present and active among

Gentiles, and God had to show them otherwise (Acts 10). And the contemporary story of William Seymour and the folks at Azusa Street is only another verse of the same song. To reiterate: the ecstatic gifts often help us see that God is present and active among peoples and situations we have written off as hopeless.

Building in Love

First Corinthians contains the most extensive teaching we have in the Bible on spiritual gifts. At its center is the famous "love chapter," which should give us some inkling of how central divine love is to any effective functioning of spiritual gifts. The section that precedes 1 Corinthians 13 may be lesser known, but it is intimately tied to it and contains great practical wisdom. I would like to focus on this passage as a summation of the essential principles we need for the exercising of spiritual gifts in such a way that they build rather than destroy community life.[54]

Taking responsibility is the first principle. "Indeed," says Paul, "the body does not consist of one member but of many. If the foot would say, 'Because I am not a hand, I do not belong to the body,' that would not make it any less a part of the body. And if the ear would say, 'Because I am not an eye, I do not belong to the body,' that would not make it any less a part of the body" (1 Cor. 12:14–16). This is a passage for all who feel that they have nothing to offer the community. The charism of helps may have small effect when compared to the charism of prophecy, but it is absolutely essential for life together. *Every* charism is needed, no matter how insignificant it may seem to us.

Accepting limitation is the second principle. "If the whole body were an eye," writes Paul, "where would the hearing be? If the whole body were hearing, where would the sense of smell be? . . . there are many members, yet one body" (1 Cor. 12:17–20). This is a passage for all who feel that they have *everything* to offer the community. No single individual contains all the charisms of the Spirit. We are limited in the good we can accomplish by ourselves. This is a divinely imposed limitation in order to defeat our egoism.

Esteeming others is the third principle. "The eye cannot say to the hand," says Paul, "'I have no need of you,' nor again the head to the feet, 'I have no need of you.' On the contrary, the members of the body that seem to be weaker are indispensable, and those members of the body that we think less honorable we clothe with greater honor, and our less respectable members are treated with greater respect; whereas our more respectable members do not need this" (1 Cor. 12:21–24a). This is a passage for all who feel that they can live independent of the community. Any proper exercise of the charisms of the Spirit is a joint effort. God has arranged the functioning of the gifts in this way so that we will always be dependent upon one another and always esteem each other.

Maintaining unity within diversity is the fourth principle. "God has so arranged the body," teaches Paul, "giving the greater honor to the inferior member, that there may be no dissension within the body, but the members may have the same care for one another. If one member suffers, all suffer together with it; if one member is honored, all rejoice together with it" (1 Cor. 12:24b–26). This is a passage for all who bring division to the community, either deliberately or inadvertently. While we are all different personalities and exercise differing gifts, we still function as a whole. We are inseparably linked together, suffering together and rejoicing together.

What a wonderful description of our life together! Spiritual gifts are given to build us up as a community of faith. But of course this way of living and relating can be done only through an all-encompassing, supernatural love, which is precisely why Paul sets *agape* at the center of his teaching on the charisms of the Spirit. Love, you see, "bears all things, believes all things, hopes all things, endures all things. Love never ends" (1 Cor. 13:7–8a).

DISCOVERING THE MAJOR STRENGTHS

The gains of embracing the Charismatic Tradition—this Spirit-empowered life—are numerous. I shall mention four.

First, the charismatic Tradition offers an ongoing correction to our impulse to domesticate God. We have a perennial tendency to manage and control the work of the Spirit. We want a nice, tidy God. But as Jesus reminds us, the Spirit blows where he wills (John 3:8). This is actually a great grace, for it reminds us that God is in charge of this enterprise, and that he is alive and active in our world. The moment we feel that we have the spiritual-life business all figured out, God surprises us with outbreaks of the Spirit we could never have imagined. All our little attempts—both personally and historically—to institutionalize the Holy Spirit ultimately fail. For this we should thank God. How much better to move day by day in joyful surrender to the leading of the Spirit, in which "the soul, light as a feather, fluid as water, innocent as a child, responds to every movement of grace like a floating balloon."⁵⁵

Second, it offers a constant rebuke to our anemic practice. How easily we become satisfied with mere religious talk. How quickly we accommodate ourselves to "business as usual." How soon we forget that we are to "abound in hope by the power of the Holy Spirit" (Rom. 15:13b). The Charismatic Tradition constantly reminds us that "the kingdom of God depends not on talk but on power" (1 Cor. 4:20).

Third, it offers a continuing challenge toward spiritual growth and development. The Christian virtues are, after all, the fruit of the Spirit. It is by the Spirit that we defeat the "works of the flesh," and it is by the Spirit that we develop the holy habits of love and joy and peace and patience and kindness and generosity and faithfulness and gentleness and self-control (Gal. 5:19–23). The nurturing fruit of the Spirit makes the empowering gifts of the Spirit a blessing and not a curse.

Fourth, it offers a life of gifting and empowering for witness and service. Signs and wonders, miracles and healings, revelations and visions—these are all part of our walk in the Spirit. They become a witness to nonbelievers and an affirmation of hope to believers. The Spirit calls forth evangelistic fervor and accompanies it with signs and wonders. The Spirit bestows gifts of discernment and prophecy to guide the life of the community. The Spirit anoints pastors and teachers for the equipping of the people of God. These (and many other) giftings make manifest the structure of love for building up the body of Christ so that we may "grow up in every way into him who is the head, into Christ, from whom the whole body, joined and knit together by every ligament with which it is equipped, as each part is working properly, promotes the body's growth in building itself up in love" (Eph. 4:15b–16).

UNDERSTANDING THE POTENTIAL PERILS

Perils there are aplenty. As with the strengths, I will confine myself to discussing four—you, no doubt, can think of others.

The first peril is the danger of trivialization. It is so easy for us to be titillated by various phenomena. We can quickly turn signs and wonders into superstition and "magic religion." Without thinking, we often focus on the gift rather than the Giver. This problem is dealt with by effective pastoral care and teaching. Such care demands loving oversight and patience, however. At times we must bear with certain excesses for the greater good. At other times firm guidance is necessary. Throughout, a clear teaching must emerge that the gifts are not an end in themselves, but are for the greater good of the Christian fellowship and for our ongoing formation in the way of Christ.

The second peril is the danger of rejecting the rational and the intellectual. This can easily happen, because the charismatic emphasis is so focused upon the emotive side of our faith. And it *should* be. But it must never reject reason or the mind as a consequence. Emotion and reason are not opposites that we must choose between. The language of Christian conviction here is "both/and" rather than "either/or." The charisms of the Spirit do not offend our rational facilities even though they are not confined to them. We love God with both mind and heart.

The third peril is the danger of divorcing the gifts of the Spirit from the fruit of the Spirit. This was the problem of the Christian community at Corinth, and Paul dealt with it forthrightly. So should we. To be sure, it is possible to move in the realm of spiritual gifts without the maturing that the fruit of the Spirit brings, but to do so will almost always get us in trouble. How much better to see that both proceed from the same Spirit, and that when both are working together, they give balance and wholeness to our lives.

The fourth peril is the danger of linking our walk in the Spirit to highly speculative end-time scenarios that lack theological foundation. Why this tends to be a problem for charismatically oriented groups, I do not fully understand. There have been exceptions—notably the Franciscan movement in the thirteenth century and the Quaker movement in the seventeenth century—but the more common pattern has been for groups stressing the charismata to tie themselves to decidedly unorthodox views of eschatology. Perhaps this has something to do with an overreliance upon visions and prophecy. Most certainly it is tied to the isolation of many of these groups from the other great streams of teaching—most particularly the Social Justice Tradition. But whatever the reason, we need to watch for this pitfall and avoid it at every turn.

PRACTICING THE CHARISMATIC TRADITION

We experience the Charismatic Stream in many different ways and through many different venues. Who can confine the Spirit? Here are a few commonsense suggestions to foster charismatic living.

Draw near to those who have some history and experience in this area of life and learn from them. My own movement in this direction came first from a friend whom I trusted for his wisdom and discernment. Maybe you will experience one of the "shout circles" that are common in African-American Pentecostal groups. In this tradition people gather in a worship circle, and when God rests upon a given person in the group, the rest urge on what God is doing by shouting out their encouragement. Or perhaps you will feel drawn to invite someone to lay hands upon you and pray for you to enter more of the life and joy of the Spirit. Or maybe you will deepen your experience of charismatic worship by attending services known for their strength in this area.

Another suggestion: rest easy with your fears that some aspect of what you are doing is in the flesh. I can guarantee you there will be flesh in it! We will not be totally free from that problem until heaven. But God can still use us in our fumbling, bumbling ways. To be sure, we never want to manipulate others or be manipulated by others. But we should not be afraid to step out and exercise the gifts that we feel God has given us. God will receive us, flesh and all, and teach us how to walk more and more in the power of the Spirit.

A further suggestion: follow your leadings without fear of being misled. If your spirit is teachable, God will show you the way. Press in where you feel the need for more, especially in the area of spiritual gifts. Have a kind of dissatisfied satisfaction—glad for all the good God has given you and yet longing for more. More love. More power. More grace. More gifting. Paul himself urges us to "strive for the greater gifts" (1 Cor. 12:31a).

Perhaps you feel drawings to pray for someone. Or to prophesy, or to bring a healing touch. If so, step out confidently knowing that God is with you and will be your strength.

A final suggestion: regularly test your leadings and experiences in the Spirit with those you trust. Allow their spiritual discernment to encourage, correct, and refine you. And you them. In this way we will fulfill the words of the great Apostle of the Spirit: "Since you are eager for spiritual gifts, strive to excel in them for building up the church" (1 Cor. 14:12).

THE CALL TO SPIRIT-EMPOWERED LIVING

QUESTION: What is the Charismatic Tradition?
ANSWER: A life immersed in, empowered by, and under the direction of the Spirit of God.
QUESTION: Why should we explore it?
ANSWER: Because through it we are empowered by God to do his work and to evidence his life upon the earth.

While the particular manifestations will be tailored to our individual needs and personalities, we are all to enter into life in the Spirit. In 1907 C. H. Mason, founder of the African-American Church of God in Christ, gave us this witness of his own experience at the Azusa Street Mission: "The Spirit came upon the saints and upon me. . . . Then I gave up for the Lord to have His way within me. So there came a wave of Glory into me and all of my being was filled with the Glory of the Lord. So when He had gotten me straight on my feet, there came a light which enveloped my entire being above the brightness of the sun. When I opened my mouth to say 'Glory,' a flame touched my tongue which ran down to me. My language changed and no word could I speak in my own tongue. Oh! I was filled with the Glory of the Lord. My soul was then satisfied."[56]

May we too know such movements of the Spirit upon our lives that we are enabled to say, "My soul was then satisfied."

Chapter 5

❧

The Social Justice Tradition: Discovering the Compassionate Life

Let justice roll down like waters,
  and righteousness like an everflowing stream.
                                    —*Amos 5:24*

True godliness does not turn men out of the world,
but enables them to live better in it and excites
their endeavors to mend it.
                                    —*William Penn*

THE SOCIAL JUSTICE TRADITION*

Notable Figures   *Significant Movements*

0
Jesus of Nazareth
(c. 4 B.C.- c. A.D. 29)

Deacons (1st century to the present)
Order of Widows (1st–4th centuries)
Helena (c. 248–c. 327)
Paulinus (c. 353–431)
Sabas (c. 438–532)
Germanus (c. 496–576)

John the Almsgiver (?–c. 619)
Aidan of Lindisfarne (?–651)
Chad (?–672)
Adamnan (c. 625–704)

Swithun (c. 802–862)
John Gualbert (?–1073)

1000

Vladimir Monomakh (?–1125)
Catherine of Genoa (1447–1510)
Vincent de Paul (c. 1581–c. 1660)   Vincentians
Roger Williams (1603–1683)   (17th century to the present)
John Woolman (1720–1772)
Tikhon of Zadonsk (1727–1783)   Sunday School Movement
Robert Raikes (1735–1811)   (18th century to the present)
William Wilberforce (1759–1833)
Elizabeth Fry (1780–1845)   Abolition Movement
Jean-Baptiste Vianney (1786–1859)   (18th century to the present)
Sojourner Truth (c. 1797–1883)
Anthony Ashley Cooper Shaftesbury (1801–1885)
David Livingstone (1813–1873)
Susan B. Anthony (1820–1906)   Suffrage Movement
Florence Nightingale (1820–1910)   (19th century to the present)
Harriet (Moses) Tubman (c. 1820–1913)
Catherine Mumford Booth (1829–1890)   Salvation Army
William Booth (1829–1912)   (19th century to the present)
Albert Schweitzer (1875–1965)
Toyohiko Kagawa (1888–1960)
Dorothy Day (1897–1980)
Mother Teresa (1910–1997)
Rosa Parks (1913–)
Paul Jewett (1919–1991)
Martin Luther King, Jr. (1929–1968)   American Civil Rights Movement
Desmond Tutu (1931–)   (20th century to the present)
Jean Vanier (1928–)

*See Appendix B for brief biographies and histories.

T HE POWER TO BE the kind of people we were created to be and
the power to do the works of God upon the earth places us on
solid ground to engage the demands of the social arena. And no
place is in greater need of people full of the Holy Spirit and divine
love. The Social Justice Stream of Christian life and faith focuses
upon justice and shalom in all human relationships and social structures. This compassionate way of living addresses the gospel imperative for equity and magnanimity among all peoples.

SEEKING A HISTORICAL PARADIGM

I am eager to introduce John to you. Three reasons cause me to
see him as a powerful example of the Social Justice Tradition. First,
of all the social prophets—those men and women throughout history
who have been advocates for the powerless—he was among the most
contemporary, for he dealt substantively with issues such as racism,
consumerism, and militarism. Second, he brought the power of
"Divine Love" directly into the fray of one of the most volatile social
issues in human history. And third, he labored smack in the midst of
raw humanity, demonstrating a well-nigh amazing humility, compassion, and sensitivity to what he called "Divine Breathings."

Born 19 October 1720 in a modest New Jersey village, John was
destined to stand at the head of a groundswell of antislavery conviction that would assail and eventually conquer slaveholding, first in
his own denomination, the Quakers, and ultimately throughout the
Western world.

"The Operations of Divine Love"

Even as a youth John was deeply sensitive toward matters of the
Spirit. An early journal entry reads, "Before I was seven years old, I
began to be acquainted with the operations of Divine Love."[1] At

twenty-one John left the family farm and was apprenticed to a shop owner in nearby Mount Holly. Here he learned the trade of a tailor as well as becoming qualified to draft legal documents. As a young employee he was soon confronted with the institution of slavery: his employer instructed him to write a bill of sale for his slave. Even at this young age John was so struck by the inherent inconsistency of writing an "Instrument of Slavery" for one of his "fellow creatures" that he told his employer that he "believed Slavekeeping to be a practice inconsistent with the Christian Religion."[2] This was the beginning—the loosened rock before the avalanche.

John soon took over his employer's dry-goods business, added an orchard business of his own, and became moderately prosperous. Soon, however, he became concerned that his business was taking an inordinate amount of his time and energy. "A way of life," he writes, "free from much Entanglements, appeared best for me."[3] As a result, he voluntarily and deliberately pared down his business enterprises in order to give ample time to an itinerant ministry—a ministry he indulged in lavishly.

On one early ministry trip to the South he saw slavery firsthand. He described it as "a dark gloominess hanging over the Land," and more than a hundred years before the Civil War he prophetically saw that in the "future the Consequence will be grievous to posterity."[4]

The focus of John's itinerant labors soon became the abolition of the institution of slavery. He had unusual success with slaveholders because his tough nature was wedded to a gentle spirit. It would be hard to overestimate the power of this combination. His toughness is seen in his refusal to use the products of slave labor, eventually including sugar and dye for clothing. His gentleness is seen in the "inward suffering" he experienced at knowing that his decisions would distress and anger those who opposed him. Often, when entertained in a slaveholder's home, he insisted upon paying the slaves for their services. You can imagine the offense this seemed to his host!

John's tender yet tough concern can be seen in a situation with a Quaker Friend who had had a bad accident. Fearful that he might not live, this man sent for John to write his will. John wrote, "I took notes and amongst other things he told me to which of his children he gave his young Negro woman. I considered the pain and distress he was in, and knew not how it would end, so I wrote his Will save only that part concerning his Slave, and, carrying it to his bed-side read it to him, and then told him in a friendly way, that I could not write any Instruments by which my fellow creatures were made slaves without bringing trouble on my own mind. I let him know that I charged nothing for what I had done, and desired to be Excused from doing the other part in the way he propos'd. We then had a serious conference on the Subject, and at length, he agreeing to set her free I finished his will."[5]

Often John spoke as powerfully through his actions as through his words. A revealing example occurred on 18 November 1758. John, after preaching powerfully against slavery at the Quaker meeting, was taken to the home of Thomas Woodward for dinner. Upon entering the house, he saw servants and inquired as to their status. When he was told that they were slaves, he quietly got up and left the home without a word. The effect of this silent testimony upon Thomas Woodward was enormous. The next morning he freed all of his slaves, in spite of his wife's vigorous objections.[6]

"Some Considerations"

These incidents, however, were at best successful personal encounters. While important, they were not sufficient in themselves, and John knew it. But events were looming on the horizon that would afford John a unique opportunity to attack slavery, at least among Quakers. In 1754 fierce fighting—part of the French and Indian War—broke out on the Pennsylvania frontier. As a result Friends withdrew from Pennsylvania's General Assembly en masse rather than support a vote for troops and war taxes. Denied an effective political platform, Quakers began searching for new ways to express their moral concern.

John seized this opportunity in sermon after sermon, pamphlet after pamphlet. In 1754, with Yearly Meeting* approval, he published "Some Considerations on the Keeping of Negroes: Recommended to the Professors of Christianity of Every Denomination." No anti-slavery document had received such extensive circulation as this little volume, nor had any had as profound an effect. It paved the way for the later vigorous pamphleteering by John Wesley and his Methodists in England.

John's message was devastatingly clear—complete abolition of slavery—but it was communicated in such a modest spirit that it seemed to disarm even the most adamant slaveholder. He argued persuasively that to give freedom to the slave is our Christian duty; even more, it is to our benefit!

> Our Duty and Interest are inseparably united; and when we neglect or misuse our Talents, we necessarily depart from the heavenly Fellowship, and are in the Way to the greatest Evils.
>
> Therefore to examine and prove ourselves, to find what Harmony the Power presiding in us bears with the Divine Nature, is a Duty not more incumbent and necessary, than it would be beneficial.[7]

At this same time Philadelphia Yearly Meeting devoted its annual Epistle to the subject of slavery. John actually wrote this Epistle for the Yearly Meeting, and it was circulated to all other Friends bodies:

> We entreat you to examine whether the purchasing of a Negro, either born here or imported, doth not contribute to a further importation, and consequently to the upholding all the evils above mentioned, and promoting manstealing, the only theft which by the Mosaic law was punished with death. . . . We

*The Yearly Meeting constitutes the major legislative and administrative body among Friends. It covers a particular geographic region and exercises spiritual authority over its members in that region. John was a member of Philadelphia Yearly Meeting.

entreat you in the bowels of gospel love, seriously to weigh the cause of detaining them in bondage. If it be for your own private gain, or any other motive than their good, it is much to be feared that the love of God and the influence of the Holy Spirit is not the prevailing principle in you, and that your hearts are not sufficiently redeemed from the world.[8]

For the next six years John undertook vigorous writing and speaking campaigns. London Quakers added their authority to the cause with an uncompromising stand against slavery. Various Friends of rank voluntarily released their slaves. The groundswell was gaining momentum!

The Great Watershed

The Philadelphia Yearly Meeting Sessions of 1758 became the great watershed for Friends on the slavery question. John Greenleaf Whittier declared that these Sessions "must ever be regarded as one of the most important religious convocations in the history of the Christian Church."[9] Certainly it was a significant gathering, and perhaps it could serve as an instructive model for us today as we seek to grapple with the many social questions plaguing modern society.

The preliminary debates over the slavery issue had been intense and emotional, and John went to the Yearly Meeting Sessions of 1758 resolved to see the issue through to the end. At the Sessions various compromises were proposed to avoid conflict and division. Some Friends proposed that restrictions should be placed on future slavebuying, thus avoiding the volatile subject of present slaveowning. Others said that, due to the weightiness of the matter, a decision should be delayed.

John sat through all these Sessions in total silence, head bowed and eyes brimming with tears. Finally he rose and spoke:

My mind is led to consider the purity of the Divine Being and the justice of His judgment, and herein my soul is covered with awfulness. . . . Many slaves on this continent are oppressed and

their cries have entered into the ears of the Most High. Such
are the purity and certainty of His judgments that He cannot be
partial in our favour. In infinite love and goodness He hath
opened our understandings from one time to another concerning our duty towards this people; and it is not a time for delay.
Should we now be sensible of what He requires of us, and
through a respect to the private interests of some persons, or
through a regard to some friendships which do not stand upon
an immutable foundation, neglect to do our duty in firmness
and constancy, still waiting for some extraordinary means to
bring about their deliverance, God may by terrible things in
righteousness answer us in this matter.[10]

The effect of this timely, prophetic word was profound and total.
To John's compassionate appeal the Yearly Meeting responded, without a single dissent, to remove slavery from its midst.

This was the decisive step. No other religious body—indeed, no
other body of any kind—had taken such dramatic and universal
action against the institution of slavery. To be sure, years of hard work
remained. Many slaveholders needed to be helped to follow the
Yearly Meeting's decision. Other Yearly Meetings had to be convinced to follow the lead of Philadelphia. And much more.

John was deeply involved in these efforts. At times he struggled
long and hard with Friends who were "entangled with the spirit of
this world." At other times he was in great distress over the horrors of
the slave trade; "My Belly trembled, my lips quivered, [my appetite
failed and I grew outwardly weak,] and I trembled in myself that I
might rest in the day of trouble."[11] But always he pressed on. Justice
demanded no less; "Divine Love" demanded no less.

As difficult as it was for the northern Yearly Meetings to rid themselves of slavery, that challenge could not be compared to the obsta-
cles that had to be overcome in the South. North Carolina Quakers
especially had to struggle under the burden of oppressive state laws.
A thousand-dollar bond had to be posted for every slave, and each
one had to be escorted out of the state. To this injustice Friends

appealed in vain to the courts of law. Not only were the petitioners turned down, but sometimes, in apparent defiance, the legislatures and courts passed new laws "to amend, strengthen, and confirm" the previous acts against emancipation.[12]

As a result of this constant harassment, North Carolina Friends took a step unparalleled by any other Quaker body. After consultation with some of the best legal talent in the state, the Yearly Meeting itself became a slaveholder in order to release her individual members from the evil. Friends accomplished this by employing an interesting legal technicality. They used a law that allowed a religious society to become the trustees of donated real estate or personal property; and since the law stated that slaves were merely property, they could be legally donated to the society. This gave *virtual* freedom when *actual* freedom was not recognized by the state.[13]

Institutional Righteousness

As a result of the energetic activity of John and others following the Philadelphia Yearly Meeting decision of 1758, Quakerism—except in rare cases—had freed itself from the institution of slavery by the time the American colonies had declared their independence from English domination! Not one of the antislavery Revolutionary leaders—Washington, Jefferson, or Patrick Henry—was willing to take this step of freeing their slaves, a step that Quakers undertook voluntarily. In light of the difficulty of bringing religious bodies to unity on controversial social issues, it is astonishing that Friends were able to uniformly liquidate human bondage from their ranks. On the other hand, in light of the contradiction between slavery and the spirit of the gospel, it is heartbreaking that Friends ever involved themselves in such oppression in the first place.

Their action was not only bold but costly. Quakers were the *only body* that asked slaveholders to reimburse their slaves for their time in bondage. England paid West Indian planters for their losses when slavery was abolished there. Lincoln proposed the same for southern plantation owners. Friends alone believed that justice demanded exactly the opposite. No hard figures are available on how much was actually paid out or how many Friends complied with the request of their Yearly Meeting. For those who did pay their slaves, it was common to use the yearly wage of the day. We do know that one Mr. F. Buxton, in an appeal before the British House of Commons to abolish slavery, said that it had cost North Carolina Friends fifty thousand pounds to release their slaves.[14] For some southern Friends emancipation of their slaves meant financial bankruptcy; for many, if not most, it meant eventual migration to the North.

Perhaps by now you have recognized that the "John" of my story is John Woolman. I have been quoting from his *Journal*, which has received high praise indeed. The British literary figure Charles Lamb said, "The only American book I ever read twice was the *Journal* of Woolman. . . . Get the writings of John Woolman by heart."[15] Ralph Waldo Emerson declared, "I find more wisdom in these pages than in any other book written since the days of the apostles."[16] In 1797 Samuel Taylor Coleridge commented, "I should almost despair of that man who could peruse the life of John Woolman without an amelioration of heart."[17] To these eminent authors may I add a personal witness, for no book outside of the Bible has influenced me more than *The Journal of John Woolman*. I am endlessly moved by how Woolman wrestled with the knotty issues of war and peace, race and equality, wealth and simplicity, with a striking blending of compassion with courage, tenderness with firmness. And he did this not in some detached, academic way, but right in the midst of the vicissitudes of life. John Woolman was a prophet for his day, a prophet who took the Quaker testimonies for equality, simplicity, and peace and forged them into instruments of social revolution, ever tempering them in the stream of "Divine Love." D. Elton Trueblood has rightly observed that "all who read Woolman have a chance to realize that the best thing in the world is a really good person."[18]

SEEKING A BIBLICAL PARADIGM

The story of Amos is a deeply challenging depiction of the Social Justice Tradition, the compassionate life. The first in a great line of pre-Exilic prophets, Amos declared in no uncertain terms that sacrifices, ceremonies, propitiations, and other externalities of religion were insufficient for a life with God. He insisted that social righteousness—that is, justice in the social realm—was absolutely central to a life that is pleasing to God.[19]

Amos's human credentials for this prophetic work were all on the negative side of the ledger. He had never been to the school of the prophets, yet his prophetic message is among the most incisive ever recorded. He was a southerner from Tekoa in Judah, yet he was sent to Israel in the north. He was a country worker—"a herdsman, and a dresser of sycamore trees"—yet he exercised his prophetic ministry in the most sophisticated of cities: Samaria and Bethel and Gilgal. From a human point of view nothing qualified him for this most unusual prophetic ministry of social righteousness.

But of course Amos's work did not depend upon human credentials or human resources. The *debar Yahweh*, the word of the Lord, had come and he had no option but to proclaim the message given to him. "The lion has roared; / who will not fear? / The Lord GOD has spoken; / who can but prophesy?" (Amos 3:8).

Blatant Injustices

The trumpet call of Amos was a single note: justice, justice, justice. He was scandalized by the blatant injustices that had become so commonplace that no one seemed to notice. And what were these injustices? Listen:

They sell the innocent[20] for silver,
*   and the needy for a pair of sandals—*
they . . . trample the head of the poor into the dust of the earth,
*   and push the afflicted out of the way;*
father and son go in to the same girl,
*   so that my holy name is profaned;*
they lay themselves down beside every altar
*   on garments taken in pledge;*

and in the house of their God they drink
   wine bought with fines they imposed. (Amos 2:6–8)

Ferocious injustices these: selling the poor into slavery, perverting the justice of the oppressed, engaging in illicit sexual intercourse, taking financial advantage of the helpless. All these acts of injustice exhibit a single common denominator: *the abuse of power.*[21] Power here was being used to manipulate, to control, to destroy.

"They sell the needy for a pair of sandals"—creditors selling the weak and vulnerable into slavery even when the debt owed was as trivial as a pair of sandals.

"They trample the poor into the dust"—the powerbrokers of the day using brutal, callous oppression over those who were without power and influence.

"Father and son go in to the same girl"—fathers taking advantage of the cultural inability of women to stand up for their rights and forcing their daughters-in-law into sexual intercourse.

"They lay themselves down on garments taken in pledge"—the wealthy exploiting the destitute by refusing to return a coat that was given in pledge, even though the coat was desperately needed for warmth against the cold night.

"They drink wine bought with fines"—kangaroo courts assessing exorbitant fines and then carousing with the money instead of using it for restitution.

So Amos repudiated and condemned these abuses of power— abuses that allowed the elite of society to "oppress the poor," to "crush the needy" (Amos 4:1).

There is more. Amos also takes the merchants and business leaders of the day to task for theft, graft, and so much more. Listen:

Hear this, you that trample on the needy,
   and bring to ruin the poor of the land,
saying, "When will the new moon be over
   so that we may sell grain;

and the sabbath,
  so that we may offer wheat for sale?
We will make the ephah small and the shekel great,
  and practice deceit with false balances,
buying the poor for silver
  and the needy for a pair of sandals,
  and selling the sweepings of the wheat." (Amos 8:4–6)

It is important for us to hear these stern words of Amos, because it is important for us to know how much God cares about justice in the business arena. Israel at this period was in a golden age. It was mid–eighth century B.C., Jeroboam II was on the throne, and Israel had extended its borders nearly to where they had been in Solomon's day. Political security and economic prosperity abounded, and the people believed that all this abundance was a sign of God's favor.

But Amos came with a different perspective: all their wealth and affluence were the result of the sacrilegious oppression of the poor. To be sure, Israel was a religious people in every way. But their impatience with the religious holidays of sabbath and new moon when commerce had to be suspended revealed their heart. And when they could legitimately engage in the business of commerce, they used crooked weights and measurements. The ephah—a dry measure slightly larger than a half-bushel—was reduced by lining the basket. The shekel—a metal weight of about eleven grams—was enlarged so that it took more gold or silver to balance it on the scales. Beyond all this, the balance itself was bent out of kilter in favor of the seller, so that the poor buyers, impoverished to begin with, ended up paying more to get less. And finally, to add insult to injury, the wheat they sold in shrunken quantities and at inflated prices had "filler" in it, "the sweepings" from the threshing floor. These crooked market practices, these injustices to the weak and the poor, were an offense to God.

But there is *still* more. Amos aimed his verbal accusations at Israel's elite, who were trying to corrupt the legal system and use it to their own advantage. The very system designed to provide justice for all equally was being perverted. Listen:

> They hate the one who reproves in the gate,
>   and they abhor the one who speaks the truth.
> Therefore because you trample on the poor
>   and take from them levies of grain,
> you have built houses of hewn stone,
>   but you shall not live in them;
> you have planted pleasant vineyards,
>   but you shall not drink their wine.
> For I know how many are your transgressions,
>   and how great are your sins—
> you who afflict the innocent,[22] who take a bribe,
>   and push aside the needy in the gate. (Amos 5:10–12)

"The gate" of the city was the center of judicial decision making, the place where the elders gathered to hear witnesses, arbitrate disputes, decide controversies, and dispense justice. Alcoves in the gate area were used as courtrooms. Amos's condemnation of those who hate the person who "reproves in the gate" and abhor the person who "speaks the truth" evidenced a total disdain for Hebrew judicial process. In another passage Amos was even more pointed,

> Ah, you that turn justice to wormwood,
>   and bring righteousness to the ground! (Amos 5:7)

The reference to taking "levies of grain" from the poor spoke of the crime of overcharging tenant farmers for the use of the land. Likely the land had been stolen from the tenant farmers by fraud in the first place, and now harsh practices of taxation were being added to their already overburdened lives.

"The gate" was supposed to be the place where every member of society could expect to receive a fair hearing. But now, declared

Amos, illegal actions were being used to intimidate the "innocent" and reject the valid claims of the poor. Specifically, regular bribery was denying the poor their legitimate rights—and not just now and again, but repeatedly.[23]

Justice and Liturgical Worship

On numerous occasions Amos took aim at the liturgical life of Israel, but no outburst was more scathing than this first-person diatribe against their vain worship:

> I hate, I despise your festivals,
>   and I take no delight in your solemn assemblies.
> Even though you offer me your burnt offerings and grain
>   offerings,
>   I will not accept them;
> and the offerings of well-being of your fatted animals
>   I will not look upon.
> Take away from me the noise of your songs;
>   I will not listen to the melody of your harps.
> But let justice roll down like waters,
>   and righteousness like an everflowing stream. (Amos 5:21–24).

The intensity and passion of this passage is breathtaking! God is the speaker now, and in powerful parallelisms he scorns the empty worship of the people and demands that they give a ceaseless exhibition of justice. All three elements of Israel's liturgical worship come under review here, and all three are soundly rejected.

Israel gloried in her joyous festivals and solemn assemblies. (Actually, the word *solemn* is not the best translation of the adjective here; *ceremonial* would catch the sense better.) These events were exuberant, noisy celebrations filled with color and pageantry. But God's rejection of these festive events is stated in the strongest language possible: "I hate, I despise . . . I take no delight." Why would God so utterly repudiate these great festival events in his honor?

The religious rituals of the sacrifices and the offerings are likewise rejected. The burnt offering, in which the animal sacrifice was completely consumed on the altar, represented a total giving of the person to God. The grain offering, in which tribute from the harvest was paid to God, represented the giving of life and resources to God. The peace offering, in which part of the animal sacrifice was burnt and part was shared as a meal between the priests and the worshipers, represented devotion to God and communion with each other. But God will not accept them, will not even look upon them, declares Amos. Why would God so completely reject these offerings made in his name?

Finally, God declares his displeasure with the community's songs of worship. What a contrast that denunciation of song is to the call to worship issued by the Psalmist:

> Praise the LORD with the lyre;
>   make melody to him with the harp of ten strings.
> Sing to him a new song;
>   play skillfully on the strings, with loud shouts. (Ps. 33:2–3)

Why would God turn a deaf ear to the worship music of his people?

The circle has been completed. Each major area of Israel's liturgical worship—festivals, sacrifices, music—has been evaluated and soundly condemned. But why? Why would these acts of devotion be so utterly spurned? Was it because of ritual impurity? Was it because of compromise with Canaanite religious practices? Was it because of a lack of zeal in religious exercises? No, no, and no. One reason, and one reason alone, accounted for God's forthright rejection of their religious devotion: all of the festivals, all of the sacrifices, all of the instruments and music of worship failed because they were not accompanied by acts of justice and righteousness. And so the word of the Lord thunders forth:

> Let justice roll down like waters,
>   and righteousness like an everflowing stream.

For Israelites this was graphic imagery. Living in the desert, they knew well the characteristics of the wadi, the streambed. Much of the year the wadi is bone-dry and of no benefit to anyone, but when the rains come, the first rushing wall of water flows with such force that anyone caught in the wadi will surely be swept away and drowned. And so Amos calls for justice *(mishpat)* to roll down like the raging torrent in a freshly fed wadi. Yet unlike that water in the wadi, which often dwindles to nothing, this righteousness is to be an everflowing stream, flowing day after day, year in and year out, under good circumstances and bad:

> *Let justice roll down like waters,*
> *and righteousness like an everflowing stream.*

God, you see, demands something more revolutionary than festivals and sacrifices and worship songs. And that "something more" is social righteousness: impartiality in judicial decisions, equity in business dealings, justice for the poor and the oppressed. Because social righteousness is a divine mandate, liturgical life can never be divorced from it.

This is the message of Amos. It is not a popular message today. It was not a popular message then. Amaziah, the presiding priest of Bethel's sanctuary, appeared on the scene and tried to put a stop to Amos's damming prophecies against Israel, saying, "O seer, go, flee away to the land of Judah, earn your bread there, and prophesy there; but never again prophesy at Bethel, for it is the king's sanctuary, and it is a temple of the kingdom" (Amos 7:12–13). No doubt this threat simply brought to the surface the smoldering antipathy between Amos and the religious and political bureaucracies of Israel. It was not, however, an idle threat: it was, in fact, a death threat if Amos refused to comply.

But refuse he did, and we see prophetic conviction and courage in his words: "I am no prophet, nor a prophet's son; but I am a herdsman, and a dresser of sycamore trees, and the LORD took me from following the flock, and the LORD said to me, 'Go, prophesy to my people Israel'" (Amos 7:14–15). Amos first made it clear to Amaziah that he was not a professional prophet whose livelihood depended upon his ministry; he earned his living another way. Then he pointed out that his prophetic call and the assigned audience were of one piece.

Following this exchange, we have the only judgment speech in the book aimed at a single individual. In so doing, Amos was following in the prophetic tradition of Nathan, Elijah, and Elisha. Amaziah had sinned in two ways when he commanded Amos to stop prophesying to Israel: challenging God's authority by stifling the prophetic word, and failing in his priestly duties by becoming the king's puppet. The punishment, though severe, fit the crime: the total destruction of Amaziah's priestly line and his own death in an "unclean land"—that is, in a ceremonially defiled land, a horrifying rebuke to all Amaziah's priestly instincts (Amos 7:16–17).

Visions of Judgment and Hope

Having mentioned the judgment against Amaziah, I want to make a few comments about the judgment oracles in the book of Amos.

The first thing that needs to be said is that these were judgments against Israel, and we cannot universalize them. We must not try to apply these exact judgments to other settings—say, the United States or Russia or South Africa or Argentina.

But the second thing we must say is that these dreadful judgments show God's deep passion for justice in society, and we must not presume upon divine patience. If we fail to provide justice and equity, do we think that God will turn a deaf ear to the cries of the poor and dispossessed?

My third comment is in defense of Amos. Because he was called to deliver judgment oracles, it is easy for us to caricaturize him as a sign-carrying, doom-loving prophet. But such was not the case. Amos himself wished that the matter could be otherwise, and he pleaded with his hearers:

> *Hate evil and love good,*
>   *and establish justice in the gate;*
> *it may be that the* LORD, *the God of hosts,*
>   *will be gracious to the remnant of Joseph. (Amos 5:15)*

In fact, Amos struggled against his own judgment oracles. In the midst of his prophetic work God gave Amos a vision of judgment, depicted by locusts destroying the "latter growth"—that is, coming at a time when Israel's crops were the most vulnerable. Amos cried out against the vision:

> *O Lord* GOD, *forgive, I beg you!*
>   *How can Jacob stand?*
>   *He is so small! (Amos 7:2)*

And divine judgment was restrained in response to Amos's pleas.

Then God showed Amos a second vision, this one a "shower of fire" that consumed not only everything on the arable land but the "great deep" as well—that is, the underground water supply used to replenish crops following a fire. Again, Amos pleaded for the hand of judgment to be held back:

> *O Lord* GOD, *cease, I beg you!*
>   *How can Jacob stand?*
>   *He is so small! (Amos 7:5)*

And a second time God relented.

But in the third vision the focus shifted from the *fact* of judgment to the *basis* for judgment. Amos was shown a plumb line, the covenant standard of obedience to God's call for justice and righteousness. And Israel failed to measure up; her life was too crooked to warrant either pardon or relief. This time Amos was the one who had to relent. Judgment *had* to come. But it was only the overwhelming, divinely given conviction that justice cannot be separated from litur-

gical life that allowed Amos to carry out the judgment pronounce-
ments that he did.

One more comment. Judgment was not the last word for Amos,
nor is it the last word for us. How surprising that a book dominated by
doom should end with such hope. As David Allan Hubbard has written, "The sword of judgment gives way to the trowel of reconstruction. The day of darkness . . . is replaced by a day of light."[24] Listen to
Amos's final oracle, an oracle of hope and promise:

> *The time is surely coming, says the LORD,*
> *when the one who plows shall overtake the one who*
> *reaps,*
> *and the treader of grapes the one who sows the seed;*
> *the mountains shall drip sweet wine,*
> *and all the hills shall flow with it. (Amos 9:13)*

If the book of Amos is the story of the complete reversal of Israel's
fate from covenant people to humiliated outcasts, then the ending
Amos speaks of is "the healing reversal of tragic reversal."[25] God's
covenant commitment, which made Israel's crimes so unspeakable
and divine judgment so necessary, is ultimately expressed in *hesed*,
God's everlasting covenant love. And it is that covenant love which
closes the book of Amos in words of brilliant hope: "I will restore the
fortunes of my people Israel" (Amos 9:14).

Amos walks across the prophetic scene as a shadowy figure. We know
virtually nothing about him, unlike many of the other prophets. But
perhaps this anonymity has worked to our advantage, for it has forced us
to focus all of our attention upon the message he brings: the message of
justice and social righteousness. It is a message we do well to heed.

SEEKING A CONTEMPORARY PARADIGM

The people I have been writing about move me endlessly. Often I
have to brush away tears so that I can see to write. Dorothy Day, and
the story of her life among the poor, is no exception.

Dorothy Day has been called a saint, a prophet, a legend in her own time. She was most certainly all of these things, though she herself would have fought the labels; they make it too easy to dismiss her, she would say. I would like to suggest another title, one that might make it more difficult to dismiss her as irrelevant to our lives: Dorothy Day was, and is, "a living reproach" to a Church that has become self-satisfied with its affluence and privileged position.[26] She was, and is, a living reproach to us who care more about the number of shopping days until Christmas than we care about the poor. She was, and is, a living reproach to us who love status more than we love justice and shalom. She was, and is, a living reproach to us who set aside the concerns of social justice in favor of evangelism. She was, and is—quite simply—a living reproach.

Growing

The third child of John and Grace Day, Dorothy was born 8 November 1897 in New York City. The city of her birth is important. While she lived in other places—San Francisco, Chicago, New Orleans, Mexico City—New York was where she always returned, and New York was where her most enduring work occurred. New York City was in her blood.

Her most vivid childhood memory, however, came from the San Francisco Bay Area (Oakland) rather than New York. She was only seven years old when her family moved to the Bay Area in 1904—two years before the famous 1906 earthquake. The devastation from that earthquake forced the family to move almost immediately, first to Chicago's South Side and later, when Dorothy's father took a newspaper job, to the North Side.

These were the tender years for Dorothy, years filled with sensitivities toward beauty and thoughts of a God whose strength and grace could fill her with joy and make her "Christlike." At fifteen she wrote of long walks through the multicultural streets of Chicago, enraptured by its sights and sounds and smells. And lovely walks in the park, drinking in its solitude and beauty: "How I love the park in winter! So solitary and awful in the truest meaning of the word. God is there. Of course, He is everywhere but under the trees and looking over the wide expanse of lake He communicates Himself to me and fills me with a deep quiet peace."[27]

Seeking

The innocence of childhood, however, must always give way to the ambiguity of adulthood, and for Dorothy this occurred in 1913 with her entrance at sixteen into the University of Illinois in Urbana. Thoughts of God now faded into the background as her dream of becoming a journalist and writer came to the fore—a dream that would be fulfilled many times over throughout her prodigious life. It was also a time of vigorous political ferment as Dorothy interacted with the popular socialist ideologies of that era. The passionate discussions she heard and participated in struck a responsive chord in this young student tender to issues of justice and poverty.

By 1916 Dorothy was back in the city of her birth, New York, working as a reporter for *The Call*, a socialist newspaper. Quickly she immersed herself into the radical Greenwich Village scene and soon was working for *The Masses*, a monthly magazine whose editors and contributors were the intellectual aristocracy of America's left. Here she was thrust into the brilliant New York intellectual scene with writers such as Mike Gold, Max Eastman, and Floyd Dell. It was a heady time: a time of socialist and communist and anarchist sympathies, a time of interviewing Trotsky and reporting on child labor and investigating munitions makers, a time of picket lines and labor strikes and anticonscription rallies.

Dorothy's later assessment of herself during this period was brutally honest: "I was not a good radical; I was not worthy of respect like those great figures in the movement who were fighting the issues of the day."[28] Perhaps. But to say the least, she was deeply immersed in the sufferings of the poor and passionately involved in causes of justice. To be sure, Dorothy was by no means a Christian yet, but her young, energetic heart-cry against injustice expressed Christian concern.

Work as a reporter was so intently focused upon things immediate and temporal that it squeezed out any space for reflection on things immutable and eternal. "Life on a newspaper," she observed, "whether radical or conservative, makes one lose all sense of perspective at the time. You are carried along in a world of events, writing, reporting, with no time at all for thought or reflection."[29]

In 1917, as an idealistic twenty-year-old, she experienced her first arrest and imprisonment (far from her last), having marched with the suffragettes in Washington, D.C. It was a horrifying thirty days, and the ugliness of that event never left her: "I would never be free again, never free when I knew that behind bars all over the world there were women and men, young girls and boys, suffering constraint, punishment, isolation and hardship for crimes of which all of us are guilty. . . . I would be utterly crushed by misery before I was released. Never would I recover from this wound, this ugly knowledge I had gained of what men were capable in their treatment of each other."[30]

This was also a promiscuous period in her life—she called it her "Bohemian life." She had a sad love affair with an ex-newspaperman, Lionel Moise, got pregnant, and endured a heart-wrenching abortion.[31] (Ever after she was a staunch foe of abortion.) On the rebound she married Barkeley Tobey, a founder of the Literary Guild. It was a bad marriage from the start, and after a year together in Europe it ended.

But even through this period of emotional upheaval and shifting political loyalties, nascent spiritual yearnings continued to mingle with her deep commitment to social justice. Since adolescence she had had an enduring love for *The Imitation of Christ*, calling it the book that "followed me through my days."[32] Pascal's *Pensées* stirred her, and the Russian writers Dostoyevsky and Tolstoy awoke in her enduring passions for suffering humanity and social righteousness. She was particularly taken with the compassionate Father Zossima in *The Brothers Karamazov*, who "spoke glowingly of that love for God which resulted in a love for one's brother. The story of his conversion to love is moving, and that book, with its picture of religion, had a lot to do with my later life."[33] After sitting all night in taverns, she would sometimes slip into an early-morning Mass at St. Joseph's Church on Sixth Avenue and kneel at the back, "not knowing what was going on at the altar, but warmed and comforted by the lights and silence, the kneeling people and the atmosphere of worship."[34]

Dorothy became friends with the playwright Eugene O'Neill, who introduced her to Francis Thompson's poem "The Hound of Heaven." Eugene knew the poem by heart, and in a back room of a saloon nicknamed "Hell Hole," amid drink and smoke, he "would sit there, black and dour," recounting the soul's flight from divine love and God's unrelenting pursuit.[35]

> I fled Him, down the night and down the days;
> I fled Him, down the arches of the years;
> I fled Him, down the labyrinthine ways
>   Of my own mind; and in the mist of tears
> I hid from Him, . . . [36]

Of those recitations Dorothy said, "The idea of this pursuit by the Hound of Heaven fascinated me. The recurrence of it, the inevitableness of the outcome made me feel that sooner or later I would have to pause in the mad rush of living and remember my first beginning and my last end."[37]

Finding

Dorothy Day did indeed come to remember that "first beginning" and "last end." It happened in this way.[38] With money—five thousand dollars—from the movie rights to her first novel, The Eleventh Virgin, she purchased a small house on a Staten Island beach, intending to settle down and write. Here in 1926 she met and fell in love with Forster Batterham, a biologist, anarchist, and committed atheist. The love was mutual, and they entered "a common-law marriage," Forster's hostility toward "all man-made institutions" making any other marriage arrangement out of the question.[39] Forster's work took him into New York through the week, but he returned to be with Dorothy on the weekends. That made the Staten Island cottage a perfect writer's hermitage. It was a happy time for the two of them.

Forster teased Dorothy away from her books and her causes and into his love of nature: slow hours of fishing and long walks on the beach and endless gathering of driftwood for the fireplace. She said that Forster "used to insist on walks no matter how cold or rainy the day, and this dragging me away from my books, from my lethargy, into the open, into the country, made me begin to breathe . . . a new experience entirely for me, one which brought me to life, and filled me with joy."[40]

This love of all things natural awakened in Dorothy yearnings for all things eternal. She was happy, blissful. And out of sheer joy she began praying once again—praying her gratitude and thanksgiving, praying the Te Deum as she walked the beach. Ironically, though, the very events that were breathing life into Dorothy's soul were also erecting a wall between her and Forster: "The very love of nature, and the study of her secrets which was bringing me to faith, cut Forster off from religion."[41]

And then Dorothy became pregnant. For her the news was a "blissful joy." She was enraptured with the awareness of how utterly good God is and how filled with everlasting love. The pregnancy was truly a converting experience for Dorothy: "I read the *Imitation of Christ* a great deal during those months. I knew that I was going to have my child baptized, cost what it may. . . . For myself, I prayed for the gift of faith. I was sure, yet not sure."[42]

She was coming to faith—institutional Catholic faith at that! And that journey was erecting an insurmountable barrier between her and Forster: "Becoming a Catholic would mean facing life alone and I clung to family life. It was hard to contemplate giving up a mate in order that my child and I could become members of the Church. Forster would have nothing to do with religion or with me if I embraced it. So I waited."[43]

The decision was agonizing for both of them: "He stayed out late on the pier fishing, and came in smelling of seaweed and salt air; getting into bed, cold with the chill November air, he held me close to him in silence. I loved him in every way . . . I loved him for the odds and ends I had to fish out of his sweater pockets and for the sand and shells he brought in with his fishing. I loved his lean cold body as he got into bed smelling of the sea, and I loved his integrity and stubborn pride."[44] In the end, however, baby Tamar Teresa was baptized into Christ's church. Dorothy too. And Forster left. It was late December 1927.

Serving

Dorothy Day was now thirty years of age: fending for herself, caring for her daughter, maturing in her newfound faith. She moved into an apartment on New York's West Fourteenth Street "in order to be near Our Lady of Guadalupe Church,"[45] took a job with the Fellowship of Reconciliation, and eked out a living, as did most people during those early years of the Great Depression. It was during this time that she heard the lament of Pope Pius XI: "The workers of the world are lost to the Church."[46] Those words put fire in her bones, and she determined that she would devote the rest of her life to working against the assumptions of that utterance. But how?

On 8 December 1932, at the height of the Depression, Dorothy was in Washington, D.C., reporting on a "hunger strike" being staged by a small army of desperately impoverished demonstrators who were pleading for food and the chance to work. Saddened and angered at the brutal treatment of these demonstrators and at the conditions that made them so vulnerable, Dorothy went to the National Shrine of the Immaculate Conception at Catholic University to pray. The upper church was still under construction, so she went into the crypt beneath, with its low vaulted ceilings and dark chapels lit by the flickering of vigil candles. "There," she wrote, "I offered up a special prayer, a prayer which came with tears and with anguish, that some way would open up for me to use what talents I possessed for my fellow workers, for the poor."[47]

Returning to her New York apartment, she found a stranger waiting to meet her. "I am Peter Maurin," he said in a thick French accent. "George Shuster, editor of *The Commonweal*, told me to look you up. Also, a red-headed Irish Communist in Union Square told me to see you. He says we think alike."[48] It was the beginning of a lifelong collaboration that proved to be the vivid answer to Dorothy's desperate prayer. Dr. Robert Coles, who knew Dorothy well, wrote, "On many occasions Dorothy made it quite clear that for her Peter's 'spirit and ideas' were utterly essential to the rest of her life. She was inspired by his struggle to make the principles of Jesus incarnate in the kind of life he lived, to rescue them from those who had turned Him into an icon of Sunday convenience. The Catholic Worker Movement would become their shared initiative."[49] As they talked for days that became weeks and then months, Dorothy realized that "Peter's spirit and ideas" paralleled her own heart and vision.

"Peter's spirit" spoke of a radical embodiment of the gospel call to love God and neighbor. It meant embracing voluntary poverty through living with the poor and suffering with the poor; it meant engaging in a radical pacifism as a witness to loving all people, especially enemies; it meant doing the "corporal works of mercy" by feeding the hungry, clothing the naked, and housing the homeless; it meant doing the "spiritual works of mercy" by consoling the afflicted, bearing wrongs patiently, and, as Dorothy wrote, "we have always classed picket lines . . . among these works."[50] And more.[51]

"Peter's ideas" were strategies of action aimed at social reconstruction. Idealistic, visionary strategies: like a radical newspaper to publicize Catholic social teaching; like hospitality houses where the affluent could personally serve the poor and afflicted; like communal farms where manual labor, prayer, and the "green revolution" could flourish; like roundtable discussions where people of all occupations, backgrounds, and social situations could come together to seek out a common future; like "agronomic universities" where the worker could become a scholar and the scholar a worker; like spiritual retreats where solitude, silence, and faith could deepen and grow. And more. Throughout, Peter aimed at producing, as he put it, "a society where it is easier for men to be good."[52]

Dorothy's whole life had revolved around journalism, so the newspaper came first. They called it *The Catholic Worker*, the very name showing Dorothy's determination to overcome the pope's lament about workers being "lost to the Church."[53] "Workers" were defined in a broad sense, to be sure, but the focus from the beginning was upon "the poor, the dispossessed, the exploited."[54] From their own resources and what was offered them from two priests and a nun, they scraped together fifty-seven dollars—just enough to print up 2,500 copies of the first edition. On May Day 1933, walking from New York's Lower East Side to Union Square, they peddled their paper for "a penny a copy." By 1936 it had a circulation of over 150,000. To this day it still sells for "a penny a copy."

From the beginning it was a newspaper with a sting. In her first editorial Dorothy declared that this paper was

> For those who are huddling in shelters trying to escape the rain,
>   For those who are walking the streets in the all but futile
> search for work,
>   For those who think that there is no hope for the future, no
> recognition of their plight . . . [55]

Peter's unique blend of radical manifesto and "prose poetry" also found its way into the first issue:

Christ drove the money lenders
out of the Temple.
But today nobody dares
to drive the money lenders
out of the Temple . . .
because the money lenders
have taken a mortgage
on the Temple.[56]

The Catholic Worker reflected in unambiguous terms Dorothy's conviction that following Jesus required the renunciation of hatred and killing. Many Catholics found this line of teaching shocking, perhaps even heretical. The Spanish Civil War of 1936 brought the issue to a head. Nearly every bishop and Catholic publication rallied behind Franco and his fascist party, who presented themselves as defenders of the Catholic faith. *The Catholic Worker* refused to toe the line and even came out with articles warning readers of the anti-Semitism that was characteristic of fascism. Furious letters poured into *The Catholic Worker*. Dorothy's editorial reply: "We all know that there is a frightful persecution of religion in Spain. . . . [Even so,] we are opposed to the use of force as a means of settling personal, national, or international disputes."[57]

The issue became even more volatile for Americans following the Japanese attack on Pearl Harbor and the United States' declaration of war. The next issue of the newspaper carried this headline: WE CONTINUE OUR CHRISTIAN PACIFIST STAND. Inside, Dorothy's editorial was as uncompromising as ever: "We will print the words of Christ, who is with us always even to the end of the world. 'Love your enemies, do good to those who hate you.' . . . Our manifesto is the Sermon on the Mount, which means that we will try to be peacemakers. Speaking for many of our conscientious objectors, we will not participate in armed warfare or in making munitions, or by buying government bonds to prosecute the war, or in urging others to these efforts."[58]

You can imagine the wave of subscription cancellations that followed. But Dorothy would not budge. For her it was an issue of love: she was fond of quoting St. John of the Cross: "Love is the measure by which we shall be judged." All through the Second World War and all through the Korean War she was a lonely voice crying in the wilderness, crying for the ways of peace. Only with the Vietnam War did other voices join with her.

The houses of hospitality were Peter and Dorothy's central strategy for engaging in the "works of mercy." They began these houses in the simplest way possible: renting a place, buying bread and butter, making coffee, preparing soup, and inviting the poor to eat. Whenever possible they provided the homeless with a place to sleep; and most important, they sat with the poor, talking with them and offering friendship and affection. In time there were over thirty "houses of hospitality" throughout the nation. Some floundered; others flourished; all gave love and tangible aid.[59]

The farming communes were utopian efforts at radical Christian community. Dorothy articulated the dream: "There could be, I believe, groups of families on the land, surrounding a chapel, disciplined by family life and daily attendance at Mass, all subject to one another, with a division of skills and labor and accepting too the authority of one coordinator."[60] But like many utopian dreams these farm communities struggled against the hard realities of human selfishness and individualism. They did give a toehold on the land and allowed for energetic experiments in "the green revolution," however. They were also places where Catholic Workers could forge a Christian philosophy of work: "God is our creator. God made us in His image and likeness. Therefore we are creators. He gave us a garden to till and cultivate. We become co-creators by our responsible acts, whether in bringing forth children, or producing food, furniture or clothing. The joy of creativeness should be ours."[61] In the end the majority of these farming experiments failed. "We aimed high, too high," said Dorothy. "But at least we were able, as Peter said, 'to arouse the conscience.'"[62]

The Maryfarm Retreat House in upstate New York was probably the most successful of these community farms, in part because it became tied to another of The Catholic Worker visions: retreat.

Daily life in The Catholic Worker communities involved constant and inescapable crises: fights on the picket lines, life-threatening encounters with structures of injustice, the heartbreaking human needs of malnutrition and sickness and mental breakdown and drunkenness and hysterical, despairing individuals. Something was needed to strengthen and sustain those working in such desperate circumstances. That "something" was The Catholic Worker involvement in the Lacouture Retreat Movement. "The Retreat," as it came to be called, was an adaptation of the classical Ignatian Retreat.

Dorothy's first introduction to this experience came through Father Pacifique Roy, a priest who, like Dorothy, believed that the

Gospels called people to a way of life that was profoundly revolution-ary. Of that first experience Dorothy wrote, "We were sitting in the dining room having our morning coffee when Father Roy started to talk to us about the love of God and what it should mean in our lives. He began with the Sermon on the Mount, holding us spellbound, so glowing was his talk, so heartfelt. People came and went, we were called to the telephone again and again, but still Father Roy went on talking to all who would listen. The men came in from the soup ket-tles in the kitchen which were being prepared for the soup line and stayed to listen, tables were set around us and the people came in and were fed and went out again, and still Father talked. . . . He . . . filled us with the spirit of joy while he talked."[63]

In time these retreats became a regular feature of Catholic Worker life. They had retreats of "silence and recollection," study retreats, prayer retreats. In 1937 they had a "retreat for the unemployed" led by Monsignor Fulton J. Sheen.[64] The retreats were a wonder and a strength to Dorothy: "Those were beautiful days. It was as though we were listening to the gospel for the first time. We saw all things new. There was a freshness about everything as though we were in love, as indeed we were."[65]

The life and work of Dorothy Day speak to us on many levels. Her radical identification with the poor, her vigorous championing of the cause of the worker, her works of mercy to the homeless, her willing-ness to be spent in the cause of Christ—all stand as a living reproach to we who are "at ease in Zion."

Not long before Dorothy's death Dr. Robert Coles visited her for one last time. "It will soon be over," she told him, then added, "I try to think back; I try to remember this life that the Lord gave me; the other day I wrote down the words 'a life remembered,' and I was going to try to make a summary for myself, write what mattered most—but I couldn't do it. I just sat there and thought of our Lord, and His visit to us all those centuries ago, and I said to myself that my great luck was to have had Him on my mind for so long in my life!"[66]

For nearly fifty years Dorothy had written a column in *The Catholic Worker* entitled "On Pilgrimage." Well, on 29 November

1980, at 5:30 P.M., that pilgrimage ended. "It was a death," wrote her colleague Jim Forest, "as quiet as the turning of a page."[67]

A huge checkerboard of humanity gathered for the funeral Mass: well-known writers and editors and the homeless from the streets, believers and atheists, left and right. Some had traveled thousands of miles. Among the sea of mourners on that sad day stood Forster Batterham, the man whom, in spite of over a half-century's separation, Dorothy still called "husband."[68]

DEFINING THE SOCIAL JUSTICE TRADITION

Social justice is where the central issue in the Holiness Tradition—love—meets the road. Dag Hammarskjöld wrote, "The road to holiness necessarily passes through the world of action."[69] And so the supernatural resources to live appropriately—to live the virtuous life—now extend out into our relationships with people and with social structures and even with the earth itself.

Two Sweeping Movements

The fulcrum for the Social Justice Tradition is Matthew 22:37–40: "'You shall love the Lord your God with all your heart, and with all your soul, and with all your mind.' This is the greatest and first commandment. And a second is like it: 'You shall love your neighbor as yourself.' On these two commandments hang all the law and the prophets."[70]

In Jesus' day there were 613 commandments of Jewish law—365 negative and 248 positive. And Jesus gathers them all together into two sweeping movements of the heart. Love of God is the vertical movement and love of neighbor the horizontal. They are separate commandments, to be sure, but inseparable really. White-hot love of God compels us into compassionate love of neighbor.

In Luke's rendering of this teaching a lawyer asks Jesus, "Who is my neighbor?" (Luke 10:29b). That is a good question. The common view of that day was that "neighbor" meant "cultural equivalent": the person who looks like me, dresses like me, thinks like me. To explode that common view of neighbor, Jesus tells the now-famous story of a Samaritan—someone who is definitely not the Jew's cultural equivalent—who showed compassion on a beaten and broken Jew, the avowed enemy of the Samaritan. That's it! Neighbor, says Jesus, is "nigh-bor," the person near us, the person in need. Jesus refuses to put walls around the word *neighbor*. No national heritage, no racial origin, no ethnic background, no barriers of class or culture can separate us from our neighbor.

Paul gives this same issue memorable expression when he says, "There is no longer Greek and Jew, circumcised and uncircumcised, barbarian, Scythian, slave and free; but Christ is all and in all!" (Col. 3:11). I especially like this listing because Paul includes the Scythian in it. The Scythians were the barbarian's barbarians—Josephus called them "wild beasts." But in Jesus even the Scythian is my neighbor, whom I am to love as myself.

In his Sermon on the Mount Jesus pushes the horizontal movement of love of neighbor to the nth degree. In this teaching he reminds us that loving our "cultural equivalent" is nothing new; the unrighteous do as much. Instead, he says, "Love your enemies and pray for those who persecute you" (Matt. 5:44). Here we come to an understanding of neighbor that few can handle: our *enemy* is our neighbor.

Now, loving our enemies is simply not in us in natural human strength. Most of us cannot view it as a good thing, much less carry it out. Even to want to love our enemies demands a power outside of us, which is precisely why the vertical movement of love is so essential to the horizontal movement of love. Love of God makes love of neighbor possible.

Three Great Themes

The Social Justice Tradition embraces three great themes— themes that are wonderfully summed up in three Hebrew words: מִשְׁפָּט (mishpat), חֶסֶד (hesed), and שָׁלוֹם (shalom).[71]

Technically *mishpat* means "justice," but it is an expansive word rich in meaning, carrying social, ethical, and religious connotations. It involves a morality over and above strict legal justice; it includes observance of good custom or established practice, especially the practice of an equitable distribution of the land. It is used so constantly in conjunction with the Hebrew word for righteousness (צדק) that the biblical scholar Volkmar Herntrich believes the two concepts should be viewed as virtually synonymous.[72]

We are told that God "executes justice [*mishpat*] for the orphan and the widow, and . . . loves the strangers, providing them food and clothing" (Deut. 10:18). And again the Psalmist declared, "The LORD works vindication and justice [*mishpat*] for all who are oppressed" (Ps. 103:6).

This justice involved the wisdom to bring equitable, harmonious relationships between people. When Solomon prayed for the wisdom to govern the people justly, God responded, "You . . . have asked for yourself understanding to discern what is right [*mishpat*]" (1 Kings 3:11).

Political leaders were expected to exercise this quality of ethical compassion, of justice, on behalf of all the people. Micah accused the rulers of Israel of economic cannibalism for their brutal injustice:

> Should you not know justice? —
>   you who . . .
> eat the flesh of my people,
>   flay their skin off them,
> break their bones in pieces,
>   and chop them up like meat in a kettle,
>   like flesh in a caldron. (Micah 3:1b–3)

Jeremiah was brokenhearted that justice could not be found anywhere in all Jerusalem, though a person would "run to and fro" through every street (Jer. 5:1).

God had institutionalized a system of compassionate justice through such things as the law of gleaning and the Year of Jubilee,

but political leaders in Israel had institutionalized a system of hard-
ened injustice. "Woe to those who decree iniquitous decrees,"
lamented Isaiah, "and the writers who keep writing oppression" (Isa.
10:1, RSV). God, we are told, abhors all Judah's pious rituals because
they lack social relevance. The fast God desires is for people to "loose
the bonds of injustice" and to "let the oppressed go free." God's justice, God's *mishpat*, is for the people to "share your bread with the
hungry, / and bring the homeless poor into your house" (Isa. 58:5–7,
RSV). This is social justice.

Hesed holds before us the great theme of compassion. It is a word
so laden with meaning that translators struggle to find an English
equivalent, often rendering it "loving kindness" or "steadfast love." It
is a word most frequently used in reference to God's unwavering
compassion for his people. God's wonderful *hesed* love is "from everlasting to everlasting," declared the Psalmist (Ps. 103:17). It is a
"steadfast love" that "endures forever" (Ps. 106:1).

But the great challenge for us is that this covenant love, this
durable mercy that is so central to the character of God, is to be
reflected in us as well. Through Hosea the prophet, God declares, "I
desire steadfast love [*hesed*] and not sacrifice, / the knowledge of God
rather than burnt offerings" (Hos. 6:6).

Sprinkled throughout the Hebrew Scriptures are grace-filled laws
of compassion, of *hesed*. The law of gleaning, mentioned earlier, is a
prime example. Farmers were to leave some of the crop along the
borders and the grain that fell on the ground during harvest so that
the poor could gather it (Lev. 19:9–20). Likewise the vineyards and
the olive groves were not to be stripped bare, in order to make provision for the needy. There seemed in this law to be an almost holy
indifference as to whether the poor deserved their poverty; the simple
fact of need was sufficient reason to provide for them.

Think of the tender compassion in the old Hebrew laws of giving
and taking a pledge. If someone borrowed your oxcart and left his
coat in pledge, you had to be sure to give the coat back before sunset
even if he hadn't finished with the oxcart. Why? Because the night
air was cold, and he would need his coat for warmth. The rule was

doubly binding if the person who made the pledge was poor, for in all likelihood he had no other coat with which to keep warm (Deut. 24:12). A widow's coat could not be taken as a pledge, because she was helpless enough as it was (Deut. 24:17). A millstone was never to be taken in pledge; after all, it was a person's livelihood (Deut. 24:6). No one was ever to barge into a neighbor's house to retrieve what had been loaned; rather, the lender was to wait at the front door for it to be brought out (Deut. 24:10–11). Graciousness, courtesy, compassion—this is *hesed*.

Hesed is a quality that extends even to the animals and the land. The sabbath rest principle of Hebrew law included the needs of the livestock (Exod. 23:12). After seven years of planting and harvesting, the land itself needed "a year of complete rest" (Lev. 25:5). Even the soil of the vineyards was not to be overtaxed by planting other crops between the rows (Deut. 22:9). The oxen that trod out the grain were not to be muzzled so that they could eat while they worked (Deut. 25:4). And so on. The whole point of this instruction was that our dominion over the earth and the little creatures that creep upon it is to be filled with compassion. We should not rape the earth but manage and care for it—kindly, lovingly, tenderly. This too is social justice.

Most amazing of all is the way the biblical writers wove together the justice of *mishpat* with the compassion of *hesed*. To give people justice—what is due them—that is one thing; but the spirit out of which we give and the way we relate to people in our giving, well, that is another thing altogether. In what must be considered one of the most powerful summations of our task in all Hebrew Scripture, we see the blending of the demands of justice with the spirit of compassion.

> He has showed you, O people, what is good.
>   And what does the LORD require of you?
> To act justly [mishpat] and to love mercy [hesed]
>   and to walk humbly with your God. (Mic. 6:8, NIVI)

If *mishpat* and *hesed* are spotlights illuminating various dimensions of the Social Justice Tradition, then *shalom* is a great beacon. A full-bodied concept that gathers in but is much broader than peace, *shalom* means wholeness, unity, balance. *Shalom* embodies the vision of a harmonious, all-inclusive community of loving persons. The great vision of *shalom* begins and ends our Bible. In the creation narrative, God brings order and harmony out of chaos; in the Apocalypse of John people from all the nations form a loving community in "the holy city, the new Jerusalem," which has no temple, "for its temple is the Lord God the Almighty and the Lamb" (Gen. 1, Rev. 21).

The messianic child to be born is the "Prince of Peace," and justice and righteousness and peace are to characterize his unending kingdom (Isa. 9:6–7). Central to the dream of *shalom* is the magnificent vision of all nations streaming to the mountain of the temple of God to be taught his ways and walk in his paths:

> They shall beat their swords into plowshares,
>   and their spears into pruning hooks;
> nation shall not lift up sword against nation,
>   neither shall they learn war any more. (Isa. 2:2–4)

Shalom conveys the idea of a harmonious unity in the natural order as well: the wolf and the calf become friends, the lion and the lamb lie down together, "and a little child shall lead them" (Isa. 11:1–9). We are in harmony with God; faithfulness and loyalty prevail. We are in harmony with our neighbor; justice and mercy abound. We are in harmony with nature; peace and unity reign. This is the vision of *shalom*.

Economically and socially, the vision of *shalom* means a caring and a consideration for all peoples. The greed of the rich is tempered by the need of the poor. Justice, harmony, and equipoise prevail. Under the reign of God's *shalom* the poor are no longer oppressed, because ravaging greed no longer rules.

In a particularly tender scene, Jeremiah lamented the fraud and greed of his day, saying, "They have treated the wound of my people carelessly, saying 'Peace, peace,' when there is no peace" (Jer. 6:14). In essence, Jeremiah had filed a malpractice suit against self-styled religious quacks. They had put a Band-Aid over a gaping social wound and said, "*Shalom, shalom*—all is well." But Jeremiah thundered back, "*En shalom*—all is not well. Justice is spurned, the poor are oppressed, the orphan is ignored. There is no wholeness, no healing here!"

But the healing *shalom* of God will not be spurned forever, for Jeremiah could see a day when God would make a new covenant with his people: "I will put my law within them, and I will write it on their hearts; and I will be their God, and they shall be my people. No longer shall they teach one another, or say to each other, 'Know the LORD,' for they shall all know me, from the least of them to the greatest, says the LORD; for I will forgive their iniquity, and remember their sin no more" (Jer. 31:33b–34).

Mishpat, hesed, shalom—these are perspectives that inform our vision of the Social Justice Tradition. May the day soon come when "steadfast love and faithfulness will meet; righteousness and peace will kiss each other" (Ps. 85:10).

Three Great Arenas

We work for social justice within three great arenas, and we are given weapons of the Spirit specifically designed for effective use in the context of each of these arenas.

The first arena in the struggle for social justice is the personal arena. This is critical, for we cannot work for justice and live injustice; we cannot work for peace and live war; we cannot work for racial reconciliation and live bigotry. So we stand against all forms of pride, envy, anger, sloth, greed, gluttony, and lust within ourselves, for these destroy the good we would do in the world. We take the issues of sexual purity and rectitude with utter seriousness, for sexual distortion dehumanizes ourselves and others. We repudiate and crucify the self-sins within: self-promotion, self-pity, self-sufficiency, self-righteousness, self-worship. We attack the inner citadels of arrogance and independence.

Then too we pursue and embrace the cardinal virtues of temperance, prudence, fortitude, and justice, along with the theological virtues of faith, hope, and love. We commit ourselves to honesty in all business dealings, integrity in all words and deeds, purity in all matters of morality, generosity of spirit in all things, and divine love toward all peoples.

Many weapons of the Spirit are employed in this work, but the one most specifically useful in the personal arena is prayer. In prayer we wait in the power of God for the evil to dissipate and the good to rise up. By prayer we receive spiritual enabling to overpower the egoism that drives us so relentlessly. Through prayer we develop the longing, the yearning to sink down deep into the things of God. From prayer we discern the actions we are to take to overcome evil with good. All this we will need to sustain us in the struggle for social righteousness.

The second arena is the social arena. This begins on the level of interpersonal relationships: marriages and families and friends and neighbors and work associates and all those who curse us and spitefully use us. As much as it lies within us, we live in peace with all people. This is the work of healing and reconciliation, of compassion and shalom.

You may remember that the first internal controversy the early church faced after Pentecost was an issue of social justice. The widows of the Greek-speaking Jews were being discriminated against in the daily food distribution. This was at its heart a spiritual problem, and the apostles used an organizational means to solve it. Deacons who were "full of the Spirit and of wisdom" were appointed to oversee the food distribution (Acts 6:3). And just look at the grace and compassion of the community in solving this problem of discrimination: all those chosen had Greek names, meaning that they were from the aggrieved group. May we have the same grace and compassion in dealing with justice in our churches.

This work of social justice extends on out to the larger social context of our culture: school boards and community clubs and civic organizations and city commissions, and much more. Into all these social networks we bring love and joy and peace and patience and kindness and generosity and faithfulness and gentleness and self-control (Gal. 5:22–23).

We feed the hungry. We help the helpless. We reach out to the orphan, the widow, the weak, the shoved aside. We take the struggle for justice into the American slums and the Brazilian barrios and the Indian sweathouses and the Cambodian houses of prostitution.

As before, we engage in the work of reconciliation and healing, but we do more too. We look for those who are excluded or neglected because of their social status, or their race, or their background, or their gender, or their age, or any number of other things. And we lobby for their acceptance and welcome and embrace into the social network. We also look to see if there are social networks that are destructive to human life—networks that manipulate and control, networks that exclude and reject. These are not difficult to identify if we have eyes to see. Then, depending upon the situation, our task is either to work for their transformation or their defeat.

In addition, we look for any relationships or networks that need to be established for the health and welfare of the community—a new group to foster healthy families, perhaps, or to counter child abuse or to combat racism. Whatever, wherever, whoever.

Our major weapon in this work is Christian community. Now, when I speak of "Christian community," I am referring not just to the work of churches, and certainly not churches as they are often manifest today. I am speaking of an alternative way of living that shows forth social life as it is meant to be lived. Communities of love and acceptance. Fellowships of freedom and liberation. Centers of hope and vision. Societies of nurture and accountability. Little pockets of life and light so stunning that a watching world will declare, "See how they love one another!"

The third arena in our work for social justice is the arena of institutional structures. Demonic powers can be incarnated in the structures of any society, becoming part of the public policy and laws of the land. When Jesus cleansed the temple in Jerusalem, he was defeating an institutional structure that had become destructive.

Justice and goodness too can be built into institutional structures, within limits. I say "within limits" because just laws, while right and necessary, can never guarantee the spirit out of which those laws will be administered.

In the institutional arena we engage in "the cultural mandate." Our task is to envision and work to realize a society where it is easier to do good and harder to do evil; a society with institutions and laws and public policies that provide justice for all and enhanced life for all.

Where structures perpetuate poverty, we work to change them. Where structures dehumanize, we work to make them more responsive to human need. In addition, we welcome and work for all institutions that enhance art and beauty. It is instructive that all through Dorothy Day's intense ministry among the poor, she never lost her love of beauty or her love of the theater and the arts.

Now, the battlefronts in the institutional arena are myriad, and some of them are terribly complicated, for they become all tangled up in historical allegiances and cultural traditions and political interests. But face them we must. The plight of the unborn. Problems of poverty and housing. Issues of nationalism and militarism. Of war and peace. Of racism. Of sexism. Of ageism. Of consumerism. Of environmentalism.

I warned you that some of these matters would get complicated. I certainly have here neither the space nor the wisdom to stake out a position on all the areas I have just listed (not to mention the areas I have not listed). But I would encourage us all to struggle with these issues in the light of the principle of a consistent life ethic, whereby we seek to discern what position and what approach will be the most life-giving to all people. We look for ways to break the horns of cruel dilemmas. We seek out the ways most expressive of love of God and love of neighbor, the touchstone of the Social Justice Tradition.

Prophetic witness is the weapon most useful in the institutional arena. We are the conscience to the various expressions of institutional life, most particularly the state. We commend the state when it provides justice for all, and we bring prophetic critique when it fails.

This is done in many ways. John Woolman wrote and spoke and petitioned against the institution of slavery. He also refused to wear dyed clothing that was the product of slave labor. Later many Quakers engaged in civil disobedience against the Fugitive Slave Law of 1793, which made it illegal to help runaway slaves. They felt that a higher law compelled them to disobey the unjust laws of human government. Some people have been drawn into similar protests today. When we are so drawn, we must act in a manner consistent with the commandments to love God and love neighbor: we must conduct peaceful, nonviolent, prophetic protest. This too is the work of social justice.

Obviously the nature and kind of prophetic witness varies greatly depending on whether the state is participatory or totalitarian. William Wilberforce labored in a participatory state, Aleksandr Solzhenitsyn in a totalitarian state.[73] Both gave effective prophetic witness. Both understood by experience the penetrating words of Donald Bloesch: "The Gospel is a stick of dynamite in the social structure."[74]

DISCOVERING THE MAJOR STRENGTHS

It is of genuine importance that we stress the strengths of the Social Justice Tradition so that we may have hope for the task.

First, the Social Justice Tradition is constantly calling us to a right ordering of society—right relationships and right living. It envisions the social order as it was meant to be. What an important value this is! Many people, you understand, have the uneasy feeling that the concerns of social justice succeed only in making their lives rather dull and uncomfortable. If only they could dispense with these concerns—so the thinking goes—they would finally be able to relax and enjoy life. But the call of social justice is to a life that, because it functions well, makes peaceful social evolution possible. How important this is, for if we make peaceful social evolution *im*possible, we make violent revolution inevitable.

Second, a focus on social justice enhances our ecclesiology, our doctrine of the Church. It helps make our faith real, not merely theoretical. It puts names and faces on the work of justice. No longer are we people separated by nationality and social class and race and gender; "no longer Jew or Greek . . . no longer slave or free . . . no longer male and female; for all of you are one in Christ Jesus" (Gal. 3:28).

Social justice promotes harmony in relationships between peoples so that we can learn to live together not just with civility but with genuine appreciation. Human beings are infinitely precious beings because we are created in the image of God, but also because of the way we can enrich one another. If we are a people rich in social relationships, we are rich indeed. Whenever we develop significant friendships with those who are not like us culturally, we become broader, wiser persons. Social justice teaches us that we can be infinitely diverse culturally and still live as one people.

At the great Jerusalem council described in Acts 15, it was decided once and for all that faith in Christ demands no cultural presuppositions. We can receive one another in our own cultural "vessel." Gentiles do not need to become cultural Jews to be disciples of Jesus, nor do Jews need to become cultural Gentiles. Eskimos can remain Eskimo and Samoans can remain Samoan. Norwegians can worship and serve Christ in Norwegian ways and Zambians in Zambian ways.

Each culture, of course, has elements in it that are discontinuous with the gospel message and life, and these we repudiate. But seldom are these the things we imagine at first. Besides, much within every culture is either continuous with the gospel or not offensive to it, and these cultural ways we accept and receive as rich expressions of the human family. We are the body of Christ together, and individually members of it.

Third, social justice concerns provide a bridge between personal ethics and social ethics. Too many of us separate the two—with disastrous results. When, for example, we faithfully read our Bible and at the same time develop racist public policy, we are a scandal to the gospel. This must not be.

God cares about whether we individually lie or speak the truth, but he cares equally about companies that run advertising campaigns claiming more than is actually the case. We cannot speak of love and at the same time be part of institutional structures that perpetuate injustice. It is not enough for us to care for individual cases of hunger if we are part of multinational corporations whose policies continually impoverish Two-Thirds World* countries.

Fourth, social justice gives relevance and bite to the language of Christian love. Too often our talk about love is sentimental and soft. It needs to be toughened by the hard realities of absentee landlords and prostitute rings and drug smugglers and industrial spies and political pettifoggers. We cannot speak with integrity of loving our neighbor until we are prepared to face the structural violence that is built into many of our policies and institutions.

Fifth, a theology of social justice gives us a foundation for ecological concerns. The shalom we seek extends to the earth itself, as Paul reminds us: "The whole creation has been groaning in labor pains until now" (Rom. 8:22). We have been given stewardship over the environment, and may God help us to exercise it wisely. We are still struggling to know what it means to have a just and sustainable world. David Orr of Oberlin College writes, "Many things on which our future health and prosperity depend are in dire jeopardy: climate stability, the resilience and productivity of natural systems, the beauty of the natural world, and biological diversity."[75]

Sixth, and finally, Christian social witness continuously holds before us the relevance of the impossible ideal. It points us to the new heaven and the new earth. It reminds us that "God can make a way where there is no way." It keeps alive the prophetic imagination. It never lets us forget the redemptive power of the active, self-sacrificial love that is imaged in the cross. *Vicit agnus noster, eum sequamur.* Our Lamb has conquered, let us follow him.

---

*As used by sociologists the term "Two-Thirds World" deals with geography, population, and economics. The underdeveloped countries comprise two-thirds of the population covering two-thirds of the earth's land mass. It is certainly worth pondering whether these are truly "underdeveloped countries" or whether the remaining one-third are "overdeveloped countries."

UNDERSTANDING THE POTENTIAL PERILS

By now you have a well-rehearsed sensibility to the fact that all the Traditions can be distorted and used in destructive ways. Social justice is no exception. Let's consider some of its most prominent perils.

Perhaps the greatest danger is the tendency for the Social Justice Tradition to become an end in itself. Though regrettable, this tendency is understandable. The needs of poverty are so immediate and the demands of justice are so great that they can consume all our energies. Besides, spiritual realities are often less pressing and less visible, and thus we tend to set them aside. The value systems of the world in which we live do not help. They may be able to appreciate our works of mercy and compassion, even to give them recognition and praise. But modern sensibilities consider spiritual realities to be irrelevant, even suspect.

It is, of course, a genuine danger for the Holiness Tradition to operate on a pietistic level that never engages the social dimensions of its work, or for the Evangelical Tradition to preach a gospel that fails to understand the larger context of its message. But these dangers pale when compared to the pitfall in the Social Justice Tradition of caring for social needs without reference to the condition of the heart. Organizations without number have begun with a wholehearted commitment to minister to both physical and spiritual needs, only to end up severing the spiritual underpinnings of their efforts. The only thing these organizations have left is a kind of social salvation that leaves people rooted in spiritual despair and alienated from God.

We must face the fact that, on a strictly human level, the state has more resources for providing social services than the Church does. And we should most certainly urge the state in just such efforts. But the Church has deeper reasons for its existence and ministry, reasons that are fundamentally spiritual in nature. For Christians social justice concerns must always be rooted in profound spiritual realities.

A second peril is that of strident legalism. This is a surprise to many, because the Social Justice Tradition is the stream with the least obvious religiosity, and it is the most deeply rooted in human need. But after the Holiness Tradition it is the stream most prone to rigidity and judgmentalism. This is because it operates primarily on the level of action and lifestyle, people can easily be judged on the most superficial of outward standards. People's level of commitment to a simple lifestyle, for example, is often based upon the kind of housing they live in or the transportation they use or the clothing they wear.

In addition, the concerns of social justice are so critical to human life that we often cannot bring ourselves to allow the same latitude of differences that we might in other matters. We quickly and harshly condemn people who differ with us on matters, say, of abortion or capital punishment or racism or militarism or any number of other issues. Standards of who is in and who is out, who is right and who is wrong become more and more narrowly defined. It is a danger we tend to fall into because the stakes are so high.

A third arena of peril emerges whenever we become too closely identified with any particular political agenda. Our faith is political, and it does make value judgments on political concerns. But this political link needs to be handled in such a way that we are never co-opted by any political persuasion or for any political agenda. The Church must forever stand as the conscience of the state, insisting that it fulfill its divinely appointed function of providing justice and order in society. Too cozy a relationship with any political entity will blunt our prophetic edge. Now, this describes the task of those who stand outside the political process and bring prophetic critique to that process.

Those who are called to the body politic have a somewhat different task. They will, most certainly, take firm political positions — positions that prayerfully grow out of Christian conviction and are legitimate within the context of a pluralistic society — and they will initiate legislation and sponsor bills based on those political positions. But even here Christ's disciples must maintain sufficient distance to speak prophetically to political agendas or to the very political structure itself, even to the point of resignation if necessary. Earlier in this chapter I mentioned the Quakers' 1756 resignation from the Pennsylvania General Assembly, and perhaps that action can be a helpful model for us.[76]

Other perils exist; we could never cover every circumstance. But we will be guided rightly if we, with purity of heart, ever keep before us the vision of loving God furiously and loving our neighbor as ourselves.

PRACTICING THE SOCIAL JUSTICE TRADITION

It is easy to feel that these issues are far beyond our small abilities, and most certainly they are. But even so, there is much that we can do. First, we can open ourselves to the possibility that God may want to use us in a significant way. History is full of ordinary people who, like Amos, were called to positions of influence far beyond their intentions. Second, we can get the facts. We become global citizens when we care enough to be informed about what happens to our neighbors in Belfast and Sarajevo, in Santiago and Johannesburg. Third, we can become advocates for the powerless and exploited. Our comfortable dinner parties need to hear the whimpering, moaning "songs from the slums."[77] Our soft love needs the backbone of justice.

Fourth, we can support relief agencies in their good work both financially and through volunteer efforts. Such agencies *need* our help. Fifth, we can go beyond relief and become involved politically. Life is political, and if we refuse to influence public policy, someone else will. Sixth, we can use our literary skills in the cause of the poor. Letters to the editor, newsletters, magazine articles, substantive books, and good television and movie scripts are all needed. Our hymns and contemporary gospel music desperately need tough social content. Seventh, we can take the work of prayer into the social arena. It is necessary work if we are to defeat the demonic principalities and powers incarnated in so many institutional structures.

I conclude these brief comments on *praxis* with a word of caution: do not try to answer every cry of human need or respond to every instance of injustice. It would simply do you in. While it is important for us to take up *some* task of justice, we are not to take up *every* task of justice. God knows that we are finite human beings and does not ask us to do more than we can bear.

The Call to Compassionate Living

QUESTION: What is the Social Justice Tradition?
ANSWER: A life committed to compassion and justice for all peoples.
QUESTION: Why should we explore it?
ANSWER: Because through it God develops in us the compassion to love our neighbor freely and develops in our world a place where justice and righteousness prevail.

God calls us to a life of social justice whose circumference embraces 360 degrees: personal, social, institutional. It is a life that receives all peoples: enemies and friends, poor and rich, illiterate and educated, whomever and whomever. It is a life that engages in outward conflict with all social, economic, and civil injustices of society, judging down wickedness and building up the good, the true, and the beautiful.

In the seventeenth century James Nayler was a vigorous protagonist in the cause of social justice across the length and breadth of England. In 1660, a year after his release from prison for his religious activity, he headed for home to see his wife and children. On his way he was attacked by bandits who robbed and beat him and left him for dead. Friends found Nayler in a field, mortally wounded. They took him to a nearby home and watched over him until he died. Fortunately, they recorded his words in the hours before his death—words that remain to this day a classic manifesto to the life of compassion and justice and shalom.

Perhaps Nayler's dying words can be living words for you and for me:

> There is a spirit which I feel that delights to do no evil, nor to revenge any wrong, but delights to endure all things, in hope to

enjoy its own in the end. Its hope is to outlive all wrath and contention, and to weary out all exaltation and cruelty, or whatever
is of a nature contrary to itself. It sees to the end of all temptations. As it bears no evil in itself, so it conceives none in
thoughts to any other. If it be betrayed, it bears it, for its ground
and spring is the mercies and forgiveness of God. Its crown is
meekness, its life is everlasting love unfeigned; and takes its
kingdom with entreaty and not with contention, and keeps it by
lowliness of mind. In God alone it can rejoice, though none
else regard it, or can own its life. It's conceived in sorrow, and
brought forth without any to pity it, nor doth it murmur at grief
and oppression. It never rejoiceth but through sufferings: for
with the world's joy it is murdered. I found it alone, being for-
saken. I have fellowship therein with them who lived in dens
and desolate places in the earth, who through death obtained
this resurrection and eternal holy life.[78]

Chapter 6

~

The Evangelical Tradition: Discovering the Word-Centered Life

Jesus says, "I am the resurrection and the life. Those who believe in me, even though they die, will live, and everyone who lives and believes in me will never die."

—*John 11:25–26*

The monument I want after I am dead is a monument with two legs going around the world—a saved sinner telling about the salvation of Jesus Christ.

—*D. L. Moody*

THE EVANGELICAL TRADITION*

Notable Figures   *Significant Movements*

0
Jesus of Nazareth
(c. 4 B.C.- c. A.D. 29)

Peter the Apostle (1st century)
Ignatius of Antioch (c. 35–107)

Athanasius (c. 295–373)
Basil the Great (c. 330–379)
Ambrose of Milan (c. 339–397)
Jerome (c. 347–420)
John Chrysostom (c. 347–407)
Ninian (c. 360–c. 432)
Patrick (c. 390–c. 461)
Augustine of Hippo (354–430)
Peter Chrysologus (c. 400–c. 450)

Benen (?–467)
Columba (521–597)
Wilfred (634–709)

Willibrord (658–739)
Boniface (680–754)
Constantine (826–869)
Methodius (c. 815–884)

1000

Sigfrid (?–c. 1045)
Dominic (c. 1170–1221)   Dominicans
                                 (13th century to the present)
Thomas Aquinas (1225–1274)

John Wycliffe (c. 1329–1384)

Martin Luther (1483–1546)   Protestant Reformation
Huldrych Zwingli (1484–1531)   (16th century to the present)
Francis Xavier (1506–1552)
John Calvin (1509–1564)   Roman Catholic Missionary Movement
                                 (16th century to the present)
George Whitfield (1714–1770)
William Carey (1761–1834)   Great Awakenings
Charles Finney (1792–1875)   (18th–19th centuries)
John Veniaminov (1798–1879)
Ivan Nicolai (Kasatkin) (c. 1836–1912)
Charles Haddon Spurgeon (1834–1892)   Protestant Missionary Movement
Dwight L. Moody (1837–1899)   (18th century to the present)
Mary Slessor (1848–1915)
Billy Sunday (1862–1935)
John R. Mott (1865–1955)   Student Volunteer Movement
C. S. Lewis (1898–1963)   (19th–20th centuries)

Billy Graham (1918–)

*See Appendix B for brief biographies and histories.

T HE WORK OF SOCIAL JUSTICE is most complete when it is intricately connected to authentic evangelical witness. These two Traditions—the Social Justice Tradition and the Evangelical Tradition—are at their best when they function together. The Evangelical Tradition of Christian life and faith focuses upon the proclamation of the evangel, the good news of the gospel. We are enabled by the power of God to take the word of the gospel into our hearts in such a transforming way that others, seeing this, want it for themselves. This faith stream addresses the crying need for people to see the good news lived and hear the good news proclaimed.

SEEKING A HISTORICAL PARADIGM

When, in *The Waste Land*, T. S. Eliot writes, "To Carthage then I came / Burning burning burning burning . . . ,"[1] he is alluding to the person who is my number-one choice as a paradigm for the Evangelical Tradition: Aurelius. Aurelius was a North African, born Sunday, 13 November A.D. 354, in Thagaste (modern-day Souk Ahras, in eastern Algeria), a city bounded by the Mediterranean to the north and the Sahara to the south. Eliot's mention of Carthage refers to Aurelius's years of academic training there. In Carthage, by his own admission, Aurelius was thrust into "a hissing cauldron of lust."[2] Longing for genuine love but unable to separate it from lust, he dipped into this cauldron more than once: "I polluted . . . the stream of friendship with the foulness of lust, and clouded its purity with the dark hell of illicit desire."[3] During those years Aurelius took to himself a concubine, and she bore them a son, Adeodatus.

An Arduous Search

But that Carthage period was not all "a whole frying-pan of wicked loves,"[4] for through his studies the teenage Aurelius discovered

Cicero and his *Hortensius*. This was the beginning of a long and arduous search for the good, the true, the beautiful—indeed, the search for God. The writings of Cicero were a fortunate initial discovery, for they aroused in Aurelius a love of wisdom and an ardent pursuit after truth: "That book inflamed me with the love of wisdom. . . . I was not encouraged by this work of Cicero's to join this or that sect; instead I was urged on and inflamed with a passionate zeal to love and seek and obtain and embrace and hold fast wisdom itself, whatever it might be."[5] And so, at the very time he was "sinking down to the depths" of the "lower beauties" of sexual promiscuity, he continued to be drawn to the higher beauties of virtue and justice.

Now, Cicero was not a Christian—he did not have the full revelation of God in the face of Jesus Christ—but his writing did serve as a vital pre-evangelism for Aurelius. In fact, Cicero's penetrating questions on life actually turned Aurelius to the Bible to see what answers he could find there. Unfortunately, the only Bible available to him at the time was a badly flawed Latin translation with inept style. "To me," he said, the Scriptures "seemed quite unworthy of comparison with the stately prose of Cicero."[6]

Rejecting the Bible, Aurelius turned to the raging intellectual fad of the day, Manichaeism, a philosophy that postulated an absolute dualism of good and evil. (This viewpoint is quite popular today, incidentally. The *Star Wars* movie trilogy, for example, is decidedly Manichaean in its presentation of good and evil.) Aurelius was enthralled with Manichaeism for some time, but eventually he began to see through its obvious intellectual weaknesses. His disillusionment with Manichaean philosophy was all but sealed when he met its chief spokesman—one Faustus—whom Aurelius described as a "wordy dish" (that is, a person who has nothing at all to say but can say it extremely well).

For a time Aurelius was attracted to "the Academics," a group that embraced agnosticism. He deemed these people "wiser than the rest because they held that everything should be considered doubtful."[7] He knew that honest doubt was far superior to superstitious belief. This period of skepticism was essential to Aurelius, for he needed to examine rigorously the various philosophies of his day. And examine them he did—all the way to "the deceitful fortune-telling and wicked lunacies of the astrologers"—and he found them all wanting.[8]

The great intellectual hurdle for Aurelius was the problem of evil. How could a good God allow a universe that was filled with evil, with pain, with suffering? "Where then is evil? What is its origin? How did it steal into the world? What is the root or seed from which it grew?"[9]

These were his questions, and they are our questions too whenever we go through the wringers of life. For Aurelius the first hints of an answer came when he discovered the writings of the Neoplatonists, who viewed evil as the absence of good. In addition, intellectually the Neoplatonists opened the window onto the Bible for Aurelius so that he could look at its claims once again, this time with a more docile heart. He was later to witness that "whatever I had read in the Platonists was said in Paul's writings."[10]

But all of Aurelius's high-minded ideals seemed constantly contradicted by his moral ineptitude. He was trapped, as he put it, in "the swirling mists of lust," which thrust him into "the whirlpools of vice."[11] Try as he might, he could not break the chains that held him a moral prisoner: "The enemy held my will and made a chain out of it and bound me with it. From a perverse will came lust, and slavery to lust became a habit, and the habit, being constantly yielded to, became a necessity."[12]

Actually, his sexual escapades only underscored the more profound reality that the character of sin taints all the affections. As a child Aurelius had stolen some pears, and his later prolonged musings on that seemingly trivial event reveal his penetrating understanding of how evil works its way into the very warp and woof of all our motives. Aurelius knew by bitter experience that all of us have tasted of the tree of the knowledge of good and evil.

The deeply ingrained nature of evil even tainted his professional life, where he had embraced the accepted canons of academia: pride, social advancement, education as an end in itself, and more. By now he had been a professor of rhetoric in Carthage, written a first book (*Beauty and Proportion*), traveled to Rome seeking the larger world of power and influence, and accepted an appointment in Milan as professor of literature and elocution. But all this only threw him into an intolerable moral contradiction. Here he was— "an ardent searcher for the blessed life" consumed with "a burning zeal for truth and wisdom"—and at the same time enslaved to lust and power and pride. He had "panted after honours," and it had corrupted his moral sensibilities. He had turned his profession of rhetoric into a "talking-shop" where he showed students how to toy with truth and pervert justice. Words became propaganda to be maneuvered at will. By his own admission he had become a teacher in "the arts of deception." (I imagine you can readily think of modern parallels.) Desperately Aurelius needed something more; he needed the power to live as he knew he should.

And here, in the midst of his moral quandary, Aurelius met Ambrose, the famous Bishop of Milan. Initially Aurelius was intrigued with Ambrose not out of any spiritual concern, but simply out of a professional interest in observing his skills in rhetoric. And he was not disappointed: "I was delighted with the sweetness of his discourse."[13] But ultimately it was the content of that discourse that gripped Aurelius, for Ambrose forthrightly declared that Jesus Christ had the power to break the bonds of moral failure. No one had offered that kind of power before—not the Manichaeans, not the Academics, not even the Neoplatonists, who had been so helpful to him. Only Christ gave the ability to live the virtuous life for which he longed so ardently. Further, Ambrose opened the spiritual meaning of Scripture to Aurelius in a way that released him from a wooden literalism and allowed him to come to the Bible prayerfully, seeking the illumination of the Spirit. Even so, Aurelius was not certain he was quite ready for such soul-shaping commitment. "Give me chastity and self-control," he prayed, "but not yet."[14]

All of this was such a mighty struggle for Aurelius because he did not believe, as is so common today, that one could be a convert to Christ without being a disciple of Christ. For him conversion and discipleship were two sides of the same door—and both were necessary to get through the door. In counting the cost, he understood that turning to Christ meant turning from the intellectual pride that had driven him so fiercely and embracing a lifestyle free of sexual promiscuity. Conversion for Aurelius was no easy assent to a few propositions; it was the restructuring of his whole life. He not only understood that the grace of God was "costly grace"; he was unaware of any other kind of grace.

A small garden in Milan became Aurelius's valley of decision. He wrote, "To this garden the tumult in my heart had driven me, as to a place where no one could intervene in this passionate suit which I had brought against myself until it could be settled. . . . I tore my hair, beat my forehead, locked my fingers together, clasped my knee. . . ."[15] There, in that Milan garden on a summer's day in A.D. 386, Aurelius probed the hidden depths of his soul.

What occurred next was so overwhelming an experience that it is best given in Aurelius's own words:

> Then a huge storm rose up within me bringing with it a huge downpour of tears. . . . Suddenly a voice reaches my ears from a nearby house. It is the voice of a boy or a girl (I don't know which) and in a kind of singsong the words are constantly repeated: "Take it and read it. Take it and read it." At once my face changed, and I began to think carefully of whether the singing of words like these came into any kind of game which children play, and I could not remember that I had ever heard anything like it before. I checked the force of my tears and rose to my feet, being quite certain that I must interpret this as a divine command to me to open the book and read the first passage which I should come upon. . . . I snatched up the book, opened it, and read in silence the passage upon which my eyes first fell: "Not in rioting and drunkenness, not in chambering and wantonness, not in strife and envying; but put ye on the Lord Jesus Christ, and make not provision for the flesh in concupiscence." I had no wish to read further; there was no need to. For immediately [when] I had reached the end of this sentence it was as though my heart was filled with a light of confidence and all the shadows of my doubt were swept away.[16]

What a moving example of the living Word of God bringing healing and saving grace through the means of the written Word of God—in this case, Paul's Epistle to the Romans. Years later Aurelius wrote, "Late it was that I loved you, beauty so ancient and so new, late I loved you! . . . You called, you cried out, you shattered my deafness: you flashed, you shone, you scattered my blindness: you breathed perfume, and I drew in my breath and I pant for you: I tasted, and I am hungry and thirsty: you touched me, and I burned for your peace."[17] In a garden in Milan Aurelius at last found this peace.

Have you by now realized that I am telling you the story of Aurelius Augustine, later to become the famous bishop of Hippo? I thought it would be futile to disguise his identity any longer, for what occurred in that Milan garden is, outside of Scripture, perhaps the most well-known conversion story in Christian history. But the story is really only at its beginning; let me continue.

Preacher of the Faith

Following this transforming experience, Augustine, along with several friends, retreated to a country villa at the foot of the Italian Alps for six months of reflection, prayer, and writing. This allowed generous space for Scripture study and endless discussions as Augustine and his friends sought to integrate the reality of this new life into their thinking. As he wrote during this time, "Really great things, when discussed by little men, can usually make such men grow big."[18] The time was also a vital preparation for his baptism on Easter Sunday, A.D. 387. Augustine was thirty-two years old.

A whole new life lay ahead for Augustine. Perhaps wanting to make a clean break with the professional arrogance and sexual promiscuity that had dominated his life in Italy, he decided to return to North Africa, to Thagaste, the city of his birth. As he and his friends made their way to the coast, an event of enormous sadness occurred. Augustine told of it simply and elegantly in his *Confessions*: "When we had got as far as Ostia on the Tiber, my mother died."[19]

Back in Thagaste Augustine set about establishing a lay community that would allow ample time for contemplation and Scripture study. No doubt he thought he would spend the rest of his days in this obscure setting, but that was not to be. On a trip to the coastal city of Hippo to counsel a seeker, the local congregation seized him and brought him before the bishop, eagerly shouting for his ordination by acclamation, a not uncommon practice in that day. So it was that Augustine was snatched from the life of reflection and catapulted into the life of protagonist for the Christian faith. Hippo was thereafter the center of his vast ministry and prodigious activities.

Augustine was supremely the preacher with a passion for souls. "Preach wherever you can," he declared, "to whom you can and as you can."[20] Possidius, a contemporary and biographer of Augustine, wrote, "No one can read what he wrote on theology without profit. But I think that those were able to profit still more who could hear him speak in church and see him with their own eyes."[21]

Here Augustine's extensive training in rhetoric and elocution was put to excellent use. No one was more at home in public discourse. Augustine saw himself supremely as a rhetorician for Christ, and he believed that his calling as a bishop was above all else a calling to the apostolic proclamation of the gospel, the very heart of the Evangelical Tradition.

We today can still read many of Augustine's sermons exactly as he preached them in the basilica of Hippo. This fortunate circumstance came about because of the practice in that day of designating shorthand writers in the congregation to record the message for the further edification of the people—an ancient version of our sermon audiocassette. Even more exciting was the interactive nature of preaching in that day. It was common for the congregation to break into the sermon—applauding when they were pleased, interrupting when they were confused, shouting and heckling when they disagreed. At one point, when Augustine was preaching on Psalm 88, he shouted back to the people, "So you know what I am about to say, you anticipate it by your crying out."[22] Remember too that there were no pews in that day; people stood throughout the service, crowding in tightly together. All this provided a dynamic that made the sermon a preaching *event*. Augustine clearly understood this when he wrote, "To teach is a necessity, to please is a sweetness, to persuade is a victory."[23]

As a master of the spoken word Augustine would reach out to his people with analogy, metaphor, and illustration, calling them to a living obedience: "It is easy to hear Christ, easy to praise the gospel, easy to applaud the preacher: but to endure unto the end is peculiar to the sheep who hear the Shepherd's voice."[24] In his biography, *Augustine: The Bishop*, Frederick van der Meer wrote, "Through his genius for the right word he surpasses all the Church Fathers. Never once does he fail to make an idea unforgettable. . . . Everyone who reads a number of his sermons will carry away the same impression as the men of his day, for no words from the pulpit have ever so fully come from the heart or combined that quality with such brilliance as did the words spoken by this one man in this remote corner of Africa."[25]

But Augustine's proclaiming work was in deeds as well as words: he lived the gospel as fully as he preached it. We find this most fully expressed in his famous Rule,* which to this day is the foundation for the Augustinian order. Even before his return to North Africa, Augustine and his friends had formed a community of faith, naming themselves *Servi Dei*, "Servants of God." Now at Hippo he was able to bring this vision of community life into full flower. And until his death he lived a simple life, following his own Rule among the Christian community in Hippo, which he affectionately referred to as *Familia Dei*. "He was always hospitable," noted Possidius, his contemporary. To preclude malicious gossip, Augustine placed on his dining table an inscription written in Latin and large enough for all to see:

Whoever thinks that he is able
To nibble at the life of absent friends
Must know that he is unworthy of this table.

*Roman Catholic religious orders typically have a Rule—that is, a formal expression of the regulations to be observed by members.

Possidius observed that "his clothes and food, and bedclothes also, were simple and adequate, neither ostentatious nor particularly poor."[26] And each year, on the anniversary of his ordination, he gave a banquet for the poor. The actions of his daily living are well summed up by his own words in another context: "One loving heart sets another on fire."[27] Thus Augustine sought to be just as eloquent for the evangelical counsels of Christ in the way he lived as in his words from the pulpit.

Apologist for the Faith

The warm-heart experience of Augustine's conversion most certainly exemplifies evangelical faith, as does his evangelistic proclamation of the good news of the gospel. But equally important is how his vigorous defense of orthodox Christian belief helped to explicate and clarify the gospel message. Over his lifetime he took up the Christian cause against three major opposing views—Manichaeism, Donatism, and Pelagianism—views that continue to be popular to this day.

We have already encountered Manichaeism and its dualism of good and evil. Quickly upon his ordination by acclamation Augustine challenged the local Manichaean priest, Fortunatus, to a formal debate in the hall of a public bathhouse in Hippo. A huge crowd gathered, and Possidius tells us that "the shorthand reporters opened their notebooks as Augustine threw down the gauntlet." As a professional in the art of public speaking, debate, and communication, Augustine completely humiliated Fortunatus. "The result was that this man, whom everybody had thought so great and learned, was considered to have entirely failed in the defense of his sect. His embarrassment was such that, when soon afterwards he left Hippo, he left it never to return."[28]

What Augustine had accomplished in one fell swoop was to completely discredit the notion of absolute dualism: two kingdoms of equal power, eternal and completely separate—the kingdom of Light and the kingdom of Darkness. Instead, he held high the Christian belief in one true God, the Almighty, the Maker of heaven and earth.

In creation, Augustine insisted, there was no evil anywhere; what we now call evil is but the absence of good. Evil, he insisted, is degradation, a lack of goodness, a decline from our God-given created rank. Augustine's teaching here, which interpreted the biblical witness in the light of Neoplatonic thought, may have had its weaknesses, but it clearly was a huge advance over the dualism of the Manichaeans.

The struggle with the Donatists was somewhat more complicated. The issue here concerned the moral character of the priesthood and the treatment that the Church should accord to those Christians who repented after having been guilty of serious lapses. The Donatists were actually the purists in this debate, insisting that those clergy who had renounced their faith during the Diocletian persecution had thereby rendered themselves invalid as ministers of the Word and could therefore no longer validly celebrate the sacraments. As a result, the Donatists went on to declare themselves the only pure and holy church, seeing all others as the church of Judas. Hence a genuine concern for purity turned into a cultic mentality of exclusion.[29]

The Donatists were especially strong in North Africa, Donatus himself being the bishop of Carthage. When Augustine took over as bishop of Hippo, the Donatist cathedral nearby was the largest church in the city. Indeed, as Augustine's congregation worshiped, they could hear music coming from the Donatist cathedral—the "roaring of lions," said Augustine. Although he could, no doubt, appreciate some of the Donatist scruples, Augustine became their sworn enemy. For him the issues were substantive. The legalism of the Donatists, he thought, tended to deny the free gift of God's grace. Furthermore, he felt that the seeking after a "pure church" was fundamentally misdirected, for in this world the wheat and the tares of the church grow up together (Matt. 13:24–30). Most of all, he utterly rejected the Donatist cultic claim to be the only true church: "The clouds roll with thunder, that the house of the Lord shall be built throughout the earth: and these frogs sit in their marsh and croak—we are the only Christians!"[30]

But as important as the controversies with Manichaeism and Donatism are, they pale next to Augustine's battle against Pelagianism. Pelagius, a genteel British layman, was a popular writer and teacher in the early decades of the fifth century. He had a vastly more optimistic outlook on human nature than Augustine—*too* optimistic, as it turned out. He wanted people to advance into perfection, letting go of the debilitating doctrines of the fall and our inherent sinfulness. He wrote a pamphlet titled *On Nature*, which played down human depravity and sin and played up human strengths and virtues—in modern terms, an optimistic picture of human potential, a picture of the human race come of age.

Augustine was enraged. He responded with a major treatise, *Nature and Grace*, in which he insisted that confidence in human potential only insulates us from an accurate diagnosis of human depravity. Thus he established the foundation for his famous teaching on original sin—namely, the conviction that human beings are utterly incapable of virtuous action within themselves and are desperately in need of saving grace from outside themselves.[31] The answer to the problem of original sin, Augustine maintained, was not more education or better environment or enhanced self-improvement; rather, it was God-initiated, grace-filled salvation—redemption and justification and sanctification in Jesus Christ alone.

Now, in his emphasis upon sin and depravity and grace Augustine never rejected human response to and cooperation with the divine initiative. He confidently cut a path between unaided human initiative and total passivity, succinctly stated as follows:

Without God we cannot,
Without us, he will not.

On the one side of this path is the abyss of quietism and antinomianism—the conviction that we can do nothing at all and that we accept the process of redemption in complete passivity. On the other side is the abyss of Pelagianism and moralism—the contention that everything depends upon us and that human growth in virtue comes in our own strength. Between those abysses is the path of disciplined grace: the initiative and work come entirely from God, and we act in response to and in cooperation with God. Once, when preaching on grace, Augustine declared, "He who created you without your help, will not save you without your cooperation."[32]

The battle with Pelagius was protracted and complicated, but Augustine ultimately emerged victorious. Pelagian beliefs about the innate goodness of human nature were condemned as heretical in church councils at Carthage and Mileve in A.D. 416 and reaffirmed at a second council at Carthage in 418. Augustine was a triumphant, albeit battle-scarred, defender of Christian orthodoxy. (I hope you noticed how utterly contemporary all three of these "isms" are. We fight much the same battles today.)

A Tale of Two Cities

Throughout the major part of Augustine's forty years of ministry the Roman Empire was coming apart at the seams. Augustine was fully aware of this disintegration, as well as of the charge by the neo-pagan intelligentsia that the Christians were to blame for its decline because they had abandoned the gods who had made Rome great. Provoked by the sack of the Eternal City by the Goths in 410, Augustine knew that he must answer the challenge issued by the neo-pagans. Within three years he had begun work on his magnum opus, a brilliant work that would take thirteen years to write: *The City of God*. It was, however, far more than a refutation of the neo-pagan charge; it was a positive and comprehensive philosophy of history. Departing radically from the Greek notion that history was an endless series of meaningless cycles and deeply informed by the biblical vision, Augustine saw history (under the sovereign hand of God) as having purpose and direction, having a beginning and moving to a culmination. Flatly contradicting many of his contemporaries—those who prized the Roman Empire as the citadel of order in the midst of a chaotic world and were deeply dismayed at its decline— Augustine regarded the passing of the Empire with confident hope in God, who was building a city not made with human hands.

His contrast between the earthly city, formed by the love of self, and the heavenly city, formed by the love of God, is masterful. The earthly city is not all bad, in Augustine's view. Consider Babylon and Rome—the highest representatives of that city—which out of self-interest brought about a certain peace and order. But the earthly city will fade—indeed, *must* fade—as the heavenly city grows. And all of history, directed and governed by God, is moving toward a climax in the creation of an all-inclusive community of love, a heavenly city in which God's will is done perfectly. We enter this heavenly city here and now, although its fulfillment in that eternal "felicity, which shall be tainted with no evil, which shall lack no good" is not fully realized here and now, but only in the age to come.[33] The heavenly city is presently represented by the Church of Jesus Christ—though not perfectly, for not all who are in the Church are citizens of the heavenly city, and not all actions and activities of the Church are actions and activities of the heavenly city.

It is fitting that Augustine should have penned his *Confessions* near the beginning of his ministry and *The City of God* near the end. The first was his personal autobiography; the second, the autobiography of the Church universal. He opened the first with his confessional prayer to God: "You made us for yourself, and our heart is restless until it find rest in you."[34] He closed the second with the beatific vision of perpetual sabbath rest: "There we shall rest and see, see and love, love and praise. This is what shall be in the end without end. For what other end do we propose to ourselves than to attain to the kingdom of which there is no end?"[35]

The complete collapse of the "earthly city" of Roman Africa coincided almost to the day with the death of Aurelius Augustine. On 28 August A.D. 430, as the Vandals were laying siege to the city of Hippo, Augustine left this life for the greater Life of the City of God.

We can be immensely grateful for the life and work of Augustine. He modeled evangelical faith for us through his effective proclamation of the gospel, his vigorous defense of the faith, and his faithfulness to the Scriptures.

SEEKING A BIBLICAL PARADIGM

For a biblical paradigm of the Evangelical Tradition I choose the Apostle Peter. The reason is simple: above all else Peter was a proclaimer of the evangel, a preacher of the good news of the gospel. Peter was everywhere and in every way a fisher of men and women. He understood his supreme task to be the winning and making of disciples for Jesus Christ.

We see him doing this most wonderfully and most powerfully on the day of Pentecost. The disciples—now 120 strong—*had waited* as instructed. The Spirit *had come* as promised—accompanied with the sound of heavenly wind and the sight of tongues as of fire. And the disciples *did speak* in other tongues so that the crowds gathered from the nations of the world heard them in their own languages boldly praising God. What under heaven did it all mean?

Seizing the moment, Peter explains exactly what it means. Luke records Peter's sermon in considerable detail, and with good reason: it is a masterful piece of gospel proclamation. He first explains the supernatural behavior going on as a fulfillment of Joel's prophecy that the Spirit will be poured out upon all flesh. Next he confronts his hearers with three great facts. Fact 1: God commended Jesus by "deeds of power, wonders, and signs." Fact 2: In spite of this, Jesus was murdered "by the hands of those outside the law." Fact 3: God raised Jesus from the grave, "having freed him from death," an event that King David himself prophesied. Finally, he draws the irrefutable conclusion: "Therefore let the entire house of Israel know with certainty that God has made him both Lord and Messiah, this Jesus whom you crucified" (Acts 2:14–36). Pointed, powerful, penetrating gospel proclamation.

Well, the Spirit strikes home with Peter's message: the people are "cut to the heart" and cry out, "What should we do?" Peter is ready with an answer: "Repent, and be baptized every one of you in the name of Jesus Christ so that your sins may be forgiven" (Acts 2:38). That day three thousand receive saving grace and immediately move into God's new community: "They devoted themselves to the apostles' teaching and fellowship, to the breaking of bread and the prayers" (Acts 2:42). It is hard to improve upon this witness and these results.

Essential Training

Peter did not always possess the spiritual resources to speak as he did at Pentecost, however. Oh, he spoke often enough, for he was the titular head of the apostolic band. But more often than not his speaking was what the old preacher of Ecclesiastes graphically described as "the sacrifice offered by fools"—humanly initiated talk, no more (Eccles. 5:1, RSV).

Consider Peter on the Mount of Transfiguration, for example. Jesus has taken his three closest disciples—Peter, James, and John—with him up the mountain to pray. As Jesus prays, he is transfigured before them, and Moses and Elijah appear with him. An overwhelming experience, to say the least. Peter, unable to contain himself, blurts out, "Master, . . . let us make three dwellings, one for you, one for Moses, and one for Elijah." Though he is attempting, I am sure, to express a sense of devotion, he speaks (as Luke notes) "not knowing what he said" (Luke 9:33b). What, after all, would Moses and Elijah do with a dwelling? Sadly, Peter is offering the sacrifice of fools.

We should not be too hard on Peter here, for often we do much the same thing—perhaps out of fear, out of the need to control a situation, or out of a desire to impress others. We speak "not knowing what we said," and in so doing we too offer the sacrifice of fools.

On other occasions Peter speaks both rightly and wrongly at the same time. At Caesarea Philippi Jesus gives a midterm exam, asking the disciples, "Who do you say that I am?" Peter speaks right up: "You are the Christ, the Son of the living God" (Matt. 16:16, RSV). Jesus commends him for speaking out of a source deeper than himself and uses the occasion to change his name from Simon to Peter, "the Rock." Jesus then explains how the Messiah must "undergo great suffering . . . and be killed, and on the third day be raised." Immediately Peter jumps into the fray: "God forbid it," he exclaims. As Jesus had commended Peter a moment ago, he must now correct him: "Get

behind me, Satan! You are a stumbling block to me; for you are setting your mind not on divine things but on human things" (Matt.
16:13–23). It is as James reminds us: "From the same mouth come
blessing and cursing" (James 3:10a).

At times Peter's impulsive speech gets him into serious trouble.
When the disciples see Jesus walking on the water, they are terrified.
But Peter jumps right into the situation: "Lord, if it is you, command
me to come to you on the water." Jesus welcomes this budding faith.
As it turns out, though, Peter has enough faith to get out of the boat
but not enough to keep himself afloat. "Lord, save me!" he cries out;
and, gracious as always, Jesus comes to Peter's aid (Matt. 14:25–31).

Throughout this process Peter is on a steep learning curve. Every
time he runs ahead of the Spirit—he seldom lags behind—he grows
from the experience. He is deepening, growing, becoming established. As the pace of events increases, irrevocably moving toward
their divine yet tragic climax, so does the training of Peter.

In the Upper Room Jesus washes his disciples' feet, and in what
Peter thinks of as an act of supreme humility, he retorts, "You will
never wash my feet." After Jesus helps Peter see the arrogance in his
remarks, Peter's reflex action then goes to the other extreme: "Lord,
not my feet only but also my hands and my head!" (John 13:9).
Again, the sacrifice of fools.

Patiently Jesus shows Peter the larger context of the struggle
(reverting here to Peter's pre-Caesarea Philippi name): "Simon,
Simon, listen! Satan has demanded to sift all of you like wheat, but I
have prayed for you that your own faith may not fail." Peter responds,
"Lord, I am ready to go with you to prison and to death!" Now, this is
no idle boast; Peter genuinely means it. But once again he simply
does not know what he is saying. He overestimates his own spiritual
resources and underestimates the spiritual forces pitted against him.
Jesus, you understand, knows the reality of the situation in a way
Peter does not: "I tell you, Peter, the cock will not crow this day, until
you have denied three times that you know me" (Luke 22:31–34).

To his credit Peter does try, but the spiritual substance of his life
has not yet matured. Jesus takes the Twelve with him across the

Kidron Valley to the Mount of Olives and then takes Peter, James, and John a little further into the Garden of Gethsemane so that they can be with him in his moment of greatest agony. "Watch," he says, and "pray" that you do not "enter into temptation." I have no doubt but that they try to do exactly what Jesus has asked of them, but sleep becomes a ready way to avoid their own pain and grief. So they *do not* "watch" and they *do not* "pray" and they *do* "enter into temptation" (Matt. 26:41, KJV).

Finding them asleep, Jesus diagnoses Peter's situation this way: "The spirit indeed is willing, but the flesh is weak" (Matt. 26:41). But Jesus does not intend for this situation to continue for Peter, and later in the stories in Acts we see that it did not. From Pentecost onward we discover that the flesh had come into a working harmony with the spirit, enabling Peter to speak both boldly and appropriately. But we are not at that point yet. Here, now, Peter has a willing spirit, but his flesh needs further training in matters spiritual.

Peter's flesh does take bold action by cutting off the ear of the high priest's servant. (No doubt he was aiming for the nearest neck and was able to catch only an ear.) But Jesus has to help Peter see that bold action is not necessarily appropriate action; and once Peter is denied recourse to the power of the flesh, he simply has no other resources.

I am sure I do not need to recount for you the sad story of Peter's triple denial. Deplorable, heartrending, curse-filled denial. And then the cock crows. At that sound Jesus' eyes meet Peter's, and in that instant Peter realizes, perhaps for the first time in his life, what he has said. "And he went out and wept bitterly" (Matt. 26:75).

Sufficient Love

Fortunately, this is not the end to Peter's story. There is more. There is great tenderness in the angel's resurrection instruction for the disciples "and Peter" to meet Jesus in Galilee: "Tell the disciples and especially tell Peter, make sure Peter knows Jesus wants him there too" (Mark 16:7). There is great sensitivity in the word given from the shore for Peter and those fishing with him to cast their nets

on the other side, for in their supernatural catch they are able to recognize that it is Jesus speaking to them. There is great kindness in
Jesus' preparation of a warm fire and a fish breakfast for his bone-
weary, heartbroken disciples. But the truly great work in Peter is yet
to come.

Following this breakfast by the Sea of Tiberias, Jesus takes Peter
aside and asks him, "Simon son of John, do you love me more than
these?" Perhaps Jesus is referring to the fishing trade, perhaps to the
other disciples by the fire—we do not know for sure. Whatever or
whoever the object of the comparison, we do know for sure that Jesus
is searching the depths of Peter's love and loyalty (John 21:15).

Now, you must allow me a small digression into the Greek language, for precise language is of critical importance to an understanding of this dialogue between Jesus and Peter. Greek has four words
for *love*. The first, *storge*, refers to human affection, especially between
parents and offspring—a mother nursing her baby or a cat with her
litter, for instance. The second word, *philia*, deals with human friendship and describes a quality highly valued among the ancients—a
quality that Aristotle classified among the virtues. *Eros*, the third
Greek word for love, deals with the relationship between lovers—that
is, erotic love, which frequently includes the heights of sexual experience. The fourth, *agape*, used to be translated "charity," but that was
when the word charity was able to bear a lot more weight than it can
today. Today, perhaps we could use a term such as "divine love" or
"supernatural love"—that is, the kind of love that becomes a part of
human experience only by action from beyond and above it. Paul's
catalog of the attributes of *agape* in 1 Corinthians 13 helps us see
something of its character.

In this exchange between Jesus and Peter there is an important
play on two of these words—*agape* and *philia*. Jesus begins by asking,
"Simon son of John, do you *agapas* me?"—that is, "Do you love me
with God's eternal, ever-receiving, ever-giving, ever-forgiving love?"
Now, there was a time when Peter would have quickly answered,
"Absolutely!" But not this time. Now, humbled by his recent failures
and disciplined by his training under the Master, Peter responds far

more modestly (and more accurately): "Yes, Lord; you know that I *philo* you"—that is, "Yes, I genuinely and deeply care for you as a friend." Jesus responds by commissioning him with the words, "Feed my lambs."

A second time Jesus asks, "Simon son of John, do you *agapas* me?"—"Do you love me with that grace-filled, God-kissed love?" A second time Peter humbly responds, "Yes, Lord; you know that I *philo* you"—"Lord, you know I am your loyal friend." Again, Jesus responds with the commission, "Tend my sheep."

Then a third time. . . . Do you see what Jesus is doing? Three times Peter denied his Master; three times he is being brought to confess his love and loyalty. I rather think that Jesus is also healing Peter's heart, which was wounded beyond imagining from the grief of his denials.

But on the third time Jesus changes the word he uses for love: "Simon son of John, do you *phileis* me?"—"O Simon, dear Simon, do you even love me as a friend?" Scripture tells us that Peter is "grieved" because this time Jesus probes all the more deeply, questioning even Peter's friendship and loyalty. Finally, Peter confesses, "Lord, you know everything." The word "to know" here refers to instinctive knowledge. "Lord, you know the depths of my heart. I cannot hide from you. You know that I *philo* you, that I love you as a friend."

Peter at this juncture may well feel that he possesses very little love. But his yes is a true yes; he has not embellished or overstated the case. He shares what is truly in his heart. Now, perhaps for the first time, he knows what he is saying. And Jesus sees this in Peter and for a third time commissions him for evangelical ministry with the words, "Feed my sheep" (John 21:15–19).

And, as we say, the rest is history. From this point on we see a different Peter. Not that he is perfect; he still makes mistakes. At one point, for example, Paul has to rebuke him for withdrawing from the Gentile Christians at Antioch (Gal. 2:11–14). But the spiritual substance of his life has been established. He has a new firmness of life-orientation, and we see this most clearly in Peter's ability to proclaim the good news of the gospel. Whether he is preaching in Solomon's Portico or before the Sanhedrin or in the home of Cornelius, we see someone who is constantly and consistently "holding forth the word of life" (Phil. 2:16, KJV). This is what commends Peter to us as a faithful representative of the Evangelical Tradition.

In the two Epistles that have been traditionally attributed to the pen of Peter, we see the same faithfulness in gospel proclamation. "By his great mercy," he writes, "[God] has given us a new birth into a living hope through the resurrection of Jesus Christ from the dead" (1 Pet. 1:3b). And consistent with the Great Commission stipulations, he calls all peoples to faithful discipleship to Jesus Christ, walking, ever walking "in his steps" (1 Pet. 2:21b).

If the traditions are true, and there is good reason to believe them, then this man who began as a fisherman on the Sea of Galilee ended up fishing for men and women in the greatest urban center of the world, Rome. And it was there, just as Jesus had foretold, that Peter was bound and taken "where you do not wish to go" (John 21:18).

So many years ago and so many miles away Peter had declared his willingness to die for Christ. Then, in that Upper Room, he had spoken naïvely, "not knowing what he said." But now, in Rome, he was indeed able to give final witness by death on a cross. His only request was to be crucified upside down, for he believed himself unworthy to die in the same position as his Lord and Master.[36]

SEEKING A CONTEMPORARY PARADIGM

In considering a contemporary model for the Evangelical Tradition, one name rises head and shoulders above all the others: Billy Graham. In a debate at Cambridge University Dr. Graham declared, "The proclamation of the Gospel lies at the very heart of our mission to the world."[37] Yes indeed, and Billy Graham himself has clearly fulfilled the demands of that mission, proclaiming the gospel to monarchs and millions alike all over the world. He has traveled to more places and preached to more persons than anyone in history.

The life story of Billy Graham has been well documented, and so the barest outline here will be sufficient, allowing us to give more detailed attention to his key contributions to the work of evangelism and the Evangelical Tradition in our day.[38]

We can be grateful for the sturdy home environment that nurtured Billy Graham during his growing-up years on a farm near Charlotte, North Carolina. Born 7 November 1918, he experienced a second birth—"born from above," as Jesus put it—as a teenager under the fiery evangelistic ministry of Mordecai Ham. After that decisive event it was not long before Graham's course was set: he sensed a call to preach while a student at Florida Bible Institute, trained in the liberal arts at Wheaton College, preached and pastored at "the Tab" (United Gospel Tabernacle) and Western Springs Baptist Church, and experienced the wider world as the "international organizer" for Youth for Christ before becoming evangelist to the world after the historic Los Angeles meetings in 1949.

Crusades in Abundance

The number and size of Graham's crusades, the multiplicity of countries and cultures he has preached in, and the reach of his elongated ministry simply stagger the imagination. Out of his more than three hundred crusades, several stand out as great high-water marks.

The 1949 "Campaign" (a term later abandoned in favor of "Crusade") in Los Angeles gave Graham his first national exposure. Held in a tent, the meetings had virtually no advance publicity from the media. But then God began moving in wondrous ways: country singer Stewart Hamblen made a "decision for Christ," William Randolph Hearst issued his famous "Puff Graham" memo to his newspaper conglomerate, and underworld wiretapper Jim Vaus and Olympic track star Louis Zamperini came to faith in Christ. Those meetings, slated to run for three weeks, were extended to a full eight weeks because of the clear blessing of God upon them. Overnight Graham was transformed from a little-known itinerant evangelist to the central figure in mass evangelism.

If the Los Angeles meetings of 1949 gave Graham a national platform, the Greater London Crusade of 1954 catapulted him onto the international stage. Filled to overflowing with divine blessing, that crusade had a power and strength that simply cannot be overstated. "This campaign," wrote William Martin, "so defied expectations, so triumphed over skepticism and opposition, and so captured the attention and imagination of the English-speaking world . . . that participants found it easy to believe they were living in the days foreseen in the rousing revival standard: 'From vict'ry unto vict'ry / His armies shall he lead / Till ev'ry foe is vanquished / And Christ is Lord indeed.'"[39]

Mention must be made of the longest crusade ever held by Billy Graham: New York, 1957. Meeting in Madison Square Garden, Graham preached for sixteen bruising weeks with a closing rally at Times Square. It was the most broadly sponsored event Graham had had up to that point, and though it precipitated the final break with fundamentalist leaders unhappy with his growing ecumenism, nothing could take away the thrill of proclaiming the gospel to overflow crowds in what Billy believed was "the most strategic center in the world."[40]

Nor should I fail to mention the million-plus souls who gathered on Yoido Island in Seoul, Korea, in 1973. With Billy Kim as an enormously effective translator, Billy Graham preached the gospel message of salvation in Jesus Christ as that solid block of humanity listened quietly, attentively, reverently. Nearly a year and a half after the event Sam Moffett, son of the first Protestant missionary to Korea, commented that he was "stunned by the emotional impact of that many people on that island. It's still with me."[41]

Finally, I must note the 1995 Crusade in San Juan, Puerto Rico. This crusade may be the most extensive single evangelistic outreach in the history of the Church — an outreach made possible by satellite technology that transmitted the meetings into 185 countries and territories. Graham's messages were simultaneously translated into forty-eight languages as people listened in literally thousands of venues, from sports stadiums to refugee camps.

Intentional Focus

Anyone who looks at the life ministry of Billy Graham cannot help but be struck by how focused it is. The charism of the evangelist is a highly specific and intently focused ministry. Graham wrote, "An evangelist is called to do one thing, and one thing only: to proclaim the Gospel."[42] He penned these words in the midst of admitting his own failure to live up to this high standard of intentional focus, but whatever his shortcomings in this regard, the more amazing fact is how much he achieved the standard.

This life focus had its beginnings with Billy's own sense of call to gospel ministry—a call that came, as I noted, during his student days at Florida Bible Institute. The school was a nurturing place that offered a variety of opportunities to test his preaching skills—from street corners and rural churches to his favorite audience at "Tin Can Trailer Park." The results were most encouraging, but the question that plagued Billy was, "Did I want to preach for a lifetime? I asked myself that question for the umpteenth time on one of my nighttime walks around the golf course. The inner, irresistible urge would not subside. Finally, one night, I got down on my knees at the edge of one of the greens. Then I prostrated myself on the dewy turf. 'O God,' I sobbed, 'if you want me to serve you, I will.'. . . In my spirit I knew I had been called to the ministry. And I knew my answer was yes."[43]

Billy honed his preaching skills by paddling a canoe over to a little island where he proclaimed gospel truths to alligators and birds and cypress trees. This hidden preparation was crucial for his future ministry, which was destined to include audiences the size and scope of which he could never have imagined back then.

His varied Florida preaching experiences were crucial preparation in another way also, a way that helped focus and direct his entire life. Florida Bible Institute had only one real curriculum: the Bible. Now, this curricular focus certainly had its limitations, but it also had its strengths, and the greatest strength for Billy was the way it encouraged him to immerse himself in the content of the Bible. Most academic settings, even many religious ones, force students to keep the biblical message at arm's length. Not Florida Bible Institute. There Billy Graham soaked himself in Scripture: reading Scripture, studying Scripture, pondering Scripture, preaching Scripture, applying Scripture. He so imbibed the biblical worldview during those years

that "Bible" simply flowed from his every pore thereafter. He thought
Bible, he spoke Bible, he prayed Bible. As he later said of those days
in Florida, "I came to believe with all my heart in the full inspiration
of the Bible."[44]

Billy had to face the issue of the Bible as the focus of his life again
just prior to the famous 1949 Los Angeles Crusade. Chuck Templeton,
a close friend and able preacher in his own right, had been attending
Princeton Seminary and was challenging some of Graham's most
cherished beliefs about the inspiration and authority of Scripture.
Graham indicated little inclination or patience for abstract intellectualism. "Bill," Templeton retorted, "you cannot refuse to think. To
do that is to die intellectually." The rebuke stung, and the debate in
his soul intensified. Finally, the issue came to a head at Forest Home,
a Christian retreat center in the San Bernardino Mountains near Los
Angeles. Struggling over the intellectual questions his friend had
raised, Billy went out alone into the pine forest to think, to pray.
With his Bible spread open on a tree stump he dropped to his knees.
"O God!" he prayed, "There are many things in this book I do not
understand. There are many problems with it for which I have no
solution. . . . Father, I am going to accept this as Thy Word—by *faith!*
I'm going to allow faith to go beyond my intellectual questions and
doubts, and I will believe this to be Your inspired Word."[45]

He rose from the ground, eyes stinging with tears, sensing the
presence of God in a new and living way. This conscious resolution
settled the battle in his soul and galvanized his faith. Since that day
the singular focus of biblical authority has given unusual power and
authority to his preaching.

The evangelistic focus of Graham's life was almost detoured once
when, under obligation to an old friend and mentor, he accepted the
presidency of Northwestern Schools, a combination Bible school,
college, and seminary. At first he felt that he could build an institution with a passion for evangelism. He even came up with an evangelistic motto for Northwestern: "Knowledge on fire." But even at an
idealistic twenty-nine years of age he quickly learned that he had little stomach for the detailed educational development and adminis-

tration needed to make such an institution thrive. Never having felt fully comfortable in the presidency, he tried to resign in 1950, but the board of trustees refused to accept his resignation. Finally, in 1952, he was able to make his resignation stick. In retrospect he notes simply, "I was called by God to be an evangelist, not an educator."[46]

And evangelist he was! As the realization deepened that his gift was in evangelism, this focus became all the more sharp. After the great success of Los Angeles in 1949, he never looked back. Once, when Paramount Pictures tried to lure him into an acting career, he answered bluntly, "God had called me to preach the Gospel and . . . I would never do anything else as long as I lived."[47]

The charism of the evangelist is to proclaim the good news of the gospel and, by means of the convicting work of the Holy Spirit, call people to enter saving faith based upon that message. The temptations to stray from this clear-cut task are many, and they are often far more subtle than the offer of an acting career. In 1955 at Cambridge University Graham tried for three nights to make his preaching academic and erudite, but his efforts had no effect. Finally, realizing that his gift was not to present the intellectual side of faith, he abandoned his prepared texts and in utter simplicity preached the gospel message of our alienation from God because of sin and our reconciliation to God through the cross of Christ. The results were astonishing: hundreds of sophisticated students responded to this clear proclamation of the gospel. It was a lesson in clarity and simplicity that he never forgot.

Even more complex were temptations in the political arena. Here the pressures to lose his evangelistic focus were constant and sustained as Graham cultivated relationships with numerous presidents and other heads of state. And it was not just the temptation of endorsing one political candidate over another; it was also the more knotty problem of advocating religious nationalism of some sort. The pressures here were exceedingly great because they played directly into Graham's own natural impulses toward patriotism. As a result, particularly in the early years, the Bible often got wrapped in the flag of nationalistic interests.[48] In later years Graham became much more circumspect in these matters. Frankly, it is never easy to be both pastoral and prophetic to the powerful while being courted by them.

As I mentioned earlier, whatever shortcomings Billy Graham may have had in evangelistic focus, they are eclipsed by the amazing clarity of direction that has permeated his entire life and ministry. When he was first thrust into national prominence, with its attendant multidimensional opportunities, he stayed true to his evangelistic focus: "All I knew how to do was to preach the essential Gospel as revealed in the New Testament and experienced by millions across the centuries."[49] When establishing the Billy Graham Evangelistic Association, he set into its charter a simple and direct statement of purpose: "To spread and propagate the Gospel of the Lord Jesus Christ by any and all . . . means."[50] This same clarity of focus has permeated all of Graham's preaching, regardless of the announced sermon topic or any special emphasis used to attract attention. As Graham noted, "People soon found out that my theme was always the same: God's redemptive love for sinners, and the need for personal repentance and conversion."[51]

The calling of the evangelist, as we have seen, is to an intentional, disciplined focus upon one thing: the proclamation of the good news of the gospel. Billy Graham has most certainly shown us what such a singular focus looks like.

Major Contributions

The contributions that Billy Graham has made to the evangelistic enterprise in general and the Evangelical Tradition in particular are many and varied. I would like to especially highlight five.

First of all, he has brought moral and fiscal integrity to itinerant evangelism. Graham himself had an unimpugnable moral character, and he did not want any moral failures in his burgeoning organization. Furthermore, he was deeply concerned over the entrenched cultural stereotypes of evangelists as "Elmer Gantry" charlatans. He dealt forcefully with these matters early on in what later came to be known as "The Modesto Manifesto."

Calling his team together during a November 1948 campaign in Modesto, California, he said to them, "God has brought us to this point. Maybe he is preparing us for something that we don't know. Let's try to recall all the things that have been a stumbling block . . . to evangelists in years past, and let's come back together in an hour and talk about it and pray about it and ask God to guard us from them." When they regathered an hour later, they found that their lists of abuses were remarkably similar: money, sex, exaggerating results, and criticism of local churches and pastors.

To deal with the financial abuses, they developed strict accounting procedures and eventually went to a salary support system instead of the common "love offering." To deal with sexual immorality, they pledged to avoid any situation that would have even the appearance of evil. On that day Graham himself established a rule never to meet, travel, or eat alone with a woman other than Ruth, his wife. To guard against the problem of exaggerated results, they decided that instead of generating their own statistics, they would accept the crowd estimates given by police or arena managers. To avoid an antichurch and anticlerical spirit, they determined never to publicly criticize local clergy and to cooperate with them everywhere possible.[52]

These simple guidelines reflect the integrity of the Graham team and their determination to have an evangelistic ministry that is above reproach. In this objective they have succeeded immensely, escaping even the slightest hint of scandal in over five decades.

The second major contribution is Graham's advocacy of "cooperative evangelism"—in other words, working with a broad spectrum of the Christian community in evangelistic efforts.[53] This pragmatic ecumenism is actually in the best of the Evangelical Tradition. Whitfield, Wesley, Moody, Finney, Sunday, and others freely cooperated with church leaders of widely differing persuasions in order to proclaim the gospel to all peoples. But in the early twentieth century this Tradition was stunted by bitter controversies between "modernists" and "fundamentalists," the latter heeding the call to "come out from among them, and be ye separate" (2 Cor. 6:17, KJV).

Graham himself largely escaped the harshness of fundamentalist separatism. At Florida Bible Institute he found "a wondrous blend of ecumenical and evangelical thought that was really ahead of its time."[54] In 1948 Graham went to the founding assembly of the World Council of Churches as an observer. Though uncomfortable with its dominantly liberal theology, he was deeply impressed by the council's secretary, Dr. Willem Visser 't Hooft; and the experience instilled in him "a greater desire to work with as many churches as possible."[55]

He was beginning to catch a vision of united efforts that could bring together as many churches as possible around the common mission of evangelism. In preparation for the 1949 Los Angeles Crusade Graham challenged the sponsoring committee to broaden its base of churches supporting the event. The results were electrifying. From this point on he worked long and hard to deepen and broaden the base of sponsoring church groups. Key fundamentalist leaders, however, viewed such alliances as a compromise of the gospel itself.

The showdown came in conjunction with the great 1957 New York Crusade. Graham had already turned down two invitations (in 1951 and 1954) to hold crusades in New York because he felt that the sponsoring constituency was too narrow. But when he got an invitation from the Protestant Council of the City of New York, he agreed. It was the last straw for the three leading fundamentalists of the day—Carl McIntire, Bob Jones, and John R. Rice. They came out against Graham in article after vitriolic article. Graham gave a spirited defense: "I would like to make myself clear. I intend to go anywhere, sponsored by anybody, to preach the Gospel of Christ if there are no strings attached to my message. I am sponsored by civic clubs, universities, ministerial associations, and councils of churches all over the world. I intend to continue."[56] The controversy, however, was distressing to Graham, for it pained him to lose the support and affection of those who had worked by his side. In spite of the division—which was complete and irreparable—Billy for his part pledged, "I shall continue to preach the Gospel of Jesus Christ and not stoop to mudslinging, name-calling, and petty little fights over nonessentials."[57]

The fundamentalism of McIntire, Jones, and Rice and the evangelicalism of Graham took two different paths to gospel proclamation. Graham, in my opinion, chose the better path—certainly the path more true to the Evangelical Tradition and, I would venture to say, more true to biblical revelation. For this those who come after him are ever in his debt.

The third contribution I would like to mention is Graham's quiet work for racial reconciliation—work that has gone almost unnoticed in the rush of stadium events and meetings with heads of state. The foundation for this push toward reconciliation was, as we should expect, Scripture: "Most influential . . . was my study of the Bible, leading me eventually to the conclusion that not only was racial inequality wrong but Christians especially should demonstrate love toward all peoples."[58]

It was, however, an "eventual conclusion," because Billy, as a son of the South, had inherited some of its discriminatory views. As he struggled toward a Christian view of racial justice, he accepted, for example, the common practice of segregated seating in his southern crusades. But by 1953 he had reached that "eventual conclusion," and at the Chattanooga, Tennessee, Crusade he personally tore down the ropes separating the white and black sections. In protest the head usher of the crusade resigned on the spot. It was a critical turning point.

One year before the Supreme Court decision of 17 May 1954 outlawing segregated schools, Graham (perhaps lamenting his own reluctance to take a firm stand earlier) wrote in *Peace with God*, "The church should have been the pace-setter." He went on to insist that when true Christians look at others, they should see "not color, nor class, nor condition, but simply human beings with the same longings, fears, needs and aspirations as our own."[59]

From this point on Graham's integrated crusades were a quiet testimony for racial justice. At the 1957 New York Crusade he asked Martin Luther King, Jr., to lead a prayer, and he later invited King to a team retreat to help the crusade staff understand the racial situation more fully. When the Little Rock Central High School desegregation crisis erupted, President Eisenhower called Graham at Madison Square Garden, asking for his advice about sending in federal troops. "Mr. President," Graham responded, "I think that is the only thing you can do. It is out of hand, and the time has come to stop it." An hour later Vice President Nixon called to get a second reading and received the same counsel. That afternoon a thousand federal troops rolled into Little Rock, Arkansas.[60] Later the Little Rock Ministerial Association asked Graham to help unite the city by preaching in the Memorial Stadium. He did (albeit a year later), to fully integrated seating.

His trip to South Africa in 1973 also furthered racial reconciliation. Invited several times before, he had always refused since the government policy of apartheid would have meant segregated audiences. But in 1973, to everyone's surprise, he was able to gain permission for two fully integrated evangelistic rallies—one in Johannesburg and the other in the coastal city of Durban. About the Durban rally, Billy wrote, "I will never forget . . . when 45,000 people of all races—half the people non-white—jammed King's Park Rugby stadium and spilled over most of the playing field. Some of the committee members were almost overcome with joy by the sight of white ushers escorting nonwhites to their seats."[61] As biographer John Pollock noted, "Those South African rallies hold a special niche in history for their contribution to racial reconciliation."[62]

A quiet witness, to be sure. Even so, these simple acts of racial justice at home and abroad were noticed, garnering Graham his share of threats and hate mail from white citizen councils (especially through the 1950s) and changing not a few minds. Thus as a witness for truth, a witness for justice, they had their effect.

A fourth contribution is the way in which Billy Graham has used literally every communications tool at his disposal in the task of evangelism. This pragmatism in utilizing the media is, to use the words of Charles Finney, "the right use of the constituted means."[63]

Graham's use of media goes all the way back to the beginnings of his ministry. In 1944 Torrey Johnson, a well-known preacher in the Chicago area, offered Graham a weekly radio program, "Songs in the

Night." Graham seized the opportunity, and "with a confidence bordering on gall" persuaded the well-known soloist George Beverly Shea to become the show's primary musical performer.[64] That was his first use of media technology; it was far from his last.

The foundation of his use of media has been the printed page. Since 1950 he has written (or had his staff write) a daily syndicated newspaper column, "My Answer." In 1953 he published *Peace with God*, the first of several books. In 1956 he launched a new magazine, *Christianity Today*, which sought to set forth evangelical concerns in a positive and constructive way. Wisely he turned the editorship and management of the magazine over to other hands. Next came *Decision* magazine in 1960, which sought to do for the lay reader what *Christianity Today* was doing for Christian leaders. With a circulation of over four million, it is by far the farthest-reaching of his publications.

On that foundation have been built other media technologies: radio, with "The Hour of Decision"; film, with the establishment of World Wide Pictures; television, with an average of four primetime specials each year; and cutting-edge communication, with satellite and Internet technology.

Every decision made by Graham and his colleagues to move into a new medium has been a challenging story in itself—a story of faith ventures combined with human foibles, superintended throughout by divine Providence. Because these endeavors have been enormously expensive, great care and wisdom have been needed to keep faith-filled exuberance from bankrupting the organization. Most interesting of all is the way Graham has embraced these technologies not just to promote his own ministry, but for the task of worldwide evangelism itself.

Which leads me to the fifth and, in my opinion, the greatest of Graham's contributions to evangelism in our day: the training of itinerant evangelists worldwide. While this work had been going on in many ways over the years, the concern to train itinerant evangelists became the focused objective of a pair of conferences held at Graham's initiation in Amsterdam in 1983 and 1986.[65]

In one sense this enormous undertaking is the unknown story of the Billy Graham Evangelistic Association. No one had ever attempted anything like this before, and leading thinkers to this day do not quite know what to make of it all. It was exactly the opposite of the modern mind set of exerting a worldwide influence by going to the famous, the powerful, the influential. This, in contrast, was an effort to discover and train the most obscure, and, to many, the most insignificant of people: itinerant evangelists. In the eyes of modern opinion makers there could hardly be a more irrelevant vocation. Not to Billy Graham, though.

Before these conferences were held no one had the slightest idea how many itinerant evangelists there were in the world. No one, you understand, had ever tried to find out. These were people who were mostly from Two-Thirds World countries and mostly unknown to ecclesiastical leaders—people who labored in total obscurity, often traveling on foot from village to village, preaching the gospel. Many of them had never been outside the borders of their own country, much less to an international conference. With diligent work, organizers were able to assemble a list of ten thousand evangelists from one hundred thirty-three countries. In time that number swelled to sixty-two thousand from virtually every corner of the globe. Of these, Amsterdam '83 was able to accommodate nearly four thousand, and Amsterdam '86 somewhere between eight and nine thousand. A tremendous effort really, but only a fraction of the total. Fortunately, the Amsterdam gatherings have spawned many regional conferences. In 1988 there were twenty-six "mini-Amsterdams" in Latin America alone. By 1990 the Graham organization had helped organize eighty-eight such conferences with an aggregate attendance of over forty-six thousand evangelists from ninety-seven countries.[66]

If I were to compare this enormous effort to anything in history, it would be the great ecumenical councils in the first centuries of the Church. And the "Amsterdam Affirmations" that grew out of these gatherings are not unlike the creedal confessions that emerged from those historic councils. From the perspective of heaven, these gatherings may well be the greatest contribution Billy Graham and his team have given the Church of Jesus Christ for the fulfillment of the Great Commission upon the earth.

We can be thankful to God for these varied contributions. They are all deeply rooted in the Evangelical Tradition and have contributed richly to it.

DEFINING THE EVANGELICAL TRADITION

The Evangelical Tradition is comprised of three great themes: first, and foremost, the faithful proclamation of the gospel; second, the centrality of Scripture as a faithful repository of the gospel; and third, the confessional witness of the early Christian community as a faithful interpretation of the gospel.

A Faithful Proclamation

The evangel message is the good news of redemption and reconciliation, powerfully captured in the words of the Apostle Paul: "If anyone is in Christ, he is a new creation; the old has gone, the new has come! All this is from God, who reconciled us to himself through Christ and gave us the ministry of reconciliation. . . . We are therefore Christ's ambassadors, as though God were making his appeal through us. We implore you on Christ's behalf: Be reconciled to God" (2 Cor. 5:17–20, NIV).

This evangel, this *euangelion*, this wonderful good news is that we no longer have to stand outside, barred from nearness to God by our sin and rebellion. Knowing that we are a stiff-necked and hard-hearted people, God has provided us a way into his heart. And that way is through him who says, "I am the way, and the truth, and the life" (John 14:6). Jesus Christ is the door that opens into God's great grace and mercy.

The evangel message is rooted in the person of Jesus Christ, the Word of God living. In the Christ event—Jesus' birth, life, death, and resurrection—the way has been opened for us to be reconciled to God.

Jesus himself announced this good news of the gospel in his cryptic call, "Repent, for the kingdom of heaven has come near" (Matt.

4:17). The word *repent* here means literally "to turn around in your mind." In other words, we should reevaluate our whole way of living in light of this great fact: in the person of Jesus Christ the kingdom of heaven has been made accessible to human beings.[67]

What does this mean? It means that we *can* be reconciled to God. It means that we *can* be made new. It means that we *can* be born from above. It means that we *can* experience the forgiveness of sins through the atoning death of Jesus on the cross.[68] It means that we *can* enter a loving, living, eternal relationship with God the Father, through Jesus Christ the Son, by the power of the Holy Spirit. Surely this is great, good news!

Listen to Jesus' grand invitation of grace: "Come to me, all you that are weary and are carrying heavy burdens, and I will give you rest. Take my yoke upon you, and learn from me; for I am gentle and humble in heart, and you will find rest for your souls. For my yoke is easy, and my burden is light" (Matt 11:28–30).

So we are invited into a new life in Christ. And that new life is ours by faith alone. There are no things we do to get good enough to receive this life. It is all grace and all gift: "For by grace you have been saved through faith, and this is not your own doing; it is the gift of God—not the result of works, so that no one may boast" (Eph. 2:8–9). In the words of P. T. Forsyth, "Christianity is not the sacrifice we make, but the sacrifice we trust; not the victory we win, but the victory we inherit. That is the evangelical principle."[69]

Please understand, we are not here talking exclusively (or even primarily) about how we may get into heaven when we die. Getting into heaven is a matter of genuine consequence (and it does, in fact, come as part of the total package), but the evangel of the gospel is that abundant life in Christ begins *now*, and death becomes only a minor transition from this life to greater Life.

So the evangel, the good news of the gospel, is that we enter into life in Christ as his disciple right now. It is not that we believe now, enrolling as his disciple at some later point if we are so inclined (as if it were possible to believe without being his disciple). Believing in Jesus and discipleship to Jesus are part of the same action. We accept

Jesus Christ, the living Word of God, as our life. He then promises to be yoked to us as we are yoked to him, and to teach us how to live our life as he would live it if he were in our place. He is alive and among us in all his offices: as our Savior to redeem us, as our Teacher to guide us, as our Lord to rule us, and as our Friend to come alongside us. In this way we grow ever more into Christlikeness, "for those whom [God] foreknew he also predestined to be conformed to the image of his Son" (Rom. 8:29a).

Even more, we are given the honor of sharing this good news of ongoing life in Christ with all peoples: "Go therefore and make disciples of all nations, baptizing them in the name of the Father and of the Son and of the Holy Spirit, and teaching them to obey everything that I have commanded you" (Matt. 28:19–20a).

Now, we do not do this without the working of this transforming life in ourselves. We cannot preach the good news and be the bad news. So, making the necessary cultural adjustments, we step into the life of the Gospels and do what they did and live as they lived. As we take the words of Christ into our hearts, and those around us— seeing the transforming power of God in us—say, "We need to get in on this." What we are offering the world is life as it was meant to be.

Remember, we are calling people not merely to accept a set of beliefs about Jesus that will somehow trip the divine lever and get them into heaven when they die. Oh, no! We are calling people to turn to Jesus as their life. We are inviting people to believe in Jesus by becoming his disciples, and as his disciples (or apprentices) to enroll in his school of living. Thus people become trained in the Way, increasingly taking into themselves Jesus' hopes, dreams, longings, habits, and abilities. This is how they learn "to obey everything that I have commanded you." There simply is no other way.

A Faithful Repository

This evangel message has been faithfully preserved and presented to us in Scripture. The Bible is the Word of God written, just as Jesus is the Word of God living. Evangelical faith is biblical faith. The Gospels—

Matthew, Mark, Luke, and John—stand at the heart of the biblical witness, for they faithfully give us the Christ event. The Epistles are the interpretative record of the Christ event, and we receive the Hebrew Scriptures as the written Word of God because Jesus did. And Paul's confessional statement is ours as well: "All scripture is inspired by God and is useful for teaching, for reproof, for correction, and for training in righteousness, so that everyone who belongs to God may be proficient, equipped for every good work" (2 Tim. 3:16–17).

Many and varied are the apologetic witnesses to the inspiration and authority of Scripture, and beyond affirming their validity, we need not go into them here. But alongside them we can add what the old writers called the *indicia*, the inward testimony of Scripture, for it is the uniform witness of the Church that, as illuminated by the Spirit, Scripture authenticates itself.

The evangelical witness affirms the primacy of Scripture as the only infallible rule of faith and practice. This cannot be stressed enough. Scripture has primacy over other writings; primacy over church tradition; primacy over individual religious experience; primacy over the individual conscience; primacy over individual revelations, dreams, and visions; primacy over culture.[70] As the Protestant reformers put it, *Sola Scriptura*, the Scripture alone.

This important confession gives us a standard or a norm for discerning faith and practice. Theologians, in fact, call Scripture the "formal norm" (just as Jesus and his message are the "material norm") for Christian faith and practice. This by no means solves all of our problems, for huge questions of interpretation (hermeneutics) remain, but it does give us a basis upon which to work on the various problems that confront us almost daily.

A Faithful Interpretation

The evangel message of new life in Christ spread rapidly to virtually every culture and people group in the known world of that day. Soon, however, competing views began to emerge, some claiming to replace or even surpass the good news of the gospel. Clarification

was needed. In the New Testament Epistles, especially those attributed to Paul, we see the beginnings of this clarification and interpretation of the Christ event. We cannot, for example, read Paul's great
christological statement in Colossians 1:15–20 without the deepest
admiration and thanksgiving to God for it:

> He is the image of the invisible God, the firstborn of all cre-
> ation; for in him all things in heaven and on earth were created,
> things visible and invisible, whether thrones or dominions or
> rulers or powers—all things have been created through him
> and for him. He himself is before all things, and in him all
> things hold together. He is the head of the body, the church; he
> is the beginning, the firstborn from the dead, so that he might
> come to have first place in everything. For in him all the full-
> ness of God was pleased to dwell, and through him God was
> pleased to reconcile to himself all things, whether on earth or in
> heaven, by making peace through the blood of his cross.

This clarifying and interpreting work continued on for some
time—roughly five centuries. Several great "ecumenical councils"
were held during those years to hammer out as clear an understanding of the Christ event as possible.[71] A precursor to these councils, as
you may know, is recorded in our Bible—the momentous Jerusalem
Council of Acts 15, convened to clarify the grounds of salvation for
Gentile disciples. (We might wish that all of the subsequent gatherings had the same Spirit-driven unity.)

The debates at these ecumenical councils were highly significant, for
opposing positions abounded: Gnosticism and Marcionism and Montanism and Arianism and Nestorianism and Pelagianism and more.[72] Perhaps
the three most important councils were Nicea in A.D. 325 (which confessed Christ as fully divine), Constantinople in A.D. 381 (which confessed
Christ as fully human), and Chalcedon in A.D. 451 (which confessed the
unity of Christ—two natures, one person).

These were matters of no small consequence, and what the councils concluded in regard to them has defined and clarified the Christ

event for the Church ever after. For example, the Christian community has for fifteen hundred years looked to the Council of Chalcedon as providing the foundation of the doctrine of salvation in the unique God-man, Jesus Christ.

Probably the most famous of the clarifying statements from these ecumenical councils is the Nicene Creed, which grew out of and was named after the Council of Nicea. In its words we can see how carefully and forthrightly it was correcting the Arian notion that Christ was a created being and the Nestorian idea that Christ was two distinct beings. This statement is so powerful and so foundational to Christian conviction that it is best quoted in full:

> We believe in one God the Father All-sovereign, maker of heaven and earth, and of all things visible and invisible;
> And in one Lord Jesus Christ, the only-begotten Son of God, Begotten of the Father before all the ages, Light of Light, true God of true God, begotten not made, of one substance with the Father, through whom all things were made; who for us men and for our salvation came down from the heavens, and was made flesh of the Holy Spirit and the Virgin Mary, and became man, and was crucified for us under Pontius Pilate, and suffered and was buried, and rose again on the third day according to the Scriptures, and ascended into the heavens, and sitteth on the right hand of the Father, and cometh again with glory to judge living and dead, of whose kingdom there shall be no end:
> And in the Holy Spirit, the Lord and the Life-giver, that proceedeth from the Father, who with Father and Son is worshipped together and glorified together, who spake through the prophets:
> In one holy Catholic and Apostolic Church:
> We acknowledge one baptism unto remission of sins. We look for a resurrection of the dead, and the life of the age to come.[73]

These affirmations and creeds, which seek to interpret and clarify the Christ event, must never carry the same weight and authority as Scripture, for evangelical conviction always calls for the primacy of

Scripture as the formal norm in matters of faith and practice; but they are confessional statements of immense importance. Authentic evangelical witness is rooted in doctrinal fidelity as well as the transforming experience of conversion. What we believe matters, and the Evangelical Tradition has always concerned itself with clarity in belief. (Did you notice how much of this clarifying work Augustine did throughout his ministry?)

Such doctrinal concerns as the deity and humanity of Christ, his resurrection from the dead, and the doctrine of the Trinity are of prime interest to evangelical witness. Why? Because they, and other doctrinal beliefs like them, hold us to a faithful interpretation of the Christ event. This in turn enables us to proclaim the good news of the gospel, the evangel, with fidelity and integrity.

DISCOVERING THE MAJOR STRENGTHS

We can be thankful for the many strengths of the Evangelical Tradition. I shall mention four here.

First, let's thank God for the evangelical call to conversion. We have constant tendency to hold any real faith commitment at arm's length, and so we need to hear the call to decide for Christ. We need to hear the invitation to be born from above. We need to hear the witness to experience converting grace.

Such evangelistic fervor is often associated with the explosive revivalism of the Great Awakenings in America and beyond. These revival experiences of grace help to keep our faith warm and personal. They press us past theoretical mental assent toward personal heart-faith.

Lifting high the existential call to commitment, evangelical witness gives us a clear theology of salvation. It is a doctrine of *sola gratia*, grace alone. It is a doctrine of *sola fide*, faith alone. It is a doctrine of *solus Christus*, Christ alone.

Second, let's thank God for the evangelical stress upon Christ's missionary mandate to disciple the nations. This is not something peripheral or incidental to who we are and what we are about. As disciples of

Jesus Christ we do not have mission efforts; our very life is mission. Emil Brunner put it well: "The Church exists by mission as fire exists by burning."[74]

The mood of contemporary culture is not congenial to the missionary mandate. This lack of receptiveness has its roots in the modern absolutizing of tolerance and relativizing of belief. Every lifestyle is to be tolerated. Every belief is to be accepted—unless, of course, it is an exclusive-truth claim that challenges the beliefs of anyone else. These unquestioned assumptions of our day undercut any serious mission conviction.

Such assumptions need to be challenged directly and when we do so, they evaporate immediately. Tolerance for people and diverse cultures is surely a good thing, until it is made absolute. Frankly, not all lifestyles and customs should be tolerated. Some are clearly destructive—human enslavement, for example, and other similar forms of dehumanization. Likewise, certain beliefs need to be challenged because they are clearly false. All religious beliefs are *not* equal. Some are dangerous and destructive to human life. Racism, for example, or militarism. Nor can all religious beliefs stand together. Certain beliefs, by their very nature, exclude other beliefs. The law of contradiction holds that a thing cannot both be and not be at the same time.

Therefore, in spite of its lack of appeal to the mood of contemporary society, we can take up Christ's missionary mandate with confidence. As his disciples this is not an option; Jesus, our sovereign Lord, calls us to go into all the world and disciple the nations. And he promises to be with us, even to the end of the age (Matt. 28:20).

Jesus uses several striking metaphors to describe our mission mandate—metaphors such as "light," "salt," and "leaven." On the surface these metaphors seem quite different from one another, but with a little reflection we see that they all speak of penetration. Light exists to penetrate the darkness; salt exists to penetrate the meat; leaven exists to penetrate the dough. And we exist to penetrate the world! May I encourage you in this good work with the challenging words of

George Fox: "Let all nations hear the word by sound or writing. Spare no place, spare not tongue nor pen; but be obedient to the Lord God and go through the work and be valiant for the Truth upon earth."[75]

Third, let's thank God for the evangelical commitment to biblical fidelity. The authority of the written Word gives us the criterion by which we test for error. This is utterly essential, for if we cannot test for error, we cannot claim truth. The knowledge of truth presupposes the distinguishing of it from error.

The Christ event is the heart of Scripture. Everything in the Bible either looks forward to Christ or flows from Christ. And the Bible is a faithful record both of God's dealings with his children in preparing them for the coming of Christ and of their response to his advent. It is important to know that the Christ event is an incarnational reality rooted in history. It is important to know the historical and grammatical context for his teachings. It is important to know that his death was a literal death on a Roman cross outside the city gates. His burial, his resurrection, his ascension—these were actual historical events witnessed by scores of people living at the time. The Christ of faith *is* the Jesus of history who walked the dusty roads of Palestine—healing the sick, giving sight to the blind, and teaching the reality of the kingdom of God. "Christ died . . . he was buried . . . he was raised on the third day . . . he appeared to Cephas, then to the twelve. Then he appeared to more than five hundred brothers and sisters at one time. . . . Then he appeared to James, then to all the apostles. Last of all, as one untimely born, he appeared also to me" (1 Cor. 15:3–8). This is Paul's confessional witness, a holy witness deeply rooted in history. And Scripture is the faithful record of this holy history.

Fourth, let's thank God for the evangelical witness to sound doctrine. Beliefs are important. The gospel of the kingdom does have content. Now, the propositional truths of theology may not be everything, but they are something. We do not know many things about God and the life of faith, and many of the things we do know we probably understand imperfectly. But we do want to think as rightly about God as finite human beings can. We do seek to love God with all our mind. We do endeavor to rightly divide the word of truth. This is our intention.

Right belief, "true truth," as Francis Schaeffer liked to put it—is important to us. Most assuredly we hold these doctrines with great humility of heart, for "we know only in part," as Paul reminds us (1 Cor. 13:9). We can have it wrong. Our understanding can be defective. We are willing to be instructed. But in our learning and struggling and growing, the words of Martin Luther should ever be ours: "It is impossible for me to recant unless I am proved to be wrong by the testimony of Scripture. My conscience is bound to the Word of God."[76]

UNDERSTANDING THE POTENTIAL PERILS

As with all the others, the Evangelical Tradition has its own set of perils. As in the other Traditions, these are potential pitfalls rather than convictions inherent to the Tradition itself. They often emerge when the points of strength in the Tradition are distorted.

The first peril is the tendency to fixate upon peripheral and nonessential matters. This danger emerges when, out of a proper concern for truth and sound doctrine, people are unable to distinguish matters of primary importance from matters of secondary importance. All doctrines are important, but not all doctrines are of primary importance. Frankly, it makes a huge difference whether the issue we are debating is the divine/human nature of Christ or the pretribulation rapture.[77] The first issue is of primary importance; the second is not.

It is critical that we learn to discern between primary and secondary issues if we are to keep from majoring in minor matters. Old-fashioned common sense is sufficient to show us the difference in most cases, but the following principle can also help: the closer the issue comes to the heart of the Christ event—Jesus' birth, life, death, and resurrection—the more it becomes a matter of primary importance. Using that standard, we see that if we are discussing whether the book of Job is literal history or a literary device to teach religious truth, we are considering a matter of secondary importance—important, certainly, but secondary. But if we are discussing Jesus' resurrection from the dead, we are addressing an issue of primary importance, for it is right at the heart of the Christ event.

Now, you and I may have strong opinions on double predestination, supralapsarianism, and biblical inerrancy, but these should not be considered evangelical essentials. Even issues as pressing as women in ministry or glossolalia—and I have strongly held positions on both matters—must not be made a test of evangelical orthodoxy. We must never allow pious convictions to be elevated into central dogmas of the Church. In these matters the old saying, first articulated by Augustine, can serve us well: *In necessariis unitas, in dubiis libertas, in omnibus caritas.* "In essentials unity, in doubtful questions [or nonessentials] liberty, in all things charity."

The second peril (which closely parallels and in some measure grows out of the first) is the tendency toward a sectarian mentality. I say that this peril in some measure grows out of the first because when minor doctrines are elevated to the place of primary importance, they can then become grounds for separation.

Now, a proper concern generally underlies this separatist or sectarian impulse, a concern for the purity of the Church—purity of doctrine, purity of conviction, purity of practice. But problems arise when the impulse turns legalistic, for then it becomes narrow, rigid, and doctrinaire. Nor is it balanced by the equally important biblical concern for the unity of the Church (John 17).

Sectarian groups sometimes take on a cultic mentality by insisting that they are the only true church and that everyone else is apostate. When this occurs, the center of gravity shifts from a warm-heart experience of saving grace to an intolerant, censorious spirit. This can even take the form of guilt by association, as if merely associating with people of differing beliefs would somehow compromise a person. Billy Graham, you may remember, was accused of this very thing when he insisted that the local sponsoring committees for his crusades be drawn from a broad spectrum of the Christian community.

Sectarian groups often break with history with a wave of the hand. They declare, in essence, that no one besides the early Christians and themselves have been faithful to God. This break with history can even get tangled up in specific historical battles. The Protestant Reformation is a case in point. Some groups, going far beyond the corrective teaching of the reformers (and not realizing how deeply their own positions are rooted in Augustine and others), have decided that everything between the end of the book of Acts and the nailing of Luther's ninety-five theses on the door of the castle church in Wittenberg is doctrinally corrupt and must be rejected.

The answer to this problem is not to break with the history of the Church, but to discriminate between truth and error in church tradition in the light of Scripture. Luther himself linked the two when he spoke of Scripture as the light and church tradition as the lantern.[78] An authentic evangelical witness is rooted in the heritage of the Church as well as in Scripture.

A third peril is the tendency to present too limited a view of the salvation that is found in Jesus Christ. There are two aspects to this problem. One is the ellipse of the whole of a person's life in favor of the sole issue of getting into heaven; the other is a pronounced individualism that neglects social responsibility and prophetic insight.

Now, this pitfall emerges because of a valid concern that we never lose sight of the evangelistic call for commitment to Christ—a commitment that must extend all the way down to the most personal and individual level. We should affirm the concern, but we must also affirm that the call to commitment extends out as well as down. It must encompass, first, our entire discipleship before God and, second, our community and institutional life. Christ came to break the shackles of both personal sin and social sin. The salvation that is in Jesus Christ impacts all levels of human existence: personal, social, institutional.

A fourth peril, and the last I shall mention here, is the tendency toward bibliolatry. I describe this as a "tendency" because seldom do people plunge headlong into a literal worship of the Bible. But many people have practices and beliefs that lean in that direction. Some groups, for example, hold views of the inspiration of the Bible that are nothing short of magic religion, as if God had simply dictated the words of the Bible to Moses and Paul and the others, or dropped it out of the sky. Other groups tend to proclaim the Bible more than they do Jesus Christ. Now, the open Bible is certainly a good symbol, but for the Christian it is a secondary symbol. Our primary symbol must ever be Jesus Christ in his life, death, resurrection, ascension, session, return, and reigning forever and ever. One institution I know of has a mural of a thirty-foot Jesus holding out a Bible. Now, I hope that image gives you pause as you consider whether our primary mission is to give the world the Bible or give the world Jesus. Perhaps that artist would have done better to have painted a thirty-foot Bible holding out Jesus.

Now, this problem emerges out of an evangelical strength— namely, the desire to hold a high view of Scripture. But we are to worship God, not the Bible. Donald Bloesch writes, "The ultimate, final authority is not Scripture but the living God himself as we find him in Jesus Christ. Jesus Christ and the message about him constitute the material norm for our faith just as the Bible is the formal norm. The Bible is authoritative because it points beyond itself to the absolute authority, the living and transcendent Word of God."[79]

The *euangelion*, the good news of the gospel, is not that we have a Holy Book—most religions have as much. The good news of the gospel is that God entered history in the person of Jesus Christ and did for us what we could not do for ourselves. The Bible is ever the normative interpretation of this great redemptive event, and for this we thank God. But the Christ event is the foundation for the normative interpretation, not the other way around.

We should always affirm a high view of Scripture, recognizing at the same time that salvation is not in the Book but in Jesus Christ. To avoid the heresy of bibliolatry, we would do well to remember the classical formulation of Christian theology: *Christus Rex et Dominus Scripturae*. "Christ is King and Lord of Scripture."

PRACTICING THE EVANGELICAL TRADITION

I cannot imagine that you need much instruction in the actual practice of the Evangelical Tradition. For most of us the problem is not *knowing* what we are to do; it is *doing* it. "Just do the stuff" is the challenge John Wimber gave people again and again. It is a well-aimed challenge. May God give us the strength and courage to do what we already know to do.

Rather than detailed instruction, then, I offer here two simple, practical suggestions.

First, let us get to know our Bible. I recommend that we make a really good friend of Scripture, reading it in substantial doses. It is far better to devote one hour once a week to Bible reading than ten minutes every day. The popular devotional practice of a brief Bible reading each morning is a little like trying to take a shower one drop at a time. Just as we simply cannot get a shower that way, we simply cannot become a biblically saturated person that way. So read entire sections of books of the Bible in one sitting. This is not nearly as difficult as you might think once you develop the habit.

One caution: our souls will never grow in God if we read the Bible solely to get ammunition to defend ourselves or to defeat others. No. We read the Bible to be fed. We read it to be converted, to be strengthened, to be taught, to be rebuked, to be counseled, to be comforted. As we sit under the Bible for sustained periods, we will be formed by the experience.

Second, let us get to know those around us. I am thinking of those we live near and those we work with and those we meet at the grocery store and the gas station. Now, if we really pay attention to those around us—learning their interests, needs, hopes, hurts, dreams, fears—we will be given what we need to say. Our lives will preach Christ, and our words will confirm and make specific the message of our lives.

One caution: we must never confuse witnessing with "soul-winning." Jesus made it unmistakably clear that it is the domain of the Holy Spirit to convict the world "of sin, and of righteousness, and of judgment," and we must never abrogate the work of the Holy Spirit

(John 16:8, KJV). God alone "wins the soul." We are simply and solely witnesses to how good God is and to what transforming things he has done in us. No more, no less.

THE CALL TO WORD-CENTERED LIVING

QUESTION: What is the Evangelical Tradition?
ANSWER: A life founded upon the living Word of God, the written Word of God, and the proclaimed Word of God.
QUESTION: Why should we explore it?
ANSWER: Because through it we experience the knowledge of God that grounds our lives and enables us to give a reason for the hope that is in us.

Every one of us is called to a Word-centered life. Jesus Christ is among us as the Word of God living. He teaches us, guides us, rules us, comforts us, corrects us, nurtures us, strengthens us. The Bible is given to us as the Word of God written. Through the illuminating, guiding ministry of the Spirit, Scripture is for us the infallible rule of faith and practice. In addition, the doctrinal fidelity of the early Christian witnesses helps to guide our understanding and interpretation of the Christ event. And we have the evangel, the good news of the gospel, as the Word of God proclaimed. In obedience to Christ's Great Commission and in the mighty power of the Spirit, we call all people everywhere to be reconciled to God through the atoning sacrifice of Christ Jesus. This leads, of necessity, to lifelong discipleship to Christ, through which we learn from him how to live the abundant life of "righteousness and peace and joy in the Holy Spirit" (John 10:10; Rom. 14:17).

Chapter 7

~

The Incarnational Tradition: Discovering the Sacramental Life

We have this treasure in earthen vessels.
—*2 Corinthians 4:7*

We are creatures of sense and of spirit, and we must live an amphibious life.
—*Evelyn Underhill*

THE INCARNATIONAL TRADITION*

Notable Figures   *Significant Movements*

0
Jesus of Nazareth
(c. 4 B.C.- c. A.D. 29)

Flavia Domtilla (?–c. 100)

Origen (c. 185–254)
Monica (c. 331–c. 387)   Eastern Orthodox Iconography (4th
                                     century to the present)
Aurelius Prudentius Clemens (348–c. 410)

Oswald (c. 605–642)
Hunna (?–c. 679)
Caedmon (658–680)
Vincent Madelgarius (c. 615–c. 687)
Waldetrude (?–c. 688)
John of Damascus (c. 675–749)
Gottschalk (c. 803–869)
Alfred the Great (849–899)
Adelaide (?–999)
Olga (c. 890–969)
Vladimir the Prince (979–1015)
Stephen of Hungary (c. 970–1138)

1000

Isidore the Farmer (1070–1130)

Dante Alighieri (1265–1321)
Geoffrey Chaucer (c. 1340–1400)   Renaissance
Leonardo da Vinci (1452–1519)   (14th–16th centuries)
Nicolas Copernicus (1473–1543)
Michelangelo (1475–1564)
Rembrandt Harmenszoon van Rijn (1606–1669)

John Milton (1608–1674)
Isaac Newton (1642–1727)   Classical Movement
Susanna Wesley (1669–1742)   (17th–18th centuries)
Johann Sebastian Bach (1685–1750)
George Frideric Handel (1685–1759)
Samuel Johnson (1709–1784)   Romantic Movement
Samuel Taylor Coleridge (1772–1834)   (18th–19th centuries)
John Henry Newman (1801–1890)
Fyodor Dostoyevsky (1821–1881)   Russian Novelists
James Hudson Taylor (1832–1905)   (19th century)
Pilgrim (19th century)
T. S. Eliot (1888–1965)
Dag Hammarskjöld (1905–1961)   Professional Christian Societies
Aleksandr Solzhenitsyn (1918–)   (20th century to the present)
Flannery O'Connor (1925–1964)

*See Appendix B for brief biographies and histories.

WE HAVE LEARNED how a prayer-filled life lays the foundation for both the virtuous life and the Spirit-empowered life, and how these in turn give us the ability to engage in social justice and the proclamation of the good news of the kingdom. The one element remaining is to understand how all of these components function in ordinary life, which is the task of the Incarnational Tradition.

The Incarnational Stream of Christian life and faith focuses upon making present and visible the realm of the invisible spirit. This sacramental way of living addresses the crying need to experience God as truly manifest and notoriously active in daily life.

SEEKING A HISTORICAL PARADIGM

At Susanna's baptism her father, Dr. Samuel Annesley, was asked how many children he had. He replied, "Two dozen, I believe, or a quarter of a hundred."[1] The last guess was the correct one: Susanna was the twenty-fifth child of the renowned Puritan divine. Born 20 January 1669 in London, England, Susanna is my choice for a historical model of the Incarnational Tradition.

I chose Susanna because of her complete immersion in the details of daily life: finding God in the details and serving God through these same details. Susanna represents the millions of people who have learned to do ordinary things with a perception of their enormous value. Later in her life Susanna prayed, "Help me, Lord, to remember that religion is not to be confined to the church, or closet, nor exercised only in prayer and meditation, but that everywhere I am in Thy presence. So may my every word and action have a moral content. . . . May all the happenings of my life prove useful and beneficial to me. May all things instruct me and afford me an opportunity of exercising some virtue and daily learning and growing toward Thy likeness. . . . Amen."[2] This prayer, by the by, is one of the finest expressions of the Incarnational Tradition you will ever find.

Susanna was a precocious child. Even though, as a female, she could not attend college, she received a substantial education at home. Her father, known for his intellectual acumen (M.A. and LL.D. from Queen's College, Oxford), took an active part in her education. Under his tutelage she studied logic, metaphysics, anatomy, French, and possibly Greek and Latin.[3] She has been called "a theologian in short dresses,"[4] and for good reason. By the time she was thirteen she had carefully weighed the doctrinal debates between the Nonconformist groups (her father was known as "the St. Paul of the Nonconformists") and Established Anglicanism and had decided in favor of the Church of England. Whatever Samuel Annesley's inward anguish over his daughter's decision, he gave Susanna his blessing, and she remained a favorite daughter, receiving all his letters and papers upon his death.[5]

The next major event in Susanna's life was marriage, and the moment I tell you who she married, you will recognize the Susanna I am talking about. Not that her husband ever became well known— he did not—but two of their children were among the most famous figures in all of England. The two children I speak of were John and Charles Wesley, the founders of Methodism; their father was Samuel Wesley; and their mother—the Susanna of this story—was Susanna Wesley.

The diminutive Reverend Samuel Wesley had also left the Nonconformist cause in favor of the staid and stately Church of England, so their interest in one another is not surprising. They married at St. Marylebone Parish Church, London, on 12 November 1688. Samuel became curate of two small parishes, rector at one other, and chaplain on a man-o'-war ship for a brief time, but by far the bulk of his ministerial life was spent as rector of Epworth Parish Church in Lincolnshire. And it was at Epworth that Susanna lived and worked and showed the world how sacred are the duties of living and working.

Mother and Educator

Susanna was first and foremost a mother. For her, motherhood was a calling—a *vocatio*—and she took up this work with a seriousness that is hard for people to comprehend today. The fact that she had nineteen children in a span of twenty years is, by itself, difficult for us moderns to wrap our minds around. To be sure, nine of these children did not survive infancy, but the remaining ten received a loving care that was special even in that day. And training—did they ever receive training! Susanna has received universal acclaim for the way she undertook to educate all of her children in a kind of "home schooling" environment.

This commitment to teaching her children was no small undertaking. She, in essence, set up a small private boarding school. All the children—there were seven girls and three boys—on their fifth birthday were taught the alphabet, and then they started immediately on the first chapter of Genesis. From there the homemade syllabus included grammar, history, mathematics, geography, and theology. Samuel, the father, occasionally helped Susanna with lessons in the classics.

The teaching schedule went from nine in the morning until noon and from two in the afternoon until five. Despite all the ups and downs of their eventful life Susanna kept up this six-hour-a-day schedule for twenty years. Each day she would watch over her children doing their lessons, all the while nursing the newest baby, keeping the household accounts, writing her letters, doing her sewing. In addition, she met individually with each child once a week. John's tutorial was on Thursday nights, and all through his influential ministry he expressed his indebtedness for those Thursday night sessions. Susanna maintained this regimen, as I said, for twenty years, instilling into her children something of her rare personality in the process.

One aspect of that personality was an exceptional patience. Observing his wife teaching on one particular day, Samuel counted twenty times that she repeated a single piece of information. "I wonder at your patience," he commented; "you have told that child twenty times that same thing." Susanna, looking up, smiled and said, "If I had satisfied myself by mentioning it only nineteen times I should have lost all my labour. It was the twentieth time that crowned it."[6]

Another of her personality traits was an exceptional love of learning. That Susanna passed this trait on to her children is apparent in the zeal with which they pursued learning when they went out into the wider world after the "home schooling" years. The three brothers all went on to advanced degrees, John becoming a fellow of Lincoln College, Oxford. In that day, of course, formal college training was not an option for the girls. But even so, John said of his sister Emily that she was the best reader of Milton that he had ever heard. Another sister, Martha, became a respected member of the great Samuel Johnson's literary circle.

A third sister, Hetty, excelled even more. Samuel, recognizing this daughter's extraordinary qualities, gave her special training in the classics, and by the time she was nine, she was able to read Greek and Latin. She also possessed "an exquisite poetic genius," a gift that both she and her brother Charles inherited from their father. A contemporary described her as "Hetty of the high spirits, the clear eye, the springing gait; Hetty, the wittiest, cleverest, mirthfullest of them all."[7]

"The Calamities of Life"

But everything, as I am sure you can imagine, was not all sweetness and light, and the mention of Hetty causes me to comment on the sadness, even tragedy, that struck Susanna and her household more than once.

Hetty was said to be the most attractive of the seven sisters. But Epworth was far from the most favorable environment for finding suitable young men. Hetty, in fact, once wrote these words to her sister Emilia:

Fortune has fixed thee in a place
Debarred of wisdom, wit and grace:
High births and virtue equally they scorn,
As asses dull on dunghills born . . . [8]

There was one man, John Romley by name, who was interested in Hetty. Oxford educated, he was a schoolteacher in a nearby village. Unfortunately, he offended Samuel Wesley by ridiculing the way Samuel changed his Tory and Whig loyalties to fit the prevailing political wind. Samuel ordered Romley out of the house and forbade Hetty from ever associating with him. She obeyed. Soon after, however, a young lawyer came courting Hetty, and when Samuel forbade that relationship too, she ran off with the young man. Her lover had given her every assurance that they were running away to be married; but the next morning he was gone, and she soon found that she was pregnant. Hetty was devastated, and Samuel was scandalized. If not for Susanna's pleas, Samuel would have ordered Hetty out of the house immediately. With his only thought to avoid the disgrace of a fatherless child, Samuel arranged a marriage for Hetty with the first man they could find—an illiterate plumber who happened to be traveling through the countryside.[9] The marriage was a complete disaster, of course, and Hetty suffered a lifetime for her one night of indiscretion. Compounding her sorrow, Hetty, the daughter who had showed such literary promise, was disowned by her father. They were never reconciled.[10]

This incident shows the rigid, self-righteous side of Samuel Wesley. It was a dark character flaw in an otherwise faithful and diligent husband, father, and minister. It did not surface often, but whenever it did, it caused misery in the Wesley family.

Susanna was herself the recipient of Samuel's rigidity on one occasion. It seems that once during evening prayers she did not say Amen to her husband's petition for William of Orange, then King of England. (Susanna had sympathies toward the minority who believed that the deposed James II still remained king by divine right.) Susanna recorded what happened next: "He retired to his study, and calling me to him asked me the reason of my not saying Amen to the Prayer. I was a little surprised at the question and don't well know what I answered, but too too well I remember what followed: He immediately kneeled down and imprecated the divine Vengeance upon himself and all his posterity if ever he touched me more or came into a bed with me before I had begged God's pardon and his, for not saying Amen to the prayer for the K[in]g."[11]

Susanna, refusing to be intimidated, stood her ground. Samuel left in a huff for London and did not return for six months—and then only because a tragic fire had destroyed two-thirds of the Wesley home. The fire brought them back together again, and the most visible result of their reconciliation arrived the next June, a baby boy named John.

If one fire gave them their son John, another fire nearly took him from them. That is the well-known fire of Methodist lore in which John is said to have been "a brand plucked from the burning." The night was Wednesday, 9 February 1709. Near midnight a fire, perhaps the latest mischief of the rector's enemies, engulfed the house. In the frantic moments that followed, everyone was able to make his or her way out—everyone, that is, except five-year-old John (or Jacky, as he was known then). Susanna wrote that her husband heard Jacky "miserably crying out in the nursery and attempted several times to get upstairs, but was beat back by the flame; then he thought him lost and commended his soul to God and went to look after the rest."[12] But unknown to the father, young Jacky had climbed to the edge of the nursery window, where he again called for help. "Fetch a ladder!" shouted one man—but there was no time. One large man braced himself against the wall while a slender man climbed onto his shoulders. At the first try the slender man tumbled to the ground. But the second try was successful: he pulled little Jacky out of the window just as the flaming roof caved in—truly "a brand plucked from the burning." Overjoyed, Samuel gathered his shivering family together beside the charred ruins of their home: "Come neighbours, let us kneel down! Let us give thanks to God! He has given me all my eight children: let the house go, I am rich enough!"[13]

Rich in family perhaps, but totally destitute in possessions. Everything had been lost: their home, their furnishings, Samuel's library, all Susanna's early letters, Dr. Annesley's precious papers— everything.

This was not the only occasion when they had to go without, however. Samuel, while a diligent minister, was an extremely poor manager of his worldly affairs. He was constantly in debt and at one point was even thrown into debtors' prison. On that particular occasion Susanna brought her wedding ring to him in the hope that it could be used to release him. Samuel—here we see his tender side—could not take it, preferring to stay in prison rather than have his Susanna deprived of her wedding ring. The bishop finally came to the rescue, clearing Samuel's debts.

These incidents give you a sampling of "the calamities of life" that Susanna endured.[14] And endure she did. The secret of her endurance was a *faith* that could see everything in light of God's overriding governance for good, a *hope* that could carry her through the most difficult of circumstances, and a *love* that could overcome evil with good.

Listen to how Susanna sought to make tragedy a cause for spiritual formation: "Help me, O Lord, to make a true use of all disappointments and calamities in this life, in such wise that they may unite my heart more closely with Thee. Cause them to separate my affections from worldly things and inspire my soul with more vigour in the pursuit of true happiness."[15] Listen to her tough realism in these words: "Since I must expect to meet with many difficulties, much opposition, many disappointments and daily trials of faith and patience in my passage through this world, may it be my highest wisdom to disengage my affections as much as I lawfully may from all transitory, temporal enjoyments, and to fix them on those more rational and spiritual pleasures which we are to enjoy when we enter upon our state of immortality."[16] Listen to her wisdom (won, no doubt, by many years of difficulty) in these words: "The best preparation I know of for suffering is a regular and exact performance of present duty."[17]

"A Preacher of Righteousness"

John Wesley declared that his mother "had been in her measure and degree a preacher of righteousness."[18] Susanna was never ordained or appointed to a parish. Why would John say this of her?

The most obvious reference is to Susanna's famous kitchen services. When Samuel was away in London on church matters for an extended period one time, his assistant did a poor job of nurturing the congregation. Consequently, Susanna decided to have Sunday evening services at home for the family, in order to bring some added spiritual influence. They gathered in the kitchen to sing psalms, pray, and read a short sermon selected from Mr. Wesley's library shelves. Soon friends and neighbors asked to join in, and before anyone knew it, two hundred souls were crowding into Susanna's home.

Mr. Inman, the church assistant, was insulted and scandalized, mainly because the Sunday night gatherings were outdrawing Sunday mornings. He contacted Samuel Wesley in London and protested these irregular worship services. Mr. Wesley, in turn, wrote his wife, asking her to desist. Her response was a masterful balance of deference and defiance.

Susanna began by responding to his three major objections to the meetings: these were "first, that it will look particular; secondly, my sex; and lastly, your being at present in a public station and character." She took up each objection with the most careful deference, providing an extended and definitive answer. She then concluded, "If you do after all think fit to dissolve this assembly, do not tell me any more that you desire me to do it, for that will not satisfy my conscience; but send me your positive command in such full and express terms as may absolve me from all guilt and punishment for neglecting this opportunity of doing good to souls, when you and I shall appear before the great and awful tribunal of our Lord Jesus Christ."[19]

Need I say that the meetings continued unabated? Interestingly, Susanna referred to her kitchen congregation as "our Society." John was nine years old at this time, and scholars generally feel that these meetings had a pronounced influence upon his eventual development of the Methodist Societies. Certainly the meetings offer the most obvious explanation for his designation of Susanna as "a preacher of righteousness."

But there is another reason for that designation, and I think it is equally significant. It is the rich legacy Susanna left in her letters, journals, and catechetical writings. In Susanna Wesley's letters, she continued her preaching role with family members who had left home. Throughout John's tenure at Oxford his mother continued as his tutor in "practical divinity." In one letter she carried on an extended discussion with him about zeal, prudence, and charity. In another she commented on William Sherlock's book A *Discourse Concerning the Divine Providence*. In others she functioned as a de facto adviser to the Oxford "Holy Club."[20] And more.

Some of her writings were intended for an even wider audience. She wrote an essay—at her son John's request—on her method of educating her family, and John published it. She wrote a commentary on the Apostles' Creed and an exposition on the Ten Commandments. She wrote a dialogue called "A Religious Conference" (obviously intended for publication) that sought to reconcile Christian faith with the emerging new science represented by Isaac Newton. Finally, toward the end of her life, Susanna entered the arena of public disputation in "Some Remarks on a Letter from Mr. Whitfield." In this essay she waded into the complicated Calvinist-Arminian debate over predestination and showed that she could hold her own against a formidable public figure. All of this indicates that in Susanna Wesley we do indeed find "a preacher of righteousness" who knew how to articulate and defend her faith. The assessment of Adam Clarke—while in language that is antiquated for us today— remains telling: "If it were not unusual to apply such an epithet to a *woman*, I would not hesitate to say she was an able divine!"[21]

"Holy Living and Holy Dying"

Susanna Wesley lived sacramentally in the most common ventures of life. The details of her living were the arena for her interaction with God and the place where she built a history with God. And what was true of her living was also true of her dying.

Susanna brought from her Puritan heritage the conviction that dying as much as living was holy work—an opportunity to give glory to God and build up others in the faith. Her father, Dr. Annesley, great Puritan divine that he was, died with these words on his lips: "I will die praising thee, and rejoice that others can praise thee better. I shall be satisfied with thy likeness. Satisfied! Satisfied! Oh my dearest Jesus! I come!"[22]

Susanna had to leave her home at Epworth after Samuel's death, for the new rector and his family were on their way. She was, therefore, dependent upon her own children in the declining years of her life. They cared for her graciously, and her final years were spent with her son John at "the Foundery," a London center for Methodist activity.

It was there at the Foundery that Susanna performed one of her finest services for the burgeoning Methodist movement. Whenever John and Charles were out on their evangelistic missions, a layman, Thomas Maxfield, was left in charge of the gatherings of the Bands and the Societies at the Foundery. Not being an ordained clergyman, Maxfield was not allowed to preach, but on one occasion zeal ran away with him and he did indeed preach to the congregation at the Foundery. Catching wind of this, John rushed back to London. When he arrived at the Foundery, Susanna was the first to meet him. "Thomas Maxfield has turned preacher, I find," John said curtly. Susanna (perhaps remembering her own experience with her kitchen congregation) replied, "John, you know what my sentiments have been. You cannot suspect me of favoring readily anything of this kind. But take care what you do with respect to that young man; for he is as surely called of God to preach as you are. Examine what have been the fruits of his preaching, and hear him yourself."

John followed his mother's counsel, and after hearing Maxfield preach, declared, "It is the Lord! . . . What am I that I should withstand God!"[23] This decision changed the whole course of Methodism. One of the great marks of that movement was in the multiplied thousands of itinerant lay evangelists who fanned the flames of renewal worldwide.

On 30 July 1742 Susanna's children gathered around her, for she was "on the borders of eternity." John chronicled the event in his

Journal: "I sat down on the bed-side. She was in her last conflict; unable to speak, but, I believe, quite sensible. Her look was calm and serene, and her eyes fixed upward, while we commended her soul to God. From three to four [in the afternoon] the silver cord was loosing and the wheel breaking at the cistern; and then, without any struggle, or sigh, or groan, the soul was set at liberty. We stood round her bed, and fulfilled her last request, uttered a little before she lost her speech: 'Children, as soon as I am released, sing a psalm of praise to God.'" Holy living, holy dying—that was Susanna Wesley.

Perhaps now, after learning something of Susanna's story, we are in a better position to appreciate Adam Clarke's moving tribute: "I have traced her life with much pleasure, and received from it much instruction; and when I have seen her repeatedly grappling with gigantic adversities, I have adored the grace of God that was in her, and have not been able to repress my tears."[24]

SEEKING A BIBLICAL PARADIGM

When we turn to the biblical roots of the Incarnational Stream, we immediately think of the example that stands above them all, Jesus Christ. Nothing can ever approach the perfect and unrepeatable reality of Jesus' incarnation. Jesus, the Christ, is incarnation itself. We bow under the mystery of it.

Nor should we neglect to mention the role of Mary, mother of Messiah, who was given astonishing news: "The Holy Spirit will come upon you, and the power of the Most High will overshadow you; therefore the child to be born will be holy; he will be called Son of God" (Luke 1:35). What a revelatory, incarnational word! A virgin, conceiving in her womb and bearing a son—a son who shall be called Emmanuel, God with us. God made manifest to the world through a simple Jewish girl from an obscure village in the backwater of society. And Mary's word of obedience must ever be our word, we who seek to live sacramentally: "Here am I, the servant of the Lord; let it be with me according to your word" (Luke 1:38).

Jesus and Mary, who made present and visible the realm of the invisible spirit, express the Incarnational Tradition in its fullness and utter beauty. We do well to linger on these incarnational mysteries long and often, pondering them in our heart. But frankly, they are unrepeatable events in holy history. We shall never express the Incarnational Stream in the way Jesus and Mary did. Never.

In order, therefore, to give a paradigm that we can look to and apply to our own experience, I want to take us back in time—way back. Back to the Exodus, where God, with a mighty hand and an outstretched arm, delivered the children of Israel from the land of Egypt, the house of bondage. Back to Moses, who led the Israelites through the Sea of Reeds to Sinai, the mountain of God. Here the people received the Decalogue, the Ten Commandments. And here they built the Tabernacle and the Ark of the Covenant.

Divine Aesthetics

This is where I want us to pause and focus our attention. Up to this point the people had seen the manifest presence of God almost by divine fiat: the cloud by day and the pillar of fire by night, tablets of law hewn out by the finger of God, and so forth. But now God orders human activity, intense activity, skilled activity—the building of the Tabernacle and, inside it, the Ark of the Covenant. Then, as if in divine cooperation with this human effort, God allows his glory to be "housed" in the Tabernacle.

What a sight! There they are, a homeless, nomadic multitude, camping out in the wilderness of Sinai for nearly a year, building a strange-looking portable contraption that serves no apparent military or civic purpose. Can you imagine what the lizards and the ravens were thinking as they watched these unusual events?

Right at the center of this strange scene is one individual, Bezalel by name. In fact, he is called out by name: "The LORD spoke to Moses: See, I have called by name Bezalel . . . and I have filled him with the spirit of God, with ability, intelligence, and knowledge in every kind of craft, to devise artistic designs, to work in gold, silver, and bronze, in cutting stones for setting, and in carving wood, in every kind of craft" (Exod. 31:1–5).

The crucial point for us to see is this: God chose a skilled artisan and had him use his artistry to show forth God's manifest presence to the people. Bezalel worked as an artisan—this was his job, his profession—and it was through his vocation that he was to demonstrate the presence of God. And note this: he was described not only as a skilled artisan but also as one "filled with the spirit of God." Now, this statement is all the more impressive when we realize that Bezalel was the first person in the Bible described in this way. "Filled with the spirit of God" is a description first used, not of a priest or prophet or patriarch, but of an artisan, a "blue-collar" worker. Perhaps this will give us a hint of how much God values the work of our hands.

But Bezalel was not alone in his work. He had an assistant, Oholiab, who was described as an "engraver, designer, and embroiderer in blue, purple, and crimson yarns, and in fine linen" (Exod. 38:23). And God inspired Bezalel to teach other skilled workers so that a goodly number were involved in the building of the Tabernacle (Exod. 35:34). In addition, the people were urged to help by bringing "gold, silver, and bronze; blue, purple, and crimson yarns, and fine linen; goats' hair, tanned rams' skins, and fine leather; acacia wood, oil for the light, spices for the anointing oil and for the fragrant incense, and onyx stones and gems to be set in the ephod and the breastpiece" (Exod. 35:5b–9). This the people did, "both men and women; all who were of a willing heart" (Exod. 35:22).

So we see many people involved in this construction project. Bezalel, the general contractor; Oholiab, the job foreman; skilled workers, the subcontractors; and the people, the owners who paid for the construction project. Yes, and they paid lavishly. In fact, the people gave so much that Moses had to send out a command for them to stop: "'No man or woman is to make anything else as an offering for the sanctuary.' So the people were restrained from bringing; for what they had already brought was more than enough to do all the work" (Exod. 36:6–7).

When Bezalel and the others had finished their work, Moses, seeing their exquisite craftsmanship, "blessed them" (Exod. 39:43). Then came the final benediction over their efforts: "The cloud covered the tent of meeting, and the glory of the LORD filled the tabernacle" (Exod. 40:34).

What a wonderful model of the Incarnational Stream Bezalel is. A person of skill, intelligence, and knowledge in every kind of craft. A person able to work artistically with gold, silver, bronze, stone, and wood. Most of all, a person filled with the spirit of God. And what he produced gave the people a continual vision of God throughout their wanderings in the wilderness. In the midst of a stark, barren landscape, the Tabernacle was a magnificent aesthetic experience. Worshipers could absorb the faith, not just by hearing about it, but by reliving it through the cherubim overshadowing the mercy seat and the table of acacia wood for the shew bread and the lampstand of pure gold and the altar of incense of acacia wood and the holy anointing oil and the pure fragrant incense and the altar of burnt offering of acacia wood and the court of the Tabernacle of hangings of fine twisted linen and the entrance screen of embroidered needlework in blue, purple, and crimson yarns and fine twisted linen.

Accomplishing the building of the Tabernacle took not only special skills in craftsmanship, but unusual personality qualities as well. Just look at some of the qualities Bezalel possessed.

First, he was imaginative. He caught the vision for what this project could be. He had to see it as a thing of beauty in his mind's eye before he could build it.

Second, he was articulate. He had to communicate this vision of what the Tabernacle could be to his subcontractors. They had to see it as he saw it and work with the same kind of imagination and skill.

Third, he was an effective administrator. He had to choose the right workers and organize them. He had to set priorities and make sure the work was done in the right order—curtains, standards, furniture, and so forth. He had to delegate well, because any worker who did poorly reflected on the entire project.

All of these qualities, and more, gave Bezalel the ability to oversee the building of the Tabernacle—making present and visible the realm of the invisible spirit.

At the beginning of this Scripture study into the Incarnational Tradition, I mentioned Jesus and Mary. I would like to conclude with them as well. When we reflect on the Tabernacle in the wilderness and all that it represents, we realize that in the fullness of time Mary's womb became the dwelling place, the "tabernacle" of God. Even more, we see that in Jesus Christ, God has truly "tabernacled" among us. And, as if that were not enough, we are to be the dwelling place of the Holy Spirit, making the reality of God visible and manifest everywhere we go and in everything we do.

SEEKING A CONTEMPORARY PARADIGM

Around midnight on 17 September 1961, in the heart of Africa, the airplane of the secretary-general of the United Nations crashed in circumstances that forever will be shrouded in mystery. In that flaming instant the world lost one of its greatest leaders, Dag Hammarskjöld. "Hammarskjöld was the greatest statesman, and the best 'matched with his hour', since Abraham Lincoln," suggests Philip Toynbee.[25]

Within days of that fateful night a former aide, Per Lind, flew from Stockholm to New York to care for Hammarskjöld's personal effects and private papers. In the bedroom of the secretary-general's spacious East 73rd Street apartment he discovered a buff-colored folder, worn and faded by age and use. Paper-clipped to the top of the folder was a small envelope of United Nations Secretariat stationery. Typed on the envelope was the name "Leif Belfrage," and in the lower left-hand corner was the Swedish word *Personligt*—"Personal."

Without opening it, Per Lind took the folder and attached envelope to Sweden and handed it to Dr. Leif Belfrage, a colleague of Hammarskjöld and an intimate friend of many years' standing. Inside the envelope was an undated note typed in Swedish:

Dear Leif:

Perhaps you may remember I once told you that, in spite of everything, I kept a diary which I wanted you to take charge of someday.

Here it is.

It was begun without a thought of anybody else reading it. But, what with my later history and all that has been said and written about me, the situation has changed. These entries provide the only true "profile" that can be drawn. That is why, during recent years, I have reckoned with the possibility of publication, though I have continued to write for myself, not for the public.

If you find them worth publishing, you have my permission to do so — as a sort of white book concerning my negotiations with myself — and with God.

Dag[26]

Belfrage did indeed recall such a conversation some years back and naturally assumed that the folder contained something in the nature of a political memoir of Hammarskjöld's achievements at the United Nations. Imagine his astonishment when, on turning the cover of the folder, he saw over six hundred individual entries revealing Hammarskjöld's most private reflections covering a period of more than thirty-six years. The entire manuscript, introduced on the title page by the single word "Vägmärken,"[27] had been typed by the Secretary-General himself on an ancient machine he kept in his apartment. No other person had seen a page of it — indeed, no one had even been aware of its existence.

And so it happened that the enduring spiritual classic *Markings* was given to the world. Interestingly, in all 175 meticulously typed pages Hammarskjöld does not make a single direct reference to his distinguished career as an international civil servant; neither does he mention the many presidents, kings, and prime ministers with whom he had dealings, or the dramatic historical events in which he played so central a role. Instead, with merciless scrutiny and absolute honesty, he plots the intricate and sometimes tortured path of "God's marriage to the soul."[28]

Markings would be a remarkable book if it had emerged from the prolonged meditations of the monastic retreat. But it becomes an even more astonishing piece of writing when we realize that it was penned in the midst of modern civilization's most volatile international stage. W. H. Auden, in his foreword to *Markings*, calls it a "historical document of the first importance as an account—and I cannot myself recall another—of the attempt by a professional man of action to unite in one life the *via activa* and the *via contemplativa*."[29]

And so the author of this slender volume provides us with a shining contemporary model for the Incarnational Tradition. Hammaskjöld's vocation became the supreme place for living out his deepest spiritual convictions. In so doing he bridged the chasm between the world of devotion and the world of work. His political work was sacramental living of the deepest sort. Indeed, he himself used the language of "calling" and "vocation" to describe the work he had been given. And the unflinching inner struggle through which he traveled formed in him a rock-solid character capable of supreme moral leadership—what his biographer called "moral magistracy."[30]

Dag Hammarskjöld was a man of international affairs, thoroughly schooled in contemporary intellectual thought, and close friends with avant-garde leaders in literature and drama and philosophy. At the same time he possessed a living faith that he quietly and unobtrusively brought to bear upon this most exacting and responsible office for peace and good order. At the very apex of his international diplomacy[31] he wrote, "In our era, the road to holiness necessarily passes through the world of action."[32]

Deep Roots

For more than three centuries the Hammarskjöld family has been known in Sweden for outstanding civil service. Dag's father, Hjalmar Hammarskjöld, had a distinguished political career that included posts as minister of justice, minister of education, ambassador to Copenhagen, governor of Uppland at Uppsala, and prime minister of Sweden. "On my father's side," wrote Dag, "I inherited a belief that no life was more satisfactory than one of selfless service to your country—or humanity. This service required a sacrifice of all personal interests, but likewise the courage to stand up unflinchingly for your convictions."[33] The elder Hammarskjöld's paternal influence can be summed up in the single word "duty"—indeed, an exacting and relentless devotion to duty—a theme that would pervade Dag Hammarskjöld's entire life. His respect, even reverence, for his father had a far-reaching impact on his mind and life.

However, two unfortunate legacies from his father persisted throughout Dag's life. The first was a tendency to feel like an outsider, remaining aloof and distant. Hjalmar Hammarskjöld was a forbidding figure, autocratic and authoritarian. Forty years after the fact Dag recorded this painful childhood memory:

A box on the ear taught the boy
That Father's name
Was odious to them.[34]

The second legacy contributed to Dag's decision to lead a single life. We learn of it from the Queen Mother of Sweden, who (while visiting the UN headquarters in New York) asked Dag Hammarskjöld why he had never married: "He explained that having watched his mother suffer so much from his father's absences on public business he did not feel that he wanted to subject a woman to such a life."[35]

By contrast Dag's mother, Agnes Almqvist, was warm, radically democratic, and enormously generous to friends and strangers alike. She was able to transform the ancient and foreboding governor's castle at Uppsala into a comfortable home for Dag and his three brothers: Bo, Ake, and Sten. She had a great influence on Dag as well: "On my mother's side I inherited a belief that, in the very radical sense of the Gospels, all men were equals as children of God, and should be met and treated by us as our masters in God."[36] In a simple

but moving tribute to his mother, Dag wrote to a friend, "My mother
. . . had the qualities I admire most: she was courageous and good."[37]

After his parents, perhaps the most formative influence upon the
young Hammarskjöld was mountain climbing, a sport he engaged in
often. For him mountaineering was far more than a source of pleasure or physical exercise or even intellectual camaraderie; it was a
means of character formation. Upon his arrival in New York to
assume his new responsibilities as UN Secretary-General, he spoke
to reporters at the airport of how mountaineering developed the
qualities most needed in public office: "Mountaineering calls . . . for
endurance . . . perseverance and patience, a firm grip on realities,
careful but imaginative planning, a clear awareness of the dangers
but also of the fact that fate is what we make it and that the safest
climber is he who never questions his ability to overcome all difficulties."[38]

After earning a bachelor's degree in 1924 from Uppsala University
at the early age of nineteen,* Hammarskjöld moved quickly into government service. His positions included secretary of a Royal Commission on Unemployment, undersecretary in the Ministry of
Finance, and secretary and later chairman of the Bank of Sweden,
the oldest bank of issue in the world. Following the Second World
War, he was drawn more and more into foreign affairs: renegotiating
Sweden's trade agreement with the United States, serving as vice
chairman of the Organization for European Economic Cooperation,
serving as secretary-general and then vice minister in the Ministry of
Foreign Affairs, serving in the Swedish Cabinet as a nonparty "minister without portfolio," and more.

During these years of growing prominence Hammarskjöld began
recording his private inner reflections, his "markings." In his very first
notation (written at the age of twenty) we see a foreshadowing of the
kind of intense self-scrutiny that pervades *Markings*:

---

*His areas of concentration were in the history of literature, philosophy, French,
and political economy. He later completed a doctorate in economics. His dissertation was entitled "The Spread of Boom and Depression."

I am being driven forward
Into an unknown land. . . .
Shall I ever get there?
There where life resounds,
A clear pure note
In the silence.[39]

These lines also foreshadowed the great darkness to come.

The Darkest Night

In 1950, at age forty-five, Hammarskjöld was at the apex of Swedish public service. He was viewed by friends and colleagues as the epitome of the successful man of affairs. Yet his "markings" show us another man—a man of acute solitariness, of deep anguish, of near despair.

By now Hammarskjöld had been writing his "markings" for twenty-five years, but those notations comprise less than one-sixth of the book. In the next three years his reflections intensify and deepen, together comprising fully one-fourth of *Markings*. They are a key to his internal struggle and to understanding all that comes after. Those reflections show that he is entering a "dark night of the soul"—one that will last for three years.

In 1950 Hammarskjöld initiates a practice that he will follow for six of the next eight years. The first entry—typed in capitals and likely written on New Year's Day—is a line from an 1814 Swedish hymn: "SNART STUNDAR NATTEN"—"NIGHT APPROACHES NOW."[40] Hammarskjöld's mother has read this hymn—titled "The Little While I Linger Here"—to the family circle every New Year's Eve as a meditation on the brevity of life. Following this startling reminder of life's transience, Hammarskjöld writes:

In a whirling fire of annihilation,
In the storm of destruction
And deadly cold of the act of sacrifice,
You would welcome death.

But when it slowly grows within you,
Day by day,
You suffer anguish
Anguish under the unspoken judgment which hangs
  over your life
While leaves fall in the fool's paradise.[41]

One year later, New Year's Day 1951, he writes, "'Night Approaches Now—' So another year it is. And if this day should be your last. . . . The pulley of time drags us inexorably forward towards this day. A relief to think of this, to consider that there is a moment without a beyond."[42] And his cryptic notation at the beginning of 1952: "'Night Approaches Now—' How long the road is."[43]

But on New Year's Day 1953 the mood changes dramatically:

"—Night is drawing nigh—"
For all that has been—Thanks!
To all that shall be—Yes![44]

And a few notations later he writes, "Not I, but God in me."[45] From this point on this affirming tone dominates his reflections. Why? Why the striking contrast between the brooding darkness of 1950–1952 and the expectant outlook of 1953 and beyond? Is it possible to discern what caused such a dramatic transition?

Yes, most assuredly.[46] Far and away the most significant single entry in *Markings* occurs on Whitsunday 1961, when Hammarskjöld is looking back to that decisive period in his life.

> I don't know Who—or what—put the question, I don't know when it was put. I don't even remember answering. But at some moment I did answer Yes to Someone—or Something—and from that hour I was certain that existence is meaningful and that, therefore, my life, in self-surrender, had a goal.
> From that moment I have known what it means "not to look back," and "To take no thought for the morrow."

Led by the Ariadne's thread of my answer through the labyrinth of Life, I came to a time and place where I realized that the Way leads to a triumph which is a catastrophe, and to a catastrophe which is a triumph, that the price for committing one's life would be reproach, and that the only elevation possible to man lies in the depths of humiliation. After that, the word "courage" lost its meaning, since nothing could be taken from me.

As I continued along the Way, I learned, step by step, word by word, that behind every saying in the Gospels stands *one* man and *one* man's experience. Also behind the prayer that the cup might pass from him and his promise to drink it. Also behind each of the words from the cross.[47]

"I did answer *Yes*." Those words parallel his affirmation on that first day of 1953: "To all that shall be—Yes!" New Year's Day 1953 is the first occurrence of this confessional-like affirmation—this *Yes*—but it is far from the last. Hammarskjöld repeats it often, frequently in italics, and with growing meaning and precision. In fact, it becomes a refrain echoing through the rest of the book. After his election as United Nations Secretary-General, he writes jubilantly, "To be free, to be able to stand up and leave *everything* behind—without looking back. To say *Yes*—." Then two entries later, "To say Yes to life is at one and the same time to say Yes to oneself. Yes—even to that element in one which is most unwilling to let itself be transformed from a temptation into a strength."[48]

In 1956 he writes:

You dare your Yes—and experience a meaning.
You repeat your Yes—and all things acquire a meaning.
When everything has a meaning, how can you live anything but
    a Yes.[49]

Again after his re-election as Secretary-General: "Yes to God: yes to Fate: yes to yourself."[50] And finally, only weeks before his tragic death:

Asked if I have courage
To go on to the end,
I answer Yes without
A second thought.[51]

How providential that three months before his election as the leader of the United Nations, Dag Hammarskjöld passed through the most profound spiritual crisis of his life—a crisis that became a vital interior preparation for all that he was to face on that international stage.

And, as we say, the rest is history. Others have documented thoroughly the many accomplishments of Dag Hammarskjöld in his eight-and-a-half-year tenure at the helm of the United Nations, so rehearsing them here is unnecessary.[52] Suffice it to say that, from his first bold mission to Peking in 1955 to his intervention in the Suez Crisis in 1956 to his mediation in the Congo in 1961—the mission that claimed his life—he transformed the United Nations from a forum for conference and controversy into an agency of creative action for peace. As Henry Van Dusen has written, "Probably no other individual in history has effected so large a work of mediation and pacification among nations."[53]

We can be profoundly grateful for this man's immense contribution toward world peace. Further, we can be grateful that he experienced devotion and work as a seamless garment.

One of the finest statements we have on the Incarnational Tradition, the sacramental life, was penned by Hammarskjöld on Christmas Eve 1956, when the resolution of the Suez Crisis finally was assured: "Your own efforts 'did not bring it to pass,' only God—but rejoice if God found a use for your efforts in his work."[54] And again two days later, "We act in faith—and miracles occur."[55]

If his life had not been cut short, how much more could he have accomplished? We will never know. His untimely death is a genuine loss to us, but perhaps he spoke more prophetically than he knew when he wrote these words:

For him who has faith,
The last miracle
Shall be greater than the first.[56]

DEFINING THE INCARNATIONAL TRADITION

The Incarnational Tradition concerns itself with the relationship between spirit and matter. In short, God is manifest to us through material means.

Now, the spiritual and the material are not in opposition to one another, but are complementary. Far from being evil, the physical is meant to be inhabited by the spiritual. We are created so as to receive life from God, who is Spirit, and to express that life through our bodies and in the physical world in which we live. The material world is created, in part, so as to make visible and manifest the realm of the invisible spirit.

God loves matter. In his original creative acts God affirmed matter again and again, declaring it good at every point along the way. We, therefore, should take the material world quite seriously; it is the "icon" of God, the epiphany of his glory. We must not dismiss material things as inconsequential—or worse yet, as genuinely evil. The stuff of the material world—what Pierre Teilhard de Chardin called "holy matter"—has been created by God and again he declared it to be good, very good (Gen. 1:25, 31). The material world is intended to enhance human life.[57]

It is also the realm or the place where we are to develop our spirit under God. One of the main functions of matter is to mediate the presence of an infinite God to finite minds. The Ark of the Covenant and the Tabernacle were divinely appointed arrangements so that God could be with human beings without destroying them. The same is true of the coming of the Messiah as a babe in a manger. These material realities are all graciously designed to allow for the necessary space between us and God. In this way God can come to us and we, in turn, can come to God. Divine realities are thus mediated to us through the finite realities of our personal histories, our social experiences, our physical bodies.

Now, there are fundamentally two arenas or dimensions of incarnational life. The first is what we, from a human point of view, would identify as the specifically religious dimension. The second is the arena of everyday life.

The Religious Dimension

The specifically religious dimension is most fully expressed in our corporate worship. Here we utilize the physical and the material to express and manifest the spiritual.

In this dimension of our life together it is important to underscore that all of us are liturgical. That is to say, we all use material and human "forms" to express our worship of God. There simply are no nonliturgical churches. Monastics rising to recite the Night Office and Quakers waiting in silent assurance upon the Spirit, Catholics praying the rosary and revivalists singing hymns of devotion to the name of Jesus, Russian Orthodox ritualists bowing amid incense and icon and Salvation Army evangelists marching to drum and tambourine—all are engaged in liturgy. We have a choice of liturgy, but we do not have a choice of whether to use liturgy. As long as we are finite human beings, we must use liturgy; we must express ourselves through forms of worship.[58]

Liturgy—*liturgia*—simply means "the people's work." Our task in liturgy is to glorify God in the various aspects of our worship life. We are to let the reality of God shine through the human or physical forms. This is true whether we are singing hymns or burning candles, dancing in ecstatic praise or bowing in speechless adoration.

It is useful here to draw upon the Apostle Paul's imagery of "the treasure in earthen vessels" (2 Cor. 4). The treasure is "the glory of God in the face of Jesus Christ," as Paul put it (v. 6). The earthen vessel is the human body, along with the various cultural forms we use to manifest the treasure. To apply Paul's imagery to the issue at hand, the "earthen vessel" is, very simply, our form of worship. We must always remember that the form itself is not the treasure; we worship God, never the form.

Understanding this imagery helps us appreciate others who do not worship in our way. We can recognize the treasure they are showing forth even though they worship in a different earthen vessel from us. Many earthen vessels, one treasure; many forms, one God and Father of us all.

We can even learn to rejoice in the beautiful variety of worship forms among the people of God. Evelyn Underhill (along with many others) speaks of forms of worship as "sacramentals," by which she means that they are "more than symbols and less than sacraments."[59] In other words, these physical and material forms are efficacious signs helping the worshiping soul apprehend spiritual reality. In the eighth century John of Damascus argued in exactly this manner for the icons of Eastern Orthodox faith as signs or reflections of the eternal and spiritual reality.

This discussion of forms refers, of course, to far more than the icons of Eastern Orthodoxy. Consider the music of J. S. Bach and Charles Wesley and Fanny Crosby. Consider the profound silence of Quaker worship—the silence is itself a form, a liturgy of worship. Consider the rich tapestry of Anglican worship. Consider the warm vibrancy of Pentecostal worship. Consider foot-washing in the Brethren services or the laying on of hands in Charismatic circles or the Love Feast in House churches. The list could go on and on. Our worship becomes a magnificent, all-encompassing aesthetic experience. We see, we smell, we touch, we taste, we hear. We absorb the faith by reliving the gospel and the passion in the liturgy. In short, God is manifest to us through material means.

The Sacraments of the Church most completely demonstrate God's use of matter to make present and visible the invisible realm of the spirit. They are, in fact, often called, "visible means of an invisible grace." Sacraments are concrete actions by which we are marked and fed in such a way that the reality of God becomes embedded in our body, our mind, our spirit. The Holy Spirit grafts us into the

Trinitarian life by burying and then raising us up in baptism. And the Holy Spirit continually feeds us by enacting the death and resurrection of Christ in the Communion service, or Eucharist.[60]

The Arena of Everyday Life

But the religious dimension is the beginning, not the end. We are to take this life and incorporate it into all we are and all we do. We bring it into daily life: into our homes, into our work, into our relationships with children and spouse and friends and neighbors and, yes, even enemies. Here we come to the most fundamental arena for the Incarnational Tradition: the arena of everyday life. It is the place, par excellence, in which we make visible and manifest the invisible realm of the spirit.

To move into this sacramental way of living, we must take deep into our heart and mind Paul's words, "And whatever you do, in word or deed, do everything in the name of the Lord Jesus, giving thanks to God the Father through him" (Col. 3:17).

The most basic place of our sacramental living is in our marriages and homes and families. Here we live together in well-reasoned love for everyone around us. Here we experience "the sacrament of the present moment," to use the phrase of Jean Pierre de Caussade. We miss the point of this way of life if we are off conducting prayer meetings and other churchly enterprises when the duty of the present moment is to be home, playing with our children or caring for other domestic responsibilities. C. S. Lewis wisely observed, "The great thing, if one can, is to stop regarding all the unpleasant things as interruptions of one's 'own' or 'real' life. The truth is of course that what one calls the interruptions are precisely one's real life—the life God is sending one day by day: what one calls one's 'real life' is a phantom of one's own imagination."[61]

Work is another everyday place—perhaps the most substantive place—for incarnational living. By "work" I am referring not merely to our job; I am referring to what we do to produce good in our world. I am referring to our *vocatio*, our vocation or calling.

Now, I really must bear down on this point of our work as the place for living sacramentally. While some have a special calling to pastoral or priestly work in order to equip the people of God, the calling or vocation for most of us is smack in the midst of the workaday world. And even here we often miss the point of a sacramental life. One business leader piously announced, "I instruct my secretary to set aside one noon hour a week when, instead of going out to some power lunch, I close the door on the dog-eat-dog world of business, open my Bible, and spend time alone with my Lord." Now, this may well be a wise practice, but it is not yet sacramental living. The real issue is how we live and act and react *in the midst* of the dog-eat-dog world of power lunches and business dealings and board meetings. Or the dog-eat-dog world of restaurant managers and servers, of contractors and subcontractors, of middle management and office staff. Or the dog-eat-dog world of law and education and entrepreneurship. This is where people desperately need to see the reality of God made visible and manifest.

And this is where we learn to do our work as Jesus would do our work if he were in our place. Now, in understanding how this works, we need to underscore Jesus among us in his office as resurrected and exalted Lord, free from all the localizations of time and space, geography and history, gender and race, nationality and vocation. For he *is* in our place. He continually moves among us as our ever-present Teacher. He is, you see, the Lord of all vocations, and he really can teach us how to fulfill our calling. If you are a dentist, Jesus can teach you to do dentistry as he would do it if he were you. The same is true if you are a court stenographer, a computer programmer, a research scientist, a janitor, or the CEO of a multinational corporation. It is just as true if the thing you do to produce good in the world is raise a family or paint pictures or create stained-glass windows or peel potatoes. Whoever, whatever, wherever—he will teach you. Learn from him.

The third place—in addition to home and work—that we learn to live sacramentally is in society at large. Here we are to bring the reality of God to bear upon cultural, political, and institutional life. The theologians call this "the cultural mandate," a teaching that is deeply rooted in the creation narrative, where God gives the human pair stewardship authority to care for and manage the earth (Gen. 1–3). And so we do. We work to lift our culture, not just through the commonsense moral standards of decency and honesty, but through art and literature and drama, justice and beauty and shalom. We nurture "the good, the true, the beautiful" throughout society—through the person-centered caring of the schools we run, through the beauty of the parks we build, through the entrepreneurial empowerment we offer the poor, through the imaginative and redeeming literature we write, through the ecological sensitivity we bring to land use and development, and so much more.

Family, work, society—these comprise the arena of everyday life. Now, it is of utmost importance that we keep a constant and intimate link between the specifically religious dimension and the arena of everyday life. This connection, incidentally, is seen in many of the "sacramental" passages in our New Testament—passages that carry this double reference to both the religious dimension and everyday life. In the sixth chapter of John, for example, where Jesus gives an extended teaching on "eating the flesh of the Son of Man and drinking his blood," we immediately see both the reference to Communion and the call to our continual feeding on his life. As Jesus says, "The words that I have spoken to you are spirit and life" (John 6:63b). The same thing can be seen in Jesus' discourse on "living water" with the woman at the well, where baptism stands in the background of his teaching on the sustaining life that he gives to all who trust in him.[62]

Martin Luther profoundly linked the religious sphere with common life when, in writing about baptism, he said, "For as long as we live we are continually doing that which baptism signifies, that is, we die and rise again. . . . [T]hat which baptism signifies should swallow up your whole life, body and soul, and give it forth again at the last day, clad in the robe of glory and immortality. We are therefore never without the sign of baptism nor without the thing it signifies."[63] This bridge is also seen in the Reformation principle of "the priesthood of all believers." To be sure, this principle teaches us that "the plow boy and the milk maid" can do priestly work. But even more profoundly it teaches us that the plow boy *in his plowing* and the milk maid *in her milking* are in fact doing priestly work.

Have I given enough substance for you to grasp the concept of the Incarnational Tradition? I could say more, but my guess is that you have the sanctified imagination to take the central insight of this sacramental way of living and contextualize it into the many situations you face day in and day out.

DISCOVERING THE MAJOR STRENGTHS

The strengths of the Incarnational Tradition are myriad. I shall briefly mention seven.

First, it underscores the fact that God is truly among us in the warp and woof of our very earthy existence. God is not distant, nor is he disinterested. "The world is charged with the grandeur of God," writes Gerard Manley Hopkins; "Christ plays in 10,000 places."[64] We, you understand, are not alone. God stoops to our need and allows himself to be glimpsed in the material world.

Second, it roots us in everyday life. It saves us from a spirituality divorced from the stresses and strains of ordinary living. We cannot retreat from the "secular" world in the hopes of finding God elsewhere. Indeed, the very presence of God is manifest in the smallest, most mundane of daily activities.

Third, it gives meaning to our work. We have a heightened sense of the sacramentality of work. We work to "the audience of One." We are becoming co-laborers with God as we bring good into the world. We get beyond ourselves and, in so doing, become more of what we were meant to be.

Fourth, it is a valuable corrective to Gnosticism. The central Gnostic heresy is that spiritual things are wholly good and material things are wholly bad. This Gnostic dualism is just as appealing today as it was in earlier centuries, for people gravitate toward ideas that are clear-cut and uncomplicated even when those ideas are clearly false. But the Incarnational Tradition reminds us again that our God created a good world, that "the earth is the LORD's and all that is in it" (Ps. 24:1).

Fifth, it constantly beckons us Godward. We are often weak and forgetful, distracted and confused. But, in the religious dimension especially, the visible signs of worship are a constant Ebenezer reminding us that "hitherto the LORD has helped us" (1 Sam. 7:12, RSV). Most particularly the Sacraments shock us back into reality by making specific and concrete our Christian identity.

Sixth, it makes of our body a portable sanctuary through which we are daily experiencing the presence of God; learning, ever learning, to work in cooperation with God and in deepening dependence upon God.

Seventh, it deepens our ecological sensitivities. We grow in our stewardship of the earth, for we know that it is God's good creation. We plant evergreens and compost garbage, we clean a room and put coasters under glasses, and in these ways we help to tidy up Eden.

These are some of the strengths of the Incarnational Tradition. Perhaps you can think of others.

UNDERSTANDING THE POTENTIAL PERILS

Dangers abound. Two stand head and shoulders above the rest. The first of these is the pitfall of idolatry. It comes at us from several directions. When we confess that God is made manifest to us in and through the created universe, for example, we can be tempted to take that next easy step of identifying God with the universe. It is not difficult to see why. Frankly, this material universe is so stunning, so spectacular, so beyond us that we can understand why people would want to worship it. This helps explain why pantheism is experiencing something of a revival in our day.

This problem also crops up when people fail to distinguish between a sacred object and the spiritual reality it signifies. Idolatry is the inevitable result. No doubt this is why the Bible has such strict prohibitions against making any graven image of God.

These are issues that Christians have wrestled with constantly through the last two millennia. Earlier I mentioned the great theologian John of Damascus and his argument for icons as a kind of window between the earthly and the spiritual worlds. Many, however, disagreed with him, fearing that people would end up worshiping the icon rather than God. This difference of opinion precipitated the great iconoclastic controversy of the eighth century. In the seventeenth century the Puritans under Oliver Cromwell sought to purify the Anglican Church of its objects of veneration by defacing the statuary in the cathedrals and throwing out candles and other objects of "popery." The Quakers took the matter even further by rejecting all outward symbols, including baptism and Eucharist, as a testimony against the superstitious religious practices they saw around them.

The point is that the danger of idolatry is a genuine danger. Constant vigilance is needed. It is almost as if we should write in bold letters across all icons, symbols, and liturgical exercises, "Beware of worshiping the creation rather than the Creator." But such vigilance must be accompanied by great humility of heart, for there is no absolute line of demarcation between the proper use of rite and ritual to reflect spiritual reality and the idolatrous use of these material things.

The second great peril lies in the way we seek to manage God through externals. Cain with his grain offering was the first to try this strategy, but he certainly was not the last. The story of Ananias and Sapphira's land deal (recorded in the fifth chapter of Acts), is only another verse of the same song.

Perhaps this peril reaches its highest expression in religious structures that seek to confine and control the work of God through ritual systems. We encounter this peril when a particular group declares its religious system to be the only system that can ensure the full blessing of God. If you want God, *really* want God, you must come through that church and its ritual system to find him. Statements like the following—and their number is legion—are warning signals that we just might be trying to manage God through externals. "You must become a member of our church [or denomination or prayer group or whatever] if you really want the blessing of God." "If you haven't responded to an altar call, you haven't responded to God." "Our baptism is the only efficacious baptism."

This, you may remember, is one of the major dangers Jesus dealt with in his famous Beautitudes in the Sermon on the Mount. People in those days were bound to a temple ritual system in order to receive the blessing of God, and Jesus, in effect, said, "This temple and all its rites can dry up and blow away and your blessedness under God will remain."

You see, all these little systems of blessedness only succeed in binding people all the more tightly to us rather than freeing them to God. Indeed, one of the best signs that we are *avoiding* this danger is seeing in people an ever-decreasing dependence upon us and an ever-deepening dependence upon God.

PRACTICING THE INCARNATIONAL TRADITION

The first action in practicing the Incarnational Tradition is the invocation of God's manifest presence into this material world of ours. Here the initiative rests squarely upon us (even though we know that we are only responding to God's prior initiation upon our heart). God, you see, will not enter many areas of our life uninvited. So we invite God to enter every experience of life. We invite God to set our spirit free for worship and adoration. We invite God to animate our preaching and singing and praying. We invite God to transform the bread and wine of Communion.[65] We invite God to heal our bodies. We invite God to inform our minds with creative ideas for our business enterprises. We invite God to touch broken relationships and resolve conflicts at work or home. We invite God to make our homes holy places of worship and study and work and play and love-making. We invite . . . we invite. Perhaps we could speak of this as "invited grace"—the grace of God coming in loving response to our invocation.

A second action comes as we recover a Christian spirituality of work. We are helped in our thinking by the Benedictine notion of the dignity of manual labor and the Franciscan ideal of serving the poor as a way of worshiping God. We can add to this Martin Luther's conviction that "the menial housework of a manservant or maidservant is more acceptable to God" than the work of monks or priests.[66] And we can learn much from the Puritan notion of *calling* or *vocation*.

In our day special emphasis needs to be placed upon the sacredness of the work of our hands and our mind. If ours is God's world, any true work for the improvement of human life is a sacred undertaking. As Elton Trueblood has noted, "We should see the ordination to the priesthood as a sacrament; but we should likewise see ordination to any worth-while human task as a sacrament."[67] You see, we can never confine the "call" to "full-time Christian service" to clergy-related vocations. Farmers and plumbers and secretaries can be equally "called" and equally "full-time" and equally "Christian," and they can equally render "service." The really crucial decision comes, not when we decide to be a pastor rather than a biologist, but when we decide to allow our entire life to be a channel of divine love.

So what does a Christian spirituality of work look like? I can give only the barest essentials here.[68] We have a sense of *calling*, a God-given ability to do a job linked with a God-given enjoyment in doing it. We have a sense of *responsibility* to do something in our own time that has value. We have a sense of *freedom* from the burden of the workaholic, for we are not asked to do more than we can. We have a sense of *creativity* that enables us to place the autograph of our souls on the work of our hands. We have a sense of *dignity*, for we value people over efficiency. We have a sense of *community*, for we know that our life together is more important than the end product. We have a sense of *solidarity with the poor* to empower them to do what they cannot do by themselves. And we have a sense of *meaning and purpose*, for we know that we are working in cooperation with God to bring the world one step closer to completion.

A third action comes through the recovery of marriage and family life. From prison Dietrich Bonhoeffer wrote to his fiancée Maria, "Our marriage shall be a yes to God's earth; it shall strengthen our courage to act and accomplish something on the earth."[69] Bonhoeffer affirmed this in spite of the fact that his world—indeed, the whole world as it was then known—was crumbling. We need Bonhoeffer's courage.

Marriage is covenantal. Marriage is no marriage at all if it is conditional or partial or entered into with fingers crossed. It involves an uncalculating abandon, an utter and mutual outpouring of love and loyalty. It is a "one flesh" reality in which the two become one functional whole, not unlike the way a computer disk drive and its disk form one functioning unit or the way a bow and arrow are essential to each other. And so a home is formed and children most normally follow.

Family life should be expressed in its fullness in the home, because this is the place where the specifically religious dimension and everyday life meet. The home is intrinsically a religious institution, and the family table is the center of the home. The idea that a meal can be a sacred occasion is so deeply rooted in many religious traditions that it cannot be accidental or of passing significance. The Jewish Passover and the Christian Love Feast are among the more familiar examples of sacred meals. Of special significance for us is the fact that in the Gospel accounts the risen Christ was recognized by his disciples at the moment they began sharing in a ordinary meal (Luke 24:31–35). This leads to the hope that every common meal may be, if we are sufficiently sensitive, a time when we are conscious of the real presence of our risen Lord.

Common labor too should be found in the home. Our grandparents' farmhouse was large because it was far more than a place to eat and sleep: it was a place to work. In the past the home was a workshop, a school, a church, and a club all rolled into one. True, those days are gone forever, but it is still possible to discover work together in the home. Floors need cleaning and windows need washing. In addition, modern computer technology makes cottage industries once again a genuine possibility. It is worth our best thinking and most creative efforts to make the home not just a rooming house, but the center of family life, *the* place for work and worship and play and love-making.

THE CALL TO SACRAMENTAL LIVING

QUESTION: What is the Incarnational Tradition?

ANSWER: A life that makes present and visible the realm of the invisible spirit.

QUESTION: Why should we explore it?

ANSWER: Because through it we experience God as truly manifest and notoriously active in daily life.

All of us are called to sacramental living. Redeemed by God through Christ, we are indwelt by the Holy Spirit and experience a growing transformation of character as our bodies come into a working harmony with our spirit. Hence our embodied self becomes a habitation of the Holy—a tabernacle—where we learn throughout our daily activities to function in cooperation with and in dependence upon God. Through time and experience we discover that everywhere we go is "holy ground" and everything we do is "sanctified action." The jagged line dividing the sacred and the secular becomes very dim indeed, for we know that nothing is outside the realm of God's purview and loving care.

Afterword

EVERYTHING I HAVE SHARED with you in this book grows out of a deep conviction that a great, new gathering of the people of God is occurring in our day. The streams of faith that I have been describing—Contemplative, Holiness, Charismatic, Social Justice, Evangelical, Incarnational—*are* flowing together into a mighty movement of the Spirit. They constitute, as best I can understand it, the contours and shape of this new gathering.

Right now we remain largely a scattered people. This has been the condition of the Church of Jesus Christ for a good many years. But a new thing is coming. God *is* gathering his people once again, creating of them an all-inclusive community of loving persons with Jesus Christ as the community's prime sustainer and most glorious inhabitant. This community *is* breaking forth in multiplied ways and varied forms.

I see it happening, this great new gathering of the people of God. I see an obedient, disciplined, freely gathered people who know in our day the life and powers of the kingdom of God.

I see a people of cross and crown, of courageous action and sacrificial love.

I see a people who are combining evangelism with social action, the transcendent Lordship of Jesus with the suffering servant Messiah.

I see a people who are buoyed up by the vision of Christ's everlasting rule, not only imminent on the horizon, but already bursting forth in our midst.

I see a people . . . I see a people . . . even though it feels as if I am peering through a glass darkly.

I see a country pastor from Indiana embracing an urban priest from New Jersey and together praying for the peace of the world. I see a people.

I see a Catholic monk from the hills of Kentucky standing alongside a Baptist evangelist from the streets of Los Angeles and together offering up a sacrifice of praise. I see a people.

I see social activists from the urban centers of Hong Kong joining with Pentecostal preachers from the barrios of São Paulo and together weeping over the spiritually lost and the plight of the poor. I see a people.

I see laborers from Soweto and landowners from Pretoria honoring and serving each other out of reverence for Christ. I see a people.

I see Hutu and Tutsi, Serb and Croat, Mongol and Han Chinese, African-American and Anglo, Latino and Native American all sharing and caring and loving one another. I see a people.

I see the sophisticated standing with the simple, the elite standing with the dispossessed, the wealthy standing with the poor. I see a people.

I see a people, I tell you, a people from every race and nation and tongue and stratum of society, joining hearts and hands and minds and voices declaring,

Amazing grace! How sweet the sound—
That saved a wretch like me!
I once was lost but now am found,
Was blind but now I see.

Appendix A:
Critical Turning Points in Church History

RICHARD J. FOSTER AND
LYNDA L. GRAYBEAL

WE PRESENT THIS brief overview of the last two millennia to give you a sense of the sweep of church history. It is our hope that this will provide you with a grid through which you can evaluate the development of the six faith streams you are studying in this book. A timeline for this survey is given at the beginning of Chapter 1. Any standard church history volume will give you additional details.

People mold events, and events define history. Examples of this are innumerable: the children of Israel's exodus from Egypt, the fall of Jerusalem to Rome, the collapse of the Roman Empire, the spread of Islam, the merging of city-states into nations, the Renaissance, World Wars I and II. All were critical turning points, but none shaped or defined history like Jesus Christ.

Jesus Christ is the great continental divide* of history. Prior to his appearance, humans devised countless ways to fill the God-shaped vacuum in their lives—animal and human sacrifices, secret rituals, laws and regulations, impressive temples, and more. They were constantly struggling uphill, scouting out a clear path, looking for the light shining through the trees,

---

*A *continental divide* designates "the line separating areas drained to opposite sides of a continent." In North and South America and southern Asia, this divide is found atop mountain ranges, and this is the picture we have in mind: contiguous mountains that form a chain along which people can walk.

straining toward the crest. All to no avail. Trapped in the underbrush and darkness of the forest, they caught only an occasional glimpse of the peak.

But Jesus, who entered human history at the continental divide, fills this God-shaped vacuum and provides sure footing on the crest of the mountain range. Our struggles to reach the crest are over, and there is no need to go down the other side. Jesus has brought us up to the top of the divide, and we now travel the ridge of this divide with him as our guide. We, the Church, the people of God, work in cooperation with God to shape the events that define our history.

Birth of the Church

The Church starts its journey along the divide at an unusually high summit: "When the day of Pentecost had come, they were all together in one place. And suddenly from heaven there came a sound like the rush of a violent wind, and it filled the entire house where they were sitting. Divided tongues, as of fire, appeared among them, and a tongue rested on each of them. All of them were filled with the Holy Spirit and began to speak in other languages, as the Spirit gave them ability" (Acts 2:1–4). "It doesn't get any better than this," as the saying goes. Here they were, this ragtag band of frightened, uncertain, marginalized humans, obediently waiting for something called "power from on high" (Luke 24:49c).

These 120 people became the God-ordained, Jesus-trained, Holy Spirit–empowered charter members of the Church. That first day saw three thousand others join this embryonic movement, and "day by day the Lord added to their number those who were being saved" (Acts 2:47).

With the new movement's roots in Judaism, it would have been easier for Jesus' followers to stay in Jerusalem and its environs. But doing so would not have fulfilled his words, "You will be my witnesses in Jerusalem, in all Judea and Samaria, and to the ends of the earth" (Acts 1:7b). Something radical, something drastic had to force the believers beyond their comfort zone. That "something" was persecution. These early disciples of Jesus were "scattered throughout the countryside of Judea and Samaria" (Acts 8:1b). Then "those who were scattered went from place to place, proclaiming the word" (Acts 8:4).

On the day of Pentecost people from the shores of the Persian Gulf in the east to the Tyrrhenian Sea in the west, from the Black Sea in the north to the countries lining the Mediterranean Sea in the south heard the gospel. Next it went into the Horn of Africa via an Ethiopian eunuch (Acts 8:26–39). The apostles, coming under persecution, remained in Jerusalem until James was killed and Peter was imprisoned and escaped. Then they too started to disperse throughout the region.

Peter went to Caesarea for some time, but we later see him and Jesus' brothers traveling with their wives, presumably spreading the gospel (1 Cor. 9:5). Thomas proclaimed the gospel in India. Paul joined the ranks of the apostles and traveled to Asia Minor and Greece. Evangelist Barnabas, teachers Priscilla and Aquila, pastor Timothy, deacon Phoebe, evangelist Silas, and innumerable others proclaimed the gospel everywhere, building up the infant churches, moving from mountain peak to mountain peak along the divide.

However, Roman persecution soon began, because these followers of the Way refused to "bow the knee" of worship to Caesar. The first persecution took place in A.D. 64. Nero had used his personal monies to reconstruct Rome, but fire destroyed ten out of fourteen districts in that year. Rome's citizens suspected that he had set the fire so that he could rebuild the city more splendidly yet (early "urban renewal"). When their gossip reached Nero's ear, he knew he had been discovered and had to find a scapegoat. Fortunately for him, and unfortunately for the Christians (who were now recognized as a distinct group), he found one. This first persecution did not affect the spread of Christianity throughout the region much, but it was a harbinger of things to come: the trail along the divide would be neither smooth nor easy. Nine other persecutions were spread over approximately 250 years. Finally, with the issuance of the Edict of Toleration in the year 311, state-sponsored persecution ended. Then, when the Roman Emperor Constantine issued the Edict of Milan in 313, Christianity became an "authorized religion." Disciples now had confiscated property restored, enjoyed freedom of worship, and savored equality with other cults.

ECUMENICAL COUNCILS

Along with persecutions early Christians faced another danger on their trek along the divide: false teachings. In northern climates, wind-driven snow sometimes falls so fast that "white-out" conditions force hikers to grope their way to safety. In the early Church much the same thing happened: a proliferation of heresies obscured their vision. Major disagreements centered around the proper understanding of Christ's nature, the standing of members who had recanted their faith to escape martyrdom, the nature of human beings, which books to include in the canon of the Bible, what Jesus' death had accomplished, and more.

These debates absorbed enormous amounts of time and energy, but they were immensely important. Without the clear thinking and argumentation of such early leaders as Ignatius, Polycarp, Justin Martyr, Irenaeus, and Tertullian, the Church's body of beliefs would have been seriously compromised, perhaps beyond recognition.

Seven great ecumenical councils were convened to wrestle with these matters, the most dominant issue being the christological question. It needs to be noted that many of the teachings these councils dealt with were not necessarily false. A great variety of positions were floated during this period with a view to discovering which ones were most consistent with biblical revelation. While these gatherings were complicated by political rivalries and the growing tension between East and West, the general theological thrust is clear.

The Emperor Constantine called the First Ecumenical Council of the Church at Nicea in 325. The issue here was over the teachings of Arius, an Alexandrian priest. Arius did not hold to the full divinity of Christ, believing that there was a time in which the "Logos" did not exist and that Jesus was subordinate to God. Another priest, Athanasius, argued persuasively against Arius. The teachings of Arius were ultimately rejected and Christ was declared to be "begotten not made" and "one in being" *(homoousios)* with God. This, then, defined Christ the Son as co-equal and co-eternal with God the Father. In addition, this gathering wrote a beginning creedal statement (expanded and refined at future councils)—a statement that has ever since been called the Nicene Creed.

If the First Ecumenical Council affirmed the full divinity of Christ, the Second Ecumenical Council affirmed his full humanity. This gathering was convened in 381 by the Emperor Theodosius at Constantinople. Here was the situation: Apollinarius of Laodicea, out of a strong reaction against the teaching of Arius, went to the other extreme, emphasizing the unity of the person of Jesus Christ as one incarnate nature of the divine Logos, and thereby denied the existence of a human soul in him. This denial of Jesus' humanity was condemned at Constantinople. The council also affirmed the results of Nicea and further developed the Nicene Creed. In addition, this council effectively completed the basic outline of trinitarian theology by affirming the deity of the Holy Spirit.

The next two councils need to be discussed together. They concerned themselves with how both the divine nature and the human nature of Jesus could exist in one person. Nestorius, a monk from Antioch who became patriarch of Constantinople, stressed the distinction between Christ's human and divine nature and taught that they could never be fully united in one person. On the other side of the equation Eutyches, a leading monk of Constantinople, stressed the unity in Christ so much that he essentially had Christ's humanity swallowed up by his divinity. Both positions were condemned: Nestorius by the Third Ecumenical Council held at Ephesus in 431, and Eutyches by the Fourth Ecumenical Council held at Chalcedon in 451. The result of these council debates was a position that held in creative tension both the unity of Christ's person and the distinction of Christ's dual natures. Chalcedon affirmed that "the one and the same Christ, Son, Lord and Only begotten," has been made known in these two natures which, without detriment to their full characteristics, continue to exist "without confusion or change, and without division or separation," while belonging to one person. The phrase "without confusion or change" was intended to exclude the error of Eutyches in merging Christ's two natures. The phrase "without division or separation" was intended to exclude the error of Nestorius in separating the person of Christ. "One person in two natures" became the normative terminology after Chalcedon.

We should add that the Third Council at Ephesus declared that Mary was *Theotokos*, "God-bearer." This was all part of the christological debate over "one person in two natures." Nestorius, it appeared to his detractors, was teaching that in Christ there are two persons and that Mary is the mother of the human person of Christ but not the mother of the divine person of Christ. In order to emphasize that Jesus is "one person" and that Mary went hand in hand with the mystery of the union of divine and human in Jesus' person, the council declared her *Theotokos*. Because the Council of Chalcedon went further in clarifying christological terminology for this union, the Council of Ephesus has become associated almost exclusively with this definition of Mary as "the bearer of God."

The Fifth and Sixth Ecumenical Councils, both held at Constantinople, resulted in a further refinement of the decisions made at Chalcedon. The Fifth Council was convened by Emperor Justinian I in 553. Its main agenda was the condemnation of three individuals on the grounds that their teachings were in error in much the same manner as Nestorius's. Known as "the Three Chapters," they were Theodore of Mopsuestia, Ibas of Edessa, and Theodoret of Cyrrhus.

The Sixth Ecumenical Council (680–681) declared that Jesus possessed both a human will and a divine will that function together in perfect moral harmony. This teaching was really a deduction stemming from the affirmation of Chalcedon that Christ had two natures in one person. It effectively condemned Monothelitism, a movement that believed Christ had only a divine will.

The Seventh Council (and the last truly "ecumenical" gathering) was called by the Byzantine Empress Irene. It was held in 787 in the very same city as the First Council, Nicea. The issue it addressed, while still christological in nature, was more practical and pastoral: the place of images or icons in the life of the Christian community. This problem had been brewing for a long time. The veneration of icons had been a part of Eastern worship and spirituality since the fourth century. An important theologian, John of Damascus, defended the use of icons on the basis of the doctrine of the incarnation. He maintained, in other words, that the imaging of Jesus by Christians was part of an incarnational (or enfleshment) theology. Others—including two emperors—disagreed violently. Thus the iconoclastic ("icon-smashing") controversy soon reached fever pitch. Only a council could solve the impasse. The council's conclusion was to affirm the use of icons and other symbols as a valid aspect of Christian worship. In expressing this conclusion, the council was careful to make a clear distinction between the *veneration* of icons and the *worship* of icons.

The summary list below will help you cement these seven ecumenical councils in your mind:

1. Nicea (325): Declared that Christ is fully divine.

2. Constantinople (381): Declared that Christ is fully human.

3. Ephesus (431): Declared that Christ is a unified person and that Mary is *Theotokos*.

4. Chalcedon (451): Declared that Christ is "two natures (divine and human) in one person."

5. Constantinople (553): Reaffirmed Chalcedon and condemned "the Three Chapters."

6. Constantinople (680–681): Declared that Christ possessed both a human will and a divine will that function together in perfect moral harmony.

7. Nicea (787): Icons and other symbols are acceptable aids to worship and devotion.

Of course, many other critical issues were being debated during the centuries of the seven ecumenical councils, not the least of which was the issue of the canon of the Bible. This issue became critical when Marcion, a second-century leader, began teaching that Christians should reject the Hebrew Bible because he felt that the God of the Old Testament was radically different from the picture of God presented by Jesus. This led Christian thinkers to work hard at determining not only the collection of the Hebrew Bible but what writings from the Christian era should be considered authoritative. The first list that has come down to us of the twenty-seven books that appear in our New Testament is in a letter written by Athanasius, bishop of Alexandria, in 367. It was much later, of course, that the Church finally reached uniform agreement on the New Testament. The most important determination was whether a book was written by an apostle or a close associate. Other criteria had to do with whether the writing was in accord with the rest of biblical revelation and whether it passed the test of experience (whereby through long use the Christian community had come to a consensus regarding divine inspiration).

As we have seen, the Christian community plowed through a whole blizzard of controversies in its trek along the divide during the centuries of the ecumenical councils. We today owe a great debt to those who helped the Church through those defining events.

But if the great blizzard of theological defining had passed, two great earthquakes were yet to come—earthquakes that would irrevocably split the Church into three great branches: Eastern Orthodoxy, Roman Catholicism, and Protestantism. The Orthodox quake occurred in 1054 and the Protestant quake in 1517. Let's look individually at these three great expressions of Christian faith, first attempting to understand the background and history of each quake and then examining the strengths of each expression. We begin with the Roman Catholic Church.

ROMAN CATHOLIC CHURCH

Because the supreme authority of the pope is at the heart of the Roman Catholic Church, to understand the Roman expression of faith we must first trace the growth of the papacy.

Papal Ascendancy

In the early centuries of the Church five centers dominated Christian life: Jerusalem, Antioch, Alexandria, Constantinople, and Rome. Each of these centers had a bishop who gave spiritual and theological leadership, and all five functioned in a collegial manner. Jerusalem, however, lost much of its influence after the city's fall to the Romans in A.D. 70. Antioch and Alexandria, though intense centers of theological creativity, had difficulty competing with the political clout of Rome and Constantinople. In addition, the rise of Islam in the seventh century further eroded the influence of Jerusalem, Antioch, and Alexandria.

Rome, being the center of political power, began to dominate the life of the Church. But in 330 the center of political power shifted when the Emperor Constantine moved from Rome to Constantinople. (The city was originally called Byzantium. After the move Constantine renamed it after himself.) This set up a classic struggle between East and West, for dominance not only in theological thought but also in ecclesiastical power.

In theory, the bishops were all equal, but in practice the bishops at Rome and Constantinople grew in importance as the various church councils sought to hammer out Christian beliefs and teaching. Bishop Damasus of Rome (366–384) was the first to begin describing that part of the Church centered in Rome as "the apostolic see" and argued that "although the East sent the apostles yet because of the merit of their martyrdom, Rome has acquired a superior right to claim them as citizens." Innocent I (402–417) referred to the Roman bishop as "head and apex of the episcopate."

Leaders in Constantinople did not sit idly by. At the Second Ecumenical Council at Constantinople they asserted, "The bishop of Constantinople shall take precedence immediately after the bishop of Rome, because his city is the New Rome." Then, at the Fourth Ecumenical Council at Chalcedon, they passed a statement (Canon 28) that accorded the See of Constantinople an honor and authority equal to that of Rome.

This struggle went back and forth for some time, but it was Bishop Leo (440–461) who really turned the tide in favor of Rome. Called "Leo the Great," he saved the city of Rome twice: first from the onslaught of Attila the Hun and then from the Vandals, led by King Gaiseric. In both cases Leo succeeded not by armies but by diplomacy and persuasion. Leo also laid a biblical and theological base for papal primacy, centering his teaching squarely in the doctrine of "apostolic succession." Leo took to himself the title *Pontifex Maximus*, the greatest high priest. (The title "papa" *[pope]* originally expressed the fatherly care of any and every bishop for his flock. It began to be reserved for the bishop of Rome only in the sixth century, long after Rome's claim of primacy.) From this point on the bishops of Rome continued to gain authority over the affairs of the Church.

Crusades

The Crusades in the eleventh, twelfth, and thirteenth centuries reflected the power and dynamism of the papacy. Driven by intense religious fervor (and the love of adventure and personal profit), crusaders from western Europe attempted to expel the Muslims from the Holy Land. In one way or another all of the great and colorful figures of this era were caught up in this consuming cause, from Peter the Hermit, who sparked the First Crusade, to the saintly Louis IX, King of France, who energized the Sixth and Seventh Crusades. These Crusades also caused untold suffering and horrors beyond imagining: "It was necessary to pick one's way over the bodies of men and horses. . . . [M]en rode in blood up to their knees and bridle reins."

There was one notable exception to the continued rise and authority of the papacy. That exception is known as "the great papal schism." What happened, in short, is this. In 1305 the archbishop of Bordeaux was elected as Pope Clement V. This Frenchman never set foot in Rome, preferring instead to set up the papacy in the French town of Avignon. This marked the start of what historians call "the Babylonian captivity of the papacy." It lasted for seventy-two years. Finally in 1378 the College of Cardinals, still heavily weighted with Frenchmen, gave in to the clamor of a Roman mob and elected an Italian as pope: Urban VI. Urban quickly set up residency in Rome. Within a few months, however, the cardinals had second thoughts about Urban and announced to all of Europe that the people of Rome had forced the election of an apostate and that the proceedings were invalid. They then chose another from among their number as pope—Clement VII, who set up residency in Avignon. Now there were two popes, each condemning the other.

To solve the problem both camps agreed to a council at Pisa, on the west coast of Italy. They deposed both claimants to the papal chair and elected a third man, Alexander V. But the two deposed popes refused to be deposed! Now there were *three* claimants to the papacy. Finally in 1414 the Holy Roman emperor called together a great gathering of leaders at the German city of Constance to settle the matter. This time their efforts met with success: the three popes were effectively shoved aside and a new pope was elected, Martin V. For all practical purposes this ended the great schism, but the whole process weakened the papacy enormously. And in many ways it set the stage for the Protestant Reformation (which we will discuss presently).

The pinnacle of papal authority came under the leadership of Pius IX in the nineteenth century. To solidify papal authority he called together the First Vatican Council in 1869–1870. The central issues for this gathering were the primacy of the pope and the dogma of papal infallibility, both of which were affirmed at this council. The council further affirmed that when the pope makes a final decision in matters of faith and morals in his official capacity (*ex cathedra*), this decision is infallible and immutable and does not require the prior consent of the Church.

This action of the First Vatican Council was a major shift in favor of the authority of the papacy. For the first time the pope was placed above the process of the corporate discernment of the whole Christian community. Clearly the Church had traveled a long way from the consensual agreements of the early church councils.

Roman Catholic Mission Efforts

In the first thousand years of the Church's life enormous gains were made. The gospel was introduced into all of Western Europe, Scandinavia, the British Isles, the southern part of Eastern Europe, southern Russia, central Asia, North Africa, and the Horn of Africa. The stories of the sacrifices and gospel labors of those early evangelists for Christ are endlessly moving. But there is also a dark side to some of these efforts—imperial conquest and forced conversion at the point of the sword. Overall, though, we can say that great good came from the sacrificial labors of many.

Considerable mission activity occurred in the thirteenth century and beyond through the Franciscans, who fanned out into many places, especially China. But the great wave of Catholic missions occurred in the sixteenth century, and the key figures were Ignatius Loyola and his younger contemporary and disciple, Francis Xavier. Some historians call this period "the Catholic Reformation"; others use the term "Counter-Reformation" to emphasize its vigorous attack on the expanding Protestant movement; still others see it as a revival of spiritual piety with little concern for Protestantism. No doubt it was in some measure all of these.

Loyola founded "the Society of Jesus," or Jesuits, a highly disciplined mission-minded order of chivalrous soldiers of Jesus—mobile, versatile, and ready to go anywhere and everywhere . . . which is exactly what they did. Latin America, Africa, Asia, and beyond. Other orders—Dominicans, Franciscans, Augustinians—were also actively involved in these mission efforts.

Francis Xavier was the one who took Loyola's vision of missionary zeal to the far-flung regions of the globe, earning him the title "patron saint of Catholic missions." This "industrious missionary of indescribable gaiety" planted the Christian message in India, Japan, and China. His work in Japan is especially noteworthy, mainly because it was there that Xavier worked out his views of contextualizing the gospel message into Japanese culture. He saw that many things in Japanese life were valuable and should be preserved and brought into the context of Christian life and witness. He even wanted to add Japanese elements to the Roman liturgy. (The pope eventually rejected these changes as too much contextualization!) In 1579 the Jesuits established a new town as a home for Christian converts, calling it Nagasaki. Before the end of the sixteenth century Jesuit missionaries could count three hundred thousand Japanese converts, hundreds of churches, and two Christian colleges.

It is well known that many did not follow Xavier's emphasis upon indigenization and contextualization. Ruthless policies of imperialism, conquest, and enslavement followed much of the exploration of "the new world." The story is sad beyond describing. It would, therefore, be useful to pause briefly to remember one Bartholomew de Las Casas. A Spanish missionary whose father had accompanied Columbus on his second voyage to the West Indies, Las Casas spoke out vigorously for the equality and freedom of the Indians. The only way to seek their conversion, he argued, is by peaceful preaching of the Word and by example of holy living. Unfortunately, his voice did not win the day, but it does represent many who sought to faithfully serve Christ and just as faithfully bring the good news of the gospel to all peoples.

A major step in Catholic thinking about missions occurred at the Second Vatican Council (1962–1965). This was the first council called not to combat heresy, pronounce new dogmas, or rally the Church to stand against hostile forces. It was a council called not *against* but *for* something—for *aggiornamento*, an Italian term for "bringing up to date." "Revolutionary" is probably not too strong a term for Vatican II. What one council theologian, Canadian Father Gregory Baum, said over the proposed document on divine revelation could appropriately be said over the entire proceedings: "This day will go down in history as the end of the Counter Reformation." In Pope John XXIII's opening speech he called the Catholic Church to "rule with the medicine of mercy rather than with severity."

That statement was to be prophetic for Catholic mission thinking, for on 7 December 1965 Vatican II accepted the Declaration on Religious Freedom (*Dignitatis Humanae*) which renounced in principle any use of external force against the voice of conscience. This marked a radical break with a fifteen-hundred-year-old practice.

Two other key developments for mission came out of Vatican II. First, the Decree on Mission Activity of the Church (Ad Gentes Divinus) centered the basis for mission in the dynamic activity of the Trinity in the world, through the sending of the Son to the world in the incarnation and the sending of the Holy Spirit into the world following the resurrection. The Church then participates in this sending by being the sacrament of God in the world. As a result, the Church does not *have* missions; it *is* mission. Missionary activity is thus not the work of a designated few, but is incumbent upon all Christians. Clearly this was a major step forward in Catholic mission thinking and practice.

Second, the Declaration on the Relation to Non-Christian Religions (Nostra Aetate) stated that the good things found in others religions are to be affirmed and that those who follow those traditions, and through no fault of their own do not know Christian faith, achieve some measure of salvation. (The meaning of this latter point is unclear and has caused vigorous debate in the Catholic community. Whatever the precise meaning of the statement, it is clear that it is not teaching universalism.) Since Vatican II Pope John Paul II has issued an important encyclical on mission (Redemptoris Missio), which places particular emphasis upon proclamation as the central mode of evangelization.

EASTERN ORTHODOX CHURCH

Now, as we turn our attention to Eastern Orthodoxy, you will need to back up a bit in your mind—back to the struggles for power between Constantinople and Rome. Deep-seated dissimilarities existed between the Eastern and Western branches of Christianity. Their languages were different. Their practices were different. Their political relationships were different. And these differences produced first a rift and then a full break.

In 867 the patriarch of Constantinople declared Rome heretical for adding the *filioque* ("and the Son") to the Nicene Creed: "I believe in the Holy Spirit . . . who proceeds from the Father and the Son." Then, in the mid–eleventh century, the East accused the West of error by universalizing clerical celibacy and by celebrating the Eucharist with unleavened bread.

In 1054 Pope Leo IX sent Cardinal Humbert, a non-Greek-speaking, pro-celibate, anti–political alliance diplomat to negotiate with Constantinople. The mission was doomed from the outset. Finally, just as a worship service was about to begin in the Church of Holy Wisdom at Constantinople, Cardinal Humbert marched in, placed a papal bull of excommunication upon the altar, and marched out. A deacon, grabbing the paper, rushed after the cardinal and begged him to take it back. Humbert refused, dropping the papal bull in the street. Historians use this shattering event of 1054 to mark the break between East and West—the first great earthquake along the divide. Henceforth Eastern Orthodoxy was a separate expression of Christian faith and witness.

Understanding Eastern Orthodoxy

At present Orthodoxy has over two hundred million adherents in fifteen self-governing ("autocephalous") churches, including the four ancient centers of Constantinople, Alexandria, Antioch, and Jerusalem. The other centers are Russia, Serbia, Georgia, Romania, Bulgaria, Greece, Cyprus, Albania, Poland, former Czechoslovakia, and the United States. We have mentioned some of their differences with Rome: the conciliar authority of bishops rather than a pope, the permissibility of marriage for clergy, the insistence on leavened bread for the Eucharist, and the rejection of the *filioque* in the Nicene Creed. But none of these differences really gets at the heart of the uniqueness of Orthodoxy. Just what is Eastern Orthodoxy?

Perhaps the one word that best sums up the heart of Orthodoxy is the word *tradition*. Not the plural *traditions*, as in various and sundry customs, but *tradition*—a living continuity with the Church throughout the ages. The Eastern patriarchs put it this way: "We preserve the Doctrine of the Lord uncorrupted, and firmly adhere to the Faith he delivered to us, and keep it free from blemish and diminution, as a Royal Treasure, and a monument of great price, *neither adding any thing, nor taking any thing from it.*" John of Damascus wrote, "We do not change the everlasting boundaries which our fathers have set, but *we keep the Tradition, just as we received it.*"

For Orthodoxy tradition means more than just handing down certain beliefs and ideas to future generations. It means a living connection to the faith of the apostles and fathers of the Church. It means entering into the inner spirit of the tradition. It means creative fidelity to the past, in which the disciple always seeks to live *into* the tradition. Tradition also involves quite specific elements to Orthodox Christians: "Tradition . . . means the books of the Bible; it means the Creed; it means the decrees of the ecumenical councils and the writings of the Fathers; it means the Canons, the Service Books, the holy Icons—in fact, the whole system of doctrine,

Church government, worship and art which Orthodoxy has articulated over the ages."

Perhaps one helpful way to understand Eastern Orthodoxy is through its use of icons. "An icon," says Orthodox historian Timothy Ware, "is not simply a religious picture designed to arouse appropriate emotions in the beholder; it is one of the ways where God is revealed to man. Through icons the Orthodox Christian receives a vision of the spiritual world." Icons, then, serve as a kind of window between earth and heaven. Through the icons the heavenly world is manifest to the worshiping congregation. According to Orthodox theology the icon is the capstone of the doctrine of Incarnation: because God became fully human in Jesus Christ the invisible has become visible and can be portrayed in wood and paint. All matter has been sanctified and is able to convey the grace of God.

You may recall that the Seventh Ecumenical Council struggled with this issue and came down on the side of the use of icons, affirming that icons did not represent idolatry but were an authentic expression of incarnational worship. The argument is that, while the icon is not of the same substance as its original, it does open to us a window onto the original. By material means we receive a glimpse into the heavenly world. Further, Orthodox teaching insists that icons should not be worshiped but should be venerated—venerated in much the same way that other Christian groups venerate the Bible. Indeed, Orthodox Christians speak of the Bible as the verbal icon of Christ.

Theologically speaking, Orthodox belief would remind us that we are created "in the image of God," so that we carry the "icon" of God within us. Sin, then, is the marring of the divine likeness. When we sin we inflict a wound in the original image of God. Salvation therefore consists in God restoring the full image of God. Christ came to restore the icon of God within us. This "restoring" involves rebirth, re-creation, and transfiguration into the image of Christ.

John of Damascus, commenting on the power of icons, wrote, "When I have no books, or when my thoughts, torturing me like thorns, do not let me enjoy reading, I go to church, which is the cure available for every disease of the soul. The freshness of the images draws my attention, captivates my eyes . . . and slowly leads my soul to divine praise."

Another way of getting at the spirit of Orthodox faith is by understanding something of the approach to prayer called *hesychasm*. The word literally means "quietness," "stillness," "peace." Hesychasm has sometimes also been called "the prayer of the heart." This meditative approach to prayer was developed beginning in the fourth century, with Evagrios of Pontus (c.

344–399) as the key figure; it then experienced considerable subsequent development in the fourteenth century, with two writers having extensive influence—Gregory Palamas (1296–1359) and Gregory of Sinai (?–1346). Since the nineteenth century something of a hesychast renaissance has occurred, sparked by the publication of two books: the *Philokalia* and *The Way of a Pilgrim*. Inclusion of the "Jesus Prayer" is a prominent feature of hesychastic prayer: "Lord Jesus Christ, Son of God, have mercy on me." (Gregory of Sinai often added the phrase "a sinner" to the prayer, and more recently Orthodox believers have tended to follow his example.)

Hesychasm is prayer of the entire person. Though we may begin by praying with the lips, in time we "descend with the mind into the heart," allowing the intellect and the heart to be united. We "find the place of the heart," and our spirit acquires the power of "dwelling in the heart," so that our prayer becomes a "prayer of the heart." All of this signifies a complete state of reintegration in which, as we pray, we are totally united with the prayer itself and with our divine Companion to whom we pray. We are not so much saying a prayer as we are being turned into prayer.

This "prayer of the heart" may well be one of the finest gifts Eastern Orthodoxy has to offer to all Christians. It certainly is the most borrow-able.

Eastern Orthodox Mission Expansion

The turning of Russia to Eastern Orthodoxy is one of the great stories of history. It seems that Vladimir, prince of Kiev, while still a pagan, sent his followers to many countries in the world in search of the true religion. After visiting Muslim peoples they reported to Vladimir that "there is no joy among them, but mournfulness and a great smell; and there is nothing good about their system." Traveling on to Rome they found their worship more satisfactory, but they complained that it was without beauty. Finally they journeyed to Constantinople, and as they attended the divine liturgy in the Church of the Holy Wisdom, they discovered what they were seeking: "We knew not whether we were in heaven or on earth, for surely there is no such splendour or beauty anywhere upon earth. We cannot describe it to you: only this we know, that God dwells there among men, and that their service surpasses the worship of all other places. For we cannot forget that beauty." Thus in 988 Vladimir embraced the Eastern expression of Christianity, making it the state religion of Russia. Thus one of the great civilizations of the world was opened to evangelism by Orthodoxy.

Eastern Orthodoxy has often been criticized for not being a missionary church, and there is enough in the criticism to make it sting. Frankly, Orthodoxy has never developed anything close to the mission societies of Protestantism or the mission orders of Catholicism. Even in the above story of Russia's move into Orthodoxy Vladimir took the initiative, not a mission-minded Orthodoxy. Having said this, we must also emphasize that Orthodoxy has had shining examples of individual mission activity. The Eastern monks who brought the Christian faith to Persia, India, and Ethiopia illustrate these courageous efforts.

Special mention should be made of two brothers, Constantine (or Cyril) (826–869) and Methodius (c. 815–885). Their great work was among the Slavic peoples. Before setting out for Moravia (roughly equivalent to modern Czechoslovakia) they devised a Slavic alphabet and began translating the Bible into the Slavic language. Their work in Moravia met with some successes, though their specific mission efforts ultimately did not endure. But the great contribution of Constantine and Methodius was their translation of the Bible and the liturgical service books into Slavic. Because of their efforts the Slavic Christians from the outset heard the Bible and the services of the Orthodox Church in a tongue that they could understand. This is all the more astonishing when we realize that Christians in the western European countries did not have this same privilege, Latin being the language of the Roman Catholic Church. Building on the foundation of Constantine and Methodius, Orthodox mission efforts went forward in a language understandable to the people among the Moravians, Bulgarians, Serbs, and Russians.

Hilarion, the metropolitan of Russia, said in 1051, "The religion of grace spread over the earth and finally reached the Russian people. . . . The gracious God who cared for all other countries now no longer neglects us. It is his desire to save us and lead us to reason." So it was that Russia—that great land mass and even greater mix of ethnic groupings—became the most important mission field for Orthodoxy.

The Russian Orthodox Church, centered in Kiev, was restricted largely to the cities until the fourteenth and fifteenth centuries. In 1237 the Mongols invaded Russia, destroying Kiev. Under the most severe conditions the Orthodox Church kept the Russian national consciousness and Orthodox religious faith alive for the next two centuries of Mongol occupation.

While Orthodox missionary activity continued under the Mongol occupation, the Russian Church ultimately failed to convert the Mongols themselves. One key factor in this failure stemmed from the Orthodox practice of establishing national churches. The Russians, meeting the Mongols on Russian soil, simply could not bring themselves to encourage a Mongol national church; they did not want to give up their national customs in favor of Mongol culture.

One effective mission effort during the Mongol occupation came under the leadership and inspiration of Stephen, Bishop of Perm (c. 1340–1396). The evangelistic efforts of Stephen (and those inspired by his example) were not to the Mongols, however, but to the primitive tribes in the northeast and the far north of the Russian continent. Stephen himself worked among the Zyrian tribes. Following the example of Constantine and Methodius, these missionaries translated the Bible and church services into the languages and dialects of the people to whom they ministered.

The major evangelization of the Russian nation, however, occurred by a most unusual method of colonization devised by Sergius of Radonezh (1314–1392), a gifted leader who eventually became the greatest national saint of Russia. Sergius headed the Monastery of the Holy Trinity fifty miles north of Moscow, and he would send his monks into the surrounding forests to establish other monasteries. Communities soon grew up around these monastic centers, and by means of this colonizing process, repeated over and over, the Christian faith spread across all of northern Russia, carrying the gospel as far as the White Sea and the Arctic Circle. Sergius also influenced a deepening of the spiritual life of the Orthodox Church. (The years 1350–1550 are considered the golden age of Russian spirituality.) This rise of the Russian Orthodox Church was timed perfectly, for the Turks overran the Byzantine Empire four years after the Mongols departed Russia. Hence Russian Orthodoxy became the protector and ascendant church of the Orthodox world.

The city of Kiev never recovered from the sacking by the Mongols. Moscow, a small and relatively unimportant town at the time, took its place as religious hub when Peter, metropolitan of Russia from 1308 to 1326, settled there. Moscow came to see herself as the leader of the Orthodox world. A saying developed during the years of Moscow's ascendancy regarding that leadership role. There had been one Rome in Italy—so the saying went—but it had fallen to the barbarians. Constantinople therefore became the second Rome. Eventually it too had fallen, this time to the Turks. And so a third Rome had arisen—namely, Moscow. The Russian emperor took his title from the first Rome (*czar* is the same word as *caesar*) just as he had taken his religion from the second Rome.

PROTESTANT CHURCH

Historians use 31 October 1517—the date when Martin Luther nailed his ninety-five theses (or propositions) to the door of the castle church at Wittenberg—to mark the beginning of the Protestant Reformation. There were, of course, precursors, especially Englishman John Wycliffe and Bohemian John Huss. Coming to prominence during the papal schism, they both condemned numerous Roman practices, especially the sale of indulgences, and emphasized the primacy of Scripture over tradition. Huss was excommunicated twice, put under investigation, and finally condemned and burned at the stake in 1415. Wycliffe died in 1384, before being persecuted by Rome, but his followers—the Lollards—suffered considerable persecution, and with the death of their leader in 1417, they went underground.

Then, exactly one century later, Augustinian monk Martin Luther nailed his theses to that Wittenberg door. It was the spark that ignited the Protestant Reformation. It would prove to be the second great earthquake for travelers along the divide.

Defining the Reform

Initially Luther was working to reform the Catholic Church, not trying to start a new church. Historian Bruce Shelley notes that in these reform efforts Luther brought creative theological answers to four critical questions:

> "How can a person be saved?"
> "Where does religious authority lie?"
> "What is the Church?"
> "What is the essence of Christian living?"

Luther's reply to the question of how a person can be saved was unequivocal: "By grace through faith alone!" His own deepening understanding of this answer came as he began his work as a teaching theologian at the newly founded University of Wittenberg. In 1515 he lectured on Paul's letter to the Romans. Then for two years—1516–1517—he lectured on Paul's letter to the Galatians. The powerful message of justification by faith in these two books began to work its way into Luther's heart and soul. The great turning point came as he meditated long and hard on the words of Romans 1:17: "For therein is the righteousness of God revealed from faith to faith: as it is written, The just shall live by faith." He later recalled, "Night and day I pondered until I saw the connection between the justice of God and the statement that 'the just shall live by his faith.' Then I grasped that the justice of God is that righteousness by which through grace and sheer mercy God justifies us through faith. Thereupon I felt myself to be reborn and to have gone through open doors into paradise."

To Luther, faith was not merely intellectual assent, as it had been for most of the scholastics. Rather, it was a grateful, whole-hearted response of one's entire being to the love of God in Christ.

Thus one of the great cornerstones of the Protestant Reformation was laid: *sola fide*, faith alone. Luther knew that by emphasizing *alone* he was adding a word to Scripture, but he believed that the theological climate demanded the addition and that it was, in fact, in perfect accord with Scripture. Besides, Augustine and Ambrose had said the same thing before him.

As to the second question, about the grounds of religious authority, Luther's forthright response rested on *sola Scriptura*, the Scripture alone. During an eighteen-day debate with John Eck of Leipzig, Luther declared, "A council may sometimes err. Neither the church nor the pope can establish articles of faith. These must come from Scripture." Then, in April 1521, Luther defended his position of the authority of Scripture before the Diet of Worms. When he was told to recant what he had written, he responded, "My conscience is captive to the Word of God," adding that unless he were convicted by Scripture and plain reason, he could not recant, for he did not accept the authority of popes and councils (since they had contradicted one another). "I will not recant anything," he declared to the court, "for to go against conscience is neither honest nor safe. Here I stand, I cannot do otherwise. God help me. Amen."

By stressing the primacy of the Word of God as contained in Scripture, Luther was not rejecting the teachings of councils or the great writers of Christian thought. But he was making them subject to Scripture: any time there is a discrepancy between the two, he said, the Bible is to be regarded as the authoritative source of faith and practice.

Luther backed up his emphasis on "Scripture alone" by translating the entire Bible into German, thus making Scripture accessible to his people. That effort was clearly one of Luther's major achievements. Others had translated the Bible into German, but no one else had equaled Luther's dignity and felicity of expression (nor has anyone since). His version of the Bible became a cherished possession of Germany and did much to standardize the literary language of that country. Indeed, the effect of Luther's version upon the German language was even more profound than the effect of the King James Bible upon English.

As to the third question—What is the Church?—Luther replied that the entire community of faith are priests before God. This doctrine of the priesthood of all believers tied directly into his stress upon the primacy of Scripture, for Luther urged all Christians (as priests unto God) to read the Bible; and he insisted that they were competent, under the guidance of the Holy Spirit, to understand it aright. In taking this stance he rejected the papal claim to have the exclusive right to interpret Scripture.

Further, he rejected the supposed superiority of popes, bishops, priests, and monks over the laity, insisting that all Christians are consecrated priests by baptism and that the only difference among Christians is one of office. He maintained that the work of priests and members of the religious orders is not a whit more sacred in the sight of God than the work of a farmer in his fields or of a woman in her household duties.

This leads directly to Luther's answer to the fourth question: What is the essence of Christian living? To this he replied, serving God in any useful calling, whether ordained or lay.

While not deprecating the vows of poverty, chastity, and obedience, Luther found no grounds for them in Scripture; and by insisting that all useful work is sacred, he undercut the fundamental rationale for monastic life. He saw family life as being just as sacred as single monastic life, and he helped arrange marriages for those who left the cloistered life. He himself married a former nun, Katherine von Bora. Theirs was a happy home, and several children were born into it. When the family gathered around the table, they were typically joined by a number of Martin Luther's students, who admiringly recorded his "table talk."

All of this had a way of erasing the line between things sacred and things secular. Indeed, it was Luther's contention that all useful and good things are sacred. The thrust and logical conclusion to his teaching was that ours is a sacramental world.

Five Expressions of Reform

It is common knowledge that the Protestant Church is far from uniform. Its diversity is, in fact, one of its great strengths (however lamentable the infighting and divisions that have come from it). Perhaps it would be helpful to explain this diversity in terms of five major expressions of Christian faith and witness.

The first is the Lutheran expression, which we have already discussed to some extent. In some cases the Lutheran Church is tied to the state, as in Germany, Sweden, Denmark, and Norway. In other cases it is a self-standing denomination, as in the Evangelical Lutheran Church in America or the Lutheran Church—Missouri Synod.

Lutherans still hold high the standard of their founder by stressing justification by grace through faith alone, believing that people gain favor with God (justification) purely as a divine gift (by grace alone) to those who trust in Jesus Christ (through faith alone). Lutherans produced the first Protestant confession of faith, the Augsburg Confession (1530), and have always had a keen concern for right belief. They also pioneered congregational singing of the liturgy and hymns. As with other Protestants, Lutherans recognize two rather than seven sacraments, practice infant baptism, and teach the real presence of Christ in the Eucharist (consubstantiation). In worship Lutherans have especially stressed the importance of the preaching office—the proclamation of the Word.

One important thread of Lutheran renewal has been Pietism, with Philipp Jacob Spener and August Francke being the key figures in the movement. The pietist concern for holy living, the use of the Bible in small groups, and the care of souls has been a helpful balance to scholastic Lutheranism, with its concern for proper doctrinal formulation. Pietism is a history and an emphasis from which the entire Church could profit.

A second expression of Protestant Christian faith is called *Reformed*. Reformed Christians are reflected in the Huguenots, numerous Presbyterian groups, and a whole family of Reformed churches (e.g., the German Reformed Church, the Dutch Reformed Church, the Reformed Church of America, and the Christian Reformed Church).

No single human leader has placed a more profound stamp on the people of the Reformed family than John Calvin (1509–1564). At the age of twenty-six Calvin wrote and published what was probably the most influential single book of the Protestant Reformation, *Institutes of the Christian Religion*. *Institutes* did not owe its prominence to Calvin's originality of ideas—Calvin himself wanted only to demonstrate that Protestant beliefs were exactly what had been taught by the Church throughout the ages. It was the clarity, the comprehensiveness, the orderly arrangement of thought that commended *Institutes* to Christians throughout Europe. It was the most inclusive and systematic presentation of the Christian faith as held by Protestants that had thus far appeared. The great burden of Calvin's writing and teaching was upon the sovereignty of God, though he certainly stressed many of the beliefs that are commonly associated with his name: total depravity, election, predestination, and more. Attempts to define the essence of Reformed thinking produced a series of important confessions and catechisms, the two most prominent being the Heidelberg Catechism (1563) and the Canons of the Synod of Dort (1618–1619).

One of the best gifts the Reformed expression of faith has given the larger Christian family is a careful understanding of how the Church should relate to and interact with the culture in which it lives. The Reformed conviction is that by informing the culture with values of truth and beauty and civility, by establishing good laws and morals and government, it is possible to create a civilized society, perhaps even to effect an approximation of the kingdom of God in history.

A third expression of Protestant life and witness is the Anabaptists. The Mennonites, the Hutterites, and the Brethren are their direct descendants, and the Quakers and Baptists are distant relatives. The most famous leader of the Anabaptists was Menno Simons (1496–1561).

Their name, assigned to them by their enemies, means "rebaptizers." The Anabaptists themselves rejected any notion of "rebaptism," for they did not consider the ceremonial sprinkling they received in infancy to be valid baptism. For them Christian baptism was a conscious adult action experienced upon confession of personal faith in Jesus Christ. They were severely persecuted for this position, an unusual one in that day.

Anabaptists were the "radicals" of the Protestant Reformation, voices crying in the wilderness urging the moderate reformers to strike even more deeply at the roots of the old order. While Luther would allow whatever the Bible did not prohibit, the Anabaptists rejected whatever the Bible did not prescribe. Hence they tended to strip away more of the traditional symbols of the Roman Church than did either Luther or Calvin—statues, pictures, candles, even music. Their goal was the "restitution" of apostolic Christian faith, a return to communities of radical faithfulness to Jesus Christ as reflected in the book of Acts.

They took the task of Christian community with great seriousness, forming a communal life of love, support, and economic sharing called the *Bruderhof*. Even to this day we can find thriving Bruderhof communities that trace their roots back to those early Anabaptist experiments in Christian community. They remind us that it *is* possible to establish communal ways of living that are not monastic in character.

Perhaps we can learn most from the Anabaptist insistence upon radical discipleship to Jesus Christ. Because Anabaptists have worked harder than most groups to translate the Sermon on the Mount into daily practice, we can be instructed in obedience and faithfulness by their example.

A fourth expression of Protestantism is the Anglican Church, which has created the historic background for several Anglo-American denominations. Actually, it is a matter of historical debate whether the family of Anglican churches should even be classed as part of the Protestant Reformation. Many Anglican leaders like to speak of their communion as the *via media*, the middle way between Catholicism and Protestantism. After all, the Anglican break with Rome was far more political than it was theological, having to do with Henry VIII's desire to head a national English church (with the archbishop of Canterbury as its religious leader). All of this got rather complicated by Rome's refusal to annul Henry's marriage to Katharine of Aragon, and Henry's subsequent marriage to Anne Boleyn, and more. No doubt you have read all about it in undergraduate history courses. The point is that Henry merely wanted an *English* Catholic Church rather than a *Roman* Catholic one.

Be that as it may, it can be argued that the Anglican Church over time did initiate numerous reforms that stand in continuity with the concerns of the Protestant Reformation. Perhaps the two most important reforms were (1) to have an English Bible installed in all the churches and (2) to replace the Latin service of worship with Archbishop Thomas Cranmer's *Book of Common Prayer*. These two acts are contributions from which the entire Church has benefited.

The "Great Bible" that Henry VIII commissioned was in reality a compilation of the earlier translation work of William Tyndale (c. 1494–1536) and Miles Coverdale (1488–1569). A pioneer in translation efforts, Tyndale was imprisoned and ultimately died at the stake in Belgium. Interestingly, his dying prayer was, "Lord, open the king of England's eyes." The simple step of making the Bible accessible in the language of the people encouraged other reforms and increased interest in accurate translation work. A century later this resulted in the finest English translation of the Bible ever produced: the Authorized Version, commonly called the King James Bible. It is a treasure that has been given to all English-speaking Christians. In a similar manner, *The Book of Common Prayer* has become a rich source of worship and devotion to groups far beyond its Anglican and Episcopalian roots.

The fifth (and last) expression of Protestant witness we shall mention here is a little more difficult to name than the others. "Nonconformists" is the term usually given by historians to groups in this fifth category—a term that underscores the refusal of these Christians to conform to established church bodies. They have also been described as "free churches," to distinguish them from state churches. "Dissenters," "Independents," and "Separatists" are other labels that have been used to accent one aspect or another of these groups. The Puritans were among the most influential of the early Nonconformist groups. Other Nonconformist Protestant bodies include Quakers, Baptists, Congregationalists, Methodists, Plymouth Brethren, and the Salvation Army. Nonconformists are also the taproot of a vastly branching tree of denominations and evangelical parachurch groups that have developed in the United States and beyond.

Strong preaching has historically been one of the distinguishing marks of the Nonconformists. Charles Haddon Spurgeon (1834–1892) represents this emphasis well. The most famous English Baptist preacher of the nineteenth century, Spurgeon was warmly evangelistic, a Liberal in politics (and a friend of Prime Minister William Gladstone), the editor of a monthly magazine, the founder of orphanages and a training school for ministers, and the author of many books. At nineteen he took over an old church in London, and before he was thirty his preaching had attracted such crowds that in 1861 the Metropolitan Tabernacle was built, seating over five thousand. His book on preaching, *Lectures to My Students*, is filled with striking expressions and evangelical passion. It is used to this day.

Perhaps the finest contribution of the Nonconformist groups to the Church worldwide has been to hold high the vital importance of warmhearted conversion, effective evangelism, and cross-cultural mission. These themes tie in so completely with the next section that it would be best to integrate them into that larger story.

Protestant Missionary Explosion

During the four-hundred-year period of 1600–2000, Christian faith and witness went from being European-centered to becoming the first real worldwide religion, with a substantial presence in every major culture on earth. The first half of this period was dominated by Roman Catholic mission efforts, as we noted earlier. But by the year 1800 Catholic missionary efforts had been forced into decline: the Jesuit order had been abolished in 1773 (the pope acting under monarchical pressure), and European financial support had been curtailed because of the French Revolution and the ensuing chaos. At this point Protestants picked up the slack, equipping themselves with structures of mission societies comparable to the Catholic orders.

That Protestant effort grew into the greatest explosion of missionary activity in the history of the Church.

Precursors included first the Quaker "Valiant Sixty," who in the mid–seventeenth century fanned out from northern England in evangelistic efforts to many parts of the globe. Then, in 1732, the Moravian Brethren set out in missionary passion for the West Indian island of St. Thomas. In the subsequent twenty years they commissioned missionaries to Greenland, Suriname, South Africa, the Samoyed peoples of the Arctic, Algiers, Ceylon, China, Persia, Abyssinia, Labrador, and the American Indian territories. Nor should we forget John Wesley, who in 1739 declared, "The world is my Parish." Under the leadership of Francis Asbury and Thomas Coke, Wesley's Methodist lay evangelists took the gospel worldwide.

But, as we say, those were precursors. When in 1792 a self-educated teacher, shoemaker, and pastor wrote *An Enquiry into the Obligations of Christians to Use Means for the Conversion of the Heathens*, an utter explosion of missionary zeal resulted, and the "means" that he wrote about stimulated the founding of countless mission societies. This little book became the Magna Carta of the Protestant mission movement and earned its author, William Carey (1761–1834), the title "Father of Protestant Missions." Carey's vision, combined with the spiritual fervor of the First Evangelical Awakening, propelled the Church into what Yale historian Kenneth Scott Latourette has called "the great century" of unprecedented missionary expansion.

Missiologist Ralph Winter has divided Protestant mission efforts into three great eras. The First Era focused primarily on the coast lands of the great continents of Asia and Africa (and other coast lands, to a lesser extent). William Carey's work in India is a good representative of these pioneering efforts. This period was marked by remarkable sacrifice on the part of those who went out. For example, in the first sixty years few missionaries to Africa survived more than two years. Winter writes, "The gruesome statistics of almost inevitable sickness and death that haunted, yet did not daunt, the decades of truly valiant missionaries who went out after 1790 in virtually a suicidal stream cannot be matched by any other era or by any other cause."

The Second Era focused upon the inland areas and is well represented by J. Hudson Taylor (1832–1905). Many assumed that with a Christian presence in the coast regions the mission task was over, but Taylor saw the need to push on to the interior. Consequently, he established the China Inland Mission, which eventually served in one way or another over six thousand missionaries, predominantly in the interior of China. As with the First Era, a whole host of new societies sprang up to respond to the challenge to move inland: Sudan Interior Mission, Unevangelized Fields Mission, Africa Inland Mission, Regions Beyond Missionary Union, Heart of Africa Mission, and more. The greatest student missionary movement in history, the Student Volunteer Movement for Foreign Missions, arose during this period and responded to the call to the interior. Twenty thousand volunteers went overseas, and another eighty thousand stayed at home to rebuild the foundation of the missions endeavor.

The Third Era of Protestant missions focused upon "hidden people groups," a difficult-to-define nongeographical category of peoples who are socially isolated. Two leaders represent that new mission frontier of hidden people groups: Cameron Townsend (1896–1982) and Donald McGavran (1897–1990).

Townsend established Wycliffe Bible Translators to respond to the need he saw in the neglected tribal peoples. At the same time McGavran worked to analyze the problem of social barriers, and through his writings and efforts spawned the frontier mission movement, devoted to deliberate approaches to reach unpenetrated social groups. What Townsend and McGavran helped us see is that there are numerous "hidden peoples" that are defined by ethnic or sociological traits, people so different from the cultural traditions of any existing church that mission (rather than evangelism) strategies are necessary to plant indigenous churches within their particular traditions.

At the International Congress on World Evangelization in 1974 some 16,750 hidden people groups were identified. These groups comprise roughly 2.5 billion men, women, and children. This is the great remaining task of the Third Era of missions.

FINIS

Much more could be written, but we hope that this brief survey will give you the tools needed to go on from here. We would like to conclude this thumbnail sketch of church history by drawing on the International Congress on World Evangelization's analysis of the 16,750 hidden people groups still in need of a viable Christian witness in their own ethnic and cultural setting. To be sure, many organizations have arisen since 1974 to address this need; even so, a massive task still lies before us—*all* of us: Protestant, Eastern Orthodox, and Roman Catholic. It is our contention that these three great branches of the Christian family are all valid expressions of

Christ's Church. We worship one God and Father of us all. We confess Jesus Christ to be Savior and Lord. However divided and separated we may be in ecclesiastical structure, we walk the continental divide of history together. It is our hope and prayer that God will help us find ways to join hearts and hands in bringing the good news that Jesus Christ is "the way, the truth and the life" to these remaining hidden people groups representing some 2,500,000,000 precious people—people for whom Christ died.

Appendix B:
Notable Figures and Significant Movements in Church History

RICHARD J. FOSTER AND
LYNDA L. GRAYBEAL

A WORD FROM RICHARD

This appendix provides you with a sampling of the key figures and significant movements in the Traditions you have just read about (Contemplative, Holiness, Charismatic, Social Justice, Evangelical, and Incarnational)—figures and movements that correspond with the timelines found at the beginning of Chapters 2 through 7. I know that some readers will protest that their favorite person or movement is not listed. To this objection I can only say that this listing is meant to be suggestive, not exhaustive. I tried to list not fewer than thirty and not more than forty people for each Tradition, along with half a dozen movements. In some cases this self-imposed restriction was excruciating—a little like cutting off a finger or an ear. Over seventy of my favorites did not make the cut! But I believe enough are included to give you a sense of each Tradition.

In addition, the categories are far from perfect. For instance, certain individuals could be listed under several different Traditions. This should be expected, for every great spiritual movement has included many, if not all, of these great "streams of living water." A good case could be made, for example, for placing John Wesley in the Evangelical Tradition rather than

Holiness, or for placing John Woolman in the Incarnational Tradition rather than Social Justice. The same is true of the movements: the Franciscans could be in the Charismatic *and* the Social Justice *and* the Evangelical Traditions, for example. But I have tried to accent the major contribution of each person and movement.

The compiling of this appendix has been a collaborative effort between me and my Administrative Associate, Lynda L. Graybeal. Lynda has done the lion's share of research and virtually all of the descriptive writing.

A WORD FROM LYNDA

While working on the thumbnail sketches, I was impressed by the uniqueness of the people profiled. Some of them were brilliant, original thinkers; others borrowed ideas, only systematizing their predecessors' work. Some were educators and scholars; others were homemakers and farmers. Some were monks and nuns; others were married with children. Some were nobility; others were commoners. But their stories are all different, all original. Their unique humanness inspires me.

I also rediscovered how much Jesus' followers interacted with the world around them and with each other. Even in the early centuries of the Church an amazing amount of cross-pollination took place. Christianity was born in the midst of culture and people, not in a vacuum, and many times an idea that we today think is new and original is only a rediscovery of an earlier one.

Other qualities that impressed me were the perseverance, courage, and love of God these people displayed. For the first eighteen centuries of the life of the Church, conditions for human survival were perilous at best. Each person lived precariously, for an illness, broken bone, or failed crop could mean calamity, even death. In spite of this, they were truly alive to God, preaching, teaching, serving, traveling, and more. Some died while young; others lived to a great age. In either case, the kingdom of God went forward.

One more comment. You may wonder why we place a person who develops liturgy in the Charismatic Stream, or someone who translates the Bible into another language in the Evangelical Stream. The Charismatic Stream emphasizes worship renewal as well as Spirit-empowerment. With regard to the Evangelical Stream, because languages arise, change, and die, it is vital to evangelism to have the Scriptures available in the everyday language of the people.

For easy reference, the listing is alphabetical. I hope you enjoy these tiny glimpses into the lives and movements that make up the living history of the Church.

Abolition Movement (18th century to the present) — Social Justice

The Quaker example of freeing slaves and their campaign to ban slavery awakened the conscience of two key figures: William Wilberforce in England and William Lloyd Garrison in the United States. With other reformers Wilberforce, a member of Parliament, worked unstintingly to abolish slavery in the British Empire. It happened in two stages: a bill outlawing the slave trade was passed in 1807, and in 1833 slavery itself was abolished.

In the United States Garrison published the antislavery newspaper *The Liberator*, which brought the issue before a wide audience. He was joined in his antislavery efforts by many others, including Levi Coffin, James Russell Lowell, John Greenleaf Whittier, Wendell Philipps, Lucretia Mott, and freed slaves James Forten, Robert Purvis, Frederick Douglass, and Sojourner Truth. Sadly, it took a Civil War, the Emancipation Proclamation, untold deaths, and the passage of the Thirteenth Amendment to the Constitution to end slavery. Most of the activity to ban slavery during the eighteenth and nineteenth centuries took place in the U.S. and England, but now movements to ban it worldwide are arising.

Adamnan (or Eunan) (c. 625–704) — Social Justice

Born in the county of Donegal (Ireland), Adamnan followed in the footsteps of Columba, the founder of the monastery at Iona, by living at that monastery. He is remembered for negotiating the release of captives from the Northumbrians (Britains) and for persuading participants of the Council of Birr to exempt women from active participation in warfare and to protect them and their children from being killed or taken prisoners of war. Far ahead of its time, this decision became known as "Adamnan's Law."

Adelaide (?–999) — Incarnational

The Italian mother of the German emperor, the gentle, peace-loving, forgiving, and gracious Adelaide survived numerous politically motivated misfortunes to become regent of Germany in 991. As one of few West European women monarchs ever, she was able to bring the work of the kingdom of God directly into the press of human need by founding and restoring monasteries for monks and nuns and urging the conversion of the Slavs.

Aelred (or Ailred) of Rievaulx (c. 1110–1167) — Contemplative

Aelred is best known for his influential and poetic spiritual writings, which include *Speculum Caritatis* (Mirror of Love) and *Spiritual Friendship*. The latter book has had a significant influence on forming the context for healthy and abiding friendships within contemplative communities. A Cistercian abbot, Aelred was raised in the Scottish court, and from the Rievaulx Abbey in Yorkshire he advised English kings and bishops, influencing public policy for decades.

Aidan of Lindisfarne (?–651) — Social Justice

When the king of Bernicia (Northumbria/Britain) requested aid from the monastery at Iona to Christianize northeastern England, the abbot sent a monk who was soon replaced by Aidan. Establishing monasteries and churches from his base on the island of Lindisfarne just off the coast, Aidan helped children and slaves; and (in a time when slavery was accepted unquestioningly) he purchased the freedom of slaves with gifts he received. This important work was carried forward at Aidan's death by twelve youths he had trained.

Alcuin of York (c. 732–804) — Charismatic

A scholar in the court of Charlemagne (Charles the Great), Alcuin is known as the most prominent figure in the continental Carolingian renaissance (the revival of classical training) during the early Middle Ages. Educated at the York Cathedral school (England), which had one of the best libraries in Christianity, he became an influential though unoriginal writer in several fields: history, poetry, education, and theology. A concern close to Alcuin's heart — liturgical reform and worship — continues to be emphasized in an English society known as the Alcuin Club.

Alfred the Great (849–899) — Incarnational

In spite of his Wessex authority being interrupted in three cycles by wars with the Danes, Alfred helped revive learning in England by gathering together notable scholars. From them Alfred learned Latin, which he used to translate several books into Anglo-Saxon (including Gregory the Great's *Pastoral Care*). He also founded a palace school and monasteries. In adulthood, Alfred tried to give half of his time and money to religious endeavors. His was a life that wed work and faith.

Ambrose of Milan (c. 339–397) — Evangelical

Ambrose is most often remembered for his lasting influence on his most famous catechumen, Augustine of Hippo. Trained in rhetoric and law with a background in the Roman government prior to ordination as bishop of Milan, he served as counselor and guide to several emperors. In addition to evangelizing in Milan and encouraging missionary efforts, Ambrose was an effective preacher and writer. The ethical treatise *On the Duties of the Church's Servants* was his most influential work.

American Civil Rights Movement (20th century to the present) — Social Justice

Passed after the Civil War, the Thirteenth Amendment to the United States Constitution abolished slavery; the Fourteenth Amendment gave African-American men their citizenship; the Fifteenth Amendment prohibited the states from denying any man the right to vote based on race. Though social and political equality was codified, the reality was much different: blacks were denied basic rights by fiat and forced to contend with assigned seating in public places (always at the back or least desirable location), "colored" restrooms and water fountains, exclusion from social clubs and top-level jobs, and (in the South) extra restrictions attached to voting. The contemporary movement toward correcting these injustices started in 1954, when the U.S. Supreme Court ruled in *Brown* v. *Board of Education of Topeka* that segregation in public schools was unconstitutional — hence all "separate but equal" and exclusionary practices against women, the disabled, racial groups, and more were open to challenge.

Anabaptists (16th century to the present) — Holiness

The Anabaptists ("rebaptizers," an oxymoron; see below) trace their spiritual ancestry to several humble groups of the Middle Ages — groups that, convinced by the New Testament record, tried to reproduce the simplicity and commitment of first-century Christians. They rejected the association between church and state prevalent in sixteenth-century Europe, accepted the Bible as the sole law of the Christian Church, practiced pacifism, and believed in adult baptism as a sign of conversion to Christ. Significant leaders include Menno Simons, Felix Manz, Conrad Grebel, Balthasar Hubmaier, Hans Denck, and George Blaurock. Setting up separate, free communities, the Anabaptists expanded into most of Europe by the end of the Protestant Reformation. Their legacy includes Mennonite, Brethren, and Amish churches, and Bruderhof communities.

Anthony, Susan B. (1820–1906)—Social Justice

First joining the temperance movement (where she was not allowed to serve in a leadership role), Anthony, a Massachusetts (United States) Quaker, dropped out and started the Woman's State Temperance Society of New York. Heading up the effort, she became increasingly aware that women had limited rights. Upon meeting in 1851, she and Elizabeth Cady Stanton formed a fast friendship. Both worked in the abolition movement during the Civil War but left soon after it ended to focus their energies on women's suffrage. (Though leaders of the abolition movement supported the right of black men to vote, they showed little interest in helping secure the same right for women.) Working tirelessly, Anthony published a weekly journal, co-edited *History of Woman Suffrage*, co-founded the International Woman Suffrage Alliance, and served as president of the National American Woman Suffrage Association. She died fourteen years before the Nineteenth Amendment to the Constitution gave women the right to vote.

Antony of Egypt (c. 251–356)—Contemplative

See Chapter 2.

Antony of Kiev (or Anthony of Pechersky) (?–c. 1073)—Contemplative

Although monastic life in Russia already existed before the eleventh century, Antony is considered its founder. He first experienced monastic life at Mount Athos in Greece. When he returned home to Russia, he found himself unable to settle down in any of the established monasteries. Finally settling in a cave overlooking the city of Kiev, he, like his namesake Antony of Egypt, relished his solitude and contemplation. But others gathered around him and proceeded to build a church and enlarge nearby caves, founding the Monastery of the Caves (or Pechersky Lavra).

Aquinas, Thomas (1225–1274)—Evangelical

Considered by many to be the greatest philosopher and theologian of the Middle Ages, Aquinas's *Summa Theologica* and *Summa Contra Gentiles* are authoritative, systematic, intellectual statements of Christian faith. Putting forth Aquinas's distinctive natural theology and natural law ethic, they have influenced the development of theology, philosophy, ethics, and other issues in Western government and society. Italian by birth, Benedictine by fate, Dominican by choice, he carried the nickname "Dumb Ox" because of his physical bulk and silence at debates.

Asbury, Francis (1745–1816)—Holiness

English-born Francis Asbury was converted at fourteen, began preaching at sixteen, became a lay preacher at twenty-one, and volunteered to go as a missionary to the American Colonies at twenty-six. Upon arrival, he assumed leadership of four Methodist Episcopal missionaries, hence becoming the father of U.S. Methodism, a "holiness" denomination. As the first American "itinerant" preacher, he traveled by horseback an estimated quarter of a million miles, helping spread Methodism to every state east of the Mississippi.

Athanasios of Constantinople (c. 1230–c. 1323)—Holiness

Twice serving as patriarch of Constantinople, Athanasios worked fearlessly for reform in the Byzantine Empire. According to John L. Boojamra, Athanasios believed that only a centralized government "could serve the needs of the people and maintain good order in state and church." He consequently condemned officials for taking presents, seeking compensation, unfairly judging the cases of orphans, "milking" the people through inequitable tax collection, expecting bribes, and more. He also worked for reform within the Orthodox Church, fiercely attacking leaders who had betrayed their duties. Practices he uncovered and denounced in leaders included using church monies for their own gain, taking bribes, working to get a higher rank, and loaning church monies but keeping the interest for themselves. With his emphasis in two areas—Social Justice and Holiness—

Athanasios stands as an example of integrating more than one Tradition into the fabric of life.

Athanasius (c. 295–373) — Evangelical

Bishop of Alexandria (Egypt) and "Champion of Orthodoxy," Athanasius was exiled five times by four different emperors during his forty-five-year struggle to defeat state-sponsored Arianism. A trained theologian, he accompanied Bishop Alexander to the Council of Nicea (325) and succeeded him upon Alexander's death. Athanasius used his power and visibility to openly defend the trinitarian formulation in the Nicene Creed in a treatise titled *On the Decrees of the Nicene Synod*, which complemented an earlier work, *On the Incarnation*. As he had laid the groundwork for the Nicene party's eventual triumph, victory over Arianism came in 381 at the Council of Constantinople.

Augustine of Hippo (354–430) — Evangelical

See Chapter 6.

Bach, Johann Sebastian (1685–1750) — Incarnational

Trained on violin and organ, Bach became cantor at St. Thomas's School, Leipzig (Germany), and organist and music director at two Lutheran churches in 1723. In these established positions he composed pieces that reflect his Christian faith and were first used during worship services. Most people are familiar with *The Passion of St. John, Christmas Oratorio*, and his most famous choral work, *Mass in B Minor*. Capping almost one thousand years of Christian music, he composed some of the most technically brilliant pieces ever written and became the father of modern music.

Baillie, John (1886–1960) — Contemplative

Best remembered for his devotional classic, *A Diary of Private Prayer*, John Baillie was also a theologian, educator, and ecumenical leader. He served on the faculties of seminaries and colleges, moderated the Church of Scotland (Presbyterian) General Assembly, and attended the first gathering of the World Council of Churches. With "prayers for all the mornings and evenings of the months," Baillie's *Diary* provides windows into his heart and leads us into worship.

Basil the Great (c. 330–379) — Evangelical

Basil, Gregory of Nazianzus, and Gregory of Nyssa were known as "the three Cappadocian fathers"—religious leaders in Cappadocia (present-day Central Turkey) who helped shape eastern Christian thought. Basil was occupied primarily with four tasks: getting monasticism recognized as a normal part of church life, mending the schism caused by Arianism, continuing charitable works, and, most important, defending the orthodox Nicene understanding of the Trinity. As bishop of Caesarea, he organized Eastern monasticism, emphasizing seven periods of prayer per day and giving aid to the poor and sick. After Athanasius's death, Basil co-led the "new Nicene" party. But he died before seeing the schism healed and Arianism defeated.

Baxter, Richard (1615–1691) — Holiness

Baxter was ordained by the Church of England but allied himself with the Puritan cause two years later. Though self-educated, he was eloquent, and his preaching drew large crowds. His moderate stance led him to seek reconciliation between political and theological enemies, even though that stance led to imprisonment. Of his two hundred writings, *The Saints' Everlasting Rest,* one of the most widely read books of the seventeenth century, continues to provide motivation, assurance, and a method of meditation (which he borrowed from Puritan Joseph Hall) to those people of God seeking "rest" (Heb. 4:9, KJV).

Benedict of Aniane (c. 750–821) — Contemplative

Beginning his career in the Holy Roman Empire under Pepin and Charlemagne, the Burgundian Benedict left the court and became a monk. Discontented after practicing the Rules of Benedict of Nursia, Pachomius, and Basil, he founded a monastery at Aniane (Germany), where he systematized the Benedictine Rule. Emperor Louis, recognizing Benedict's talents for organization, appointed him to the Empire's court and provided inspectors to check on the implementation of the Rule, a great help in bringing constancy to ninth-century European monastic life.

Benedict of Nursia (c. 480–c. 547)—Contemplative

Founder of the movement that bears his name, Benedict established the model for monastic communal life at Monte Cassino (Italy). His Rule had the effect of gathering the roving prophets of the time into communities of loving, nurturing accountability. He provided connectedness to the past with his rule of "spiritual reading," simple accountability with his rule of "stability," and rootedness to common life with his rule of "daily manual labor." Born in Nursia and educated in rhetoric and law in Rome, he died at Monte Cassino.

Benedictines (6th century to the present)—Contemplative

Founded by Benedict of Nursia in the sixth century, the Benedictine way of life became the norm for Western monasticism. Each monastery is stable and self-supporting, and its members are devoted to following Christ. Each person is required to renounce personal possessions, practice continence, and stay in the community for life. And each member has three tasks: praising God in corporate worship, working in the fields, and practicing *lectio divina* ("spiritual reading").

Benen (or Benignus) (?–467)—Evangelical

According to legend, as a child in Ireland Benen attached himself to Patrick (the Christian missionary who was later canonized) and became his disciple. Though this story may not be true, he certainly had some connection with Patrick, because their names are coupled in the civil, military, and criminal code of laws Senchus Mór, and he is known as "Patrick's psalmodist." Also attributed to Benen are the evangelization of Clare and Kerry and part of Connaught, the first pastorate at Drumlease Church in Kilmore diocese, and, after Patrick's death, the bishopric of the church in Ireland.

Bennett, Dennis (1917–1991)—Charismatic

On 3 April 1960 the Holy Spirit fell on St. Mark's Episcopal Church in Van Nuys, California (United States), changing forever the dynamics of twentieth-century mainstream Christianity. When compared with accounts of the events at the Azusa Street meetings earlier in the century, the account told by Bennett in *Nine O'Clock in the Morning* appears small and insignificant. But it was a pivotal event in the Pentecostal/Charismatic movement, and Bennett became a significant leader.

Bernard of Clairvaux (1090–1153) — Holiness

A key figure in the Cistercian movement, which sought to bring reform to the monastic system, French-born Bernard was the most influential figure of his age. His motto—"To Know Jesus and Jesus Crucified"—has been adopted by Christians throughout the ages, and his outstanding life, hymns, and practical mystical piety have been appreciated by Christians worldwide. In *Twelve Steps to Humility* he outlined a way to gain harmony with God, and in *On Loving God* he gave classic expression to the mystic contemplation of Christ.

Bonhoeffer, Dietrich (1906–1945) — Holiness

See Chapter 3.

Boniface (680–754) — Evangelical

"Apostle to Germany" is the title given to Boniface, a native of Crediton, Devonshire (England), who continued the work of his predecessor, Willibrord. Great miracles in overcoming animistic religions accompanied his evangelizing efforts as he destroyed idols, baptized converts, and established churches and monasteries. After being consecrated bishop at age forty-two, Boniface continued to evangelize, but he also worked with civil powers to bring reform to the whole Frankish (German) church. (He is also known by another name, which can be spelled three ways: Wynfrith, Wyfrid, or Winfrith.)

Booth, Catherine Mumford (1829–1890), and William (1829–1912) — Social Justice

Co-founders of the Salvation Army, the Booths married in 1855, left the Methodist New Connection denomination (where William was a minister) five years later, and started a philanthropic and evangelistic mission in the East End (Whitechapel district) of London in 1865. Basic to their ministry was first meeting physical needs through a network of social relief and rehabilitation agencies and then filling spiritual voids through gospel preaching and lively worship. They named the organization the Salvation Army in 1890. Both William and Catherine were effective preachers, and William served as the Army's general.

Bridget (or Birgitta) of Sweden (c. 1303–1373) — Charismatic

Wife at fourteen, mother of eight, lady-in-waiting to the Swedish queen, visionary, prophetess, founder of the Brigittines—all these roles testify to Bridget's personal strength and spiritual power. Not involved in monastic life until her husband, Ulf, died at the Cistercian monastery in Alvastra, Bridget stayed on at the monastery four more years. During this time her visions and revelations became so insistent that she asked for help in discerning if they were from God. Assured of their authenticity, she became famous when her recorded revelations and prophecies came true.

Brother Lawrence (or Nicholas Herman) (1611–1691) — Contemplative

Living most of the seventeenth century—"the century of genius"—he wrote *The Practice of the Presence of God*. This "loving gaze upon God" is powerfully crystallized in his comment, "The time of business does not with me differ from the time of prayer; and in the noise and clatter of my kitchen, . . . I possess God in as great tranquility as if I were at the blessed sacrament." Working as a cook in his Discalced ("barefooted") Carmelite community was a mid-life career change for Lawrence; earlier he had served in the French army and civil service.

Brothers and Sisters of the Common Life (14th and 15th centuries) — Contemplative

Launched in the eastern Netherlands during the fourteenth and fifteenth centuries by Dutch scholar Gerard Groote, this movement spread further and had more influence than any other of the time. The communities that were established lived a practical piety centered around Groote's *devotio moderna* ("modern devotion")—inner spirituality and charitable service. Their work included copying books, distributing religious literature, and providing pastoral care for schoolboys. Reformer Martin Luther and scholar Desiderius Erasmus received spiritual direction from community members.

The most influential writing to come out of the community was *The Imitation of Christ*.

Caedmon (658–680)—Incarnational

Everything we know about Caedmon is recorded in the English historian Bede's *Ecclesiastical History*. From it we learn that he was an illiterate Anglo-Saxon herdsman from Whitby who had a vision in which he was commanded to write verse. The next day, remembering that he had recited verses in the vision, he repeated them and added others. This led to a job at the local abbey, where he continued to put biblical stories and events into poetic form. Though considered the first Old English Christian poet, only his poem on creation, "Caedmon's Hymn," survives.

Caesarius of Arles (?–543)—Holiness

Twenty years old when he entered the monastery of Lérins, Caesarius devoted himself to bringing "holy habits" into his own life and the lives of those he served. When ordained as a deacon, he was transferred to a nearby monastery that had a very relaxed discipline. After putting in place a Rule that made the monastery a model of piety and order, he drew up a comparable Rule for women. When appointed bishop of Arles (France), Caesarius imposed his two Rules on all the religious houses under his jurisdiction. Later a metropolitan, he presided over several synods, energetically opposing semi-Pelagianism at Orange in 529.

Calvin, John (1509–1564)—Evangelical

Educated in theology and law in his native France, reformer Calvin experienced a "sudden conversion" sometime between 1532 and 1534. With his faith taking first place in his life, he quit his job and moved to Basel (Switzerland), where he wrote the first draft of *Institutes of the Christian Religion*. Originally written to defend slandered believers, *Institutes* was the most ordered, systematic presentation of Christian life and doctrine that the Protestant Reformation produced. Calvin became one of that movement's key figures, spending most of his time in Geneva, where he developed the "presbyterian" model of church polity that "reformed" churches still use today. This model also influenced many social institutions established in the sixteenth century, along with later representative democracies. Congregationalist, United Church of Christ, Presbyterian, and Reformed churches trace their beginnings to Calvin.

Carey, William (1761–1834)—Evangelical

The "Father of Protestant Missions" was also botanist, linguist, and pioneer missionary to India. Carey's passion to take the gospel to the whole world, expressed in sermons and writings, led to the formation of an English Baptist missionary effort in 1792. In less than a year he fulfilled his lifelong call and left Leicester for Calcutta. The actions and vision of this shoemaker from Northamptonshire sparked the greatest missionary movement the world has ever seen and continue to influence Protestant evangelism efforts today.

Cassian, John (c. 360–c. 435)—Holiness

In Egypt Cassian spent thirteen years studying the ascetic life. From there he went to Constantinople, where he was befriended by John Chrysostom and ordained as a deacon. When Chrysostom was banished, Cassian left too, eventually establishing a monastery and convent in Marseilles (France). Of his writings—all of which have been preserved—*The Institutes* and *The Collations* (or *Conferences*) have been the most influential. Eastern monastic patterns became familiar to the Western Church through *The Collations*.

Catherine of Genoa (1447–1510)—Social Justice

Well-educated, Catherine married at age sixteen and in her mid-twenties had a profound conversion experience. Simultaneously, her husband, Guiliano, suffered financial reverses that brought about his transformation. Together they moved into a humble section of the city and devoted the rest of their lives to caring for the orphaned, the sick, and the dying. She became director of a hospital, and her influence spread far and wide. From Catherine's most famous book—*Spiritual Dialogues*—we learn about the power behind her life of service, prayer, and fasting.

Catherine of Siena (c. 1347–1380)—Contemplative

Choosing to become a Dominican lay sister at sixteen, Catherine spent her early years in the solitude of her home. Embarking later on a more public life, she worked for ecclesiastical reform; cared for the poor, sick, and imprisoned; and served as an ambassador to popes and other leaders, working for reconciliation. All these efforts were undergirded by times of solitude and contemplation. *The Dialogue* is the spiritual testament of Catherine, the best-known Italian mystic of her time.

Chad (or Ceadda)(?–672) — Social Justice

One of the youths trained by Aidan of Lindisfarne to continue his work of helping children and slaves and purchasing the freedom of slaves, Chad (with his brother Cedd) served well. Bede, the English historian, reported that "he was one of Aidan's disciples and tried to instruct his hearers by acting and behaving after the example of his master [Jesus]." He is also credited with bringing the gospel to the kingdom of Mercia (central England) and with establishing over thirty churches.

Charismatic Renewal (20th century to the present) — Charismatic

When the early-twentieth-century Pentecostal movement failed to penetrate mainstream Christianity, a new work of the Holy Spirit arose in the late 50s and early 60s. This movement spread the news that life in the Spirit is meant for all Christians of all times. Two special emphases of the movement were meaningful worship and exercising the gifts of the Holy Spirit. A list of a few of its leaders reflects the diversity of the movement: Dennis Bennett (Episcopalian), Francis MacNutt (Roman Catholic), Jane Hansen (Christian Missionary Alliance), Jamie Buckingham (Southern Baptist), Catherine Marshall (Presbyterian), C. Peter Wagner (Conservative Congregational), Cindy Jacobs (Baptist), Reinhard Bonnke (German Pentecostal), Oral Roberts (United Methodist).

Chaucer, Geoffrey (c. 1340–1400) — Incarnational

Chaucer is not remembered for his service in the English army, court, and civil service, but rather as the author of the classic *Canterbury Tales*. The prologue to the *Tales* describes thirty-one pilgrims who are on their way from London to Canterbury to visit the shrine of Thomas à Becket; the tales are told by the travelers as they try to amuse themselves during the pilgrimage. All but one of the twenty-four *Canterbury Tales* are set in verse, and with the prologue they give us a wonderful picture of fourteenth-century

English life. They also contributed to the call for reformation of the Church in England but failed to give a clear glimpse of what some believe was Chaucer's own ambiguous, skeptical faith.

Cho, David Yonggi (1936–)—Charismatic

Converted from Buddhism as a young man, Cho, pastor of the Yoido Full Gospel Church in Seoul, knows the full import of the Great Commission and relies on prayer, home cell groups, and lay ministers to carry it out. All members undergird with prayer the outreach of lay ministers who lead home cell groups organized by geographic area. In the power of the Holy Spirit, neighbor takes the gospel to neighbor. This winning combination has not only helped give birth to the dynamic Korean prayer movement, but has grown the largest single Christian fellowship in the world.

Chrysologus, Peter (c. 400–c. 450)—Evangelical

Peter was known for his short sermons—he was afraid of losing the congregation's attention—many of which are still extant. Very articulate, he earned the name Chrysologus ("golden-worded"), and he preached with such vehemence that he occasionally lost his breath from excitement. Though born in Imola, a town in eastern Emilia (northern Italy), Peter spent his adult years as bishop in Ravenna (also northern Italy).

Chrysostom, John (c. 347–407)—Evangelical

Regarded by the Protestant reformers as a church father second only to Augustine, Chrysostom ("golden-tongued") studied logic, philosophy, and rhetoric, hoping to become a lawyer. This training stood him in good stead when, after his ordination by the bishop of Antioch (Syria) in 386, he was instructed to engage in preaching only. (He had damaged his health by following a severe Syrian monastic rule for approximately ten years.) A popular and gifted preacher, Chrysostom combined sound biblical exposition with practical application. Opposed to the allegorical method of interpreting Scripture, he sought the exact, literal meaning of each verse after carefully examining the Greek text, a method that the reformers revived eleven hundred years later.

Cistercians (12th century to the present)—Holiness

With the first community started by Robert of Molesme and a small band of monks in 1098 at Cîteaux (in Latin *Cistercium*, hence Cistercian), they dominated Western monastic life during the twelfth century. Following the Rule of Benedict to the letter, members cultivated a strenuous self-denying life that contained elements—a rigorous moral code combined with withdrawal to wild, uninhabited areas—of eremitism (living as hermits). Both monasteries and nunneries sprang up—though the women residents had no official standing—and were deeply involved in the reformation of monastic life. The Cistercians' most famous member, Bernard, was part of the Cîteaux community before he founded the monastery at Clairvaux.

Clare of Assisi (c. 1193–1253)—Contemplative

After hearing Francis of Assisi's message of peace and penance, Clare—thirteen years his junior—left home and joined the Franciscans. Francis and the friars escorted the nineteen-year-old Clare to a Benedictine monastery, where she was welcomed by the nuns. As other women joined her, they eventually moved into San Damiano, the first church Francis had restored. There for the rest of her life Clare gave attention to the interior life of prayer and devotion. A brief biography and writings are available in *Francis and Clare: The Complete Works*.

Classical Movement (17th–18th centuries)—Incarnational

The opposite of romanticism, classicism emphasizes order, balance, and simplicity. These elements are expressed in, for example, reason and analysis; the true, the good, and the beautiful; conformity to society; and compliance with musical composition rules. The first "classicists" were the ancient Greeks (400s–300s B.C.), followed by the Romans (80 B.C.–A.D. 14), and then by the Western Europeans. Mathematician Blaise Pascal, musician Johann Sebastian Bach, and writer Samuel Johnson are good examples of classicists from different disciplines.

Coleridge, Samuel Taylor (1772–1834)—Incarnational

An English poet, Coleridge was a student at Cambridge twice, though he never earned a degree. His poetic career started when he met William

Wordsworth. That association resulted in a collaborative publication, *Lyrical Ballads*. Coleridge's most significant contribution to the work was "The Rime of the Ancient Mariner." A supernatural, eerie ballad, the piece ends on an ecological note: the ancient mariner's destiny is to teach reverence for all of God's creation. Active in philosophical and religious reflection, Coleridge was attracted to Unitarism and German mystical pantheism but returned to the faith of his birth, Christianity, in his latter years.

Columba (or Columban) (521–597) — Evangelical

Of noble blood, Columba spent his first forty-two years in his Irish homeland, serving the cause of Christ. Because of a controversy surrounding a manuscript of the Gospels he had copied without permission and an ensuing battle in which three thousand men were killed, he went into self-imposed exile on the small island of Iona off the western coast of Scotland in 563. There he set up an outpost that became a beehive of missionary activity. When he secured the independence of the Scots from the Picts, it opened the door for monks from Iona to penetrate all of Scotland and northern England with the gospel. In addition, Columba revived learning and introduced a written Gaelic language, which provided the base for Celtic literature.

Constantine (or Cyril) (826–869) and Methodius (c. 815–884) — Evangelical

Missionaries to both southern Russia and the region around the Danube River (Moravia), Constantine and Methodius became known as "apostles to the Slavs." Both were scholars and theologians in their own right; Constantine translated the Bible into Slavic after inventing an alphabet, and they introduced a Slavic liturgy. These efforts met strong opposition from German Catholic missionaries in Moravia and were eventually banned by Rome. But when Moravian Christianity spread northward, Constantine and Methodius's disciples carried with them copies of the Slavic Scriptures and liturgy.

Copernicus, Nicolas (1473–1543) — Incarnational

Europeans in the sixteenth century accepted the Ptolemaic explanation that all heavenly bodies revolved around the earth, making it the center of the universe. Copernicus, a canon at the Frauenberg Cathedral and an astronomer educated at the University of Cracow (Poland), based his conclusion that the planets revolved around the sun not on observation, but on mathematical calculations. The theory, which was later validated and corrected by other scientists (Johannes Kepler, Galileo Galilei, and Isaac Newton), forms the foundation of modern astronomy.

Corbinian (670–725) — Holiness

Several miracles and good spiritual advice made Corbinian famous in Châtres, near Melun (France)—so much so that people who wanted a more rigorous spiritual life attached themselves to him. He let several people stay, and they formed themselves into a community under his discipline. Already a bishop and wanting relief from supervising the group, he asked permission to again live in obscurity. Instead, he was sent to Bavaria to evangelize. The long years of spiritual discipline and holy living bore fruit as he took the gospel to Bavaria and founded a monastery at Obermais.

Cuthbert (634–687) — Contemplative

As a shepherd Cuthbert had ample time to practice solitude, but at fifteen he had a religious experience that changed his life's direction. After that experience he adopted the religious life, serving at various times as a prior, missionary, bishop of Hexham (England), and bishop of Lindisfarne. Following in the steps of Aidan, he preached, taught, gave money to the poor, and administered the diocese with compassion and talent. But at the heart of his long ministry were solitude and prayer.

Cyprian of Carthage (c. 200–258) — Holiness

The first martyr-bishop of the North African churches, Cyprian fought for the purity of the Church and was known for his strong position on church order and discipline. A careful student of the presbyter Tertullian, he became a bishop at forty-eight and was a significant figure in the controversies surrounding readmission of the "lapsed" to church fellowship and rebaptism. His view that the unity and holiness of the Church depended upon the bishops led directly to group oversight of churches by bishops. And rebaptism, which Cyprian opposed, prevailed when Augustine supported it.

Dante Alighieri (1265–1321)—Incarnational

Hailed as the greatest Italian poet, prose writer, moral philosopher, and political thinker ever, Dante is remembered by most for his epic poem *The Divine Comedy*. A theological, moral, and political allegory, the poem was written in the common language of Florence and laid the foundation for a standardized Italian language. Less well known is his work *De Monarchia (On Monarchy)*, in which he argues for a one-world government and the separation of church and state.

Day, Dorothy (1897–1980)—Social Justice

See Chapter 5.

Deacons (1st century to the present)—Social Justice

In Acts 6:1b Luke reports that "the Hellenists complained against the Hebrews because their widows were being neglected in the daily distribution of food." This is the first reported instance where the early Christian Church had to deal with injustice. The problem was solved rather simply: seven Greeks (Hellenists) were selected to oversee the allocation of food. With this solution the Church took a proactive stance toward treating everyone equally and defined διακαηος (transliterated "deacon"; sometimes translated "minister"): one who serves others without showing preference.

Desert Fathers and Mothers (4th century)—Contemplative

This movement cannot be traced to one particular person, though Antony of Egypt was its most famous leader. At the beginning of the fourth century leaders and contemplative communities started settling in the desert—first in the desert of Nitria (southwest of Alexandria and the Nile Delta) and then in the desert of Scete and the area known as "the Cells." By the middle of the fourth century Antony's followers and thousands of other ascetics were devoting themselves to prayer and following Christ while living in the desert.

Doherty, Catherine de Hueck (1900–)—Contemplative

Foundress of Madonna House Apostolate in rural Combermere, Ontario (Canada), Catherine de Hueck Doherty is known best for the book *Poustinia*, which makes Russian Christian spirituality accessible to the West. She writes, "One is forever immersed in the silence of God, forever listening to the word of God, forever repeating it to others in word and deed. . . . It is through this inner, total identification with humanity and with Christ that every Christian should be living in a state of contemplation."

Dominic (c. 1170–1221)—Evangelical

When Dominic accompanied Bishop Diego to Denmark, they came into contact with the Albigensians, whose leaders were well educated, versed in Scripture, and persuasive at preaching, but who lived in poverty. This so profoundly affected the noble-born Spaniard that, to better evangelize, he adopted a simple lifestyle and lived among the people. Like many other leaders of the time, he soon attracted others who wanted to help but who also needed discipline and unity. In 1216 Dominic got permission to start the Order of Friars Preachers (Dominicans).

Dominicans (13th century to the present)—Evangelical

The *fratres predicatores* ("preaching brothers") are dedicated to world evangelization and the cure of souls. Founded in the thirteenth century by Dominic and named the Order of Friars Preachers, the brothers adopted mendicancy (begging) and corporate poverty so that they could preach more effectively among the growing population of urban poor. This evangelistic emphasis naturally led the Dominicans to take an active part in the conversion of South and Central America. The order counts German theologian Albertus Magnus and his student, French philosopher Thomas Aquinas, among its members.

Domtilla, Flavia (?–c. 100)—Incarnational

Domtilla married the first cousin of the Roman Emperor Domitian, Titus Flavius Clemens, who was put to death by Domitian in 95. We do not know if Titus was a Christian, but Domtilla (who was banished to the island of Pandateria after Flavius's death) was and allowed her land to be used as a burial place for Christians.

Dostoyevsky, Fyodor (1821–1881)—Incarnational

Early in life Dostoyevsky was interested in literature. After serving in the Russian Engineering Corps, he resigned to devote himself to writing. But his plans were cut short when he was imprisoned in Siberia for four years for reading the works of a utopian socialist. Allowed to read the one book that had significantly influenced his early education—the Bible—he emerged from prison a Christian and a member of the Russian Orthodox Church. His first novel, *Poor Folk*, published prior to imprisonment, had been a tremendous success, but it is his last novel, *The Brothers Karamazov*, that most Westerners are familiar with. Concerned with the justice of God, *The Brothers Karamazov* witnesses to Dostoyevsky's incarnational life.

du Plessis, David (1905–1987)—Charismatic

South African David du Plessis, whom *Time* magazine called "one of the Christian giants of our age," was one of the best-known leaders in the twentieth-century Pentecostal movement. Ordained by the Assemblies of God, in the World Council of Churches he worked for unity between Christians (the first Pentecostal to do so), and he attended the third session of the Second Vatican Council as an observer in 1963. His persistent attempts to advance unity truly made him a "world Christian."

Eastern Orthodox Iconography (4th century to the present)— Incarnational

An icon is a pictorial representation. In Eastern churches icons consist of images of Christ, the Virgin Mary, angels, leaders, and saints painted on a flat surface, usually wood or ivory, sometimes small enough to be carried in processions. After the Edict of Milan in 313 allowed Christians to worship legally, they could acquire land and build places of worship without fear of confiscation. In the basilicas various pictures—frescoes, mosaics, and icons—became integral to the worship experience. The pictures are full of symbolism, and historian Williston Walker states that the veneration of icons is seen as "an affirmation of the Chalcedonian doctrine of the full and distinct human nature of Christ."

Eliot, T. S. (1888–1965)—Incarnational

American-born poet Eliot's faith journey followed a roundabout path. He was brought up Unitarian but went through an agnostic period, which is reflected in his early poetry. His first poem of note, "The Love Song of J. Alfred Prufrock," utilized a style that became a landmark in modern poetry.

But it was not until Eliot became a British citizen and was confirmed in the Church of England that his poetry took on serious religious themes. His last major poem, entitled *Four Quartets*, meditates on the relationship between time and eternity. He won the Nobel Prize for Literature in 1948.

Ephraem (or Ephraim) the Syrian (c. 306–c. 373)—Charismatic

Ephraem is recognized in both Western and Eastern Christianity as a deacon who could not only write and do biblical exegesis but could compose hymns. Early in his Nisibis (Turkey) ministry, when he recognized the value of including music in worship services, he set about writing hymns that were theologically sound. These hymns, which he introduced through a women's choir in his church, supplanted the Gnostic songs (syncretizing pagan philosophy and astrology with Christianity) that had been introduced by a previous leader. Ephraem wrote most of his hymns at Edessa, his home after the Persians overran Nisibis.

Euthymius the Great (c. 378–473)—Contemplative

Sixty-eight of Euthymius's ninety-five years were spent in the desert practicing solitude. In the early years, after being ordained as a priest in Melitene (Armenia), he spent whole nights in prayer on a mountain close to one of the monasteries he supervised, St. Polyeuctus. Then he went to a monastery near Jerusalem, where he made and sold baskets to support himself and the poor. In his last years he lived near Jericho, where he spent weekdays in prayer and met on weekends with those seeking spiritual advice. He was known for performing miracles, converting Arabs, and helping the needy.

Fénelon, François (1651–1715)—Contemplative

Fénelon followed the path trod by many Frenchmen who respond to their religious impulses: education and ordination as a priest. But his life took an unusual turn when in 1688 he met and became acquainted with mystic Madame Guyon. At first he approved and defended the quietism she espoused—a brand of mysticism asserting that people could attain perfection through contemplation of God—but later he signed the Thirty-Four Articles of Issy, which condemned that movement. After that controversy he wrote articles that defended mysticism—articles officially condemned by the Church. In spite of these difficulties, his *Christian Perfection*, which illumines his mastery of the spiritual life, has become a devotional classic. (His full name was François de Salignac de la Mothe Fénelon!)

Finney, Charles (1792–1875)—Evangelical

Trained as a lawyer, Finney was converted at twenty-nine and became a full-time Presbyterian evangelist, working as a missionary in upstate New York under the auspices of the Female Missionary Society of the Western District. These "western revivals," which used "new measures"—the "anxious seat," protracted meetings, and women pray-ers at meetings—brought Finney national fame. When several evangelical leaders disapproved of his methods, they met with him, discussing their concerns, and Finney emerged as the new leader and "father" of evangelical revivalism. Tuberculosis forced him to curtail his travels in 1832. Thereafter he served as a pastor, taught at Oberlin Collegiate Institute in Ohio (now Oberlin College), and in 1851 became Oberlin's president.

Flavian (c. 320–404)—Charismatic

From history we see that Flavian was embroiled in several controversies from the date of his selection as presider at the Council of Constantinople to the end of his tenure as bishop of Antioch (Syria). But these controversies passed, as all do. What lasted was his introduction of singing the psalms antiphonally by church choirs. This responsive style of singing has enhanced the worship of the Church through the ages.

Fox, George (1624–1691)—Charismatic

It took three years for George Fox to find an answer to his spiritual quest: "There is one, even Christ Jesus, that can speak to thy condition." This prompted him to abandon the formalities of the Anglican Church and actively share his newfound faith through preaching. Though not formally educated, he traveled not only in England but also in Holland, North America, the West Indies, and elsewhere, establishing congregations centered around Christ as living Teacher, the priesthood of believers, the empowering word of the Holy Spirit, and equality of all. The "Quaker" (a judge's jibe aimed at Fox, who had urged the bench to "tremble at the word of the Lord") worship services he introduced were "unprogrammed"; that is, they followed no formal order and often included long periods of silence. Fox was known for his charismatic preaching and miracle-working power. Besides the Society of Friends, he left Christendom *The Journal of George Fox*, a record of his life and magnetic personality.

Francis of Assisi (1182–1226) — Charismatic

See Chapter 4.

Franciscans (13th century to the present) — Charismatic

The Order of Friars Minor (*fratres minores*, "little brothers") owes its existence to Francis of Assisi, who imparted not only his name but also his character to the order. Living under the power of the Spirit, caring for outcasts, praying, and practicing poverty, chastity, and obedience are central to both the Franciscans and their "second order," the Poor Clares (or Poor Ladies). Historians believe that Francis did not intend to start an order, but he was so winsome that people were attracted to him and his way of life. The order prepared its final Rule in 1223. Along with the Dominicans, the Franciscans are the best-known of the mendicant (begging) orders.

Fry, Elizabeth (1780–1845) — Social Justice

Of devout Quaker stock from Norwich (England), Elizabeth Fry married Joseph John Gurney at twenty and became a minister of the Society of Friends at thirty-one. Receiving strong support from her husband and family of eleven, Elizabeth ministered to the needy and established an institution to train nurses: the "Nursing Sisters of Devonshire Square." But she is best remembered for working to improve the lives of female inmates at Newgate Prison in London. She also traveled to northern England, Scotland, France, and northern Europe, working for prison reform; and her influence reached into Italy, Denmark, and Russia.

Germanus (or Germain) (c. 496–576) — Social Justice

First as abbot of St. Symphorian and then as bishop of Paris, Germanus was recognized for his work in the Frankish (German) church at large, but that work never diverted him from his concern for the poor. He was known for entertaining beggars at his own table and giving generously to benevolent causes. This interest was complemented by his austere life, which freed him to found numerous religious houses and participate in councils.

Gildas the Wise (?–c. 570)—Holiness

"The miseries, the errors and the ruin of Britain" constantly grieved Gildas, a man animated by a zeal for holy living and the spiritual life. Not much is known about his early years other than what we learn from his book *De Excidio et Conquestu Britanniae,* which indicts laypeople and clergy for their immoral lives. We do know that the last years of his life were spent in Brittany, where he trained disciples.

Gottschalk (c. 803–869)—Incarnational

Most often remembered for adopting and preaching fourth-century theologian Augustine's double predestination teaching, the Saxon Gottschalk was condemned and imprisoned. But he also wrote poetry that historian Allen Cabaniss considers "some of the most beautiful poems of the Carolingian (French dynasty) renaissance." His writing prepared the way for later medieval poetry.

Graham, Billy (1918–)—Evangelical

See Chapter 6.

Great Awakenings (18th–19th centuries)—Evangelical

Englishmen George Whitfield and brothers Charles and John Wesley are the most recognized leaders of what is called the Evangelical Revival in England and the First Great Awakening in America—a movement that lasted approximately fifty years. First signs of an awakening appeared around 1714 in Scotland and spread southward, transforming English society and crossing oceans to all English-speaking countries. In America historian Williston Walker calls it "the most far-reaching and transforming movement in . . . eighteenth-century religious life." "Conversion" or regeneration became the criterion for becoming a member of the church, not infant baptism and confirmation.

The Second Great Awakening, beginning in the early 1790s, cropped up on both sides of the Atlantic off and on into the mid to late 1800s. Charles Finney evangelized the northern U.S. frontier during this awakening, becoming a leading figure in America in the early part of the nineteenth century. This second awakening prompted the formation of the first American Bible and tract and missionary societies. Among the missionaries sent by these societies were Adoniram Judson and Luther Rice, who served in India. In the 1870s American evangelist Dwight L. Moody played a significant role in England, influencing the birth of the Keswick Movement. The lay Haldane brothers, Robert and James Alexander, and Thomas Chalmers led the effort in Scotland. On the Continent the awakening took several forms: evangelism and pietism in Germany, creativity in Denmark, pietism in Norway, and evangelism in the Reformed churches of Switzerland, France, and the Netherlands. And in all countries touched by the awakening, the formation of missionary societies was stimulated.

Gregorian Liturgical Movement (7th century to the present) — Charismatic

This movement owes its life to Pope Gregory the Great, who (along with Pope Celestine I and Pope Sixtus III) organized and codified Roman liturgy and its music. Casting the liturgy in a three-year cycle and incorporating plainsong (also known as Gregorian chant, after Gregory) into the liturgy, this movement—in conjunction with using Latin as the primary ecclesial language—gave the Western Church a unified body of rites. This allowed the liturgy to cross all political and ethnic lines.

Gregory of Nazianzus (c. 330–389) — Holiness

Gregory, along with brothers Gregory of Nyssa and fellow student Basil ("the three Cappadocian fathers"), worked tirelessly for the doctrinal purity of the Church by defending the Nicene Council's view of the Trinity at the Council of Constantinople (381). Twice others tried to get him to accept a public office, and twice he refused in favor of leading a contemplative life, though that life was interrupted from time to time by church ministry. Gregory's father (also named Gregory) was bishop of Nazianzus, and his mother, Nonna (or Emmelia), greatly influenced his spiritual life.

Gregory of Nyssa (330–c. 395) — Contemplative

Enlisted by Gregory of Nazianzus to help oppose Arianism, he was also one of "the three Cappadocian fathers." Well equipped by a classical education, Gregory was a teacher of rhetoric when his brother Basil forced the bishopric of Nyssa upon him. There, in spite of huge responsibilities, he maintained a life of communion with God. Also a writer (and the brother of Macrina), he produced numerous treatises on theological subjects, ascetic piety, and prayer. Gregory's mystical writings especially his *Life of Moses* were seminal for the subsequent Christian mystical tradition.

Gregory Palamas (c. 1296–1359) — Contemplative

Refining the teachings of Simeon the New Theologian, Gregory vigorously defined and defended the practice of hesychasm in the Eastern Church. Gregory based his argument that the whole body should be involved in prayer in a good material world blessed by God. (At that time the view that the physical world was evil dominated Christian teachings.) While reciting the "Jesus Prayer," Orthodox historian Timothy Ware says hesychasts carefully regulate their breathing and sit with "head bowed, chin resting on chest, eyes fixed on the place of the heart." For his teachings Gregory was excommunicated. Though he was later vindicated, he died before hesychasm became an accepted practice.

Gregory Thaumaturgus (c. 213–c. 270) — Charismatic

As a member of a wealthy family in Pontus (Turkey), Gregory Thaumaturgus ("miracle-worker") was converted under the teaching of Origen and became Origen's disciple. Returning from Palestine to Pontus and becoming bishop, he utilized his aristocratic heritage and position to substitute Christian festivals for pagan ones and to convert people en masse. But at the heart of Thaumaturgus's ministry were miracles — healings, stopping the flow of a river, and visions. One legend reports that only seventeen people in Pontus remained unconverted at his death.

Gregory the Great (c. 540–604) — Charismatic

"Father of the medieval papacy," Gregory I's list of achievements before and after becoming pope is lengthy. Gregory mastered legal studies, founded monasteries, contributed time and money to good works, consolidated power in Rome, regulated and reformed bishoprics, codified the liturgy, dispatched missionaries to England, and more. One of his most influential works, *Pastoral Rule*, set the standard for understanding the role of bishops in the Western Church. And his namesake, the Gregorian chant, has survived the centuries and is now being used in churches of numerous traditions worldwide.

Gualbert, John (?–1073) — Social Justice

When his brother was murdered, John vowed revenge; but he found that he could not kill the murderer when they met in a narrow passage. John repented of his hate and embraced his enemy, and they parted peacefully. This event changed his life, and he gave the rest of his days to starting monasteries and meeting the needs of the poor. All of his monasteries were modest; all the poor who approached him received help; all instances of simony (the buying or selling of church offices) in his area were stopped to the best of his ability.

Guyon, Madame (Jeanne Marie Bouvier) (1648–1717) — Contemplative

Madame Guyon has had an extensive influence through her writings, the most important of which include the voluminous *Autobiography of Madame Guyon*, *Experiencing the Depths of Jesus Christ*, and *Union with God*. Embroiled in a seventeenth-century controversy over quietism, which she practiced, she was censored and imprisoned, but her message continued to spread as leaders as diverse as evangelist John Wesley, hymn writer and poet William Cowper, and church leader and writer Watchman Nee translated her works and recommended them to their followers. An accomplished poet, she wrote these words from prison:

> Strong are the walls around me
>   That hold me all the day;
> But they who thus have bound me
>   Cannot keep God away;
> My very dungeon walls are dear
>   Because the God I love is here.

Hammarskjöld, Dag (1905–1961) — Incarnational

See Chapter 7.

Handel, George Frideric (1685–1759)—Incarnational

With Johann Sebastian Bach and Wolfgang Amadeus Mozart, Handel dominated the music produced in the so-called classical period. He gained his fame initially for his vocal works. Born in Germany, Handel received his musical training there and in Italy. In 1712 he emigrated to England, where there was a growing taste for opera. But it was the oratorio—"sacred" opera performed without costumes and sometimes without scenery—that built his popularity. Handel's most famous oratorio is *The Messiah*, a work that combines his mastery of the English choral tradition with his gift for the dramatic.

Helena (or Helen) (c. 248–c. 327)—Social Justice

Thought to be the daughter of an innkeeper, Helena was the mother of Roman Emperor Constantine the Great, who issued the Edict of Milan in 313 with co-emperor Licinius. Formerly deposed by Emperor Constantius, she had been restored to honor at sixty-three when Constantine came to power, and she became a Christian at the same time as her son. Using her influence, Helena gave liberally to the poor and established many basilicas (including the Church of the Nativity in Bethlehem and Eleona on the Mount of Olives).

Hermas (2nd century)—Holiness

Hermas's only surviving work is *The Shepherd*, a description of five visions. With repentance followed by forgiveness as a major theme, *The Shepherd* gives us insight into second-century Christian life and morality. Simultaneously, it reveals that Hermas was a former slave who married, started a business, almost lost everything, saw his children "backslide," and repented to reunite his family. Some early church leaders considered *The Shepherd* worthy of becoming part of the New Testament; others viewed it as only a tool to help Christians deepen their lives in holiness and virtue. External evidence suggests that *The Shepherd* was respected and read widely in the early Christian Church.

Hildegard of Bingen (1098–1179)—Charismatic

Hildegard's German parents sent her to a Benedictine convent at a young age to be educated. Entering the order at fifteen, at thirty-two she was persuaded to write down the visions of God that she had experienced from the age of three on. These she recorded in *Scivias*, a classic of medieval mysticism, and it and her letters made her famous. Widely regarded as a prophetess, Hildegard also established a Benedictine convent at Rupertsberg near Bingen and wrote both words and music to numerous hymns, canticles, and anthems.

Holiness Movement (18th century to the present) — Holiness

When Oxford-educated Anglicans Charles and John Wesley became involved in the Evangelical Revival in England and First Great Awakening in America, they were concerned only to "reform the nation," not to start a new denomination. But start one they did—and then some. Out of their itinerant ministries and emphasis on "holy living" came a "method"—societies, class meetings, and bands that emphasized mutual accountability—and Methodism was born. Other groups that claim the holiness heritage include Free Methodist, Wesleyan Methodist, Church of God (Anderson, Indiana), Church of the Nazarene, Methodist Episcopal Church, and the Salvation Army.

Hsi, Pastor (1830–1896) — Charismatic

Wanting to enter a literary contest sponsored by a Methodist minister, forty-nine-year-old Hsi read the required Gospel of Matthew and was converted to Christ. Formerly a Confucian scholar, he worked with the China Inland Mission and became a spiritual giant, his influence spreading far beyond his native province of Shanxi. His simple faith spoke of a God who became real, a Bible that came alive, promises that came true, and prayers that were effective. A former opium addict, he helped deliver other addicts from their habit at rehabilitation centers and prayed for the deliverance of people possessed by demons. In the power of the Holy Spirit he became one of China's greatest preachers.

Hunna (or Huva) (?–c. 679) — Incarnational

Little is known of the noble-born Hunna's background other than that she was from the French province of Alsace and married a nobleman, Huno, who was from the village of Hunnaweyer in the diocese of Strasbourg (France). Her importance stems from her willingness, though she was of noble birth, to do wash for her needy neighbors. This willingness earned her the nickname "the Holy Washer-Woman." In this menial activity she helped define incarnational living.

Hyde, John (1865–1912) — Contemplative

It seemed that John Hyde was going to follow in his minister father's footsteps and accept an assignment in Illinois (United States), but instead he went with a group of missionaries to India. Assigned by the Presbyterian Church to the Punjab region, he labored as an itinerant preacher for years — learning several local languages and taking the gospel to remote villages — without seeing many converts. Discouraged, he turned to prayer — vigilant, persistent prayer — which became his greatest work and his greatest legacy. Sometimes spending over forty hours on his knees, he became known as "praying Hyde"; through that ministry of prayer and example, he saw people converted to the way of Christ.

Ignatius of Antioch (c. 35–c. 107) — Evangelical

The only thing we know for certain about Ignatius's life before he was arrested for his faith during the reign of Trajan is that he was bishop of Antioch (Syria). During the trip to Rome under armed guard, he wrote seven letters — six to churches and one to Polycarp, bishop of Smyrna. From these we learn that he opposed the Ebionite heresy (a teaching that asserted that for salvation believers must keep the Jewish regulations) and Docetism (a teaching that asserted that Christ only *appeared* to have lived, died, and been resurrected). We can assume that Ignatius, who called himself "the bearer of God," arrived in Rome and was martyred.

Ignatius of Loyola (1491–1556) — Holiness

"By the term 'Spiritual Exercises' is meant every method of examination of conscience, of meditation, of contemplation, of vocal and mental prayer, and of other spiritual activities." So starts Ignatius's *Spiritual Exercises*, the book that stands at the center of both his life and the Society of Jesus (Jesuits), which he founded. This book has been a powerful tool for devotion in the Roman Catholic Church and beyond. Born of a knightly family, Ignatius served in the Spanish army until he received severe leg wounds and was discharged. During his long recovery, he read Ludolph the Carthusian's *Life of Christ* and biographies of other Christians, decided to become a knight for Christ, and with single-minded devotion set his heart to the task.

Isidore the Farmer (1070–1130) — Incarnational

Named after the archbishop of Seville, Isidore was born to poor parents in Madrid and was employed as a farm laborer as soon as he was old enough to work. He married a girl as poor as himself, and they had one son who died young. Isidore was a farmer all of his life, but he served God by going to church early every day, praying while he worked in the fields, visiting churches, and giving generously to the poor. There was no division between sacred and secular in his life.

James the Apostle (1st century) — Holiness

See Chapter 3.

Jerome (or Eusebius Hieronymus) (c. 347–420) — Evangelical

Jerome is remembered by the average person not for his winning personality—he was testy, quarrelsome, and vindictive—but for translating the Bible from the original Hebrew and Greek into Latin. Schooled in grammar, rhetoric, and Latin classical literature at Rome, he went on a twenty-year pilgrimage of the Roman Empire, during which he learned Hebrew. Returning to Rome in about 382, he served as Pope Damascus's personal secretary. He left when the pope died, eventually settling in a Bethlehem monastery. It was there—during his most productive period—that Jerome finalized the Vulgate Bible, the translation that was used almost exclusively by the Roman Catholic Church until recent times. Though Jerome's methods of translation set the pattern for those of succeeding eras, the Vulgate received its share of criticism. Since it changed some of the people's favorite texts, historian Justo L. Gonzalez writes that "many demanded to know who had given Jerome authority to tamper with Scripture."

Jesus of Nazareth (c. 4 B.C.–c. A.D. 29)

See Chapter 1.

Jewett, Paul (1919–1991) — Social Justice

As professor of systematic theology at Fuller Theological Seminary (United States), Paul Jewett left a legacy of writings and students that exhibit clear, consistent evangelical thinking. This thinking is best represented in his book *Man as Male and Female*, in which he "sought to gather together in a single essay what has been said by the theologians about Man as male and female, both that which reflects the traditional view and that which seeks to go beyond it. In doing so, I take the position that the 'woman question' is a 'man/woman' question which has its roots, theologically speaking, in the doctrine of the *imago Dei*." He went beyond the emotional arguments and centered on "all the counsel of God," the Bible, to reach his conclusions. With this book, Jewett established himself as a leading proponent for the equality of women in the Church.

Joan of Arc (1412–1431) — Charismatic

Joan of Arc's life has been told in numerous books, plays, and movies, and her story continues to fascinate. Born into a devout peasant family, early in life Joan experienced visions and voices that told her to lead the king's eldest son (the dauphin) and his troops into battle against the British siege at Orleans (France). She kept the revelations to herself initially but then spoke up. After passing rigorous testing by a panel of theologians, she got the dauphin's consent to accompany him. The Orleans assault was successful, and she stood with the dauphin at his crowning as Charles VII. But the war dragged on, and Joan was captured and sold to the English by their Burgundian allies. In a trial for sorcery that lasted three months, Joan answered the English examiners' questions but denied the voices when told she faced death by fire—a denial she soon retracted. Burned at the stake as a lapsed heretic, "the Maid of Orleans'" last words were "Jesus, Jesus."

John Climacus (or John of the Ladder) (579–649) — Contemplative

An Eastern hermit and later abbot of the Monastery of Saint Catherine at Mount Sinai, John Climacus wrote *The Ladder of Paradise*, which has become a spiritual classic. John was a contemporary of Maximus the Confessor, who helped form Eastern Orthodox theology and spirituality. With Maximus he also is considered a spiritual forerunner of Simeon the New Theologian, a leader in the contemplative practice of hesychasm.

John of Damascus (or John Damascene) (c. 675–749) — Incarnational

Succeeding his father as the Christians' representative in the Muslim caliph's court, John resigned and entered the monastery of St. Sabas near Jerusalem. From there John wrote theological works, beautiful poetry, and hymns. His greatest work was *The Fountain of Knowledge*; this document, with his other writings, provided a systematic theology of Eastern Christianity and defended the use of icons in Christian devotion. His writings, which influenced Italian theologian Peter Lombard and French philosopher Thomas Aquinas, endure today.

John of the Cross (1542–1591) — Contemplative

John was a powerful figure in the Carmelite movement of Teresa of Ávila, which was part of the Roman Catholic Reformation, but his most noteworthy contribution is the writing of several of Christianity's greatest spiritual classics: *The Ascent of Mount Carmel, Spiritual Canticle, The Living Flame of Love,* and *The Dark Night of the Soul.* Written in Spanish rather than Latin, all are world literature masterpieces and all are important markers in the history of Spanish spirituality. Particularly in *The Dark Night of the Soul,* John provided keen insight into human nature and guided readers in the soul's journey with God:

> O guiding light!
> O night more lovely than the dawn!
> O night that has united
> the Lover with His beloved,
> transforming the beloved in her Lover.

John the Almsgiver (?–c. 619) — Social Justice

Of a noble and wealthy family, John used his money to help the poor after his wife and children died. After his actions became known, he was appointed patriarch of Alexandria (Egypt) when approximately fifty years old. In that position John did all he could to protect the oppressed: he ordered merchants to use just weights and measures, he forbade all his officers and servants to take presents, he distributed all the money in the church treasury to hospitals and monasteries, he dedicated the revenues of the see to the poor, he gave shelter to refugees, and more.

John the Apostle (1st century)—Contemplative

See Chapter 2.

Johnson, Samuel (1709–1784)—Incarnational

For the last twenty years of his life, Samuel Johnson so dominated the literary life of London that those years were called "the Age of Johnson." The son of a Litchfield, Staffordshire, bookseller, Johnson attended Pembroke College, Oxford, but dropped out. Moving to London two years later, he started writing essays and poetry and published two short-lived periodicals. His first major work, *Dictionary of the English Language*, was the best dictionary of its day, and his *Prayers and Meditations*, published posthumously, reveal a man of humble spirit and continual self-examination. A faithful Anglican, historian P. M. Bechtel calls Johnson "one of England's most pious writers."

Jones, E. Stanley (1884–1973)—Holiness

A four-day experience of being "flooded by the Spirit" propelled the Methodist Jones into missionary service in India, but a ruptured appendix and tetanus cut short his appointment. Reappraising his career, he changed direction, focusing instead on serving as an evangelist to Indian intellectuals. The rest of his life he combined "holy living" with moving comfortably among world leaders and working for peace and harmony. Twice he was nominated for the Nobel Peace Prize. He also developed Christian ashrams (centers for meditation and group worship) and wrote *With the Christ of the Indian Road*, his first and best-known book.

Julian of Norwich (c. 1342–c. 1413)—Contemplative

Julian's importance rests on a single book, *Showings*—her mature reflections upon sixteen visions that were given to her on 13 May 1373. This first book written by a woman in the English language contains some of the most passionate love language in all of devotional literature. In her most famous passage she says that God, in tender love, comforts all those trapped in pain and sin by speaking over them, "But all shall be well, and all shall be well, and all manner of thing shall be well."

Kagawa, Toyohiko (1888–1960) — Social Justice

Born to a single geisha in Kobe (Japan), Kagawa's childhood was lonely and bitter, and his family disinherited him when he converted from Buddhism to Christianity. But in spite of the hardships, he entered Christian service, becoming an evangelist—he began the Kingdom of God and Million Souls movements (mass evangelism crusades); social reformer—he started labor unions, relief works, and cooperatives; and political activist—he became a leader in the democratic and pacifist movements. Imprisoned three times for his activities, he wrote almost 170 books on religion, sociology, and science.

Kelly, Thomas R. (1893–1941) — Contemplative

Kelly, an extraordinary Quaker philosopher, educator, and speaker, wrote *The Eternal Promise, Reality of the Spiritual World*, and *A Testament of Devotion*. He said, "Life from the Center is a life of unhurried peace and power. It is simple. It is serene. It is amazing. It is triumphant. It is radiant. It takes no time, but it occupies all our time." Born in Ohio (United States) and educated at leading American colleges and universities, he is known for his dogged pursuit of the divine Center. He died prematurely of a heart attack.

Keswick Movement (19th–20th centuries) — Holiness

Operating out of two English centers—Mildmay and Keswick—this movement was a child of the Second Great Awakening and the ministries of the American evangelist Dwight L. Moody and singer/composer Ira Sankey. Moody, at the invitation of Anglican vicar William Pennefather, led the first meeting designed to deepen the spiritual life at Mildmay in 1870 in a hall especially built for the occasion. The Keswick Center was begun in 1875 by T. D. Harford-Battersby, a Church of England clergyman, and was the site of annual meetings that were attended by both Anglicans and Nonconformists (that is, persons who did not conform to the Church of England) into the twentieth century.

King, Martin Luther, Jr. (1929–1968) — Social Justice

When Rosa Parks refused to give up her bus seat to a white man in 1955, her action inspired the African-American population of Montgomery,

Alabama (United States), to boycott city buses. Lasting about a year (until segregation on public transportation was ruled unconstitutional by the Supreme Court), the bus boycott spawned the civil rights movement. Martin Luther King, Jr., became that movement's most visible leader. A Baptist minister from Atlanta, Georgia, he adopted the nonviolent protest approach used by Mahatma Gandhi in gaining India's freedom from England and led numerous protests before his assassination.

Kuhlman, Kathryn (c. 1910–1976) — Charismatic

Describing herself as "Missouri" cornbread, Kuhlman experienced a conversion at age fourteen that was as definite as her call to ministry. First speaking before small groups — "Name any town in Idaho, and you'll discover that one time, years ago Kathryn Kuhlman came through trying to evangelize it" — she later spoke before filled arenas in the United States and beyond. Her ministry also used the media — radio, television, books — to spread her message of faith in God and divine healing. People at her meetings experienced an overpowering sense of the Holy Spirit, and many claimed miraculous healings. Kuhlman's motivation is best explained in her own words: "The goal of every Christian, every born-again man and woman, should be helping people."

Laubach, Frank (1884–1970) — Contemplative

See Chapter 2.

Law, William (1686–1761) — Holiness

William Law lost his fellowship at Emmanuel College, Cambridge, along with his right to preach in the Church of England when he followed his conscience and refused to take the oath of allegiance at the enthronement of George I. But his A Serious Call to a Devout and Holy Life, which spoke to the hearts of evangelist John Wesley, writer Samuel Johnson, and Catholic Cardinal John Henry Newman, has lasted much longer than his sermons. Indeed, it continues to speak today: "Devotion signifies a life given or devoted to God. . . . The devout [person] . . . lives . . . to the sole will of God, . . . considers God in everything, . . . serves God in everything, . . . makes all the parts of common life parts of piety by doing everything in the name of God and under such rules as are conformable to His glory."

Leonardo da Vinci (1452–1519)—Incarnational

This Italian artist, inventor, and scholar is best known among Christians for his painting *The Last Supper*. Early on he collaborated with his teacher, Andrea del Verrocchio, on *The Baptism of Christ*, and on his own he started *Adoration of the Three Kings*. So when he started *The Last Supper* in a monastery dining hall about 1495, Christian themes were not new to him. But Leonardo did try a new technique—coating the wall with a self-created compound so that he could revise his work before it dried. It failed. The painting, which created a more centralized and active design than other artists had achieved, and which shows the humanity of Jesus and his disciples, started flaking soon after its completion and is in poor condition today.

Lewis, C. S. (1898–1963)—Evangelical

A "happy atheist" at fourteen, "surprised by joy" at thirty, tutor and fellow at Magdalen College, Oxford, Lewis wrote some of the most popular and creative books of the twentieth century. But it is in *Mere Christianity*, which explains and defends "the belief that has been common to nearly all Christians at all times," that Lewis shines. Originally four different series of radio talks that were broadcast once a week starting in August 1941 (two months after the nightly German bombing raids on England ended), these writings can be read separately. However, they are best read under the *Mere Christianity* title, since in that volume Lewis edited and expanded the talks. Besides Lewis's own writings (and third-party analyses of them), there are numerous biographies and two movies—an English and an American version of *Shadowlands*—that can help you get acquainted with this twentieth-century giant.

Livingstone, David (1813–1873)—Social Justice

Most of us are acquainted with Henry Morton Stanley's famous greeting, "Dr. Livingstone, I presume," and probably know that the Scottish Livingstone "discovered" Victoria Falls in Africa. But few know that as a leader in the eighteenth-century Protestant missionary movement he advocated using indigenous peoples in African evangelism efforts and preached against the white exploitation of blacks. Livingstone's tombstone at Westminster Abbey bears this epitaph: "For thirty years his life was spent in an unwearied effort to evangelize the native races, to explore the undiscovered secrets, to abolish the desolating slave trade of Central Africa."

Lutgarde of Aywieres (1182–1246) — Charismatic

A contemporary of Francis of Assisi, Lutgarde was known for her "power of healing," in which her very touch had the effect of instantly curing those who came to her. She also experienced ecstatic gifts of visions, prophecies, and miracles. The authoritative biography of her life — *Vita Lutgardis* — is not available in English, but Thomas Merton wrote a sympathetic interpretation of her interior life and mystical experiences, *What Are These Wounds? The Life of a Cistercian Mystic.*

Luther, Martin (1483–1546) — Evangelical

Luther is most remembered for nailing his ninety-five theses to the Wittenberg Castle church door on 31 October 1517. Though discontentment against extravagant fiscal practices of the Roman Catholic Church had been rumbling through Germany for some time, Luther's listing of the specific abuses connected with the selling of indulgences (led at that time by Johann Tetzel, who in his fund-raising used the rhyme "As soon as the coin in the coffer rings, / The soul from purgatory springs") launched a revolt, and he became the father of the German Reformation and a key figure in Protestantism. Roland Bainton's biography *Here I Stand* gives a clear picture of Luther's life and times.

Macrina the Younger (c. 330–379) — Contemplative

Macrina, eldest of ten children, counted Basil the Great, Peter of Sebastea, and Gregory of Nyssa among her brothers. Their mother, Nonna, acted as spiritual guide to her husband and the children. After Basil returned from school he secured an estate for his mother and Macrina, and they were joined by other women seeking to live in community. It is said that the contemplative Macrina taught Basil humility and was "father, teacher, guide, mother, giver of good advice" to Peter.

Mason, C. H. (1866–1961) — Charismatic

Expelled by the National Baptist Convention in 1899 because he preached Wesleyan holiness and retained and defended black worship practices, Mason attracted thousands in the early 1900s. After receiving the baptism of the Holy Spirit under William Seymour at the Azusa Street Revival in 1907, he integrated this new understanding into his teaching and practice, becoming the founder of the Church of God in Christ. Under Mason's powerful spiritual leadership, the Church of God in Christ became the largest Pentecostal denomination in the United States, and, according to Ithiel C. Clemmons, it continues to hold "in tension the dynamics of holiness, spiritual encounter, and a prophetic Christian social consciousness."

Maximus the Confessor (c. 580–662) — Contemplative

Deeply spiritual, Maximus cultivated a three-step approach that leads toward God and insisted that contemplation and love are inseparable; we become spiritually mature only through love of neighbor (the practical) and love of God (the contemplative). As a theologian Maximus, along with John Climacus, was a forerunner of Simeon the New Theologian, a leader in the theological movement that favored the contemplative practice of hesychasm, and he was a vigorous opponent of the Monothelite belief that Christ has only one will—a divine will—and no human will.

McPherson, Aimee Semple (1890–1944) — Charismatic

Converted during the Pentecostal movement in the early 1900s, "Sister Aimee" held a series of revival tours across the United States shortly after World War I. An early pioneer in radio evangelism, she delivered messages emphasizing sanctification (a life set apart to God), divine healing, the baptism of the Holy Spirit (evidenced by speaking in tongues), and Christ's imminent return. She settled in California in 1922 and preached each week to thousands at her church, the Los Angeles Temple, out of which arose a new denomination in 1927: the International Church of the Foursquare Gospel.

Medericus (or Merry) (?–c. 700) — Holiness

Merry, a monk, became abbot of his monastery in Autun (France) against his will, but that did not keep him from living a virtuous life. He was such a good example that the monks and people who came for spiritual advice started to idolize him. Fearing that he would become vain, Merry resigned and hid in a forest a few miles away. But the people learned where Merry was living, and at about the same time he got sick, so Merry had to return to the monastery where he again helped his brothers live holy lives.

Merton, Thomas (1915–1968) — Contemplative

French-born Trappist monk Thomas Merton was a poet and author of many books, including *The Seven Storey Mountain, New Seeds of Contemplation,* and *Spiritual Direction and Meditation.* Merton has been the most influential proponent of traditional monasticism in the twentieth century. "Contemplative prayer is not so much a way to find God," he wrote, "as a way of resting in him whom we have *found,* who loves us, who is near to us, who comes to us to draw us to himself."

Michelangelo (1475–1564) — Incarnational

Italian Renaissance artist and sculptor Michelangelo is best known for his statues *David,* the *Pieta,* and *Moses,* and the creation story fresco on the ceiling of the Sistine Chapel in the Vatican. One of the most technically gifted artists and intellectuals of the time, Michelangelo produced art that centered around God and humans. By his own testimony, God was his greatest influence and source of ideas. Michelangelo felt that in God-centered art the beauty of the piece is not an end in itself; rather, it is a reflection of spiritual reality, lifting the viewer's mind beyond the material. (His full name was Michelagniolo di Lodovico Buonarroti-Simoni!)

Milton, John (1608–1674) — Incarnational

Milton was one of England's greatest poets, and his life and works followed the same rhythm. During the first period of his life he became a Puritan and wrote poetry in Latin, Italian, and English. He was a political Independent, serving in the Cromwell government during the second period and writing mostly polemical and scholarly essays. Milton's last period, beginning in 1660, was his greatest, even though he was blind, he had suffered the death of two wives and two children, and he had lost his government position. During that final period he wrote the epic poems *Paradise Lost, Paradise Regained,* and *Samson Agonistes.*

Modern Liturgical Renewal (20th century to the present) — Charismatic

By the 1960s a liturgical renaissance—an outgrowth of the ecumenical movement—was underway. Those from free church backgrounds wanted to incorporate liturgical elements such as processions into their services. Those from liturgical churches wanted to add elements such as intimate worship choruses to their liturgies. As a result, interest in the theology and practice of worship mushroomed. Many free churches adopted liturgical elements, a number of denominations revised their liturgies, and a Vatican II document titled *The Constitution on the Sacred Liturgy* hastened liturgical reform in Roman Catholic churches.

Monica (c. 331–c. 387)—Incarnational

Born near Hippo (North Africa), where later her son, Augustine, was bishop, Monica was a Christian with Christian parents. She married a man who received Christ before he died, and she left an indelible mark on everyone her life touched. Augustine wrote of her, "All of them who knew her found in her good reason to praise and honor and love you [God], because on the evidence of the fruit of her holy conversation they could feel your presence in her heart. . . . [S]he gave to each one of us the care that a mother gives to her son and to each one of us the service which a daughter gives to her father."

Montanist Movement (2nd–3rd centuries)—Charismatic

Named after its founder Montanus, Montanism arose in about 170 among the Phrygians (residents of the Roman province in Asia Minor), who emphasized Spirit-directed prophetic utterance and prized celibacy. They believed that Montanism was the beginning of a new—or newer—age and restricted the definition of a church to a group of charismatic, "spiritual" persons. Spreading rapidly through Asia Minor, Montanism reached Syria, Antioch, North Africa, and Rome and the West. Though it kept alive the prophetic tradition, it was eventually condemned by a synod because of certain excesses (and also, no doubt, because it was a threat to the church power structure).

Montanus (2nd century)—Charismatic

Seeking to retain the charismatic, prophetic tradition in the Church, Montanus started the Montanist movement. Its adherents counted among their number two women prophetesses, Priscilla and Maximilla, and possibly women bishops. According to historian Kenneth Scott Latourette, Montanus taught that he got "direct messages from the Spirit, that the age of the Spirit foretold in the

Gospel of John had returned, and that the second coming of Christ was at hand." There is no reason to believe that prophetic gifts had ceased in the Church at large by the latter part of the second century, but the popularity of Montanism most likely hastened ways to control such movements.

Moody, Dwight L. (1837–1899) — Evangelical

A former shoe salesman, evangelist Dwight L. Moody continued one emphasis of Great Awakening revivalism — salvation of souls through verbal proclamation of the gospel. Though earlier he had worked in the slums of Chicago, Illinois (United States), he backed away from another emphasis — involvement in poverty relief efforts. He believed that the poor first needed to come into the kingdom of God; then their physical needs would be met. This shift coincided with the premillennial movement in which he and many of his close friends and associates — R. A. Torrey, C. I. Scofield, and others — were deeply involved. Moody did, however, refuse to become embroiled in theological debates and set a policy of cooperating with many denominations in his revival campaigns. The Student Volunteer Movement was born at a Moody-sponsored Mount Hermon Bible Conference held in Northfield, Massachusetts; and several educational institutions, including Moody Bible Institute, owe their existence to him.

Moravian Movement (16th century to the present) — Contemplative

With their roots in the Anabaptist movement, the Moravian Brethren had been fractured by persecution and disagreements between leaders until survivors sought refuge on the estate of Count Nikolaus Ludwig von Zinzendorf in 1722. Joined by German pietists and other zealous followers, they formed the village of Herrnhut and were transformed into the *Unitas Fratrum* (or Moravian Church) under Zinzendorf's spiritual leadership. Herrnhut became a center of missionary activity with outposts in Suriname, Guiana, Egypt, and South Africa. All Moravian activities were undergirded by daily prayer and worship, and it was the serenity of Moravian missionaries during a storm at sea that started John Wesley on the path to a deeper faith.

Mother Teresa (1910–1997) — Social Justice

Albanian by birth, Mother Teresa knew that she wanted to be a missionary early in life. Joining the Sisters of Loretto, she initially taught school in

Calcutta. Soon, though, she felt drawn to found a new order and received permission to start the Missionaries of Charity. Joined by other dedicated workers, she added a fourth vow to poverty, chastity, and obedience—whole-hearted free service to the poor—and set to work helping the "poorest of the poor": lepers, abandoned infants, starving families, and disabled beggars. Her ministry has since spread throughout the world, and at her death she received a state funeral from the nation of India.

Mott, John R. (1865–1955)—Evangelical

The first person to sign a Student Volunteer Movement (SVM) pledge to serve as a missionary, Mott got his start in the Young Men's Christian Association. In fact, it was while he was secretary of the Intercollegiate YMCA that he organized the SVM. Dividing his time between administration and evangelism, he kept those two interests tightly integrated. From the platform of the SVM the American Mott organized the 1910 World Missionary Conference at Edinburgh (Scotland), his first involvement in the ecumenical efforts to which (along with mission work) he devoted the rest of his life. Co-receiver of the Nobel Peace Prize in 1946 and honorary chairman of the World Council of Churches in 1948, he chose to remain a Methodist layperson as he undergirded his work with prayer.

Newman, John Henry (1801–1890)—Incarnational

Newman experienced a spiritual awakening after reading William Law's *A Serious Call to a Devout and Holy Life* and coming under the influence of a Calvinist teacher. After attending Oxford University, he was ordained and served at St. Mary's, Oxford. There he became a leader in the Oxford (or Tractarian) Movement, which sought to interpret the Church and the Protestant Reformation in Anglo-Catholic terms. Increasingly the publication of the group, *Tracts for the Times*, adopted views more closely associated with the Roman Church than the Anglican, and Newman joined the Catholic Church after his *Tract Ninety* brought severe criticism from the bishop of Oxford and others. He was elevated to the College of Cardinals in 1879.

Newton, Isaac (1642–1727)—Incarnational

Popularly known for his "discovery" of gravitation, which he explained in *Principia Mathematica*, Newton also is credited with "the discovery of the differential calculus, and the first correct analysis of white light." Deeply religious and interested in theology, he was a conforming Church of England member and had a particular fascination for the biblical prophetic books—especially Daniel and Revelation—and suggested a way to interpret them meaningfully. Ironically, his validation of the Copernican theory that the planets revolved around the sun was used by some to deprecate Christianity.

Nicodemus the Hagiorite (1748–1809)—Contemplative

Nicodemus the Hagiorite ("holy mountain") is recognized as the primary force behind the eighteenth- and nineteenth-century Orthodox spiritual revival. From the Mount Athos (Greece) monastic republic he co-edited the *Philokalia*, adapted and popularized the most useful Roman Catholic works and practices for the East (e.g., Lorenzo Scupoli's *Spiritual Combat* and *Road to Paradise* under the title *Unseen Warfare*), wrote the important *Manual of Advice on the Custody of the Five Senses and on the Imagination of the Spirit (Noûs) and the Heart*, promoted monastic reform, and helped spread a spirituality of renewal through the Eastern Church. Nicodemus is especially recognized in the Orthodox Church for reintroducing traditional sources that are free of imposed cultural and political influences.

Nicolai (Kasatkin), Ivan (c. 1836–1912)—Evangelical

Sent to Japan as the chaplain to the Russian diplomatic consulate in Nagasaki, Ivan Nicolai mastered the Japanese language and then translated the Eastern Orthodox liturgical books from Russian. Expanding his original mandate in Japan, Nicolai worked to introduce Orthodoxy into Japan, utilizing an evangelistic method used by the Eastern Church since the fourteenth century: with support and students from Russia, he helped establish communities throughout Japan and helped build a cathedral in Tokyo, around which he located a seminary, a girls' school, and other administrative support houses. Today the Orthodox Church in Japan is independent, national, and indigenous in character.

Nightingale, Florence (1820–1910)—Social Justice

Born of English parents in Florence (Italy)—after which she was named—Florence Nightingale is recognized as the founder of modern nursing. "Home-schooled" by her father and called to nursing by God, she studied the methods of the Sisters of Charity and was trained at the Institute of Protestant Deaconesses in Germany. While the superintendent of a women's hospital in London, Florence was recruited by the British secretary of war to go to Constantinople to care for Crimean War wounded. There she initiated procedures that reformed hospital administration and nursing worldwide. She was the first woman to receive the British Order of Merit.

Nil Sorsky (or Nil of Sorsk) (1433–1508) — Contemplative

Schooled in traditional Russian monasticism, Nil Sorsky practiced solitude and hesychasm as a means to become totally detached from the world. Sorsky also allowed companions who joined him to build a monastery, for which he wrote a body of spiritual advice. But he is best remembered for opposing the "possessor" movement led by Joseph of Volokolamsk. The "possessors" believed that it was proper for monasteries to own buildings and land, while the "nonpossessors" taught that communities should be free of any possessions. Since the possessors' position fit with the climate of the times — the czars supported the prosperity of the Russian church, and monasteries owned huge tracts of land — the possessors eventually won. The nonpossessors' emphasis upon an interior, personal, spiritual life was too intangible.

Ninian (c. 360–c. 432) — Evangelical

Bede's *Ecclesiastical History* reports that Ninian was a Briton who had been "accurately instructed" at Rome. He was consecrated as bishop of Galloway by the pope — who must have taken a personal interest in him — and sent back to his homeland to spread the gospel. With the help of stonemasons, Ninian built Candida Casa ("white house" — a church at what is now Whithorn, Scotland) on the shores of Solway Firth. This church became the base for the evangelization of the Southern Picts. Ninian and his preachers laid the foundation for later efforts by Columba and Kentigern (Mungo).

Nouwen, Henri (1932–1996) — Contemplative

Gaining world recognition as a teacher at several universities, the Dutch-born Henri Nouwen spent the last years of his life as a member of the l'Arche Daybreak Community (a home for the mentally retarded) near

Toronto, Ontario (Canada). His numerous books continue to be best-sellers, especially the spiritual journal *The Genesee Diary*. Written during his seven-month stay in a Trappist monastery in upstate New York, it contains Nouwen's honest, transparent meditations on his time at Genesee and challenges Christians to seek a deeper spiritual life through the practice of solitude.

O'Connor, Flannery (1925–1964)—Incarnational

O'Connor's novels and short stories bring together two traditions: the Georgian South (United States) and Roman Catholicism. A tragic figure in her own right—she suffered from systemic lupus and died prematurely—her writings are filled with characters who struggle with physical deformity, emotional problems, spiritual disturbance, and religious obsession. The collection *Flannery O'Connor: The Complete Works* won a National Book Award for fiction in 1972. Her collected letters, *The Habit of Being*, offer intriguing insight into her personality.

Olga (c. 890–969) and Vladimir the Prince (979–1015)—Incarnational

It is unclear when Olga became a Christian, but we know from evidence gleaned from her grandson's life that she lived an incarnational life. As regent of Kiev she had a huge influence on Vladimir who became czar of Russia (after his father and then his brother were killed in battle). Though there is evidence of Russian Christianity prior to Vladimir, he and his son, Yaroslav, are responsible for the Russian state's officially making the transition from paganism to Christianity. Of Swedish Viking descent, Vladimir erected monasteries; promoted education; helped the poor, orphaned, and sick; and built churches. The evidence suggests, however, that he may have converted some of his subjects at the point of a sword.

Order of Widows (1st–4th centuries)—Social Justice

"The real widow . . . continues in supplications and prayers night and day. . . . Let a widow . . . be well attested for her good works, as one who has brought up children, shown hospitality, washed the saints' feet, helped the afflicted, and devoted herself to doing good in every way" (Tim. 5:5, 9–10). The Order of Widows, though not universal in the first- and second-century Christian Church, involved itself in the pastoral ministries of appropriating church discipline and repentance, teaching and baptizing new converts, receiving revelations, instructing the faithful, visiting the sick and needy, praying, and fasting. After the guidelines in the *Didascalia* (a third-century manual on church organization) were implemented, however, they were allowed only to care for the needy, pray, and fast.

Origen (or Origenes Adamantius) (c. 185–254) — Incarnational

Considered by historians to be the best scholar of the Church during the first half of the third century, Origen was a student of another Alexandrian, Clement. He tried to join his father and teacher in martyrdom during a persecution of Christians, but the effort failed. To address the burden of caring for his family, he began teaching school. He was soon in such demand that he had to divide the classes and hire assistants. Origen's legacy includes bringing the best of Greek philosophical thinking to Christian apologetics, compiling the *Hexapla*—a six-column parallel Bible with Hebrew, a Greek transliteration of the Hebrew, and four other Greek translations side by side—and writing *De Principiis*—one of the first efforts to systematize theology.

Oswald (c. 605–642) — Incarnational

Oswald, raised among the Scots and Picts of Christian Caledonia (Scotland), was converted to Christianity during the heat of a battle. During his reign as king of Bernicia (northeastern England), he endowed monasteries and appealed to the monastery at Iona for help in Christianizing his people, an indication that he did not separate faith from work. Aidan of Lindisfarne responded to Oswald's appeal.

Pachomius (290–346) — Contemplative

Pachomius was a contemporary of Antony of Egypt, and like him he lived an eremetic (hermit) life for some time. But unlike Antony, Pachomius left the solitary life and founded a monastery on the banks of the Nile at Tabbenisi in Egypt. Centering the group on love and sharing, he became the founder of cenobitic (communal) monasticism. He developed a Rule for the community—a rule that Benedict of Nursia practiced and used as a resource for his own Rule over two centuries later. Pachomius is considered one of the greatest of the monastic founders.

Palmer, Phoebe (1807–1874)—Holiness

See Chapter 3.

Parks, Rosa (1913–)—Social Justice

In 1955 Rosa Parks, sometimes called the mother of the modern civil rights movement, refused to follow the convention of segregated bus-riding. Blacks were expected to pay their fare at the front door of the bus and then exit, entering again through the rear to find a seat. Rosa Parks entered, paid her fare, and then sat down in the front; and she refused to give her seat up to a white man when asked to by the driver. Her action against injustice in Montgomery, Alabama (United States), spurred people of conscience to protest the denial of rights to African-Americans, and it continues to be an example of how one person can inspire positive, lasting change.

Pascal, Blaise (1623–1662)—Holiness

A "classical" mathematician and inventor by trade, but a Christian apologist by choice, Pascal is most widely known for his posthumously published devotional classic *Pensées*. As a youth he became acquainted with the intellectuals of his day; as a young man he converted to Jansenism (a reform movement in the Catholic Church); as an adult he experienced a "definitive," purifying conversion. From that point on he became a champion of God's truth and holiness and worked to overcome the corrupt alliance between the French monarchy and the Society of Jesus (Jesuits).

Patrick (c. 390–c. 461)—Evangelical

The birthplace of Patrick is shrouded in mystery—along with most of his life and work. We do know that he was British and that at sixteen he was captured with many others by Irish pirates. Sold as a slave, he served as a shepherd in Ireland for six years before hearing a supernatural or divine voice and escaping to Gaul (France/Belgium). Eventually reunited with his family, at about twenty-three he heard voices again, beckoning him once again to go to Ireland. From that point on his life is again shrouded in mystery, but it is believed that Patrick and his followers, including Benen, evangelized Ireland. Today Patrick is known as the "patron saint of Ireland" and the founder of Irish monasticism.

Paul the Apostle (1st century)—Charismatic

See Chapter 4.

Paulinus (c. 353–431)—Social Justice

Born of a noble, wealthy Bordeaux (France) family, Paulinus gave his time to public service before becoming a Christian. Later, greatly influenced by Martin of Tours and Ambrose of Milan, he and his wife, Therasia, decided to give away their wealth to the Church and the poor. After Paulinus was ordained, they settled at Nola (central Italy) ministering to the needy there while living an austere life. Later ordained bishop of Nola, Paulinus corresponded widely with Christians leaders and counted Martin, Ambrose, and Augustine of Hippo among his friends. He was also a talented Latin poet.

Pentecostal Movement (20th century to the present)—Charismatic

Twentieth-century Pentecostals trace their origins to Bethel Bible College in Topeka, Kansas (United States), where students spoke in tongues and the Azusa Street Revival in Los Angeles, which began in 1906. Coming from Baptist and Holiness backgrounds, the early leaders of this movement emphasized justification, sanctification, and the gifts (in Greek *charis*) of the Holy Spirit. Initially participants stayed in their own churches, since the movement was not sharply defined doctrinally. But soon Pentecostal churches and then denominations formed, shaped by three controversies: (1) baptism of the Holy Spirit as the "third blessing," (2) integration of races, and (3) the understanding of the Trinity. The Assemblies of God rejected the "third blessing" as essential to salvation and to this day remains mostly white; the black Church of God in Christ continues to teach that the "third blessing" is essential; the major Jesus Only movement (which teaches that there is only one personality in the Godhead) split from the Assemblies of God, formed the Pentecostal Assemblies of the World, and is largely nonwhite, as are its spin-off denominations. Since its birth, Pentecostalism has spread worldwide. In recent years it has grown rapidly, particularly in South America.

Perpetua (c. 180–203)—Charismatic

The Martyrdom of Perpetua and Felicity is a record of the visions Perpetua had when she was imprisoned in Carthage (Egypt). A well-to-do nursing mother of about twenty-two, she was a catechumen at a time when Christians were being persecuted. She was baptized during her confinement, along with five others arrested with her. The five included Felicity, Perpetua's slave. An eyewitness to Perpetua's martyrdom added an introduction and conclusion to Perpetua's own record, and her catechist added some chapters, making *The Martyrdom of Perpetua and Felicity* a reliable martyrology.

Peter the Apostle (1st century) — Evangelical

See Chapter 6.

Pietist Movement (17th century to the present) — Contemplative

One of the reasons that German Pietism arose was the rejection of scholastic Lutheranism, which intellectualized Christian faith. (Scholastic reformer Philipp Melanchthon, for example, saw belief as "an assent by which you accept all articles of the faith.") Pietism, which arose less than seventy years after the birth of the Protestant Reformation, centered on an inward, heartfelt, experiential Christian life rather than on correct dogma. Its most influential leaders were Philipp Jacob Spener and August Hermann Francke. Spener formed the basis of the movement when he set up *collegia pietatis*—small groups of pastors and laypeople—who gathered for prayer and Bible study. Francke, from his faculty position, established the University of Halle as the center of Pietism. From that center missionaries were sent to India and Greenland. Spreading throughout the Lutheran world— Germany, Sweden, Norway, and Denmark—Pietism's "warm heart" reinvigorated the Moravian movement through its patron, Count Nikolaus Ludwig von Zinzendorf, and deeply influenced German settlers in America.

Pilgrim (19th century) — Incarnational

All we know about the Pilgrim is contained in *The Way of a Pilgrim* and *The Pilgrim Continues His Way*, a summation of classical Russian Orthodox spirituality. The record of a simple peasant's spiritual journey, these two documents chronicle his quest to "pray without ceasing." Given the advice to "acquire the habit of prayer and it will be easy for you to do good" by a spiritual teacher, the Pilgrim set his heart to the task with the aid of the "Jesus Prayer" ("Lord Jesus Christ, have mercy on me, a sinner") and the *Philokalia* (an anthology of writings from the fourth to fourteenth centuries on prayer and the spiritual life).

Poor Clares (or Poor Ladies) (13th century to the present)— Contemplative

Unintentionally founded by Clare of Assisi, the Poor Clares (or Poor Ladies) are part of the Franciscan (or Order of Friars Minor) movement. The first group was based at San Damiano (Italy), the first church Francis renovated, and soon similar communities spread throughout Europe. Since members could not participate in the Franciscan public ministries of helping the poor and preaching, they focused on the interior or spiritual life. This focus manifested itself in the formation of a loving community. Using the poverty of Christ as its model, each monastery depended upon the work of the sisters and freewill offerings to survive.

Professional Christian Societies (20th century to the present)— Incarnational

Since World War II Christians in the marketplace have felt a special burden to bring the life of God into their life of work. To help each other in this task, philosophers, writers, dentists, doctors, lawyers, and more have joined together and formed professional organizations that meet regularly for encouragement, worship, and training. The Christian Medical and Dental Society is one such group.

Protestant Missionary Movement (18th century to the present)— Evangelical

During the hundred years prior to the formation of the Baptist Society for Propagating the Gospel Among the Heathen and William Carey's departure for India, Protestant missionary activity was limited to home countries and colonial territories. Carey's example and letters inspired others to form mission boards—London Missionary Society, Netherlands Missionary Society, American Board of Commissioners for Foreign Missions, and more—which dispatched volunteers committed to fulfilling the Great Commission throughout the world. What started as one man's vision radically changed the focus of Protestant Christian missions.

Protestant Reformation (16th century to the present) — Evangelical

Several influences came together to produce the Protestant Reformation. The Catholic Church was in disarray after undergoing a split papacy and was guilty of serious abuses. The Renaissance had revived classical learning (including the study of Hebrew and Greek biblical texts and early Christianity), and its teachings spread beyond the rich. Throughout Europe monarchies that were growing stronger and promoting nationalism started opposing the papacy, and some even broke away. Economically, cities that included a wealthy merchant class were growing larger and becoming independent. Then Martin Luther nailed his ninety-five theses to the Wittenberg Castle church door, and the rest is history. American historian Martin Marty divides the reform period that followed, with its many movements and branches, into five general parts: conservative reform movements (1500s), radical reform movements (1500s and 1600s), free church movement (1500s and 1600s), Methodist movement (1700s), and unity movement (1800s and 1900s).

Prudentius Clemens, Aurelius (348–c. 410) — Incarnational

Prudentius was trained in law and served in the Spanish civil service until he quit at age fifty-seven. Devoting the rest of his life to Christ, he published his Latin writings, which greatly influenced Christian poetry and hymnology. His work *Psychomachia* (the story of a soul's spiritual warfare) was the first Christian allegorical epic, and his hymns are still sung today:

Of the Father's love begotten
Ere the worlds began to be,
He is Alpha and Omega
He the source, the ending he,
Of the things that are,
that have been,
And that future years shall see,
Evermore and evermore!

Puritan Movement (16th–18th centuries) — Holiness

With their hearts in the Reformation and their roots in the Church of England, adherents of the Puritan movement sought to "purify" the Anglicanism inherited from Henry VIII. The movement's leaders sympathized with the Reformation, accepting the Bible as authority and relying on a spiritually minded, preaching minister in every parish. They objected to the Anglican-prescribed clerical dress, kneeling during Eucharist, exchanging rings at marriage ceremonies, and using the sign of the cross in baptism. After a controversy over wearing vestments that resulted in a crackdown by the archbishop, they concluded that the New Testament pattern for church government was presbyterian (that is, elders overseeing a local church), not episcopal (bishops overseeing numerous churches). As in many other movements, some Puritans wanted to stay in the Church of England and try to reform it from within; others— known as Separatists—wanted to leave. Both happened. Heirs of the Puritan movement include Baptists, Congregationalists, and Quakers.

Raikes, Robert (1735–1811) — Social Justice

An English publisher, Robert Raikes used his newspaper, the *Gloucester Journal*, to publicize his benevolent causes. First he focused on prison reform; then, in 1780, he founded the Sunday School movement. After conferring with the vicar of a neighboring parish, he set the school up in his own parish and paid teachers to teach reading, writing, and the principles of the Christian faith to the children of the poor. Though the movement spread rapidly (a Society for Promoting Sunday Schools was organized in London in 1785 and a similar society in Philadelphia in 1791), the work met some opposition from clergy who felt that Sunday was being "desecrated." But Sunday School outlasted the critics (though paid teachers gave way to volunteers), becoming a normal part of Protestant church life.

Rembrandt Harmenszoon van Rijn (1606–1669) — Incarnational

The Netherlands' greatest artist, Rembrandt is known worldwide for dramatic pieces that use light and shadow to heighten the drama of his subject. Rembrandt's range included portraits, landscapes, nudes, stories from the Old and New Testaments, and more. The biblical pictures created during the last years of his life (1640–1669) seem to glow from within, the shadows intense and vibrant. Christians are especially familiar with *Christ at Emmaus*.

Renaissance (14th–16th centuries) — Incarnational

Beginning in Italy, the Renaissance (in Italian, *Renascimento*) consisted of a "rebirth" of culture in general and classical Greek and Roman culture in particular. Viewing the past thousand years as the "Middle Ages" (or intermission between the classic civilizations and their time), the leaders of this movement tried to shed all of the influence of that intermission by going back to original sources. In truth, though, they drew from both. For Western civilization the Renaissance is important because it gave birth to individualism, which allows a person to be judged on merit rather than on birth. Church historians take keen interest in this time because during the Renaissance the power of the Roman Catholic Church was weakened by the Protestant Reformation.

Roberts, Evan John (1878–1951)—Charismatic

Six years of formal education, twelve years of working in mines, and two years as a blacksmith's apprentice did not give Evan Roberts the credentials to lead the 1904–1908 revival in Wales; the Holy Spirit did. At twenty-six Roberts felt called to the ministry, and between his acceptance and his entry into the Ministers' Training College he was visited by God nightly. During his first year of training, the appearances stopped for some time and then began again. Later, while on retreat, he was anointed by the Holy Spirit and commissioned to preach Jesus Christ. People spontaneously responded to his first efforts, and a revival spread through all of Wales and into northern England.

Roberts, Oral (1918–)—Charismatic

As a young man Oral Roberts was healed of tuberculosis under miraculous circumstances, and this event shaped his life. With an emphasis on "seed-faith"—"Each act of faith is a seed planted and will be multiplied many times"—he has become a well-known leader in the twentieth-century Pentecostal/Charismatic movement. An ordained United Methodist minister who grew up in rural Oklahoma (United States), he continues to influence the direction of two namesakes—an evangelistic association and a university, both based in Tulsa, Oklahoma.

Rolle, Richard (c. 1300–1349)—Charismatic

Richard Rolle spent most of his life as a hermit and become part of the flowering of mystical piety. Born in Yorkshire and educated at Oxford, he wrote numerous tracts; the one for which he is known most widely is *The*

Fire of Love. On almost every page he explores the love of God: "There must be a serious intention . . . to long continually for the love of God. . . . God the Holy Trinity is to be loved for himself alone. . . . It behooves us to make sure that the love of Christ is in us. . . . No creature can love God too much." Rolle served as a spiritual director for Cistercian nuns at Hampole during his last years.

Roman Catholic Missionary Movement (16th century to the present)—Evangelical

The revival of missionary zeal within the Roman Church was a direct outgrowth of the sixteenth-century Roman Catholic Reformation. Central to the execution of the Catholic Reformation was Ignatius of Loyola and the Society of Jesus (Jesuits) that he founded. The secret to their crucial role was Ignatius's decision to place every Jesuit at the pope's disposal, an original and very expedient idea. This allowed the order to be assigned to missions crucial to Rome, and the pope sent that small, totally dedicated, highly gifted band of men throughout the world. With the Franciscans and Dominicans, the Jesuits evangelized and made converts from the Philippines in the east to the New World in the west.

Roman Catholic Reformation (16th century)—Holiness

A mid-sixteenth-century effort that brought reform to the Catholic Church, the Roman Catholic Reformation streamed from such movements as the Brothers and Sisters of the Common Life and the efforts of earlier leaders—preacher Girolamo Savonarola, Spanish Dominican Vincent Ferrer, preacher Bernardino of Siena, and Catherine of Siena. During the Roman Catholic Reformation, revival radiated from its two main centers in Spain and Italy; "oratories" composed of clergy and lay members cultivated personal piety and charitable actions; orders of clerks emphasized spirituality, clergy reform, and charity; monastic orders caught a vision for missions; and mystical piety flourished.

Romantic Movement (18th–19th centuries)—Incarnational

Romanticism valued emotion over reason, imagination over comprehension, inspiration over logic, spontaneity over restraint, and freedom over order in the arts and literature. Its opposite was classicism. Poets Johann

Wolfgang von Goethe, Samuel Taylor Coleridge, and William Wordsworth were part of the Romantic movement.

Russian Novelists (19th century) — Incarnational

Count Leo Tolstoy and Fyodor Dostoyevsky are Russia's two greatest novelists. Writing during the age of realism, when the novel—their chosen genre—was the principal literary form, they focused on the human condition. In *War and Peace* and *Anna Karenina*, Tolstoy explored such universal themes as birth, love, marriage, moral duty, and death. Dostoyevsky's characters in *Crime and Punishment* and *The Brothers Karamazov* experience violent spiritual struggles between their pride and self-centeredness and their belief in God.

Sabas (c. 438–532) — Social Justice

Living to the age of ninety-four, Sabas is remembered for intervening with the Emperor Justinian on behalf of the Palestinians who were suffering under Samaritan control. In negotiations Sabas agreed to help free Palestine if Justinian lowered taxes, built a hospital for pilgrims, constructed a fort to protect monks and hermits from raiders in Jerusalem, and granted the monks religious freedom. Justinian agreed. Earlier Sabas had built three hospitals and a monastery with his inheritance.

Salvation Army (19th century to the present) — Social Justice

Founded by Catherine Mumford and William Booth, the Salvation Army was not a significant movement in Christianity until the publication of the book *In Darkest England and the Way Out* in 1890. Bearing William Booth's name and containing his ideas, it describes the ills of English society and prescribes cures. After the release of the book, the Army quickly expanded, spreading the world over, and is one of the most respected Christian benevolent efforts ever. It continues to minister to the neediest of people—body and soul.

Samson (c. 485–c. 565) — Charismatic

A miraculous "child of promise," Samson was dedicated to God and placed in a Welsh monastery at age five by his parents. After ordination, he reluctantly returned home to administer last rites to his father, who recovered and decided to join Samson in the monastery. Unhappy as abbot of first one monastery and then another, Samson saw a vision that told him to go beyond the seas. Traveling across Cornwall, where he restored to health a boy who had been thrown from a horse, he took a ship to Brittany. There he became known for performing miracles, evangelizing, and establishing churches and monasteries.

Savonarola, Girolamo (1452–1498) — Holiness

A Dominican friar and member of the San Marco monastery, Savonarola was a spiritual grandson of Catherine of Siena, a contemporary of Catherine of Genoa, and one of Italy's greatest late-Renaissance preachers and reformers. His efforts to correct the evils of Florentine society centered in powerful, prophetic sermons that garnered the loyalty of the citizens. When several predictions came true and the ruling Medici family fled after an invasion by France, he became the de facto ruler and put in place tax and judicial reforms and programs to help the poor. However, his story ends unhappily: Savonarola was executed by the city government of Florence after unpopular political views eroded his popularity and enemies mounted an offensive.

Schweitzer, Albert (1875–1965) — Social Justice

As a medical doctor Albert Schweitzer established a missionary hospital and medical station at Lambaréné, French Equatorial Africa (now Gabon). As a philosopher Schweitzer formulated his "reverence for life" in a book of the same title that was published posthumously. As a theologian he wrote *The Quest of the Historical Jesus* and other works. As a musician he interpreted the music and life of Johann Sebastian Bach and was an expert organist and authority on organ construction. But Schweitzer centered most of his energy at Lambaréné, tending to the medical needs of the Congolese for fifty-two years.

Seraphim of Sarov (1759–1833) — Charismatic

Described by historian Louis Bouyer as a combination of Francis of Assisi and Jean-Baptiste Vianney, Seraphim radiated joy, made friends with God's creatures, detached himself from the world, eased souls into serenity, devotedly gave to charity, and periodically saw visions. Possibly the most luminous and winsome figure of recent Russian Orthodoxy, he has been the subject of many stories—stories so richly embellished that truth is hard to distinguish from fiction. However, this ascetic monk from Kursk, a man who loved solitude, seemed to live with one foot in the natural world and one foot in the supernatural.

Sergius of Radonezh (1314–1392)—Contemplative

Sergius's life followed a pattern we are now familiar with: as a young man he felt drawn to solitude, which he found in the forests near Radonezh (Russia). There he stayed, but others joined him and built a monastery and church. He was so beloved by the people that his reputation spread, and he became the spiritual leader of the nation. Sergius is also credited with uniting the feuding Russian princes who marched against the Tartars at Kulikovo Pole. Prior to the battle the princes had sought the advice of the saintly Sergius, and he had said, "Go forward and fear not. God will help thee." His words were prophetic. The princes won the battle, starting the long process of throwing off two hundred years of Mongol occupation.

Seymour, William (1870–1922)—Charismatic

See Chapter 4.

Shaftesbury, Anthony Ashley Cooper (or Lord Shaftesbury) (1801–1885)—Social Justice

A vigorous social reformer Shaftesbury campaigned on such matters as the treatment of the mentally ill; the terms of employment for workers in factories, mills, and mines; and the use of boys as chimney sweeps. As a member of the House of Lords he consistently called for improvement of the living conditions of industrial workers. As a landowner he built a model village in Dorset. In addition, he was president of numerous philanthropic and missionary societies, including the Ragged School Union, the National Society for the Prevention of Cruelty to Children, and the British and Foreign Bible Society.

Shakarian, Demos (1913–)—Charismatic

Descended from Armenian Christians, Demos Shakarian was filled with the Holy Spirit at age thirteen in his home church in Los Angeles (United

States). But Shakarian was a thirty-eight-year-old dairyman before he started the Full Gospel Business Men's Fellowship International. From a group of twenty-one people meeting during lunch in a room over a cafeteria in 1951, the organization grew to over seventeen hundred chapters worldwide and reached one billion people yearly with the gospel. Intentionally organized to appeal to the ordinary businessman, it has been joined by similar efforts: Christian Women's Clubs, Women's Aglow, and others.

Sigfrid (?–c. 1045) — Evangelical

Sigfrid and two other missionary bishops were sent by the English king, Ethelred, to Norway at the request of King Olaf Tryggvason. But they did not stop permanently in Norway; they went on to Sweden, where Sigfrid settled at Växjö and built a church. He is credited with converting the Swedish king, Olaf Skötkonung, and with preaching the gospel in Denmark.

Simeon (or Symeon) the New Theologian (949–1022) — Contemplative

Coming from the tradition of Maximus the Confessor and John Climacus, Simeon was the earliest proponent of hesychasm. He taught that theology transcends reason. Rather than knowing God with the intellect, God is perceived through the continual living of faith. Since God is beyond comprehension, we must be caught up in the "light" — God's self-communication or divine energy, which flows from him and is uncreated. This teaching, further refined by the fourteenth-century monk Gregory of Palamas, stands as the key difference between Greek/Eastern and Latin/Western theology.

Simons, Menno (1496–1561) — Holiness

A former Catholic priest, the moderate Menno Simons is credited with helping save the Anabaptist movement by his emphasis upon purity of life and discipleship to Christ. Radical millennialism had almost ruined the movement, but Simons's wise, moral, devotional ministry helped rehabilitate it. To preserve church purity, he introduced the "ban" or "shunning," to be exercised by the community against offenders until they repented. Under his guidance, the movement practiced foot-washing as a sign of humility, strongly opposed war, and believed in the separation of church and state. Menno Simons traveled for twenty-five years throughout Germany and the

Netherlands, preaching and planting churches. Today Mennonite churches follow his teaching.

Slessor, Mary (1848–1915) — Evangelical

Reared in a poor working-class Scottish home and given little education, Mary Slessor had only her experience as a Sunday School teacher and missions helper to prepare her for service in Calabar (Nigeria). There she faced constant danger from warring, witchcraft-practicing tribes, but she finally won over the tribal chiefs and their people. Besides bringing the gospel to West Africa, Slessor encouraged trade, opposed slavery, improved conditions for women, ended the killing of twins at birth, and guided the opening of the Hope Waddell Institute, a job-training center.

Smith, Hannah Whitall (1832–1911) — Holiness

Smith is most often remembered for her book *The Christian's Secret of a Happy Life*. First published in 1870, this spiritual classic explores why followers of Christ lack joy and invites them to lead a full and blessed life. "I saw, as in a flash, that the religion of Christ ought to be, and was meant to be, to its possessors, not something to make them miserable, but something to make them happy; and I began then and there to ask the Lord to show me the secret of a happy Christian life."

Solzhenitsyn, Aleksandr (1918–) — Incarnational

Many elements contributed to the collapse of Eastern European and Soviet communism, but novelist Aleksandr Solzhenitsyn's writings played a significant role in undermining communism's moral authority. While serving in the Soviet army, Solzhenitsyn was falsely accused of a political crime and imprisoned. His first novel, *One Day in the Life of Ivan Denisovich*, describes that prison life, and *Cancer Ward* takes place in a hospital. The stories contrast revolutionary ideals with harsh political reality and describe heroes whose human dignity triumphs over tyranny and suffering. The trilogy known as *The Gulag Archipelago, 1918–1956* studies the Soviet prison-camp system. In response to the publication of the first book in that trilogy in 1973, the Soviet Union revoked Solzhenitsyn's citizenship and deported him. After the collapse of communism he returned to his beloved Russia in 1994 and continues to live there.

Spurgeon, Charles Haddon (1834–1892) — Evangelical

One of the most magnetic and successful preachers in nineteenth-century England, Spurgeon began preaching at age sixteen. By age twenty he had been asked to pastor a Baptist church in London, and his preaching drew such large crowds that the church had to build an addition. He preached at a public hall while the space was being added, but it soon proved too small. Finally, the church built a five-thousand-seat tabernacle to accommodate the large crowds, and Spurgeon preached there until just before his death.

Stephen of Hungary (c. 970–1038) — Incarnational

The son of Geza, duke of the Magyars, Stephen was baptized with the rest of his family and became governor when his father died. As Hungary's first king, he consolidated his rule and gradually established sees with churches and monasteries at their centers. He exercised his kingly rights, commanding that people pay tithes to support a church and priest in every tenth town, repressing public crimes such as blasphemy and murder, abolishing tribal divisions, dividing the land into "counties," and limiting the accumulation of wealth by nobility. The architect of an independent Hungary, his example of virtue inspired the people under his rule.

Student Volunteer Movement (19th–20th centuries) — Evangelical

With the motto "the evangelization of the world in this generation," and with John R. Mott as leader, the Student Volunteer Movement became the greatest student missionary force in history. Created at a Dwight L. Moody–sponsored Mount Hermon Bible Conference, it formed the base for the World Student Christian Federation organized in 1895 in Sweden. Nondenominational student chapters prophetically pioneered in the evangelistic training of men and women worldwide. As adults the student volunteers went on to lead other ecumenical efforts.

Suffrage Movement (19th century to the present) — Social Justice

Broadly defined, suffrage is the right of voting or the exercise of such right. In most Western countries the controversy over suffrage has centered on the right of women to vote in local and national elections. In the original American Colonies some women were able to vote, but by 1807 all states had rescinded that right. In the 1830s new conditions—women in the labor force, men needing the help of women in social reform efforts—created the women's suffrage movement, but it took almost ninety years to get women's right to vote included in the U.S. Constitution. New Zealand granted women the right to vote in 1893, followed in quick succession by Finland, Norway, Australia, Denmark, Iceland, Russia, and others. At present only a half-dozen countries deny women the right to vote; one country also denies the right to certain classes of people.

Sundar Singh (c. 1889–1929)—Charismatic

As a member of a wealthy Sikh family, Sundar was expected to become a sadhu (Indian holy man), but after a dramatic vision he became a Christian. He adopted the dress of the sadhu and traveled throughout India and beyond, preaching the gospel to huge audiences, trying to live as Christ did, and experiencing many visions and miracles. He failed to return from an evangelistic trip to Tibet in April 1929 but left behind numerous writings, including *At the Feet of the Master*, his best-known work in the West.

Sunday, Billy (or William Ashley) (1862–1935)—Evangelical

An estimated one million people responded to Billy Sunday's evangelistic messages and walked the tabernacle "sawdust trail." An Iowan whose Union father was killed in the American Civil War before he got to see his son, Billy became self-sufficient at age fourteen. Over the next nineteen years he earned a high school education, played professional baseball, came to Christ, got married, worked full-time at the YMCA, and helped evangelist J. Wilbur Chapman. When Chapman left mass evangelism in 1895, Sunday began holding meetings on his own. Periodically coming under criticism for various reasons—lack of follow-up and social action, ministerial failings, sensationalism—he persevered. One of his innovations, the "love offering," became the usual way to pay evangelists. By 1919 Sunday's popularity had waned, but he continued to lead meetings until his death. Never traveling beyond the United States, he left no institution to carry on his work.

Sunday School Movement (18th century to the present)—Social Justice

The first systematic effort to educate children came as a direct result of the Evangelical Revival in England. Founded by newspaper publisher

Robert Raikes and named the Ragged School, the first Sunday School had as its purpose the teaching of reading, writing, and the Christian faith to children of the poor on the only day they were free. Piggybacking on the Protestant missionary movement, the concept of Sunday School spread quickly to all parts of the world, and the model was adopted by the Roman Catholic Church as well as by other faiths. With the advent of tax-supported public education, the focus changed from general education of children only to religious instruction for all ages, as a complement to Sunday worship services.

Swithun (or Swithin) (c. 802–c. 862) — Social Justice

As prince of Wessex and counselor and chaplain to two kings of the West Saxons, Swithun became known for his concern for the needy, his humility, and his dedication to church building programs. He was named bishop of Winchester in 852. In the church calendar, Swithun's feast day is July 15, and in England it is a weather indicator similar to America's Groundhog Day. But instead of predicting how much winter remains, it predicts rainfall: if it rains on July 15, there will be rain every day for forty days; if the weather is fair, then it will be fair for forty days.

Taylor, James Hudson (1832–1905) — Incarnational

James Hudson Taylor's grandparents were influenced by John Wesley, his father had a deep concern for the spiritual needs of China, and his mother prayed unceasingly. By age five Taylor had indicated an interest in being a missionary to China, and, though with frail health, he studied medicine, theology, Latin, and Greek as a young man. Upon arrival in China he adopted local customs and dress and worked tirelessly to enculturate the gospel into Chinese life. When he discovered that his sponsoring mission organization was operating on borrowed money, he founded the interdenominational China Inland Mission (CIM). With half of the missionaries in China affiliated with the CIM by the turn of the century, Taylor's contribution to the church in China is immense.

Taylor, Jeremy (1613–1667) — Holiness

The "Shakespeare of English divines," Taylor is best known for two books, *The Rule and Exercises of Holy Living* and *The Rule and Exercises of*

Holy Dying (sometimes published in one volume). Containing practical, down-to-earth advice for Christians, these books continue to guide us into a life of sacrifice and humility for the good of our own souls. "It is not sufficient to think of the service of God as an optional work. Rather it is to be done as God intended it—with great earnestness and passion, with much zeal and desire. . . . Humility is the great ornament and jewel of Christian religion by which it is distinguished from all the wisdom of the world."

Teresa of Ávila (or Teresa of Jesus) (1515–1582)—Holiness

Discontent with the laxness of her Carmelite monastic life, Teresa of Ávila sought new depths of contemplation and experienced a spiritual awakening at forty. Resolving to found a reformed order, Teresa received permission seven years later. After establishing the first convent, St. Joseph of Ávila, Teresa started sixteen other Discalced ("barefooted") Carmelite communities. Though a semi-invalid, she traveled extensively throughout Spain, becoming a leader of the Catholic Reformation. In spite of her infirmity and busy schedule, she wrote *Life* (or *Autobiography*), *The Way of Perfection*, *Book of Foundations*, and the book most widely known, *Interior Castle*.

Thérèsa of Lisieux (1873–1897)—Contemplative

Known to us as "the Little Flower," Thérèsa entered a convent at fifteen, taking seriously the principal Carmelite duty of praying for the clergy and the "lapsed." Even though her health was delicate, she was able to fulfill all of her obligations (other than fasting) under the austere Rule. She also wrote the widely read devotional classic *The Little Way* and her autobiography, *The Story of a Soul*. Soon after volunteering to join missionaries in Hanoi (Vietnam)—and before she could make the trip—she contracted tuberculosis and died. She was only twenty-four.

Tertullian (c. 160–c. 225)—Holiness

Converted sometime in his late thirties, Tertullian became a leading third-century apologist for the Christian faith, along with Origen and Cyprian. Key works in which he defended Christianity include *Against Marcion*, *Against the Valentinians*, and *Against Praxeas*. He also wrote voluminously in the areas of Christian theology, morality, and practice. His systematic formulation of the doctrine of the Trinity (the term *Trinitas* was first applied to the Deity by Tertullian) influenced later expositions by church fathers—Athanasius and Augustine among them—and the Councils of Nicea and Chalcedon. Tertullian was often perceived as rigid because his writings on marriage, penance, baptism, and other issues emphasize that the Church is composed of people whose faith separates them from the world. He urged Christians not to participate in anything that comes into contact with the "gods" of the pagan world: army, government, educational institutions, public amusements, and even some businesses. He seemed to become more moralistic with age, joining the Montanists, a separatist group that emphasized sexual purity and holy living. Eventually he left even the Montanists and started his own sect. In spite of these digressions, Tertullian is viewed as the founder of Latin (Western) Christian doctrine, giving it its vocabulary and basic agenda.

Thomas à Kempis (1379–1471)—Holiness

Thomas à Kempis, ordained a priest by a Windesheimer "congregation" in the Netherlands, was the best-known member of the renewal movement known as the Brothers and Sisters of the Common Life. Author of sermons, chronicles, and devotional works, he distilled the holiness teaching of this *devotio moderna* ("modern devotion") movement in *The Imitation of Christ*. Excluding the Bible, that volume is the most widely read book of Western Christianity.

Tikhon of Zadonsk (1727–1783)—Social Justice

Tikhon's story sounds strange to our ears: appointed superior of a monastery and then resigning; living the rest of his life in a small, squalid hut in the woods; reading Roman Catholic and Protestant books on contemporary Western piety; spending whole nights in prayer; suffering through a dark night of the soul. In context, though, his is a heartwarming story: Tikhon distributed to the poor the entire pension given to him by the Russian empress. He denied himself the necessities of life so that he could give to those who flocked to him. And when he had given all away and could no longer personally give anything to the poor, he carried on a voluminous correspondence. Fyodor Dostoyevsky may have based Father Zossima, a character in *The Brothers Karamazov*, on Tikhon of Zadonsk.

Truth, Sojourner (or Isabella Van Wagenen) (c. 1797–1883)— Social Justice

Isabella Van Wagenen was born from below as a slave in New York (Unites States). In 1843, in her middle years, she was born from above as a child of God. She then took a new name—Sojourner Truth—and hit the road as an itinerant preacher. Highly intelligent, though with no formal education, "Truth had great presence. She was tall, some 5 feet 11 inches, of spare but solid frame. Her voice was low, . . . and her singing voice was powerfully beautiful. No one ever forgot the power and pathos of Sojourner Truth's singing, just as her wit and originality of phrasing were also of lasting remembrance. . . . Truth was first and last an itinerant preacher. From the late 1840s through the late 1870s, she traveled the American land, denouncing slavery and slavers, advocating freedom, women's rights, woman suffrage, and temperance."

Tubman, Harriet (Moses) (c. 1820–1913)—Social Justice

A generation younger than Sojourner Truth, Harriet Tubman was born a slave in Maryland (United States), married a free man, and escaped and went to Philadelphia via the Underground Railroad in 1849. Having vowed to return and assist other slaves, she went back one year later; over the next ten years she helped over three hundred people gain their freedom. During the Civil War she served as a Union army nurse, scout, and spy, still helping countless slaves escape to freedom via the Underground Railroad. Returning to New York after the war, Tubman raised money for black schools and established a home for needy and elderly blacks. She and Sojourner Truth are America's most famous nineteenth-century African-American women.

Tutu, Desmond (1931–)—Social Justice

Wanting to be a teacher but unable to pursue that dream because of the Bantu Education Act that limited learning opportunities for blacks, Tutu, inspired by white priests working in the slums of South Africa, entered the Anglican Church and was ordained. With gifts for speaking and diplomacy, he rapidly advanced, becoming the first black Anglican archbishop of Cape Town in 1986. In that position he worked tirelessly against apartheid. Profoundly religious—he fasts, prays, meditates, and withdraws for times of silence—Tutu has been a key figure in the disassembly of apartheid and continues to work for harmony and peace as chair of the Truth and Reconciliation Commission.

Underhill, Evelyn (1875–1941)—Contemplative

Evelyn Underhill was a widely acknowledged English scholar in Christian mysticism, writing such pioneering works as *Mysticism*, *Abba*, *The Ways of the Spirit*, and her much-praised *Worship*, a study of the liturgical practices of a number of church traditions. With Baron Friedrich von Hügel as her spiritual director, she deepened and grew in her understanding of the Christian life and witness and was a pioneer in the British retreat movement.

Vanier, Jean (1928–)—Social Justice

Jean Vanier believes that he was "just a catalyst" in the life of the l'Arche communities. At their heart is love—love for the mentally retarded, "who have been excluded from society" and who "can become instruments of God's love." He writes, "The essential way then is not to *do* things *for* the poor but rather to *be with* them in a covenant of love. It is to grow with them, to celebrate with them, to pray with them, to hope with them. L'Arche thus becomes a means and a channel whereby the poor can give their message to the church and to the world."

Veniaminov, John (1798–1879)—Evangelical

John Veniaminov placed Alaskan Orthodox mission efforts on a firm basis. Working from 1824 until 1853, he developed the work started by a group of monks who had established the first mission in 1794. Veniaminov's accomplishments include translating the Gospels and liturgy into Aleutian, founding a native priesthood, opening a seminary in Sitka, showing interest in native customs and beliefs about which he wrote extensively, and undertaking year-long evangelistic journeys to remote islands. He is regarded by the Russian Orthodox Church as the greatest of its nineteenth-century missionaries, and Veniaminov is honored by American Orthodox members as their chief "apostle."

Vianney, Jean-Baptiste (or John Baptist) (1786–1859)—Social Justice

Jean-Baptiste Vianney's life reminds "ordinary" people that God does not require perfection to accomplish his purposes. As a child Vianney faced one obstacle after another—extreme poverty, a lack of formal education and religious instruction, political upheaval, and more. As a young man he joined the army but lost his way. Technically a deserter, he went into hiding for almost two years. Finally accepted into a minor seminary, he had to drop out because the studies were too hard. And on it goes. But as priest of the 250-person parish of Ars-en-Dombes (France), the servant Vianney met the needs of the people. He started a free school for girls. He chided the people until they quit drinking and dancing. Though other clergy made fun of him, nonetheless he became so famous that people went to Ars by the thousands to confess their sins. Today the Curé d'Ars is honored as the patron saint of parochial clergy.

Vincent de Paul (c. 1581–c. 1660)—Social Justice

The fact that Vincent de Paul was born a peasant at Ranquines (France) and was condemned to two years as a slave by pirates undoubtedly contributed to his compassion and sense of justice in later life. He studied the humanities and prepared for ordination, thereby moving out of a life of poverty. After his capture by Turkish pirates while on a trip to Narbonne and subsequent escape, he came under the influence of Pierre de Bérulle, who further awakened his concern for the downtrodden. In his position as a parish priest he ministered to the poor, and in 1625 he was appointed superior of the order known as the Congregation of the Mission (also known as the Vincentians, or Lazarists).

Vincent Madelgarius (c. 615–c. 687) and Waldetrude (or Waudru) (?–c. 688)—Incarnational

Vincent and Waldetrude, both from France, raised four children who served the cause of Christ. Immersion in everyday life did not deter them from following their spiritual impulses. In their latter years both started communities—Vincent the monastery of Hautmont, Waldetrude the convent at Chateaulieu. They are a wonderful example of ordinary people living incarnationally, first as a couple with children, then in community with other Christians.

Vincentians (or Lazarists) (17th century to the present)—Social Justice

Formally known as the Congregation of the Mission, the Vincentians were founded by Vincent de Paul in 1625. A congregation of secular priests, they take four vows—poverty, chastity, obedience, and stability—and are employed in missions, especially among the poor. They also conduct retreats, start hospitals, and found seminaries. At Vincent's urging and with the help of Louise de Marillac, an order of enclosed women dedicated to serving the sick and poor—the Daughters of Charity—was established in 1633. Other non-resident members, wealthy women, collect funds and assist the Vincentians in their charitable work.

Vladimir Monomakh (?–1125)—Social Justice

This Russian prince wrote to his children, "Praise God, and love men.... Forget not the poor, but feed them.... Do not bury your wealth in the ground; this is against the precepts of Christianity. Be fathers to orphans, be judges in the cause of widows and do not let the powerful oppress the weak. Put to death neither the innocent nor the guilty, for nothing is so sacred as the life and the soul of a Christian. Do not desert the sick. ... Drive out of your heart all suggestions of pride and remember that we are all mortal, to-day full of hope, to-morrow in the coffin. Abhor lying, drunkenness and debauchery."

von Hügel, Friedrich (1852–1925)—Contemplative

Born in Florence (Italy) this noble son of an Austrian diplomat received a cosmopolitan education from private tutors. He came to a deeper faith when an attack of typhus left him deaf and with permanently damaged health at age eighteen. Subsequently moving to England, he became a friend of several leaders in the turn-of-the-century Roman Catholic modernist movement and spiritual adviser to many in cultured social circles, including Evelyn Underhill. Though highly critical of certain developments within the Roman Catholic Church, he avoided being excommunicated, probably because of his lay status. Baron von Hügel wrote several books, among which is the classic *Selected Letters*.

Vulmar or (Wulmar) (?–c. 700)—Contemplative

Married, but forced to separate from his wife because of her earlier betrothal to a noble Frank, Vulmar entered a monastery. There he took care of the cattle and hewed the wood. Known for his prayer life, he was ordained a priest but promptly left to spend time in solitude. Some years later he founded the abbey of Samer near Calais (France) and a nunnery at Wierre-aux-Bois.

Wesley, Charles (1707–1788) — Charismatic

The younger brother of John Wesley, Oxford-educated Charles was converted three days before John and was as indispensable as his brother to the Methodist or "holiness" movement. Like John he preached in England and America. His greatest impact, though, came through the approximately eight thousand hymns he wrote — hymns that teach Christian doctrine and witness to his rich personal faith. Following in the tradition of hymn writer Isaac Watts, he wrote songs that were meant to be read *and* sung. It is no small wonder that "O, For a Thousand Tongues to Sing," "Hark, the Herald Angels Sing," "Christ the Lord Is Risen Today," and more have endured these two hundred plus years.

Wesley, John (1703–1791) — Holiness

On 24 May 1738, after a disastrous missionary and pastoral trip to the United States, the Anglican Wesley went to a Moravian meeting on Aldersgate Street, London. With a soul prepared by discussions about the nature of faith with Moravian Peter Böhler and a peculiar heaviness of heart, John had a life-changing experience: "I felt my heart strangely warmed. I felt I did trust in Christ, Christ alone for salvation." What followed was a life poured out in service to God. Wesley's efforts — traveling over a quarter-million miles to preach over forty-two thousand sermons, publishing over two hundred books, pioneering or participating in most of the social causes of the day — helped save England from the chaos of a revolution like the one that devastated France.

Wesley, Susanna (1669–1742) — Incarnational

See Chapter 7.

Whitfield, George (1714–1770) — Evangelical

With the two Wesleys, Whitfield was a leader of the Evangelical Revival in England and the First Great Awakening in the Colonies. He preached whenever and wherever possible: in open fields, at religious society meeting houses, in public halls, in barns, and more. Though Anglican, he freely worked with other denominations, refusing to let doctrinal differences affect where he preached and enlisting the help of laypeople. In America he inspired Jonathan Edwards and Gilbert Tennet, and historian Chris Mitchell writes that in the British Isles Whitfield "fanned into flame the revival fires that swept through Scotland and Wales in the early 1740s." Some have called him the founder of American revivalism.

Wilberforce, William (1759–1833)—Social Justice

Despite having been born into the merchant class (which was despised by the aristocracy and landed gentry), Wilberforce became a member of the British House of Commons at twenty-one. An eloquent orator and the best friend of Prime Minister William Pitt, he wielded enormous influence. Two years before Pitt asked Wilberforce to "give a notice of a motion on the subject of the Slave Trade," he had experienced a time of spiritual turmoil, and ex-slaver John Newton had led him to a "rededication" to Christ. Pitt asked and Wilberforce was ready—in soul and position—to spearhead the effort to ban slavery. Abolishing slavery became the great passion of his life. A bill to end the slave trade was passed in 1807, though it took another eighteen years to finally abolish slavery.

Wilfred (634–709)—Evangelical

Wilfred was sent to the monastery at Celtic Lindisfarne as a young teenager and later learned Christian ideas and traditions at Canterbury and Rome. Preferring Roman practice to Celtic, he spent his life embroiled in the struggle to make Roman traditions the official practice of the church in Northumbria (one of seven kingdoms in ancient Great Britain). Alternately appointed to church offices, deposed, exiled, then reappointed, Wilfred spent seven years during one exile in southern England, where he evangelized the Saxons of Sussex (also teaching them better methods of fishing during a famine). From there he promoted the evangelization of the Isle of Wight, the last area in England to hear the gospel.

Williams, Roger (1603–1683)—Social Justice

A clergyman and Dissenter (and briefly a Baptist), Williams graduated from Cambridge University and immigrated to New England when the Dissenters came under persecution. Refusing an invitation to become a minister of the only Boston church because it did not acknowledge its separation from the Church of England, he finally accepted a position at the Salem church. Then he ran afoul of authorities when he disputed their right to take land from the Native Americans without compensation. Under threat of deportation, he escaped into the wilderness, secured land from the Native Americans, and founded Providence, the capital of Rhode Island. Williams's tracts—*The Bloody Tenant of Persecution* and *The Bloody Tenant Yet More Bloody*— defended religious liberty and the separation of church and state, main tenets of the American experience.

Willibrord (658–739)—Evangelical

A native of Northumbria (Britain) educated at the monastery of Ripon (near York), Willibrord devoted his life to bringing the gospel to the Frisian Islands (the Netherlands and northern Germany). In alliance with the new Frisian king he received official permission from Rome and began to see mass conversions and acceptance of Christianity in northwestern Europe. He suffered hardship when the previous ruler retook the Frisias, however, fleeing to Scandinavia and Germany for safety. Upon that ruler's death, Willibrord returned and rebuilt the churches and monasteries with the help of Boniface, his own successor; and people again began to come to Christ.

Wimber, John (1934–1997)—Charismatic

Before he came to Christ in 1963, John Wimber was a professional musician and founding member of the Righteous Brothers, an American rock group. His "baptism" by the Holy Spirit about a year after his conversion propelled him into the worldwide Christian community, where he became known as an evangelist, pastor, Bible teacher, composer, founder of the Vineyard movement, and conduit for the power of the Holy Spirit. When this "gentle giant" prayed, things happened—people were made whole, relationships were healed, souls were saved—and observers caught a glimpse of what could happen when someone wholeheartedly became, as John put it, "a fool for Christ."

Woolman, John (1720–1772)—Social Justice

See Chapter 5.

Wycliffe, John (c. 1329–1384) — Evangelical

Once the Catholic Church had controlled the expansion of two Central European sects, it found itself faced with two new threats to its control: John Wycliffe in England and John Huss (or Jan Hus) in Bohemia. The foremost scholar of his day at Oxford, Wycliffe boldly criticized and questioned major practices and dogmas of the Church, eventually rejecting its whole medieval structure. Named by some the "Morning Star of the Reformation," he and his followers (later called Lollards) translated the entire Bible from Latin into English, making it available to many in Britain. Wycliffe's writings came into Huss's possession — and thereby into wider circulation on the Continent. A century later Martin Luther was also influenced by Wycliffe's writings.

Xavier, Francis (1506–1552) — Evangelical

Francis Xavier, one of the first Jesuit missionaries, is the foremost Roman Catholic missionary of contemporary times. One of the founding members of the Society of Jesus, in ten years of work the noble-born Spaniard carried Catholicism to Goa and southern India, the Malay Archipelago, the Molucca Islands (part of Indonesia), and Japan. He is credited with seven hundred thousand converts — but not without controversy: he was intolerant of Oriental religions, urged the Portuguese king to institute the Inquisition in Goa, and used government pressure to convert people. In spite of the controversies, he was a superb organizer and pioneer in the use of common languages in mission work.

Zinzendorf, Nikolaus Ludwig von (1700–1760) — Contemplative

Passionate personal devotion to Christ marked the life of Count Zinzendorf. Relatives urged him to go into public service in Dresden (Germany), yet he preferred to cultivate "heart religion"; so he opened his home to anyone seeking spiritual guidance. Buying a large estate — that included the village of Berthelsdorf — he appointed a friend to the pastorate, and this opened the door to his life's work. When asked to give the remnants of the *Unitas Fratrum* (or Moravians) sanctuary on the estate, he let them found a village, Herrnhut. Under his leadership Herrnhut became a center of Pietism. To avoid trouble with the authorities, he became a Lutheran pastor, but the movement he sponsored ultimately challenged the nominal faith of German Lutheranism.

Zwingli, Huldrych (1484–1531)—Evangelical

Probably the third most important figure in the Protestant Reformation (following Martin Luther and John Calvin), Huldrych Zwingli came under the influence of humanist Desiderius Erasmus's teaching. He agreed with the other reformers on many issues, including salvation by faith, the Bible as the sole authority for the Church, and the priesthood of all believers. But he disagreed with them on the Eucharist and was more concerned for the "renaissance of Christendom" than for individual salvation. As he studied and came under Augustinian and biblical influence, Zwingli modified some of his teachings, which were being spread through much of German-speaking Switzerland. According to church historian Geoffrey Bromiley, Zwingli's reform alternative, though more radical than Martin Luther's, was adopted by Calvin in Geneva and influenced the development of Reformed and Presbyterian polity and theology.

Endnotes

Chapter 1

1. I am well aware of the various "quests for the historical Jesus"—especially the three rounds of "quest" studies that have gone on in the twentieth century. These studies are clearly uneven: some reflect serious scholarship, others reflect philosophical presuppositions that are firmly anti-Christian, and still others merely reflect deep longings for notoriety. Still, I am glad for any light that these studies can shed on the history and sociology of first-century Judaism and on how the four Gospels came to be written. For the most part, however, I find that these "quest" studies ignore the issue that the Gospel writers themselves viewed as central—namely, our living as Jesus himself lived.

2. For an elaboration of this line of thinking see Donald B. Kraybill's *The Upside-Down Kingdom* (Scottdale, PA: Herald, 1978), especially chaps. 2–4.

3. The concept of the Hebrew Year of Jubilee is found in Leviticus 25. To understand the theological and exegetical background for the conviction that Jesus was proclaiming the inauguration of a perpetual Jubilee, I turn you to two sources: André Trocmé, *Jesus and the Nonviolent Revolution* (Scottdale, PA: Herald, 1973), and John Howard Yoder, *The Politics of Jesus* (Grand Rapids, MI: Eerdmans, 1972).

4. See Ephesians 2:8–10. There is an entire theology of the cross behind this—a theology of redemption and justification and reconciliation. But that theology comes after the Christ event. I am seeking here to describe Jesus' own proclamation of the good news of the gospel.

Chapter 2

1. Athanasius, *The Life of Antony and The Letter to Marcellinus*, in *The Classics of Western Spirituality*, trans. and intro. Robert C. Gregg (New York: Paulist, 1980), p. 33. Whenever the name "Antony" is used in the text

I have substituted the Latin spelling "Antonius" in the hopes of keeping you, the reader, guessing a bit as to who I am writing about. Of course, if you have checked these endnotes, you already know, and the ruse is up!

2. Athanasius, *The Life of Antony*, pp. 33–35.

3. Athanasius, *The Life of Antony*, pp. 37–39.

4. Other disciplines engaged in—sleeping on the ground, rough clothing, etc.—involved excesses unnecessary for the task of training in righteousness.

5. Athanasius, *The Life of Antony*, p. 81.

6. Athanasius, *The Life of Antony*, pp. 80–81.

7. Athanasius, *The Life of Antony*, p. 66.

8. Athanasius, *The Life of Antony*, pp. 66, 89.

9. Athanasius, *The Life of Antony*, p. 77.

10. Athanasius, *The Life of Antony*, p. 74.

11. Athanasius, *The Life of Antony*, p. 73.

12. Athanasius, *The Life of Antony*, pp. 83–84.

13. Athanasius, *The Life of Antony*, pp. 84–89.

14. Athanasius, *The Life of Antony*, p. 64.

15. Athanasius, *The Life of Antony*, p. 94.

16. Everett F. Harrison, *Jesus and His Contemporaries* (Grand Rapids, MI: Baker, 1949), p. 242.

17. I am well aware of the scholarly debates over the authorship of the Gospel of John, the Epistles that bear his name, and the book of Revelation. These are important issues in other contexts. Here, however, our only concern is to illustrate the contemplative life as a model for our living. In doing so I am following the record of church tradition that the Apostle John is the author of each of these writings.

18. A.H.N. Green-Armytage, *John Who Saw: A Layman's Essay on the Authorship of the Fourth Gospel* (London: Faber & Faber, 1952), p. 45.

19. Green-Armytage, *John Who Saw*, p. 47.

20. There are large and complicated debates over the identification of "the disciple whom Jesus loved." For the sake of this study I am following the view secured in church history by Irenaeus and others who identified this person as the Apostle John. If you want to look at alternative positions, I recommend three books: *The Beloved Disciple: Whose Witness Validates the Gospel of John?* by James H. Charlesworth (Valley Forge, PA: Trinity, 1995); *The Beloved Disciple: His Name, His Story, His Thought,* by Vernard Eller (Grand Rapids, MI: Eerdmans, 1987); and *The Secret Identity of the Beloved Disciple,* by Joseph A. Grassi (New York: Paulist, 1992). The book that in my opinion gives the best overall discussion of the Johannine issue is *John, the*

Son of Zebedee: The Life of a Legend, by R. Alan Culpepper (Columbia, SC: University of South Carolina Press, 1994).

The contemporary wonderings about whether these passages might be referring to a homosexual relationship are a commentary on modern culture, not on the biblical passages.

21. We can reasonably assume, from the two Greek words used in verses 23 and 25, that John bolted upright when Jesus announced that someone would betray him. In verse 23 the disciple "was reclining" on Jesus breast. Verse 25 reads literally, "falling back" on Jesus breast, which gives the clear impression that he had risen. We can further assume that John said nothing of what he had learned about Judas from the fact that the other disciples were left guessing as to why Judas left the room (John 13:27–30).

22. Harrison, *Jesus and His Contemporaries,* p. 249.

23. I am developing only one of the many themes in John's writings. All of the themes in his writings are multilayered, which helps explain why he has been called John the Theologian. The three most prominent themes in John could be gathered around the key words *light, life,* and *love.*

24. John also had other reasons for insisting on the confession "Jesus Christ has come in the flesh." Most specifically, he was concerned about the teachings of Gnosticism (with its dualism of spirit and flesh), which had already made inroads into the early Christian communities.

25. A. T. Robertson, *Epochs in the Life of the Apostle John* (New York: Revell, 1935), p. 21. Irenaeus expressly states that John spent his later years in Ephesus. This Irenaeus tradition is followed by Apollonius, Polycrates, Clement of Alexandria, Origen, Tertullian, Eusebius, and Jerome.

26. Jerome, *Commentary on Galatians,* 6.10 (J. Migne, *Patroligia latina* 26:462), trans. E. Glenn Hinson, as cited in Culpepper, *John, the Son of Zebedee,* p. 165. Jerome is the source of this story, though he obviously received it from others. The famous text reads: "The blessed evangelist John, when he delayed at Ephesus up to the highest old age and could scarcely be carried to church in the hands of disciples and was not able to put together a statement of several words, used to offer in different sayings nothing but: 'Little children, love one another.' At last the disciples and brethren who were present, tired of the fact that they always heard the same thing, said, 'Teacher, why do you always say this?' John made a worthy response: 'Because it was the Lord's precept, and if it alone is done, it is enough.'"

27. Karen A. Norton, *Frank C. Laubach: One Burning Heart: A Biography of Frank C. Laubach* (Syracuse NY: Laubach Literacy International, 1990), p. 11.

28. Frank C. Laubach, *Thirty Years with the Silent Billion: Adventuring in Literacy* (Old Tappan, NJ: Revell, 1960), pp. 26–28.

29. Frank C. Laubach, *Letters by a Modern Mystic* (Syracuse, NY: New Readers Press, 1979), pp. 23–24.

30. Laubach, *Letters by a Modern Mystic*, p. 38.

31. Laubach, *Letters by a Modern Mystic*, p. 25.

32. Laubach, *Letters by a Modern Mystic*, pp. 18–19.

33. Frank C. Laubach, *Learning the Vocabulary of God: A Spiritual Diary* (Nashville, TN: The Upper Room, 1956), p. 5.

34. Laubach, *Learning the Vocabulary of God*, pp. 22–23.

35. Laubach, *Learning the Vocabulary of God*, p. 20.

36. Laubach, *Learning the Vocabulary of God*, p. 36.

37. Laubach, *Learning the Vocabulary of God*, p. 47.

38. Laubach, *Learning the Vocabulary of God*, p. 62.

39. Laubach, *Learning the Vocabulary of God*, p. 62.

40. Norton, *Frank C. Laubach*, p. 15.

41. Laubach, *Thirty Years with the Silent Billion*, pp. 195–200.

42. Laubach, *Learning the Vocabulary of God*, p. 9.

43. These phrases are taken from many sources, including John of the Cross, Blaise Pascal, and Richard Rolle.

44. *The Life: The Collected Works of St. Teresa*, vol. 1, trans. Kieran Kavanaugh and Otilio Rodriquez (Washington, DC: ICS Publications, 1976), chap. 8, no. 5, p. 67, as cited in Thomas Dubay, *Fire Within: St. Teresa of Avila, St. John of the Cross, and the Gospel—On Prayer* (San Francisco: Ignatius, 1989), p. 58.

45. Those who have read the great masters of contemplative prayer will recognize that I am describing in my own way the ancient triad of illumination, purgation, and union. Some of the items in this list were suggested to me by Thomas Dubay in his book *Fire Within*. This book is a good resource for a full discussion of these matters, especially his chapter entitled "What is Contemplation?"

46. As quoted in Dubay, *Fire Within*, p. 61.

47. As quoted in Dubay, *Fire Within*, p. 62.

48. As quoted in Dubay, *Fire Within*, p. 62.

49. *Thomas Merton: Spiritual Master*, ed. Lawrence Cunningham (New York: Paulist, 1992), p. 426.

50. *Sing Joyfully* (Carol Stream, IL: Tabernacle Publishing, 1989), no. 409.

51. *The Art of Prayer*, comp. Igumen Chariton of Valamo, trans. E. Kadloubovsky and E. M. Palmer (London: Faber & Faber, 1966), p. 51, as cited

in *The Lord of the Journey: A Reader in Christian Spirituality*, ed. and comp. Roger Pooley and Philip Seddon (San Francisco: Collins Liturgical, 1986), p. 225.

52. Brother Lawrence, *The Practice of the Presence of God*, trans. E. M. Blaiklock (London: Hodder & Stoughton), p. 44.

53. I am not referring here to the monastic vocations, for in them the monks and nuns are often more redemptively engaged in the world than many of us. No, I am dealing rather with the notion that says, for example, that praying about sexism absolves me from dealing with the specific issues of gender discrimination at the office.

54. The phrase "consuming asceticism" is Dallas Willard's, and this issue is discussed at length in his book *The Spirit of the Disciplines* (San Francisco: Harper & Row, 1988). See especially his chapter "History and Meaning of the Disciplines."

55. Will Durant, *The Age of Faith*, vol. IV of *The Story of Civilization: A History of Medieval Civilization from Constantine to Dante—A.D. 325–1300* (New York: Simon & Schuster, 1950), p. 60.

56. Willard, *The Spirit of the Disciplines*, pp. 142–143.

57. Thomas Vincent, *The Shorter Catechism of the Westminster Assembly Explained and Proved from Scripture* (Aylesbury, UK: The Banner of Truth Trust, 1980), p. 1.

58. "The Inner Experience," *Cistercian Studies* 19 (1984), p. 145f, as cited by M. Basil Pennington, "The Call to Contemplation," *Weavings* (May/June 1996), p. 34.

CHAPTER 3

1. Charles Edward White, "Phoebe Palmer and the Development of Pentecostal Pneumatology," *Wesleyan Theological Journal* (23:1987), pp. 198–212.

2. *Phoebe Palmer: Selected Writings*, ed. Thomas C. Oden (New York: Paulist, 1988), p. 99

3. *Phoebe Palmer: Selected Writings*, pp. 99–100.

4. John Wesley, *A Plain Account of Christian Perfection* (London: Epworth, 1952), p. 52.

5. Charles Edward White, *The Beauty of Holiness: Phoebe Palmer as Theologian, Revivalist, Feminist, and Humanitarian* (Grand Rapids, MI: Zondervan, 1986), p. 15.

6. *Phoebe Palmer: Selected Writings*, p. 115.

7. In this teaching Phoebe amended Wesley's theology regarding the "witness of the Spirit." Wesley had stressed this as a subjective experience of an inner witness of the Spirit. Phoebe objectified the witness of the Spirit, teaching that assurance of "entire sanctification" derived from the objective word of Scripture, and that seeking a subjective inner witness of the Spirit was to question God and thus dishonor him. Her concern was a practical one: she did not want believers to suffer needlessly, waiting—as she had—for signs of assurance that were unnecessary.

8. Melvin E. Dieter, "The Development of Nineteenth Century Holiness: The Historical Milieu," *Wesleyan Theological Journal* (20:1985), pp. 61–77.

9. It is generally recognized that the modern Pentecostal doctrine of the Holy Spirit has its roots in the thought of John Wesley. Many have credited Charles Finney and his friends at Oberlin College with the shifts in Wesley's teaching that facilitated the emergence of Pentecostal pneumatology. However, essential elements of the Pentecostal teaching are missing in Finney's formulations: in particular, the strong emphasis on power, the initiatory nature of sanctification, and the simple three-step process for attaining sanctification. This has led recent scholarship to turn to the work and writings of Phoebe Palmer (who stressed all three elements) to explain the transition from Wesleyan to Pentecostal pneumatology.

10. *The Promise of the Father* is the first extensive defense of women testifying publicly in the church. It has been recognized as the prototypical exegetical-historical defense of women in ministry. In order to extend the message of this book, Phoebe later edited it down into a slender booklet entitled *Tongue of Fire on the Daughters of the Lord*. The entire text of that work can be found in *Phoebe Palmer: Selected Writings*, pp. 31–56.

11. *Phoebe Palmer: Selected Writings*, p. 42.

12. White, *The Beauty of Holiness*, pp. 67–90.

13. *Phoebe Palmer: Selected Writings*, pp. 1–2.

14. The meaning of "brothers of Jesus" is disputed. There are three major interpretations: (1) The word means "cousins." This position was championed by Jerome and is the officially recognized view of the Roman Catholic Church. (2) The four "brothers" were children of Joseph by a former wife. This is the explanation held by the Greek Orthodox Church and certain Protestant groups. (3) "Brothers" refers to Joseph and Mary's four boys born after the birth of Jesus. James, Joses, Judas, and Simon are named, while the "sisters" remain unnamed (Mark 6:3, Matt. 13:55). This is the majority interpretation among Protestants and the position I am taking here.

The question of the authorship of the New Testament book of James is also hotly debated. Dr. James B. Adamson, in *James: The Man and His Message* (Grand Rapids, MI: Eerdmans, 1989), reviews all the relevant data in a scholarly and quite readable manner. His arguments are, for me, quite convincing, and he concludes that "James the Just," the leader of the Jerusalem church, was indeed the author of the Epistle that bears his name. For alternate interpretations see W. G. Kümmel, *Introduction to the New Testament*, trans. Howard Clark Kee (Nashville, TN: Abingdon, 1975), and A. H. McNeile, *Introduction to the Study of the New Testament* (Oxford: Clarendon, 1953).

15. Eusebius, *Ecclesiastical History*, vol. 1, trans. Kirsopp Lake, the Loeb Classical Library (Cambridge, MA: Harvard University Press, 1965), p. 171 (II.23.3–9). See also Kent Hughes, *James: Faith that Works* (Wheaton, IL: Crossway, 1991), p. 16.

16. The conspiracy group of which Bonhoeffer was a part had made two earlier assassination attempts on Hitler. On 13 March 1943 a bomb was planted on Hitler's plane, but the fuse failed to ignite. Then on 21 March 1943 one of the conspirators armed himself with a bomb and attempted to get close enough to Hitler, who was scheduled for a thirty-minute walk-through of a war museum, to detonate the Führer as well as himself. But Hitler was uninterested in the museum and rushed through in ten minutes, leaving before the armed conspirator could get near him. Interestingly, Bonhoeffer's arrest came not from the assassination attempts (which had remained undetected), but from a daring and successful initiative to smuggle a small group of Jews out of Germany.

17. Translated from *Widerstand und Ergebung*, pp. 403–4, as cited in *A Testament to Freedom: The Essential Writings of Dietrich Bonhoeffer*, ed. Geffrey B. Kelly and F. Burton Nelson (San Francisco: HarperSanFrancisco, 1990), pp. 542–43.

18. Dietrich Bonhoeffer, *Gesammelte Schriften, I*, 2nd ed. (Munich: Kaiser Verlag, 1958–74), as cited in *A Testament to Freedom*, p. 25.

19. Dietrich Bonhoeffer, *The Cost of Discipleship*, trans. R. H. Fuller (New York: Macmillan, 1963), p. 47.

20. Dietrich Bonhoeffer, *Letters and Papers from Prison* (London: Collins/ Fontana, 1953), p. 173.

21. Dietrich Bonhoeffer, *Letters and Papers from Prison*, enlarged ed., ed. Eberhard Bethge, trans. R. H. Fuller, John Bowden, et al. (New York: Macmillan, 1971), pp. 361–62.

22. Bonhoeffer, *Letters and Papers from Prison*, p. 11.

23. A *Testament to Freedom*, p. xi.

24. Albrecht Schoenherr, "Dietrich Bonhoeffer: The Message of a Life," *Christian Century* (27 Nov. 1985), p. 1091.

25. Eberhard Bethge, *Dietrich Bonhoeffer: Man of Vision, Man of Courage*, ed. Edwin H. Robertson, trans. Eric Mosbacher et al. (New York: Harper & Row, 1970), p. 164.

26. Dietrich Bonhoeffer, *Christ the Center*, trans. Edwin H. Robertson (New York: Harper & Row, 1960), pp. 62–65.

27. Bonhoeffer, *Christ the Center*, pp. 35–36.

28. More recently some scholars have called into question certain aspects of Bonhoeffer's Christology. Those wanting to explore this issue further might consider Richard Weikart's book *The Myth of Bonhoeffer: Is His Theology Evangelical?* (Bethesda, MD: International Scholars, 1997) and Bruce Demarest's essay "Devotion, Doctrine, and Duty in Dietrich Bonhoeffer" (*Bibliotheca Sacra* [Oct.–Dec. 1991]).

29. Dietrich Bonhoeffer, *Gesammelte Schriften, III*, 2nd ed. (Munich: Kaiser Verlag, 1965–69), pp. 24f., as cited in Bethge, *Dietrich Bonhoeffer*, p. 155.

30. Bonhoeffer, *The Cost of Discipleship*, pp. 45, 47.

31. Bonhoeffer, *The Cost of Discipleship*, p. 47.

32. Bethge, *Dietrich Bonhoeffer*, p. 360.

33. Bonhoeffer, *Letters and Papers from Prison*, enlarged ed., pp. 275–76.

34. In Bonhoeffer's speech at an ecumenical conference in Fano, Italy, in 1934 he rejected all human means of security and called for a Christian council of all churches to reject war. Even so, he was drawn into the resistance movement. One of his students, Albrecht Schoenherr, said that Bonhoeffer explained his participation in the resistance by this analogy: "If a drunken driver drives into a crowd, what is the task of the Christian and the church? To run along behind to bury the dead and bind up the wounded? Or isn't it, if possible, to get the driver out of the driver's seat" ("Dietrich Bonhoeffer," *Christian Century*, p. 1092).

35. Bethge, *Dietrich Bonhoeffer*, p. 154.

36. Bonhoeffer, *Gesammelte Schriften, III*, p. 25, as cited in Bethge, *Dietrich Bonhoeffer*, p. 380.

37. By *formation* Bonhoeffer meant a total identity with Christ. He felt keenly that the Church in his day had become triumphalist and avoided the scandal of Christ's humiliation (Bonhoeffer, *The Cost of Discipleship*, p. 341). Also see Bonhoeffer, *Letters and Papers from Prison*, enlarged ed., pp.

285–87; Bonhoeffer, *The Cost of Discipleship*, pp. 340–42; and Dietrich Bonhoeffer, *Ethics*, trans. Neville Horton Smith, rearranged ed. (New York: Macmillan, 1965), pp. 81–83.

38. *The Way to Freedom: Letters, Lectures, and Notes, 1935–1939: The Collected Works of Dietrich Bonhoeffer*, vol. II, ed. Edwin H. Robertson, trans. Edwin H. Robertson and John Bowden (New York: Harper & Row, 1966), p. 246.

39. Bonhoeffer, *Letters and Papers from Prison*, enlarged ed., pp. 217–18. The German title of *Letters and Papers from Prison* is *Widerstand und Ergebung* ("Resistance and Submission").

40. Bonhoeffer felt that this book was his major contribution to theology. At one point he wrote, "I sometimes feel as if my life were more or less over, and as if all I had to do now were to finish my *Ethics*" (Bonhoeffer, *Letters and Papers from Prison*, enlarged ed., p. 163). He now had to write on the run, as it were, as the Nazi suspicions of him were growing. Bonhoeffer was not able to finish this work, though enough was done that others were able to complete it. And in one sense—through his life and death—he did indeed finish it.

41. Bonhoeffer, *Ethics*, p. 90.

42. Bonhoeffer, *Letters and Papers from Prison*, enlarged ed., pp. 13–17. In fairness it should be noted that right at this point some have accused Bonhoeffer of advocating a situationalism lacking in timeless ethical norms.

43. Bonhoeffer, *Ethics*, pp. 110–19.

44. At this point in the talk Bonhoeffer was cut off the air in what may have been the Third Reich's first governmental action against free speech. Concerned that the talk might be distorted into an endorsement of the Führer, he privately circulated the entire script and presented a lecture incorporating the element missing from the radio broadcast (Bethge, *Dietrich Bonhoeffer*, pp. 193–94).

45. Dietrich Bonhoeffer, *No Rusty Swords: Letters, Lectures and Notes, 1939–1945*, ed. Edwin H. Robertson, trans. John Bowden and Eberhard Bethge (London: Collins, 1970; Cleveland, OH: Collins-World, 1977), pp. 224–26.

46. *Gesammelte Schriften, IV*, pp. 130–36, as cited in Bethge, *Dietrich Bonhoeffer*, p. 228.

47. Bonhoeffer, *No Rusty Swords*, pp. 240–42.

48. That challenge was taken up some time later with the Barman Confession under the leadership of Karl Barth.

49. Bonhoeffer, *Letters and Papers from Prison*, enlarged ed., pp. 380–83.

50. Bonhoeffer, *Letters and Papers from Prison*, enlarged ed., pp. 361–62.

51. Bonhoeffer, *Letters and Papers from Prison*, enlarged ed., pp. 382–83. Even so, much of Bonhoeffer's thinking on this matter remained in question form. "How can Christ become the Lord of the religionless?" "Are there religionless Christians?" "What do a church, a community, a sermon, a liturgy, a Christian life mean in a religionless world?" "What is the place of worship and prayer in a religionless situation?" "How do we speak of God—without religion, i.e., without the temporally conditioned presuppositions of metaphysics, inwardness, and so on?" And so forth . . . (Bonhoeffer, *Letters and Papers from Prison*, enlarged ed., pp. 280–81).

If you would like to study a Christian leader who devoted his entire ministry to developing one form of "religionless Christianity," I encourage you to consider the life and writings of George Fox, founder of the Society of Friends, or Quakers. Good starting places are his *Journal* and *Epistles*.

52. C. S. Lewis, *Mere Christianity* (New York: Macmillan, 1952), p. 160.

53. Lewis, *Mere Christianity*, p. 158.

54. John Flavel, *Keeping the Heart* (Grand Rapids, MI: Sovereign Grace Publishers, 1971), pp. 5, 12.

55. Thomas Merton, *Life and Holiness* (Garden City, NY: Doubleday/Image, 1964), p. 57.

56. The doctrine of "imputed righteousness," when rightly understood, assumes the ongoing work of sanctifying grace.

57. Lewis, *Mere Christianity*, pp. 160–61.

58. Lewis, *Mere Christianity*, p. 161. There are groups within the Holiness Tradition that would argue for complete transformation in this life. This is usually associated with what is called "the doctrine of sinless perfection."

59. Various names are given to these powerful experiences, and whole theologies have grown up around them. Often terms such as "the baptism in the Holy Spirit," "the filling of the Holy Spirit," "second work of grace," "entire sanctification," "victorious living," and many others are used. Great debates have raged over these terms and the ecstatic experiences that should (or should not) accompany them. While I in no way want to minimize the importance of these debates, my concern here is to show how these experiences reflect a common reality. God, in sovereign grace, will at times move individuals (and even whole groups) dramatically forward in the spiritual life. Frequently these experiences have a substantial, even hypostatic, effect on character formation.

60. Francis de Sales, *An Introduction to the Devout Life*, trans. and ed. John K. Ryan (New York: Doubleday, 1972), pp. 43–44.

61. Pelagius founded a school of thought that rejected the doctrine of original sin and stressed our inherent capacity for good. To Pelagius's credit his teaching arose out of a deep concern over the moral laxity he saw in the Christians at Rome. He urged the Church to holy living and feared that Augustine's view of divine grace (which stressed our human inability to earn salvation) contributed to this laxity. Augustine responded by denouncing the teachings of Pelagius, especially on three points that he felt were dangerously heretical: (1) the denial of original sin, (2) the belief that justifying grace is not given freely, and (3) the teaching that after baptism sinless perfection is possible. Like all such matters, this debate was complicated by diverse political considerations and personalities, especially one rather strident colleague of Pelagius named Celestius. In the end Pelagius's teaching was condemned by two African councils in A.D. 416. A modified form of his views, known as semi-Pelagianism, lingered on for many years, and echoes of it can be detected throughout church history (and even in some modern holiness groups).

62. Anthony Bloom, *God and Man* (New York: Paulist, 1971), p. 93. See also *The Lord of the Journey: A Reader in Christian Spirituality*, ed. and comp. Roger Pooley and Philip Seddon (London: Collins, 1986), p. 301.

CHAPTER 4

1. Placid Hermann, *XIIIth Century Chronicles* (Chicago: Franciscan Herald Press, 1961), as cited in *St. Francis of Assisi: Writings and Early Biographies: English Omnibus of the Sources for the Life of St. Francis*, ed. Marion H. Habig (Chicago: Franciscan Herald Press, 1973), p. 230.

2. *St. Francis of Assisi*, p. 643.

3. Brother Ugolino di Monte Santa Maria, *The Little Flowers of St. Francis*, trans. Raphael Brown (New York: Doubleday/Image, 1958), pp. 72–74.

4. Brother Ugolino, *The Little Flowers*, pp. 88–91. This was far more than a nice story about taming a wolf. It was a parable about the shalom of God coming between the created world, its creatures, humankind, and the Creator. Or, to use a concept from the Middle Ages, it sought to teach *cortesia*. We use the word "courtesy" to mean manners, but originally it spoke of the nobility, behavior, and etiquette of the knight. It was, for example, the preeminent characteristic of the knight in Chaucer's *Canterbury Tales*. *Cortesia* was a way of seeing and acting toward others. It meant honoring others, rec-

ognizing and respecting their personhood. It encompassed harmonious relationship, loving care, proper respect. Francis, who knew the courtly literature well, deepened and extended the concept of *cortesia* beyond human relationships to all of creation, including inanimate creation—sun and moon, wind and fire, water and earth.

5. *St. Francis of Assisi*, p. 553.

6. *St. Francis of Assisi*, p. 554.

7. *St. Francis of Assisi*, p. 807.

8. Francis of Assisi, *The Prayers of St. Francis*, trans. Ignatius Brady (Ann Arbor, MI: Servant, 1987), p. 119, lines 5ff. In the interest of space I have given only four stanzas. The entire prayer contains eighteen stanzas, all of which are well worth prayerful reading and meditation. Perhaps the best rendition of the prayer for study is found in *Francis and Clare: The Complete Works*, trans. Regis J. Armstrong and Ignatius C. Brady, *The Classics of Western Spirituality* series (New York: Paulist, 1982), pp. 151–52.

9. *St Francis of Assisi*, pp. 289–90.

10. *St. Francis of Assisi*, pp. 299–301. Many other stories of Francis's life and the circumstances surrounding his death are readily available to you, so I will not go into them here. I recommend to you Thomas of Celano's *First Life and Second Life of St. Francis* (Chicago: Franciscan Herald Press, 1963), St. Bonaventure's *Major Life of St. Francis* in *St. Francis of Assisi* (pp. 627–787), Brother Ugolino's *The Little Flowers of St. Francis*, and any number of the popular biographies of St. Francis.

11. See Galatians 1:17 and Acts 9:23–25. A fish basket was a large, shapeless sack that could fold around a person so that no casual observer would notice in the darkness that it hid a man.

12. The Book of Acts is the primary text. Luke, as a good historian, gives many interesting and suggestive details for each of the three missionary journeys. In the first journey Paul and Barnabas are commissioned by the leaders at Antioch and sent out to evangelize westward, and upon their return they report to the church "all that God had done with them," noting how God had opened a door of faith for the Gentiles (Acts 13:1–14:28). On the second journey Paul and Silas travel through Asia Minor and eastern Greece, evangelizing (Acts 15:36–18:22). On the third journey Paul re-traverses the area previously covered with Silas, at some point taking Luke as a companion (Acts 18:23–21:20). If you want to fill in the history and geography of the times and places, I heartily recommend three books: *St. Paul the Traveller and Roman Citizen*, by W. M. Ramsay (New York: Putnam, 1896), *The Apostle: A Life of Paul*, by John Pollock (New York: Doubleday, 1969), and

Paul: Apostle of the Heart Set Free, by F. F. Bruce (Grand Rapids, MI: Eerd-mans, 1977).

13. As a Roman citizen the Apostle Paul had three names—a *praenomen,* a *nomen gentile,* and a *cognomen.* Although the first two have been lost to history, his Roman *cognomen,* Paullus or Paul, is used here for the first time by Luke. From this point on "Paul" is the preferred designation, perhaps to underscore his increasing shift in ministry efforts from Hebrew to Gentile peoples.

14. As quoted in F. F. Bruce, *The Book of Acts,* in *The International Commentary on the New Testament* series (Grand Rapids, MI: Eerdmans, 1954), p. 265. Luke never uses words loosely, so we can assume from the phrase "a mist and darkness came over him" that Elymas did not go stone blind in a second: light faded first before total blindness set in. This detail could only have been provided by Elymas himself—presumably recovered and, at a minimum, friendly to the Christian historian.

15. We can reasonably surmise that Luke was a member of the party at Philippi, because this is one of the "we" passages in Acts.

16. That Lydia—a dealer in purple cloth (Acts 16:14)—was the head of the household is an interesting detail. We are not told the reasons behind this fact, but whatever they were, we can be certain that she was a most capable woman.

17. For many years I searched for further details of Seymour's story and learned from each of the various sources I found. But these sources were frustratingly fragmented and at times contradictory. Then I discovered the unpublished Ph.D. dissertation of Douglas J. Nelson, *For Such a Time as This: The Story of Bishop William J. Seymour and the Azusa Street Revival* (Birmingham, UK: University of Birmingham, 1981). The research in this 363-page work far exceeds anything ever done on Seymour and must be considered the standard on his life and ministry. Thus, while I have consulted other sources, I am deeply indebted to and dependent upon Nelson's work (even to the extent of some of his conclusions, which I believe are exactly on the mark). I have told Seymour's story in more detail than the others in this book because reliable sources about his life are simply not available to people today.

18. During Seymour's growing up years, black Americans endured unspeakable hostility and atrocities. To illustrate, in the spring of 1873, 150 to 200 black men were massacred about a hundred miles northwest of Centerville. On May 10 *Harper's Weekly* reported, "A general feeling of insecurity prevails among the colored people of Louisiana, and hundreds are seek-

ing safety in the swamps and forests." From 1874 through 1900 over 2,500 persons were lynched or burned at the stake; virtually all were black residents of Mississippi, Alabama, Georgia, and Louisiana (Middleton Harris and others, *The Black Book* [New York: Random House, 1974], Carter G. Woodson, *The African Background Outlined* [New York: Negro University Press, 1973], p. 304, and John Hope Franklin, *From Slavery to Freedom: A History of Negro Americans*, 4th ed. [New York: Knopf, 1974], pp. 322–23, as cited in Nelson, *For Such a Time as This*, pp. 155–56).

19. Judging from Seymour's written sermons of 1906–1908, he attained an astonishing facility with both the English language and Christian theology. A book of these sermons has been published by Lukas Wegmann under the title *The Message of Bishop William J. Seymour* (Jackson, MS: Lukas J. Wegmann, 1992).

20. "The invisible institution" is a term coined by E. Franklin Frazier in *The Negro Church in America* (New York: Schocken, 1964). See also *The Black Church Since Frazier*, by C. Eric Lincoln (New York: Schocken, 1974).

21. The name "Evening Light Saints" derived from Zechariah 14:7: "[I]t shall come to pass, that at evening time it shall be light" (KJV). Seymour wrestled with his preaching call, and during this time of hesitation and turmoil he contracted the dreaded smallpox, which killed so many in those days. He survived the disease, though he was left with facial scarring and blindness in his left eye. He accepted those physical afflictions as stemming from his disobedience to the divine call and took ordination from the "saints." He wore a beard the rest of his life to cover his facial disfigurement, and the vision in his left eye remained impaired by a partial opaque covering ("Smallpox," *Chambers' Encyclopaedia: A Dictionary of Universal Knowledge*, new ed., 10 vols. [Philadelphia: Lippincott, 1906]; *Chambers' Encyclopaedia: The Illustrated: A Dictionary of Universal Knowledge*, new ed., ed. David Patrick and William Geddie [London and Edinburgh: W. & R. Chambers Ltd., 1925]; and interview with Mattie Cummings, as cited in Nelson, *For Such a Time as This*, p. 165).

22. In a Chicago hotel room Seymour related some of his prayer experiences to John G. Lake, the man who carried the Pentecostal fires to South Africa. Seymour told Lake, "Brother, such a hunger to have more of God was in my heart that I prayed for five hours a day for two and a half years. I got to Los Angeles, and when I got there the hunger was not less but more. I prayed, God, what can I do? And the Spirit said, Pray more. But Lord, I am praying five hours a day now. I increased my hours of prayer to seven, and

prayed on for a year and a half more. I prayed to God to give me the real Holy Ghost and fire with tongues and love and power of God like the Apostles had" (Wegmann, *The Message of Bishop William J. Seymour*, p. IX).

23. Lee had earlier received a vision in which Peter and John appeared to him, lifted their hands, began to shake under divine power, and spoke in other tongues. Lee believed that this vision was given to show him what happened when the Holy Spirit fell on people. The phrase "This is that" comes from Acts 2:16, where Peter equated the ecstatic experience of believers at Pentecost with fulfillment of ancient prophecy: "This is that which was spoken by the prophet Joel . . . " (Frank J. Ewart and W. E. Kidson, *The Phenomenon of Pentecost: A History of "The Latter Rain"* [Houston, TX: Herald, 1947], p. 38, as cited in Nelson, *For Such a Time as This*, p. 189).

24. It is moving to hear the story in Jennie Moore's own words: "For years before this wonderful experience came to us, we as a family, were seeking to know the fulness of God, and He was filling us with His presence until we could hardly contain the power. I had never seen a vision in my life, but one day as we prayed there passed before me three white cards, each with two names thereon, and but for fear I could have given them, as I saw every letter distinctly. On April 9, 1906, I was praising the Lord from the depths of my heart at home, and when the evening came and we attended the meeting the power of God fell and I was baptized in the Holy Ghost and fire, with the evidence of speaking in tongues. During the day I had told the Father that although I wanted to sing under the power I was willing to do whatever He willed, and at the meeting when the power came on me I was reminded of the three cards which had passed [before] me in the vision months ago. As I thought thereon and looked to God, it seemed as if a vessel broke within me and water surged up through my being, which when it reached my mouth came out in a torrent of speech in the languages which God had given me. I remembered the names on the cards: French, Spanish, Latin, Greek, Hebrew, Hindustani. . . . [T]he Spirit led me to the piano, where I played and sang under inspiration, although I had not learned to play. In these ways God is continuing to use me to His glory ever since that wonderful day" (*Apostolic Faith* [May 1907], p. 3, as cited in Nelson, *For Such a Time as This*, pp. 226–27).

25. Interview with Morton Asbery by Russell Chandler, *Los Angeles Times* (11 Jan. 1976), pp. 4, 22; Mother Emma Cotton, "Inside Story of the Outpouring of the Holy Spirit, Azusa Street, April, 1906," *Message of the Apostolic Faith* (vol. 1, no. 1, April 1939), p. 3; Zelma Argue, "Memories of Fifty Years Ago," *Pentecostal Evangel* (22 April 1956), pp. 6–7, 29, as cited in Nelson, *For Such a Time as This*, p. 191.

26. Nelson, *For Such a Time as This*, p. 192.

27. Frank Bartleman, *Azusa Street: The Roots of Modern-Day Pentecost* (Plainfield, NJ: Logos, 1980), p. 55.

28. Bartleman, *Azusa Street*, p. 54.

29. Leonard Lovett, *Black Holiness-Pentecostalism: Implications for Ethics and Social Transformation*, Ph.D. dissertation (Atlanta, GA: Emory University, 1978), p. 63, as cited in Nelson, *For Such a Time as This*, pp. 10, 37.

30. *Apostolic Faith* (Nov. 1906), p. 1, as cited in Nelson, *For Such a Time as This*, p. 199. More than one eyewitness thought of the manger in Bethlehem when they saw the humble surroundings at Azusa Street. One such witness, Rachel Sizelove, said that "as we entered the old building somehow I was touched by the presence of God. It was such a humble place with its low ceilings and rough floor. Cob webs were hanging in the windows and joist. As I looked around I thought of Jesus when He came to earth and was born in a manger. There was no place for Him in the inn. I thought of the fine church houses in the city of Los Angeles, but the Lord had chosen this humble spot to gather all nationalities" (Rachel A. Sizelove, "A Sparkling Fountain for the Whole Earth," *Word and Work* [June 1934], p. 11, as cited in Nelson, *For Such a Time as This*, p. 71).

31. *Apostolic Faith* (Sept. 1906), p. 3, and *Apostolic Faith* (Dec. 1906), p. 1, as cited in Nelson, *For Such a Time as This*, p. 197.

32. The stories of people overcoming the color line are endlessly moving. For example, G. B. Cashwell, a holiness leader from North Carolina, traveled three thousand miles to see the Azusa Mission for himself. At first he recoiled from the black leadership, cringing inwardly when a young black man touched him while praying for him. Yet after several services he underwent a change of heart, humbled himself, and asked Seymour to pray for him. He returned home to become the "Apostle of Pentecost" to the South (*Apostolic Faith* [Dec. 1906], p. 3; Vinson Synan, *Aspects of Pentecostal Charismatic Origins* [Plainfield, NJ: Logos, 1975], pp. 122–35, as cited in Nelson, *For Such a Time as This*, p. 198). Another leader wrote, "I being southern born, thought it a miracle that I could sit in a service by a colored saint of God and worship, or eat at a great camp table and forget I was eating beside a colored saint, but in spirit and truth God was worshipped in love and harmony" (Fred J. Foster, *Think It Not Strange* [St. Louis, MO: Pentecostal Publishing House, 1965], p. 74, as cited in Nelson, *For Such a Time as This*, p. 198).

33. W. E. Burghardt DuBois, *The Souls of Black Folk: Essays and Sketches* (Greenwich, CT: Fawcett, 1961), p. 23.

34. *Apostolic Faith* (Nov. 1906), p. 1, as cited in Nelson, *For Such a Time as This*, p. 199.

35. Wayne E. Warner, "The Miracle of Azusa," *Charisma & Christian Life* (April 1996), p. 40.

36. *Apostolic Faith* (Sept. 1907), p. 3, as cited in Nelson, *For Such a Time as This*, pp. 197–98.

37. *Apostolic Faith* (June to Sept. 1907), p. 2; and *Apostolic Faith* (May 1908), p. 3, as cited in Nelson, *For Such a Time as This*, p. 205.

38. *Apostolic Faith* (June to Sept. 1907), p. 2, as cited in Nelson, *For Such a Time as This*, pp. 204–5; and *Apostolic Faith* (May 1908), p. 3, as cited in Nelson, *For Such a Time as This*, pp. 204–5.

39. B. F. Lawrence, *The Apostolic Faith Restored* (St. Louis, MO: Gospel Publications, 1916), p. 86; *Apostolic Faith* (June to Sept. 1907), p. 2, as cited in Nelson, *For Such a Time as This*, pp. 204–5.

40. Glenn A. Cook, *The Azusa Street Meeting: Some Highlights of This Outpouring* (Belvedere, CA: Glenn A. Cook, n.d.), as cited in Nelson, *For Such a Time as This*, p. 200.

41. *Apostolic Faith* (Feb. to Mar. 1907), p. 4, as cited in Nelson, *For Such a Time as This*, p. 62. Durham was to later turn against Seymour in a blatant effort to take control of the Mission.

42. Rachel A. Sizelove, "The Temple," *Word and Work* (May 1936), p. 2, as cited in Nelson, *For Such a Time as This*, p. 200.

43. Cook, *The Azusa Street Meeting*, p. 2, as cited in Nelson, *For Such a Time as This*, p. 225.

44. *The Light of Life Brought Triumph: A Brief Sketch of the Life and Labors of Florence L. (Mother) Crawford, 1872–1936* (Portland, OR: AF Publishing House, 1955), pp. 9–10, as cited in Nelson, *For Such a Time as This*, p. 200.

45. Vinson Synan, *Aspects of Pentecostal Charismatic Origins* (Plainfield, NJ: Logos, 1975), p. 110; Charles Shumway, "A Study of the 'Gift of Tongues,'" A.B. dissertation (Los Angeles: University of Southern California, 1914), p. 178; interview with Rev. Edward H. Smith; Bartleman, *Azusa Street*, p. 69; Cook, *The Azusa Street Meeting*, p. 2; as cited in Nelson, *For Such a Time as This*, p. 208.

46. Shumway, "A Study of the 'Gift of Tongues,'" pp. 178–79, as cited in Nelson, *For Such a Time as This*, p. 209. This reaction against "animalism" is a racist charge that condemned the African roots of American blacks. In an obvious reference to the Azusa meetings Parham himself later wrote, "I have seen meetings where all crowded around the altar, and laying across

one another like hogs, blacks and whites mingling; this should be enough to bring a blush of shame to devils, let alone equals, and yet all this was charged to the Holy Spirit" (Ithiel C. Clemmons, *Bishop C. H. Mason and the Roots of the Church of God in Christ* [Bakersfield, CA: Pneuma Life Publishing, 1996], pp. 47–48).

47. Mrs. Charles F. Parham, *The Life of Charles F. Parham, Founder of the Apostolic Faith Movement* (Birmingham, AL: Commercial Printing, 1930), pp. 83, 91–100, as cited in Nelson, *For Such a Time as This*, pp. 19–21, 209. One historian, noting Parham's Klan connection, says that he left the Azusa meetings because of their "disgusting similarity to Southern darkey camp meetings" (Leonard Lovett, "Black Origins of the Pentecostal Movement," in Synan, *Aspects of Pentecostal Charismatic Origins*, pp. 125–41, as cited in Nelson, *For Such a Time as This*, p. 21).

48. Shumway, "A Study of the 'Gift of Tongues,'" pp. 178–79; Parham, *Life*, p. 163; as cited in Nelson, *For Such a Time as This*, pp. 61, 210.

49. The separations were complicated by many factors, race being only one. After Parham, two additional divisions were especially crippling. Clara Lum, who oversaw the publication of *The Apostolic Faith*, opposed Seymour's marriage. (From C. H. Mason we learn that Seymour told him that Lum had privately made it clear that she had fallen in love with Seymour and wanted him to propose marriage to her. See Clemmons, *Bishop C. H. Mason*, p. 50.) She left for Portland, Oregon, taking with her the national and international mailing lists for the magazine. Denied this outlet, Seymour could not communicate with the thousands worldwide who looked to him and Azusa Street for leadership. The other separation was a doctrinal dispute with William Durham over "the finished work of Christ." In addition, it appears clear that Durham tried to usurp Seymour's leadership. Those who followed Durham's teaching eventually organized the Assemblies of God denomination in 1914. The separations of Parham, Lum, and Durham effectively ended Seymour's major role of leadership in the Pentecostal movement.

50. Nelson, *For Such a Time as This*, pp. 12–13.

51. William J. Seymour, *The Doctrines and Discipline of the Azusa Street Apostolic Faith Mission* (Los Angeles: n.p., 1915), pp. 8, 31, 40, 91, as cited in Nelson, *For Such a Time as This*, pp. 265–66.

52. Nelson, *For Such a Time as This*, p. 13.

53. *Apostolic Faith* (Nov. 1906), p. 1; interview with Frank Cummings, as cited in Nelson, *For Such a Time as This*, pp. 212–13.

54. These four principles are culled from chapter 7 of *What Shall This Man Do?* by Watchman Nee (Fort Washington, PA: Christian Literature Crusade, 1961). I also commend to you *Gifts and Graces: A Commentary on 1 Corinthians 12–14* by Arnold Bittlinger (Grand Rapids, MI: Eerdmans, 1967).

55. Jean-Pierre de Caussade, *The Sacrament of the Present Moment,* trans. Kitty Muggeridge (San Francisco: Harper & Row, 1982), p. 22.

56. Clemmons, *Bishop C. H. Mason,* p. 146.

CHAPTER 5

1. *The Journal and Essays of John Woolman,* ed. Amelia Mott Gummere (New York: Macmillan, c. 1922), p. 151.

2. *The Journal and Essays of John Woolman,* ed. Gummere, p. 161.

3. *The Journal and Essays of John Woolman,* ed. Gummere, p. 164.

4. *The Journal and Essays of John Woolman,* ed. Gummere, p. 167.

5. *The Journal and Essays of John Woolman,* ed. Gummere, pp. 180–81.

6. D. Elton Trueblood, *The People Called Quakers* (New York: Harper & Row, 1966), p. 162.

7. *The Journal and Essays of John Woolman,* ed. Gummere, p. 346.

8. Thomas E. Drake, "Cadwaler Morgan—Antislavery Quaker of the Welsh Tract," *Friends Intelligencer* (vol. 98, no. 36:1941), p. 576.

9. *The Journal of John Woolman,* ed. John G. Whittier (London: Headley Brothers, 1900), p. 13 of introduction.

10. As quoted in Rufus M. Jones, *The Quakers in the American Colonies* (New York: Norton, 1921), p. 517.

11. *The Journal and Essays of John Woolman,* ed. Gummere, p. 234.

12. Stephen Beauregard Weeks, *Southern Quakers and Slavery: A Study in Institutional History* (Baltimore, MD: Johns Hopkins Press, 1896), p. 222.

13. Weeks, *Southern Quakers,* pp. 223–25.

14. *The Friend: A Religious and Literary Journal* (vol. 1:1828), p. 384.

15. As quoted on the back cover and p. 3 of *The Journal and Major Essays of John Woolman,* ed. Phillips P. Moulton, A *Library of Christian Thought* series (New York: Oxford University Press, 1971).

16. As quoted on the back cover of *The Journal and Major Essays of John Woolman,* ed. Moulton.

17. *Collected Letters of S. T. Coleridge,* ed. E. L. Griggs (London: n.p., 1956), I, 302, as cited in *The Journal and Major Essays of John Woolman,* ed. Moulton, p. 3.

18. Trueblood, *The People Called Quakers*, p. 167.

19. This vision of justice and peace for all people swept across the face of the earth during this period. The worldwide revelation of this message is an actual, historical event. In Israel we find it in the pre-Exilic prophets (750–586 B.C.), Amos being the first. It is also found in India with the Upanishads (800–600 B.C.), Gautama, the Buddha (560–480 B.C.), and Mahavira (599–527 B.C.); in China with Confucius (551–479 B.C.) and Lao Tze (604–517 B.C.); and in Persia with Zarathushtra (660–583 B.C.).

20. I use the word innocent here rather than *righteous* because I think contextually it is a more appropriate translation of *saddiq*.

21. David Allan Hubbard, *Joel and Amos: An Introduction and Commentary, Tyndale Old Testament Commentaries* series, ed. D. J. Wiseman (Leicester, UK: Inter-Varsity, 1989), p. 142.

22. Again I am translating *saddiq* here as *innocent* rather than *righteous* (the latter being the preference of the New Revised Standard Version).

23. The New English Bible translates *sumim* in verse 12 *countless* ("countless sins"). This, I think, more accurately conveys the sense of Amos's concern that these were not just occasional violations, but a firm pattern of behavior aimed at thwarting justice.

24. Hubbard, *Joel and Amos*, p. 236.

25. Walter Brueggemann, *The Land* (Philadelphia: Fortress, 1977), p. 133.

26. The phrase "a living reproach" grew out of a conversation I had with Emilie and Henry William Griffin about Dorothy Day. I believe it was Bill who first employed the phrase, though Emilie wholeheartedly concurred in the assessment. Bill and Emilie are writers who live in New Orleans, Louisiana.

27. *The Long Loneliness: The Autobiography of Dorothy Day* (San Francisco: HarperSanFrancisco, 1980), pp. 33–34.

28. *The Long Loneliness*, p. 59.

29. *The Long Loneliness*, p. 65.

30. *The Long Loneliness*, pp. 78–79.

31. This, of course, was at a time when abortions were illegal, secretive affairs. In her book *The Eleventh Virgin*, an autobiography with a thin fictional veneer, the operation occurred in an apartment on the Upper East Side. A surgical instrument cut the child from the lining of her womb. For several hours there were painful contractions, one spasm every three minutes. Finally, a dead six-month-old fetus was born.

32. As quoted in Bridgid O'Shea Merriman, *Searching for Christ: The Spirituality of Dorothy Day (1897–1980)* (Ann Arbor, MI: University Microfilms International, 1989), p. 52.

33. *The Long Loneliness,* p. 87.

34. *The Long Loneliness,* p. 84.

35. *The Long Loneliness,* p. 84.

36. Francis Thompson, "The Hound of Heaven" (New York: McCracken, 1993).

37. *The Long Loneliness,* p. 84.

38. I am skipping over many moving events: her time as a nurse at Kings County Hospital, her sojourn in Europe, her work in Chicago with Robert Minor at *The Liberator,* her experiences in the French Quarter working with the *New Orleans Item,* and more. If you want to fill in the details, I recommend three sources: Dorothy's own autobiographical writings, especially *The Long Loneliness; Dorothy Day: A Radical Devotion,* by Robert Coles, *Radcliffe Biography* series (Reading, MA: Addison-Wesley, 1987); and *Love Is the Measure: A Biography of Dorothy Day,* by Jim Forest (New York: Paulist, 1986).

39. *The Long Loneliness,* pp. 113, 120.

40. *The Long Loneliness,* p. 135.

41. *The Long Loneliness,* p. 134.

42. *The Long Loneliness,* p. 136.

43. *The Long Loneliness,* pp. 136–37.

44. *The Long Loneliness,* p. 148.

45. Coles, *Dorothy Day,* p. 9.

46. *The Long Loneliness,* p. 159.

47. *The Long Loneliness,* p. 166, and Forest, *Love Is the Measure,* p. 75.

48. *The Long Loneliness,* p. 169.

49. Coles, *Dorothy Day,* p. 13.

50. *The Long Loneliness,* p. 220.

51. Peter Maurin's vision stands very much within the Catholic Christian tradition. Many of the monastic orders were founded with these very same values. Peter, then, was speaking of spiritual practices that had deep historical roots. His passion, however, was to take those practices, that way of living, out of a monastic setting and place it in the middle of urban society.

52. *The Long Loneliness,* p. 181.

53. Peter had wanted to call the paper *The Catholic Radical,* noting that the word *radical* comes from the Latin *radix,* meaning root—hence a paper that goes to the root of personal and social problems. Dorothy insisted that

the name must refer to the class of its readers rather than the attitude of its editors. As was often the case, Dorothy won the debate.

54. *The Long Loneliness*, p. 204.

55. *The Catholic Worker* (vol. 1, no. 1:1933), p. 4.

56. Peter Maurin, "Easy Essay," *The Catholic Worker* (vol. 1, no. 1:1933), p. 8.

57. "Explains CW Stand on Use of Force," *The Catholic Worker* (vol. 6, no. 4:1938), pp. 1, 4.

58. "We Continue Our Christian Pacifist Stand," *The Catholic Worker* (vol. 9, no. 3:1942), p. 1.

59. Coles, *Dorothy Day*, pp. 14–15.

60. *The Long Loneliness*, p. 234.

61. *The Long Loneliness*, p. 227.

62. As quoted in Forest, *Love Is the Measure*, p. 96.

63. *The Long Loneliness*, pp. 246–48.

64. Merriman, *Searching for Christ*, p. 234. This book, a Ph.D. dissertation, has an extensive section on the Lacouture Retreat Movement and the Catholic Worker participation in it. It details the theological controversy surrounding this movement—a controversy that hinged on an understanding of the relationship between nature and grace. Many ecclesiastical authorities were concerned over "the supposed rigors that the retreat introduced." Dorothy never felt competent to enter these theological debates, but she followed them closely in *The American Ecclesiastical Review* and continued to support the Lacouture Retreat Movement both in public and in private.

65. *The Long Loneliness*, pp. 250–51. In the fall of 1944 Dorothy took a prolonged private retreat, seeking to go deeper into spiritual realities than she could in the brief retreats. She intended the retreat to last one year, but after six months she was ready to return to the hectic community life she found so invigorating.

66. Coles, *Dorothy Day*, p. 16.

67. Forest, *Love Is the Measure*, p. 199.

68. Forest, *Love Is the Measure*, pp. 200–201.

69. Dag Hammarskjöld, *Markings*, trans. Leif Sjöberg and W. H. Auden (New York: Ballantine, 1993), p. 103.

70. Jesus is here drawing from two Hebrew traditions: Deuteronomy 6:5 and Leviticus 19:18.

71. I have written more extensively on these matters in my book *Freedom of Simplicity* (San Francisco: Harper & Row, 1981). The section here is a summation of that teaching.

72. See the article "The OT Term מִשְׁפָּט" in *Theological Dictionary of the New Testament* (Grand Rapids, MI: Eerdmans, 1975). Expanded information on the use of *mishpat* in the Hebrew Scriptures can be found in this excellent article.

73. William Wilberforce was a British statesman who labored tirelessly to abolish the slave trade in England. Aleksandr Solzhenitsyn (1918–) is a Russian writer whose book *The Gulag Archipelago* is a devastating critique of Stalin's totalitarianism.

74. See Donald Bloesch, *Essentials of Evangelical Theology*, vol. 1 (San Francisco: Harper & Row, 1978), p. xi.

75. As quoted by James M. Wall, "In Jeopardy," *Christian Century* (3 Dec. 1997), p. 1115.

76. The issue was more complicated than I have space for here. To explore that historical question further, I would direct you to Jack D. Marietta, *The Reformation of American Quakerism, 1748–1783* (Philadelphia: University of Pennsylvania Press, 1984), pp. 150–68.

77. *Songs from the Slums* is the title of a book by Toyohiko Kagawa, a Japanese Christian leader who was well known for his work in some of the worst slums of Japan (Nashville, TN: Cokesbury, c. 1935).

78. Kenneth Boulding, *There is a Spirit: The Nayler Sonnets* (New York: Fellowship Publications, 1945), p. x.

CHAPTER 6

1. T. S. Eliot, *The Waste Land*, 1922, in *Collected Poems* (New York: Harcourt, Brace & World, 1970), p. 64.

2. *The Confessions of St. Augustine*, trans. R. S. Pine-Coffin (Baltimore, MD: Penguin, 1961), III.1, p. 55. Throughout this section I use three different translations of Augustine's *Confessions*: the above by Pine-Coffin, a translation by E. M. Blaiklock (Nashville, TN: Thomas Nelson, 1983), and one by Rex Warner (New York: New American Library/Mentor, 1963).

3. *Confessions*, Blaiklock, III.I, p. 58.

4. *Confessions*, Blaiklock, III.I, p. 58.

5. *Confessions*, Warner, III.4, pp. 56–57.

6. *Confessions*, Pine-Coffin, III.5, p. 60. It is sobering to realize that the Church almost lost one of the greatest theological thinkers of all time because of an inferior translation of the Bible. We might well ponder this in the midst of today's constant hankering after simplified, grammar school–level translations.

7. *Confessions*, Warner, V.10, p. 104.

8. *Confessions*, Blaiklock, VII.VI, pp. 160–61.

9. *Confessions*, Pine-Coffin, VII.5, p. 138.

10. *Confessions*, Blaiklock, VII.XXI, pp. 176–77.

11. *Confessions*, Warner, II.2, pp. 40–41.

12. *Confessions*, Warner, VIII.5, p. 168.

13. *Confessions*, Blaiklock, V.XIII, p. 120.

14. *Confessions*, Blaiklock, VIII.VII, p. 196.

15. *Confessions*, Warner, VIII.8, pp. 175–76.

16. *Confessions*, Warner, VIII.12, pp. 181–83.

17. *Confessions*, Warner, X.27, p. 235.

18. Augustine, *Against the Academicians [Contra Academicos]* (Milwaukee, WI: Marquette University Press, 1957), 1.2.6, as cited in Michael Marshall, *The Restless Heart: The Life and Influence of St. Augustine* (Grand Rapids, MI: Eerdmans, 1987), p. 71. Augustine wrote two books during this period: *Contra Academicos*, his first apologetic work, in which he rejects the skepticism and agnosticism of the academics, and *Beata Vita* ("On the Happy [or Blessed] Life"), in which he insists that true happiness is found only in the knowledge of God.

19. *Confessions*, Warner, IX.8, p. 195. I have not had space to write about the enormous influence that Augustine's mother, Monica, had upon him. The story of Monica's intense prayers and absolute refusal to give up on her wayward son is genuinely moving. Only days before her death she said to Aurelius, "There was only one reason why I wanted to stay a little longer in this life, and that was that I should see you a Catholic Christian before I died. Now God has granted me this beyond my hopes; for I see that you have despised the pleasures of this world and are become his servant. So what am I doing here?" (IX.10). Her story is told in some detail in Augustine's *Confessions*, and I urge you to read it for yourself. Please don't miss the marvelous mystical vision that God gave Monica and Aurelius just a few weeks before her death (IX.10).

20. Augustine, *Sermons*, 19.2, as cited in Marshall, *The Restless Heart*, p. 110.

21. Possidius, *Life of St. Augustine*, trans. F. H. Hoare, *The Western Fathers* series (London: Sheed & Ward, 1954), p. 31, as cited in Marshall, *The Restless Heart*, p. 108.

22. Augustine, *On the Psalms*, 88.1.10, as cited in Marshall, *The Restless Heart*, p. 110.

23. Augustine, *Epistolae*, 21.5, as cited in Marshall, *The Restless Heart*, p. 110. Augustine goes on to say: "It is necessary . . . for the ecclesiastical orator, when he urges that something be done, not only to teach that he may

instruct, and to please that he may hold attention, but also to persuade that he may be victorious." Solid homiletical advice even today.

24. Augustine, *On St. John's Gospel*, 45.13, as cited in Marshall, *The Restless Heart*, p. 110.

25. Frederick van der Meer, *Augustine: The Bishop: The Life and Work of a Father of the Church* (London: Sheed & Ward, 1961) p. 412.

26. Possidius, *Life of St. Augustine*, p. 22, as cited in Marshall, *The Restless Heart*, pp. 105–6.

27. Augustine, *De Cat. Rud.*, 13.19.209, as cited in Marshall, *The Restless Heart*, p. 110.

28. Possidius, *Life of St. Augustine*, p. 6, as cited in Marshall, *The Restless Heart*, p. 95.

29. A specially convened council at Arles clearly and resolutely declared that the sacraments are not dependent for their validity upon the moral character of the one through whose hands they are administered. Ever able with the apt metaphor Augustine said, "The spiritual value of the sacraments is like light: although it passes among the impure it is not polluted."

30. Augustine, *On the Psalms*, 95.11, as cited in Marshall, *The Restless Heart*, p. 118.

31. Augustine's teaching on original sin, in brief, is as follows. Only angels and human beings have rational free will. While they can exist without being evil, only they can *be* evil (since they alone possess rational free will). Adam, the first human, chose evil—a deliberate choice made through the use of reason. On its most fundamental level his was the sin of pride— the desire of the creature to be at the center rather than God. And Adam's sin has tainted all human beings with sin. We all share in Adam's fallenness, his loss of status, his inability to choose God, his desire for him to be at the center rather than God. This falling away is not something we can recover from by our own efforts, for every effort to extricate ourselves is nullified by the fact that it arises from our continuing concern for ourselves; thus we are mired ever-more deeply in the morass of pride. We are still free, but now we are free only to sin, not to turn to God. We can be rescued from our helplessness only by the grace of God acting on our behalf. Thus we are born from above, a divine action accomplished only in and through Jesus Christ, who is God incarnate, fully God and fully human.

32. Augustine, *Sermons*, 169.13, as cited in Marshall, *The Restless Heart*, p. 135.

33. Augustine, *The City of God*, trans. Marcus Dods (New York: The Modern Library, 1950), XXII.30, p. 864.

34. *Confessions*, Blaiklock, I.1, p. 15.

35. Augustine, *The City of God*, XXII.30, p. 867.

36. Peter's death has been placed variously between A.D. 64 and 68, the most generally accepted date being July of 67. The greetings from "the church in Babylon" in 1 Peter 5:13 are the closest thing we have to biblical evidence of Peter's presence in Rome. There is, however, fairly strong evidence of that presence (as well as the manner of his death) in the writings of Clement, Eusebius, Origen, Tertullian, and Jerome.

37. Billy Graham, *Just As I Am* (San Francisco: HarperSanFrancisco, 1997), p. 695.

38. For those wanting to read more of the Graham story, and I hope you will, I recommend three sources. The first is Dr. Graham's own autobiography, *Just As I Am*, which will give you numerous glimpses into his passion for souls. The well-known biographer John Pollock has written two fine books on Graham: the first titled simply *Billy Graham: The Authorized Biography* (New York: McGraw-Hill, 1966) and the second an authorized biography of the decisive years titled *Billy Graham: Evangelist to the World* (San Francisco: Harper & Row, 1979). The third source is a substantial biography by William Martin titled *A Prophet With Honor: The Billy Graham Story* (New York: Morrow, 1991).

39. Martin, *A Prophet with Honor*, p. 173.

40. Graham, *Just As I Am*, p. 298.

41. As quoted in Pollock, *Billy Graham: Evangelist*, p. 54.

42. Graham, *Just As I Am*, p. 724.

43. Graham, *Just As I Am*, p. 53.

44. Graham, *Just As I Am*, p. 46.

45. Martin, *A Prophet with Honor*, pp. 111–13 and Graham, *Just As I Am*, pp. 137–39.

46. Graham, *Just As I Am*, p. 117. Graham has had a long-standing interest in education and in 1967 set up a nonprofit group to look into the feasibility of establishing a university. Insurance magnate John D. MacArthur offered a thousand acres of prime property in Florida, along with major financing to build and endow the university. He wanted Graham to be president of the proposed school, but Billy (perhaps remembering his near–vocational detour at Northwestern) was not interested. Graham was also concerned that the effort would become too much of a drain on his time and on the resources of the Billy Graham Evangelistic Association, so he backed out of the deal (Martin, *A Prophet with Honor*, pp. 341–42 and Graham, *Just As I Am*, p. 472).

47. Graham, *Just As I Am*, p. 175.

48. This can be seen most vividly in Graham's close friendship with Richard Nixon, which bordered on outright support of his political agenda, and in his enthusiastic support of the interests of America in Southeast Asia, particularly the Vietnam War.

49. Graham, *Just As I Am*, p. 171.

50. Graham, *Just As I Am*, p. 182.

51. Graham, *Just As I Am*, p. 160.

52. Martin, *A Prophet with Honor*, pp. 106–8, and Graham, *Just As I Am*, pp. 127–29.

53. Robert O. Ferm, a researcher for the Billy Graham Evangelistic Association, wrote an entire book entitled *Cooperative Evangelism* (Grand Rapids, MI: Zondervan, 1958) in order to present the historical and theological case for Graham's methods. In that book he insisted that "no major evangelist in history has ever too closely analyzed the orthodoxy of his sponsors," p. 31.

54. Graham, *Just As I Am*, p. 46.

55. Graham, *Just As I Am*, p. 125.

56. Martin, *A Prophet with Honor*, p. 222.

57. Martin, *A Prophet with Honor*, p. 223.

58. Graham, *Just As I Am*, p. 426.

59. Billy Graham, *Peace with God* (Garden City, NY: Doubleday, 1953). I would have wished for a more prophetic position, and an earlier one, but it is easy to state such things in hindsight. Furthermore, I must realize that I am from a denominational tradition that has struggled for racial justice since its inception and encourages its members to take a stand on these matters, while Graham is from a denominational tradition that has had a checkered history on racial justice. For the sake of the Christian cause worldwide we can be grateful that he did eventually take a firm position on racial justice.

60. Martin, *A Prophet with Honor*, p. 247.

61. Graham, *Just As I Am*, pp. 430–31.

62. Pollock, *Billy Graham: Evangelist*, p. 42.

63. As quoted in Martin, *A Prophet with Honor*, p. 543.

64. Martin, *A Prophet with Honor*, p. 86.

65. There were three conferences that served as vital preparation for the Amsterdam meetings. The first was a modest 1960 gathering of thirty-three key leaders in Montreux, Switzerland, with the theme, "God's Strategy in Missions and Evangelism." The next two were major assemblies of Christian leaders: the World Congress on Evangelism held in Berlin, Germany, in

1966, and the International Congress on World Evangelization held in Lausanne, Switzerland, in 1974. These gatherings set forth the critical theological foundation for evangelism, especially "The Lausanne Covenant." These were, however, gatherings of major leaders, and Graham longed to reach beyond the recognized leadership to those evangelists, most of them in Two-Thirds World settings, who faithfully proclaimed the gospel year in and year out in total obscurity.

66. Martin, A *Prophet with Honor*, pp. 530–41.

67. The word we translate *repent* is *metanoeo*. "Meta," in this context, means to turn around or to go in a different direction, while "noeo" or "nous" means the mind, the understanding, the intellect—hence "turn around in your mind." Jesus is telling us to reevaluate everything we have understood about life, for his presence and his message of the kingdom change absolutely everything.

68. Some may wonder why I do not say more about the vicarious, substitutionary death of Christ on the cross for the forgiveness of sins. The answer is not that I feel these matters are unimportant, but that I do not want people to mistake a theory of the atonement for the experience of saving grace. Personally, I hold that Christ's death on the cross satisfied the justice of God and opened the way for our reconciliation with God, dependent upon our repentance and acceptance of the free gift of salvation. But again, this is one theory of the atonement, and many people have no doubt experienced saving grace and abundant life with Christ as his disciple without believing every jot and tittle of this particular theory. Of course, if I were writing a theology of the cross, I would delve into the doctrine of the atonement in detail.

69. As quoted in Donald G. Bloesch, *Essentials of Evangelical Theology*, vol. 1 (San Francisco: Harper & Row, 1978), p. 7.

70. This primacy list is taken from Donald G. Bloesch, who has an extended discussion of each item listed. See *Essentials of Evangelical Theology*, vol. 1, chap. 4.

71. For a listing and discussion of each of the seven ecumenical councils, see Appendix A.

72. In brief: Gnosticism held to a strict dualism of spirit as good and matter as evil. Of necessity, then, it denied that God was creator of the material world and that Jesus was incarnated in the flesh. Marcionism posited a radical disjunction between God as revealed in the Hebrew Scriptures and God as revealed in Jesus Christ, resulting in a rejection of the Hebrew Scriptures. Montanism held to an eschatology which taught that the new Jerusalem would soon be established in Phrygia. Arianism insisted that Christ, the Son,

was a created being, hence undercutting his divinity. Nestorianism insisted upon two distinct beings in Christ—one human, one divine—which diminished the sense of the unity of Christ. Pelagianism rejected Augustine's notion of "original sin" and insisted upon sufficient human free will to respond to God, thus opening the door to a foundational theology of righteousness by means of human works.

As you can imagine, these single-sentence definitions are necessarily simplified. Any good church history book will help you explore the various arguments in more detail.

73. *Documents of the Christian Church*, 2nd ed., sel. and ed. Henry Bettenson (London: Oxford University Press, 1963), p. 26. The Nicene Creed went through several stages of development, from the gathering at Nicea (A.D. 325) to Constantinople (A.D. 381) to Chalcedon (A.D. 451), where the creed took the form that is quoted in the text. If you compare this statement to the creed as we find it today, you will note some further development, although the substance is the same.

There are four "ecumenical" creeds:

1. The Apostles' Creed, attributed to the original apostles but most likely adapted from an ancient Roman baptismal creed of the second century. The present form of the creed appeared around the sixth century.

2. The Nicene Creed, given in the text.

3. The Chalcedonian Creed, formulated in A.D. 451 to clarify the two natures of Christ—the relationship between his humanity and his divinity.

4. The Athanasian Creed, wrongly attributed by tradition to Athanasius. Though the real author and origin are unknown, this creed was probably written between the fifth and seventh centuries. The doctrines of the Trinity and the incarnation are developed in it.

Still other faith statements have been developed through the centuries, such as the Augsburg Confession (Lutheran), the Westminster Confession of Faith (Reformed), and the Richmond Declaration of Faith (Quaker). These should be thought of as ancillary teachings reinforcing particular denominational distinctives rather than as essential to evangelical faith and witness.

74. As quoted in D. Elton Trueblood, *The Validity of the Christian Mission* (New York: Harper & Row, 1972).

75. *The Journal of George Fox*, rev. edition ed. John L. Nickalls (Cambridge: University Press, 1952), p. 263.

76. As quoted in Bloesch, *Essentials of Evangelical Theology*, vol. 1, p. 51.

77. Those who make the pretribulation rapture a test for orthodoxy would probably be shocked to realize that this view cannot be found in the thinking of the Protestant reformers and that it was also generally alien to early Puritan and Pietist groups. After examining Philip Schaff's *Creeds of Christendom* (New York: Harper, 1919), Edward John Carnell notes that "the church has *never* made the details of eschatology a test of Christian fellowship" (*The Case for Orthodox Theology*, p. 118).

78. Bloesch, *Essentials of Evangelical Theology*, vol. 1, p. 58.

79. Bloesch, *Essentials of Evangelical Theology*, vol. 1, pp. 62–63.

CHAPTER 7

1. John Pudney, *John Wesley and His World* (Norwich, UK: Thames and Hudson, 1978), p. 7.

2. Donald L. Kline, *Susanna Wesley: God's Catalyst for Revival* (Lima, OH: C.S.S. Publishing, 1980), p. 42.

3. Rita F. Snowden, *Such a Woman: The Story of Susanna Wesley* (London: Epworth, 1963), p. 7. We cannot be certain about the Greek and Latin. Some scholars state that Susanna was well versed in these languages, but I have found no evidence of this in her letters. Also, her husband once wrote to their oldest son, who was away at Westminster School, urging him to share freely with him his inmost thoughts, adding, "I will promise you so much secrecy that even your mother shall know nothing but what you have a mind she should; for which reason it may be convenient you should write to me still in Latin" (Rebecca Lamar Harmon, *Susanna: Mother of the Wesleys* [New York: Abingdon, 1968], p. 19).

4. Harmon, *Susanna*, p. 20.

5. *Susanna Wesley: The Complete Writings*, ed. Charles Wallace, Jr. (New York: Oxford University Press, 1997), p. 5.

6. Snowden, *Such a Woman*, p. 21.

7. Arnold A. Dallimore, *Susanna Wesley: The Mother of John and Charles Wesley* (Grand Rapids, MI: Baker, 1993), p. 111.

8. George J. Stevenson, *Memorials of the Wesley Family* (Partridge, UK: n.p., 1876), p. 158, as cited in Dallimore, *Susanna Wesley*, p. 110.

9. The plumber was William Wright, and the marriage occurred in 1725. Before the wedding Hetty, realizing that they were completely unsuited for each other, tried to back out, but her father compelled her to go through with it. The child that had been conceived on that unfortunate night died soon after birth. Mr. Wright, completely unable to appreciate Hetty's intellect and sensibilities, spent more time in taverns than he did at home. Hetty tried desperately all her life to win him over, but in vain. She once wrote these tragic lines:

> Unkind, ungrateful, as thou art,
> Say, must I ne'er regain thy heart?
> Must all attempts to please thee prove
> Unable to regain thy love?

It is entirely possible that Susanna's grief and inner conflict over Hetty were responsible for her near-fatal illness during this period—a period that she called her "sad defection when I was almost without hope" (Adam Clarke, *Memoirs of the Wesley Family* [New York: Carlton & Porter, n.d.], pp. 535–36, 539).

10. John Wesley tried repeatedly to bring about a reconciliation between father and daughter. On 28 August 1726 he preached a sermon entitled "Universal Charity." He noted, "One great reason for my writing the above-mentioned sermon was to endeavour as far as in me lay, to convince them that even on the supposition that she [Hetty] was impenitent, some tenderness was due to her still which my mother, when I read it to her, was so well aware of that she told me as soon as I had read it, 'You writ this sermon for Hetty. . . .'" His efforts were to no avail, however; Samuel Wesley went to his grave estranged from his most gifted daughter (Harmon, *Susanna*, pp. 124–25).

11. *Susanna Wesley*, ed. Charles Wallace, p. 35.

12. *Susanna Wesley*, ed. Charles Wallace, p. 65.

13. Pudney, *John Wesley and His World*, p. 53, and Harmon, *Susanna*, p. 13.

14. The phrase "the calamities of life" actually comes from a letter Hetty wrote to her father in a futile bid for reconciliation (Stevenson, *Memorials of the Wesley Family*, p. 306, as cited in Harmon, *Susanna*, p. 133). Susanna knew more "calamities" than I have mentioned here. For example, one child died accidentally when a nurse fell asleep on top of her, suffocating her. Another child, Kezia, died at thirty-two after a lingering illness.

15. Kline, *Susanna Wesley*, p. 51.

16. Kline, *Susanna Wesley*, p. 49.

17. Harmon, *Susanna*, p. 166.

18. Harmon, *Susanna*, p. 80.

19. *Susanna Wesley*, ed. Charles Wallace, pp. 79–83.

20. *Susanna Wesley*, ed. Charles Wallace, pp. 118–22, 133–41, 144–54.

21. Clarke, *Memoirs*, p. 420.

22. Clarke, *Memoirs*, pp. 297–98, originally published as "The Excellency of A Publick Spirit: Set forth in a Sermon preach'd . . . at the Funeral of that late Reverend Divine Dr. Samuel Annesley, 1697," by Daniel Williams, p. 146, and republished by John Wesley in the *Arminian Magazine*, vol. XV, p. 248.

23. Harmon, *Susanna*, pp. 160–61.

24. John Kirk, *The Mother of the Wesleys*, 4th ed. (London: Jarrold & Sons, 1866), p. x.

25. Henry P. Van Dusen, *Dag Hammarskjöld: The Statesman and His Faith* (New York: Harper & Row, 1967), p. 4.

26. Dag Hammarskjöld, *Markings*, trans. Leif Sjöberg and W. H. Auden (New York: Ballantine, 1993), p. v.

27. A good translation of *Vägmärken* is "Trail Marks." Hammarskjöld explained the title in one of the book's entries: "These notes?—They were signposts you began to set up after you had reached a point where you needed them, a fixed point that was on no account to be lost sight of." The image is from his own extensive experience in mountain climbing. He had learned of the practice of piling up stones to mark progress on an uncharted mountain. The stones not only helped the original climber but also served as a guide for future climbers. Hammarskjöld hinted at just such a reason for his notes: "Perhaps it may be of interest to somebody to learn about a path about which the traveler who was committed to it did not wish to speak while he was alive (Hammarskjöld, *Markings*, p. 124).

28. Hammarskjöld, *Markings*, p. 143.

29. Hammarskjöld, *Markings*, pp. xix–xx.

30. Joseph P. Lash, *Dag Hammarskjöld: Custodian of the Brushfire Peace* (London: Cassell, 1961), pp. 206, 209, as cited in Van Dusen, *Dag Hammarskjöld*, p. 210.

31. In eight-and-a-half years at the United Nations Hammarskjöld undertook seventy-six diplomatic missions, including an early trip to China; six trips to the Near East; three trips to Moscow, Prague, and other Eastern European capitals; two trips to southern and eastern Asia; one trip around the world via Australia and the central Pacific Islands; two trips to South

America; and six trips to virtually every part of the African continent. For a detailing of these and other missions see Lash's *Dag Hammarskjöld*.

32. Hammarskjöld, *Markings*, p. 103.

33. *Servant of Peace: A Selection of the Speeches and Statements of Dag Hammarskjöld*, ed. Wilder Foote (New York: Harper & Row, 1963), fore-word, as cited in Van Dusen, *Dag Hammarskjöld*, p. 46.

34. Hammarskjöld, *Markings*, p. 158.

35. Van Dusen, *Dag Hammarskjöld*, p. 80. The issue is, of course, more complex than this. Hammarskjöld penned his most significant "marking" on the subject after a 1952 visit with a friend of his youth—a woman who in earlier days the young Dag considered a possible fiancée.

> *Incapable of being blinded by desire,*
> *Feeling I have no right to intrude upon another,*
> *Afraid of exposing my own nakedness,*
> *Demanding complete accord as a condition for a life together:*
> *How could things have gone otherwise?*

In this poem of penetrating self-understanding (*Markings*, p. 72) we find the four reasons Hammarskjöld himself gave for his lifelong celibacy: (1) a firm refusal to give in to impulse, (2) the deepest respect for the privacy of others, (3) an extreme modesty in revealing himself, emotionally and physi-cally, and (4) an unrealistic and unattainable ideal of mutual understanding. As he put it, "How could things have gone otherwise?" Even so, Ham-marskjöld suffered terribly from the media's insinuations of sexual devia-tion—insinuations for which there was never a shred of evidence. In one of his late *haiku* (*Markings*, p. 170), he wrote:

> *Because it never found a mate,*
> *Men called*
> *The unicorn abnormal.*

36. *Servant of Peace*, ed. Wilder Foote, foreword, as cited in Van Dusen, *Dag Hammarskjöld*, p. 46.

37. Van Dusen, *Dag Hammarskjöld*, p. 18.

38. Van Dusen, *Dag Hammarskjöld*, p. 6.

39. Hammarskjöld, *Markings*, p. 1.

40. The translators of *Markings*, in seeking an equivalent hymn line that would be meaningful to English readers, chose the phrase "Night is drawing nigh" from the Baring-Gould evening hymn "Now the Day Is Over." Despite the superficial similarity of the lines, the two hymns are utterly different in

character. "Now the Day Is Over" is a simple evening hymn reminding us of the end of the day, and it concludes on a hopeful note of the new morning to come. In contrast, the Swedish hymn "The Little While I Linger Here" is a powerful contemplation upon the transitoriness of life, and its closing lines anticipate and welcome death. The "NIGHT APPROACHES NOW" that Hammarskjöld quotes is the night of death, not the end of the day.

41. Hammarskjöld, *Markings*, p. 28. These meditations upon death may strike the American mentality as a bit strange, even morbid. The Scandinavian mind would not find it unusual in the least, however; nor would most cultures throughout history. Indeed, one of the well-established Spiritual Disciplines is to contemplate one's own demise.

42. Hammarskjöld, *Markings*, p. 50.

43. Hammarskjöld, *Markings*, p. 68.

44. Hammarskjöld, *Markings*, p. 74.

45. Hammarskjöld, *Markings*, p. 75.

46. It has been commonly assumed that this radical alteration in outlook came because of Hammarskjöld's election as secretary-general of the United Nations. Without a doubt this played a role in consolidating the transformation, but I am arguing here that the real change was far deeper and more interior and that it preceded his UN election by several months. In doing this, I am following the line of argumentation of Henry Van Dusen, which to my mind is quite convincing. For an enlargement of Van Dusen's position see *Dag Hammarskjöld: The Statesman and His Faith*, particularly chaps. 4 and 5.

While the change in outlook is fundamental and pervasive, we must not give the impression that the dogging questions and spiritual anguish utterly disappear from the reflections. They do not. Expressions of loneliness, interior suffering, sacrifice, and death continue to the very end, but they never again dominate his thinking.

47. Hammarskjöld, *Markings*, p. 180.

48. Hammarskjöld, *Markings*, p. 76.

49. Hammarskjöld, *Markings*, p. 106.

50. Hammarskjöld, *Markings*, p. 136.

51. Hammarskjöld, *Markings*, p. 181.

52. A host of books and articles are available through libraries. I especially call your attention to the following: Joseph Lash, *Dag Hammarskjöld: Custodian of the Brushfire Peace*; Israel Levine, *Champion of World Peace: Dag Hammarskjöld* (New York: J. Messner, 1962); Stephen Myron Schwebel, *The Secretary-General of the U.N.: His Political Powers and Prac-*

tices (Cambridge, MA: Harvard University Press, 1952); Adlai Ewing Stevenson, *Looking Outward: Years of Crisis at the United Nations* (New York: Harper & Row, 1963); and Sven Stolpe, *Dag Hammarskjöld: A Spiritual Portrait* (New York: Scribner, 1966).

53. Van Dusen, *Dag Hammarskjöld*, p. 104.

54. Hammarskjöld, *Markings*, p. 122.

55. Hammarskjöld, *Markings*, p. 124.

56. Hammarskjöld, *Markings*, p. 172.

57. Today we encounter the material world in its fallen state. It is "a good world gone bad," as C. S. Lewis put it. Therefore, on a practical level, we are constantly dealing with the many distortions of the material universe—the ways it can lead us into sin—and I will address some of these under the "perils" of the Tradition. But that constant pastoral and practical struggle must never keep us from affirming the goodness of matter as created by God.

58. What is often called the liturgical movement began almost simultaneously in different parts of the Christian world in the years following the First World War. It has had different forms and colorings in each of the Christian confessions, and within these confessions it has developed in a variety of ways in various countries. While it is true that this movement has been most prominent among the "high churches," hardly a group has been left untouched by it. And the liturgical flow moves both ways: many of the spontaneous liturgies of the "low churches" have been adapted into more sacramental settings with great benefit.

59. Evelyn Underhill, *Worship* (Guildford, Surrey, UK: Eagle, 1991), p. 33.

60. Throughout history different Christian groups have had various lists of official Sacraments. By the twelfth century the Roman Catholic Church had solidified its number at seven: baptism, confirmation, Eucharist, penance, extreme unction, holy orders, and matrimony. Sacraments in the Orthodox Church are officially called "holy mysteries," and they usually list a similar seven. The idea of counting, however, may be misleading, for the more ancient practice of the Orthodox Church has been to consider *everything* that is in and of the Orthodox Church as sacramental or mystical. Protestants have tended toward two Sacraments—baptism and Eucharist—though they have often also stressed the sacramental quality of preaching. Quakers and the Salvation Army are the two groups that have done away completely with outward and visible Sacraments. Even these groups, however, stress the sacramental character of life and the need for a visible enfleshment of that life. This notion is well expressed in the following hymn written by Albert Orsborn, a general in the Salvation Army:

My life must be Christ's broken bread,
My love his outpoured wine,
A cup o'erfilled, a table spread
Beneath his name and sign.
That other souls, refreshed and fed,
May share his life through mine.

61. C. S. Lewis, *They Stand Together: The Letters of C. S. Lewis to Arthur Greeves* (1914–1963), ed. Walter Hooper (New York: Macmillan, 1979), p. 499.

62. See John 4:1–26. For an extended exegesis of this "double meaning" see Oscar Cullmann, *Early Christian Worship* (Philadelphia: Westminster, 1953).

63. "Babylonian Captivity," *Luther's Works*, trans. A.T.W. Steinhauser, Frederick C. Ahrens, and Abdel Ross Wentz (Philadelphia: Muhlenberg, 1959), XXXVI, 57, as cited in James F. White, *A Brief History of Christian Worship* (Nashville, TN: Abingdon, 1993), p. 114.

64. "God's Grandeur" and #34 (untitled), *Prose and Poetry of Gerard Manley Hopkins*, ed. W. H. Gardner (New York: Penguin, 1953), pp. 27, 51.

65. The exact nature of the transformation is beyond the scope of this book. I have convictions on the eucharistic debate over transubstantiation, consubstantiation, and memorial, but they are irrelevant here. The key point is that in all three understandings we invite God to manifest his presence among us.

66. Martin Luther, "The Babylonian Captivity," in *Three Treatises* (Philadelphia: Muhlenberg Press, 1960), p. 203.

67. D. Elton Trueblood, *The Common Ventures of Life: Marriage, Birth, Work, Death* (New York: Harper & Row, 1965), p. 86.

68. For those who would like to pursue this matter further, I suggest a few sources: *Work and Leisure in Christian Perspective*, by Leland Ryken (Portland, OR: Multnomah, 1987); *The Biblical Doctrine of Work*, by Alan Richardson (London: SCM, 1952); *Working*, by Studs Terkel (New York: Avon, 1975); *Your Other Vocation*, by D. Elton Trueblood (New York: Harper, 1952); *Business as a Calling*, by Michael Novak (New York: Free Press, 1996); and *Why America Doesn't Work*, by Charles Colson and Jack Eckerd (Dallas, TX: Word, 1991).

69. *A Testament to Freedom: The Essential Writings of Dietrich Bonhoeffer*, ed. Geffrey B. Kelly and F. Burton Nelson (San Francisco: HarperSanFrancisco, 1990), p. 512.

Subject Index

Scripture Index